*The Columbia Companion
to Modern Chinese Literature*

The Columbia Companion to Modern Chinese Literature

EDITED BY

Kirk A. Denton

COLUMBIA UNIVERSITY PRESS

NEW YORK

Columbia University Press
Publishers Since 1893
New York   Chichester, West Sussex
cup.columbia.edu
Copyright © 2016 Columbia University Press
All rights reserved

Library of Congress Cataloging-in-Publication Data
The Columbia companion to modern Chinese literature /
edited by Kirk A. Denton.
pages cm
Includes bibliographical references and index.
ISBN 978-0-231-17008-6 (cloth : acid-free paper) — ISBN 978-0-231-17009-3
(pbk. : acid-free paper) — ISBN 978-0-231-54114-5 (electronic)
1. Chinese literature—20th century—History and criticism. 2. Chinese
literature—21st century—History and criticism.
I. Denton, Kirk A., 1955- editor.
PL2303.C5996 2016
895.109'005—dc23
2015019156

Columbia University Press books are printed
on permanent and durable acid-free paper.
This book is printed on paper with recycled content.
Printed in the United States of America

c 10 9 8 7 6 5 4 3 2 1
p 10 9 8 7 6 5 4 3 2 1

Cover design: Noah Arlow

References to websites (URLs) were accurate at the time of writing.
Neither the author nor Columbia University Press is responsible for URLs
that may have expired or changed since the manuscript was prepared.

CONTENTS

Preface and Acknowledgments   ix
Chronology of Major Historical Events   xi

PART ONE   Thematic Essays

    1. Historical Overview   3
        Kirk A. Denton
    2. Modern Chinese Literature as an Institution:
        Canon and Literary History   27
        Yingjin Zhang
    3. Language and Literary Form   38
        Charles Laughlin
    4. Literary Communities and the Production of Literature   46
        Michel Hockx
    5. Between Tradition and Modernity: Contested Classical Poetry   55
        Shengqing Wu
    6. Diaspora in Modern Chinese Literature   62
        Shuyu Kong
    7. Sinophone Literature   72
        Brian Bernards

8. Chinese Literature and Film Adaptation   80
Hsiu-Chuang Deppman

PART TWO   Authors, Works, Schools

9. The Late Qing Poetry Revolution: Liang Qichao, Huang Zunxian, and Chinese Literary Modernity   89
Jianhua Chen

10. The Uses of Fiction: Liang Qichao and His Contemporaries   97
Alexander Des Forges

11. Late Qing Fiction   104
Ying Hu

12. Zhou Shoujuan's Love Stories and Mandarin Ducks and Butterflies Fiction   111
Jianhua Chen

13. Form and Reform: New Poetry and the Crescent Moon Society   121
John A. Crespi

14. Reconsidering the Origins of Modern Chinese Women's Writing   128
Amy D. Dooling

15. The Madman That Was Ah Q: Tradition and Modernity in Lu Xun's Fiction   136
Ann Huss

16. Romantic Sentiment and the Problem of the Subject: Yu Dafu   145
Kirk A. Denton

17. Feminism and Revolution: The Work and Life of Ding Ling   152
Jingyuan Zhang

18. The Debate on Revolutionary Literature   159
Charles Laughlin

19. Mao Dun, the Modern Novel, and the Representation of Women   163
Hilary Chung

20. Ba Jin's *Family*: Fiction, Representation, and Relevance   169
Nicholas A. Kaldis

21. Chinese Modernism: The New Sensationists   176
Steven L. Riep

22. Shen Congwen and Imagined Native Communities   183
Jeffrey Kinkley

23. Xiao Hong's *Field of Life and Death*   189
Amy D. Dooling

24. Performing the Nation: Chinese Drama and Theater   195
    Xiaomei Chen

25. Cao Yu and *Thunderstorm*   205
    Jonathan Noble

26. The Reluctant Nihilism of Lao She's *Rickshaw*   211
    Thomas Moran

27. Eileen Chang and Narratives of Cities and Worlds   217
    Nicole Huang

28. Literature and Politics: Mao Zedong's "Yan'an Talks" and Party Rectification   224
    Kirk A. Denton

29. Qian Zhongshu and Yang Jiang: A Literary Marriage   231
    Christopher Rea

30. Revolutionary Realism and Revolutionary Romanticism: *Song of Youth*   237
    Ban Wang

31. The Hundred Flowers: Qin Zhaoyang, Wang Meng, and Liu Binyan   245
    Richard King

32. Cold War Fiction from Taiwan and the Modernists   250
    Christopher Lupke

33. Nativism and Localism in Taiwanese Literature   258
    Christopher Lupke

34. The Cultural Revolution Model Theater   267
    Di Bai

35. Martial Arts Fiction and Jin Yong   274
    John Christopher Hamm

36. Taiwan Romance: Qiong Yao and San Mao   280
    Miriam Lang

37. Misty Poetry   286
    Michelle Yeh

38. Scar Literature and the Memory of Trauma   293
    Sabina Knight

39. Culture Against Politics: Roots-Seeking Literature   299
    Mark Leenhouts

40. Mo Yan   307
    Yomi Braester

41. Avant-Garde Fiction in Post-Mao China   313
    Andrew F. Jones

42. Contemporary Experimental Theaters in the People's Republic of China, Taiwan, and Hong Kong 320
Rossella Ferrari

43. Modern Poetry of Taiwan 327
Michelle Yeh

44. Homoeroticism in Modern Chinese Literature 336
Thomas Moran

45. Contemporary Urban Fiction: Rewriting the City 345
Robin Visser and Jie Lu

46. Xi Xi and Tales of Hong Kong 355
Daisy S. Y. Ng

47. Writing Taiwan's Fin-de-Siècle Splendor: Zhu Tianwen and Zhu Tianxin 363
Lingchei Letty Chen

48. Wang Anyi 371
Lingzhen Wang

49. Wang Shuo 379
Jonathan Noble

50. Commercialization of Literature in the Post-Mao Era: Yu Hua, Beauty Writers, and Youth Writers 386
Zhen Zhang

51. Popular Genre Fiction: Science Fiction and Fantasy 394
Mingwei Song

52. Word and Image: Gao Xingjian 400
Mabel Lee

53. Hong Kong Voices: Literature from the Late Twentieth Century to the New Millennium 407
Esther M. K. Cheung

54. Avant-Garde Poetry in China Since the 1980s 414
Maghiel van Crevel

55. Taiwan Literature in the Post–Martial Law Era 422
Michael Berry

56. Speaking from the Margins: Yan Lianke 431
Carlos Rojas

57. Internet Literature: From YY to MOOC 436
Heather Inwood

Index 441

PREFACE AND ACKNOWLEDGMENTS

The essays in this volume are not meant to constitute a comprehensive history of modern Chinese literature, and there are, of course, gaps in coverage. My motivation was primarily pedagogical: to put together a resource that could be used fruitfully in university classrooms as a companion to readings of works of modern Chinese literature. In selecting topics for the essays, I have sought to focus on the most significant literary trends, styles, and writers, as well as some larger, macro issues related to language, literary institutions, media, and socioeconomic transformations. The first eight essays are of a general thematic nature and serve as background for the remaining forty-nine essays, which focus on specific authors, works, or schools and which are organized into rough chronological order. The volume treats fiction, poetry, and drama from the late nineteenth century to the present. I have chosen not to include the essay (散文) in its purview because of space limitations and because the essay is not often taught in the West in courses on modern Chinese literature, not because I see it as a marginal literary genre in China. Indeed, in certain periods—the war against Japan and the 1980s, for instance—prose writing was an extremely popular and influential literary form.

Many of these essays originally appeared in the China section of the *Columbia Companion to Modern East Asian Literature*, edited by Joshua Mostow (Columbia, 2003). They have been updated and revised to take into account the literary output in the decade since that book's publication. All other essays are new.

I wish to thank, first and foremost, the authors who contributed to this book. It is their vast knowledge and clarity of mind and expression that have made this book possible. I am also grateful to the external reviewers for their highly constructive criticisms. Jennifer Crewe and Jonathan Fiedler of Columbia University Press were extremely supportive throughout the process of revising the book. Jia Shi lent her valuable time to help with final preparations.

CHRONOLOGY OF MAJOR HISTORICAL EVENTS

1839–1842	Opium War (鸦片战争)
1842	Nanjing Treaty (南京条约) and the British occupation of Hong Kong
1860s–1880s	Self-strengthening Movement (洋务运动)
1894–1895	First Sino-Japanese War (甲午战争)
1895	Treaty of Shimonoseki; Japan occupies Taiwan
1905	Abolishment of the civil service examination
1911	Xinhai Revolution (辛亥革命)
1915–1920	New Culture movement (新文化运动)
1919	May Fourth movement (五四运动)
1926–1928	Northern Expedition (北伐)
1927–1936	First Nationalist/Communist Civil War
1937–1945	Second Sino-Japanese War (抗日战争)
1941–1945	Hong Kong occupied by the Japanese
1946–1949	Second Nationalist/Communist Civil War
1947	February 28th Incident (二二八事件)
1949	Founding of the People's Republic of China
1950–1987	White Terror in Taiwan (白色恐怖)
1956–1957	Hundred Flowers movement (百花运动)
1957–1958	Anti-Rightist Campaign (反右运动)
1958–1961	Great Leap Forward (大跃进)
1966–1976	The Cultural Revolution (文化大革命)

1987	End of martial law in Taiwan
1989	June Fourth Protest movement (六四)
1992	Deng Xiaoping's Southern Tour (南巡)
1997	Retrocession of Hong Kong to China
2000	Democratic Progressive Party wins Taiwan election

The Columbia Companion to Modern Chinese Literature

PART I

Thematic Essays

1

HISTORICAL OVERVIEW

KIRK A. DENTON

The question of the origins of modern Chinese literature is very much intertwined with politics and politicized definitions of modernity. The conventional view, initially promoted by May Fourth movement literary critics and later propagated by their Marxist inheritors before and after the 1949 revolution, is that modern Chinese literature erupted suddenly in 1918 with the publication of Lu Xun's 鲁迅 short story "Diary of a Madman" (see "The Madman That Was Ah Q"). The "birth" of this socially and culturally engaged literature was portrayed as an origin leading to the revolutionary literature of the late 1920s and 1930s and the establishment of a class-based literature in Yan'an, the Communist base during the war against Japan, which in turn became the model for literature in the People's Republic of China (PRC). Since the early 1980s, however, literary historians in China have assailed this canonical May Fourth/Maoist view of the origin of modern Chinese literature and consciously sought to "rewrite literary history" (重写文学史) (see "Modern Chinese Literature as an Institution"), a project that has restored many writers excluded or marginalized from the Maoist canon and has created a far more diverse and heterogeneous picture of literary development. Chinese and Western critics have questioned the narrative of May Fourth as origin and its faith in "enlightenment" and have looked to "alternative modernities" repressed by its hegemonic voice, including late Qing fiction (D. Wang 1997), popular Butterfly fiction (Chow 1991:34–83), and modernism.

Although any periodization of literary history will whitewash tensions, complexities, and ambiguities, delineating distinct periods is still a useful framework for making sense of the past and understanding how and why literature evolves and changes. At the same time, we should recognize that the very structure one uses to divide literature into periods—and, for that matter, into schools and styles—is never empty of political and ideological motive (see "Modern Chinese Literature as an Institution"). In what follows, I sketch a history of modern Chinese literature that draws from conventional PRC representations while at the same time focusing attention on and questioning the politics of that representation.

LATE QING: IMAGINING THE NATION (1895–1911)

Two important and intertwined forces shaped the history of nineteenth-century China: imperialism and internal social disintegration. To a great degree, though of course by no means absolutely, these forces determined the nature of literary production in the late Qing and through the rest of the twentieth century. As the sovereignty of their country was increasingly threatened by Western and Japanese imperialism, particularly economic imperialism, over the course of the nineteenth century, Chinese intellectuals began to look for explanations for their country's weakness relative to the global powers of the day. Initial responses—such as borrowing Western science and technology in order to increase Chinese "wealth and power"—were grounded in a faith that Western materiality would not destroy the essence of Chinese spiritual and cultural values. With the humiliating defeat by Japan in the Sino-Japanese War (1894–1895), however, intellectuals began to extend this reflection to the sacrosanct realm of ideas and culture. Was there something inherent in Chinese culture, they asked, that inhibited national strength and prevented China from acting on equal terms with other nations?

For the most part, late Qing intellectuals questioned aspects of tradition from within a traditional set of assumptions; their goal was not to destroy tradition but to invigorate it by stripping it of its negative aspects and renewing it with an infusion of Western ideas. The effect of their labors, however, was often to make tradition appear even less relevant. A good example of someone who sought this revamping of tradition is Kang Youwei 康有为 (1858–1927), whose reinterpretations of Confucian texts transformed Confucius from someone who looked back nostalgically on a lost golden age to a forward-looking, progressive reformer, a transformation that could not have occurred without the influence of Darwinian, evolutionary thought. Tan Sitong 谭嗣同 (1865–1898), another late Qing reformer, sought to place "benevolence" (仁) at the core of the Confucian value system by attacking the ethics of *li* (礼, the prescriptive ethical guidelines for human relations).

Central to the dissemination of Western thought in China was, of course, translation. Two translators, Lin Shu 林纾 (1852–1924) and Yan Fu 严复 (1854–1921), stand far above the rest. Yan Fu translated a host of Western works of sociology, economics, and philosophy, including Adam Smith's *Wealth of Nations*, Montesquieu's *The Spirit of Laws*, John Stuart Mill's *On Liberty*, and most influential of all, Thomas Huxley's *Evolution and Ethics*. As these works were read and discussed by intellectuals in the crisis atmosphere of the late Qing, their ideas were appropriated and shaped into a Chinese discourse of modernity centered on such concepts as evolution, progress, individualism, liberty, law, nation, and national character. Lin Shu's translations of more than two hundred, mostly Western European, novels were extremely popular in intellectual circles. They seemed to give narrative form to aspects of this discourse of modernity, presenting tales of individualist heroes, for example, and to offer a new, more politically engaged role for fiction in nation building (Hill 2013).

The spread of this discourse of modernity could not have occurred without the rise of a commercial print culture, which blossomed especially after 1905 when the civil service examination system was abolished and intellectuals were forced to search for new careers. Western-style newspapers, literary journals and literary supplements to newspapers, popular magazines, women's magazines, and the like became national forums for the shaping and dissemination of this discourse of modernity. Key to this new print culture was the figure of Liang Qichao 梁启超 (1873–1929), who founded and edited many newspapers and journals and contributed his own very influential writings to them. These writings introduced to a national Chinese readership knowledge of the West, critiqued aspects of the Chinese tradition and the national psychology it instilled, and promoted political, social, and literary reform. Although professional writers had certainly existed in earlier times (for example, Li Yu 李渔 [1610–1680]), their broad-scale emergence as a class occurred during the late Qing. Writers could potentially live off the proceeds of their writing, though in reality this was seldom the case and most relied on more steady incomes from teaching or jobs as editors in publishing houses.

Interconnected with these events in the intellectual and print spheres were important developments in literature. Even within the dominant Tongcheng 桐城 and Wenxuan 文选 schools, which advocated traditional styles of classical prose, important changes were occurring. The Tongcheng school of prose, of which the translators Yan Fu and Lin Shu were a part, sought to revive traditional values through a restoration of "ancient-style prose" (古文) modeled on the prose masters of the Tang and Song dynasties. When Lin Shu translated Western novels into Chinese, he did so not in the vernacular but in ancient style. He did this to make the Western novel respectable to his literati peers, but also because he wanted to reinvigorate the ancient style with the dynamism that the Western novel seemed to offer. Ultimately, readers were far more interested in the exotic content of the novels than the prose style into which they were translated (Huters 1987, 1988). Moreover, as Michael Hill (2013) argues, Lin Shu's prose incorporates many modern lexical terms and in that sense is not nearly as purely "ancient" as it is often made out to be. The Wenxuan school promoted a highly ornate parallel prose as the embodiment of an indigenous national culture and as a revolutionary stance against the Qing, a foreign dynasty. Outside these traditional literary schools, more profound changes were taking place. A "poetry revolution" (诗界革命) led by Liang Qichao and Huang Zunxian 黄遵宪 proposed reinvigorating classical poetry by incorporating Western terms, folk motifs, vernacular language, and new themes. In prose, Liang was instrumental in developing a style called "new style prose" (新文体), a blend of classical syntax, vernacular language, and foreign loanwords, that would exert an important influence on the formation of a modern vernacular language in the May Fourth period.

Liang Qichao's most influential contribution to literature was his promotion of fiction as an instrument of national reform (see "The Uses of Fiction"). With its particular power of immersing the reader in its world, Liang believed that fiction could "renovate" morality, politics, social customs, learning and arts, and the human mind itself (Denton 1996:74). In seeing fiction as a vehicle for moral and social transformation, Liang was both traditional and modern. His modernity lies in promoting fiction—traditionally a genre on the low end of the literary hierarchy—for the serious moral and political purposes conventionally ascribed to poetry and prose. Following Liang's call for a new "political" novel was an unprecedented boom in fiction writing (see "Late Qing Fiction"). Thousands of novels in many styles and on a wide variety of themes were produced in the final decade of the Qing: sentimental love stories, detective novels, satires of corruption, science fiction, allegories about China, political novels (Yeh 2015), and so on. Strikingly different from the premodern novel in terms of its focus on contemporary society, these novels also bear some of the structural properties of their premodern progenitors, although some scholars argue that they also experimented with narrative modes and plot structures borrowed from the Western novel (Doleželová-Velingerová 1980). Of course, the novels produced during this period were tremendously varied in form and content; some embodied Liang's call for a new political novel, but many were far more concerned with entertaining and titillating.

Broadly speaking, the late Qing was a transitional period in which there was a gradual move away from traditional concepts of *wen* (文)—writing in a wide variety of prose genres and poetic forms performed by literati not for profit but for their own moral self-cultivation or that of civilization as a whole—to a modern, Western-influenced concept of *wenxue* (文学)—a belletristic view of literature as a field distinguished from other areas of society and limited to the genres of fiction, poetry, and drama (Huters 1987).

MAY FOURTH: ICONOCLASM AND THE DISCOURSE OF MODERNITY (1915–1925)

The meaning of "May Fourth" and its relation to the formation of literary modernity is so contested as to provoke at least one scholar (Hockx 1999) to question its validity as a category for understanding literature of the early Republic. But May Fourth is still a necessary tool with which to discuss literary modernity in China. The term derives from the May Fourth Incident of 1919, when in response to the humiliating stipulations of the Treaty of Versailles, which would have ceded control to Japan parcels of Chinese territory in Shandong Province, thousands of university students in Beijing marched to Tiananmen Square in protest. The term "May Fourth" is also used to describe a broader cultural movement, sometimes also called the New Culture movement (新文化运动), that was both different from and closely related to the anti-imperialist nationalism expressed in the student demonstrations and nationwide patriotic movement that followed.

The May Fourth cultural movement deepened and enhanced the discourse of modernity conceived by late Qing intellectuals such as Liang Qichao and Yan Fu. Antitraditionalism, democracy, science, enlightenment, individualism, evolution, nation, and revolution, a hodgepodge of sometimes conflicting concepts derived from a range of Western cultural-historical periods, were the rhetorical tools with which these intellectuals attempted to pry themselves and their compatriots free from what Lu Xun would refer to as the "iron house" (铁屋) of tradition. Central to this discourse was iconoclasm, a totalistic attack on tradition. Wu Yu 吴虞 (1871–1949), Lu Xun (1881–1936), Chen Duxiu 陈独秀 (1880–1942), Gao Yihan 高一涵 (1885–1968), Yi Baisha 易白沙 (1886–1921), and other Westernized intellectuals focused their iconoclasm on the Confucian ethical system (礼教), which they saw as deadeningly hierarchical and oppressively authoritarian. Lost in the constricting web of Confucian social relations was the individual; liberating the individual would unleash a new dynamic force that would serve society and the nation well. Key to May Fourth iconoclasm was the question of language. Denying the significant vernacularization that had already occurred in the final years of the Qing, May Fourth intellectuals like Hu Shi 胡适 and Chen Duxiu (in Denton 1996) made grand appeals for an end to the hegemony of the classical language—the very bearer of tradition—and for the adoption, in all forms of writing, of a modern vernacular language. Because it was closer to what people actually spoke, these language reformers tell us, the vernacular could better portray social and emotional realities and serve as the new national language (see "Language and Literary Form").

The literary production that emerged following these calls for reform was highly diverse and heterogeneous. Poets were among the first to respond (see "Form and Reform"). Working against the powerful force of a long and glorious poetic tradition that favored highly structured forms, Hu Shi, Zhou Zuoren 周作人 (1885–1967), Xu Yunuo 徐玉诺 (1893–1958), Xu Zhimo 徐志摩 (1897–1931), Bing Xin 冰心 (1900–1998), Yu Pingbo 俞平伯 (1899–1990), and Guo Moruo 郭沫若 (1892–1978), for example, experimented with the vernacular in free-verse forms (Hockx 1994). In fiction, some writers wrote in a style they labeled "realism," exposing a reality that traditional ideology concealed as a way of demystifying the naturalness of that ideology's worldview. Lu Xun's fiction, especially his first collection of stories, *Call to Arms* (呐喊), is often seen in this light. Others painted themselves in the romantic mode of literature as self-expression; Yu Dafu 郁达夫, in fiction, and Guo Moruo, in poetry, became the icons of this romantic position. The romantic and realist positions—and the Creation Society (创造社) and Literary Association (文学研究会) that promoted them, respectively—were not nearly so at odds as conventionally thought; more often than not, the romantic and realist ethos coexisted within individual writers or across the boundaries set by polemical debates between literary societies. Still other writers in the May Fourth period placed emphasis not so much on writing about reality or expressing the self as on developing language, style, and form—the aesthetics of the literary text. All writers in this early period were experimenting with the new national literary language—a hybrid of premodern vernacular, Liang Qichao's "new style," Western and Japanese grammatical forms, foreign loanwords, and remnants of classical Chinese.

May Fourth writers, in all their variety, shared a disdain for entertainment fiction, which was extremely popular at the time and which they deprecatingly labeled "Mandarin Ducks and Butterflies" (鸳鸯蝴蝶派) fiction. Butterfly fiction came in many forms, including knight-errant novels (see "Martial Arts Fiction and Jin Yong"), detective fiction, comedic satires, and sentimental love stories. Even as they denounced the didactic tradition of "literature conveys the Way" (文以载道), May Fourth writers asserted their own serious high-mindedness by positioning themselves apart from popular writers—and their commercialism and cultural entrepreneurship—with whom they competed for an urban readership (Hockx 1998). They also differed from the Butterfly writers in terms of language and literary form: whereas the latter retained some of the narrative and rhetorical forms of premodern fiction, the former developed a highly Westernized, or Japanized, prose style and experimented with the narrative modes, poetic forms, and dramatic styles of the modern West (Gunn 1991).

As Michel Hockx discusses in his essay (see "Literary Communities and the Production of Literature"), literary societies (and their journals) were important phenomena of the early twentieth century (see also Hockx 2003; Denton and Hockx 2008). These journals offered a stable venue for publication of members' writings and were forums for manifestos and polemics that declared to the literary world a society's position. Societies debated among themselves, sometimes vociferously and with venom, as they vied for positions within the literary field.

Another important phenomenon of this period was the "emergence" of women writers (see "Reconsidering the Origins of Modern Chinese Women's Writing"). Although Dorothy Ko (1994), Susan Mann (1997), and others have shown us that women writers were active in the late imperial period—a fact that undermines received views, largely created by the May Fourth movement itself, that women had been completely silenced by a patriarchal tradition—it is nonetheless true that women writers emerged on the May Fourth literary scene to a much greater degree and in a much more public way than ever before. Not surprisingly, this first generation of modern women writers were from the economic and social elite, daughters of wealthy families whose parents allowed them access to Western-style education. Bing Xin, Chen Hengzhe 陈衡哲 (1893–1976), Lu Yin 庐隐 (1898–1934), and Ling Shuhua 凌叔华 (1900–1990) are among the most significant. Unlike their male counterparts, they tended to write about love and domestic life, perhaps because they felt excluded from the new male discourse of modernity or because they consciously struggled against its patriarchal implications.

LITERARY DIVERSIFICATION IN THE 1920S AND 1930S: LEFTIST LITERATURE, MODERNISM, AND NATIVISM

Although the degree to which writers adhered to the leftist revolutionary cause has been dramatically overemphasized by Marxist literary historians, it is true that many May Fourth writers and a new generation of younger writers willingly embraced a political role for literature by the 1920s and into the 1930s. This turn to the left has everything to do with political and historical circumstances: the success of the revolutionary Northern Expedition (which united much of Chinese territory in 1928 after years of warlord domination), the rise of Japanese imperialism after 1931, and Guomindang (GMD) fascism and its inattention to social problems. This leftward swing in literature began with a critique of the May Fourth movement by such leftists as Qu Qiubai 瞿秋白 (1899–1935), who perceptively attacked the May Fourth writers for their elitism, particularly their use of Westernized language and literary forms, which Qu labeled "Western eight-legged essays" (洋八股), referring to the abstruse and formulaic essay of the late imperial examination system. Qu promoted the use of street vernacular and favored popular performance arts that would be more accessible to the masses and hence more effective as tools of social change (see "Language and Literary Form"). Some of these radical critics went so far as to attack Lu Xun, widely regarded as the father of modern literature and the embodiment of May Fourth enlightenment values, as no longer in sync with the times. Qian Xingcun 钱杏邨 (1900–1977), for example, claimed that the "age of Ah Q" (the protagonist in a Lu Xun novella) was "bygone" (Denton 1996: 276–288) and that what China needed was not the gloomy and difficult moods of Lu Xun's prose poems in *Wild Grass* (野草, 1927) but a more positive and optimistic literature that pointed to a bright revolutionary future.

The critics promoting "revolutionary literature"—written about the masses and in their interests—and the writers they addressed were mostly from bourgeois or gentry backgrounds. According to the logic of Marxist determinism, bourgeois writers could not but write in the interest of their own class, a predicament critics circumvented by claiming that bourgeois writers could "transcend" or "sublate" their class backgrounds by entering into and experiencing the lives of the lower classes. Many of the debates that arose in the leftist camp in the 1930s centered on this question of what role the bourgeois writer could have in the production of a revolutionary literature (Denton 1996: 48–49).

Attempting to end the rhetorical battles in the leftist literary world, the Chinese Communist Party (CCP) established the League of Left-Wing Writers (左翼作家联盟; 1930–1936), which promoted Marxist literary theory and published leftist literature in its many official journals. Not surprisingly, the literary practice of left-leaning writers was an imperfect realization of Marxist theoretical prescriptions. The generally engaged nature of this writing can be seen in the dominance of the literary modes of realism and satire. Writers such as Mao Dun 茅盾, who had since the May Fourth period promoted "naturalism," wrote realistic novels and short stories about, for instance, the economic hardship of peasants or the inner workings of capitalism in Shanghai. Zhang Tianyi 张天翼 (1906–1985) and Wu Zuxiang 吴组缃 (1908–1994) offered satirical portraits of a decadent gentry class. Romantic writers of the Creation Society, who were the most histrionic in their "conversions" to the revolutionary cause, publicly decried their former individualism, only to continue to uphold a romantic view of the power of literature to contribute to the revolutionary movement and to transform the world. The modern spoken drama (话剧) (see "Performing the Nation"), a new form that developed in the 1910s and 1920s against a powerful operatic tradition, came into its own in the 1930s, particularly in the hands of Cao Yu 曹禺 (1910–1966), and was largely associated with the leftist movement.

Leftist literature was, of course, only one element of the literary field in the late 1920s and 1930s. Butterfly fiction continued to be highly popular. Writers like Zhang Henshui 张恨水 reached a readership unimaginable to most of the progressive writers, the one exception being Ba Jin 巴金, whose novel *Family* (家, 1933) reached a wide readership, although precisely because it contains many tropes from the Butterfly tradition. A small group of writers associated with the journal *Les Contemporains* (现代) promoted and wrote literary works that were self-consciously at odds with those demanded by the proponents of revolutionary literature. These writers have been referred to as the New Sensationists (新感觉派), after the Japanese modernist school (the Shinkankakuha) that one of its members, Liu Na'ou 刘呐鸥 (1900–1939), followed while in

Japan. Modernist tendencies were also very strong in poetry. Dai Wangshu 戴望舒 (1905–1950), who was connected with *Les Contemporains*, and Li Jinfa 李金发 (1900–1976), for example, experimented with symbolist modes of poetry. Much ink has been spilled on the question of whether these Chinese modernists constitute true modernism. One scholar (Lee 1990) argues that modernism, at least as it was formulated in Western Europe and America, could not develop fully in China because of the radically different historical circumstances: "cultural modernity" arose in the West as a critique of "historical modernity" (capitalism, science, progress, civilization, and the like); in China, however, culture was usurped by the cause of bringing about historical modernity. Although others have sought to decenter the study of modernism away from Western Europe and the United States to allow it to include alternative forms, this view is nonetheless valuable in delineating how and why literature was made to serve the cause of nation building in China.

The 1930s also gave rise to writers like Shen Congwen 沈从文 (1902–1988) and Feng Wenbing 冯文炳 (1901–1967), whose works depict life in rural areas in a lyrical and nostalgic mode. These works are void of the political jargon and the heroic revolutionary themes being promoted by leftist critics; instead, their language exudes a folk quality, even as it is studiously modern, and their plots have the universal appeal of primitive themes. Literary historians have often depicted Shen as a "nativist" writer whose work consistently recounts his native region, West Hunan. But Shen also wrote romantic short stories (in the manner of Yu Dafu) and more explicitly modernist fiction. In any case, his body of work resisted, sometimes quite self-consciously, the literary prescriptions emanating from the leftist camp, which is one of the reasons it is so popular today.

With the historical pressures of the war against Japan and the increasingly strident calls for social realism from the revolutionary camp, these various attempts to steer literature away from politics faded, but did not disappear, by the late 1930s.

WAR PERIOD: LITERATURE AND NATIONAL SALVATION (1937–1945)

The war period, during most of which China was divided into three distinct political regions (the Communist-controlled area around Yan'an in the northwest, the Japanese-occupied coast, and the GMD-held southwest), has been seriously misrepresented in literary histories. Marxist literary historians in the PRC have often portrayed the war period as one of great homogeneity: writers happily abandoned their personal motivations for writing and devoted themselves and their pens to the political cause of national salvation. They arrived at this view by emphasizing the theory and practice in Yan'an and ignoring or underemphasizing work produced in the GMD-held areas and in territory under Japanese control. When one takes all three areas into consideration, however, the Chinese literary scene during the war appears quite heterogeneous. Yet, at the same time, the war period also marked a shift toward cultural homogenization: realism, romanticism, modernism, regionalism, and popular literature seemed to be making their "last stands" against the tide of revolutionary and national salvation literature (Anderson 1989). The May Fourth notion of the writer as the voice of "critical consciousness," an ideal embodied in the figure of Lu Xun, also came under assault during the war, especially in Yan'an during the Rectification Campaign (整风运动).

In the early years of the war, writers caught up in the euphoria of resistance devoted themselves to propaganda work. The All China League of Resistance Writers (and its many local branches)—an umbrella organization established in Wuhan in 1938 to unite cultural workers from all political persuasions—directed this promotion of anti-Japanese propaganda work. Writers were encouraged to produce works that were readily accessible to a mass audience (see "Language and Literary Form"). This meant using "national forms" (民族形式) or "old forms" (旧形式)—literary, oral, and visual forms that had indigenous roots and were appealing to a rural as well as urban audience. These forms included storytelling, ballads, New Year's prints, local opera, and Peking drum singing. New forms such as "street plays" (街头剧), short propaganda dramas performed in villages around the country, were also developed; the most famous was *Put Down Your Whip* (放下你的鞭子, 1936). The war was also a period in which the modern spoken drama flourished and came to maturity (see "Performing the Nation").

That writers willingly engaged in propaganda work is not to say that there was no debate in literary circles during the war, or that literary practice was homogeneous. In the face of what they saw as a degrading retreat from the May Fourth ideal of a modern, cosmopolitan literature, some critics such as Hu Feng 胡风 (1902–1985) denounced "national forms." Other voices (Shen Congwen and Liang Shiqiu 梁实秋) even criticized as destructive the usurpation of culture by politics and political figures. By the early 1940s, moreover, the national literary scene became increasingly heterogeneous. In GMD-controlled areas, realism and romanticism returned as writers shifted their attentions away from the war (which had stalemated by this time) and the external enemy toward social and cultural issues. Writers such as Sha Ting 沙汀 (1904–1992) wrote fiction that exposed the social problems under GMD rule. Lu Ling 路翎 (1923–1994) wrote in a radically subjective style about the psychological effects of oppression on the individual.

In Beijing and Shanghai, the Japanese occupiers sought to stem political dissent and largely succeeded. Although historical costume dramas were occasionally used allegorically to promote resistance, popular-entertainment fiction and escape were the rule of the day. This is not to say that there were no serious writers. Eileen Chang's 张爱玲 (1921–1995) *Romances* (传奇, 1943), a collection of short stories, is among the most sophisticated and important works of modern Chinese literature. Although the war does not, for the most part, figure directly in them and Chang seems to be self-consciously reacting against the heroic historical narratives that dominated the literary scene outside Shanghai, her fiction nonetheless reveals in subtle ways how history imprints itself on the psyche. Shi Tuo 师陀 (1910–1988) wrote lyrical essays and experimental fiction that further belie the stereotype of war literature as uniformly propagandistic. Costume dramas—plays with historical settings—were popular in occupied Shanghai, but other playwrights, such as Yang Jiang 杨绛, wrote contemporary comedies that satirized intellectual pretension and social climbing.

In Yan'an, CCP cultural policy promoted "national defense literature" (国防文学) and the use of "national forms." Urban, bourgeois writers like Ding Ling 丁玲, who had idealistically made their way to Yan'an to participate in the revolution, found life there far from the promise they had held for it and experienced difficulty abandoning May Fourth notions of the role of literature. With CCP backing, in the spring of 1942 they began to publish essays and short stories that exposed problems in Yan'an society: party privilege, the unequal place of women, thought reform of intellectuals, absence of freedom of speech, and the like. Mao Zedong, who had since 1935 been head of the CCP but whose political position was not completely secure, was surprised by the depth and extent of the criticism that he himself had unleashed. He decided to hold a conference for cultural workers, at the end of which he gave two speeches, collectively called the "Yan'an Talks," that summed up party cultural policy: literature is subservient to political interests, and writers should write for and about the masses of workers, peasants, and soldiers. Even as he invoked his name in the Talks, Mao countered everything Lu Xun stood for: intellectual autonomy and the critical consciousness of the writer. The Talks are significant for setting the draconian national cultural policy after the establishment of the PRC in 1949.

Although often skipped over in literary histories, the brief period after the war and before the establishment of the PRC was highly active and saw the appearance of many excellent full-length novels, including Qian Zhongshu's 钱钟书 (1910–1998) satirical *Fortress Besieged* (围城, 1946), although film and drama were perhaps the most important cultural forms.

EARLY POSTREVOLUTIONARY PERIOD: REVOLUTIONARY ROMANTICISM (1949–1966)

After the revolution, the CCP began to impose systematically the dictates of the Yan'an Talks. Although many writers enthusiastically embraced the cultural policy of the new regime, others balked at abjuring their roles as cultural critics. The party attempted to impose literary uniformity in two primary ways: institutions and cultural campaigns. The publishing industry was nationalized and journals were brought under state control. Writers were organized into the Chinese Writers Association (中国作家协会), which "served the complementary functions of providing the party with a means of monitoring and controlling creative writing and of establishing a clear-cut ladder of success for writers within the socialist literary system" (Link 2000: 119). The pluralist literary field of the Republican period—with its privately owned journals and publishing houses, competing literary societies, and stylistic heterogeneity—was effectively destroyed. Censorship (see "Literary Communities and the Production of Literature") was exerted by not approving manuscripts for publication, but more often than not writers internalized party guidelines (as best they could interpret them in the ever-changing political climate). When writers crossed the line, public criticism could follow. The 1950s, even before the radical excess of the Great Leap Forward and the Cultural Revolution, were dotted with periodic campaigns against wayward writers and intellectuals (for example, the campaign against the Hu Feng clique in 1955). The effect of these campaigns was to break down intellectuals' lingering sense of autonomy and critical consciousness and instill a notion of what the party would and would not tolerate.

Even under such effective means of control, the literary products of the first "seventeen years" of the PRC, as they are often called on the mainland, were not just uniform political propaganda. There were moments of relaxation in cultural policy, such as the Hundred Flowers (1956–1957), when writers were encouraged to write about problems in the new socialist society. This they did with a forthrightness that Mao, who launched the movement in 1956, could never have foreseen. After just a few short months, the CCP reversed its policy and attacked the very writers and intellectuals it had encouraged to speak out. At least one hundred thousand writers and intellectuals were targeted during the subsequent Anti-Rightist Campaign (1957–1958), the most virulent cultural campaign to date and a harbinger of the radicalism and anti-intellectualism of the Cultural Revolution to come.

In terms of literary production, writers were expected to follow the "worker, peasant, soldier" formula established by Mao in his Yan'an Talks. Socialist realism and then "revolutionary realism combined with revolutionary romanticism" were the prescribed literary models. Although much of the resulting literary practice was dull and uninspiring, readers sincerely enjoyed and were moved by some of the better works. Novels such as Yang Mo's 杨沫 *Song of Youth* (青春之歌, 1958), Zhou Erfu's 周而复 *Morning in Shanghai* (上海的早晨, 1958), Qu Bo's 曲波 *Tracks in the Snowy Forest* (林海雪原, 1957), Liu Qing's 柳青 *The Builders* (创业史, 1959), and Luo Guangbin 罗广斌 and Yang Yiyan's 杨益言 *Red Crag* (红岩, 1961) were extremely popular with readers for varying reasons, including sentimental description of love and revolution (*Song*), sense of adventure (*Tracks*), heroic sacrifice (*Red Crag*), and optimism for building a new society (*The Builders*), themes that derive in part from the popular literary tradition (Link 2000: 210–248). Poetry—much of it narrative—was promoted by the state, as was traditional-style operatic theater, but neither gained the wide audience enjoyed by fiction.

CULTURAL REVOLUTION: CLASS STRUGGLE (1966–1976)

Although the core of Mao Zedong's motivation for launching the Cultural Revolution in 1966 was bald politics—he had lost control of the vast CCP bureaucracy to the more pragmatic wing of the party leadership—there was also a sincere desire to radically revamp a culture that had, Mao felt, become complacently mired in bourgeois values. The Cultural Revolution was an attempt to destroy remnants of both the feudal culture of China's past and Western bourgeois culture. The campaign attacking the "four olds"—ideas, culture, customs, and habits—carried out sometimes by marauding Red Guards burning library books or destroying temples, was one element of this revamping of culture. Many writers associated with the May Fourth tradition were attacked, sometimes physically, and their works were disparaged. Lu Xun, poster boy for the leftists, was one of the few Republican era intellectuals to escape critique during the radicalism of the Cultural Revolution. During this time, educational and cultural institutions were mostly closed. Swept up in the political fervor of the times or simply trying to survive, most writers stopped writing. Those who did write and publish generally belonged to a younger generation. They churned out short stories, essays, and reportage that praised the Cultural Revolution and supported its class-struggle ideology. Hao Ran 浩然 is the best known of the Cultural Revolution novelists, and his *Bright and Sunny Days* (艳阳天, 1965) and *The Golden Road* (金光大道, 1972–1974) exemplify the Cultural Revolution aesthetics of heroism and class struggle (King 2013).

By far the most important form of cultural production in the Cultural Revolution was the model theater (样板戏): Peking operas (for example, *Taking Tiger Mountain by Strategy* [智取威虎山] and *The Red Lantern* [红灯记]) and ballets (such as *The White-Haired Girl* [白毛女] and *Red Detachment of Women* [红色娘子军]) designed to embody the class-struggle values of the radical leftist position. The model theater was the domain of Jiang Qing 江青, Mao Zedong's wife; through it, she supported Maoism, exerted herself in the cultural and political fields, and, some scholars argue, propounded a feminist agenda through strong revolutionary heroines. Stylized and propagandistic as they are, with their colorful costumes and set designs, songs, dance, and acrobatics, these plays were genuinely enjoyed by audiences. As Mittler (2012) argues, the propagandistic culture of the Cultural Revolution is not as anomalous as critics make out: it is part of a "continuous" history that dates back to at least the late Qing.

Mostly in the form of hand-copied manuscripts, works of popular fiction circulated among friends throughout the Cultural Revolution. That people would take the serious risk of being caught with these "dregs" of bourgeois culture attests to the powerful appeal of literature as pure entertainment (Link 2000: 193–197). Similarly, elite poetry also thrived underground during the later years of the Cultural Revolution (see "Misty Poetry").

POST-MAO: THE RETURN OF MODERNITY (1977–1989)

The death of Mao, the end of the Cultural Revolution, and the subsequent liberalization of party cultural policy unleashed a flowering of Chinese literature that has often been compared to the May Fourth movement. The parallels are striking. Like the May Fourth writers, who portrayed themselves as emerging from the shackles of a deadening Confucian tradition, post-Mao writers saw themselves as struggling against the legacy of an equally oppressive Maoist system. Early post-Mao writers, like their May Fourth counterparts, discovered and experimented with romantic self-expression, modernist literary styles, critical realism, and the avant-garde; they did so at least in part to pry themselves from the Maoist discourse and its ideological constraints. Just as May Fourth writers saw a need to develop a new vernacular language free of traditional ideology, so too did post-Mao writers attempt to develop a language untainted by Maoism. As in the May Fourth movement, women writers (the most famous of whom is Wang Anyi 王安忆) reemerged on a large scale in the post-Mao period.

The development of post-Mao literature has often been seen in terms of literary movements: Misty poetry (modernist-style poetry that was intensely personal and lyrical in contrast to the highly politicized narrative poetry that dominated the Maoist era), scar literature (fiction that depicted the psychological wounds suffered during the Cultural Revolution), roots-seeking literature (fiction that sought a return to China's indigenous cultures, though often marginalized ones, in reaction to a century of rupturing iconoclasm), and the avant-garde (postmodern fiction that questions modernity's basic discourse of self, progress, realism, and enlightenment in a language self-consciously denuded of Maoist tropes). Of course, not all writing produced in the 1980s fit neatly into these movements, and some literary genres were more closely associated with movements than others. As a whole, the development from movement to movement shows an intensification of criticism of the socialist system: whereas scar literature in the late 1970s and early 1980s was superficial in its treatment of the Cultural Revolution, often laying blame with the Gang of Four and falling back on the stereotypical representation of characters seen in Cultural Revolution writing, by the late 1980s the avant-garde, with its radical formal and linguistic experiments, questioned the values at the heart of socialist ideology. This gradual radicalization in the cultural sphere contributed to the 1989 protest movement.

Another significant phenomenon in the 1980s was the arrival on the mainland of Taiwan and Hong Kong commercial culture (film, pop music, television programs, and fiction). Qiong Yao 琼瑶 and San Mao 三毛—women writers of popular romance—led the way in the Taiwan literary invasion. Their novels and shorts stories were extremely popular on the mainland and helped usher in the commercialization of cultural production of the 1990s. Similarly, the liberalization led to the rediscovery of Republican era writers who had been banned during the Mao era, most notably Eileen Chang and Shen Congwen.

POST-TIANANMEN: THE RISE OF CONSUMER CULTURE (1989–)

The violent crackdown on the 1989 Tiananmen movement was followed by what Barmé (1999) describes as a "soft" cultural suppression. Wang Meng 王蒙 (b. 1934), an important writer of fiction in the 1980s who had risen in the cultural bureaucracy to become minister of culture, was removed from his post and, eventually, criticized for allowing cultural pluralism to flourish during his tenure. Conservative cultural figures crawled out of the woodwork and began to call for a return to the socialist culture that the late 1980s had so effectively erased. Some writers involved in the 1989 movement were arrested; others fled the country. Exile literature, or a literature of the PRC diaspora, emerged at this time: *Today* (今天), an underground journal associated with the Democracy Wall movement of 1978–1979, was resurrected abroad and became the leading venue for the publication of exile writing. Exiles also published in journals and newspapers in Hong Kong and Taiwan.

But by far the most significant phenomenon of the 1990s cultural scene was the commodification of culture (see "Commercialization of Literature in the Post-Mao Era"). Because of market reforms and the influx of capital from Taiwan and Hong Kong, PRC cultural institutions (journals, publishing houses, film studios, and the like) were forced to turn a profit and compete in the cultural marketplace. Some writers responded by popularizing their work. The literary figure who best embodies this commercialization is the novelist and scriptwriter Wang Shuo 王朔 (b. 1958). Credited with establishing *pizi wenxue* 痞子文学 or *liumang wenxue* 流氓文学 (punk literature), fiction about hooligans, punks, the laid-off, and the disenfranchised, Wang Shuo both made use of popular fiction forms and tapped into a social discontent that made him extremely popular with young readers, as well as with intellectuals. This is not to say that all writers succumbed to commercialization and gave in to popular culture. To the contrary, some poets have created a cult of poetry, an elite bastion from the relentless onslaught of commercial culture (Yeh 1996). Poets like Xi Chuan 西川 (b. 1963), for example, position themselves as purveyors of pure art against the stench of the popular (van Crevel 1999: 2008). Gao Xingjian 高行健

(b. 1940), who worked mostly in experimental theater until 1987, when he relocated to Paris, has over the years upheld a staunchly humanist view of literature as the voice of the individual and a vaguely Daoist-inspired belief that the artist should retreat from politics. In 2000, Gao became the first Chinese-language writer to win the Nobel Prize in Literature. Still other writers, such as Su Tong 苏童 (b. 1963) and Yu Hua 余华 (b. 1960), have attempted to negotiate a position somewhere between the avant-garde and the popular (Xu 2000). The protagonist in Jia Pingwa's 贾平凹 (b. 1952) controversial novel *City in Ruins* (废都, 1993), notorious for its explicit description of sex, is emblematic of intellectuals' struggle to find a new role in the rapidly changing society of 1990s China.

The 1990s also saw a return to realist fiction that both reflected and responded to the new market economy. Liu Heng 刘恒 (b. 1954), He Dun 何顿 (b. 1958), Chen Ran 陈染 (b. 1962), Qiu Huadong 邱华栋 (b. 1969), and others have created a new urban fiction that attempts to describe realistically the problems of living and coping in the freewheeling capitalism of postsocialist China, a stark change from the largely rural orientation of much socialist era writing. Other writers are more assertive in their social and political critique. Foremost among them is Yan Lianke 阎连科, whose "mythorealist" novels, such as *Dream of Ding Village* (丁庄梦) and *Lenin's Kisses* (受活), satirize the excesses of the market economy and its invasive exploitation of the poor and disenfranchised.

One of the most significant developments in recent literature on the mainland (and also in Taiwan and to a lesser extent Hong Kong) has been the emergence of Internet literature (Inwood 2014; Hockx 2015). China has arguably the most active and creative literary presence on the Internet of any nation. The Internet is both a vehicle for elite avant-garde poets to disseminate their work and argue over poetics and the meaning of poetry in an age of "mind, mayhem and money," as van Crevel (2008) puts it, and for the proliferation of popular-genre fiction, including such distinctive genres as time travel fiction and grave robbery fiction, as well as romance (Feng 2013) and science fiction. Writers like Han Han 韩寒 and Guo Jingming 郭敬明 (see "Commercialization of Literature in the Post-Mao Era") have first gained immense readerships online and then translated that capital into the more conventional world of print publication.

The granting of the Nobel Prize in Literature to Mo Yan 莫言 in 2012—greeted with glee by most in China and with scorn by some in the West who derided the writer as a CCP toady—reflects a new boon for contemporary Chinese literature outside China, where it has always had trouble reaching an audience through translation. Penguin has launched a translation series that is both reprinting Republican era fiction (for example, Lao She's 老舍 *Cat Country* [猫城记]) and introducing the work of younger writers (Sheng Keyi's 盛可以 *Northern Girls* [北妹]), and new translation journals such as *Pathlight* have been established to disseminate the work of young up-and-coming writers.

TAIWAN

Literature in Taiwan and Hong Kong developed along paths independent of, but not disconnected from, that of the mainland. Unlike the mainland, Taiwan and Hong Kong were colonies, the former of Japan and the latter of Britain. Taiwan (with Korea) was given over to Japanese control under treaty terms following the defeat in the 1894–1895 Sino-Japanese War. It remained under Japanese occupation until the end of World War II. Under the influence of the May Fourth movement and literary developments on the mainland, "new literature" emerged in Taiwan around 1924 and developed as a form of Chinese and Taiwanese nationalist resistance to Japanese colonialism. This first generation of modern writers, represented by Lai He 赖和 (1894–1943), was more Chinese than Taiwanese in its cultural consciousness (Chang 1999: 269). The next generation, having been educated primarily in Japanese, was more culturally hybrid. Many wrote in Japanese. *Kominka* (皇民化) literature, or literature written by Chinese in Japanese during the war years (1937–1945), has been conventionally treated very unkindly by Taiwan literary historians, who have equated it with political or cultural collaboration. Recently, however, some have begun to find in these texts subtle forms of agency and resistance to colonial oppression (Chang 1997). The colonial government banned Chinese-language publications outright during World War II.

Not long after the Japanese left Taiwan, the Nationalists, defeated by the CCP in the civil war on the mainland, retreated there. Many Taiwanese view this as yet another colonial occupation, especially after the GMD brutally suppressed a Taiwanese protest movement on February 28, 1947, which ushered in a period of four decades of martial law and the suppression of intellectual dissent. Those writers who had matured under Japanese colonialism and could write only in Japanese were now banned from writing in the language of the former colonizers, and it was only in the 1960s that Taiwanese writers would emerge in force on the literary scene. Not surprisingly, in the 1950s, mainlanders, writers who had come to Taiwan with the GMD, dominated. Because of GMD censorship, writers in Taiwan no longer had access to the leftist literary tradition of the previous three decades and had only the more lyrical strand of May Fourth writing (Xu Zhimo, Zhu Ziqing 朱自清, and others) as indigenous literary models. The GMD actively promoted anti-Communist literature and tolerated popular romances, which dominated the literary scene. T. A. Hsia upheld realism in the pages of the journal he edited, *Literary Review* (文学杂志, 1956–1960), but had difficulty attracting works for publication, as well as readers. In the politically repressive environment of the 1950s and 1960s, writers turned for inspiration to the West and to a particularly aesthetic form of Western modernism. The leading journal in the promotion of modernism was *Modern Literature* (现代文学, 1960–1973), founded by students of T. A. Hsia: Bai Xianyong 白先勇 (b. 1937), Wang Wenxing 王文兴 (b. 1939), Ouyang Zi

欧阳子 (b. 1939), and Chen Ruoxi 陈若曦 (b. 1938). The journal systematically introduced Western modernist writing and promoted experimentation in literary form (see "Cold War Fiction from Taiwan and the Modernists"). Nationalist critics attacked this modernism as empty imitation of the West. In defense of the modernist position, Wang Wenxing wrote:

> If someone would say that this Chinese effort to experiment with modernism betrays a mentality of adulating foreign things, we cannot tolerate [this charge]. Are Chinese not permitted to create new forms? . . . In the opinion of some people, Chinese cannot write psychological or symbolist fiction or novels of fantasy, nor should they experiment with surrealism or accept existentialism. These people are like fathers who forbid their children's activities—no ball-playing, no running, no singing, no riding bicycles, no listening to radios—all because of one reason: that they are foreign things. Dear reader, if you meet such a father, please give him some good advice.
>
> (in Faurot 1980: 16)

The criticism of modernist literature was in some sense a natural reaction to the Westernization of literature, but it was also the product of an abrupt shift in global politics. Nations around the world, including the United States, were beginning to recognize the government on the mainland as the sole legitimate "China," leaving Taiwan in a state of diplomatic limbo. This contributed to the Taiwanese nationalist movement, which in turn gave rise to a "nativist" (乡土) literature that was realist in its focus on rural Taiwan society and that attempted to capture in language and form a Taiwanese consciousness. The 1970s literary scene was dominated by such nativist writers as Huang Chunming 黄春明 (b. 1935), Wang Zhenhe 王祯和 (b. 1940), and Chen Yingzhen 陈映真 (b. 1937), though it should be stressed that the politics and literary styles of these writers varied greatly.

The lifting of martial law in 1987 and the remarkable democratization of Taiwan political life that followed has led to a heterogeneous literary scene. As in post-Mao China and contemporary Hong Kong, recent writing in Taiwan has become so varied as to undermine any attempts to impose on it neat literary categories. This heterogeneity has much to do with capitalism and the global commercialization of culture, as well as with a more general postmodern or postcolonial decentering of culture. Tied to an ever-changing and volatile market, writers have had to find a niche that makes them identifiable and marketable. Some writers, such as Li Yongping 李永平, have gone the avant-garde route taken by the likes of Su Tong, Ge Fei 格非, and Yu Hua on the mainland. Popular culture found its way into elite literature in the works of women writers such as Qiong Yao (b. 1938) and San Mao (1943–1991), whose romances were widely read in the 1980s and 1990s. Indeed, one characteristic of recent writing in Taiwan (and on the mainland) is the breakdown of clear distinctions between elite and popular literature. Others like Zhang Xiguo 张系国 have used satire to draw attention to problems in Taiwan's urban society. Although serious literature in Taiwan, as everywhere, faces the challenge of a marketplace dominated by popular, commercial culture, in its heterogeneity Taiwan literature has perhaps never been healthier.

Much Taiwan literature in the post-martial law era has sought to restore memories repressed by the Nationalist regime, most notably the February 28 (1947) Incident and the White Terror of the 1950s and 1960s. Rather than "counter" Nationalist era memory with a new monolithic memory, however, some writers have tended to problematize memory itself, stressing the difficult relationship between the present and the past and the inadequacy of writing to recapture the past (Braester 2007). Issues of identity—what it means to be Taiwanese—recur in post–martial law fiction and are often intertwined with questions of historical memory. The lifting of martial law has also led to the unleashing of voices of repressed social groups and the emergence of a self-conscious queer literature (see "Homoeroticism in Modern Chinese Literature"), aboriginal literature, and feminist fiction (for example, Li Ang 李昂 [b. 1952]).

HONG KONG

Hong Kong's cultural development, like Taiwan's, is inseparable from its colonial history and from its close proximity to the mainland. The British were colonial overlords of Hong Kong from the end of the Opium War (1839–1842) until 1997, when it "returned" to the mainland to much media fanfare. Unlike the Japanese in Taiwan, the British took a laissez-faire approach to the production of culture in Hong Kong (Tay 1995). Although some writers and editors were influenced by the new literature being produced on the mainland in the 1920s and 1930s and attempted to develop this realist, engaged literature in Hong Kong (the journal *Red Beans* [红豆, 1933] being its most important forum), writers who identified with tradition and traditional literary forms dominated the literary scene. This traditionalism was perhaps a product of the colonial environment: writers resisted the colonial government by asserting their Chineseness through upholding and recreating their literary tradition, but in its apolitical stance it was inherently conservative.

Over the years, Hong Kong has been greatly influenced by writers who came from either Taiwan or the mainland. An influx of writers from the mainland during the war against Japan and again during the civil war stirred up the literary scene, and Hong Kong became a hotbed of modern, often leftist, literature. Some critics argue that this period marks the real birth of Hong Kong modern literature, but this reflects a mainland-centric perspective. Many of these mainland writers stayed only temporarily, and Hong Kong did not figure substantially in their works. Others, such as Liu Yichang 刘以鬯 (b. 1918), an émigré from the mainland, and Yu Kwang-chung 余光中 (b. 1928), from Taiwan, integrated Hong Kong settings and issues of Hong Kong identity into their writing, and they have consequently been adopted as Hong Kong writers. The postwar period also saw the rise of martial arts fiction, whose most famous exemplar is the prolific Jin Yong 金庸.

Hong Kong's cultural scene flourished with the city's development as a major global metropolis in the 1970s. By the 1980s, new writing, much of it vaguely modernist in its experimentation with form, proliferated. Writers were beginning to concern themselves with issues of Hong Kong identity—what it means to live in a space that is neither Chinese nor British and is on the "margins" of the nation-state (see "Hong Kong Voices"). A Hong Kong-oriented literature developed further, ironically, following the 1984 agreement to return Hong Kong to the mainland in 1997. Writers such as Xi Xi 西西 (b. 1938), Dung Kai-cheung 董启章 (b. 1967), and Leung Ping-kwan 梁秉鈞 (1949–2013) self-consciously wrote about Hong Kong in their works. Leung's poetry collection *A City at the End of Time* (1992) beautifully conveys a sense of Hong Kong's spatial marginality—between the mainland and Taiwan—and its cultural hybridity—Chinese, colonial, British, cosmopolitan. "We need a fresh angle, / nothing added, nothing taken away, / always at the edge of things and between places," wrote Leung, expressing Hong Kong's search for identity in the postcolonial period. In some sense, Hong Kong's marginal status as a "city at the end of time" can be taken as a metaphor for the postmodern condition itself, a condition Hong Kong shares with both China and Taiwan. The outpouring of commemorations when Leung died in 2013 belies the myth that Hong Kongers care only about money, as does a movement to push the Hong Kong government to build a museum dedicated to the literature of Hong Kong.

The extent to which the "return" of Hong Kong to the mainland has affected the cultural sphere remains uncertain, but clearly a difficult transition is under way that involves negotiating between local interests and the mainland market. Events of 2013 and 2014 suggest that Hong Kongers generally will not stand silent as mainland shoppers, mainland culture, and mainland politics engulf their city. Indeed, writers have been active in local politics, in particular in struggles to preserve the historical heritage of Hong Kong's colonial past. Hong Kong writers are also reimagining Hong Kong identity in terms of their relations to the culture of the mainland, the British colonial past, and the culture of the rest of the world. Perhaps the larger threat to Hong Kong literature comes from the economic sphere and its neoliberal ideology of the market.

THE SINOPHONE AND THE GLOBAL

One of the most important trends in the study of modern Chinese literature to emerge in the past decade has been a move away from the nation-state as the principal lens through which to understand and appreciate literary developments. Shu-mei Shih (Shih, Tsai, and Bernards 2011) has led the way in emphasizing language—the "Sinophone" (see "Sinophone Literature")—as a new critical paradigm; others (Tsu and Wang 2010) have adopted the term "global Chinese literature" to stress the transnational nature of Chinese-language literary production and consumption. Such scholarship has drawn attention to writers working in Chinese who either live outside the mainland, Hong Kong, or Taiwan or who in their lives and in their works cross over national boundaries. Scholars have introduced the work of Malaysian writers writing in Chinese (Groppe 2013), for example, or applied a Sinophone or transnational framework to earlier writers, such as Lao She, Eileen Chang, and Lin Yutang 林语堂, who lived multicultural, transnational lives and embodied that experience in their writing. Though some have argued for the continuing importance of the nation-state (and its particular history and particular culture) as a lens for understanding Chinese-language literary development, the Sinophone/global offers a promising new critical framework that helps situate that literature in the larger context of the global flow of culture.

Bibliography

Note: For extensive bibliographies of translations and studies of modern Chinese literature, see the MCLC Resource Center (http://u.osu.edu/mclc).

Anderson, Marston. "Realism's Last Stand: Character and Ideology in Zhang Tianyi's *Three Sketches*." *Modern Chinese Literature* 5, 2 (Fall 1989): 179–196.

Barmé, Geremie. *In the Red: On Contemporary Chinese Culture*. New York: Columbia University Press, 1999.

Braester, Yomi. "Taiwanese Identity and the Crisis of Identity: Post-Chiang Mystery." In Wang and Rojas, ed., *Writing Taiwan: A New Literary History*, 213–232. Durham, NC: Duke University Press, 2007.

Chang, Sung-cheng Yvonne. "Beyond Cultural and National Identities: Current Reevaluation of the Kominka Literature from Taiwan's Japanese Period." *Journal of Modern Literature in Chinese* 1, 1 (1997): 75–107.

——. "Literature in Post-1949 Taiwan, 1950s to 1980s." In Murray A. Rubenstein, ed., *Taiwan: A New History*, 403–418. Armonk, NY: M. E. Sharpe, 1999.

——. *Modernism and Native Resistance: Contemporary Fiction from Taiwan*. Durham, NC: Duke University Press, 1993.

Chang, Sung-cheng Yvonne, Michelle Yeh, and Ming-ju Fan, eds. *The Columbia Sourcebook of Literary Taiwan*. New York: Columbia University Press, 2014.

Chow, Rey. *Woman and Chinese Modernity: The Politics of Reading Between West and East*. Minneapolis: University of Minnesota Press, 1991.

Chu, Yui-Wai. *Lost in Transition: Hong Kong Culture in the Age of China*. Albany: State University of New York Press, 2013.

Denton, Kirk A., ed. *Modern Chinese Literary Thought: Writings on Literature, 1893–1945*. Stanford, CA: Stanford University Press, 1996.

Denton, Kirk A., and Michel Hockx, eds. *Literary Societies of Republican China.* Lanham, MD: Lexington Books, 2008.

Doleželová-Velingerová, Milena, ed. *The Chinese Novel at the Turn of the Century.* Toronto: University of Toronto Press, 1980.

Faurot, Jeannette L. *Chinese Fiction from Taiwan: Critical Perspectives.* Bloomington: University of Indiana Press, 1980.

Feng, Jin. *Romancing the Internet: Consuming and Producing Chinese Web Romance.* Leiden: Brill, 2013.

Groppe, Alison. *Sinophone Malaysian Literature: Not Made in China.* Amherst, NY: Cambria Press, 2013.

Gunn, Edward. *Style and Innovation in Twentieth-Century Chinese Prose.* Stanford, CA: Stanford University Press, 1991.

Hayot, Eric. "Modernisms' Chinas: Introduction." *Modern Chinese Literature and Culture* 18, 1 (Spring 2006): 1–7.

Hill, Michael Gibbs. *Lin Shu Inc.: Translation and the Making of Modern Chinese Culture.* Oxford: Oxford University Press, 2013.

Hockx, Michel. *Internet Literature in China.* New York: Columbia University Press, 2015.

———. "Is There a May Fourth Literature? A Reply to Wang Xiaoming." *Modern Chinese Literature and Culture* 11, 2 (Fall 1999): 40–52.

———. "The Literary Association and the Literary Field of Early Republican China." *China Quarterly* 153 (March 1998): 49–81.

———. *Questions of Style: Literary Societies and Literary Journals in Modern China, 1911–1937.* Leiden: Brill, 2003.

———. *Snowy Morning: Eight Chinese Poets of Early Modern China.* Leiden: CNWS, 1994.

Hong, Zicheng. *A History of Contemporary Chinese Literature.* Trans. Michael Day. Leiden: Brill, 2007.

Hsia, T. A. *The Gate of Darkness: Studies on the Leftist Literary Movement.* Seattle: University of Washington Press, 1968.

Hung, Chang-tai. *War and Popular Culture: Resistance in Modern China, 1937–1945.* Berkeley: University of California Press, 1994.

Huot, Claire. *China's New Cultural Scene: A Handbook of Changes.* Durham, NC: Duke University Press, 2000.

Huters, Theodore. "From Writing to Literature: The Development of Late Qing Theories of Prose." *Harvard Journal of Asiatic Studies* 47, 1 (June 1987): 50–96.

———. "A New Way of Writing: The Possibility for Literature in Late Qing China, 1895–1908." *Modern China* 14, 3 (1988): 243–276.

Inwood, Heather. *Verse Going Viral: China's New Media Scenes.* Seattle: University of Washington Press, 2014.

Kaldis, Nicholas. *The Chinese Prose Poem: A Study of Lu Xun's* Wild Grass (Yecao). Amherst, NY: Cambria Press, 2014.

King, Richard. *Milestones on a Golden Road: Writing for Chinese Socialism, 1945–1980.* Vancouver: University of British Columbia Press, 2013.

Kinkley, Jeffrey, ed. *After Mao: Chinese Literature and Society, 1978–1981.* Cambridge, MA: Harvard University Council on East Asian Studies, 1985.

———. *Corruption and Realism in Late Socialist China: The Return of the Political Novel*. Stanford, CA: Stanford University Press, 2007.

Ko, Dorothy. *Teachers of the Inner Chambers: Women and Culture in Seventeenth-Century China*. Stanford, CA: Stanford University Press, 1994.

Larson, Wendy. *Literary Authority and the Modern Chinese Writer: Ambivalence and Autobiography*. Durham, NC: Duke University Press, 1991.

———. *Women and Writing in Modern China*. Stanford, CA: Stanford University Press, 1998.

Laughlin, Charles. *Chinese Reportage: The Aesthetics of Historical Experience*. Durham, NC: Duke University Press, 2002.

———. *The Literature of Leisure and Chinese Modernity*. Honolulu: University of Hawai'i Press, 2008.

Lee, Leo Ou-fan. "In Search of Modernity: Some Reflections on a New Mode of Consciousness in Twentieth-Century Chinese History and Literature." In Paul Cohen and Merle Goldman, eds., *Ideas Across Culture: Essays on Chinese Thought in Honor of Benjamin I. Schwartz*, 109–135. Cambridge, MA: Harvard University Council on East Asian Studies, 1990.

———. *The Romantic Generation of Modern Chinese Writers*. Cambridge, MA: Harvard University Press, 1973.

———. *Shanghai Modern: The Flowering of a New Urban Culture in China, 1930–1945*. Cambridge, MA: Harvard University Press, 1999.

Link, Perry. *Mandarin Ducks and Butterflies: Popular Fiction in Early Twentieth Century Chinese Cities*. Berkeley: University of California Press, 1981.

———. *The Uses of Literature: Life in the Socialist Chinese Literary System*. Princeton, NJ: Princeton University Press, 2000.

Liu, Lydia. *Translingual Practice: Literature, National Culture, and Translated Modernity—China, 1900–1937*. Stanford, CA: Stanford University Press, 1995.

Mann, Susan. *Precious Records: Women in China's Long Eighteenth Century*. Stanford, CA: Stanford University Press, 1997.

McDougall, Bonnie, and Kam Louie. *The Literature of China in the Twentieth Century*. London: Hurst, 1997.

Mittler, Barbara. *A Continuous Revolution: Making Sense of Cultural Revolution Culture*. Cambridge, MA: Harvard University Asia Center, 2012.

Shih, Shu-mei. *The Lure of the Modern: Writing Modernism in Semicolonial China, 1917–1937*. Berkeley: University of California Press, 2001.

Shih, Shu-mei, Chien-hsin Tsai, and Brian Bernards, eds. *Sinophone Studies: A Critical Reader*. New York: Columbia University Press, 2011.

Tang, Tao. *History of Modern Chinese Literature*. Beijing: Foreign Languages Press, 1993.

Tay, William. "Colonialism, the Cold War Era, and Marginal Space: The Existential Conditions of Four Decades of Hong Kong Literature." In Sung-sheng Yvonne Chang and Michelle Yeh, eds., *Contemporary Chinese Literature: Crossing the Boundaries*, 141–147. Austin, TX: Literature East and West, 1995.

Tsu, Jing, and David Der-wei Wang, eds. *Global Chinese Literature: Critical Essays*. Leiden: Brill, 2010.

van Crevel, Maghiel. *Chinese Poetry in Times of Mind, Mayhem, and Money*. Leiden: Brill, 2008.

———. "Xi Chuan's 'Salute': Avant-Garde Poetry in a Changing China." *Modern Chinese Literature and Culture* 11, 2 (Fall 1999): 107–149.

Wang, Ban. *The Sublime Figure of History: Aesthetics and Politics in Twentieth-Century China*. Stanford, CA: Stanford University Press, 1997.

Wang, David Der-wei. *Fictional Realism in Twentieth-Century China: Mao Dun, Lao She, Shen Congwen*. New York: Columbia University Press, 1992.

———. *Fin-de-Siècle Splendor: Repressed Modernities of Late Qing Fiction, 1849–1911*. Stanford, CA: Stanford University Press, 1997.

Wang, David Der-wei, and Carlos Rojas, eds. *Writing Taiwan: A New Literary History*. Durham, NC: Duke University Press, 2007.

Wang, Jing. *High Culture Fever: Politics, Aesthetics, and Ideology in Deng's China*. Berkeley: University of California Press, 1996.

Wang, Xiaoming. "A Journal and a Literary Society: A Reappraisal of the May Fourth Tradition." *Modern Chinese Literature and Culture* 11, 2 (Fall 1999): 1–39.

Wang Yao 王瑶. *Zhongguo xiandai wenxue shi gao* 中国现代文学史稿 (A draft history of new Chinese literature). Hong Kong: Bowen shuju, 1972 [1951].

Woesler, Martin, ed. *The Modern Chinese Literary Essay—Defining the Chinese Self in the 20th Century*. Bochum: Bochum University Press, 2000.

Xu, Jian. "*Blush* from Novella to Film: The Possibility of Critical Art in Commodity Culture." *Modern Chinese Literature and Culture* 12, 1 (Spring 2000): 115–163.

Yeh, Catherine Vance. *The Chinese Political Novel: Migration of a World Genre*. Cambridge, MA: Harvard University Asia Center, 2015.

Yeh, Michelle. "The 'Cult of Poetry' in Contemporary China." *Journal of Asian Studies* 55, 1 (1996): 51–80.

2

MODERN CHINESE LITERATURE AS AN INSTITUTION: CANON AND LITERARY HISTORY

YINGJIN ZHANG

Literary history is a reconstruction of the past in writing, an interpretative practice informed in varying degrees by the literary historian's chosen theoretical paradigm as well as his (rarely her in modern China) ideological purpose at a specific historical moment (Y. Zhang 1994: 348). Different artistic or ideological agendas, as well as changing sociopolitical circumstances, often determine the model of literary development and the selection of literary writers and works in literary histories.

The first phase of the formation of a modern Chinese literary history, from the 1920s to the 1940s, I call the "experimental phase." This phase is characterized by efforts to institute modern literature as a legitimate subject worthy of special attention due to its close tie to contemporary life. In 1922, Hu Shi 胡适 published a survey of Chinese literature from the previous fifty years and instituted an evolutionary paradigm by endorsing "new literature" (新文学) as "living literature" that would replace "dead" or "half-dead" classical literature (Hu Shi 1953: 165–166). Contrary to Hu's model of a linear development toward a certain telos, a new model emerged in 1934 when Zhou Zuoren 周作人 proposed a pattern of wavelike movement in which literature "conveys the Way" (文以载道) and literature as an "expression of intention" (言志) are two alternating currents that rise and fall with literary developments. With the publication of Wang Zhefu's 王哲甫 1933 history, Chinese literary historiography embarked on a genuine search for methodology. In subsequent years, most literary historians adopted Wang's narrative method of combining theoretical discussion, historical account, and detailed analysis of individual writers. Li Helin's 李何林 1939 book signaled the starting point from which issues of periodization and the ideological "nature" of modern Chinese literature became polemical. For Li, the first period began with the May Fourth movement (1919); all other periods were similarly demarcated by significant sociohistorical events, such as the Japanese invasions of Manchuria and Shanghai. Li's model implies that literary development is directly affected by historical events, which must be subject to correct political interpretation. Another notable work of this period is A Ying's 阿英 1937 study of late Qing fiction, which proposed a sociological model by classifying fiction along social themes and treating literature as "reflecting" social conditions.

Scholarship on modern Chinese literary history from the 1920s to the 1940s may be characterized as experimental in that it rarely aspired to a comprehensive coverage of all aspects of literary developments and sought, instead, to develop certain historical visions, theoretical paradigms, or narrative methods. In other words, a full-scale institutionalization of literary history was not attempted until after the founding of the People's Republic of China (PRC) in 1949, which marks the beginning of phase two in the formation of modern Chinese literary historiography. One immediate cause of the new efforts at canon formation was pedagogical: leading universities were in urgent need of curriculum material for their Chinese programs. The official release of the first volume of Wang Yao's 王瑶 comprehensive history in 1951 marked a founding moment in this sense. Wang Yao adopted Li Helin's periodization scheme and improved Wang Zhefu's methodology. Like Hu Shi before him, Wang Yao also implemented an evolutionary paradigm, but this time modern Chinese literature was shown to "progress" toward the ends legitimized by Mao Zedong's 1942 "Yan'an Talks"—namely, that literature must serve party politics and appeal to the masses.

In spite of its ideological orientation, Wang Yao's history was harshly criticized in 1952 for neglecting revolutionary writers and proletarian leadership, and official intervention led to the increasing politicization of modern Chinese literature. Ding Yi's 丁易 1955 history, which soon became available in English translation (Ding 1959), defined realism as the mainstream, integrated class analysis into its discussion, and clearly labeled writers as "revolutionary" (for example, Jiang Guangci 蒋光慈 and Hu Yepin 胡也频), "progressive" (for example, Lao She 老舍 and Ba Jin 巴金), and "bourgeois" (for example, Xu Zhimo 徐志摩 and Shen Congwen 沈从文). The prerogative of political correctness was evident in subsequent literary histories, such as Liu Shousong's 刘绶松 (1956), which reclassified writers into two opposing camps, the "enemy's" (敌) and "ours" (我) and devoted three chapters to Lu Xun 鲁迅, redefined as "a great Communist" writer. Compared with the experimental spirit that characterized the founding phase of literary historiography, the second phase in the PRC was marked by a monolithic voice and by extreme intolerance. For instance, women's writings and stories about private or "humanistic" concerns were denounced as petit bourgeois and written out of standard history. Toward the mid-1960s, only a handful of "revolutionary" writers (for example, Lu Xun, Guo Moruo 郭沫若, and Mao Dun 茅盾) survived rigid political scrutiny, and scholars such as Wang Yao and Liu Shousong were severely criticized during the Cultural Revolution (see sample criticisms collected in Wang Yao 1972).

The historiography of phase three focuses on canon revision, and its beginnings can be traced back to the 1970s. Outside the PRC, scholars slowly began to revise the canon set up by the Communist ideological apparatuses. While Li Huiying's 李辉英 history—published in Hong Kong in 1970—attempted to reclaim the tradition of intellectual openness of the first phase, Liu Xinhuang's 刘心皇—published in Taiwan—redirected attention to the New Literature movement and expanded coverage to include Taiwan literature. It was not until 1975–1978 that a substantial challenge to the Communist canon was posed by Sima Changfeng's 司马长风 three-volume history, which is distinguished by its meticulous documentation, its nonpartisan position, its wide selection of "marginal" writers and women writers (for example, Mu Shiying 穆时英 and Xu Xu 徐訏, or Luo Shu 罗淑 and Lin Huiyin 林徽因, respectively), and its organic model of literary development from "birth" through "fruition" to "decline" and "stagnancy." Although sharing Sima's pessimism by declaring that modern Chinese literature had turned into a "wasteland" by the 1960s, Zhou Jin 周锦 (1980: 9) nonetheless launched an ambitious forty-volume book series in 1980 with Taiwan Chengwen Books. The project covered or "rediscovered" neglected literary schools and societies (such as Crescent Moon), writers (for example, Qian Zhongshu 钱钟书, Xiao Hong 萧红, and Su Xuelin 苏雪林), and "conservative" intellectuals (for example, Lin Shu 林纾, Wu Mi 吴宓, and Mei Guangdi 梅光迪). The fact that Zhou Jin's series openly deals with the Creationists (many of them Communists), for instance, reveals the increasing freedom Taiwan scholars were allowed in the early 1980s.

The 1980s also witnessed a proliferation of literary histories in the PRC, most of them fruits of collective efforts, and nearly all of them intended for use as college textbooks. As represented by Tang Tao's 唐弢 three-volume work, this new crop of histories inherited certain "genetic" traits from its precursors, and periodization was strictly in accordance with the sociohistorical paradigm. Gradually, however, a revision of the canon was under way, particularly in the project of "rewriting literary history" (重写文学史) in the late 1980s (Y. Zhang 1994: 371). Three separate works by Beijing University professors are worth mentioning: Qian Liqun 钱理群 and his colleagues' 1987 history of modern literature reclaimed the tradition of intellectual openness, though political jargon still pops up from time to time; Chen Pingyuan's 陈平原 1989 history of late Qing fiction returned to A Ying's pioneering exploration of the late Qing as the beginning period of modern Chinese literature; and Yan Jiayan's 严家炎 1989 history of modern fiction recommended a new historiographic paradigm, one that traces the formation, divergence, and convergence of various literary schools or trends (流派) in modern China (see Y. Zhang 1991 for a review).

Two other points regarding literary historiography merit further attention. First, in the 1980s, periodization schemes were greatly loosened up, and starting dates of modern Chinese literature were pushed back to the late Qing (see D. Wang 1997). Second, from studies of literary schools initiated by Yan Jiayan and pursued by many others (for example, Shi Jianwei 1986), the Chinese modernism of the Beijing and Shanghai schools of the 1920s and 1930s, which had been proscribed in most previous PRC literary histories, emerged as a viable alternative to mainstream realism. Rather than grouping writers according to their alleged political or ideological affiliations, which had been the practice, literary historians paid more attention to other connections in terms of gender (for example, women writers), geographical area (for example, northeastern writers), and literary styles and themes (for example, the New Sensationists [新感觉派] and psychoanalytic fiction). To a great extent, Yang Yi's 杨义 three-volume history of modern Chinese fiction represents the best product of the canon revision taking place in this third phase of literary historiography, and Huang Xiuji's 黄修己 (1995) history of modern Chinese literary historiography provides an overview of major books, historians, and problems.

Starting around the turn of the twenty-first century, phase four tends to favor diversification. Multivolume textbooks of literary history have appeared in greater numbers in the PRC, and some new concepts have been proposed. A 1,991-page general history coedited by Zhu Defa 朱德发 and Wei Jian 魏建 (2012) constructs "a singular system of heterogeneities" (多元一体) and tracks its transformation over three extended periods, 1900–1929, 1930–1976, and 1977–2010, as represented by major modes (形态) of literature shaped by four contending types of culture—political, new wave, traditional, and commercial. Chen Sihe's 陈思和 textbook (1999) integrated new keywords—"multidimension" (多层面), "concealed writing" (潜在写作), "folk realm" (民间), and "consensus" (共名) versus "nonconsensus" (无名)—to reinterpret contemporary Chinese literature. Like Zhu Defa's and Wei Jian's history, Chen Sihe's book offers close readings of individual works as case studies. Similarly searching for new conceptualization, Chen Xiaoming's 陈晓明 history of contemporary Chinese literature (2013) emphasizes modernity (in particular socialist modernity) and historicization (including rehistoricization and dehistoricization) in his depiction of a literary mainstream from Mao's Yan'an Talks to current diversification in the postliterary era. Tao Dongfeng's 陶东风 and He Lei's 和磊 history of thirty years of literature in the new era (1978–2008) delineates a clear picture of diversification by tracing the movement from "eliticization" (精英化)—as in modernist poetry and avant-garde fiction—to "de-eliticization" (去精英化)—as in hooligan (痞子) literature, parodist (大话) writing, and body writing (身体写作). In general, in phase four, historical research on contemporary literature seems to be livelier than that on modern literature because the former covers over sixty years and its ongoing development in the age of globalization offers more possibilities for diversification.

LITERARY HISTORY OF TAIWAN AND HONG KONG

In quantity and quality, scholarship on Taiwan and Hong Kong literatures pales in comparison to that for mainland literature. This unfortunate situation may have resulted not just from the geopolitically (though not economically) marginal status of Taiwan and Hong Kong but also from other factors, such as the Nationalist Guomindang (GMD) government's investment in the revival of traditional Chinese culture in Taiwan and the British colonial government's discouragement of reflections on local culture and history in Hong Kong.

In spite of the flourishing of "nativist literature" (乡土文学), modernist poetry, and popular fiction (for example, Qiong Yao 琼瑶), the history of Taiwan literature did not receive much scholarly attention until the 1970s. Chen Shaoting's 陈少廷 1977 work represents one of the earliest book-length treatments of the subject. Years of archival research and critical discussion have made the picture of the Japanese colonial period—when writers published in both Chinese and Japanese—clearer. In a 1987 history of Taiwan literature, Ye Shitao 叶石涛, a long-time advocate for nativist literature, starts his discussion with the influence of traditional Chinese literature on the island and the development of the New Literature movement in the 1920s and the 1930s. Ye periodizes the years from the 1940s to the 1980s by decade and examines literary and sociohistorical events. A development from the 1990s was the debate on Taiwanese identity, with scholars drawing on theories of postmodernism and postcolonialism to inform their historical research. One example is Chen Fangming 陈芳明, whose *Postcolonial Taiwan* (2002) includes his view of the peculiar position of Eileen Chang (Zhang Ailing 张爱玲) in Taiwan literature and his three replies (2000–2001) to Chen Yingzhen 陈映真, a Taiwan nativist writer who had repeatedly criticized Chen Fangming's de-Sinicization position a decade before publication of the latter's *New History of Taiwan Literature* (2011). Two other books deserve special attention: *Rewriting Taiwanese Literary History* (2006), edited by Zhang Jinzhong 张锦忠 and Huang Jinshu 黄锦树, collects articles on topics such as identity, diaspora, and Sinophone literature; and *Essays on the History of Taiwan Fiction* (2007), coauthored by Chen Jianzhong 陈建忠 and four other scholars, revisits the colonial period, the 1950s, the 1960s–1980s, and post–martial law fiction.

Several histories of Taiwan literature have been published in the PRC, among which Gu Jitang's 古继堂 *History of the Development of New Poetry in Taiwan* (1989) also appeared in a Taiwan edition. Like Ye Shitao, Gu also adopts decades as his periodizing scheme and surveys the rise of fiction in Taiwan (for example, Lai He 赖和 as "Taiwan's Lu Xun"), its uneven developments through anti-Communist fiction of the 1950s, modernist fiction of the 1960s, nativist fiction of the 1970s, and diversification in the 1980s. As is true of most other PRC histories, the two-volume history compiled by Liu Denghan 刘登翰 and his associates in 1991 aspires to a comprehensive treatment, tracing roots to ancient Taiwanese culture, to the oral literature of the aboriginals, through the Ming and Qing dynasties, to the early occupation period.

In the United States, relatively few book-length studies of Taiwan literary history are available. Years after Jeannette Faurot's collection of critical studies (1980), Yvonne Chang contributed two books, *Modernism and the Nativist Resistance* (1993) and *Literary Culture in Taiwan* (2004), covering the transition, in her words, "from martial law to market law." Chang and her collaborators (2014) have also published a valuable sourcebook of English translations of primary sources related to the history of Taiwan literature. As with her Taiwan counterparts, Emma Teng moves back to the colonial period by tracing early travel writings in *Taiwan's Imagined Geography* (2004). A more ambitious project on literary history is David Wang and Carlos Rojas's *Writing Taiwan* (2007), a collection of essays that as a whole offer a broad vision of Taiwan literature and an in-depth examination of critical issues in a fashion similar to that of the volume coedited by Pang-yuan Chi and David Wang (2000), which covers the second half of the twentieth century but does not focus solely on Taiwan.

Even more underdeveloped than research on Taiwan literary history is research on the history of Hong Kong literature. According to Leung Ping-kwan, a noted Hong Kong poet and scholar, only in the 1990s did the study of Hong Kong literature emerge with the appearance of book-length studies, yet most are "compiled by mainland Chinese scholars" and informed by "a predominantly mainland Chinese perspective" (Leung 1998: 78). One such example is Yuan Liangjun's 袁良骏 *History of Hong Kong Fiction* (1999).

DEVELOPMENTS IN THE WEST

In 1961, C. T. Hsia published the first history of modern Chinese fiction written in English and explained that his "main intention has been to contradict rather than affirm the communist view of modern Chinese fiction" (Hsia 1961: 498). Focusing on the art of individual writers, Hsia elevated Shen Congwen, Eileen Chang, Qian Zhongshu, and Shi Tuo 师陀 to a level comparable to, if not better than, PRC canonized writers such as Lu Xun, Mao Dun, Lao She, and Ba Jin. Hsia's radical challenge to the PRC canon triggered a polemical exchange between him and Jaroslav Průšek over the ideological functions of literature and literary study (Průšek 1961; Hsia 1963; see Y. Zhang 1993: 820–821). From his firm Marxist stance, Průšek denounces Hsia's preference for minor writers over socially committed masters. Although Hsia's author-centered approach to literary history might have influenced Leo Ou-fan Lee's (1973) study of the romantic generation of Chinese writers, Hsia's interest in New Criticism finds echoes in Edward Gunn's (1980) close readings of some "minor" writers—labeled as "unwelcome muses"—marginalized by PRC scholars for years. Perhaps not originally intended as such, Perry Link's (1981) study of popular urban fiction of the Butterfly school has also challenged the rigid divide between "serious literature" and popular urban culture. In fact, decades later, images of the city and urban culture have come to great prominence in literary-historical research (Y. Zhang 1996; Lee 1999; Shih 2001; DesForges 2007; Visser 2010), and the blurring of high and low culture has legitimized the inclusion of late Qing fiction (D. Wang 1997), as well as martial arts fiction (Huss and Liu 2007), and has fundamentally changed the institution of literary history in modern China. This revisionism has even led to the inclusion of classical-style poetry (Wu 2014) (see "Between Tradition and Modernity") in the purview of modern Chinese literature.

Other works contributed to the paradigm shift during the 1990s. Marston Anderson (1990) interrogates the canonical practice of realism in modern Chinese literature by revealing the social and moral impediments to pure representation, whereas Rey Chow (1991) proceeds from the margins of literary history and redirects attention to textual details that challenge entrenched habits of interpretation in modern Chinese literature. Although itself more a critical intervention than a historical study, Lydia Liu's 1995 book seeks to replace the influence model of comparative literature with one squarely situated in modern Chinese history. Also related to literary history of modern China is Kirk Denton's 1996 anthology of modern Chinese literary criticism, which contains an extensive introduction to major problematics in literary study from 1893 to 1945. In the new century, a more comprehensive historical landscape has taken shape as scholars have moved to address previously ignored or neglected subjects, such as literary journals and schools (Hockx 2003; Denton and Hockx 2008), literary genres like autobiography (L. Wang 2004) and the prose essay (Laughlin 2008), and marginalized writers like Jin Yong 金庸 (Hamm 2005), Lin Yutang 林语堂 (S. Qian 2011), and Zhou Zuoren (Daruvala 2000), as well as Sinophone or global Chinese literature (Shih 2007; Tsu and Wang 2010).

However, despite an increasing number of English books on modern Chinese literature, the only ambitious historical survey in English to follow Hsia's is the 1997 book coauthored by Bonnie McDougall and Kam Louie, which while wide-ranging in its coverage, including poetry and drama from 1900 to 1989, is nevertheless limited by its lack of in-depth critical analysis of representative writers and works. Individual chapters on modern Chinese literature are included in two general histories of Chinese literature (Mair 2001; Chang and Owen 2010: vol. 2), but for a single-volume history of modern Chinese literature we have David Wang's edition (forthcoming) in Harvard's new literary history series and the present *Columbia Companion to Modern Chinese Literature*. Literary history is an ongoing project of constructing the past in literary production and reception. As a result, canon formation and revision is an open-ended process through which generations of literary critics and historians compete in verifying evidence, supplying interpretations, and negotiating their own production and distribution of knowledge and power.

Bibliography

A Ying 阿英. *Wan Qing xiaoshuo shi* 晚清小说史 (A history of late Qing fiction). Beijing: Renmin wenxue, 1980 [originally published in 1937].

Anderson, Marston. *The Limits of Realism: Chinese Fiction in the Revolutionary Period*. Berkeley: University of California Press, 1990.

Chang, Kang-i Sun, and Stephen Owen, eds. *The Cambridge History of Chinese Literature*. 2 vols. New York: Cambridge University Press, 2010.

Chang, Sung-cheng Yvonne. *Literary Culture in Taiwan: Martial Law to Market Law*. New York: Columbia University Press, 2004.

——. *Modernism and the Nativist Resistance: Contemporary Fiction from Taiwan*. Durham, NC: Duke University Press, 1993.

Chang, Sung-cheng Yvonne, Michelle Yeh, and Ming-ju Fan, eds. *The Columbia Sourcebook of Literary Taiwan*. New York: Columbia University Press, 2014.

Chen Fangming 陈芳明. *Houzhimin Taiwan: wenxue shilun jiqi zhoubian* 后殖民台湾：文学史论及其周边 (Postcolonial Taiwan: Essays on literary history and its periphery). Taipei: Maitian, 2002.

——. *Taiwan xin wenxue shi* 台湾新文学史 (New history of Taiwan literature). 2 vols. Taipei: Lianjing, 2011.

Chen Jianzhong 陈建忠, Ying Fenghuang 应凤凰, Qiu Guifen 邱贵芬, Zhang Songsheng 张颂圣, and Liu Liangya 刘亮雅. *Taiwan xiaoshuo shilun* 台湾小说史论 (Essays on the history of Taiwan fiction). Taipei: Maitian, 2007.

Chen Pingyuan 陈平原. *Ershi shiji Zhongguo xiaoshuo shi* 二十世纪中国小说史 (A history of twentieth-century Chinese fiction), vol. 1. Beijing: Beijing daxue, 1989.

Chen Shaoting 陈少廷. *Taiwan xin wenxue yundong jianshi* 台湾新文学运动简史 (A concise history of the new literary movement in Taiwan). Taipei: Lianjing, 1977.

Chen Sihe 陈思和, ed. *Zhongguo dangdai wenxue shi jiaocheng* 中国当代文学史教程 (Textbook history of contemporary Chinese literature). 2nd ed. Shanghai: Fudan daxue, 1999.

Chen Xiaoming 陈晓明. *Zhongguo dangdai wenxue zhuchao* 中国当代文学主潮 (Major trends in contemporary Chinese literature). 2nd ed. Beijing: Beijing daxue, 2013.

Chen Zhaoying 陈昭瑛. *Taiwan wenxue yu bentuhua yundong* 台湾文学与本土化运动 (Taiwan literature and the nativization movement). Taipei: Zhengzhong shuju, 1998.

Chi, Pang-yuan, and David Der-wei Wang, eds. *Chinese Literature in the Second Half of a Modern Century: A Critical Survey*. Bloomington: Indiana University Press, 2000.

Chow, Rey. *Woman and Chinese Modernity: The Politics of Reading Between West and East*. Minneapolis: University of Minnesota Press, 1991.

Chow, Tse-tsung. *The May Fourth Movement: Intellectual Revolution in Modern China*. Cambridge, MA: Harvard University Press, 1960.

Daruvala, Susan. *Zhou Zuoren and an Alternative Chinese Response to Modernity*. Cambridge, MA: Harvard University Asia Center, 2000.

Denton, Kirk A., ed. *Modern Chinese Literary Thought: Writings on Literature, 1893–1945*. Stanford, CA: Stanford University Press, 1996.

Denton, Kirk A., and Michel Hockx, eds. *Literary Societies of Republican China*. Lanham, MD: Lexington Books, 2008.

DesForges, Alexander. *Mediasphere Shanghai: The Aesthetics of Cultural Production*. Honolulu: University of Hawai'i Press, 2007.

Ding Yi. *A Short History of Modern Chinese Literature*. Beijing: Foreign Languages Press, 1959.

——. 丁易. *Zhongguo xiandai wenxue shilüe* 中国现代文学史略 (A brief history of modern Chinese literature). Beijing: Zuojia, 1955.

Faurot, Jeannette L. *Chinese Fiction from Taiwan: Critical Perspectives*. Bloomington: University of Indiana Press, 1980.

Goldman, Merle, ed. *Modern Chinese Literature in the May Fourth Era*. Cambridge, MA: Harvard University Press, 1977.

Gu Jitang 古继堂. *Taiwan xiaoshuo fazhan shi* 台湾小说发展史 (A history of the development of Taiwan fiction). Taipei: Wenshizhe, 1989.

——. *Taiwan xinshi fazhan shi* 台湾新诗发展史 (A history of the development of new poetry in Taiwan). Taipei: Wenshizhe, 1989.

Gunn, Edward. *Unwelcome Muse: Chinese Literature in Shanghai and Peking, 1937–1945*. New York: Columbia University Press, 1980.

Hamm, John Christopher. *Paper Swordsmen: Jin Yong and the Modern Chinese Martial Arts Novel*. Honolulu: University of Hawai'i Press, 2005.

Hockx, Michel. *Questions of Style: Literary Societies and Literary Journals in Modern China, 1911–1937*. Boston: Brill, 2003.

Hsia, C. T. *A History of Modern Chinese Fiction*. New York: Columbia University Press, 1971 [1961].

——. "On the 'Scientific' Study of Modern Chinese Literature: A Reply to Professor Prušek." *T'oung Pao* 50, 4–5 (1963): 428–474.

Hu Shi 胡适. *Wushinian lai Zhongguo zhi wenxue* 五十年来中国之文学 (Chinese literature in the past fifty years). Taipei: Yuandong tushu, 1953 [1922].

Huang Xiuji 黄修己. *Zhongguo xin wenxue shi bianzuan shi* 中国新文学史编纂史 (A history of the historiography of modern Chinese literature). Beijing: Beijing daxue, 1995.

Huss, Ann, and Jianmei Liu, eds. *The Jin Yong Phenomenon: Chinese Martial Arts Fiction and Modern Chinese Literary History*. Youngstown, NY: Cambria Press, 2007.

Laughlin, Charles A. *The Literature of Leisure and Chinese Modernity*. Honolulu: University of Hawai'i Press, 2008.

Lee, Leo Ou-fan. *The Romantic Generation of Modern Chinese Writers*. Cambridge, MA: Harvard University Press, 1973.

——. *Shanghai Modern: The Flowering of a New Urban Culture in China, 1930–1945*. Cambridge, MA: Harvard University Press, 1999.

Leung Ping-kwan. "Two Discourses on Colonialism: Huang Guliu and Eileen Chang." *boundary 2* 25, 3 (1998): 77–96.

Li Helin 李何林. *Jin ershinian Zhongguo wenyi sichao lun* 近二十年中国文艺思潮论 (An essay on Chinese ideological currents in literature and arts over the past twenty years). Xi'an: Shanxi renmin, 1981 [1939].

Li Huiying 李辉英. *Zhongguo xiandai wenxue shi* 中国现代文学史 (A history of modern Chinese literature). Hong Kong: Dongya shuju, 1970.

Link, Perry. *Mandarin Ducks and Butterflies: Popular Fiction in Early Twentieth Century Chinese Cities*. Berkeley: University of California Press, 1981.

Liu Denghan 刘登翰, Zhuang Mingxuan 庄明萱, Huang Chongtian 黄重添, and Lin Chenghuang 林承璜, eds. *Taiwan wenxue shi* 台湾文学史 (A history of Taiwan literature). 2 vols. Fuzhou: Haixia wenyi, 1991.

Liu, Lydia. *Translingual Practice: Literature, National Culture, and Translated Modernity—China, 1900–1937*. Stanford, CA: Stanford University Press, 1995.

Liu Shousong 刘绶松. *Zhongguo xin wenxue shi chugao* 中国新文学史初稿 (A draft history of new Chinese literature). 2 vols. Beijing: Renmin wenxue, 1979 [1956].

Liu Xinhuang 刘心皇. *Xiandai Zhongguo wenxue shihua* 现代中国文学史话 (A history of modern Chinese literature). Taipei: Zhengzhong shuju, 1971.

Mair, Victor H., ed. *The Columbia History of Chinese Literature*. New York: Columbia University Press, 2001.

McDougall, Bonnie, and Kam Louie. *The Literature of China in the Twentieth Century*. London: Hurst, 1997.

Průšek, Jaroslav. "Basic Problems of the History of Modern Chinese Literature and C. T. Hsia, *A History of Modern Chinese Fiction*." *T'oung Pao* 49, 4–5 (1961): 357–404.

Qian Liqun 钱理群, Wu Fuhui 吴福辉, Wen Rumin 温儒敏, and Wang Chaobing 王超冰. *Zhongguo xiandai wenxue sanshinian* 中国现代文学三十年 (Three decades in modern Chinese literature). Shanghai: Shanghai wenyi, 1987.

Qian, Suoqiao. *Liberal Cosmopolitan: Lin Yutang and Middling Chinese Modernity*. Boston: Brill, 2011.

Shi Jianwei 施建伟. *Zhongguo xiandai wenxue liupai lun* 中国现代文学流派论 (On literary schools in modern Chinese literature). Xi'an: Shanxi renmin, 1986.

Shih, Shu-mei. *The Lure of the Modern: Writing Modernism in Semicolonial China, 1917–1937*. Berkeley: University of California Press, 2001.

——. *Visuality and Identity: Sinophone Articulations Across the Pacific*. Berkeley: University of California Press, 2007.

Sima Changfeng 司马长风. *Zhongguo xin wenxue shi* 中国新文学史 (A history of new Chinese literature). 3 vols. Hong Kong: Shaomin, 1975–1978.

Tang Tao 唐弢, ed. *Zhongguo xiandai wenxue shi* 中国现代文学史 (A history of modern Chinese literature). 3 vols. Beijing: Renmin wenxue, 1979–1980.

Tao Dongfeng 陶东风 and He Lei 和磊. *Zhongguo xinshiqi wenxue 30 nian* 中国新时期文学30年 (Chinese literature of the new era, 1978–2008). Beijing: Zhongguo shehui kexue, 2008.

Teng, Emma Jinhua. *Taiwan's Imagined Geography: Chinese Colonial Travel Writing and Pictures, 1683–1895*. Cambridge, MA: Harvard University Asia Center, 2004.

Tsu, Jing, and David Der-wei Wang, eds. *Global Chinese Literature: Critical Essays*. Boston: Brill, 2010.

Visser, Robin. *Cities Surround the Countryside: Urban Aesthetics in Post-Socialist China*. Durham, NC: Duke University Press, 2010.

Wang, David Der-wei. *Fictional Realism in Twentieth-Century China: Mao Dun, Lao She, Shen Congwen*. New York: Columbia University Press, 1992.

——. *Fin-de-Siècle Splendor: Repressed Modernities of Late Qing Fiction, 1849–1911*. Stanford, CA: Stanford University Press, 1997.

——, ed. *Harvard Literary History of Modern China*. Cambridge, MA: Harvard University Press, forthcoming.

Wang, David Der-wei, and Carlos Rojas, eds. *Writing Taiwan: A New Literary History*. Durham, NC: Duke University Press, 2007.

Wang, Lingzhen. *Personal Matters: Women's Autobiographical Practice in Twentieth-Century China*. Stanford, CA: Stanford University Press, 2004.

Wang Yao 王瑶. *Zhongguo xin wenxue shigao* 中国新文学史稿 (A draft history of new Chinese literature). Hong Kong: Bowen shuju, 1972 [1951].

Wang Zhefu 王哲甫. *Zhongguo xin wenxue yundong shi* 中国新文学运动史 (A history of the movements of new Chinese literature). Beijing: Jiecheng yinshuju, 1933.

Wu, Shengqing. *Modern Archaics: Continuity and Innovation in the Chinese Lyric Tradition, 1900–1937*. Cambridge, MA: Harvard University Asia Center, 2014.

Yan Jiayan 严家炎. *Zhongguo xiandai xiaoshuo liupai shi* 中国现代小说流派史 (A history of the schools of modern Chinese fiction). Beijing: Renmin wenxue, 1989.

Yang Yi 杨义. *Zhongguo xiandai xiaoshuo shi* 中国现代小说史 (A history of modern Chinese fiction). 3 vols. Beijing: Remin wenxue, 1986–1991.

Ye Shitao 叶石涛. *Taiwan wenxue shigang* 台湾文学史纲 (A history of Taiwan literature). Taipei: Wenxuejie zazhishe, 1987.

Yuan Liangjun 袁良骏. *Xianggang xiaoshuo shi* 香港小说史 (History of Hong Kong fiction). Shenzhen: Haitian, 1999.

Zhang Jinzhong 张锦忠 and Huang Jinshu 黄锦树, eds. *Chongxie Taiwan wenxue shi* 重写台湾文学史 (Rewriting Taiwanese literary history). Taipei: Maitian, 2006.

Zhang, Yingjin. *The City in Modern Chinese Literature and Film: Configurations of Space, Time, and Gender*. Stanford, CA: Stanford University Press, 1996.

——. "Four Recent Histories of Modern Chinese Fiction in the PRC." *Journal of Asian Studies* 50, 4 (1991): 923–925.

——. "The Institutionalization of Modern Literary History in China, 1922–1980." *Modern China* 20, 3 (1994): 347–377.

——. "Re-envisioning the Institution of Chinese Literary Studies: Strategies of Positionality and Self-Reflexivity." *positions* 1, 3 (1993): 816–832.

Zhou Jin 周锦. *Zhongguo xinwenxue jianshi* 中国新文学简史 (A concise history of new Chinese literature). Taipei: Chengwen, 1980.

Zhou Zuoren 周作人. *Zhongguo xinwenxue zhi yuanliu* 中国新文学之源流 (The sources of new Chinese literature). Beijing: Renwen shudian, 1934.

Zhu Defa 朱德发 and Wei Jian 魏建, eds. *Xiandai Zhongguo wenxue tongjian, 1900–2010* 现代中国文学通鉴 1900–2010 (General history of modern Chinese literature). 3 vols. Beijing: Renmin, 2012.

3

LANGUAGE AND LITERARY FORM

CHARLES LAUGHLIN

Modern Chinese literature emerged from a more general, sweeping cultural transformation that spanned the last decades of the Qing dynasty to the aftermath of World War I (roughly 1841–1921). This transformation was initiated largely by late Qing literati influenced by Western thought and deeply concerned about China's survival in a hostile, competitive world. In part because it was traditionally the literati who guided and governed the nation, the responses they offered to this crisis were more often intellectual than practical. The transformation culminated in the May Fourth movement, which in many ways defined the character of Chinese cultural modernity, and its principal achievements were the establishment of a standard written vernacular language, *baihuawen* (白话文), and the launching of a new Chinese literature, under the influence of European forms, that used this language as a vehicle. The standardization of *baihua* led to some unforeseen rigidity under the influence of leftism, nationalism, and war, but the inherent diversity of the Chinese language returned to fracture this conformity and bring about unprecedented formal innovation.

ESTABLISHING THE LANGUAGE AND FORMS OF MODERN WRITING

During the 1890s, the first attempts were made in literature and education to develop and use some sort of modern written vernacular language, as well as to standardize the spoken language (Doleželová-Velingerová 1977: 19–22). The classical or literary language, *wenyan* (文言), that served as the only written medium for official purposes had changed little over two millennia. It was vastly different from modern spoken Chinese in both structure and vocabulary and very difficult to learn. Moreover, many literati decried the artificiality of formal prose, the principal mode of written expression in the late imperial period. This genre had been nicknamed "eight-legged essay" (八股文) for its tight formal constraints, and the term continued to be used throughout the twentieth century to refer to slavish adherence to literary formulas and stereotypes. However, the absence of clear alternatives to *wenyan* made the development of a practical modern written language a long and difficult process.

As early as the medieval period a written vernacular much closer to the language of speech began to appear in popular literature (Buddhist sutras and short stories based on the performances of professional storytellers), and continued to develop especially in fiction and drama of the Ming and Qing dynasties. However, it was not until the end of the nineteenth century that education reformers and publishers began to publish *baihua* journals and primers on practical matters—especially for women and others just learning to read. At the same time, a group of poets emerged who attempted to combine a greatly simplified style with lively emotional, political, and social content (see "The Late Qing Poetry Revolution"). Although the still classical idiom of this poetry halted its development at the turn of the century, one of its practitioners—Liang Qichao 梁启超—turned his attention to other strategies for achieving linguistic and literary modernity.

Liang Qichao played a crucial role in linking the educational, political, and literary uses of *baihua* (see "The Uses of Fiction"). Educated in both traditional Chinese and modern European cultures, Liang was convinced that the key to cultural modernization and national strength lay in the publishing industry, in the newspaper in particular. Newspapers published by foreign missions and businesspeople had existed in treaty ports and foreign concessions throughout most of the nineteenth century; even the earliest of these modified *wenyan* by simplifying the structure and using a limited vocabulary. Observing this phenomenon and its influence, Liang Qichao entered the publishing industry, but with a nationalist mission: his newspapers would educate and enlighten their readers to become informed citizens who would help build a strong, modern China. To this end, he developed a hybrid of *wenyan* and *baihua*—called "new style prose," or 新文体—that was a more lucid means of expression than other turn-of-the-century prose forms and became the standard for newspaper Chinese for more than a generation. In addition, he joined with other prominent modernizers such as Xia Zengyou 夏曾佑 and Yan Fu 严复 to do something that would set the course of modern Chinese literature for most of the twentieth century: he promoted the use of political fiction in the popular press for the civic indoctrination of readers.

There was also experimentation with European-style poetry and drama in the 1890s (see "Performing the Nation") and 1900s, but by the 1920s fiction came to dominate modern Chinese letters. According to one literary history, the predominance of fiction over poetry and drama was intimately tied up with matters of language and form (Doleželová-Velingerová 1977: 26–31). Attempts to modernize drama were hampered by the tradition of performing in regional dialects, whereas poetry was mired in a formal legacy antithetical to vernacular expression. Late imperial fiction, however, had already been developing for two centuries in the direction advocated by the literary reformers and had a readership much broader than that of purely elite essays and poetry. By the last decades of the Qing, traditional-style novels had already incorporated themes of social critique and were often conceived by their writers as a means of public indoctrination, so as a mode of expression the novel fit right in to the ambitions of turn-of-the-century advocates of new literature.

The "literary revolution" of 1917 and the ensuing New Culture movement attempted to go much further: leading intellectuals like Hu Shi 胡适 and Chen Duxiu 陈独秀 advocated the complete abandonment of *wenyan* and set the unification of writing and speech as one of the stylistic goals of modern literature. The May Fourth movement merged with the New Culture movement and established a role for these modern intellectual reformers at the forefront of social change and at the center of a new literary arena. Translation of Western literature and creation of a new, modern vernacular literature became the principal concerns of writers in the 1920s. This set the stage for the emergence of modern China's first major writers, Lu Xun 鲁迅, Ye Shengtao 叶圣陶, and Bing Xin 冰心, as well as China's first important modern literary organization, the Literary Association (文学研究会).

Within fiction, realism took on the role of an almost ideological norm. The preference for fictional realism reveals much about the adoption of the vernacular language and what was at stake. Despite the earnest passion to modernize literature, language, and society, there was still a very traditional faith that the proper form of writing would capture the truth immanent in reality. Literature was viewed less as creative expression than as a vehicle for authors to bring their readers closer to the truth; the adoption of fictional realism was a modern phase of this age-old concern, a phase that dominated the first half of this century.

THE ENTRENCHMENT OF REVOLUTIONARY LANGUAGE AND FORM

The written vernacular of the May Fourth writers reflected their education and their social profile. It was not long before writers with revolutionary dreams of uniting with the broad masses of common people began to feel that this new vernacular was still too sophisticated to serve the needs of the general population. By the mid-1920s, further transformation was called for to forge an even more common and popular vernacular idiom. Qu Qiubai 瞿秋白 was one of the most outspoken and radical advocates of the "massification" (大众化) of the modern language and its literature (Pickowicz 1977). As left-wing writers multiplied and influenced the literary mainstream, the League of Left-Wing Writers (左翼作家联盟, est. 1930) helped direct the process by promoting activities and forums that would bring modern literature closer to the working class, linguistically and otherwise. This massification effort also involved experimentation with new forms like reportage and "wall newspapers" (壁报) in order to educate the working class and make its members not only consumers of literature but also producers in their own right.

The war against Japan (1937–1945) gave leftists the opportunity to exploit widespread anti-Japanese sentiment to popularize their literary initiatives, with their only cost being toning down the less popular themes of class struggle and social critique. Inasmuch as business as usual in the publishing industry became impossible, especially after the November 1937 fall of Shanghai, headquarters of the Chinese publishing industry, the war made unique new demands on writers. The idea that literature was a weapon for struggle gained greater popularity, and its propaganda potential became more important, at least in the short term, than issues of literary quality. The demand for moral seriousness in literature, formerly met with soul-searching complexity and profundity of thought, was under these conditions met by the sincere determination to use literature as a weapon to help resist Japan's invasion. Now even more than in the revolutionary phase of the late 1920s and early 1930s, the audience of contemporary literature had to be maximized, expanded throughout the broad public, even to the illiterate.

Modern writers confronted with this challenge put the 1930s debate on the use of national forms for revolutionary ends into high gear. National forms— premodern popular forms such as folk theater and storytelling—were important vehicles for crossing the literacy gap that had hindered the success of revolutionary literature over the past two decades. Theatrical performances with new patriotic scripts were performed to all kinds of audiences, including the rural peasantry, throughout the regions of the unoccupied rear (Holm 1991). The troupes that performed these plays, especially those dispatched from the remote Communist base areas, also penetrated into the frontline battle zones and occupied regions. These plays, as well as dramatic harangues on current events called "living newspapers" (活报), often had no texts or only a rudimentary outline. They were performing arts often rehearsed into shape in a collective and active process rather than carefully crafted beforehand. Many of the actors, directors, production assistants, and especially writers and organizers of such performances had been novelists, poets, and playwrights before the outbreak of the war. The Communist base areas were attractive and relatively safe training grounds for such cultural workers, as they came to be called, but the literary record has left behind only a fraction of their interventions into the wartime cultural scene (Hung 1994).

The prolific novelist Lao She 老舍 makes an interesting case in point. Although not regarded as a leftist writer when he assumed leadership of the newly formed All China League of Resistance Writers, Lao She confronted the need to adapt the language and the form of his creative intervention to the needs of the times. He dabbled in the creation of theatrical pieces based on traditional performing arts. By his own account, these efforts, although determined by the urgent needs of the times, had the effect of reforming his literary imagination, and his subsequent efforts clearly bore the marks of traditional popular forms (Kao 1980).

If standard *baihua*, or the "national language" (国语), was the distinctive product of the literary revolution and the May Fourth movement, further, more profound transformations of the written and spoken languages would result from massification, revolutionary literature, the war against Japan, and especially the wartime emergence of a socialist society in Communist base areas and its subsequent expansion throughout China during and after the civil war. By the late 1920s the forces of radical change—militant students, revolutionary organizers, leftist journalists, and officers and soldiers in the Red Army—began to imagine and legitimize their experience in purely military terms. Courage, determination, and even ruthlessness became exalted qualities in every field of endeavor, and written discourse among these groups became suffused with a standardized rhetoric of battle, weapons, front lines, and enemies. By the time of the outbreak of war, such rhetoric had already been available to the reading public for some years and thus rapidly spread to become a principal medium of discourse, at least for the war experience. Even writers engaged in inquiries not directly related to the war, whether writing introductions or prefaces or engaging in a public discussion, almost invariably peppered their expression with militant and patriotic catchphrases.

In the Communist base areas, militarization of everyday language blended with politically correct Maoist jargon: "class background," "bad elements," and "counterrevolutionary" all became household words. Becoming a good citizen in Mao's republic largely meant acquiring the special language and concepts of Chinese communism and being able to tell the story of one's own life adeptly using this language and these concepts. Communist Party leaders learned that perhaps the most effective way to guarantee political conformity was to recreate knowledge and language in their own image and impose it on their citizens (Apter and Saich 1994).

Regimentation of language in the Maoist era had its literary counterpart in orthodox styles such as socialist realism and "revolutionary romanticism"—in effect, modern eight-legged essays. This is an ironic development, considering that fictional realism was originally viewed in China as a vehicle through which sincere writers would bring readers closer to the truth immanent in historical experience. People learned to hide their true feelings and thoughts behind a mask of political correctness in the interest of self-preservation and the protection of their families. In the tragically frequent political campaigns that enforced conformity throughout the history of the People's Republic at least until the Cultural Revolution (1966–1976), these words and concepts (just as the accidents of one's past) became landmines that could suddenly incriminate the unwitting and weapons to attack those who had made themselves vulnerable through honesty or humanity. This strange political–linguistic process may very well have taken place unconsciously; there were probably only a few cases in the divisive campaigns from the Anti-Rightist movement to the Cultural Revolution of individuals who stood back and said to themselves, "What am I saying?"

Only years after the Cultural Revolution, after the death of Mao Zedong in 1976 and the birth of the era of reform and opening, did it occur to critics to name the use of this stilted Communist jargon in literature and life "Maoist discourse" and try hard to move beyond it. In fact, a principal goal of mainland writers since the mid-1980s has been to wrest themselves and the Chinese reading public from the stultifying shadow of Maoist discourse, to enrich the language anew and make it once again into a viable medium for the creation of modern literature (Li Tuo 1993). The trend of 1980s "roots-seeking" (寻根) literature, of which many works were made into prominent films such as *Yellow Earth* (黄土地) and *King of the Children* (孩子王), registered a profound ambivalence toward the meaning and legitimacy of Maoist discourse, critiquing it and yet still largely caught within its own terms. A more radical break was accomplished by avant-garde fiction writers such as Can Xue 残雪 and Yu Hua 余华, who launched an assault on not only conventional language but also the very moral compass and standards of intelligibility that accompanied the legacy of socialist culture. This shift unsurprisingly coincided with an unprecedented resurgence of poetry led by writers such as Bei Dao 北岛 whose defiant ambiguity led conservative critics to label them "Misty poets." Indeed, the departure from realism and the linguistic and symbolic enrichment of fiction since the 1980s should be in part attributed to the influence of "Misty" and "post-Misty" poetry.

REGIONAL SPEECH AND THE FRACTURE OF STANDARDS

The topic of regional speech involves the literatures of Taiwan and Hong Kong as well. To return briefly to the late Qing, regional dialect was a principal obstacle to the standardization of spoken and written modern Chinese and to the establishment of certain forms of modern literature. Apart from what we now call "Mandarin" (官话), which is spoken widely across the northern half of

China but is based largely on the Beijing dialect, there are also the Cantonese spoken in Guangdong Province and in Hong Kong, the Wu and Min dialects of southeastern China, Shandong dialect, Sichuan dialect, and so on. Before language reform and new literature, these dialects were used locally, especially in commerce, everyday speech, and theatrical performances, to the exclusion of official Mandarin. Even as modern language and literature were standardized, dialect-based literature persisted in its appeal to regional audiences. One example is the traditional-style vernacular novel *Flowers of Shanghai* (海上花列传), its dialogue originally written in the Wu (Shanghai) dialect. The novel later became more prominent when it was translated into Mandarin by Eileen Chang 张爱玲. These local literatures and performing arts were marginalized by the overwhelming force of standardization during the first half of the twentieth century. But in the wake of the civil war, which ended in 1949, dialects took on new significance as vehicles of regional identity resisting linguistic and literary standardization with both cultural and political overtones.

For example, the distinction between modernist and nativist literature in Taiwan, usually approached from the point of view of content or theme, can also be illuminated by the issues of language and form. Although Mandarin has been promoted as the official language on Taiwan since its retrocession to the Republic of China in 1945 after the end of the war, most people speak variations of the Min or Hakka dialects. In Taiwan this issue has become more than a linguistic one because the people indigenous to Taiwan as well as nonelite immigrants from southeast mainland China often feel alienated from the Mandarin-speaking elite associated with the nationalist Guomindang. Rural poverty and ethnic minority issues found expression in the use of dialect-inflected speech in "nativist" (乡土) literature (Gunn 1991: 154–161). And with the liberalization of the print media in 1987, regional speech became more conspicuous on the Taiwanese cultural scene. A similar inclination toward regional speech in the roots-seeking fiction of the 1980s in mainland China was instrumental in breaking the grip of standard Maoist discourse (164–176).

Similar issues surrounded the emergence of Cantonese written literature in Guangzhou and Hong Kong, particularly after World War II (Gunn 1991: 48–49). Manifestations of Cantonese inflections in the written language first appeared and continued to be most numerous in newspapers. One of the easiest places to find such special characters to represent idiomatic particles is in political cartoons: dialogue in the cartoons is often expressed in writing in heavily inflected Cantonese, almost indecipherable to a reader who does not understand the dialect and a perfect vehicle for political satire when outside government officials do not speak the local language. Cantonese popular music has become widespread throughout the Chinese-speaking world and has led to an interest in Cantonese expressions and other aspects of popular culture in Taiwan and mainland China as well.

Although a standard written and spoken vernacular based on Beijing dialect is in place throughout cultural China, and many had a stake in affirming its authority, forces inherent in actual usage and in literature undermined that authority and continued to threaten its stability throughout the twentieth century. That it has never been completely standardized is testimony to the diversity and vitality of modern spoken Chinese. Similarly, realistic fiction has loosened its hold on modern literature, making room for the proliferation of nonfictional forms and more adventurous approaches to fiction. This vital diversity will nourish the language and forms of Chinese literature as it enters a phase of unprecedented accomplishment.

Bibliography

Apter, David, and Tony Saich. *Revolutionary Discourse in Mao's Republic*. Cambridge, MA: Harvard University Press, 1994.

Bing, Sang. "The Vernacular Language During the May Fourth Period." *Twentieth-Century China* 38, 1 (January 2013): 71–93.

Doleželová-Velingerová, Milena. "The Origins of Modern Chinese Literature." In Merle Goldman, ed., *Modern Chinese Literature in the May Fourth Era*, 17–35. Cambridge, MA: Harvard University Press, 1977.

Gunn, Edward. *Rendering the Regional: Local Language in Contemporary Chinese Media*. Honolulu: University of Hawai'i Press, 2005.

——. *Style and Innovation in Twentieth-Century Chinese Prose*. Stanford, CA: Stanford University Press, 1991.

Hill, Michael Gibbs. *Lin Shu Inc.: Translation and the Making of Modern Chinese Culture*. Oxford: Oxford University Press, 2013.

Holm, David. *Art and Ideology in Revolutionary China*. Oxford: Clarendon Press, 1991.

Hung, Chang-tai. *War and Popular Culture: Resistance in Modern China, 1937–1945*. Berkeley: University of California Press, 1994.

Kao, George, ed. *Two Writers and the Cultural Revolution: Lao She and Ch'en Jo-hsi*. Hong Kong: Chinese University Press, 1980.

Li, Tuo. "The New Vitality in Modern Chinese." In Wendy Larson and Anne Wedell-Wedellsborg, eds., *Inside Out: Modern and Postmodernism in Chinese Literary Culture*, 65–77. Aarhus: Aarhus University Press, 1993.

Pickowicz, Paul. "Qu Qiubai's Critique of the May Fourth Generation: Early Chinese Marxist Literary Criticism." In Merle Goldman, ed., *Modern Chinese Literature in the May Fourth Era*, 351–384. Cambridge, MA: Harvard University Press, 1977.

Zhou, Gang. *Placing the Modern Chinese Vernacular in Transnational Literature*. New York: Palgrave Macmillan, 2011.

4

LITERARY COMMUNITIES AND THE PRODUCTION OF LITERATURE

MICHEL HOCKX

Texts of modern Chinese literature, as with those of any other modern literature, circulate within a professional community of writers, editors, publishers, booksellers, critics, educators, and readers, all of whom share and uphold the conviction that literature is a significant part of culture. In China, as in the United States, this community began to take shape in the second half of the nineteenth century as a direct result of revolutionary changes in the system of education and in the techniques of printing and publishing. However, the ways in which this community organized itself, produced literary works and defined their value, and interacted with the state and other communities have often been very different from the ways in other countries. Understanding the habits and beliefs of the members of this community is an important condition for understanding and appreciating the literary works they shared.

Working with texts has always been the trademark of the Chinese elite. Traditional Chinese education strongly emphasized the reading and memorizing of an array of canonized philosophical, historical, and literary texts. A thorough knowledge of the literary tradition and the ability to write in various literary forms were indispensable for any man wishing to pass the imperial examinations and work his way up the social ladder. Women were not allowed to take part in the examinations, but literacy was very common among upper-class women, and there have been women writers throughout Chinese history.

During the second half of the nineteenth century, the Qing government confronted mounting threats to the unity and integrity of the country because of internal problems (rebellions and uprisings) and external pressure (the onslaught of Western and Japanese imperialism). To cope with these threats, many within government and the local elites believed that the education system should be reformed to offer a wider variety of practically oriented courses. New schools were set up at all levels, offering a Western-style curriculum consisting of various topics in the sciences and humanities, including foreign languages. The importance of literary skills and the significance of the imperial examinations decreased rapidly. Finally, the system of imperial examinations was abolished in 1905 and replaced by a nationwide, state-supported system of primary, secondary, and tertiary education.

With literary skills no longer promising a successful career in government, intellectuals with an interest in textual work were forced to explore new career paths. Many of them took advantage of the mushrooming of new schools all over the country to pursue careers as educators. Many others were attracted by the booming print and publishing industry in major cities, especially Shanghai.

The Chinese, of course, pioneered the art of printing, and large-scale printing and publishing houses had existed in China from at least the Ming dynasty. However, during the second half of the nineteenth century, the introduction of new printing techniques developed in the West (for instance, steam printing and lithography) created the possibility to reproduce texts, photographs, and illustrations in very large quantities and at very low cost. These new techniques enabled the establishment of large, commercial publishing houses and the publication of newspapers, journals, and cheap books. In other words, this was the beginning of modern print culture in China. The new industry was badly in need of writers, translators, proofreaders, editors, and the like, creating many career opportunities for intellectuals.

It was in these two novel sectors of society—the new schools and the new publishing industry—that the modern Chinese literary community began to take shape. Starting out as journalists or teachers, modern Chinese literary intellectuals during the first decades of the twentieth century gradually managed to turn literature into an independent discipline by founding literary organizations, launching literary publications, and promoting literary education. Apart from periods of extreme political repression in mainland China during the 1960s and 1970s, the modern Chinese literary community in the whole of Greater China has displayed a number of stable characteristics.

ORGANIZATIONS

Modern Chinese literary practice is characterized by a high level of organization. During the first half of the twentieth century, most writers clearly preferred working in various kinds of collectives, a preference institutionalized by the authorities in mainland China after 1949 with the establishment of the Chinese Writers Association (中国作家协会).

The most common type of literary organization is the literary society or club (文学社团). These are usually small groups, mainly involved in editing a literary journal meant for the publication of members' own works. Membership is limited to those involved in running the journal. A manifesto is published in the journal's first issue. Members' financial contributions are used to fund the printing and distribution of the journal, although more successful societies of this type have tended to cooperate with publishing houses. Many Chinese writers of the Republican era (1911–1949) began their literary careers in such societies and continued to organize similar ones during later stages of their careers. An active organizer was the famous writer Lu Xun 鲁迅. In the 1920s and 1930s, there were hundreds of small societies. In later decades, societies continued to be prominent in Hong Kong and Taiwan. Nowadays, some literary groups active on the Internet display similar characteristics, combining social interaction with the editing of regular "webzines" (网刊).

Some literary groups of the Republican period developed a relatively formal structure and a public function that extended beyond the literary community. Collectives of this kind depended on a large membership or on shareholders for funding a variety of publishing projects, including literary journals, literary series (丛书), and literature textbooks. Their public visibility derived from activities such as hosting receptions and dinner parties, establishing an official location (a bookshop, printing shop, or clubhouse carrying the name of the society), publishing announcements in large newspapers, and signing general political or cultural manifestos. Organizations like these played a large role in public acceptance of new literature (新文学) and its literary scene (文坛). Important examples are the Literary Association (文学研究会, 1920–1947) and the Creation Society (创造社, 1921–1930).

A unique organization that was very large, very formally organized, yet forced to stay completely underground was the 1930s League of Left-Wing Writers (左翼作家联盟, 1930–1936), established by the then-outlawed Communist Party and chaired by Lu Xun. After the establishment of Communist rule on the mainland, literary production in its entirety became the responsibility of the Writers Association, a government organization under the auspices of the Ministry of Culture. Throughout the Mao period and well into the 1980s, the Writers Association, which has subdivisions on the provincial and local levels, coordinated and sponsored all literary activity. Its most established members were provided with a steady income, housing, and social benefits in return for their loyalty to party principles concerning literature. The system helped to consolidate the status and well-being of writers but also restricted their freedom, especially at times of extreme ideological pressure. In the 1990s, when a privatized market for literature began to develop, many writers ceased to be dependent on the union. Nowadays the association plays a largely ceremonial role, but membership remains highly sought after and provides writers with access to useful networks and funding opportunities. The association also remains responsible for several publishing houses and literary magazines, as well as for the two most prestigious literary prizes in the People's Republic of China (PRC): the Lu Xun Prize and the Mao Dun 茅盾 Prize.

PUBLICATIONS

Partly because of this preference for collective organization, the most important medium for the publication of literary works in modern China has often been the literary journal. The first literary journals appeared in Shanghai in the late nineteenth century. They were mainly commercial fiction journals aimed at a broad readership of literati and city-dwellers, although many of them included contributions in other genres written for a more limited audience. A further change occurred in the late 1910s and early 1920s, with the influx of large numbers of graduates from the new education system into the publishing business and the rapid spread of "new literature" (新文学). The new literature journals, often run by literary societies, had a more highbrow and less commercial image, although most of them were business ventures catering to the tastes of the younger generation. These new literature journals come closest to the Western definition of a "serious" literary journal. It should be kept in mind, however, that journals containing more traditional forms of (popular) literature continued to appear and draw a substantial readership throughout the twentieth century.

In China, unlike in many Western countries, books only recently replaced journals as the primary avenue for publication of literary work. Well into the 1980s, even full-length novels by famous writers were often first serialized in literary journals before being presented in book form. The dominance of this mode of literary production merits consideration, particularly of its general effects on literary writing and literary texts. For the writer, regular contribution to journals has important financial advantages (journals usually pay by the word). This can lead to a tendency to write large numbers of short works or very large works in many short installments. During the Republican era, the shorter genres were extremely popular, while somewhat longer works, such as Lu Xun's seminal "The True Story of Ah Q" (阿Q正传, 1922), clearly bear the traces of publication in installments, such as cliffhangers and other devices meant to keep the audience's attention. If financial pressure or pressure from the editors is high, journal publication can also lead to fast or sloppy writing, a phenomenon especially prevalent during the Republican era but not entirely absent in later decades, since the socialist organization of literary production required writers to be prolific in their contributions to state-supported periodical publications. Because many literary journals were either commercial or propagandistic and reached relatively large audiences, writers were often inclined to take their perception of readers' tastes and needs, or the needs of political propaganda, strongly into account, which could result in a reluctance to experiment.

The arrival of the Internet has seen a continuation of some of these habits, with Chinese entrepreneurs in the early twenty-first century developing a highly successful business model for selling popular fiction (especially romance and martial arts), based on offering readers subscriptions to ongoing serializations of very long fictional works. The most popular of these novels have also been published in print, and some websites also act as commercial intermediaries between online writers and state-owned publishers in the print-based system.

LITERARY EDUCATION

Although the introduction of a modern education system in China from the late nineteenth century onward brought about a significant drop in the cultural value of literary skills, the study of literary texts continued to be part of the school curriculum. However, emphasis in teaching shifted from memorization and reproduction to the reading and analysis of literary texts. Under the influence of the modern Western concept of literature (encompassing fiction, poetry, and drama), literary education began to include the study of vernacular genres, such as the novel.

Education was the key to the success of the new literature. Whereas the first generation of literary reformers, including people like Liang Qichao 梁启超 (1873–1929), were "journalist-littérateurs" (Lee 1973) who wielded their influence mainly through journals and newspapers and gave modern literature an audience, the second generation, including people like Hu Shi 胡适 (1891–1962), Chen Duxiu 陈独秀 (1880–1942), and Zhou Zuoren 周作人 (1885–1967), were "literary intellectuals" (McDougall and Louie 1997), active in schools and universities, who gave modern literature its status. Within years after the literary revolution of 1917 (see "Language and Literary Form"), works of new literature were being included in school textbooks and were well on their way toward canonization.

A very influential canon of modern Chinese literature was the one established in the PRC after 1949 (see "Modern Chinese Literature as an Institution"). In line with Mao Zedong's opinions on the nature and function of literature, standard textbooks from both before and after the Cultural Revolution made literary development subservient to political development (for instance, adopting periodizations based on the various stages of the "revolution") and placed great emphasis on the political correctness of the contents of literary works. Although this canon of revolutionary literature has come under increasing attack since the 1980s, the idea that mainstream modern Chinese literature should consist of socially engaged, realist writing remains commonplace among scholars and students of modern Chinese literature, in both China and elsewhere.

In post-1949 Taiwan, for various, mainly political reasons, modern Chinese literature was not commonly taught in Chinese departments of universities. Although the discipline was finally established in the 1980s, its significance has been overshadowed by more pressing concerns for the historiography of and education in modern Taiwanese literature, referring to texts written during the twentieth century by writers living on Taiwan and writing in Japanese, Taiwanese, or Mandarin Chinese. The problems involved in writing and teaching the history of Taiwanese literature continue to divide the Taiwanese literary community into "China-oriented" and "nativist" groups (see Martin 1995).

In Hong Kong under British rule, the teaching and study of Chinese literature was long marginalized. Modern Chinese literature, especially, was considered a minor subject, for unlike classical literature, it could not be employed to transmit Chinese cultural heritage. As in Taiwan, the topic of local identity, intertwined with issues of colonialism and postcolonialism and of language (English, Cantonese, Mandarin), played an important role in the study of modern literature in Hong Kong in the last two decades of the twentieth century.

Education in modern Chinese literature in all areas of Greater China strongly affirms the relationship between works of literature and sociopolitical reality, with relatively less emphasis placed on the aesthetic function of literature. Although this is an overgeneralization, it is safe to say that many Chinese readers and critics have great tolerance for political and didactic statements in literary texts and that this taste has been partly inculcated by the canonization practices of literary education.

CENSORSHIP

All literature published in China during the twentieth century and all literature published in Taiwan until the late 1980s were produced under conditions of state censorship. Thus for most modern Chinese writers, unlike for modern writers in most Western countries, censorship is the norm, and knowing how to deal with censorship authorities is an essential skill.

During the first three decades of the twentieth century, censorship of literature was normally carried out after publication, with regulations differing from region to region and censors erratically deciding to ban certain books or journals or to raid certain shops or publishing houses. In the 1930s, the Nationalist government attempted to establish a system of prepublication censorship, forcing publishers to submit all book manuscripts to censorship authorities for inspection and possible revision. One unintended result of this policy was the further rise in popularity of literary magazines, which were exempt from this form of censorship because of the time constraints on their production. Targets of censorship in the 1930s were works referring to the then-outlawed Communist movement and works critical of the government's policy toward Japanese aggression. Although the Nationalist government attempted to launch its own literary movement, its censorship system was more prohibitive than prescriptive, telling writers not what to write but what *not* to write. The 1930s were good years for apolitical, modernist writers in that the censorship system had nothing against their works, whereas it significantly limited the impact of prescriptive Communist ideology on cultural circles.

Around the same time on Taiwan, under Japanese rule, the authorities were carrying out what has become known as the "assimilation policy" aimed at fully integrating Taiwan, as well as Korea, into the Japanese empire. In the literary realm, this policy demanded writing that has since become known as *kominka* (皇民化) literature, written in Japanese and emphasizing themes such as loyalty to the Japanese emperor and the volunteering of Taiwanese men for the Japanese army, as well as coprosperity in general. Although most Taiwanese writers of the time ended up conforming to the policy in one way or the other—the alternative being not to publish at all—various expressions of resistance or ambiguity can and have been read into their works.

When the Nationalist government relocated to Taiwan in 1949, it established a prohibitive censorship system similar to that of 1930s mainland China. The main target of censorship was still leftist writing, but a second important target, especially in the 1950s and 1960s, was Taiwanese nativism. Most important literary publications were initially controlled by intellectuals who had moved from the mainland and brought along and continued the new literary tradition, but with an even greater emphasis on modernism, both through translation of Western modernist works and theories and through original creation. After the extended debates between modernists and nativists in the late 1970s, and especially after the introduction of civil rights, including freedom of speech, in 1987, nativist critics pointed out the ambiguous relationship between the modernist trend and government cultural policy. On the one hand, modernist writing was politically safe, for the censors had no interest in it. On the other hand, through its language (standard Chinese) and its background (building on mainland Chinese literary history), it also helped to further the government's attempts to suppress expressions of local Taiwanese culture.

By far the most repressive system of censorship, however, was established in mainland China by Communist authorities after 1949. Adopting Mao Zedong's "Yan'an Talks" as its basic credo, the Communist authorities assumed a prescriptive approach and installed a system of total prepublication censorship. All publishing houses were brought under state control, and all writers were assembled in the Writers Association. In theory, nothing that did not live up to the doctrine of socialist realism could be published. So many writers were persecuted and so many books were banned during the first three decades of the PRC, not because the censorship system did not work properly, but because official views of what could or could not be permitted kept changing. Many writers who were imprisoned or killed for their writing earnestly believed that they had been following the official policies and indeed enthusiastically supported them (as in the case of the Hundred Flowers movement of 1956–1957). Policies were most extreme during the Cultural Revolution (1966–1976), when cultural authorities drew up long lists of requirements for literary form and content aimed at preventing any possible confusion about, for instance, who were the heroes and who were the villains in a particular work (see "The Cultural Revolution Model Theater").

During the Cultural Revolution, literature other than the officially sanctioned types managed to survive through the apparently spontaneous development of a network of underground distribution of texts and books, which were often copied out by hand and exchanged among young intellectuals throughout the country. After the Cultural Revolution, some of these underground writers, such as the poet Bei Dao 北岛 (pen name of Zhao Zhenkai 赵振开, b. 1949) (see "Misty Poetry"), soon rose to prominence both inside and outside China. During the last two decades of the twentieth century, censorship in the People's Republic gradually became more relaxed, but occasional campaigns continued to be leveled against writers or works perceived to have directly attacked party leaders, insulted national minorities, or violated "good taste." Prepublication censorship mechanisms are still in place, and editors avoid many problems with the authorities by preemptively cutting out possibly objectionable passages from authors' manuscripts. In general, there now seems to be a status quo in which writers censor themselves, in a way, by choosing not to write on topics known to be problematic while fully exploring all the topics that were once taboo (for instance, sex) and are now permissible. Writers have relatively more freedom to experiment when they publish online, where controls are less strict and it is possible to serialize entire novels without going through official publishing channels.

Meanwhile, increased contact between the mainland and Taiwan has opened important avenues of publication for mainland authors. Many new works by leading writers from the PRC are now often first published in Taiwan or Hong Kong, which has the double advantage of freeing authors from censorship and giving them substantially higher fees and royalties. The emergence of a Greater China literary community and the increased participation of Chinese writers in a global literary community through international festivals and prizes, for instance, and of course through translation, are important developments that will no doubt influence the course of Chinese literature in the twenty-first century.

Bibliography

Denton, Kirk A., ed. *Modern Chinese Literary Thought: Writings on Literature, 1893–1945*. Stanford, CA: Stanford University Press, 1996.

Denton, Kirk A., and Michel Hockx, eds. *Literary Societies of Republican China*. Lanham, MD: Lexington Books, 2008.

Hockx, Michel. *Internet Literature in China*. New York: Columbia University Press, 2015.

—, ed. *The Literary Field of Twentieth-Century China*. Honolulu: University of Hawai'i Press, 1999.

—. *Questions of Style: Literary Societies and Literary Journals in Modern China*. Leiden: Brill, 2003.

Lee, Leo Ou-fan. *The Romantic Generation of Modern Chinese Writers*. Cambridge, MA: Harvard University Press, 1973.

Link, Perry. *The Uses of Literature: Life in the Socialist Chinese Literary System*. Princeton, NJ: Princeton University Press, 2000.

Martin, Helmut. *The History of Taiwanese Literature: Towards Cultural-Political Identity: Views from Taiwan, China, Japan and the West*. Bochum: Ruhr University, 1995.

McDougall, Bonnie, and Kam Louie. *The Literature of China in the Twentieth Century*. London: Hurst, 1997.

5

BETWEEN TRADITION AND MODERNITY: CONTESTED CLASSICAL POETRY

SHENGQING WU

In 1923, after editing twenty-four volumes of the *Collection of Modern Poetry* (近代诗钞), Chen Yan 陈衍 (1856–1937), the leading critic of classical-style poetry of the time, wrote the following poem:

> From the Han-Wei to the Tang-Song,
> There were already plenty of poetic masterpieces.
> Li, Du, Han, Bai, and Su,
> They will last just like the rivers.
> Still I must compile new works,
> And I will not pick sides.
> Even hills and valleys change,
> Thousands of shapes appear like waves.
> Pure aspiration gives rise to new scenes,
> The past and present are very different.
> Dyes produce mixed colors,
> Thousands of beautiful silks are both light and dark.
> In grafting wood and transplanting flowers,
> Appearance and type will change in an instant.
> Loving the ancient, denigrating the present,
> This is what I object to.
>
> (Chen Yan 1999: 2: 1124)

Chen Yan wrote this poem five years after Hu Shi published his manifesto "Some Modest Proposals for the Reform of Literature," which called for a literary movement to cast away old literary forms. In this influential essay, Hu characterizes Chen Sanli 陈三立 (1859–1937) and Zheng Xiaoxu 郑孝胥 (1860–1938), both poets highly regarded by Chen Yan, as being slavishly committed to tradition, illustrating "the imitative psychology of today's 'poets of the first rank'" (in Denton 1996: 127). Since the May Fourth movement, the general assumption has been that the vernacular language swept through the literary field to easily displace classical language as a more efficient tool for communication and that works written in classical language were either ideologically backward or poorly written. The political function of classical poetry had already waned with the removal of poetry questions from the imperial civil service examination in 1901 and the emergence of the vernacular language movement (see Elman 2000). Given this context, however, Chen Yan's optimism about this supposedly doomed art is striking and points to a blind spot in our understanding of literary history—that is, that a body of rhymed poetic writing coexisted with "new literature" (新文学) in the Republican era and had dynamic interactions with modern society. Invoking the image of "grafting" in the poem, Chen Yan emphasizes the innovative practice of self-consciously appropriating the distant past and incorporating it into a modern context, and thus "appearance and type will change in an instant." In many ways, this attitude toward China's textual and poetic tradition was representative of many in the intelligentsia of his generation who stood at the crossroads of tradition and modernity and witnessed the crumbling of the traditional literati culture. Stylistically speaking, this generation of poets not only made a firm commitment to form but also took their awareness of form and textual tradition to a new extreme. As a general trend, archaism and unwavering formal commitment can be understood as a response to the collapsing *wen* (文) culture, a parallel to the mounting movement for vernacularization and dismantling of established rules and conventions. Engaging with a society riven by class divisions in the tumultuous twentieth century, classical poetry was a living enterprise, rather than merely a static form handed down from the past. Nor was it defeated overnight by the so-called literary revolution, as standard scholarly narratives would have us believe. Indeed, it became a vibrant medium of much tension and contestation related to its changing social function and political significance.

The traumatic experiences of the Boxer Rebellion, the invasion of Western powers in 1900, and the fall of the Qing, as well as the changing political landscape after 1912, served as major demarcation points for many poets of Chen Yan's generation, who responded to these political and cultural upheavals with intellectually and linguistically sophisticated poems. Chen Sanli withdrew from political life in 1901 and fully devoted himself to poetry, becoming the leading classical poet of the first three decades of the twentieth century. The poetry of Chen Sanli, Zheng Xiaoxu, and Chen Yan is conventionally categorized as representative of the

"Tongguang style" (同光体), which was part of the Song-style poetry movement in the second half of the nineteenth century (Kowallis 2006). Song-style poetry, generally modeled after that of the mid-Tang, was characterized by its ethical, moral, and philosophical themes, the extensive use of allusions and scholarship, and the expansion of generic boundaries. Chen Sanli tends to use archaic words and unusual syntax, thus defamiliarizing worn-out diction, textual strategies characteristic of Song-style poetry. The intense emotional and intellectual conflicts of his time compelled him to seek new means of expression. In the following poem, Chen uses carefully chosen words to depict the snowy scene, capturing the external world's pressure on the poet's psyche. In Yoshikawa Kōjirō's (1986: 357) view, this encroachment on the viewing subject and the disintegration of unified perception are indications of the poem's modernity.

In the Garden Watching Light Snow

Early in the year, it still snows lightly;
In the garden pavilion, I feel like sighing.
On a high branch, the calls of magpies are silenced;
On a slanted rock, saliva from snails comes alive.
Cold presses on the many quiet streets;
Sorrow brightens the myriad images in front of me.
Swirling by the window, touching plum pistils,
It is too chaotic to be beautiful.

(Chen Sanli 2003: 1:154)

Apart from the eminent regulated verse (律诗) form, "song lyrics," or *ci* (词), composed of a chosen melody and metrical patterns of varied line lengths, was a form also popular in the late Qing. Often associated with romantic expression, *ci* were charged with new intellectual significance and linguistic maneuvers. In his frequently anthologized poem "To the Tune Zhe Gutian" (鹧鸪天), Zhu Zumou 朱祖谋 (1857–1931), one of the four modern masters of *ci*, presents a deceptively tranquil scene, without a single word referring to the shocking events of the Hundred Days Reform in 1898. Only the location mentioned in the short preface indicates his lament over the tragic fate of his friend Liu Guangdi 刘光第 (1859–1898), who was executed when the reforms were quashed. Moving away from immediate experience, he leads us into a mediated world of memory and reflection. Zhu's preference for allusive diction, tropes, ornamental language, and meticulous attention to the musicality of the form produces the characteristic intensity and ambiguity of his poems. *Ci*, in contrast to regulated verse's emphasis on expressing the poet's genuine intent, introduces fictionality and persona as a formal aspect of the genre, and this offers the poet greater flexibility. In response to the Boxer Rebellion disaster, Zhu Zumou, Wang Pengyun 王鹏运 (1849–1904), and others composed poems every night.

Adopting the persona of the grieving woman in the poems, they constantly employed the trope of "fragrant plants and beautiful women" (香草美人) to express an implicit critique of the political situation. In so doing, these poems reveal a profound sense of loss, sorrow, and fragile subjectivity in the wake of these national disasters.

In the aftermath of the collapse of the Qing dynasty, the last literati generation, many of whom became *yimin* (遺民, holdovers loyal to the previous dynasty), were living in cities such as Shanghai, Beijing, and Tianjin. They frequently gathered for various social occasions and exchanged verses, casting a collective nostalgia for the fallen dynasty and the disappearing literati culture (see Lin 2012). Liang Qichao 梁启超, the prominent intellectual who proposed a "poetic revolution" in 1899, also joined the group of Tongguang-style poets at their gatherings and gained a new appreciation of classical poetry. The social function of the form was further tested and amplified at this historical juncture and in a modernizing urban environment. One result that came out of such gatherings was the cultivation of the distinctive literary and cultural tastes of a younger generation of classicists, among them Long Yusheng 龙榆生 (1902–1966), who would play an important role in establishing the discipline of *ci* studies in modern universities. At the same time, a group of female *ci* poets emerged who extended the Ming-Qing women's writing tradition into new, modern contexts, challenging the male-dominated cultural enterprises. Lü Bicheng 吕碧城 (1883–1943), a feminist activist in the 1910s, reached her poetic peak in the late 1920s, when she was sojourning in Europe and writing about the Alps and cultural relics in Rome. Her geographical and literary border crossing significantly reshaped the spatial representation of *ci*. Amid the turmoil of the war against Japan, Ding Ning 丁宁 (1902–1980) and Shen Zufen 沈祖棻 (1909–1977), the latter also known for her new poetry, managed to bring gender consciousness and a range of personal and political emotions into the form, enriching the expression of "boudoir feelings" (闺情).

On the other end of the spectrum, Lu Xun 鲁迅 and Yu Dafu 郁达夫, who carried the torch of new literature, continued to write poetry in old forms, even as they produced fiction preoccupied with a sense of responsibility to effect social change (Anderson 1990). In the 1960s, the scholar Jaroslav Průšek first remarked on the close relationship between new literature and China's classical tradition, arguing that Lu Xun had inherited the dominant lyrical strain of classical Chinese poetry and extended lyricism cross-generically into short story writing. Leo Ou-fan Lee further asserts that the stylistic brevity and emotional intensity of Lu Xun's works have undoubtedly benefited from his early training and predilection for Chinese classicism. For Lu Xun, who deftly moved among a number of literary genres (short stories, polemical essays, prose poems, scholarship), classical poetry took on a new role as "a home" in the expression of anguish and "dark" visions. Late in his life, Lu Xun also turned classical poetry into another effective weapon to satirize contemporary politics. Yu Dafu, who described himself as "someone infatuated with skeletons," is also well known for his poetic talents. In his sensational story "Sinking" (沉沦), by reciting Wordsworth's "A Solitary Reaper" and composing classical poems, the protagonist fashions himself as a sentimental subject caught in an irresolvable tension between modern alienation and a comforting traditional community (Denton 1992). Lu Xun's and Yu Dafu's indebtedness to textual tradition and continued practices of classical forms contradicted their public image as iconoclastic leaders of the New Literature movement. Their use of more "conventional" poetic forms sought to avoid the pitfalls of the "transparent" representation of reality or the unmediated confession that plagued some vernacular writings in the progressive and nationalist mode. In this complex scenario, classical poetry written by both "new" and "old" writers challenges the teleological narrative of literary progress and the artificially constructed break between tradition and modernity, pointing to their mutually transformative power.

The intertwined relationship between history and lyricism, writing for oneself or for others, culminated in the poetry of two politician-poets, Wang Jingwei 汪精卫 (1883–1944) and Mao Zedong. Wang in his youth was famous for lines such as "this head should be hung over the gate of the capital city" after his failed attempt to assassinate the Qing prince Zaifeng 载沣 (1883–1951). One of his late poems, composed while he was collaborating with the Japanese occupiers during the war, reflects on the self's relationship with history and nation in a melancholic tone: "Good friends gradually disappear along with many disasters. / China is once again sinking. / Miserable, I should not sigh at being lonely. / Examining my life of unfulfilled ambition" ("On a Boat at Night" [舟夜]). Hailed as a representative of "revolutionary romanticism," Mao Zedong expressed his grandiose, personal ambition after encountering snow-capped landscapes during the Long March: "The rivers and mountains are so beautiful, / they make countless heroes bow. . . . All have passed. / The great hero looks toward the present" ("Snow" [雪]). Instead of nature encroaching on the individual psyche, as described by Chen Sanli, in Mao's grand vision the entirety of historical time and space comes under his command and encompassing power. Under Mao's rule, Chen Yinke (sometimes Yinque) 陈寅恪 (1890–1969), the prominent historian and the son of Chen Sanli, wrote deeply coded poems to express his despair in the suffocating political environment in the People's Republic (see Yu 1998). In contrast, Nie Gannu's 聂绀弩 (1903–1986) witty and humorous poetry, written during the same social upheavals, represents another attempt at negotiating literati culture and socialism, as Xiaofei Tian (2009) has shown. The political and social functions of classical poetry were reified in the Cultural Revolution when millions of Chinese recited Mao's poetry in public gatherings and on stages. This happened again in later mass protest movements in Tiananmen Square in 1976 and 1989, when young people recited and wrote poetry to vent their feelings and forge a sense of community.

The captivating power of classical poetry has once again been reaffirmed in the age of the Internet. Classical poetry, which in imperial times was often composed at social gatherings or written in response to a friend's request, has flourished in communities that form so easily over the Internet. The Internet has amplified the social elements involved in reading and writing classical poetry. On his blog and discussion forum, Chang Ta-Chun (Zhang Dachun) 张大春, a famous fiction writer in Taiwan, often posts his poems and discusses his writings with his fans. With this renewed appreciation for traditional culture, grassroots social organizations and communities of classical poetry have mushroomed. Younger poets have begun learning and publishing classical poetry in college and are engaging in competitions at the local and national levels as well as on the web. Although most educated people today, unlike in Chen Yan's generation, are unable to compose a poem in traditional forms, anyone who can do so possesses significant cultural and symbolic capital. Contrary to the hopes of new literature proponents, classical poetry continues to be an appreciated and appealing literary form because it manages to reinvigorate itself by constantly interacting with and responding to a changing world.

Bibliography

Anderson, Marston. *The Limits of Realism: Chinese Fiction in the Revolutionary Period*. Berkeley: University of California Press, 1990.

Chen Sanli 陈三立. *Sanyuan jingshe shiwenji* 散原精舍诗文集 (Poems and essays from Sanyuan's studio), ed. Li Kaijun. Shanghai: Shanghai guji, 2003.

Chen Yan 陈衍. *Chenyan shilun heji* 陈衍诗论合集 (Poetry criticism of Chen Yan), ed. Qian Zhonglian. 2 vols. Fuzhou: Fujian renmin, 1999.

Denton, Kirk A. "The Distant Shore: The Nationalist Theme in Yu Dafu's Sinking." *Chinese Literature: Essays, Articles and Reviews* 14 (1992): 107–123.

———, ed. *Modern Chinese Literary Thought: Writing on Literature, 1893–1945*. Stanford, CA: Stanford University Press, 1996.

Elman, Benjamin. *A Cultural History of Civil Examination in Late Imperial China*. Berkeley: University of California Press, 2000.

Kowallis, Jon Eugene von. *The Subtle Revolution: Poets of the "Old Schools" During Late Qing and Early Republican China*. Berkeley: University of California, Institute of East Asian Studies, 2006.

Lee, Leo Ou-fan. "Tradition and Modernity in the Writing of Lu Xun." In Leo Ou-fan Lee, ed., *Lu Xun and His Legacy*, 13–23. Berkeley: University of California Press, 1985.

Lin Li [Lam, Lap] 林立. *Canghai yiyin: Minguo shiqi Qing yimin ci yanjiu* 沧海遗音: 民国时期清遗民词研究 (Remaining sounds of the vast ocean: A study of Qing loyalist *ci* lyrics in the Republican era). Hong Kong: Chinese University Press, 2012.

Průšek, Jaroslav. *The Lyric and the Epic: Studies of Modern Chinese Literature*, ed. Leo Ou-fan Lee. Bloomington: Indiana University Press, 1980.

Tian, Xiaofei. "Muffled Dialect Spoken by Green Fruit: An Alternative History of Modern Chinese Poetry." *Modern Chinese Literature and Culture* 21, 1 (2009): 1–45.

Wang Jingwei 汪精卫. *Shuangzhaolou shici gao* 双照楼诗词稿 (Collection of poetry from the Shuangzhao Tower). Annotated by Wang Mengchuan. Hong Kong: Tiandi tushu, 2012.

Wang Pengyun 王鹏运 et al. *Gengzi qiu ci* 庚子秋词 (Song lyrics of the autumn of Gengzi). Taipei: Xusheng shuju, 1972.

Wu, Shengqing. *Modern Archaics: Continuity and Innovation in the Chinese Lyric Tradition, 1900–1937*. Cambridge, MA: Harvard University Asia Center, 2013.

Yoshikawa Kōjirō 吉川幸次郎. *Zhongguo shi shi* 中国诗史 (History of Chinese poetry). Trans. Zhang Peiheng et al. Hefei: Anhui wenyi, 1986.

Yu Yingshi [Yu, Ying-shih] 余英时. *Chen Yinke wannian shiwen shizheng* 陈寅恪晚年诗文释证 (Annotated late works of Chen Yingke). Taipei: Dongda tushu gongsi, 1998.

Zhu Zumou 朱祖谋. *Qiangcun yuye jianzhu* 彊村语业笺注 (Annotated works of Qiangcun). Annotated by Bai Dunren. Chengdu: Bashu shushe, 2002.

6

DIASPORA IN MODERN CHINESE LITERATURE

SHUYU KONG

The term "diaspora," originally referring to the exile of the Jews from the Holy Land thousands of years ago, has come to include the modern condition and experience of transnational and intercultural dispersal. Diaspora may be externally enforced or self-imposed and may involve people of any race or nation. In the booming field of diasporic studies, the application of diasporic perspectives or methodological approaches has led scholars to reconsider the established frameworks of nation and state in literary studies and germinated the new research field of Sinophone literature.

Certainly diasporas are the dominant subject and theme of Sinophone literature, "literature written in Chinese by Chinese-speaking writers in various parts of the world outside China, as distinguished from 'Chinese literature'— literature from China" (Shih 2004: 29). However, this chapter looks at representations of diasporas as "the subjective experiences of displacement, victimhood, cultural hybridity, and cultural struggles" (Ong 1999: 12) in modern Chinese literature. Born from the historical conditions and processes of modernization, revolution, mobility, and globalization, numerous works of modern Chinese literature also articulate this specific realm of fluidity and uncertainty and depict its effect on human lives and cultural identity.

Chinese diasporas, the scatterings of people from Greater China across the globe, are historical processes that began over a millennium ago but have intensified since the second half of the nineteenth century, when constant social and political upheavals sent waves of Chinese, including intellectuals and writers, abroad, fired up with the ideal of saving their nation in crisis. And though it is true that most Chinese in the diaspora have been voluntary exiles, the historical traumas of their homeland have certainly shadowed their personal journeys.

The earliest literary representation of diaspora in modern Chinese literature can be traced to the writings of a group of Chinese students in Japan between the 1910s and 1920s who were also among the enthusiastic advocates of "new literature" in the May Fourth era. Representative of this group is Yu Dafu 郁达夫 (1896–1945) and his "notorious" short story "Sinking" (沉沦, 1921). A largely autobiographical piece emulating the Japanese I-novel tradition, "Sinking" is one of the first works of modern Chinese fiction to present an alienated and troubled soul wandering in a foreign land. The protagonist, coming to Japan to study medicine, finds himself in a state of "hypochondria" due to sexual frustrations inextricably linked with his racial insecurities. He tries to escape into solitude, severing relationships with his family and fellow Chinese students, reading the Western romantics, and returning to nature. However, these attempts to escape prove futile, and after a night of sexual misadventures in a Japanese brothel, he becomes filled with such self-loathing that he decides to drown himself.

Although seldom read from a diasporic angle, this story introduces a diasporic character who reappears in many subsequent works: a wanderer whose pained self desperately seeks to resolve contradictory impulses toward individualism and nationalism. Even if the struggle of the protagonist appears at first sight more like a "libidinous crisis," there are powerful racial sensitivities and nationalist emotions seething beneath the surface. As Kirk Denton (1992: 122) points out, "paralyzed between the island and the distant shore, Yu Dafu's protagonist encapsulated the complexity of the May Fourth dilemma of the intellectual self's relation to the nation." On the one hand, Yu blames China for her weakness and the shame and humiliation that individual Chinese people must suffer by association with her: "O China, my China, you are the cause of my death. . . . I wish you could become rich and strong soon. . . . Many, many of your children are still suffering" (1981: 141). On the other hand, he cannot help turning to her for protection and love, and he sees his own salvation as dependent on a more wealthy and powerful homeland. This problematic cultural identity and tenuous relation with China reappears again and again in later writing and becomes a characteristic of the Chinese diasporic experience.

The 1920s and 1930s also saw many writers travel to the West, including poets Li Jinfa 李金发, Xu Zhimo 徐志摩, and Wen Yiduo 闻一多 and novelists Ba Jin 巴金, Lao She 老舍, and Qian Zhongshu 钱钟书. In fact, Lao She (1899–1966) started writing novels while he taught at University of London. His *Ma and Son* (二马, 1929) is a comedy of manners heavily influenced by the English literary tradition. Set in a hostile London, the novel depicts a troubled father-son relationship as it plays out in a restricting environment of cultural difference and racial prejudice. Few subsequent writers have been able to emulate the unsentimental and sardonic way Lao She treats this "expatriate Chinese syndrome" and the problematic patriotism of Chinese abroad.

Wars, revolution, and the split between China and Taiwan in 1949 shattered many Chinese lives, divided countless families, and drove thousands into exile. Literature from Taiwan best captured this experience of forced exile and separation on a national scale. One of the most ambitious and powerful works to explore this traumatic experience against the turbulent backdrop of modern Chinese history is Nie Hualing's (aka Nieh Hualing) 聂华苓 (b. 1925) *Mulberry and Peach: Two Women of China* (桑青与桃红, 1976). After losing her father and mainland home during the anti-Japanese and civil wars, Nie went to Taiwan in 1949, but she soon became disillusioned with the Nationalist government's totalitarianism and suppression of dissent. She fled again to Iowa in the early 1960s, becoming one of the founders and organizers of the International Writing Program at the University of Iowa. *Mulberry and Peach* largely resembles Nie's personal journey. It is a scattered history of a woman whose life has become a never-ending flight. Highly symbolic and psychological, the novel nonetheless has a realistic framework and contains many historical references. It is divided into four parts, each with two sections. The first sections of each part consist of letters sent by the protagonist Peach to U.S. immigration officials during her flight across America. They are arranged in chronological order, dating from January to March 1970. The other sections are notebooks that Mulberry/Peach offers to immigration officials and that record different periods of her life from 1945 to the 1960s. Occupying the main body of the novel, the notebooks reveal the protagonist's gradual transformation from Mulberry, a timid, terrified, traditional Chinese girl, to Peach, a fierce, vigorous, sexually liberated woman from "nowhere." First, we see Mulberry in a refugee boat stranded in the Yangtze Gorges during the war against Japan; then she is stranded again, this time in the besieged city of Beiping, right before the Communist takeover; the third time we see Mulberry, she and her family are trapped in an attic as a result of her husband's embezzlement in 1950s Taipei; finally, the protagonist, by now a middle-aged woman, has fled to America, leaving her old self behind and wandering from one man to another.

Nie's use of diary and epistolary structure and her symbolic treatment of the theme of exile give psychological and historical depth to the metamorphosis of the protagonist. As one critic has put it, "The author succeeds in integrating the individual's fate with the nation's destiny" (S. Yu 1993: 138). Although one can view the tragic tale of Mulberry/Peach as a "national allegory" of disorder and fragmentation, Nie's dynamic structure offers a more reflective take on the diasporic situation. By placing the bitter memories of Mulberry's past back to back with Peach's narrative of her adventures through America, Nie displays an ambivalent attitude toward exile. It is not just a painful, negative experience of escape; it can also be an opportunity to unleash liberating forces in the quest for personal identity. Mulberry's repeated entrapments in China contrast with

Peach's voluntary journey across America. This journey begins with an intense inner struggle between her two selves; finally, Mulberry is killed and a new self, Peach, independent of society and history, is born: "You are dead, Mulberry. I have come to life. I've been alive all along. But now I have broken free" (Nieh 1981: 223). In order to gain this new identity, her traumatic memories must be shrugged off, as Peach's letters to the immigration officer make clear. Thus when Peach joins a group of drifters "on the road," she embraces the spirit of adventure at the heart of American culture and shows her determination to escape her "fate" and survive: "I am a stranger wherever I go, but I'm happy, and there are lots of interesting things to see and do" (4).

Since the 1950s there has been a constant flow of Taiwanese and Hong Kong people studying and migrating all over the world, either to escape political uncertainty or attracted by the global economic market, or both. To a certain degree, this is an extension of their earlier flights from mainland China and the constant threat of communism. This connection is most evident in Bai Xianyong's 白先勇 (b. 1937) personal experience and writing. The son of a Guomindang general, Bai left mainland China with his family to go to Hong Kong (in 1948) and then resettled in Taiwan in 1952 when he was fifteen. After graduating from Taiwan National University, he went to the United States to study. Bai subsequently became a professor of Chinese literature at the University of California in Santa Barbara and has resided there ever since. Regarded as a representative of "exile literature" (Bai's own term), Bai's melancholic works feature people involuntarily losing their roots and living in their memories of a glorious past. In Bai's characters, the tension between tradition and modernity, shared by all Chinese intellectuals, has been intensified by a "Taiwanese complex," a sense of being cut off from home and roots. Seen in this light, it is no coincidence that the overseas Chinese in Bai's *New Yorkers* (纽约客, 1974) share the fate and sentiments of the former mainlanders in Taiwan from his collection *Wandering in the Garden, Waking from a Dream* (台北人, 1971) in spite of their different environments: "Deprived of his cultural heritage, the wandering Chinese has become a spiritual exile: Taiwan and the motherland are incommensurable. . . . The Rootless Man, therefore, is destined to become a perpetual Wanderer . . . sad because he has been driven out of Eden, dispossessed, disinherited, a spiritual orphan, burdened with a memory that carries the weight of 5,000 years" (Pai 1976: 208–209).

In the 1960s and 1970s, a modernizing Taiwan also witnessed great waves of students going overseas to study, many of them writers or budding writers. No doubt encouraged by the enthusiastic support of Taiwanese and Hong Kong literary magazines and newspaper literary supplements, "literature of students abroad" and "Chinese overseas literature" also became fashionable topics for scholarly study and publication in Hong Kong and Taiwan.

Yu Lihua 於梨华 (b. 1931) is a prolific novelist whose many works depict the sentimental journey of Taiwanese students abroad trying to return to a home they cannot adjust to anymore. Yu became a de facto spokesperson for this "rootless generation" after publishing her well-received novel *Again the Palm Tree, Again the Palm Tree* (又见棕榈，又见棕榈, 1967). Realistic in style yet full of lyricism, *Again the Palm Tree* presents another wanderer drifting between the United States and Taiwan, between a nostalgia for the past and alienation in the present—and this alienation pervades both the American society where he has settled and the Taiwanese society that he visits. The uprootedness and "cultural vulnerability" (Pai 1976: 208) the protagonist experiences are sentimentally explored against the backdrop of an organic image: the tree, an age-old overseas Chinese symbol of one's relationship with the homeland. The huge gap between the imagined homeland and reality becomes the core of the protagonist's tragedy.

The other side of this desperate search for roots and a homeland can be seen in the many diaspora writers who have become "nativist overseas." In the fiction of Zhang Xiguo 张系国, Liu Daren 刘大任, and Chen Ruoxi 陈若曦, political engagement and nationalist sentiments abound, and an "obsession with China" becomes both a moral strength and a burden. Chen Ruoxi (b. 1938) is representative of these nativist overseas writers committed to writing about major social and political issues. Born in Taiwan, Chen lived in mainland China during the Cultural Revolution, then in North America for more than twenty years before returning to Taiwan in the mid-1990s. Although she is best known for her stories about the Cultural Revolution (see "Nativism and Localism in Taiwanese Literature"), after 1979 she shifted her focus to the lives of Chinese intellectuals in the United States. Often her characters are sojourners whose return home is delayed by historical circumstances. Although not as dark and melancholy as Bai Xianyong's and Yu Lihua's characters, the overseas Chinese in Chen's works are nonetheless anxious to find stability in their floating lives by establishing a new relationship with China—be it Taiwan or the People's Republic of China (PRC)—and they are all concerned with the current state and future direction of their motherland. Likewise, Chen often uses characters and their relationships to represent the various cultural and political identities and commitments of Chinese overseas.

A rare exception to Taiwanese writers' nostalgic or nationalist mode is the work of Ma Sen 马森 (b. 1932). Heavily influenced by 1960s Western culture, especially existentialism, Ma Sen distinguishes himself from his compatriots by treating the isolation and alienation of the Chinese diaspora as part of a universal modern predicament. This approach is especially evident in the stories collected in *Isolation* (隔绝, 1979). Also, in his novel *Night Wandering* (夜游, 1984), Ma describes a Chinese immigrant experiencing a unique kind of self-imposed exile. The protagonist, Wang Peilin 汪佩琳, chooses to leave home and befriend a group of wandering hippies as a protest against both the middle-class lifestyle of her "white" professor husband and the Chinese cultural conventions and ethics of her parents. Her adventures in the underground world of Vancouver during the 1970s very much resemble the search of American youth for an alternative life and identity. With Ma Sen, the universal existential quest has replaced ethnic and cultural differences.

The "opening up" of the PRC under Deng Xiaoping led to another Chinese emigrant tide, especially after 1989, when many writers and intellectuals were forced into exile. Studies of "literature of students abroad" and "overseas Chinese literature" gained a new following in the PRC. *Today* (今天), a poetry magazine banned in the early 1980s (see "Misty Poetry"), then revived as a general literary journal in 1990 by the exiled poet Bei Dao 北岛, has acted as an important literary venue for mainland writers overseas.

The stories collected in Zha Jianying 查建英's (b. 1959) *Going to America, Going to America* (到美国去, 到美国去, 1990) are some of the earliest yet most promising works of mainland Chinese émigrés. Zha's world, though still dominated by Chinese students and their peripheral community, often juxtaposes them with other marginal Americans, be they southerners, Jews, or South Asians. Thus, as in the work of Ma Sen, the diasporic experience is depicted not as uniquely Chinese but as a universal condition of the modern age, "the age of anxiety and estrangement" (Said 1994, 137). In Zha's "Ice River in the Jungle" (丛林下的冰河, 1988), which describes a female student's journey to the New World and subsequent return visit to China, the Chinese and Western worlds play equally important roles in her search for the meaning of life, and both cultures are given equal space in her reflections. Unlike other stories of return, which tend to be permeated with a nostalgic tone and focus on the negative aspects of marginality, this story is filled with the adventurous spirit of being "on the road." The journey the protagonist takes to discover her destiny of living on the periphery is an exciting and open-ended one, even if occasionally confusing and full of sadness. In Zha's work, the moral dilemmas and identity crises of Chinese overseas are treated with a subtlety and complexity reminiscent of Henry James.

Before embarking on her journey to the West, Liu Suola 刘索拉 (b. 1955), an avant-garde novelist and musician, published a travel journal, "Rocking-and-Rolling on the Road" (摇摇滚滚的道路, 1987), in which her visit to the United States is presented as an exciting, eye-opening experience in a present-tense narrative of immediacy. However, in *Chaos and All That* (混沌加哩咯楞, 1991), written during her stay in the United Kingdom, Liu Suola presents a divided narrative whose memory-haunted narrator-character resembles much more a creation of Salman Rushdie than one of her previous J. D. Salinger-type protagonists. Shifting constantly between late 1980s London and Beijing of the 1950s to 1980s, this novel is like a collective autobiography of a generation growing up in the Mao era and then drifting into the global village. The hybridity and tension in which this diasporic protagonist lives are revealed by the incongruous gulf that separates her memories from her reality. To heighten this contrast, Liu chooses two different narrative modes to indicate the difference in the character's commitment to these two worlds: while a first-person monologue presents the past in Beijing as an intimate, vigorous, and complete life, despite its inherent absurdities, a third-person narrative depicts her London life as a bored, nostalgic, and isolated émigré. Ultimately, recollection of the past overwhelms the present reality. Yet having said this, we cannot help noticing that the internal exile of this generation started long before their external exile, as they grew up in a confused "revolutionary era," feeling alienated from both tradition and revolution. What makes this chaotic, hybrid life truly fresh and vivid is Liu's playful but innovative use of "disparate elements" (S. Liu 1994: 132) in her language. Emulating the literary and documentary sources of her times, Liu's narrative itself is a rich display of multiple and conflicting realities.

In Chinese, the concept of exile often connotes a negative and undesirable "banishment as a form of punishment by government" from one's homeland and people (Lee 1994: 226). The exiled intellectual Liu Zaifu 刘再复 (b. 1941) was placed in that situation when he left China after the Tiananmen massacre of 1989. During the following decade, while traveling across different continents, Liu composed three collections of travel journals that record his pilgrimage in search of a real homeland, a spiritual space that transcends cultural and geographical boundaries and that he can share with Western intellectuals. His journey starts with pain, loneliness, and anxiety in *Notes from Drifting* (漂流手记, 1992), goes through a stage of wandering and searching for freedom and new perspectives in *The Days of Traveling Afar* (远游岁月, 1995), and finally reaches a new understanding of the concept of homeland in *Searching for Homeland Westward* (西寻故乡, 1997). He writes of the last work: "This collection is my discovery of a homeland. Rootless wandering has forced me to deconstruct and alter my ideas about my homeland. . . . In my questioning, I have bid farewell to the 'nostalgic' mode and the tribal concept of land . . . and I have now given birth to a homeland within my heart" (Liu Zaifu 1997: 11, 14). In these lyrical prose works, Liu manages to combine an incisive cultural critique and scholarly breadth of knowledge with a poetic style and is especially successful in using concrete imagery to present profound philosophical reflection.

Although Chinese diasporas consist of highly heterogeneous groups from different regions with various economic, cultural, and linguistic backgrounds dispersed to different sites for divergent political and economic reasons, the literary representation of diasporas has been, as demonstrated in the foregoing discussion, limited to the relatively narrow scope of the contemporary well-educated middle class, often first-generation immigrants: students, professionals, artists, and intellectuals. This narrow focus contrasts with the depiction of Chinese diaspora by Anglophone writers, where family histories and diverse social groups of Chinese diasporas, especially women and the working classes, have been given prominent places.

In recent years, two overseas women writers from mainland China, Yan Geling 严歌苓 (b. 1958) and Zhang Ling 张翎 (b. 1957), have extended the literary horizon by representing a more varied Chinese diaspora and looking back into the depths of history. Yan's *Lost Daughter of Happiness* (扶桑, 1995) was first serialized in Taiwan and later translated into English. Set in the seedy underworld of San Francisco's Chinatown during the gold rush in the late nineteenth century, *Lost Daughter* is about the love affairs between an enigmatic Chinese prostitute, Fusang 扶桑, and an American boy, Chris, who becomes obsessed with her. Shifting the narrative between the fetishistic gaze of Chris and the cynical voice of a postmodernist narrator, a contemporary writer who claims she uses her imagination to fill in the historical gaps, the novel is highly experimental with its narrative but relatively thin in its historical content. The appealing visual quality and details of ethnic rituals and customs, from bound feet to slave auctions in Chinatown brothels, race riots, and gangster fights in the port cities of the Wild West, remind one of the tendency toward ethnography and self-orientalism in Chinese literature and films of the late 1980s and 1990s (Chow 1995: 180–181). *Lost Daughter* is less a realist representation of early Chinese immigrants than a visual spectacle of an exotic and erotic "China in the West."

Zhang Ling does a better job in representing early immigrants to Canada in her *Golden Mountain Blues* (金山, 2009). Fashioned as a family history, this epic work ambitiously chronicles a century of Chinese immigration from Canton to North America, as represented by four generations of the Fong family. Despite its clearly marked historical dimension—the author did extensive archival and field research (Zhang 2009: 5)—the novel manages to retain a fine balance between hard historical facts and an imaginative fictional world with passionate voices, a compelling plot, and intricate characters. What particularly distinguishes this novel from previous writings about diaspora, in both Chinese and English, is the transnational perspective that encompasses two continents across the Pacific. From the determined dream-chaser Fong Ah-fat to the curious root-seeker Amy Smith, from the struggle of laundry store owners in Victoria's Chinatown to the fear that haunts the family home in the village of Kaiping, and from the laboring on the Canadian Pacific Railway, which caused these immigrants to embark on their journey from home in the 1880s, to the Communist-led peasant revolution, which violently smashed traditional Chinese society in the 1940s, Zhang presents "a panoramic history of Chinese diaspora where both roots and routes are given new complex meanings in the light of epochal change and mobility" (Kong 2012: 13).

In sum, the experience of diaspora has opened up cultural space for being Chinese. Although it has brought with it constant anxiety regarding home and roots, it has also given a sense of liberation and the opportunity to develop a dual perspective on identity. Chinese diasporic narratives of the twentieth century explore this new cultural space, which transcends any single nation, and vividly describe the experience of living in it. Written within a cultural tradition where roots, home, the land, and social grouping have played a decisive role in identity formation, and under the historical shadow of a nation torn apart by war, revolution, and foreign interference, much Chinese literature depicts transnational and marginal living as emotionally traumatic, spiritually depressing, and culturally threatening. We still see in many of these works a desperate obsession with China and Chineseness. But at the same time, some diaspora writing also investigates a new kind of hybrid sensibility, which celebrates the possibilities that travel and marginal living open up, and manages to view self, identity, and homeland from a broader, more positive perspective.

Bibliography

Chow, Rey. *Primitive Passion: Visuality, Sexuality, Ethnography, and Contemporary Chinese Cinema*. New York: Columbia University Press, 1995.

Denton, Kirk A. "The Distant Shore: The Nationalist Theme in Yu Dafu's 'Sinking.'" *Chinese Literature: Essays, Articles and Reviews* 14 (1992): 107–123.

FitzGerald, Carolyn. "'Diary of a Madwoman' Traversing the Diaspora: Rewriting Lu Xun in Hualing Nieh's *Mulberry and Peach*." *Modern Chinese Literature and Culture* 26, 2 (Fall 2014): 38–88.

Kong Shuyu 孔书玉. "Jinshan xiangxiang yushijie wenxue bantu zhong de hanyu zuyi xiezuo" 金山想象与世界文学版图中的汉语族裔写作 (Imagining Golden Mountain: Chinese ethnic writing in world literature). *Huawen wenxue* 5 (2012): 5–16.

Lao, She. *Ma and Son: A Novel by Lao She*. Trans. Jean M. James. San Francisco: Chinese Materials Center, 1980.

Lee, Leo Ou-fan. "On the Margins of the Chinese Discourse: Some Personal Thoughts on the Cultural Meaning of the Periphery." In Wei-ming Tu, ed., *The Living Tree: The Changing Meaning of Being Chinese Today*, 221–228. Stanford, CA: Stanford University Press, 1994.

Liu, Suola. *Chaos and All That*. Trans. Richard King. Honolulu: University of Hawai'i Press, 1994.

Liu Zaifu 刘再复. *Xi xun guxiang* 西寻故乡(Searching for homeland westward). Hong Kong: Tiandi tushu, 1997.

Nieh, Hualing. *Two Women of China: Mulberry and Peach*. Trans. Jane Parish Yang and Linda Lappin. Beijing: New World Press, 1981.

Ong, Aihwa. *Flexible Citizenship: The Cultural Logics of Transnationality*. Durham, NC: Duke University Press, 1999.

Pai, Hsien-yung. "The Wandering Chinese: The Theme of Exile in Taiwan Fiction." *Iowa Review* 7, 2–3 (Spring–Summer 1976): 208–209.

Said, Edward. "Reflections on Exile." In March Robinson, ed., *Altogether Elsewhere: Writers on Exile*, 137–150. New York: Harcourt Brace, 1994.

Shih, Shu-Mei. "Global Literature and the Technologies of Recognition." *PMLA* 119, 1 (2004): 16–30.

Tucker, Martin, ed. *Literary Exile in the Twentieth Century: An Analysis and Biographical Dictionary*. New York: Greenwood Press, 1991.

Yu, Dafu. "Sinking." In Joseph S. M. Lau, C. T. Hsia, and Leo Lee Ou-fan, eds., *Modern Chinese Stories and Novellas, 1919–1949*, 125–141. New York: Columbia University Press, 1981.

Yu, Shiao-ling. "The Theme of Exile and Identity Crisis in Nie Hualing's Fiction." In Hsin-sheng Kao, ed., *Nativism Overseas: Contemporary Chinese Women Writers*, 127–156. Albany: State University of New York Press, 1993.

Zhang Ling 张翎. *Jinshan* 金山 (Golden Mountain blues). Beijing: Shiyue wenyi, 2009.

7

SINOPHONE LITERATURE

BRIAN BERNARDS

The term "Sinophone" denotes Chinese-speaking individuals and communities, yet it implies that their locations and histories are heterogeneous (that is, not limited to China) and the languages they speak (including dialects, topolects, creoles, and pidgins) are varied and multiple. From a linguistic standpoint, "Sinophone" refers to communities that speak Sinitic languages, which include Mandarin, Yue (Cantonese), Min (Hokkien, Teochew), Hakka, Wu (Shanghainese), and other languages typically misrepresented as dialectal varieties of a singular Chinese language. Derived from this linguistic framework, "Sinophone literature" denotes literature written in Sinitic languages, acknowledging that despite historical pressures to conform one's writing in the Sinitic script (or "Chinese characters") to a single, standardized literary medium—either the classical "literary language" (文言文) or the modern "vernacular language" (白话文)—authors still inflect their writing with other Sinitic (or even non-Sinitic) languages. The concept of Sinophone literature is therefore attentive to the sense of multilingualism conveyed by the diverse environments, experiences, and subjectivities of authors who write in the Sinitic script.

The primary purpose of the Sinophone designation—as alternative or counterpoint to "Chinese"—is to highlight commonly conflated distinctions between ethnicity, language, and nation in literary categorization. The term "Chinese" tends to collapse all three into one overarching scheme of equivalence and assumes that if one writes in Chinese, he or she is both ethnically Chinese (Han) and of Chinese (PRC or ROC) nationality. As a relatively recent concept in English-language scholarship, "Sinophone literature" represents a new translation of various terms that have rich and deeply rooted genealogies at odds with the master narrative of "modern Chinese literature" (中国现代文学) as a national literary enterprise. Most notably, "Sinophone literature" is an updated translation of 华文文学, a term that until recently had been defined as "literature in Chinese" or "overseas Chinese literature" (海外华文文学).

This Sinophone literature developed throughout the twentieth century as "minor" literary traditions in the many areas of Chinese overseas settlement around the world, but its distinction from "Chinese literature" was first given articulation among Chinese settler communities in Southeast Asia, particularly in colonial Malaya and the British Straits Settlements of Singapore and Penang, in response to the influence of the May Fourth new literature movement in China. By the 1920s, ongoing Chinese settlement in the "South Seas" (南洋), which began following the end of the First Opium War and the lifting of the Qing imperial ban on overseas emigration, had already produced economically and culturally vibrant Chinese settler societies throughout the Southeast Asian region. The 1911 Revolution, which received much logistical and financial support from these overseas societies, inspired the proliferation of Mandarin-medium schools and vernacular newspapers in Southeast Asia. Although these venues imported and propagated models and trends of the New Literature movement from China, many local writers began to resist the idea of a diasporic "overseas consciousness" (侨民意识) that demanded they orient their cultural affinities and political loyalties toward the ancestral homeland. Following a late 1920s "South Seas color" (南洋色彩) movement that advocated for more local settings and themes in creative writings from the region, these authors founded their own tradition of "Sinophone Malayan new literature" (马华新文学) in the early 1930s, decidedly anchoring their roots and orienting their cultural and political activism in the land of settlement. Following Malaysia's independence, Chinese Malaysian authors and critics such as Miao Xiu 苗秀 (1968) and Fang Xiu 方修 (1970–1972) played instrumental roles in canonizing foundational works and composing distinct literary histories for this "minor" Sinophone tradition.

The unique practices of Sinophone literature from "overseas" sites like Malaysia steadily gained visibility in the field of modern Chinese literature as Chinese Malaysian writers, marginalized by postcolonial policies of "positive discrimination" favoring Malay-language education and publication in their home country, took advantage of educational and creative opportunities in Taiwan throughout the Cold War and eventually attracted the attention of the literary establishment there. Studying, writing, and teaching in Taiwan, the Chinese Malaysian author, scholar, and literary critic Ng Kim Chew 黄锦树 not only helped introduce Sinophone Malaysian literary history to a broader transnational readership in critical works such as *Sinophone Malaysian Literature and Chineseness* (马华文学与中国性, 1998) but also theorized key differences in cultural, literary, and language politics between what he called Sinophone (华文) and Chinese (中文) writing. Ng argues that Sinophone writing is the "reinvention" of a written language by writers outside China whose spoken vernaculars do not possess standard written forms in the Sinitic script. For Ng, Sinophone writing inevitably draws attention to the medium itself as a mode of translating reality. Drawing on the example of Malaysian author Li Yongping 李永平 and his novel *The Jiling Chronicles* (吉陵春秋, 1986), which with exquisite technical virtuosity reconstructs the language of traditional vernacular Chinese fiction in order to produce a mesmerizing atmosphere of cultural "authenticity," Ng (2013: 89) argues that such pursuits of Chineseness represent only one, but not the only and inevitable, trajectory of Sinophone modernism. Other Sinophone reinventions include the type of Chinese-Malay linguistic intermixing that Ng produces in his own satirical fiction on assimilation and the diasporic Chinese psyche in postcolonial Malaysia, or the metaphorical transformation of the Chinese character by the tropical junglescape in Zhang Guixing's 张贵兴 novels. For example, in Zhang's *My South Seas Sleeping Beauty* (我思念的长眠中的南国公主, 2001), the protagonist's mother constructs an immaculate and enchanting "Garden of Eden" on her husband's frontier estate in Sarawak with garden paths resembling mysterious Chinese characters, only to see this attempted inscription of the landscape and the garden itself become virtually indistinguishable from the surrounding Borneo rainforest that conceals and eventually engulfs it (Zhang 2007: 191). Here, the Chinese settler's original language of inscription becomes lost to the jungle. Yet, as the verbosely descriptive and meticulously detailed language of Zhang's Sinophone text demonstrates, the loss of this language, as well as the history it tells, is replaced not with utter silence but, rather, with an inventive, imaginative, and enchanting language of the rainforest that renarrates the settler's history from a local perspective.

The visibility of Sinophone Malaysian literature in Taiwan owes much to the "exiled" island republic's own reassessments of its ambiguous geopolitical status and unique colonial history following its loss of international diplomatic recognition, along with its claim to mainland China, in the late 1970s and the lifting of martial law in 1987. Faced with their own repositioning outside the mainstream narrative of modern Chinese literature, writers and literary critics in Taiwan began to rewrite the island's Chinese national literary genealogy as a Sinophone one by linking contemporary developments, such as the Taiwanese "nativist" (乡土) movement, to earlier literary trends that emerged with authors who wrote (in both Japanese and Chinese) under Japanese colonial rule before the Guomindang's 1945 "retaking" of the island. In addition to the nativist trend (see "Diaspora in Modern Chinese Literature"), there was growing interest in reconstructing a multilingual indigenous literary history of Taiwan's aboriginal populations, from oral folktales in aboriginal languages collected by Japanese colonial ethnographers to Sinophone writings by indigenous authors who contest their portrayal as barbarian "savages" in imperial China's dynastic histories. Sun Dachuan's 孙大川 seven-volume *Anthology of Taiwan's Sinophone Indigenous Literature* (台湾原住民族汉语文学选集, 2003) best exemplifies this trend.

Like Sinophone writers from Malaysia, Taiwan's aboriginal writers bring their multilingual upbringings and environments to bear on their written vernacular. In his examination of Sinophone indigenous writings, John Balcom (2005: xxi) notes how "the native language of an author impacts or 'interferes' with the style and grammar of his or her writing in Chinese" (not only as the transliterated addition of indigenous vocabulary but also as a restructuring of the standard subject-verb-object order with the verb-subject-object order common to Austronesian languages) to produce an aboriginal "subversion" and "remaking" of standard Chinese writing. As for its content, much indigenous literature draws attention not only to prevalent colonizing attitudes among Taiwan's Han settler majority toward aboriginal peoples but also to ongoing processes of settler colonization, such as timber extraction, that edge communities off their traditional hunting grounds and fishing waters by reducing game, decimating indigenous livelihoods, and rendering communities dependent on government assistance. In Topas Tamapima's 田雅各 short story "The Last Hunter" (最后的猎人, 1987), for example, a national park ranger berates the protagonist, an indigenous hunter, criticizing his poor Mandarin, calling "mountain people" cruel and "lazy and dirty," and confiscating the muntjac deer caught by the hunter (Balcom and Balcom 2005: 18–20).

Aboriginal writers in Taiwan conventionally describe their Sinophone literature as "literature in the Han language" (汉语文学), which like "overseas Chinese literature" can be understood as a "minor," or minority, tradition outside the mainstream history of modern Chinese literature. Yet unlike the overseas literature, which predominately refers to a literary tradition in a language brought and/or adopted by Chinese emigrants and their descendants abroad, literature in the Han language implicates Mandarin and modern Chinese literature as a language, body of knowledge, and cultural discourse historically imposed on the largely non-Han frontiers of the Chinese nation—that is, of both the Republic of China (ROC) in Taiwan and the People's Republic of China (PRC) on the mainland. In this sense, the genealogy of modern Sinophone literature by indigenous writers in Taiwan draws direct parallels to that of Tibetan writers in China. Whereas Sinophone writers from Malaysia and other overseas sites frequently, but not universally, adopt standard Chinese out of a desire to reclaim a native language and ethnocultural identity, or Chineseness, the decision among indigenous writers in Taiwan or Tibetan authors in China to write in the Han language "often implies a sense of *loss* of ethnocultural identity" and one's native tongue (Bernards and Tsai 2013: 188). As Patricia Schiaffini (2013: 288–289) points out, renowned Sinophone Tibetan writers like Tashi Dawa 扎西达娃 and Alai 阿来, most of whom are of mixed Han and Tibetan descent, "were raised and educated in a Chinese environment," yet "it is their nominal Tibetan identity that carries more tokenized cultural capital" among Han Chinese readers, as they are "expected to write solely about Tibet." In some cases, the discovery of their "Tibetanness" leaves Sinophone Tibetan writers feeling guilty about their lack of knowledge of Tibetan culture and language. The poetry by Woeser 唯色 from the early 1990s reflects on this sense of guilt while affirming a strong desire to embark on a "homeward" journey to reclaim a Tibetan cultural heritage, particularly through Tibetan Buddhism, that was largely unknown to her growing up during the Maoist period. For example, in her poem "Of Mixed Race" (混血儿, 1993), Woeser (2008: 80) describes herself as an "offspring of those poor and secret tribes" who has finally arrived at the "aching atmosphere among the peaks and swift waters," where she "dips into her meager stock of adjectives" to produce "songs that ring like gleaming gold coins."

Western scholars of Tibetan literature such as Schiaffini (2013) and Lara Marconi (2002) first applied the term "Sinophone" to Han-language literature by Tibetan authors not only to distinguish it from Tibetan-language literature but also to underscore the complex politics of language and cultural identity in Tibetan literature as a multilingual tradition. Drawing together the distinct applications of the Sinophone moniker to the "minor" literary traditions of both Han-language literature and overseas Chinese literature in their respective locales, Shu-mei Shih (2007) gave the term "Sinophone" its first critical theorization—and inaugurated the new field of Sinophone studies—by outlining three historical processes that have produced Sinophone cultures in different parts of the world: continental colonialism (the expansion of the Qing empire into regions like Tibet and Xinjiang, territories consolidated under successive Chinese nation-states), settler colonialism (the creation of Chinese-majority settler societies in Taiwan but also Singapore), and overseas migration (leading to the formation of significant Chinese-minority communities in places like Malaysia, Indonesia, Australia, and North America). Guided by this tripartite framework, Shih (2013: 11) delineates Sinophone studies as the study of "Sinitic-language communities and cultures outside China as well as ethnic minority communities and cultures within China where Mandarin is adopted or imposed." In order to move beyond the more monolingual connotations of both Han-language literature and literature in Chinese, Shih also translated the concept of the Sinophone back into Mandarin as "Sinitic-language family" (华语语系), because she intended the concept of Sinophone literature to encompass all the "literatures of the Sinitic-language family" (华语语系文学). With her focus on minority and marginal communities, as well as linguistic multiplicity, Shih imbues "Sinophone" with critical significance beyond mere linguistic denotation ("Chinese-speaking"), akin, but not identical, to postcolonial models of Francophone literature by authors from the former French colonies in Africa and the Caribbean and sites of French settlement abroad, like Quebec.

Shih's approach has sparked robust debate about the scope of the Sinophone category and its criteria for inclusion or exclusion, particularly its critical positioning vis-à-vis mainland China and Han Chinese cultural production there (do their boundaries overlap or are they distinct?). What is often lost in these debates is that Shih (2007: 185) devised her concept of the Sinophone not so much as an objective *category* whose boundaries must be rigidly policed, but as a "place-based" *practice* of reading and interpreting literary and other cultural texts. By proposing the Sinophone as an alternative to the "overseas Chinese" diaspora model (see "Diaspora in Modern Chinese Literature"), Shih's framework compels readers to ponder how their understanding of a given text changes when they approach it not as a diasporic or overseas text, which emphasizes its sense of distance and separation from the ancestral homeland, but as a Sinophone text that is rooted in the experience of the time and place in which it is produced. For example, a "Sinophone American" reading of the short story "A Day in Pleasantville" (安乐乡的一日, 1964) by Bai Xianyong/Pai Hsien-yung 白先勇, included in the author's *New Yorkers* (纽约客, 1974) volume, might attribute the protagonist's inability to integrate in a largely white, bourgeois suburban New York neighborhood not to her lamentable "exile" from a Chinese cultural milieu and homeland, but to the racist and exclusionary practices of an Anglo-dominant American society that paradoxically orientalizes her in the role of a "stereotyped Chinese" while demanding her conformity and assimilation (Pai 1981: 187). As an American text, Pai's work issues a challenge to the assimilationist standards and racist biases of white normativity in the United States while contributing to a more broadly conceived, multilingual canon of American literature a compelling account not of what it means to be Chinese, but of what it means to be American, though not of the dominant culture.

The Sinophone designation therefore draws critical attention to the fact that there is much literature that though written in Chinese, or more precisely Sinitic languages, does not necessarily belong to China and is not inevitably "obsessed with China," but speaks to local conditions and local histories. In addition to a category of literature, the Sinophone is a "reading lens" and perspective that emphasizes and prioritizes the local production of Sinophone cultures and does not inevitably measure them against the political and aesthetic standards of the presumed cultural center or ancestral land. Just as Sinophone literature may serve as a vehicle through which an author expresses, affirms, or redefines his or her sense of Chineseness, it may also be the medium through which one constructs and expresses particular types of Tibetanness, Americanness, Malaysianness, Taiwaneseness, and so on.

Bibliography

Balcom, John. "Translator's Introduction." In John and Yingtsih Balcom, eds., *Indigenous Writers of Taiwan: An Anthology of Stories, Essays, and Poems*, xi–xxiv. New York: Columbia University Press, 2005.

Balcom, John, and Yingtsih Balcom, eds. *Indigenous Writers of Taiwan: An Anthology of Stories, Essays, and Poems*. New York: Columbia University Press, 2005.

Bernards, Brian, and Chien-hsin Tsai. "Sites and Articulations." In Shu-mei Shih, Chien-hsin Tsai, and Brian Bernards, eds., *Sinophone Studies: A Critical Reader*, 183–190. New York: Columbia University Press, 2013.

Fang Xiu 方修, ed. *Ma Hua xin wenxue daxi* 马华新文学大系 (Compendium of Sinophone Malayan new literature). 10 vols. Singapore: Xingzhou shijie shuju, 1970–1972.

Groppe, Alison. *Sinophone Malaysian Literature: Not Made in China*. Amherst, NY: Cambria Press, 2013.

Kenley, David L. *New Culture in a New World: The May Fourth Movement and the Chinese Diaspora in Singapore, 1919–1932*. London: Routledge, 2003.

Li, Yung-p'ing. *Retribution: The Jiling Chronicles*. Trans. Howard Goldblatt and Sylvia Li-chun Lin. New York: Columbia University Press, 2003.

Mair, Victor. "What Is a Chinese 'Dialect/Topolect'? Reflections on Some Key Sino-English Linguistic Terms." *Sino-Platonic Papers* 29 (1991): 1–31.

Marconi, Lara. "Lion of the Snowy Mountains: The Tibetan Poet Yi dam Tse ring and His Chinese Poetry: Reconstructing Tibetan Cultural Identity in Chinese." In P. Christian Klieger, ed., *Tibet, Self, and the Tibetan Diaspora: Voices of Difference*, 165–194. Leiden: Brill, 2002.

Miao Xiu 苗秀. *Ma Hua wenxue shihua* 马华文学史话 (A historical narrative of Sinophone Malayan literature). Singapore: Qingnian shuju, 1968.

Ng, Kim Chew. "Sinophone/Chinese: 'The South Where Language Is Lost' and Reinvented." Trans. Brian Bernards. In Shu-mei Shih, Chien-hsin Tsai, and Brian Bernards, eds., *Sinophone Studies: A Critical Reader*, 74–92. New York: Columbia University Press, 2013.

Pai, Hsien-yung. "A Day in Pleasantville." Trans. Julia Fitzgerald and Vivian Hsu. In Vivian Ling Hsu, ed., *Born of the Same Roots: Stories of Modern Chinese Women*, 184–192. Bloomington: University of Indiana Press, 1981.

Schiaffini, Patricia. "On the Margins of Tibetanness: Three Decades of Sinophone Tibetan Literature." In Shu-mei Shih, Chien-hsin Tsai, and Brian Bernards, eds., *Sinophone Studies: A Critical Reader*, 281–295. New York: Columbia University Press, 2013.

Shih, Shu-mei. *Visuality and Identity: Sinophone Articulations Across the Pacific*. Berkeley: University of California Press, 2007.

——. "What Is Sinophone Studies?" In Shu-mei Shih, Chien-hsin Tsai, and Brian Bernards, eds., *Sinophone Studies: A Critical Reader*, 1–16. New York: Columbia University Press, 2013.

Sun Dachuan 孙大川. *Taiwan yuanzhu minzu Hanyu wenxue xuanji* 台湾原住民族汉语文学选集 (Anthology of Taiwan's Sinophone indigenous literature). 7 vols. Taipei: INK yinke, 2003.

Tan, E. K. *Rethinking Chineseness: Translational Sinophone Identities in the Nanyang Literary World*. Amherst, NY: Cambria Press, 2013.

Topas Tamapima. "The Last Hunter." Trans. John Balcom. In John and Yingtsih Balcom, eds., *Indigenous Writers of Taiwan: An Anthology of Stories, Essays, and Poems*, 3–20. New York: Columbia University Press, 2005.

Tsu, Jing, and David Der-wei Wang, eds. *Global Chinese Literature: Critical Essays*. Leiden: Brill, 2010.

Woeser. *Tibet's True Heart: Selected Poems*. Trans. A. E. Clark. Dobbs Ferry, NY: Ragged Banner Press, 2008.

Zhang, Guixing. *My South Seas Sleeping Beauty: A Tale of Memory and Longing*. Trans. Valerie Jaffee. New York: Columbia University Press, 2007.

8

CHINESE LITERATURE AND FILM ADAPTATION
HSIU-CHUANG DEPPMAN

Film adaptations played many important roles in twentieth-century Chinese literature. To understand them, it helps to look at adaptation from two sides: that of the filmmakers who adapted fictional narratives and that of the writers who produced screenplays or incorporated film techniques in their literary work. I begin this essay with a historical overview of twentieth-century Chinese film-fiction interaction, giving special attention to the relationship between adaptation and popular literature. I then describe the vital decade of the 1980s, a time when political reforms spurred new literary and cinematic movements and opened up innovative exchanges between the media. I conclude with examples from Hong Kong, Taiwan, and China that illustrate some of the geographic, aesthetic, and ideological diversity of Chinese adaptation.

After the first movie screening took place as part of a teahouse variety show in Shanghai on August 11, 1896, it did not take long for film adaptations of popular fiction to kick into high gear. The first Chinese film, *The Battle of Mount Dingjun* (定军山), directed by Ren Qingtai 任庆泰 in 1905, was a recording of a Beijing opera adapted from the fourteenth-century historical novel *Romance of the Three Kingdoms* (三国演义). In the 1920s, Chinese directors were enamored of Mandarin Ducks and Butterflies fiction: Bao Tianxiao 包天笑 (1876–1973), a representative writer of this school, charted a novelist-turned-script-writer career path when he joined the famed Shanghai Mingxing Studio in 1924 and wrote ten screenplays. Bao's cinematic ventures anticipated many later writers' involvement in film production: Eileen Chang 张爱玲 (1920–1995), Qiong Yao

琼瑶 (b. 1938), Gu Long 古龙 (1938–1985), Zhu Tianwen 朱天文 (b. 1956), Wang Shuo 王朔 (b. 1958), and Liu Heng 刘恒 (b. 1954) number among the more celebrated novelists who embraced roles as screenwriters.

Prominent directors also turned to literary sources. Cheng Bugao 程步高 pioneered socially engaged filmmaking with his 1933 adaptation of Mao Dun's 茅盾 "Spring Silkworms" (春蚕), thereby paving the way for others to popularize stories of political and humanist interest. Fei Mu's 费穆 1948 adaptation of Li Tianji's 李天济 story into *Spring in a Small Town* (小城之春) is considered by some to be the greatest Chinese film of all time. Li Hanxiang's 李翰祥 1963 adaptation of the classic *The Butterfly Lovers* (梁山伯与祝英台) into *The Love Eterne* (梁山伯与祝英台) is one of the most popular Chinese films ever and a personal favorite of Ang Lee 李安 (b. 1954), whom many consider the most "literary" director in Chinese film history.

A short list of contemporary filmmakers who succeeded commercially by drawing on literary sources would include Zhang Yimou 张艺谋 (b. 1951), Jiang Wen 姜文 (b. 1963), Hou Xiaoxian 侯孝贤 (b. 1947), Wu Nianzhen 吴念真 (b. 1952), Stanley Kwan 关锦鹏 (b. 1957), and Ann Hui 许鞍华 (b. 1947). Whether it is the social tragedy of the underprivileged, as in Hou Xiaoxian's 1983 *The Sandwich Man* (儿子的大玩偶), or the widening city-country divide, as in Zhang Yimou's 1999 *Not One Less* (一个都不能少), or the politically sensitive gay love story, as in Stanley Kwan's 2001 *Lan Yu* (蓝宇), we find in many film adaptations a strategic combination of auteurist activism, populist appeal, and literary flair.

In the steady output of Chinese cinema over the last century, genre fiction generally dominated the aesthetics and marketing of adaptation. Stories of romance, martial arts, fantasy, period drama, and agitprop were especially popular with directors sensitive to political and commercial demands. In the 1980s, however, historical developments began to reshape the landscape of Chinese culture and reconfigure the relationships between film and literature. China's economic reforms and open-door policy in the 1980s coincided with the rise of fifth-generation filmmakers and roots-seeking literature. The 1984 Sino-British Joint Declaration on the principle of "one country, two systems" energized the Hong Kong New Wave. The lifting of martial law in Taiwan in 1987 expanded the political and cultural field for the innovative visions of Taiwan New Cinema. Such transformations sparked animated conversations about democracy, self-governance, and identity politics, three controversial topics that still resonate.

Adaptations in the 1980s were diverse, creative, and provocative. In China, Wu Tianming's 吴天明 1986 *Old Well* (老井; adapted from Zheng Yi 郑义), Zhang Yimou's 1987 *Red Sorghum* (红高粱; from Mo Yan 莫言), and Chen Kaige's 陈凯歌 1987 *King of the Children* (孩子王; from A Cheng 阿城) dramatized conflicts between the collective and the individual. In Taiwan, Chen Kunhou's 陈坤厚 1983 *Growing Up* (小毕的故事; from Zhu Tianwen) and Bai Jingrui's 白景瑞 1984 *The Last Night of Madame Chin* (金大班的最后一夜;

from Bai Xianyong 白先勇) analyzed a society in rapid transition. In Hong Kong, Ann Hui's 1984 *Love in a Fallen City* (倾城之恋; from Eileen Chang), Cheng Xiaodong's 程小东 1987 *A Chinese Ghost Story* (倩女幽魂; from Pu Songling 蒲松龄), and Stanley Kwan's 1988 *Rouge* (胭脂扣; from Li Bihua 李碧华) addressed new social configurations of women. To illustrate how this fecund period continues to affect the cultural discussion today, I describe three examples that adopt different modes of adaptation and represent unique cultural and geographic regions.

Ann Hui's 1984 adaptation of Eileen Chang's 1943 short story "Love in a Fallen City" is an ironic revision of the romance genre, with a political twist. Hui is attracted to the short story for its metaphorical associations of Hong Kong with marginalized characters and by its subversive feminist approach to power paradigms. The plot of the story is deceptively simple: a financially strapped divorcée, Bai Liusu 白流苏, meets a wealthy playboy, Fan Liuyuan 范柳原, in Shanghai; they carry out a courtship in Hong Kong and eventually marry when the British colony falls to Japan at the start of the Asia-Pacific War. While functioning as a classic girl-gets-boy story, the tale also envisions several ways for readers and viewers to compare the successful marriage plot to the larger history of political disaster. Near the end of the story, Chang's narrator suggests that the fall of Hong Kong may have enabled Liusu to realize her dream of marrying Fan Liuyuan. "Tens of thousands of people have died, while tens of thousands continued to suffer. What followed was an earth-shattering revolution. . . . Liusu didn't feel that the role she played in history was anything special. She just stood up with a full smile and kicked the dish of mosquito repellent under the table." Emphasizing the smile of an individual against the canvas of collective suffering, Chang challenges her readers to interpret the causality of war. For Chang, Liusu is justified in ignoring what people say about her, because history is written by patriarchal traditions that marginalize exiled figures like her and her Indian nemesis, Saheiyini. Chang's protagonist sees political disaster largely as background noise.

Sensitive to Chang's subversive depreciation of history, Ann Hui nonetheless laments the difficulty of showing it onscreen: "Eileen Chang's wonderful depictions of people's emotions and her ability to convey very subtle changes in mood and feeling are extremely complicated and almost impossible to visualize" (Berry 2005: 430). But these difficulties also energize her creativity: Hui turns Chang's controversial contrastive techniques into a composite of text and image. In the final scene, as Hui's camera pans across the destruction of the war—strewn bodies, torn flags, broken furniture—it also intersperses images of Chang's original text, printed on the screen as a pictorial supplement.

Because Hui's decision to visualize Chang's language translates her own anxiety about usurping the words of others and abstracting political events, her composite mode of adaptation can be understood as a compromise, one that allows her to balance her viewpoint with Chang's. Retrospectively, one appreciates how Hui's text-image innovation led the way for others: Stanley Kwan's 1994 adaptation of Eileen Chang's 1944 "Red Rose and White Rose" (红玫瑰与白玫瑰) and Wong Kar-wai's 王家卫 2000 adaptation of Liu Yichang's 刘以鬯 1972 Intersection (对倒) into *In the Mood for Love* (花样年华) are award-winning examples of films that prominently feature images of literary text.

If Hong Kong proved fertile ground for reimagining women and politics, Taiwan adaptations inspired complex debates over the ideological implications of an emerging local consciousness. Hou Xiaoxian and Zhu Tianwen were in a strong position to ask what it meant to be "local" because they grew up in culturally mixed households and spoke multiple languages (Hakka, Mandarin, and Taiwanese). Their partnership is uniquely close and productive in the history of Chinese adaptation: they have worked together on thirteen movies as director and screenwriter, and Zhu has revised five of the screenplays into short stories.

Zhu's 1984 adaptation of Hou's 1984 *A Summer at Grandpa's* (冬冬的假期) into "AnAn's Vacation" typifies their multifaceted approach to presenting rural Taiwan. It is the story of city boy An An 安安 (or Dongdong 冬冬 in the movie) and his younger sister Ting Ting 婷婷 who visit their Hakka grandparents in the small town of Miaoli in central Taiwan and witness conflicts among people coping with a variety of social discontents. Zhu originally wrote the screenplay for Hou to make into a movie, and after he completed the film in 1984, she wrote a companion piece to help with the promotion. By using different aesthetic approaches to the same material—Hou distant and serene, Zhu intimate and intense—the duo established an influential dialectical model for other artists.

Hou's camera avoids inciting passion. He uses long-take and immobile cameras to describe the entrapment of Dongdong's uncle Changmin 昌民, who is perceived as a burden to the family due to his aimlessness. In an emotionally charged confession, Changmin speaks to Dongdong about his troubled situation, but Hou's camera stays detached and leaves room for interpretation: he may be a victim of social pressure or a willing accomplice of oppressive tradition. Changmin's predicament represents many Taiwan youths' uncertainty about what path to take and which lead to follow.

In her story, by contrast, Zhu zooms in to write a more confrontational "close-up" of Changmin's personal failure. In the same scene, Zhu describes the young man's expression as "wearing a typical apologetic, feeble smile, as if he was ready to say sorry to anyone at any time." The apologetic mask illustrates a behavioral logic of appearing weak to disarm others, a survival instinct for those under threat. Zhu once commented that adaptation is about manifesting "a certain portion of the work" or "a certain feeling" that moves the adapter (Berry 2005; 246), and in Hou's film she isolates the paralysis of a young generation trapped between parental expectations and independence. In the 1980s, this generational divide became a structural axis for writers and directors seeking to redefine Taiwan, in its burgeoning democratic movement, as a land of many repressed voices. Ultimately Zhu and Hou create a flexible model that illustrates the fluidity of identity formation and paves the way for other successful adaptations using a comparable strategy, as in Chen Guofu's 陈国富 1998 *The Personals* (征婚启事; from Chen Yuhui 陈玉慧) and Wang Yulin's 王育麟 and Liu Zijie's 刘梓洁 2010 *Seven Days in Heaven* (父后七日; from Liu Zijie).

In China, Zhang Yimou and the 2012 Nobel laureate Mo Yan have been the indisputable leaders of cinema and literature, respectively, since the 1980s. Together they use modes of the fantastic to stylize human interactions with nature and raise thoughtful questions about individualism, collectivism, and sexual freedom. Their bold aesthetics have pioneered new ways of looking at a Chinese society transitioning between communism and capitalism.

A landmark in adaptation is Zhang's 1987 film of Mo Yan's 1986 novel *Red Sorghum*. Set in Northeast China, the story is a retrospective look at Gaomi villagers' resistance efforts during the Sino-Japanese War. Speaking from the perspective of a grandson, the narrator recounts the critical events in the lives of his father and grandparents. Mo Yan's narrative moves nonchronologically, leaping from one event or memory to another, whereas Zhang's movie reconstructs the story in a linear, distinct narrative progression. Zhang explains: "An adaptation doesn't have to be like the original work, and it should be filmic. The first thing I do is simplify its events—simplify and popularize" (Jiao 1988: 5). In particular, Zhang identifies the constructions of masculinity and female subjectivity in Mo Yan's text as filmic, sensational, and controversial, and after *Red Sorghum* these tropes drove many Chinese adaptations in the 1980s and beyond. Examples include Zhang's 1990 *Ju Dou* (菊豆; from Liu Heng), Joan Chen's 陈冲 1998 *Xiu Xiu: The Sentdown Girl* (天浴; from Yan Geling 严歌苓), and Ang Lee's 2007 *Lust, Caution* (色戒; from Eileen Chang).

A prominent example takes place in Mo Yan's description of a marriage procession when "grandma" is delivered to her leper groom. He first emphasizes her sexual scrutiny of the sedan bearers' isolated body parts—for example, "statuesque legs," "big, fleshy feet," "firm, muscular chests," and "broad shoulders." This scaled objectification makes her a voyeuristic subject whose scopophilia offers a transgressive choice: shall she begin her married life as an adulteress? While Mo's narrative takes apart a desirable male body, Zhang's adaptation puts it back together with a sequence of shot-reverse shots to contrast "grandma's" mesmerized look of ecstasy with the bearers' lewd gaze. Like most successful directors, Zhang understands what looks good on the screen. For him, the reciprocal gaze allows him to use close-ups that magnify the star power of his actors and transform their expression into an inviting text. Both Mo and Zhang are good at constructing characters seeking freedom of choice. This creative tendency arguably anticipated the 1989 Tiananmen protest against state autocracy.

For most of the century, Chinese fiction and film provided inspiration and raw materials for each other. In the 1980s, their interactions grew more intense, multifaceted, and culturally engaged. These three examples hint at some of the ways leading artists began, through adaptation, to reinterpret, represent, and even reshape their evolving social conditions. That the issues they raised are still being processed, debated, and adapted today suggests that the 1980s marked the beginning of a new era in Chinese cultural production.

Bibliography

A, Cheng. *Three Kings*. Trans. Bonnie S. McDougall. London: William Collins Sons, 1990.
Bai Jingrui 白景瑞. *Jin daban de zuihou yi ye* 金大班的最后一夜 (The last night of Madame Chin). Chuo Mou Production Company, 1984.
Bai Xianyong 白先勇. *You yuan jing meng* 游园惊梦 (Wandering in the garden, waking from a dream). Trans. by Bai Xianyong and Patia Yasin, ed. George Kao. Bloomington: Indiana University Press, 1982.
Berry, Michael. *Speaking in Images: Interviews with Contemporary Chinese Filmmakers*. New York: Columbia University Press, 2005.
Chang, Eileen. *Love in a Fallen City*. Trans. Karen S. Kingsbury. New York: New York Review Books Classics, 2006.
——. *Lust, Caution*. Trans. Julia Lovell. New York: Anchor Books, 2007.
Chen Guofu 陈国富. *Zhenghun qishi* 征婚启事 (The personals). Central Motion Pictures, 1998.
Chen, Joan 陈冲. *Tian yu* 天浴 (Xiu Xiu: The sentdown girl). Good Machine, 1998.
Chen Kaige 陈凯歌. *Haizi wang* 孩子王 (King of the children). Xi'an Film Studio, 1987.
Chen Kunhou 陈坤厚. *Xiao Bi de gushi* 小毕的故事 (Growing up). Central Motion Picture, 1983.
Chen Yuhui 陈玉慧. *Zhenghun qishi* 征婚启事 (The personals). Taipei: Eryu wenhua, 2002.
Cheng Bugao 程步高. *Chuncan* 春蚕 (Spring silkworms). Mingxing Film Company, 1933.
Cheng Xiaodong 程小东. *Qiannü youhun* 倩女幽魂 (A Chinese ghost story). Cinema City Film Production, 1987.
Deppman, Hsiu-Chuang. *Adapted for the Screen: The Cultural Politics of Modern Chinese Fiction and Film*. Honolulu: University of Hawai'i Press, 2010.
Fei Mu 费穆. *Xiaocheng zhi chun* 小城之春 (Spring in a small town). Wenhua Film Company, 1948.
Hou Xiaoxian 侯孝贤. *Dongdong de jiaqi* 冬冬的假期 (A summer at Grandpa's). Central Motion Pictures, 1984.
——. *Erzi de da wan'ou* 儿子的大玩偶 (The sandwich man). Central Motion Pictures, 1983.
Hui, Ann 许鞍华. *Qingcheng zhi lian* 倾城之恋 (Love in a fallen city). Golden Harvest Company, 1984.
Jiao Xiongping 焦雄屏. "Discussing *Red Sorghum*." In Francis Gateward, ed., *Zhang Yimou Interviews*, 3–14. Jackson: University of Mississippi Press, 2001.

Kwan, Stanley 关锦鹏. *Hong meigui, bai meigui* 红玫瑰白玫瑰 (Red rose, white rose). First Film Organization, 1994.

——. *Lan Yu* 蓝宇. Kwan's Creation Workshop, 2001.

——. *Yanzhi kou* 胭脂扣 (Rouge). Golden Harvest Company, 1988.

Mao, Dun. *Spring Silkworms and Other Stories*. Trans. Sidney Shapiro. Beijing: Foreign Languages Press, 1956.

Mo, Yan. *Red Sorghum: A Novel of China*. Trans. Howard Goldblatt. New York: Penguin, 1994.

Lee, Ang 李安. *Se, jie* 色戒 (Lust, caution). Focus Features, 2007.

Li Bihua 李碧华. *Yanzhi kou* 胭脂扣 (Rouge). Beijing: Xinxing, 2013.

Li Hanxiang 李翰祥. *Liang Shanbo yu Zhu Yingtai* 梁山伯与祝英台 (Love eterne). Shaw Brothers, 1963.

Liu Heng 刘恒. *Fuxi Fuxi* 伏羲伏羲. Beijing: Zuojia, 1992.

Liu Yichang 刘以鬯. *Duidao* 对倒 (Intersection). Hong Kong: Huoyi, 2000.

Liu Zijie 刘梓洁. *Fu hou qi ri* 父后七日 (Seven days in heaven). Taipei: Baoping wenhua, 2010.

Wang Yulin and Liu Zijie. 王育麟, 刘梓洁. *Fu hou qi ri* 父后七日 (Seven days in heaven). Magnifique Creative Media Production, 2010.

Wong Kar-wai 王家卫. *Huayang nianhua* 花样年华 (In the mood for love). Block 2 Pictures, 2000.

Wu Tianming 吴天明. *Lao jing* 老井 (Old well). Xi'an Film Studio, 1986.

Yan Geling 严歌苓. *Tian Yu* 天浴. Xi'an: Shanxi shifan daxue, 2012.

Yuan Lei 袁蕾. "Jianji bainian: xunzhao Zhongguo dianying de shengri" 剪辑百年：寻找中国电影的生日 (Editing centennial: Searching for the birthday of Chinese cinema). *Nanfang zhoumo* (May 5, 2005). http://www.southcn.com/weekend/culture/200505050017.htm.

Zhang Yimou 张艺谋. *Hong gaoliang* 红高粱 (Red sorghum). Xi'an Film Studio, 1987.

——. *Ju Dou* 菊豆. China Film Co-production, 1990.

——. *Yige dou buneng shao* 一个都不能少 (Not one less). Beijing New Picture, 1999.

Zheng Yi 郑义. *Lao jing* 老井 (Old well). Baihua wenyi, 1993.

Zhu Tianwen 朱天文. *Zhu Tianwen zuopin ji* 朱天文作品集 (Collection of Zhu Tianwen's fiction). Taipei: Keyin, 2008.

PART II

Authors, Works, Schools

9

THE LATE QING POETRY REVOLUTION: LIANG QICHAO, HUANG ZUNXIAN, AND CHINESE LITERARY MODERNITY

JIANHUA CHEN

The "poetry revolution" (诗界革命), a term that first appeared in Liang Qichao's 梁启超 (1873–1929) *Record of Travels* (汗漫录), a diary of his ocean voyage from Yokohama to Honolulu in December 1899 (Chen 1985: 321–340), has been the object of a great deal of attention by Chinese writers and literary scholars. In their pioneering works on the history of modern Chinese literature, Hu Shi 胡适 (1891–1962) and Chen Zizhan 陈子展 (1898–1990) praised the poetry revolution for its utilitarian and populist vein, and especially for its role in transforming poetic language from the classical to the vernacular, which directly contributed to the May Fourth literary revolution (Tang 2002: 256–257). Marxist literary scholarship in the People's Republic of China (PRC) has treated the poetry revolution as an important chapter in modern Chinese literary history, recognizing it as a progressive literary school with an antifeudal and anti-imperial program, but limited by a political and literary conservatism. Although the term "poetry revolution" may not have been used until 1899, most scholars agree that the revolution took place between 1894 and 1897, when reformers Huang Zunxian 黄遵宪 (1848–1905), Liang Qichao, Tan Sitong 谭嗣同 (1865–1898), and Xia Zengyou 夏曾佑 (1863?–1924) discussed and experimented with new literary forms as part of their nationalist political agenda. However, Huang Zunxian's revolutionary poetic practice preceded the "revolution" itself by several years.

The poetry revolution is inseparable from the late Qing reform movement, which was initiated out of the shock and humiliation felt by intellectuals after

China's defeat in the first Sino-Japanese war. With Kang Youwei 康有为 (1858–1927) and Liang Qichao in the lead, the reformers were a group of protean intellectuals, well armed with classical scholarship and current Western knowledge. Unlike the participants in the earlier Self-strengthening movement (洋务运动), they planned to make China wealthy and powerful by turning to the West not only for technology but also for ideas and culture. During the Hundred Days Reform (1898), they undertook a nationwide movement at all levels, making policy at the imperial court and enlightening the populace through local institutions. Their strategy was to remold the nation and its people and modernize Chinese culture. They viewed literature as a viable medium through which to awaken patriotism and forge a new national soul, yet felt its current styles too archaic and elitist to do so. The print media, which was undergoing a boom at this time, offered them a national forum in which to propose revisions to literature in terms of its social function and communicative potential. It was no accident that their first successful literary experiment was the "new-style prose" (新文体) Liang Qichao developed in his journalist writings.

Despite its casual style, Liang's *Record of Travels* is no less than a manifesto of Chinese literary modernity. It prophetically proclaims that Chinese "poetic destiny" (诗运) can be saved from doom only by accepting the modern challenge and breaking with the past. The diary is an amalgam of politics and aesthetics, nationalism and cosmopolitanism, tradition and modernity, fact and fantasy. This prophetic voice arises from a rare moment of crisis for Liang Qichao and his country, reflected in the poems he wrote during the sea journey. In "Self-Encouragement" (自立), for example, he depicts himself as a tragic hero with the mission of enlightening the Chinese by introducing Western ideas. He feels lonely in his desperate struggle against tradition and the ignorance of his four hundred million compatriots. In "A Song for the Twentieth Century on the Pacific Ocean" (二十世纪太平洋歌), his sense of destiny is more acutely expressed as he finds himself located in a particular historical time and global space: between the old and new century, and between a reformed Japan in Asia and the advanced democracy in America (Y. Huang 2008: 40–49).

The new poetic revolution signified a crucial inversion of traditional Chinese revolutionary discourse. To a reformer like Liang, talking about revolution was taboo; in Confucian political culture, *geming* meant the divine legitimization of a new dynasty usually born from violent overthrow of the old regime. In his intense study of the Meiji experience, Liang became fascinated with the Japanese translation of the English word "revolution," whose meanings include "change in all societal affairs." The term "poetry revolution" connoted complex ideas of world political revolution that had begun to exert an influence in China. Rather than advocate a poetry revolution for its own sake, Liang wanted to mobilize literary forces to rescue China. At the end of the diary, he hints at political violence when he predicts an advancing "revolutionary army" and calls new poets to join its ranks. A rumor circulated that Liang was at the time under the influence of Sun Yat-sen (1866–1925), head of the anti-Manchu revolutionary movement, and that Liang was forced to leave for America by his mentor, Kang Youwei, who feared Liang's stay in Tokyo would further involve him with the revolutionaries (Chen 1999: 366–370).

The diary begins with Liang's apology for his lack of poetic talent; these days, however, he is so inspired by the splendor of the ocean scenery that he has written many poems. Liang then describes the Chinese poetic tradition as spoiled by more than a millennium of parrot-like poets who emulate past masters and know nothing of true poetry. He calls for an end to this shame:

> Therefore, in our present age, one should not have to bother with poetry unless it is to become a Columbus or Magellan in the poetic realm. As it happened in Europe that the fertility of soils became exhausted and overly exploited, the Europeans had to seek new land in America and the Pacific coastal regions. Those who want to be a Columbus or Magellan of the poetic realm must follow three principles: first, a new world of perceptions; second, new vocabularies; and third, incorporating the two into the styles of the ancients. Only made in this way can it be poetry.... If one can satisfy these three principles, then he will become a poetic king of twentieth-century China.... Although I am not a talented poet, I will do my best to introduce European spiritual thought, so that it can serve as poetic material for future poets. In short, Chinese poetry is doomed if there is no poetry revolution. However, poetry can never die and a revolution is just around the corner. A Columbus or a Magellan will soon appear on the horizon.
>
> (Liang 1900: 2280–2281)

Liang's vision of poetry revolution clearly encompasses things beyond the poetic realm, such as colonial adventure, economics, technology, and spirituality. Liang uses foreign names and images with ingenious eloquence. Columbus and Magellan, for example, become metaphors for the kind of intrepid spirit of discovery needed for the poetry revolution. In another metaphor—the "poetic king of twentieth-century China"—poetic modernity is constructed as the promise of China's future, an imagined Chinese modernity in all its diversity and global scale. The author predicts a poetic destiny, one that implies memories of Chinese imperial history and an optimistic reception of Western enlightenment and colonialism. If modern Chinese literature was born of and nourished by national crises, then the poetry revolution was an important moment for Chinese literary modernity and its radical rupture with the past and its literary and cultural tradition.

The "poetic king" will emerge as a literary spokesman only by adhering to Liang's three revolutionary poetic principles, which form the core of his text.

Interrelated and in tension with each other, the three principles constitute a poetics based on Liang's newly accepted theoretical dichotomy of content and form. The principle of "new vocabularies" seemingly contradicts that of "ancient styles," and the "new world of perceptions" suggests a whole aesthetic effect that will occur with a synthesis of the former two principles. "New vocabularies" refer to the neologisms that came to China through Japanese translations of Western books—for instance, such terms as "freedom" (自由) and "equality" (平权). Liang strongly believes that simply using loanwords can offer a shortcut to modernization of the Chinese mind. In the poetic realm, however, the use of new vocabularies meant violating traditional poetics. In China, poetic style was considered from not only aesthetic but also political perspectives, and poetic language was governed by stylistic canons. For example, Gong Zizhen 龚自珍 (1792–1841), forerunner of the late Qing poetry revolution, emancipated poetry by using Buddhist terms, for which orthodox Confucians condemned him as a heretic. Liang's obsession with neologism can also be traced back to the mid-1890s, when he, Tan Sitong, and Xia Zengyou experimented with a kind of "new poetry" (新诗) using unintelligible terms from the translated Bible.

Although Liang did not intend to create a movement, his repetition of the phrase "poetry revolution" resulted in an efflorescence of revolutionary poems appearing in the poetry sections of *The Discussion of China* (清议报) and *New Citizen* (新民丛报), reform journals published in Yokohama. Between 1900 and 1905 thousands of poems were published, some but not all expressing revolutionary ideas. To better articulate the poetry revolution's role in his propaganda agenda, in 1902 Liang established a column called "Poetry Talks from the Ice-Drinking Studio" (饮冰室诗话), serialized in *New Citizen*, in which he developed a theory of poetry revolution. Of his comments on numerous poets, the most influential are on Huang Zunxian, Jiang Ziyou 蒋自由 (1865–1929), and Qiu Fengjia 丘逢甲 (1864–1912), whom he praised as "three masters of the poetry revolution" (Liang 1982: 30).

With the poetry revolution, a modern literary field emerged built by the interactive forces of the print industry, circulation networks, and a national literary fellowship (Chang 2010: 441). Its formation provided the necessary experience for reformers to launch a "fiction revolution" (小说界革命) (see "The Uses of Fiction" and "Late Qing Fiction") three years later, leading national literature into a new phase. The "poetic king" Liang called for became a symbol of national literature, around which poets scattered throughout mainland China, Japan, Taiwan, Hong Kong, Singapore, and Malaysia would share a poetic vision of imagined nationhood. The poetry revolution, beyond its advocates' expectations, greatly supported the anti-Manchu movement, best evidenced by Guan Yun's "Rousseau" (卢骚), which was widely cited by the revolutionaries of the time. The second quatrain of the poem says:

We do our utmost to pave the way for equality,
And shed our blood on the flower of freedom.
The day will come when our words come true,
And the revolutionary flood sweeps across the world!

(Guan Yun 1902: 100)

Huang Zunxian is generally recognized as the leading figure of the movement. Despite Huang's reservations about the slogan itself, Liang praised him as the spirit of the poetry revolution. A closer look at Huang's poetic theory and practice provides us not only with a broader historical and global perspective but also a better understanding of the controversy over poetic form and the modern spirit. Huang was born in 1848 in Meizhou, in northeastern Guangdong, which was a frontier for contact with the West in the mid-nineteenth century. He grew up in a recently established scholar-official family that was still close to its peasant roots. As a child, Huang was educated by his great-grandmother, who taught him, among other things, to sing Hakka folk songs. As his early poem "Mixed Emotions" (杂感) shows, he radically criticizes the Confucian worship of antiquity and the eight-legged essay that suffocated free thinking. He exposes the Tang and Song scholars' idea of "truth" in their exegesis of Confucian classics as simply a projection of their own desires. Ancient sages, he asserts, speak merely with a language of their own time, which then appears antique to later generations. So he boldly claims, "I intend to write in my very own language / And refuse to be limited by ancient fashions" (Z. Huang 1981: 42; Schmidt 1994: 225). With this historical sense, in his later years Huang explored new-style poetry, characterized by contemporaneity and free use of poetic language.

In 1877 Huang decided to pursue a diplomatic career rather than climb higher on the examination ladder, as his family wished, and he went to Japan to serve as an assistant in the Chinese embassy. Over the next two decades, Huang's diplomatic career took him to America, Europe, and parts of Asia, where he continuously wrote poetry and developed his new poetics. His many intellectual interests and observations of a diverse, contingent world are interwoven into his poetry, giving it a radiant and kaleidoscopic quality. The poems refract, vividly and colorfully, his curious view of the world: how he envisions and revisions China's past, present, and future within the global context; how he moves from Sinocentrism to nationalism; and how he develops a broad concern with the human condition.

During his stay in Japan, Huang wrote "Assorted Quatrains on Japan" (日本杂事诗), praising various achievements of the Meiji Reformation (Cheng 2013: 39–58). While admiring such Western-style institutions as fire departments, newspapers, and women's normal schools, he was bewildered by and skeptical of Japan's fervent embrace of Western culture (Z. Huang 1981: 1097–1159;

Schmidt 1994: 238–241). Yet, late in his life the Sinocentrism faded out of his poetic vision of historical China as he became increasingly aware of China's decline in the world. Influenced by the political and legal philosophy of Rousseau and Montesquieu, he became convinced that China would eventually follow the road of democracy. This conviction was more evident in a couplet of one of his latest poems, addressed to Liang: "People say that in the twentieth century / No one will tolerate the imperial system any more" (Schmidt 1994: 207). More than a historical mirror or social commentary, Huang's poetry serves as a medium of self-reflection. He uses satire and irony as rhetorical devices mediating his doubt, anger, or uncertainty about modern reality.

National feeling grows more poignant in Huang's poetry when he witnesses overseas Chinese living in poor conditions and appeals strongly for a China of wealth and power. But it is worth noting that his nationalist ethos tends to contradict or yield to broader humanist concerns and a cosmopolitan perspective. In poems about the Chinese government's 1881 decision to withdraw students from the United States and the American government's 1882 Exclusion Act prohibiting Chinese immigration, Huang criticizes both policies for a lack of cultural open-mindedness. His assertion that all human beings are brothers is rooted in the Confucian ideal of "great union" (大同), yet he cherishes even more an ideal of global community in harmony and diversity regardless of nation and race. In "Overseas Merchants" (番客篇), he depicts, jubilantly and sympathetically, a Chinese wedding ceremony on a South Pacific island, in which different races and cultures happily mix. He shows a larger concern with the diaspora of those minor nationalities in world history when he compares overseas Chinese to Jews (Z. Huang 1981: 608).

Perhaps what aroused Huang's contemporaries' interest the most were his passionate and creative representations of the metropolitan, exotic, and novel in foreign lands in such poems as "A Song of Cherry Blossoms" (樱花歌), "The Great London Fog" (伦敦大雾行), "On Climbing the Eiffel Tower" (登巴黎铁塔), and "The Suez Canal" (苏彝士河). These poems were unprecedented in conveying the meaning of modernity, suggesting a new fashion in pursuit of new space, individual expression, and literary creativity. In representing an "alternative poetic world" (别创诗界) with his new poetics, Huang's works invoke the tension between maintaining a traditional style and embracing the modern spirit. While successfully creating the sensation of newness by breaking with outworn poetic forms, his new poetics nonetheless exposes an incompatibility with or disturbance within traditional poetic structure, which can be attributed to the use of translated terms from Western sources. As early as the 1870s, Shanghai newspapers published numerous "bamboo twist ballads" (竹枝词) describing Western-style novelties in the foreign concessions. New words such as "balloon" (气球), "telegraph" (电报), and "gas" (地火) were highly fashionable, showing great curiosity for the modern. Fascinated by these novelties though he was, Huang was cautious about using these new terms for fear of losing traditional poetic flavor. For example, in a series of poems from 1875 that refer to Western science and technology, translated terms are excluded from the poems and yet treated in notes (Z. Huang 1981: 160–169). If those bamboo ballads were not taken seriously by literati because of their folk style, Huang's saturation with the Western modern and his poetic experiments posed a challenge to the literary mainstream of the time and to his own identity as well. It seems that by the early 1890s his new-style poetry had matured in theory and practice.

The praise for Huang's "Modern Parting" (今别离) in the early 1890s might be attributed to the then widely accepted formula of the essence (体) and means (用): most intellectuals felt that China must be modernized by adopting Western technological means and yet must keep her cultural essence (Schmidt 1994, 269). The four poems in this series describe separated lovers longing for each other, and each poem has as subject a Western innovation—the steamship, train, telegraph, and photography. In describing how the separated lover is ecstatically dramatized by means of modern communications, the poetic convention is attractively refreshed by new images and metaphors. In this work, Huang masterfully proves the potential of traditional poetics to cope with literary modernity, for it symbolically holds up the essences of both cultures: eulogizing the technological power of the modern and at the same time keeping the poetic form intact and integral.

In 1891, Huang compiled an anthology of his poems called *Poems from the Hut in the Human World* (人境庐诗草). In the preface, he emphasizes the power of poetic tradition: "Among my predecessors, well over a hundred can be considered masters of poetry. My goal is to rid myself of their flaws and free myself from their bondage. This is a difficult task indeed" (Z. Huang 1996: 69). Huang's iconoclastic claim to rid himself of the "bondage" of the past predicted the literary modernity implicit in Liang's poetry revolution, though his practical approach to poetic reform differed from the latter's. Huang was more concerned with formal and aesthetic problems of poetic modernity. In the preface, he asserts that new poetry must freely use all kinds of language, whether classical or colloquial, official or dialectical. This understanding of poetic language was more sophisticated than Liang's prioritization of new vocabularies.

Naturally enough, because Liang had always been fascinated by Western learning, he showed dissatisfaction with the lack of new thought in Huang's poems; for his part, Huang kept silent about the poetic movement, and he even expressed uneasiness at Liang's toying with the idea of revolution. A compromise seemed to take shape between them in 1902. Huang sent Liang his new poem "Military Songs" (从军歌) and other works indicative of his support for the poetic revolution. In turn influenced by Huang's warning about political radicalism, Liang removed the principle of new vocabularies; in other words, in revising revolutionary poetics, he no longer prioritized Western ideas but emphasized only the principles of a world of perceptions and ancient styles. Liang applauded Huang's poetry as the highest achievement of the poetry revolution. However, their compromise symbolized the nature of the poetry revolution. They agreed to encourage the use of colloquial language, as Huang's "Military Songs" showed, so that poetry would be more accessible to common readers. Largely for this reason, the May Fourth literary revolutionaries took the late Qing poetry revolution as a legacy.

Bibliography

Chang, Kang-I Sun, ed. *Cambridge History of Chinese Literature*. New York: Cambridge University Press, 2010.

Chen, Jianhua. "Chinese 'Revolution' in the Syntax of World Revolution." In Lydia H. Liu, ed., *Tokens of Exchange: The Problem of Translation in Global Circulation*, 355–374. Durham, NC: Duke University Press, 1999.

——. [陈建华]. "Wan Qing 'Shijie geming' fasheng shijian ji qi tichang zhe kaobian" 晚清"诗界革命"发生时间及其提倡者考辨 (A textual study of the time and advocacy of the late Qing poetry revolution). In *Zhongguo gudian wenxue congkao*, 321–340. Shanghai: Fudan daxue, 1985.

Cheng, Yu-yu. "The Geographic Measure of Traditional Poetic Discourse: Reading Huang Zunxian's Poems on Miscellaneous Subjects from Japan." Trans. Jack W. Chen and Yunshuang Zhang. *Renditions* 79 (Spring 2013): 39–58.

Guan Yun 观云. "Lusao" 卢骚 (Rousseau). *Xinmin congbao* 3 (March 1902): 100.

Huang, Yunte. *Transpacific Imagination: History, Literature, Counterpoetics*. Cambridge, MA: Harvard University Press, 2008.

Huang, Zunxian. "Hong Kong." Trans. T. C. Lai. *Renditions* 29–30 (1988): 63.

——. "Preface to *Poems from the Hut in the Human World*." Trans. Michelle Yeh. In Kirk A. Denton, ed., *Modern Chinese Literary Thought: Writings on Literature, 1893–1945*, 69–70. Stanford, CA: Stanford University Press, 1996.

—— [黄遵宪]. *Renjinglu shicao jian zhu* 人境庐诗草笺注 (Poems from the hut in the human world with annotations). Ed. Qian Zhonglian. Shanghai: Guji, 1981.

Levenson, Joseph R. *Liang Ch'i-ch'ao and the Mind of Modern China*. Berkeley: University of California Press, 1967.

Liang Qichao 梁启超. *Hanman lu* 汗漫录 (Record of travels). *Qingyi bao* 35 (February 1900): 2280–2283.

——. *Yinbingshi shihua* 饮冰室诗话 (Poetry talks from the Studio of the Ice Drinker). Beijing: Renmin, 1982.

Liu, Wei-p'ing. "The Poetry Revolution of the Late Ch'ing Period: A Reevaluation." In A. R. Davis and A. D. Stefanowska, eds., *Austrina: Essays in Commemoration of the Twenty-Fifth Anniversary of the Founding of the Oriental Society of Australia*, 188–199. Sydney: Oriental Society of Australia, 1982.

Schmidt, J. D. *Within the Human Realm: The Poetry of Huang Zunxian, 1848–1905*. Cambridge: Cambridge University Press, 1994.

Tang, Xiaobing. "'Poetic Revolution,' Colonization, and Form at the Beginning of Modern Chinese Literature." In Rebecca E. Karl and Peter Zarrow, eds., *Rethinking the 1898 Reform Period: Political and Cultural Change in Late Qing China*, 245–265. Cambridge, MA: Harvard University Press, 2002.

10

THE USES OF FICTION:
LIANG QICHAO AND HIS CONTEMPORARIES

ALEXANDER DES FORGES

Liang Qichao 梁启超 (1873–1929) is generally considered one of the most significant theorists of literature in nineteenth- and twentieth-century China. He is credited with the popularization of a literary prose style that was easy to read, a reevaluation of the function and effects of vernacular fiction in the literary sphere and in society more generally, and the establishment in 1902 of one of the earliest fiction magazines, *New Fiction* (新小说). In addition, he began but never completed a novel set in a future China, wrote extensively on his impressions of travels in the United States and Europe, and completed an influential study of Qing dynasty intellectual history. Liang is often depicted as an iconoclast: breaking decisively with long-standing conceptions of the novel and the short story as lowly literary genres, he declares in his 1902 essay "On the Relationship Between Fiction and the Government of the People" (论小说与群治之关系) that fiction is literature's "highest vehicle." A more balanced understanding of the originality of his theories of literature, however, requires careful attention to the work of Chinese commentators on fiction in preceding centuries.

In late sixteenth-century China, full-length vernacular fiction began to appear in commentary editions; over the next three hundred years, the commentaries to novels became more lengthy and more elaborate, constituting a complex system of aesthetic standards and establishing new expectations for the novel as a genre. The best-known novels of this period—not only the six considered to be classics of the genre, but many others as well—circulated in editions that included at least one and occasionally as many as three or four distinct commentaries. The insights found in these commentaries are scattered and occasionally fragmentary, but this does not mean that Qing commentators on long vernacular fiction had no coherent theories of literature. These commentators frequently discussed the ways in which novels, when read properly, could have a positive moral influence, and they reflected on the reasons for and effects of their broad appeal. In addition, they were interested in the ways in which a well-written novel could teach one to read more thoroughly and write better literary prose, including the "eight-legged" essays for the civil service examinations. Fiction could make one not only a better person but also a better reader and writer (Rolston 1997: 1–21).

Important insights into the structure, function, and effects of fiction continued to appear in prefaces and commentaries in the decades preceding Liang Qichao's writings. A preface to a narrative translated from English and printed in the newspaper *Shenbao* (申报) in the 1870s introduced "leisure" as an important component of a didactic theory of the novel: in the hustle and bustle of everyday affairs, the novel provided a chance for readers to distance themselves from ordinary worries and enter a more relaxed and receptive state. Writing in 1892, the author, journalist, and critic Han Bangqing 韩邦庆 proposed a new aesthetic of the novel in which multiple plotlines progress simultaneously throughout the work, with no single central character or group of characters, anticipating the "novels of exposure" and "social fiction" that would play a central role in Chinese literature of the first two decades of the twentieth century. In a commentary to his own novel *Lives of Shanghai Flowers* (海上花列传, 1892), Han emphasized the care with which all the narrative threads are woven together and called on his readers to read both behind and beyond the text he provides to get the full story. New commentaries and reader's guides (读法) to novels continued to appear into the early 1900s.

Liang Qichao's fiction criticism breaks with this interpretive tradition in two respects. The most obvious difference is in the format of his analysis: whereas previous critics worked primarily through commentary, alternating briefly stated general principles of fiction writing with extremely specific notes on concrete features of the text, ad hominem attacks, and lists of characters or characteristics, Liang instead develops his observations through lengthy and systematic argument. Second, he shows no interest in the specific features of narrative organization that had been understood to determine the literariness of works of fiction. Although Liang discusses narrative content and its effects in detail, he ignores the forms that structure that content, passing over with little comment textual features such as point of view, flashback and alternation, and strategic repetition. This active suppression of inquiry into literary technique conveniently erases the link that many earlier commentators had seen between quality fiction and superior organization in more orthodox genres such as the civil service examination essay, which Liang despised. It is in fact this active counterposition of fiction against more orthodox prose forms that is Liang's most radical innovation.

In addition to considering the structural features of the text, Qing commentators were interested in the broad appeal of novels and their potential as tools for moral renovation. Liang Qichao adopted both of these interests; in "On the Relationship Between Fiction and the Government of the People" and "Foreword to the Publication of Political Novels in Translation" (译印政治小说序, 1898), he emphasizes the ease with which the common person with basic literacy could pick up fiction and find it interesting, and he goes on to claim that fiction could serve as the vehicle for moral uplift. The former essay begins with the following striking assertions:

> If one intends to renovate the people of a nation, one must first renovate its fiction. Therefore, to renovate morality, one must renovate fiction; to renovate religion, one must renovate fiction; to renovate politics, one must renovate fiction; to renovate learning and the arts, one must renovate fiction; and to renovate even the human mind and remold its character, one must renovate fiction. Why is this so? This is because fiction has a profound power over the way of man.
>
> (Liang 1996: 74)

What gives fiction this power? Liang first tries two explanations—that fiction is easy to understand and is pleasurable—but he finds objections to these explanations and dismisses them as inadequate. He concludes instead that the nature of fiction's power is twofold: first, it can show individuals other worlds; and second, it can give voice to those conscious or subconscious feelings that its readers themselves cannot articulate. Novels and short stories can tell us something about the lives of others and also something about ourselves. But Chinese fiction until this point has wasted its powers, or worse, used them to persuade its readers to behave improperly; the answer is to translate healthier novels, short stories, and plays from abroad and to encourage Chinese authors to learn from these models.

The degree to which Liang Qichao reproduces ethical assessments of the nature of fiction that had already been in circulation for more than two centuries can be seen in his frequent imprecations against literature that "incites robbery and lust" (诲盗诲淫). Writing "A Warning to Novelists" (告小说家) in 1915, more than a decade after his influential campaigns on behalf of fiction as a literary form, Liang made extensive use of the rhetoric of retribution that appears in eighteenth- and nineteenth-century texts advocating censorship of fiction and drama. Authors writing novels that led the nation's youth astray were warned that they risked divine punishment visited on them or their descendants, whether in this world or the next, just as moralizing intellectuals of the previous century had delighted in detailing accounts of the afflictions visited upon the sons and grandsons of famous novelists such as Shi Nai'an 施耐庵—accounts that were as imaginative as they were lacking in textual foundation. But whereas earlier critics saw the danger of fiction that "incites robbery and lust" in its attack on the social order, with no reference to an exterior beyond that order, Liang worried instead about its effect on China as a nation among nations. The moral uplift that ethical fiction could produce refers not to the salvation of the individual, but to the relationship between the individual and a new type of social formation, the nation.

One type of fiction in particular, the "political novel" (政治小说), was to lead this transformation of Chinese subjects into citizens of a new nation (Yeh 2015). Liang based his faith in this literary form largely on the developments in Meiji era Japan: political novels first began to appear in Japan in the 1880s, when intellectuals interested in reform were inspired by translations of novels by such English public figures as Benjamin Disraeli and Edward Bulwer-Lytton. A contemporary critic wrote that these novels "mainly describe the situation in the political world, and most of them are by politicians who tacitly make propaganda for their party policies" (in Kockum 1990: 170). Several of these political novels were subsequently translated into Chinese; two of the better-known examples, *Unexpected Encounters with Beauties* (Kajin no kigû) and *Worthwhile Chats on Statecraft* (Keikoku bidan), appeared under Liang's auspices in his journal *The China Discussion* (清议报). In 1902, Liang began a political novel of his own, *An Account of the Future of New China* (新中国未来记), of which only the first few chapters appeared (Hsia 1978: 231–236, 251–256; Kockum 1990: 168–182). In his faith in the novel as a means of producing new citizens with nationalist consciousness, Liang not only echoes nineteenth-century Christian missionaries but also anticipates twentieth-century scholars of nationalism like Benedict Anderson. The condemnation of all previous works of fiction is a familiar trope in premodern introductory commentaries to vernacular fiction; Liang appropriates this evaluative maneuver but puts it more broadly. What he is interested in praising is not a single work but an entire genre in translation (the political novel) or even an entire new universe of genres that he hopes to call into existence (including the new novel and short story).

Liang Qichao was not the only turn-of-the-century intellectual to advocate fiction as a means of national salvation; in 1897, Xia Zengyou 夏曾佑 and the famous translator Yan Fu 严复 published a manifesto called "Why Our Newspaper Will Print a Fiction Supplement" (本馆复印说部缘起, 1897). Explaining that fiction preserves accounts of heroic deeds and romantic experiences that would otherwise fade from memory, these authors maintained, as Liang Qichao would in the following year, that fiction had broad social appeal and could lead its readers to more moral behavior. Although many intellectuals writing on fiction in the first decade of the twentieth century echoed Liang, Yan, and Xia's general approach, there were critical responses. Wang Zhongqi 王钟麒, writing in 1907, presented a defense of four Ming and Qing novels considered to be classics—*Water Margin* (水浒传), *Three Kingdoms* (三国演义), *Golden Lotus* (金瓶梅), and *Dream of the Red Chamber* (红楼梦)—arguing that they, too, were in fact political novels and that the value of translated fiction should not be overestimated (A Ying 1989: 34–39; Kockum 1990: 199–200). In an early attempt to read European fiction and Chinese fiction comparatively at the aesthetic level, Wang found the multiple narrative lines and characters of Chinese vernacular fiction to be more than the equal of Western fiction that he characterized as centered on a single person and single event.

Lin Shu 林纾, one of the earliest and probably the best-known translator of European and American fiction into Chinese, articulated a slightly different position on the uses of fiction in his prefaces to translations of works by Charles Dickens, H. Rider Haggard, and others. In these prefaces, fiction is represented as a mirror that reports on the failings and corruption in a given society (see Hill 2013). Whereas Liang sees fiction as the means of producing new citizens, and therefore a new nation, Lin instead sees fiction as a tool for encouraging introspection and reform at all levels of society. Whereas Liang ignores narrative structure in his discussion of the novel, Lin Shu emphasizes it, judging Dickens's *David Copperfield* according to aesthetic standards drawn from the practice of literary Chinese (including the civil service examination essay) and earlier vernacular fiction (A Ying 1989: 196–278; Lin 1996).

The most important alternative to a utilitarian theory of literature aimed at renovating the nation during this period is found in the works of Wang Guowei 王国维 (1877–1927): "A Critical Discussion of *The Dream of the Red Chamber*" (红楼梦评论, 1904), *Talks on Verse in the Human World* (人间词话, 1906–1910), and "Incidental Remarks on Literature" (文学小言, 1906). Wang (1996: 90–91, 95) argued that genuine literature inevitably "conflicts with prevailing societal and political concerns" and is a "playful enterprise" that cannot coexist with the "struggle for existence" or constitute a professional means of support. He was absolutely opposed to the idea that literature should be used as a means of consolidating national feeling or increasing a nation's power among other nations. Instead, drawing on Schopenhauer's metaphysics, he maintained that the task of literature is to express the fundamental philosophical truth that the will to live leads inevitably to suffering. In a lengthy and sophisticated discussion beginning from this premise, Wang concluded that of all Chinese novels past and present, *Dream of the Red Chamber* best captures the tragic character of ordinary human life (Bonner 1986: 81–88, 91–127).

Liang Qichao's conception of fiction as a means to remake the nation and its citizenry has had immense influence on theories of literature in twentieth-century China; from May Fourth authors to Mao Zedong (see "Literature and Politics") to the writers of scar, or wounds, literature in the late 1970s and early 1980s, the conviction that fiction works best as a tool for civic reconstruction persists. But the pervasiveness of this view of fiction at the discursive level does not necessarily entail a corresponding dominance in practice; indeed, the many and varied forms of literary production in the Chinese language over the course of the twentieth century demonstrate that alternative ideas of how and why one should write fiction continue to flourish.

Bibliography

A Ying 阿英, ed. *Wan Qing wenxue congchao xiaoshuo xiqu yanjiu juan* 晚清文学丛钞: 小说戏曲研究卷 (Anthology of late Qing literature: Research materials on fiction and drama). Beijing: Xin wenfeng chuban gongsi, 1989.

Anderson, Benedict. *Imagined Communities: Reflections on the Origin and Spread of Nationalism*. London: Verso, 1983.

Bonner, Joey. *Wang Kuo-wei: An Intellectual Biography*. Cambridge, MA: Harvard University Press, 1986.

Denton, Kirk A., ed. *Modern Chinese Literary Thought: Writings on Literature, 1893–1945*. Stanford, CA: Stanford University Press, 1996.

Hill, Michael Gibbs. *Lin Shu, Inc.: Translation and the Making of Modern Chinese Culture*. New York: Oxford University Press, 2013.

Hsia, C. T. "Yen Fu and Liang Ch'i-ch'ao as Advocates of New Fiction." In Adele Rickett, ed., *Chinese Approaches to Literature from Confucius to Liang Ch'i-ch'ao*, 221–257. Princeton, NJ: Princeton University Press, 1978.

Kockum, Keiko. *Japanese Achievement, Chinese Aspiration: A Study of the Japanese Influence on the Modernization of the Late Qing Novel*. Löberöd, Sweden: Plus Ultra, 1990.

Lee, Leo Ou-fan, and Andrew Nathan. "The Beginnings of Mass Culture: Journalism and Fiction in the Late Ch'ing and Beyond." In David Johnson, Andrew J. Nathan, and Evelyn Rawski, eds., *Popular Culture in Late Imperial China*, 360–395. Berkeley: University of California Press, 1985.

Liang, Qichao. "Foreword to the Publication of Political Novels in Translation." Trans. Gek Nai Cheng. In Kirk A. Denton, ed., *Modern Chinese Literary Thought: Writings on Literature, 1893–1945*, 71–73. Stanford, CA: Stanford University Press, 1996.

——. "Gao xiaoshuo jia" 告小说家 (A warning to writers of fiction). In A Ying, ed., *Wan Qing wenxue congchao xiaoshuo xiqu yanjiu juan* 晚清文学丛钞: 小说戏曲研究卷 (Anthology of late Qing literature: Research materials on fiction and drama), 19–21. Beijing: Xin wenfeng chuban gongsi, 1989.

——. "On the Relationship Between Fiction and the Government of the People." Trans. Gek Nai Cheng. In Kirk A. Denton, ed., *Modern Chinese Literary Thought: Writings on Literature, 1893–1945*, 74–81. Stanford, CA: Stanford University Press, 1996.

Lin, Shu. "Preface to Part One of *David Copperfield*." Trans. Yenna Wu. In Kirk A. Denton, ed., *Modern Chinese Literary Thought: Writings on Literature, 1893–1945*, 84–86. Stanford, CA: Stanford University Press, 1996.

Rolston, David. *Traditional Chinese Fiction and Fiction Commentary: Reading and Writing Between the Lines*. Stanford, CA: Stanford University Press, 1997.

Tsau, Shu-ying. "The Rise of 'New Fiction.'" In Milena Doleželová-Velingerová, ed., *The Chinese Novel at the Turn of the Century*, 18–37. Toronto: University of Toronto Press, 1980.

Wang, Guowei. "Incidental Remarks on Literature." Trans. Kam-ming Wong. In Kirk A. Denton, ed., *Modern Chinese Literary Thought: Writings on Literature, 1893–1945*, 90–95. Stanford, CA: Stanford University Press, 1996.

Wang Zhongqi 王钟麒. "Zhongguo lidai xiaoshuo shi lun" 中國歷代小說史論 (On the history of the Chinese novel). *Xin xiaoshuo* 2, 5 (1907).

Xia Zengyou and Yan Fu. "Benguan fuyin shuobu yuanqi" 本館付印說部緣起 (Why our newspaper is printing a fiction supplement). *Guowen bao* 國聞報. Serialized from October 16 to November 18, 1897.

Yeh, Catherine Vance. *The Chinese Political Novel: Migration of a World Genre*. Cambridge, MA: Harvard University Asia Center, 2015.

11

LATE QING FICTION

YING HU

The last years of the Qing dynasty were a time of tremendous social and political crisis. The empire had sustained numerous disastrous military and cultural confrontations with the Western powers since the Opium War of 1839–1842, as well as internal social strife and mass dislocation caused by the Taiping Rebellion (1851–1864) and the Boxer Rebellion (1900). The defeat at the hands of the new imperial power of Japan (1895) sent fresh shock waves across the country, further intensifying the sense of national and cultural crisis. This crisis—the Chinese experience of the crisis of modernity—is inscribed in myriad ways in the many novels and short stories of the late Qing, a period during which fiction experienced an incredible boom. From approximately 1898 to 1911, by a conservative estimate, more than a thousand fictional works were published (A Ying 1980 [1935]). Not only did regular newspapers routinely carry fiction supplements, but there were also more than twenty periodicals devoted to fiction. To understand what part late Qing fiction played in the unfolding of Chinese modernity, it is necessary first to outline three crucial historical factors that contributed to its emergence: the politicization of fiction, the translation of Western literature, and the commercialization of fiction writing.

Around the turn of the century, "revolution in the realm of fiction" was a popular phrase among intellectuals interested in political and cultural reform. In 1897, the preeminent translator Yan Fu 严复 and his friend Xia Zengyou 夏曾佑 first championed the social utility of fiction in the modern world as they set forth the power of fiction to affect the largest possible reading public. In 1902 the reformer Liang Qichao 梁启超 further politicized fiction by explicitly harnessing it for the cause of national reform: "If one intends to renovate the people of a nation, one must first renovate its fiction" (Denton 1996: 74). Liang Qichao's conclusion is in part derived from his experience in post-Meiji Japan, where translations of works such as those by the politician-novelists Bulwer-Lytton and Benjamin Disraeli had been popular. More important, it is ultimately for political advantage that Liang invoked the story of "great European intellectuals" who turn to the writing of fiction, claiming that "a newly published book could often influence and change the views of the whole nation" (Denton 1996: 73). For although Disraeli's fiction could not be said to have radically transformed public opinion and social legislation, as he himself or Liang wished it had, many nineteenth-century Anglophone novels were written with the explicit mission to reform society. Drawing from this critical realist strain, and borrowing the term "new fiction" (新小说) from Japan, reform-minded intellectuals such as Liang gave a powerful legitimization for fiction writing. As a genre, fiction was thus suddenly promoted from its previously marginal position in the Chinese literary landscape to "the highest form of literature."

It may appear strange that despite its undisguised political instrumentality, new fiction was repeatedly proclaimed "the highest form of literature." Indeed, Liang himself condemned traditional fiction for its lack of moral value, as it does nothing but "incite robbery and lust" (诲盗诲淫). New fiction, on the other hand, could ascend the generic hierarchy precisely because it was given a moral imperative as the best vehicle for national reform. In regarding literature as a tool in cultural transformation, Liang at once harkens back to the Confucian conception that "literature conveys the Way" (文以载道) and prefigures the 1920s leftists' motto Literature for Life (为人生的文学). Thus, during the late Qing, progressive intellectuals called for the translation of political fiction from abroad, and many attempted writing new fiction themselves. Typically these Chinese experiments in the political novel are set in the near future, where protagonists debate at length over the advantage of the parliamentary system or expound on John Stuart Mill's views on the equality of the sexes. The majority of fiction produced at the time is not political fiction, strictly speaking, but falls into the subgenres of social exposé, detective stories, science fiction, and courtesan tales (Yeh 2015).

The late Qing saw an unprecedented flourishing of translation. At its height—between 1902 and 1907—more than six hundred translations were published, a number that exceeded original works (Tarumoto 1998). Interest in translation was first ignited soon after the Opium War, notably by Commissioner Lin Zexu 林则徐, who ordered the translation of international law, geopolitical surveys of the world, and various topics on "Western opinions on Chinese affairs" gleaned from Western newspapers. In the 1860s government-sponsored translation houses were established. The translation of Western literature burgeoned with the immense success of Lin Shu's 林纾 translation of

Alexander Dumas's *La Dame aux camélias* in 1899. Works by Charles Dickens, Victor Hugo, and Sir Walter Scott followed. Rather than the advocated "political fiction," however, the most popular of translated fiction were Dumas's book, fiction by H. Rider Haggard, and the detective stories of Arthur Conan Doyle. In their translated—and often drastically transformed—states, these works of popular entertainment nonetheless offer new ways of imagining the modern through an allegory of individual passion and conventional censorship, for example, or through a tale of social justice and scientific investigation.

A third important factor in the sudden prosperity of fiction was the commercial printing industry. Modern letterpress technology made printing large quantities of popular reading materials cheaper and therefore commercially profitable. Beginning in the second half of the nineteenth century, newspapers also became immensely popular, thus adding a major medium for the wide dissemination of fiction (Lee and Nathan 1985). Of the many periodicals devoted to fiction, four are most important: *New Fiction* (新小说, 1902), edited by Liang Qichao; *Illustrated Fiction* (绣像小说, 1903), edited by Li Boyuan 李伯元; *Monthly Fiction* (月月小说, 1906), edited by Wu Jianren 吴趼人; and *Forest of Fiction* (小说林, 1907), edited by Zeng Pu 曾朴. All but *New Fiction*, which was launched in Yokohama, Japan, were published in Shanghai, the hub of the new printing technology and the heart of cultural production in the late Qing. That fiction was the only form of writing for which the newspaper houses recompensed authors illustrates the profitability of fiction and serves as index of the rapid professionalization of fiction writers. This is especially significant because the abrogation of the civil service examination system in 1905 effectively terminated the major professional route that had for centuries been in existence for the literati class. Indeed, many late Qing fiction writers, such as Li Boyuan and Wu Jianren, came from families of literati-officials; some, such as Liang Qichao and Zeng Pu, had themselves been reasonably successful in the examination system.

Although the heyday of new fiction did not last much longer than a decade, it produced an amazingly rich literary legacy with unparalleled diversity of subject matters and fascinating formal innovations. How to interpret this cultural phenomenon has been a matter of scholarly debate, one that is important because it concerns how we understand modernity as well as historical change. May Fourth intellectuals typically claimed their generation as the harbinger of modernity and its radical break with the past, thus consigning late Qing fiction to the dustbin of tradition (much as Liang Qichao had done a few decades earlier with fiction that preceded his generation). More recently, scholars have argued that "the crucial burst of modernity came in the late Qing" rather than in the May Fourth era (Wang 1997: 17). Certainly many of the key questions addressed in May Fourth literature had made their appearance in late Qing fiction. For example, how to balance the need for close social engagement with the demand for formal experiment in literary representation is a central problematic in late Qing and much of twentieth-century Chinese literature. How to overcome the simplistic tendencies of "imitating the West" or "adhering to pure Chinese tradition" is another difficult task with which both late Qing and May Fourth writers had to contend. In answering these questions, however, late Qing fiction often indicated "trajectories" that did not become mainstream in later developments and that may very well suggest alternative models of thinking through modernity (Wang 1997).

The rest of this essay illustrates the implications of this debate through a discussion of specific examples of late Qing fiction, including *Strange Events Eyewitnessed over Twenty Years* (二十年目睹之怪现象, 1903–1905), *A Brief History of Modern Times* (文明小史, 1903), *Flower in a Sea of Retribution* (孽海花, 1905–1907), *The Travels of Lao Can* (老残游记, 1903), and *The Sea of Regret* (恨海, 1906).

One striking characteristic, shared by many late Qing fictional works, is a satirical engagement with contemporary society. In *Strange Events Eyewitnessed over Twenty Years*, for example, the author Wu Jianren (1866–1910) portrays the decaying empire in all its putrid aspects, a world of utter moral squalor full of corrupt officials, degenerate literati, and unscrupulous businesspeople. *A Brief History of Modern Times* by Li Boyuan (1867–1906), on the other hand, exposes the pretense of those who espouse the latest trends and newest ideas, a world of fake reformers and phony progressives. Both writers made their careers in Shanghai as newspapermen, and their novels, serialized in popular fiction periodicals, have been described as social exposés in which all aspects of a corrupt society, whether the ancient regime or the new elite, are targets for satirical treatment. Lu Xun 鲁迅, the preeminent cultural critic of the May Fourth movement, condemned such writing for its superficiality, lack of subtlety, and exaggeration (1976: 352–357). This harsh proscription dominated the evaluation of late Qing fiction until recently, when scholars have tried to reverse the verdict by arguing for the thematic and formal complexity of the so-called exposé novels. Some scholars argue that these novels experiment extensively with narrative techniques, such as introducing the first-person perspective, and that this experimentation addresses the larger problem of the writing subject, a problem that continued to plague writers for generations to come (Doleželová-Velingerová 1980; Chen 1989; Huters 1997). Others favor the grotesque realism in exposé novels as an alternative to the critical realism that dominated Chinese literature for the next few decades (Wang 1997). Furthermore, Lu Xun's criticism may reflect his own inability to accept the lack of a worldview, a grand scheme that writers such as Wu Jianren did not or were unwilling to offer (Huters 1997).

Another prominent feature of late Qing fiction is its constant awareness of global geopolitics, well showcased in Zeng Pu's *Flower in a Sea of Retribution*. An ambitious novel aimed at capturing the history of the last three decades of the Qing dynasty, *Flower* recounts the diplomatic journey of a Qing ambassador and his concubine, both characters modeled after real historical figures. Although the novel met with immediate popularity upon the publication of its first twenty chapters in 1907, the next fifteen chapters took twenty-five years to appear, and the novel was never finished. The novel's attempt to capture the rapidly changing times is both its success and its failure. It is as though the crisis of modernity produced a similar crisis in narrative, a burden so great that any artistic resolution proved elusive. This lack of fictional closure, incidentally, is not uncommon among late Qing novels. Given that the author, Zeng Pu (1872–1935), was a traditionally trained man of letters and had worked hard at reeducating himself with Western learning, it is not surprising that the novel's primary concern is the role of the traditional scholar caught in a drastically changing world. This figure is represented by the scholar-ambassador Jin Wenqing 金雯青, whose erudition in traditional learning is contrasted with his utter ignorance of current affairs. This results in a catastrophic mistake: he presents the court with a questionable collection of border maps, resulting in serious territorial losses for the Qing in its border dispute with Russia. Significantly, this blunder is presented not as an unfortunate mistake but as an inevitability for the traditional scholar and the deficient and antiquated system to which he belongs. The courtesan cum concubine Fu Caiyun 傅彩云, who travels with Jin, embodies another chief undercurrent of the fictional narrative: the reconfiguration of "woman's place" in relation to the newly conceived world order and in relation to the incompetent scholar. Although in many ways a descendant of countless courtesans portrayed in traditional fiction and drama, Caiyun departs from the conventional figure through her extensive travels. In those moments when she transforms herself into a "Lady of the camellias" or is studying German with a Russian anarchist, Caiyun's literal border crossing and transgressions of gender and class boundaries are intimately intertwined, with one enabling the other. Hardly what we would now associate with the new woman of China, she nonetheless prefigures several qualities later cherished by the May Fourth generation, albeit without the sublimation to a noble cause: an eagerness for education, an appetite for all things new and Western, and a demand for sexual autonomy, to name just a few.

Even further beyond the mainstream of twentieth-century Chinese fiction, the next two novels I discuss are more difficult to categorize. Unlike most late Qing fiction writers, Liu E 刘鹗 (1857–1909), author of *The Travels of Lao Can*, was not a professional writer but a practicing physician and sometime entrepreneur, particularly known for effective flood control on the Yellow River. His novel is modeled on travelogue; we follow the footsteps of the protagonist, the intellectual-physician Lao Can, as he tries to "cure" physical as well as social ills with his many unconventional skills. In its critique of contemporary society, *The Travels of Lao Can* shares some characteristics with the typical exposé novel. At the same time, it has been lauded (and sometimes criticized) for its lyrical passages, allegorical structure, and experimentation with techniques from detective fiction. Unlike many other works of the time, *The Travels of Lao Can* exhibits the refinement of traditional literati culture, such as art connoisseurship and rhapsodic prose, but typically employs it to depict folk rather than elite culture. Similarly, the most profound moral philosophy in the novel is voiced by a courtesan-nun.

The Sea of Regret, another important novel by Wu Jianren, was perhaps the most popular novel of romance and sentimentality in the late Qing. Set against the backdrop of the tumultuous days of the Boxer Rebellion and its aftermath, it portrays a young woman's devotion to a wastrel to whom she has been betrothed since childhood. In its response to the theme of love and marriage in the modern world, the novel exhibits an ambivalent morality. Most striking are the excessiveness of the female protagonist's virtue and the melodramatic manner with which she conforms to the wifely ideals of Confucianism. Thus, a seemingly simple allegory of doomed love and female sacrifice becomes a vehicle by which to explore the advent of modernity, with its rapidly changing relations between men and women and between parents and children.

Late Qing fiction marked a reaction to the national and cultural crisis at the end of the dynasty. Spurred by the urgent need of renovating the citizenry and reinvigorating the nation, political champions of new fiction offered a heady moment of new hope. In the practice of fiction writing, however, the resulting product is far more diverse and less instrumental than the reformers would have hoped. Yet, in its unflinching ways of depicting the coming modern world in all its aspects, in its ambiguous, sometimes conflicting portrayals of the old, the new, the Chinese, and the Western, late Qing fiction exhibits an amazing richness and a creative vigor quite unparalleled before or after.

Bibliography

A Ying 阿英. *Wanqing xiaoshuo shi* 晚清小说史 (A history of late Qing fiction). Beijing: Renmin wenxue, 1980 [1935].

Chen Pingyuan 陈平原. *Ershi shiji Zhongguo xiaoshuo shi* 二十世纪中国小说史 (A history of twentieth-century Chinese fiction). Vol. 1, 1897–1916. Beijing: Beijing daxue, 1989.

Denton, Kirk A., ed. *Modern Chinese Literary Thought: Writings on Literature, 1893–1945*. Stanford, CA: Stanford University Press, 1996.

Doleželová-Velingerová, Milena, ed. *The Chinese Novel at the Turn of the Century*. Toronto: University of Toronto Press, 1980.

Hill, Michael Gibbs. *Lin Shu, Inc.: Translation and the Making of Modern Chinese Culture*. Oxford: Oxford University Press, 2013.

Hsia, C. T. "Yen Fu and Liang Ch'i-ch'ao as Advocates of New Fiction." In Adele Austin Rickett, ed., *Chinese Approaches to Literature from Confucius to Liang Ch'i Ch'ao*, 221–257. Princeton, NJ: Princeton University Press, 1978.

Hu, Ying. *Tales of Translation: Composing the New Woman in China, 1899–1918*. Stanford, CA: Stanford University Press, 2000.

Huters, Theodore. *Bringing the World Home: Appropriating the West in Late Qing and Early Republican China*. Honolulu: University of Hawai'i Press, 2005.

——. "The Shattered Mirror: Wu Jianren and the Reflection of Strange Events." In Theodore Huters, R. Bin Wong, and Pauline Yu, eds., *Culture and State in Chinese History*, 277–299. Stanford, CA: Stanford University Press, 1997.

Lee, Leo Ou-fan, and Andrew J. Nathan. "The Beginning of Mass Culture: Journalism and Fiction in the Late Ch'ing and Beyond." In David Johnson, Andrew J. Nathan, and Evelyn S. Rawski, eds., *Popular Culture in Late Imperial China*, 360–395. Berkeley: University of California Press, 1985.

Li, Boyuan (Li Po-yüan). *Modern Times: A Brief History of Enlightenment*. Trans. Douglas Lancashire. Hong Kong: Research Centre for Translation, Chinese University of Hong Kong, 1996.

Liang Qichao 梁启超. *Yinbingshi heji—wenji* 饮冰室合集：文集 (Collected writings from the ice-drinker's studio: Collected essays). 24 vols. Shanghai: Zhonghua shuju, 1936.

Liu, E (Liu T'ieh-yün). *The Travels of Lao Ts'an*. Trans. Harold Shadick. New York: Columbia University Press, 1990.

Lu, Xun (Lu Hsün). *A Brief History of Chinese Fiction*. Trans. Yang Hsien-yi and Gladys Yang. Beijing: Foreign Language Press, 1976.

Tarumoto, Teruo. "A Statistical Survey of Translated Fiction, 1840–1920." In David Pollard, ed., *Translation and Creation: Readings of Western Literature in Early Modern China, 1840–1918*, 37–42. Amsterdam: Benjamins, 1998.

Wang, David Der-wei. *Fin-de-Siècle Splendor: Repressed Modernities of Late Qing Fiction, 1849–1911*. Stanford, CA: Stanford University Press, 1997.

Wei Shaochang 魏绍昌. *Wanqing sida xiaoshuojia* 晚清四大小说家 (Four great novelists of the late Qing). Taipei: Shangwu, 1993.

Wu, Jianren (Wu Wo-yao). *The Sea of Regret: Two Turn-of-the-Century Chinese Romantic Novels*. Trans. Patrick Hanan. Honolulu: University of Hawai'i Press, 1995.

——. *Vignettes from the Late Ch'ing: Bizarre Happenings Eyewitnessed over Two Decades*. Trans. Shih Shun Liu. Hong Kong: Chinese University of Hong Kong, 1975.

Yeh, Catherine Vance. *The Chinese Political Novel: Migration of a World Genre*. Cambridge, MA: Harvard University Asia Center, 2015.

Zeng, Pu (Tseng P'u). "A Flower in a Sinful Sea." (Partial translation.) Trans. Rafe De Crespigny and Liu Ts'un-yan. In Liu Ts'un-yan, ed., *Chinese Middlebrow Fiction from the Ch'ing and Early Republican Eras*, 137–192. Hong Kong: Chinese University Press, 1984.

12

ZHOU SHOUJUAN'S LOVE STORIES AND MANDARIN DUCKS AND BUTTERFLIES FICTION

JIANHUA CHEN

The Mandarin Ducks and Butterflies school (鸳鸯蝴蝶派; henceforth Butterfly) has its origins in the mid-1910s boom in commercial periodicals. Disillusioned with Yuan Shikai's government and the 1911 Republican revolution, this new wave of popular print culture seemed to continue the reform agenda of the late Qing "fiction revolution" (see "The Uses of Fiction") advocated by Liang Qichao (1873–1929), although it was more commercially oriented and better articulated the everyday life of the metropolis (Lee 1999: 43–81). In its narrow sense, Butterfly fiction refers to the sentimental romances or love stories that blossomed during the 1910s. Most popular and representative of these romances was Xu Zhenya's 徐枕亚 (1889–1937) *Jade Pear Spirit* (玉梨魂, 1913), which describes a tragic love affair between a chaste widow and a young scholar in a linguistic style of classical parallelism. More broadly, the term came to refer to all popular literature that developed in multiple forms in the first half of the century, mostly in Shanghai.

Other writers associated with this school are Bao Tianxiao 包天笑 (1876–1973) and his *Eastern Times* (时报) circle; and Wang Dungen 王钝根 (1888–1950), Chen Diexian 陈蝶仙 (1879–1940), and Zhou Shoujuan 周瘦鹃 (1884–1968) with their weekly magazine *Saturday* (礼拜六). In addition to the love stories of Xu and Zhou, the most notable writers and genres were the social fiction of Li Hanqiu 李涵秋 (1874–1923) and Bi Yihong 毕倚虹 (1892–1926), Xu Zhuodai's 徐卓呆 (1880–1958) comic fiction, Cheng Xiaoqing's 程小青 (1893–1976) and Sun Liaohong's 孙了红 (1897–1958) detective stories, Xiang Kairan's

向恺然 (1890–1957) knight-errant fiction, and Zhang Henshui 张恨水 (1895–1967) as a master of diverse genres. According to Perry Link's (1981: 16) estimate, the volume of popular fiction, including translations, published between 1912 and 1949 must have reached the equivalent of five or ten thousand novels of average length—that is, about two hundred pages or one hundred thousand characters.

The place of Butterfly fiction in literary history has been tenuous, tied to the political vicissitudes of the century. The revival of Butterfly literature in 1990s China—with many works reprinted and with sympathetic academic reevaluations—seems to be more than a mere literary phenomenon; it signals a resurgence of popular print culture, a longing for reading pleasure and generic pluralism, a nostalgia for the bygone splendor of urban life, and a freedom from Communist ideology. In the field of literary criticism, this revival—an ironic one, given the suppression and neglect of Butterfly fiction for more than half a century—renews nonetheless the polemics of old and new, popular and literary, and forces us to confront once again basic questions about the nature of literature and Chinese literary modernity.

Butterfly fiction has not always been received so positively. The name "Mandarin Ducks and Butterflies" was coined in the late 1910s by May Fourth writers shortly after the launch of their literary revolution (see "Language and Literary Form"). The term mocked the inseparable lovers (symbolized by Mandarin ducks and butterflies) in Butterfly fiction and was later disparagingly used to refer to all popular literature rooted in late nineteenth-century courtesan novels. As a result, Butterfly fiction was canonically excluded from "new literature" (新文学), a new form of vernacular writing the May Fourth movement promoted to replace that in the classical language. This advocacy went hand in hand with the conceptual dichotomy of new and old, progressive and backward, that underpinned the May Fourth worldview. Obsessed with linear time and the notion of progressive history, May Fourth intellectuals wanted to legitimize their concept of new literature, or literature itself, in terms of the universal codes of world literature. Butterfly fiction fit poorly into this new category of literature; it was, from the May Fourth perspective, no more than a mixture of feudal and colonial cultures associated with a decadent and money-grubbing Shanghai. Zhou Zuoren 周作人 (1885–1967) and Qian Xuantong 钱玄同 (1887–1939), in particular, criticized Butterfly fiction as the residue of "old culture," backward and amoral. In a series of essays, Zhou accused *Jade Pear Spirit* and other sad love stories of "decay and absurdity" in content and form. Examining how the "Butterfly" label was invented, circulated, and interpreted reveals how "literariness" as a canonical code ideologically articulated literary fields and empowered intellectual discourses in modern China.

Feeling the pressure from the advocates of new literature, the Butterfly writers tried to raise their voices. In early 1921, after Mao Dun 茅盾 (1896–1981) took over the *Short Story Magazine* (小说月报) and turned it into a bastion of the new literature, Butterfly writers opened fire in newspapers and periodicals such as Zhou Shoujuan's *Free Talk* (自由谈), Bao Tianxiao's *Sunday* (星期), and Yu Daxiong's 余大雄 *The Crystal* (晶报). Compared with Mao Dun, Zheng Zhenduo 郑振铎 (1898–1958), and other May Fourth theorists, their orchestrated voices seemed less theoretical and combative (J. Chen 2009: 91–114). Many Butterfly writers identified themselves with the *old* stance and questioned the linguistic, literary, and cultural legitimacy of the new literature. But within their cultural conservatism lies a paradox: espousing Western literature, on the one hand, they feared losing their cultural identity, on the other. In emphasizing pleasure and happiness as the core of literary production (Denton 1996: 243–246), they endeavored to mediate Western modernity—largely on the level of quotidian materialism—through traditional literary forms, conventions, and poetics. In this sense, their literature not only functioned to create psychological comfort for the petite bourgeoisie (Link 1981, 197) but also served their politics, internalizing Western modernity through native values. Rather than endorse a utopian ideal, it catered to urban desires deeply embedded in a liberal ideology and a constitutional Republican government and emphasized social divisions and the functions of the individual, family, and state (J. Chen 2012: 47–57).

Butterfly fiction did not lose its dominance in the popular literary market until 1949, best evidenced by the sustained popularity of Zhang Henshui's *Fate in Tears and Laughter* (啼笑因缘, 1930), a love story mixed with social and knight-errant elements. Nor did Butterfly fiction give up its hallmark—the pleasure principle—until the late 1930s, when the whole nation was plunged into war. Nevertheless, after the 1920s debate between May Fourth and Butterfly writers, the latter lost their claim on literature both ideologically and institutionally. Ideologically, they were never legitimated by the "new culture," nor did they adopt notions of "progressive history" or "revolutionary literature." They were fatally labeled "old" because of their continued association with the classical language. Most Butterfly writers did not wholly embrace the new vernacular language that had come to dominate the literary field with the May Fourth movement and the officially implemented "national language movement" (国语运动). Even in the 1940s, Zhou Shoujuan claimed that his magazine *The Violet* (紫罗兰) was impartial with respect to the vernacular and classical. Institutionally, Butterfly writers seemed not to see beyond their commercial success and paid little attention to their place in literary history. In contrast, May Fourth writers tied the formation of literature to the educational field, including universities, and the production of literary history. An example of this May Fourth self-promotion is the 1935 publication of *Compendium of Modern Chinese Literature* (中国新文学大系), which erected a historical monument not only to "new" literary creation but also to the enterprise of literature as a progressive institution in modern China. Butterfly literature was, of course, nowhere to be found. In late 1950s Communist China, a younger generation of Marxist literary historians in Beijing and Shanghai universities rewrote modern Chinese literary history, severely criticizing Butterfly literature as a "reactionary countercurrent" (反动逆流) against the progressive May Fourth new literature. This view of Butterfly fiction dominated until the revisionism of the 1980s and 1990s.

Zhou Shoujuan was one of the key figures in the Butterfly school, best known as "king of the sad love story." In many ways he contributed to the formation of modern Chinese literature in its early phase: even before the May Fourth literary movement, he had experimented with using the vernacular in fiction, drama, and translations. Many of his love stories appearing in *Saturday* in the mid-1910s were infused with new narrative techniques borrowed from Western fiction and were influential in his time. He translated numerous works of Western fiction by Dickens, Maupassant, Zola, Tolstoy, Conan Doyle, and many others; his *Anthology of Famous European and American Short Stories* (欧美名家短篇小说丛刊), published in 1917 in three volumes, was praised by Lu Xun and given an award by the Education Bureau (Guo 1998: 435–441). In addition, Zhou edited many popular magazines, among which *Saturday*, *Semi-Monthly* (半月), and *The Violet* were often best sellers. From 1919 to 1932, he also edited the daily literary page "Free Talk" in *Shenbao* (申报), the largest newspaper in Shanghai, and contributed critiques on current politics.

In his early literary career, Zhou fervently assimilated Western ideas of love. His topics ranged from the love stories of world celebrities, such as Napoleon, Hugo, Byron, Lincoln, and Washington, to how to kiss, date, or write love letters. While promoting modern ideas of love, the world of love in his fiction is nonetheless shattered rather than harmonious, mirroring complexities and conflicts in semicolonial and multicultural Shanghai. In Zhou's stories, love is entangled with hatred, one that derives, perhaps, from a trauma in his childhood. As he recalled, his father died in 1900, tortured by illness and angered by national shame: having heard of the Boxer Rebellion and the Western forces invading Beijing, he jumped down from his bed and shouted to his sons, "You are men, go fight!" Then he died. Zhou writes with resentment, "So, unexpectedly, the familial disaster and national humiliation befell the six-year-old boy" (Fan and Fan 1996: 98; J. Chen 2000: 64).

The loss of his father made him love all the more his widowed mother, who single-handedly raised four children by working as a seamstress. In his early, sad love stories, women often appear as extraordinary patriots, sacrificing their lives to save the country. However, more heartrending are his descriptions of the conflicts between patriotism and women's repressed desire. The famous short story "We Shall Meet Again" (行再相见, 1914) describes a girl falling in love with a young British officer in the service of the consulate in Shanghai. As her uncle recognizes, he is the man who killed her father during the allied invasion of Beijing in 1900; finally, she obeys her uncle and murders her lover by poison. But as she is bending over his corpse, her last words, "We shall meet again," reveal that her act had been a reluctant one. The coexistence of her love and her revenge implies that nationalism and ethical responsibility are legitimate and yet horrible (Zhou 1976: 14–18).

Zhou's moral didacticism recalls Confucian ethics, but as a supreme force capable of subverting the social order, passion is equally strong in his stories. In his 1911 vernacular drama *The Flower of Love* (爱之花), female desire is represented more sympathetically. The heroine, Manyin 曼茵, who has an extramarital affair with a young military officer, curses the state that sends him to war. Influenced by Lin Shu's 林纾 (1852–1924) translation of *La Dame aux camélias* (巴黎茶花女遗事, 1898), the drama ends in tragedy when Manyin commits suicide in her bedroom after unwittingly eating her lover's heart. In this rewriting of a modern French drama, the heroine embodies the ideal of love and is victimized by the patriarchal order: depicted negatively, both her husband and her lover are identified with the power of the nation-state and alien to true love.

For Zhou, love is a discursive practice through which to reconcile tradition and modernity. Following his romantic predecessors Lin Shu, Xu Zhenya, and Su Manshu 苏曼殊 (1884–1918), he refashions the Chinese discourse of "true passion" (真情), together with the poetic tradition of sentimental-erotic literature (Hsia 1984: 199–253). But Zhou departs from them not only in using the vernacular; more significant, he also changes traditional values and codes to suit modernity. Such a merger is not always easy, as we see in his famous short story "A Gramophone Record" (留声机片, 1921), in which a young couple die "for true love" (为情而死) after a long and painful separation caused by the feudal marriage system (Lee 2007: 100–101). A grotesque effect is evoked when the woman dies next to a gramophone after listening to a record sent by her lover exiled on a Pacific island, a record that magically delivers his dying message. The broken heart–fragile record metaphor symbolizes Western technology as both optimism for and threat to China's modern fate. Another story, "In the Nine-Flower Curtain" (九华帐里, 1917), is in the form of the author's "pillow talk" to his bride on their wedding night. This comic piece contains generic elements of diary, love letter, confession, and autobiographical fiction and is representative of Zhou's early experiments with first-person narratives (Fan 1994: 177). While the narrator passionately expresses his modern ideal of love and family, the lyricism and theatricality owe much to traditional rhetoric and poetics (J. Chen 2000: 41–66).

Zhou's literary discourse reflects changing ideas of love, marriage, and family in a transitional society; he reshapes the public and private spaces in which modern technology and communication play a crucial role. His characters are no longer the stereotyped "talent and beauty" but urbanites from all walks of life. The boy and girl meet in open spaces in colorful city landscapes—at the Bund, in tramcars, public parks, shops, or medical clinics—unlike the trysts in the back gardens or inner chambers in traditional romances. "The Intimate Beauty" (红颜知己), a novella published in 1917, gave birth to the modern romance that celebrates free contact and love between man and woman in urban space, and at the same time it creates an "intimate realm" for fantasy and daydream. Yichen 一尘, a young novelist, meets Minghua 明华 (whose name sounds like "famous flower") at the Bund one night. He manages to meet her again by advertising in a newspaper. Through free contact and mutual understanding, they fall in love and finally get married. This blissful description of their relationship eulogizes modern love and free communication and departs radically from traditional modes of representation. Zhou opens up literary dimensions in which love and compassion convey new meanings by relying on modern communicative modes; at the same time, he carves out an intimate sphere in the imagined community of his public readership. Thus "intimacy" plays a crucial role in the story; the episode in which Yichen daydreams on a train about the broach Minghua gave him as a token of intimacy is also significant in evoking an erotic fantasy in urban space.

Zhou's own real-life romance was more than just a failed first love; it was intertwined with a complex of personality, collective psychology, and cultural production. As the story goes, when Zhou was eighteen he came to know a girl in his neighborhood, and they fell in love by exchanging letters. A year later, however, the girl's parents arranged for her to marry a rich man. Zhou never recovered from the loss, and for the remainder of his life he was obsessed with the violet, which was his lover's Western name. The violet becomes a prism that mirrors the split of his self into public and private spaces. Zhou embodies a paradigm shift in terms of the male attitude toward marriage: in contrast to the debauched literati who adopt concubines or frequent the pleasure quarters, he becomes a sincere monogamist in real life. As a public figure, he speaks for patriotism and family values, but privately he always lives with the fantasy and alienation related to Violet—his ideal lover. Haunted by images of Violet, Zhou is torn by the conflict of morality and passion, the real and the ideal. He enjoys a happy family life, and yet he dreams of the *other* woman in his fiction. In 1944, on his fiftieth birthday, the magazine *The Violet* published his *Confessions of Love* (爱的供状), consisting of a hundred classical poems with detailed commentaries about his love affair with Violet. Even in the mid-1950s, Zhou recalled this affair nostalgically in his essay "My Lifelong Worship of Violet" (一生低首紫罗兰, 1956).

Evoking the classical aesthetics of flowers, Violet is identified with a pretty, educated woman—a symbol of modernity. The figure of violet becomes a medium through which the female body and social norms of gender and sexuality are represented, privately and publicly. One of the phenomena unique to literary culture in 1920s Shanghai, the popular print media favored the violet as a symbol of the modern woman for its sustained power to arouse the urban imagination. An inquiry into this phenomenon in terms of sexuality, politics, and aesthetics reveals how Butterfly literature embodied the reform ideology of the early Republican nation-state. It functioned in educating, regulating, and transforming urban mentality and culture through literary production and consumption, and it created private and public space in which the autonomy of the individual was nourished and practiced. Here the central issue is how Zhou's love discourse bares his vision of gender roles in private space and his cultural politics in public space. The popularity of his writing also served to transform the private space of his own sentiment into a public space, in which women's fate was envisioned in terms of the conflict between domesticity and publicity. Zhou treated all the problems women of the time faced: abuse by the old family system, free contact with men, public education, new familial roles, social responsibility, and national identity.

Beginning with late Qing fiction, the "new woman" became the focus of various literary representations. In Zhou's stories, woman is a contested site of nationalism and romanticism, emblematic of the chasm between tradition and modernity in the early Republican period. Like most Butterfly writers, Zhou was concerned with women's roles in the domestic space, which was closely tied to his advocacy of the "small family," a new social development in urban China. Butterfly writers' reform agenda and gender politics were expressed in articles in the *Semi-Monthly* and *The Violet*, specifically in special issues on "family," "lovers," "divorce," and the "problem of prostitution."

In the late 1920s, *The Violet* presented a unique visual image of the new woman through an extra frame added around the face of a pretty woman on the magazine's cover, making the woman's image doubly shaped by the male gaze. The making of *The Violet* in social space must thus be connected to the larger issue of publicizing women through the power of visuality. On the one hand, Zhou used the female body to invoke male desire; on the other hand, his magazines greatly enhanced the social mobility of women. Many women writers were published in his magazine: for example, after Eileen Chang's 张爱玲 first story, "Aloewood Ashes: The First Incense Brazier" (沉香屑第一炉香), appeared in *The Violet* in 1943, she rose to fame overnight.

This visual *Violet*, imbued with desire for and anxiety about the modern, was indebted to the spread of photography and cinema in Shanghai. Photography and cinema often appeared figuratively in Zhou's fiction, serving diverse rhetorical purposes. The Butterfly writers had strong faith in "photographic realism," asserting that fiction should represent life as accurately as a camera does. In reality, of course, their fiction was hardly as mimetic as they intended it to be. They often toyed with frames, "camera" angles, dramatic effects, theatricality, and the seen and the unseen, best exemplified by the story "The Opposite Window" (对邻的小楼, 1924; Fan and Fan 1996: 59–66), in which the way the author looks at the changing life behind a neighbor's window comes from the idea of a movie theater.

Zhou's vision of gender roles and family values may be linked to the ideology of the new Republic and its conceptions of citizenry, privacy, and the modern nation-state. Whereas in *Free Talk* Zhou frequently satirized Republican presidents and provincial warlords for their vile deeds and scandals, he and other

Butterfly writers spread knowledge of citizenship, law, voting rights, the economy, and domestic life in the pages of *Common Sense* (常识), another supplement to *Shenbao* (Chen 2012: 36–47).

The semiotic web of violet/Violet/*The Violet* is interwoven into a complex representation of urban identities. It designates Zhou's own writing persona, his ideal goddess of love, his home, and the magazines he edited, as well as the images of women on the magazine's front cover. From such excessive use of the figure of violet arise issues about Zhou's identity and its literary representations. As a circulated commodity, *The Violet* was the object of city-dwellers' daydreams, engendering anxiety or aspiration for a better life. Linking the multiple facets of the flower and beauty, the magazine created an intimate dialogue between authors and readers, sharing the pleasure of the erotic gaze, fantasy, gossip, and secrecy. In searching for the figure of violet in Zhou's and his friends' writings, we are drawn into a semiotic labyrinth, moving from mental to textual space and from production to social space. In examining the kaleidoscopic representations of the violet in the process of circulation and mass reproduction, we cross the boundaries between literature and culture, aesthetics and politics, gender and visuality, popularity and publicity, and urban space and perception. Crossing these boundaries in turn reveals how Zhou and his fellow literati were redefining authorship and readership.

Zhou's imagined intimate sphere seemed to meet an urgent moral need. Since the late 1910s, prostitution in Shanghai had drawn serious attention from social critics as a degenerate profession that resulted in an epidemic of diseases. Although founded on the pleasure principle, *The Violet* served a moral function. Through literary and visual innovations, the magazine transformed the world of literati, courtesans, and "flowers" into an aesthetic world of love and compassion (it is interesting that Zhou's editing principle—"renewing the fashion" [花样翻新]—was borrowed from the jargon of late Qing brothels). The violet phenomenon, as a modern vision of women, sex, family, and daily life combined with the aesthetics of pleasure and intimacy, implies the author's agenda to reform urbanites' sexual tastes and behavior to save China from moral corruption.

Bibliography

Chen, Diexian. *The Money Demon: An Autobiographical Romance*. Trans. Patrick Hanan. Honolulu: University of Hawai'i Press, 1999.

Chen, Jianhua. "An Archaeology of Repressed Popularity: Zhou Shoujuan, Mao Dun, and Their 1920s Literary Polemics." In Carlos Rojas and Eileen Cheng-yin Chow, eds., *Rethinking Chinese Popular Culture: Cannibalization of the Canon*, 91–114. New York: Routledge, 2009.

——. "Formation of Modern Subjectivity and Essay: Zhou Shoujuan's 'In the Nine-Flower Curtain.'" In Martin Woesler, ed., *The Chinese Chinese Literary Essay: Defining the Chinese Self in the 20th Century*, 41–66. Bochum: Bochum University Press, 2000.

——. "Republican Constitutional Politics and Family-State Imagination." In "From Revolution to the Republic: Chen Jianhua on Vernacular Chinese Modernity," ed. Qian Suoqiao. A special issue of *Contemporary Chinese Thought* 44, 1 (Fall 2012): 36–69.

Chow, Rey. *Woman and Chinese Modernity: The Politics of Reading Between West and East*. Minneapolis: University of Minnesota Press, 1991.

Denton, Kirk A., ed. *Modern Chinese Literary Thought: Writings on Literature, 1893–1945*. Stanford, CA: Stanford University Press, 1996.

Fan Boqun 范伯群, ed. *Zhongguo jin xiandai tongsu wenxue shi* 中国近现代通俗文学史 (A history of modern Chinese popular literature). Nanjing: Jiangsu jiaoyu, 2000.

——. "Zhu, yi, bian jie jing de 'wenzi laogong'—Zhou Shoujuan pingzhuan" 著,译,编皆精的"文字劳工"—周瘦鹃评传 (A laborer of literary writing, translating, and editing: Zhou Shoujuan). In Fan Boqun, ed., *Zhongguo jin xiandai tongsu zuojia congshu* 中国近现代通俗作家丛书 (Anthologies of modern Chinese popular writers), 163–180. 10 vols. Nanjing: Nanjing, 1994.

Fan Boqun 范伯群 and Fan Zijiang 范紫江, eds. *Zhou Shoujuan daibiao zuo* 周瘦鹃代表作 (Representative works of Zhou Shoujuan). Nanjing: Jiangsu wenyi, 1996.

Guo Yanli 郭延礼. *Zhongguo jindai fanyi wenxue gailun* 中国近代翻译文学概论 (An outline of modern Chinese translated literature). Wuhan: Hubei jiaoyu, 1998.

Hsia, C. T. "Hsu Chen-ya: *Yu-li hun*: An Essay in Literary History and Criticism." In Liu Ts'un-yan ed., *Chinese Middlebrow Fiction: From the Ch'ing and Early Republican Era*, 199–253. Armonk, NY: M. E. Sharpe, 1984.

Lee, Haiyan. *Revolution of the Heart: A Genealogy of Love in China, 1900–1950*. Stanford, CA: Stanford University Press, 2007.

Lee, Leo Ou-fan. *Shanghai Modern: The Flowering of a New Urban Culture in China, 1930–1945*. Cambridge, MA: Harvard University Press, 1999.

Link, E. Perry. *Mandarin Ducks and Butterflies: Popular Fiction in Early Twentieth-Century Chinese Cities*. Berkeley: University of California Press, 1981.

Liu Yangti 刘扬体. *Liubian zhong de liupai—Yuanyang hudie pai xinlun* 流变中的流派—鸳鸯蝴蝶派新论 (The schools in change: A new study of the Mandarin Ducks and Butterfly school). Beijing: Zhongguo wenlian, 1997.

Wang, Dungen. "Remarks on the Publication of *Saturday*." Trans. Gilbert Fung. In Kirk A. Denton, ed., *Modern Chinese Literary Thought: Writings on Literature, 1893–1945*, 243–244. Stanford, CA: Stanford University Press, 1996.

Wang Zhiyi 王智毅. *Zhou Shoujuan yanjiu zilia* 周瘦鹃研究资料 (Research materials on Zhou Shoujuan). Tianjin: Tianjin renmin, 1993.

Wei Shaochang 魏绍昌. *Wo kan Yuanyang hudie pai* 我看鸳鸯蝴蝶派 (My view of the Mandarin Ducks and Butterflies school). Taipei: Commercial Press, 1992.

——. *Yuanyang hudie pai yanjiu ziliao* 鸳鸯蝴蝶派研究资料 (Research materials on the Mandarin Ducks and Butterfly school). Shanghai: Shanghai wenyi, 1984.

Zhang, Henshui. "Fate in Tears and Laughter." (Excerpt.) Trans. Sally Borthwick. In Liu Ts'un-yan, ed., *Chinese Middlebrow Fiction: From the Ch'ing and Early Republican Era*, 255–287. Armonk, NY: M. E. Sharpe, 1984.

——. *Shanghai Express: A Thirties Novel by Zhang Henshui*. Trans. William Lyell. Honolulu: University of Hawai'i Press, 1997.

Zhou, Shoujuan. "Congratulations to *Happy Magazine*." Trans. Gilbert Fung. In Kirk A. Denton, ed., *Modern Chinese Literary Thought: Writings on Literature, 1893–1945*, 245–246. Stanford, CA: Stanford University Press, 1996.

——. "We Shall Meet Again." Trans. Perry Link. In John Berninghousen and Ted Huters, eds., *Revolutionary Literature in China: An Anthology*, 12–19. New York: M. E. Sharpe, 1976.

13

FORM AND REFORM:
NEW POETRY AND THE CRESCENT MOON SOCIETY

JOHN A. CRESPI

In considering the invention of Chinese "new poetry" (新诗) in the 1910s, it is well to keep in mind that although early modern poets did indeed come up with something quite new in the context of the long history of Chinese literature, the type of poetic project they envisioned had by that time experienced a distinct global history of its own. This is a history that can be traced from German polymath Johann Gottfried Herder's revival of native poetics and folk song in the late eighteenth century on through any number of nationalist cultural revival movements that have taken place in various quarters of Europe, Africa, the Americas, the Pacific, and Asia. Loosely unifying these many poetic renaissances is an emphasis on values consonant with those of nationalist thought. Among these is the belief that poetry, like the nation itself, must be reborn through liberation. Thus, where a new nation would throw off the political and psychological shackles of a colonial power or its own premodern past, the nation's new poetry was to reassert its identity and relevance by shaking off the formalist fetters of codified prosodies and outmoded conventions.

China's classical poetic tradition lent itself well to such a program. For those who sought to emulate the poetic virtuosos of the Tang dynasty over a thousand years before, writing poetry often meant writing regulated verse (律诗) with lines of either five or seven monosyllables that adhered to fixed patterns of tonal contrast and followed set end-rhyme schemes. Another popular genre, ci (词), or lyric meters, allowed flexibility in line length, but only within the format of fixed templates that the poet filled in with his or her own selection of tonally appropriate monosyllables. By the late Qing, the mainstream of poetry being written in China was vulnerable to criticism for its reliance on a fixed repertoire of inherited forms and, within these forms, its tendency to draw from a rather narrow range of conventionalized diction, allusion, and theme. Yet most damning of all, at least in the eyes of China's twentieth-century literary reformers, was that almost without exception Chinese poetry was the domain of the archaic classical language rather than the spoken vernacular.

Like many thinkers since the era of romantic philology, the intellectuals promoting a modernized New Culture for China in the late 1910s tended to identify language with culture. Working from this premise, they underscored the difference between the learned, written register of classical Chinese and a vernacular register that approximated everyday speech. The literary program they began to formulate was conceptually parallel to those forwarded by nineteenth- and twentieth-century scholar-poet nationalists in regions with similarly "diglossic" linguistic situations. In Turkey and Greece, for example, modernizing literati made the same distinction between a "dead" written register—for them associated with cultural traits of elitism, antihumanism, and repression—and a "living" vernacular, which they promoted as the medium for a potentially modern and democratic culture to be founded upon that most primary constituent of the nation, the people. Poetry, so often understood as the quintessence of any language, represented all that was worst or best in either of these coexisting lingua-cultures.

Given the close relationship between culture, language, and poetry, it should come as little surprise that Hu Shi 胡适 (1891–1962), one of the flag bearers of the New Culture movement in China, should have been both a language reform activist and the proclaimed father of Chinese new poetry. Hu first turned his attention toward poetic renewal while he was living in New York in 1915 and 1916. At the time a graduate student, Hu was a voracious reader, an avid though amateurish poet, and a cultural cosmopolitan well acquainted with New York's intellectual elite, including the "long-haired men and short-haired women" who frequented the tea parties held at the home of Hu's scholarly mentor at Columbia University, John Dewey (Hu 1981: 92). Among the intellectual trends Hu encountered around this time was America's own literary renaissance, in particular the movement against the conventional and derivative verse of the Victorian genteel tradition.

A convincing amount of circumstantial evidence points to Hu's awareness of the poetic innovations then afoot in America. We know he was familiar with the keystone journal of Anglo-American new verse, Harriet Monroe's *Poetry*, and Hu's earliest prescriptions for Chinese new poetry, his famous "Eight Don'ts" (八不), seem at least partially inspired by Amy Lowell's "Imagist Credo" of 1915 (Wong 1988: 44–47). One of Hu's first outright declarations on poetic revival—"Where does revolution in the Kingdom of Poetry begin? Poetry must be written like prose" (诗国革命何自始，要须作诗如作文), penned into his diary while he was riding the train into New York City in September 1915—echoes Ezra Pound's assertion that "poetry should be written at least as well as prose" (Hu 1947: 790; Pound 1914: 115).

As a rule, however, Hu downplayed the influence of the foreign avant-garde on his poetic thought. For a home audience that still had to be convinced of the validity of Chinese vernacular free verse, he emphasized the new genre's supposed indigenous origins. In the 1919 theoretical essay "On New Poetry" (谈新诗), for instance, he proposed that the history of poetry in China had been one of unconscious "liberations" in line length. Thus, poetic form evolved from the four-syllabic line of the *Book of Poetry* (诗经), to five- and seven-syllabic ancient-style poetry (古诗) and regulated verse, and on through the patterned verse of Song lyric meter (宋词) and Yuan dynasty dramatic verse (曲). According to Hu, the free-verse revolution marked a conscious transcendence of tradition, a breaking of the "shackles" of the spirit that allowed "abundant material, precise observation, high ideals, and complex feeling and emotion" to enter poetry (Hu 1935: 295). The appeal of Hu's rather simplistic historical-evolutionary narrative of poetic liberation lay in how it worked rhetorically to link him and his immediate contemporaries to their poetic past even as they sought to carry the nation into a new era of historical consciousness.

After Hu's first new-style poems appeared in *New Youth* (新青年) in 1917, nearly all the intellectuals promoting the New Culture movement began to try their hand at the infant genre, thus registering a vote of confidence in Hu's program and at the same time affirming their own status as progressive men of letters. Although most of these writers produced only a handful of poems for *New Youth* and other reformist journals such as *Renaissance* (新潮) and *Young China* (少年中国), the more ambitious among them began to publish single-author collections and multiauthor anthologies. The new poets struck out in many directions. Thematically their poems ranged from social protest and sympathy with the downtrodden to nature worship, travel, love, metaphysical despair, and patriotic outrage. They eschewed fixed forms, experimenting with everything from lengthy prose poems (散文诗) to haiku-like "short poems" (小诗), allegorical narrative poems, and poems styled loosely on folk song, a genre that had begun to attract its own band of enthusiasts. Diction in these poems ranged from the colloquial to the archaic and from local dialect to the insertion of foreign words. Hu Shi's own best effort, published in his own poetry collection *Experiments* (尝试集, 1922), was perhaps "Dream and Poetry" (梦与诗):

All ordinary experience,
All ordinary images,
Surging by chance into dream,
They are transformed into many a remarkable pattern!
All ordinary feelings,
All ordinary words,

> Encountering by chance the poet,
> They are transformed into many a remarkable verse!
> Drink to know wine's strength,
> Love to know passion's intensity:—
> You cannot write my poem,
> Just as I cannot dream your dream.

"Dream and Poetry" demonstrates a restraint and structural integrity lacking in much poetry of its time. According to Hu, it describes his theory of "poetic empiricism," the idea that poetry must be grounded in concrete, individual experience. Such a message may seem banal from today's perspective, but at the time it framed the poem as a programmatic statement against what Hu and his cohort often denounced as a lack of genuine self-expression in the traditional, form-bound literary mind.

Yet the cult of self-expression that left its thematic and formal impress on so much May Fourth era new poetry is best represented not by Hu but by another poet inspired while studying abroad, Guo Moruo 郭沫若 (1892–1978). Under the influence of Bengali poet Rabindranath Tagore, Guo had in fact begun writing modern vernacular poetry at least one year before news of Hu Shi's poetic revolution reached him in Japan (Roy 1971: 65–68). Soon afterward Guo discovered another poetic soul mate in Walt Whitman. Where Whitman assumed the task of poetic spokesman for the United States, Guo established himself as the poet of an effusive, unfettered "I" in poems such as "Heavenly Hound" (天狗, 1920), with the word *"Energy"* appearing in English in the original:

> I am the Heavenly Hound!
> I swallow the moon,
> I swallow the sun,
> I swallow all the stars,
> I swallow the entire universe,
> I am I!
> I am the light of the moon,
> I am the light of the sun,
> I am the light of all the stars,
> I am X-ray beams,
> I am the amassed *Energy* of the entire universe!

The exuberant egotism, celebration of freedom, and disdain for conventional form that marked this and other poems included in Guo's *The Goddesses* (女神, 1921) won him instant fame and numerous imitators. There were, however, those who began to wonder if this new poetry could persist on raw spontaneity, undigested foreignisms, and bristling exclamation marks. In the early and mid-1920s, even as interest in the genre began to sag among some of the original new poets, others began to draw inspiration from the poetics of French symbolism, Russian revolutionary poetry, and in the case of the Crescent Moon Society (新月社), English-language verse. The society, which took its name from a poetry collection by Tagore, formed initially around 1923 at a Beijing social club for returned students, professors, and other elements of China's urban intellectual elite. Literary inclinations ran strong among members, and over the ensuing ten years the seventeen or so poets affiliated with the society and its publications generated a varied yet stylistically distinctive corpus of poetry.

A stated goal of the Crescent Moon poets was to continue the renewal of Chinese culture through poetry, but to do so through stanzaic and metric discipline. As the society's informal leader, the irrepressible poet and socialite Xu Zhimo 徐志摩 (1897–1931) wrote in 1926, "We believe that without a proper style of poetic expression the current spiritual liberation or spiritual revolution of our people will be incomplete." The poet's duty, Xu continued, was "to hammer out an appropriate form through the discovery of new patterns and prosodies," because "perfection of outer form is the means towards expressing perfection of spirit" (Xu 1935: 119).

True to this mission, the Crescent Moon poets applied themselves to inventing poetic forms amenable to the Chinese vernacular. They experimented with and improvised on the meters, rhymes, and rhythms offered by a variety of imported stanzaic patterns. The playful Xu Zhimo, for example, was not averse to setting a love poem to what an English reader would mark as the limerick, as seen in his "By Chance" (偶然, 1926). Although the Chinese version does not—and because of linguistic difference cannot—adhere precisely to the metrics of the limerick, the poem lends itself well to a "reverse" translation:

> You and I met one black night at sea,
> Our courses were set, you and me,
> You may think of it yet,
> Better, though, to forget,
> How we shone one on one brilliantly!

To be sure, the turn to strict poetic form so soon after the critique of traditional verse required a defense. Wen Yiduo 闻一多 (1899–1946), an American-trained painter and poet in whose bohemian artist's studio poets would gather to declaim and polish their work, pointedly denounced the free-verse excesses of recent new poetry in his 1926 essay "Form in Poetry" (诗的格律). Formal technique, Wen argued, was an aid to artistic expression, not an obstacle, and thus poetry can attain perfection only when the poet learns to "dance in fetters." He took care, however, to identify the difference between old forms and new forms, noting that "the format of Regulated Verse has been determined for us by our predecessors, whereas the format of New Poetry is decided upon spontaneously according to the artist's predilection" (Wen 1996: 324). Consequently, the new poet controls form, not form the new poet, leaving the modern poetic personality free to impose structure without sacrificing personal creative autonomy.

But Wen was much more than a theorist. He demonstrated his aesthetic principles throughout his poetic works, but nowhere more strikingly than in "Stagnation" (死水, 1926). In the original Chinese, each line of this five-stanza poem measures nine syllables, creating a visual effect of stanzaic "blocks" impossible to replicate in English. Wen constructs something akin to poetic feet by subdividing each nine-syllable line into two- and three-syllable semantic clusters. Such patterning begins to allow for interlinear grammatical and rhythmic parallelism, effects that Wen enhances with subtle alliteration, assonance, and internal rhyme. A partial translation that observes at least some of these features might read thus:

> A hopeless ditch of stagnation,
> Where the breeze cannot stir half a riffle.
> Just dump in scrap copper and iron,
> Or pour in slops, leavings, and offal.
> That copper may green into jade,
> Those cans rust to peach blossom petals;
> So let the grease weave a silk plait,
> And scum steam the cloud-glow of nightfall.

Opinions vary as to what Wen might be addressing here, but most commentators see in it an irony-tinged despair over China's deeply corrupt political situation. Although this may be so, Wen's deliberate blurring of the line between decay and beauty, together with the desire to contain this "noble rot" within an exacting architectonic symmetry, speaks less to the politics of warlords and imperialists than to the subtler aesthetic politics of fashioning the raw, intractable stuff of language into a self-sufficient corpus of modern national poetry.

Bibliography

Acton, Harold, and Chen Shih-hsiang, eds. *Modern Chinese Poetry*. London: Duckworth, 1936.

Guo, Moruo (Kuo Mo-jo). *Selected Poems from The Goddess*. Beijing: Foreign Languages Press, 1978.

Hockx, Michel. *Snowy Morning: Eight Chinese Poets on the Road to Modernist*. Leiden: Research School, CNWS, 1994.

Hsu, Kai-yu, ed. *Twentieth Century Chinese Poetry: An Anthology*. Ithaca, NY: Cornell University Press, 1963.

Hu Shi 胡适. *Hu Shi koushu zizhuan* 胡适口述自传 (An oral autobiography of Hu Shi). Trans. Tong Te-kong (Tang Degang 唐德刚). Taipei: Zhuanji wenxue, 1981.

——. *Hu Shi liuxue riji* 胡适留学日记 (Hu Shi's American diary). Taipei: Shangwu, 1947.

——. "Tan xinshi" 谈新诗 (On new poetry). In Zhao Jiabi 赵家璧, ed., *Zhongguo xinwenxue daxi* 中国新文学大系 (Compendium of Chinese new literature), 1:294–311. Shanghai: Liangyou, 1935.

Kaldis, Nicholas. *The Modern Chinese Prose Poem: A Study of Lu Xun's Wild Grass (Yecao)*. Amherst, NY: Cambria Press, 2014.

Lin, Julia C. *Modern Chinese Poetry: An Introduction*. Seattle: University of Washington Press, 1972.

Pound, Ezra. "Mr. Hueffer and the Prose Tradition in Verse." *Poetry* 4, 6 (1914): 111–120.

Roy, David Tod. *Kuo Mo-jo: The Early Years*. Cambridge, MA: Harvard University Press, 1971.

Wen, Yiduo. "Form in Poetry." Trans. Randy Trumbull. In Kirk A. Denton, ed., *Modern Chinese Literary Thought: Writings on Literature, 1893–1945*, 318–327. Stanford, CA: Stanford University Press, 1996.

——. *Wen Yiduo: Selected Poetry and Prose*. Beijing: Panda Books, 1990.

Wong, Yoon Wah. *Essays on Chinese Literature: A Comparative Approach*. Singapore: Singapore University Press, 1988.

Xu Zhimo 徐志摩. "*Shikan* bianyan" 诗刊弁言 (Foreword to *Poetry Journal*). In Zhao Jiabi 赵家璧, ed., *Zhongguo xinwenxue daxi* 中国新文学大系 (Compendium of Chinese new literature), 2:117–119. Shanghai: Liangyou, 1935.

Yeh, Michelle, ed. *Anthology of Modern Chinese Poetry*. New Haven, CT: Yale University Press, 1994.

14

RECONSIDERING THE ORIGINS OF MODERN CHINESE WOMEN'S WRITING

AMY D. DOOLING

The "problem" of women has been one of the more enduring hallmarks of Chinese modernity, and the problem of literary women is no exception. Beginning in 1916, with the publication of Xie Wuliang's 谢无量 pioneering *Literary History of Chinese Women* (中国妇女文学史), countless discussions have centered on the issue of women as writers. The transformative influence of women's studies on the field of Chinese literary studies, both in and outside China, coupled with the post-Mao fascination with those aspects of the literary and cultural past marginalized by dominant Communist Party historiography, is helping to fuel yet another surge of interest, and the recent proliferation of reprints and reference materials (including bibliographies, biographical dictionaries, and new translations) and a growing corpus of textual and theoretical analyses will shape the critical discourse on literary women for years to come.

Not surprisingly, one topic that has sparked renewed attention is women's writing in the May Fourth and post–May Fourth eras (1915–1937). Conventionally remembered as the time when the first generation of women were empowered with a voice of their own, May Fourth has long been privileged as a defining moment in the history of female literary experience in China. In this account, a Western-inspired movement for cultural enlightenment alerted forward-thinking male intellectuals like Lu Xun 鲁迅 to the plight of Chinese women, a cause that thereafter found extensive coverage in the articles and fiction they—and, soon, a small legion of newly emancipated women—published in the modern urban press. Recent research, though continuing to affirm the historic significance of May Fourth to Chinese women's literary practice, fundamentally alters the story of the "birth" of women's writing, revealing it as a symbolic origin embedded in the myth making of Chinese modernity. What follows does not exhaust the wealth of archival findings or critical discussions bearing on this topic; it does, however, attempt to reintroduce this pivotal historical juncture in light of revisionist scholarship of recent decades.

To begin with, greater archival accessibility has enabled researchers to unearth a rich tradition of writing by gentry women long before the early twentieth century—comprising poetic genres above all, but also drama, *tanci* (弹词), religious scriptures, essays, criticism, and fiction—that turns on its head the entrenched assumption that educated women did not participate in literary culture until modern times. In the late imperial era, anthologies of their work, compiled in some cases by female editors, reveal not only that female poets enjoyed public recognition but that a concept of women's writing as a distinct aesthetic category had begun to gain cultural salience (Widmer and Chang 1997; Fong 2008).

Meanwhile, scholars focused on the characteristics of women's literary modernity have come to recognize that the flurry of creative writing in the 1920s and 1930s has roots in the momentous cultural and political developments of the late Qing reform era. Signs of a reconfigured relationship between women and literature can be traced to new print media of the late 1890s, if not even earlier (Dooling 2005; Qian 2008). As the turbulent nineteenth century drew to a close and the Qing dynasty teetered on the brink of collapse, elite female activists like Qiu Jin 秋瑾 (1875–1907), Chen Xiefen 陈撷芬 (1883–1923), Luo Yanbin 罗燕斌 (1869–?), and He-Yin Zhen 何银珍 (1884–1920?) began launching magazines to serve as public forums to engage such issues as women's subordinate status, China's weakness vis-à-vis foreign powers, and the urgent need to find solutions to both. Because of the nationalist inflection of the contents of many early women's magazines (女报), until relatively recently they were examined primarily through the lens of late Qing politics (Beahan 1975). But from the standpoint of women's literary history, the experiments with genre, rhetorical style, and radical ideological content in these and other late Qing publications represent important antecedents to the literary innovations of May Fourth women writers. *Stones of the Jingwei Bird* (精卫石, 1907), for example, a revolutionary *tanci* Qiu Jin intended for publication in her magazine *Chinese Women's Paper* (中国女报), combines classical storytelling techniques and newly imported political terminology to tell a story of five young ladies who escape the secluded confines of their Confucian families. Wang Miaoru's 王妙如 *Flowers of the Women's Prison* (女狱花, 1904), a fantasy novel composed in deliberately simple vernacular prose addressed to a female audience, presents female education as the key to an egalitarian Chinese future. If late Qing authors tended to display a more didactic bent than those who followed, they clearly shared an understanding of print culture as a means not just for aesthetic self-expression but of social change.

By the 1920s and 1930s, women had begun to flourish in the literary marketplace as both producers and consumers of the new vernacular writing advocated by liberal reformers such as Hu Shi 胡适 and as symbolic figures animating the myriad print debates about Chinese modernity. The much-vaunted literary revolution, fueled by desires to supplant a supposedly decrepit traditional order with a brand-new textual practice, designated femininity as an integral part of the "new knowledge." Concubinage, prostitution, female morality, foot binding, domesticity, and myriad other topics identified as "women's problems" (妇女问题) were fervently discussed in the press, and women themselves increasingly asserted their own authority in these matters. Social reforms, including initiatives dating back to the mid-nineteenth century to expand female literacy, also helped pave the way for the proliferation of women's literary expression in the May Fourth and post–May Fourth eras. Advances in education, for instance, spawned a much larger pool of educated young women capable of reading and writing modern vernacular texts and, to the extent that newly founded schools provided an alternative to the sheltered domesticity of orthodox Confucian women, bred an entire generation of self-styled "new women" (新女性). Through modern academic institutions, which soon encompassed coed universities, a growing number of urban middle- and upper-class women came to interact socially and politically with a broader range of people, and they were exposed to the new magazines and foreign literature that espoused the key ideas and ideologies of the day. Hence, when young women began venturing into the burgeoning literary scenes of Beijing and Shanghai as creative writers—or journalists, translators, critics, editors, and publishers—they came well equipped to collaborate in the making of China's "new culture" (新文化), bringing to the enterprise a profoundly altered sense of feminine roles and an unprecedented confidence that included writing as a legitimate modern vocation.

Among the most salient themes these women writers tackled was the nature of the "new" womanhood itself. Bing Xin 冰心 and Lu Yin 庐隐, the first to have work featured in the prestigious May Fourth literary journal *Short Story Magazine* (小说月报), dramatized the quest of educated, semi-Westernized heroines for independence and meaningful lives. Social obstacles, including Confucian mothers (Feng Yuanjun's 冯沅君 "Separation" [隔绝, 1923]), financial constraints (Chen Xuezhao's 陈学昭 *Dream of Southern Winds* [南风的梦, 1929]), deceitful lovers (Bai Wei's 白薇 play *Lin Li* [琳丽, 1926]), and unwanted pregnancy (Chen Ying's 沉樱 "Woman" [女性, 1929]), loom large in the realist narratives female authors favored at this time, but psychological factors were increasingly explored as impediments to the new women's happiness. Lu Yin's novel *The Heart of Women* (女人的心, 1934) features a depressed young heroine stuck in an emotionally barren arranged marriage and wracked by guilt when she falls in love with a classmate. In "Miss Sophie's Diary" (莎菲女士的日记, 1928), the short story that brought Ding Ling 丁玲 overnight fame, the protagonist's ambivalence over what (or whom) she desires plunges her to the depths of loneliness, despair, and self-loathing. And Shi Pingmei 石评梅, in a story that challenged the increasingly prevalent dichotomy between the traditional and the modern woman, probes with great empathy the internal moral struggle of a duty-bound wife who admires her self-sufficient sister-in-law yet remains psychologically trapped by her own internalized sense of filial obligation ("Lin Nan's Diary" [林楠的日记, 1928]).

Central to the emergent and highly textualized conceptions of the modern female self was the notion of literary authority itself. The 1920s and 1930s witnessed a concerted effort to weld more positive links between women and literature and to overcome cultural paradigms of the literary as a fundamentally masculine domain (Larson 1998). In countless works of fiction and autobiography, the literary act figures prominently in the new woman's resistance to inherited gender roles by emphasizing connections between writing and self-definition, authorship, and autonomy. Feng Yuanjun's "Separation," for instance, following the popular epistolary structure, comprises a letter by a young woman whose parents have locked her up lest she defy her impending betrothal. In addition to containing a spirited defense of her disobedience, the letter represents the key to her escape, for it is to be delivered to the lover who will supposedly rescue her. Conceptions of modern women's writing were further consolidated by publishers' marketing devices that highlighted the author's gender, as well as by women's histories and literary histories that delimited female literature (女性文学; 妇女文学) in terms of gender difference. Paradoxically, though, the May Fourth discourse on women's writing was also partially responsible for painting a bleak portrait of women's literary past; for in the process of applauding the creative freedoms women were thought to enjoy in the present, critics and theorists often dwelled on the restrictions women writers faced in earlier times, rather than their creative accomplishments. Contrasting the "authentic" voice of the liberated new woman was the increasingly common stereotype of the repressed poetess of the past who survived hostile cultural conditions by confining herself to private poetic forms or by upholding orthodox Confucian views. Yi Zhen 毅真, a contributor to *On Contemporary Women Writers* (当代中国女作家论, 1933), for instance, begins with a quotation from the famous Song poetess Zhu Shuzhen 朱淑真 on the incompatibility between women and writing to illustrate the extent to which traditional patriarchal values were internalized by women themselves:

When a woman dabbles in literature, that is truly evil
How can she "intone the moon" or "chant into the wind"?
Wearing out the ink stone is not our business
Let us rather be skilled at needlework and embroidery.

Given such views and women's limited access to literary training, it is not altogether surprising, according to Yi Zhen, that so few women "writers" emerged in the course of China's long literary tradition. (Yi Zhen and the many others who echoed his view fail to acknowledge the sharp irony that underlies Zhu's poem, which flouts the very message it ostensibly delivers.) The popular notion that modern literary culture gave birth to women's writing, in other words, is a myth that originated in the specific context of May Fourth debates on gender reform.

Just as research on late imperial literary history is helping to better contextualize May Fourth discourses on women's writing, a broader engagement with authors and texts excluded by the modern canon has also begun to challenge prevailing views of the period and to uncover forgotten dynamics. Names such as Bai Wei (1894–1987), Lu Yin (1898–1934), Shi Pingmei (1902–1928), Lu Jingqing 陆晶清 (1907–1993), Su Xuelin 苏雪林 (1897–1999), Luo Shu 罗淑 (1903–1938), Chen Xuezhao (1906–1991), and Chen Ying (1907–1986)—popular and in many cases prolific authors who had virtually vanished from the historical record—are again surfacing in discussions of women's writing (Larson 1998; L. Wang 2004; Dooling 2005; Yan 2006; J. Wang 2008). Such recoveries are valuable not merely because they revise the picture of a meager literary output by women writers of this era, but because they offer the chance to interrogate the assumptions underlying the critical paradigms that led to their marginalization in the first place. They reveal, for example, that fiction—the form most typically hailed as the preeminent modern form—was but one of multiple genres with which women writers experimented. Chen Xuezhao, who paid for graduate studies in France from her writing, published numerous essay collections, many of which went into multiple printings. Bai Wei and Lu Yin collaborated with male partners to produce collections of love letters, a new genre that tapped into the wide public fascination with new-style romance. And Xie Bingying 谢冰莹, Xiao Hong 萧红, and Bai Wei, to name just a few, all wrote full-length autobiographies that were well received by contemporary readers. In addition to these forms, drama, poetry, reportage, travel writing, children's fiction, and translation were all part of the literary practices of "modern" women writers.

If formal diversity attests to a high degree of creative experimentation, more important is the cultural import of this diversity, especially in relation to the recurring subject around which most of it swirled—namely, the female self. The aforementioned developments undoubtedly enabled women to speak with unprecedented authority about their experiences. Yet women's literature competed with other emergent cultural discourses as a site where gendered knowledge and identities were produced (Barlow 1994; Larson 1998). Visual media, most notably cinema and advertising, textbooks, and foreign publications, also provided enormously important channels through which alternative representations and theories of femininity were introduced. Intellectuals such as Zhou

Zuoren 周作人 hailed the new women writers as the emancipated voice of the hitherto repressed and silenced "female self," but in fact they were more complex than this formulation implies: they were beings whose identities were in the process of being reconfigured by China's new urban culture at the same time as they themselves actively rewrote gender as a category (Dooling and Torgeson 1998: 1–38).

The horizon of gender representations expanded dramatically during the early twentieth century as social, political, and cultural roles beyond those sanctioned by orthodox Confucianism became possible in both the real and ideal worlds. The newness of May Fourth discourse, however, had limits. In spite of their progressive stance on the "woman problem," the literary output of many male intellectuals evinced startling continuities with traditional gender assumptions (M. Yue 1993: 54). Fictional accounts of female suffering that appeared to contest repressive social practices often relied on rhetorical strategies that supported, rather than subverted, masculine authority. Throughout the 1920s and 1930s, moreover, conspicuous male advocacy of women's liberation and the formation of male mentor–female protégé relationships (between, for instance, Lin Yutang 林语堂 and Xie Bingying, Zheng Zhenduo 郑振铎 and Lu Yin, and Lu Xun and Xiao Hong) suggest a deeply paternalistic logic underlying the new gender order. Yet women were never merely empty signifiers of male debate. In the essays and fiction they published, literary women of the early twentieth century reveal a high degree of self-consciousness about their authority, or lack thereof, in inscribing women and the meanings of feminine experiences. In a series of articles in *The New Woman* (新女性), Chen Xuezhao accused China's "new" men of hypocritically spouting feminist rhetoric. In addition, though women undoubtedly benefited from ties to prominent men, women intellectuals also increasingly took on mentor roles for women themselves. For example, as joint editors of a widely read newspaper supplement in the 1920s, Shi Pingmei and Lu Jingqing, both students at the newly founded Beijing Women's Normal, recruited female friends and readers to contribute. And in the early 1930s, one of the most active presses to promote writing by and about women was the Women's Bookstore (女子书店) in Shanghai, whose early members included Huang Xinmian 黄心勉, Chen Baibing 陈白冰, and Zhao Qingge 赵清阁 (Zhao 1999).

The legacy of May Fourth women's writing has yet to be appreciated fully. In a view first promoted by leftist critics and perpetuated by mainstream literary historians, the May Fourth generation of women writers ultimately failed to live up to their full historic potential. Specifically, they became so narrowly fixated on the realm of personal experience that they missed the boat when literature veered toward the left and assumed a revolutionary course in the late 1920s and 1930s. Scholars of women's literary history, citing writers such as Ge Qin 葛琴 (b. 1907), who wrote about laborers and bosses in the Jiangsu pottery kilns, and Luo Shu, whose stories provided vivid sketches of the Sichuan salt works, have disputed this finding, yet they also regard May Fourth as the thwarted beginning of modern women's literature; for no sooner had women begun to use literature to explore issues of female sexuality, subjectivity, and feminism than the national emergency dictated that they suppress questions of gender difference. In this view, not until the post-Mao era has China witnessed a second "blossoming" of women's literature (Yue Shuo 1989). Insofar as both accounts rest on predetermined assumptions about what constitutes women's writing, important questions remain unanswered: What does the abiding interest in the domestic and personal among women writers of that generation suggest about their relationship to the national sphere? How did new definitions of revolutionary literary practice render invisible the work of women writers at a specific moment in history? How much can the archive be reimagined to account for such elisions?

Bibliography

Barlow, Tani, ed. *Gender Politics in Modern China: Writing and Feminism*. Durham, NC: Duke University Press, 1993.

——. "Theorizing Woman: *Funü, Guojia, Jiating*." In Angela Zito and Tani Barlow, eds., *Body, Subject and Power in China*, 253–289. Chicago: University of Chicago Press, 1994.

Beahan, Charlotte. "Feminism and Nationalism in the Chinese Women's Press, 1902–1911." *Modern China* 1, 4 (October 1975): 379–416.

Bing, Xin. *The Photograph*. Beijing: Panda Books, 1992.

Chen Jingzhi 陈敬之. *Xiandai wenxue zaoqi de nüzuojia* 现代文学早期的女作家 (Early modern women writers). Taipei: Chengwen, 1980.

Chow, Rey. *Woman and Chinese Modernity: The Politics of Reading Between West and East*. Minneapolis: University of Minnesota Press, 1991.

Ding, Ling. *I Myself Am a Woman: Selected Writings of Ding Ling*. Ed. Tani Barlow and Gary Bjorge. Boston: Beacon Press, 1989.

Dooling, Amy. *Women's Literary Feminism in Twentieth Century China*. New York: Palgrave MacMillan, 2005.

——, ed. *Writing Women in Modern China: The Revolutionary Years, 1936–1976*. New York: Columbia University Press, 2005.

Dooling, Amy, and Kris Torgeson, eds. *Writing Women in Modern China: An Anthology of Women's Literature from the Early Twentieth Century*. New York: Columbia University Press, 1998.

Feng, Jin. *The New Woman in Early Twentieth-Century Chinese Fiction*. Lafayette, IN: Purdue University Press, 2004.

Ferry, Megan. "Chinese Women Writers of the 1930s and Their Critical Reception." Phd diss., Washington University, 1998.

——. "Women's Literary History: Inventing Tradition in Modern China." *Modern Language Quarterly* 66, 3 (September 2005): 299–328.

Fong, Grace. *Herself and Author: Gender, Agency, and Writing in Late Imperial China*. Honolulu: University of Hawai'i Press, 2008.

Fong, Grace, et al. *Beyond Tradition and Modernity: Gender, Genre, and Tradition: Cosmopolitanism in Late Qing China*. Leiden: Brill, 2004.
Larson, Wendy. "The End of Funü Wenxue: Women's Literature from 1925 to 1935." In Tani Barlow, ed., *Gender Politics in Modern China: Writing and Feminism*, 58–73. Durham, NC: Duke University Press, 1993.
——. "Female Subjectivity and Gender Relations: The Early Stories of Lu Yin and Bing Xin." In Liu Kang and Xiaobing Tang, eds., *Politics, Ideology and Literary Discourse in Modern China*, 124–143. Durham, NC: Duke University Press, 1993.
——. *Women and Writing in Modern China*. Stanford, CA: Stanford University Press, 1998.
Liu, Lydia, Rebecca Karl, and Dorothy Ko, eds. *The Birth of Chinese Feminism: Essential Texts in Transnational Theory*. New York: Columbia University Press, 2013.
Lu, Tonglin, ed. *Gender and Sexuality in Twentieth-Century Chinese Literature and Society*. Albany: State University of New York Press, 1993.
Ma, Yuxin. *Women Journalists and Feminism in China, 1838–1937*. Amherst, NY: Cambria Press, 2010.
Meng Yue 孟悦 and Dai Jinhua 戴锦华. *Fuchu lishi dibiao* 浮出历史地表 (Emerging on the horizons of history). Zhengzhou: Henan renmin, 1989.
Ng, Janet, and Janice Wickeri, eds. *May Fourth Women Writers: Memoirs*. Hong Kong: Renditions Press, 1997.
Qian, Nanxiu, et al. *Different Worlds of Discourse: Transformations of Gender and Genre in Late Qing and Early Republican China*. Leiden: Brill, 2008.
Qiao Yigang 乔以钢. *Zhongguo nüxing de wenxue shijie* 中国女性的文学世界 (The literary world of Chinese women). Wuhan: Hubei jiaoyu, 1993.
Wang Jialun 王家伦. *Zhongguo xiandai nüzuojia lungao* 中国现代女作家论稿 (A discussion of modern Chinese women writers). Beijing: Zhongguo funü, 1992.
Wang, Jing M. *When "I" Was Born: Women's Autobiography in Modern China*. Madison: University of Wisconsin Press, 2008.
Wang, Lingzhen. *Personal Matters: Women's Autobiographical Practice in Twentieth Century China*. Stanford, CA: Stanford University Press, 2004.
Widmer, Ellen, and Kang I-sun Chang. *Writing Women in Late Imperial China*. Stanford, CA: Stanford University Press, 1997.
Xiao, Hong. *Selected Short Stories of Xiao Hong*. Trans. Howard Goldblatt. Beijing: Chinese Literature Press, 1982.
Xie, Bingying. *Autobiography of a Chinese Girl*. Trans. Tsui Chi. London: Pandora Press, 1986.
Yan, Haiping. *Chinese Women Writers and the Feminist Imagination, 1905–1948*. Routledge, 2006.
Yue, Mingbao. "Gendering the Origins of Modern Chinese Fiction." In Tonglin Lu, ed., *Gender and Sexuality in Twentieth-Century Chinese Literature and Society*, 47–66. Albany: State University of New York Press, 1993.
Yue Shuo 乐铄. *Chidao de chaoliu: Xin shiqi funü chuangzuo yanjiu* 迟到的潮流：新时期妇女创作研究 (Belated trend: Research on women's writing in the new era). Zhengzhou: Henan renmin, 1989.
Zhao Qingge 赵清阁. *Changxiang yi* 长相忆 (Forever recalling each other). Shanghai: Xuelin, 1999.

15

THE MADMAN THAT WAS AH Q: TRADITION AND MODERNITY IN LU XUN'S FICTION

ANN HUSS

A comparison of Lu Xun's 鲁迅 "Diary of a Madman" (狂人日记, 1918) and "The True Story of Ah Q" (阿Q 正传, 1921)—both published in Lu Xun's first collection of short fiction, *Call to Arms* (呐喊, 1923)—yields a compelling portrait of the modern Chinese intellectual's problematic of self. Ah Q is the May Fourth notion of the trapped traditional self that does not act but reacts to the calamities and consequences of the outside world without memory or vision. A symbol of China's diseased national character and tradition, he suffers from a malady that leaves him hypersensitive to the outer world and empowers society and tradition to interfere with and mold his actions. Selfless, he exists only in orientation to the other. The Madman, on the other hand, is the enlightened savior, the model of the modern Western independent self. He is the archetypal romantic cure for that debilitating disease called tradition. In Lu Xun's paradoxical moral vision, however, there is no precise dichotomy between tradition and modernity. The conclusions to "True Story" and "Diary" illustrate this ambiguity: Ah Q emerges a victim and the Madman realizes that he too may be a cannibal (Denton 1998: 58–59).

Although "Diary" and "True Story" may best illustrate the paradox of tradition versus modernity, Lu Xun's other fictional works, "Kong Yiji" (孔乙己, 1919), "Medicine" (药, 1919), "In the Wine Shop" (在酒楼上, 1924), and the stories in *Old Tales Retold* (故事新编, 1936), also engage with the problematic self and renegotiate the past in order to contextualize and assess the dilemmas of the modern world.

Lu Xun (Zhou Shuren 周树人, 1881–1936) may be understood against the backdrop of the concept of literary modernity that prevailed in the May Fourth era. May 4, 1919, represents a watershed in modern Chinese literary history. On this day, student representatives in Beijing drew up five resolutions in response to the Versailles Treaty, which had transferred Germany's rights to parts of China's Shandong Province to Japan. The nationalism of the student movement, accompanied by a growing discussion of Social Darwinist ideas and the rise of interest in Communist ideology, were symptomatic of a cultural upheaval that was spreading throughout China. The term "May Fourth movement" refers to both the demonstrations that took place on May 4, 1919, and the complex cultural and political developments that preceded and followed them.

The most striking change brought about by the May Fourth movement was that writers discarded native literary language in favor of a language explicitly based on the grammatical construction, sentence cohesion, narrative forms, and rhetorical invention of Western models. The discourse of Chinese literature since the May Fourth period dwells on the notion of a singular, belated modernity that is at once at odds with the classical Chinese literary tradition and in awe of it. Hailed as the first *modern* fiction in Chinese history, short stories such as Lu Xun's "Diary" represented Chinese tradition, with its linguistic and literary forms, as an iron house, and Chinese history as cannibalistic. "Diary" begins with a preface written in classical Chinese, the written language of the literati, and continues in the vernacular in the diary proper. The ironic juxtaposition of these two languages in the story was revolutionary: the Madman's vernacular diary, with its enlightenment discourse, implicates the classical language of the preface for blinding the Chinese to the violent reality of their cannibalistic tradition (Lee, 1987: 49–68).

First published in *New Youth* (新青年), "Diary" reveals Lu Xun's attitude toward tradition. Suffering from a "persecution complex," the Madman imagines that all those around him, including his family members, are plotting to kill him and consume his body. To authenticate his suspicions, he turns to the pages of a Chinese history book:

> In ancient times, as I recollect, people often ate human beings, but I am rather hazy about it. I tried to look this up, but my history has no chronology, and scrawled all over each page are the words: "Virtue and Morality." Since I could not sleep anyway, I read intently half the night, until I began to see words between the lines, the whole book being filled with the two words—"Eat people."
>
> (Lu Xun 1977: 10)

Although the rhetoric of virtue and morality echoes through the annals of Chinese history, that rhetoric is undermined by a tradition of cannibalism. Officials feast on the flesh of lower officials who cannibalize those beneath them, and so on. Even the Madman, the reader is told in the preface, "recovered some time ago and has gone elsewhere to take up an official post" (Lu Xun 1977: 7); regaining sanity means that the Madman rejoins a cannibalistic society. The Madman may be the curative for the disease of tradition, but he himself cannot break free from its power. Lu Xun is nevertheless not completely hopeless. At the conclusion to the story, the Madman makes the now famous plea: "Perhaps there are children who have not eaten men? Save the children" (1977: 18).

Ah Q, the protagonist of "The True Story," represents the very disease the Madman diagnoses. Living in the final years of the Qing dynasty, Ah Q is poor and homeless. Rather than sympathize with him though, Lu Xun uses Ah Q as a symbol of what is wrong with the Chinese national character (国民性). For example, Ah Q invents "spiritual victories" as a way of rationalizing defeat at the hands of those who bully him; he then turns around to torment those weaker than he is. He wallows in a physically abusive but mentally oblivious world of self-deception, consoling himself after each catastrophe and claiming victory in the face of glaring defeat. "True Story" is, then, a scathing reminder of China's weakened position in world politics and the encroachment of Western modernity. It is also, however, a cunning criticism of how revolution, particularly the Republican revolution, forced tradition into a binary and ultimately unsuccessful relationship with modernity.

At the end of the story, Ah Q's longing to join the revolution leads to his death. After angering the most powerful family in the village, he travels to the city and drifts among a gang of thieves, where he hears rumors of the anti-Manchu revolution. Each time he returns to the village to sell his stolen goods, he boasts about the revolution as if he were a soldier himself. He does this both to amplify his reputation and to intimidate those who have abused him. He naively masquerades as a revolutionary because he is superficially aware that revolution changes things—it produces new opportunities and resolves old grievances. Ironically, however, when the revolutionary forces enter the village, they collude with the local gentry to try Ah Q for his suspected part in a robbery. The hero dies a victim of the revolution, but the "Ah Q spirit" lives on to haunt a feudal society that ignores the potential of Ah Q and those like him. These contradictions between the traditional and the modern illustrate Lu Xun's ambiguous stance; the "traditional" Ah Q embodies more revolutionary potential than his revolutionary accusers epitomize modernity.

Lu Xun's paradoxical moral vision, his constant probing of the tortuous relationship between tradition and modernity, and attempts to understand what to him was the misguided, defective Chinese national character are reflected in other stories. "Kong Yiji" and "Medicine" ridicule traditional society while casting an equally critical eye at revolution. "Kong Yiji" is a poignant yet perfunctory portrayal of a minor literati-turned-thief. Narrated by a man recalling twenty years earlier when as a boy he warmed drinks in a tavern, the story recounts how Kong Yiji, dressed in a tattered scholar's gown, lectures to tavern customers in highbrow language on the differences between stealing and stealing books. Although he failed the civil service examination, Kong Yiji considers himself a scholar, albeit a scholar who steals to support his drinking and his laziness. Kong Yiji (who shares a surname with Confucius, Kongzi 孔子) clings desperately to the image of the Confucian literati class whose demise he represents. As such, the story criticizes feudal society and the intellectual's complicity in it. Yet the story is not without sympathy for Kong; as Kong grows increasingly pitiful, Lu Xun seems to shift his satirical scorn away from Kong and toward the tavern crowd, which shows no compassion for Kong's suffering, and toward the narrator, who remains unmoved by it.

"Medicine" is both a realistic interpretation of traditional life and a symbolic parable on revolution and modernity. A youth named Xia 夏 has been beheaded for participating in the anti-Qing revolution. Meanwhile, a young boy surnamed Hua 华 is dying of consumption. Hua's aged and superstitious father buys a piece of bread soaked in the dead revolutionary's blood from the executioner in the belief that this blood will cure his ailing son. Hua the younger eats the bread but dies nonetheless. The two boys have died very different deaths: Xia as a revolutionary martyr and Hua as a victim of ignorance. Their mothers, however, feel a common pain. One cold, early spring morning, as they visit adjacent graves to mourn their dead sons, the mothers face each other in shared sorrow.

Lu Xun speaks to the complexity of nation, tradition, revolution, and the modern in "Medicine." As indicated by their names, *Huaxia* 华夏 being a poetic synonym for China, the two young men represent the hope and failure of Chinese society. Hua's failure to survive even after he has drunk Xia's blood symbolizes the demise of the feudal order, but it also represents Lu Xun's desolate view of modernization by revolution. Lu Xun allows Xia's grief-stricken mother an enduring protest over her son's unjust execution. Upon visiting his grave, his mother is baffled to find a Western-style wreath of red and white flowers on the burial mound. Although his revolutionary comrades probably placed it there, she interprets the wreath as a sign that her son's soul is not yet at rest. The mother laments, "I know . . . they murdered you. But a day of reckoning will come, Heaven will see to it. Close your eyes in peace. . . . If you are really here, and can hear me, make that crow fly on to your grave as a sign" (Lu Xun 1977: 32–33). A mother's desperate belief in the justice of Heaven becomes a symbolic inquiry into the meaning and future of the revolution. "The crow, his head drawn back, perched among the straight boughs as if it were cast in iron," is completely unresponsive to the mother's cries.

"In the Wine Shop" is based on a visit Lu Xun made to his hometown, Shaoxing, during the winter of 1919–1920. While sipping wine alone in a restaurant, the narrator encounters an old classmate and former colleague at the Shaoxing middle school. No longer an energetic, youthful reformer, Lü Weifu 吕纬甫 has returned home from a distant province to carry out his mother's request to move her younger son's grave, which has been flooded. Although his brother's remains could not be located, Lü "wrapped up in some cotton some of the clay where his body had been, . . . put it in the new coffin, moved it to the grave where father was buried, and buried it beside him" (Lu Xun 1977: 149). Lü Weifu goes on to recount that he has also returned, again at the request of his mother, to give a gift of red and pink artificial velvet flowers to Ah Shun 阿顺, the daughter of a boatman he once knew. The girl has died, so Lü gives the flowers instead to her sister. Upon his return, he will tell his mother "that Ah Shun was delighted with them, and that will be that" (1977: 153). A little deception seems worth the price of his mother's happiness.

Conscious that had he maintained his faith in the new culture he would not have been quite as nostalgically filial, Lü Weifu is unable to hide his shame as he reveals his adventures to the narrator. Lu Xun portrays the old classmate as a failure who had abandoned the revolution and bargained with the enemy, the old society. "When I have muddled through the New Year I shall go back to teaching the Confucian classics as before," concludes Lü. "I could never have guessed that you would be teaching such books," the narrator retorts (1977: 154). Yet, although Lü Weifu appears a failure, his compassion and piety affirm the positive aspects of traditional society, traditional strengths that enchanted a nostalgic Lu Xun in spite of his nonconformist beliefs. "In the Wine Shop" is both a critique of compromise and a fictional affirmation of the author's own ambivalence and hesitation, a microcosm of Lu Xun's paradoxical moral vision.

The collection of eight stories entitled *Old Tales Retold* includes fiction begun during the early 1920s as well as Lu Xun's only fiction written after 1926. Although labeled by critics as "marking the sad degeneration" (C. T. Hsia 1971: 46) of his talent, the project reflects Lu Xun's ongoing revision of the relationship between tradition and modernity. "As for historical stories," Lu Xun (1961: ii–iii) begins in his 1935 preface to the collection, "those based on extensive research with sound evidence for every word are extremely hard to write, even though they are sneered at as 'novels smacking of the schoolroom' (*jiaoshou xiaoshuo*); whereas not much skill is needed to take a subject and write it up freely, adding some coloring of your own." It is by reading the void between professorial fiction (教授小说) and "adding some color" that the reader arrives at an understanding of the complexity and meaning of "old tales retold."

The tales in this collection recount events taken from ancient texts, including *Book of History* (尚书), *Huainanzi* (淮南子), *Classic of Mountains and Seas* (山海经), *Imperially Reviewed Encyclopedia of the Taiping Era* (太平御览), *Mencius* (孟子), *Mozi* (墨子), *Zhuangzi* (庄子), *Arrayed Marvels* (列异传), and *Records of the Search for Spirits* (搜神记), but in a style that is self-consciously anachronistic. They make use of modern language, with words such as *youdai* (优待), meaning "to give preferential treatment to," and Western phrases such as "good morning" and "how do you do." There are also frequent allusions to Lu Xun's contemporaries: a former student, Gao Changhong 高长虹, in

"Flight to the Moon" (奔月, 1926), the Creation Society in "Gathering Vetch" (采薇, 1935), and several well-known scholars and writers in "Curbing the Flood" (理水, 1935).

Tales negotiates its most powerful ironic effects through allusions and references to traditional Chinese texts. But reading, writing, and decoding earlier texts no longer have the same significance they had in Lu Xun's iconoclastic "Diary of a Madman" phase. Why, on the one hand, did Lu Xun attack New Sensationist author Shi Zhecun 施蛰存 for his fascination with the "skeleton" while, on the other hand, returning to the world of classical legends and fables to contextualize contemporary predicaments? As Eileen Cheng (2013, 12) has suggested, his radical reworking of old tales may be read as "textual reenactments of the dilemma of cultural displacement—that is, of being inscribed by yet alienated from tradition, while being out of place in the modern world."

Published first in 1922 under the title "Buzhou shan" (不周山), the first story in the collection, "Mending Heaven" (补天), presents the mythological character of Nüwa 女娲 and her tale of repairing heaven. The details of the original story can be traced to a number of texts: the narrative of how Nüwa created humans from mud can be found in the *Taiping yulan* (ca. A.D. 990); Nüwa repairing heaven with five-colored stones exists in the Han dynasty *Huainanzi*; and the particulars of Gong Gong 共工 cracking his head against the mountain, the fire in an ancient forest on Kunlun Mountain, and the many search parties ordered by a succession of emperors to find the Fairy Mountains are all chronicled in the *Records of the Grand Historian* (史记), Sima Zhen's 司马贞 *Supplement to the Records of the Grand Historian* (补史记), the *Classic of Mountains and Seas*, and Qu Yuan's 屈原 poems (Cheng 2013: 199). What separates Lu Xun's rewriting of the Nüwa myth from those original tales is his complicated portrayal of Nüwa. "I've never been so bored!" Nüwa claims upon waking. She bends down and kneads some mud to create her first humans. Satisfied with her creations and lulled by their laughter, Nüwa falls off to sleep again, only to be awakened by a crash. Zhuan Xu 颛顼, a descendant of the Yellow Emperor, and the giant Gong Gong, in their struggle for power, had cracked heaven and split earth. Nüwa begins mending heaven, expending all her energy and eventually taking her last breath as her mission is concluded. The humans she had created had "covered their bodies in the most curious fashion, and some of them had snow-white beards growing from the lower part of their faces." Another was hung "from head to foot . . . with thick folds of drapery, with a dozen or more supernumerary ribbons at his waist." A creature held forth a black oblong board that stated, "Your lewd nakedness is immoral, an offence against etiquette, a breach of the rules and conduct fit for beasts!" The creatures that she had forged now stood in judgment of her nakedness. Only later, on a bitterly cold day, does a group of soldiers encamp on Nüwa's stomach, announcing themselves to be the "true descendants of the goddess" and altering their standard to read "The Entrails of Nüwa" (Lu Xun 1961: 1–13).

This radical rewriting of the traditional story of creation obscures a critique of the relationship between the old vanguard and later generations, between Lu Xun and younger revolutionaries. Such commentary pervades the collection, at times more obviously than at others. When in "Gathering Vetch," for example, Lu Xun (1961: 78) recounts the travels of Boyi 伯夷 and Shuqi 叔齐, a story that can be traced to the *Book of History*, *Records of the Grand Historian*, and so on, he cannot resist criticizing the Creation Society aesthetic of "art for art's sake" in the words of Lord Xiaoping: "They went to the Old People's Home . . . but they wouldn't steer clear of politics. They came to Shouyang Mountain . . . but they would insist on writing poems. They wrote poems, all right! But they would express resentment, instead of knowing their place and producing 'art for art's sake.'"

In "Curbing the Flood," Lu Xun appropriates the classics in a biting criticism of Pan Guangdan 潘光旦 (a well-known eugenicist), Gu Jiegang 顾颉刚 (a scholar and expert on folk songs), Lin Yutang 林语堂 (an advocate of a return to the classics and their inherent "spiritual values"), Chen Xiying 陈西滢, the poet Xu Zhimo 徐志摩, and Du Heng 杜衡 (coeditor of the Shanghai journal *Les Contemporains*). Though the story appears to be a superficial reworking of the myth of Yu, the curber of the floods and founder of the Xia dynasty, Lu Xun turns attention away from the "flood," toward the scholars assembled on Mount Culture, a reference to a group of scholars who, in 1932, had petitioned the Guomindang to declare Beijing a "city of culture" and to move all military institutions out of the capital. Lu Xun (1993: 5:12–13) first discussed the folly of such a plan, as well as what he believed to be the Guomindang's betrayal of the nation, in a 1933 essay entitled "Notes on False Freedom." "Curbing the Flood" jabs at scholars' responses to the catastrophes of the time: returning from a trip to the flooded areas, a group of officials settles in for dinner and drink, coming close to blows over a few samples of calligraphy. First place is finally granted to the inscription "The state is prosperous, the people at peace." "For not only was the calligraphy so ancient as to be almost undecipherable, with a rude antique flavor about it, but the sentiments were thoroughly appropriate, worthy to be recorded by imperial historians" (Lu Xun 1961: 43), even as the country drowns in the floodwaters.

The philosopher Mozi, in "Opposing Aggression" (非攻, 1934), successfully saves the state of Song from Chu, only to be stopped and interrogated by "National Salvation Collectors" (1961: 135–136). Laozi 老子, in "Leaving the Pass" (出关, 1935), laments the departure of Confucius: "He will never come back nor ever call me master again. He will refer to me as 'that old fellow,' and play tricks behind my back" (1961: 110). Laozi's fate is no better at the pass when asked to lecture to the guards. When a combination of his accent and his toothless diction make his words difficult to understand, he spends a day and a half recording his ideas for the pass guards. Laozi leaves in a cloud of yellow dust, abandoning the warden, copyist, and accountant to a discussion of what to do with the manuscript. What is the fate of Laozi's day and a half of writing? "Warden Xi dusted his desk with his sleeve, then picked up the two strings of tablets and put them on the shelves piled high with salt, sesame, cloth, beans, unleavened bread and other confiscated goods." The musings of the philosopher, whether Laozi or Lu Xun, are no longer worthy of recording for posterity but are instead relegated to the dusty corners of the storeroom of time.

The same conflict that Lu Xun denigrated in the likes of Shi Zhecun and Lin Yutang—their fascination with the "skeleton"—haunts Lu Xun in his retelling of old tales. As the author mirrors himself in Mozi and Laozi, he also renounces their philosophies. This attachment to and profound alienation from the past exposes a complexity of experience and understanding that surpasses that evidenced in "Diary of a Madman." Lu Xun's historical rewrites "expose the gaps inherent in the writing of history"; his return to the world of myths and legend may have been a "private obeisance to traditional practices that he himself was helping to bury" (Cheng 2013: 186–190).

After years of adulation during the Mao era, the publication of his sixteen-volume complete works, and numerous scholarly manuscripts dedicated to analyzing his life, philosophy, and writing, Lu Xun remains for many not only the father of modern Chinese literature but also the greatest modern Chinese writer. When Mao Zedong claimed in *The New Democracy* (1940) that "the direction of Lu Xun is the direction of the new Chinese culture," he was making a powerful prediction. Although the Madman seemed to be the modern curative for a diseased traditional Ah Q, Lu Xun in his constant probing of old and new in stories such as "Kong Yiji," "Medicine," and "In the Wine Shop" and in *Old Tales Retold* reminds readers that modernity is never the true antithesis of tradition and that the Madman was also an Ah Q.

Bibliography

Anderson, Marston. "Lu Xun's Facetious Muse: The Creative Imperative in Modern Chinese Fiction." In David Wang and Ellen Widmer, eds., *From May Fourth to June Fourth: Fiction and Film in Twentieth-Century China*, 249–268. Cambridge, MA: Harvard University Press, 1993.

Cheng, Eileen J. *Literary Remains: Death, Trauma, and Lu Xun's Refusal to Mourn*. Honolulu: University of Hawai'i Press, 2013.

Chou, Eva Shan. *Memory, Violence, Queues: Lu Xun Interprets China*. Ann Arbor, MI: Association for Asian Studies, 2012.

Davies, Gloria. *Lu Xun's Revolution: Writing in a Time of Violence*. Cambridge, MA: Harvard University Press, 2013.

Denton, Kirk A. *The Problematic of Self in Modern Chinese Literature: Hu Feng and Lu Ling*. Stanford, CA: Stanford University Press, 1998.

Hsia, C. T. *A History of Modern Chinese Fiction*. New Haven, CT: Yale University Press, 1971.

Hsia, Tsi-An. *The Gate of Darkness: Studies on the Leftist Literary Movement in China*. Seattle: University of Washington Press, 1968.

Lee, Leo Ou-fan. *Lu Xun and His Legacy*. Berkeley: University of California Press, 1985.

——. *Voices from the Iron House: A Study of Lu Xun*. Bloomington: Indiana University Press, 1987.

Lin, Yü-sheng. *The Crisis of Chinese Consciousness: Radical Antitraditionalism in the May Fourth Era*. Madison: University of Wisconsin Press, 1979.

Lu, Xun. *Diary of a Madman and Other Stories*. Trans. William Lyell. Honolulu: University of Hawai'i Press, 1990.

——. *Lu Xun quanji* 鲁迅全集 (Collected works of Lu Xun). 16 vols. Beijing: Remin wenxue, 1993.

——. *Old Tales Retold*. Beijing: Foreign Languages Press, 1961 [1935].

——. *The Real Story of Ah-Q and Other Tales of China: The Complete Fiction of Lu Xun*. Trans. Julia Lovell. London: Penguin, 2009.

——. *Selected Stories*. Trans. Yang Hsien-yi and Gladys Yang. New York: Norton, 1977.

Lyell, William A. *Lu Hsün's Vision of Reality*. Berkeley: University of California Press, 1976.

Pollard, David. *The True Story of Lu Xun*. Hong Kong: Chinese University Press, 2002.

Wang Xiaoming 王晓明. *Wufa zhimian de rensheng: Lu Xun zhuan* 无法直面的人生: 鲁迅传 (A life that cannot be faced directly: A biography of Lu Xun). Taipei: Yeqiang, 1992.

16

ROMANTIC SENTIMENT AND THE PROBLEM OF THE SUBJECT: YU DAFU

KIRK A. DENTON

One of the principal characteristics of late nineteenth- and early twentieth-century literature in China is its emotionality, its emphasis on subjective expression. What makes this modern phenomenon different from the premodern tradition of "poetry expresses intention" (诗言志) or "poetry expresses feelings" (诗缘情) is primarily the type of emotions expressed as well as the lack of restraint in their expression. How do we account for this dramatic and obsessive interest in exposing the self? How do we deal with the sentimental, melodramatic, and sometimes maudlin character of these works? What cultural and historical motivations drive this obsessive desire to emote and express the self? These questions can be looked at in terms of a larger problem of subjectivity in Chinese modernity, but first some background.

In the crisis atmosphere of the late Qing and early Republican periods, intellectuals searched for causes to China's national impotence. Many explained this weakness in cultural terms: traditional culture had emasculated the Chinese people by rigorously enforcing submission to authority and rigidly codifying ethical behavior. The heart of this transitional generation's construction of the past was Confucianism and its concept of *li* (礼), or ritualized ethical behavior, which intellectuals from Tan Sitong 谭嗣同 to Liang Qichao 梁启超 to Chen Duxiu 陈独秀 fashioned into the central problem of Chinese culture. Of course, premodern conceptions of self were in reality never so simplistic as these and other reformers and iconoclasts made out. The heterogeneity of the past—its many contending intellectual and philosophical schools, its regional variations, and its class disparities—was reduced to a monolithic and all-powerful Confucianism—the better to attack it by. This ethical system created a nation of passive individuals, so the discourse went, subordinated to familial and state authority, whose very identities were constructed through hierarchical social relations, and who thus lacked the dynamic, willful, aggressive, and autonomous personalities needed to build a strong nation and repel the advance of imperialism. Whereas tradition was portrayed in feminine terms, modernity and the new self were seen as masculine. One of the central crises intellectuals in the early twentieth century faced, then, was how to recreate the self so that it could participate in national renovation and the global march to modernity. From the beginning of Chinese modernity, self and nation were inextricably tied together (Liu 1995: 87–89), and literature was one important means of exploring new modes of selfhood and its relation to imagined national and global communities (H. Lee 2007).

For many radical thinkers of the transitional generation, the Chinese tradition offered no models for this new masculine selfhood, so they sought models from outside. Precedents for this modern anti-Confucianism can be found in late Ming individualism and its cult of *qing* (情; love, emotion, sentiment), suggesting perhaps that traumatic historical moments give rise to reconceptualizations of the self, but the radical quality of the late Qing and early Republican writers' attack on Confucian hierarchy and authoritarianism was unprecedented. As Leo Lee (1973: 46) has shown, Lin Shu 林纾 and Su Manshu 苏曼殊 were at the forefront of this new interest in sentiment, although to Lin "sentiment . . . is more than the inner reflection of propriety (礼) as prescribed in the *Analects*; sentiment is morality." Rather than draw from late Ming antecedents, however, Lin Shu looked to graft the models of the colonizing West onto traditional Chinese ethics, forging Dickens's sentimentality, for example, onto traditional Confucian conceptions of filial piety. Su Manshu was an early romantic poet and with Chen Duxiu China's first translator of Byron, who became in the May Fourth movement an emblem of a dynamic and revolutionary—and masculine—romantic individualism China was seen to lack.

Whereas late Qing thinkers such as Lin Shu were still attached to the Confucian tradition, by the May Fourth period that tradition had lost resonance for many intellectuals. They turned instead to a wide variety of Western thought and literature as a way of resolving the problems of a rapidly changing society practically and psychologically. Science and democracy were the buzzwords of this generation, but these were merely two of many Western terms to enter the cultural vocabulary of May Fourth China. "Self" (我), another key term, was refashioned along the lines of Western individualism (Liu 1995: 77–99). Central to this new self was the concept of "self-consciousness" (自觉), sometimes translated as "autonomy" (Schwarcz 1986: 26). Self-consciousness meant developing a sense of intellectual and political autonomy from the power and authority of the state, but it also meant recovering the fullness of one's humanity repressed by tradition.

By exposing new areas of the heart and mind, writers of fiction such as Yu Dafu 郁达夫, Guo Moruo 郭沫若, Mao Dun 茅盾, and Ba Jin 巴金 broadened conceptions of self, reimagined the self's relation to the cultural whole (now called "nation"), and rewrote the national character. Love and eros, for example, were discussed and expressed in May Fourth literary works as a reaction, at least in part, to the relative denial of these things in the elite literary tradition (H. Lee 2007). Excavating dark recesses of the mind set modern writers apart from their traditional counterparts, who likely had no conception of the unconscious; the latter were more interested in the social and moral part of the mind, linked to other minds through the divine.

Yet Chinese writers seeking to rewrite the self appropriated this Western model of an autonomous self with difficulty. At the heart of the experience of modernity is a profound anxiety, made vividly apparent in the writing of Yu Dafu, arguably the representative voice in the male May Fourth strain of sentimental fiction. Yu was a founding member of the Creation Society—a literary group formed in Japan in 1921 with Cheng Fangwu 成仿吾, Guo Moruo, Zhang Ziping 张资平, and Tian Han 田汉—and shared with these writers a romantic-aesthetic view of literature that emphasized self-expression and promoted notions of the writer as genius. Yu Dafu's fiction sought to lay bare the private, to expose what had been traditionally repressed: sexual desire, alienation, despair, guilt, anxiety, insecurity, and paranoia. "My heart is thus inclined," Yu wrote in 1923, "to discharge myself once and for all of the sin of insincerity, I can only reveal my inner self in all its nakedness" (Yu Dafu 1982: 7:155–157). His fiction consistently sought to make a public display of the private and psychological, what Leo Lee (1985) has called the "externalization of the self," and as such it exposes the very deepest levels of Chinese intellectuals' experience of modernity. Here is how Yu described the origin of his early stories:

> In youth, one always passes through a romantic lyrical period, when one is still a mute bird but wants nonetheless to open one's throat and sing out, especially people who are full of emotion. This lyrical period was spent in that sexually dissolute and militarily oppressive island nation [Japan]. I saw my country sinking, while I myself suffered the humiliations of a foreigner. Everything Yufu felt, thought, experienced, was essentially nothing but despair and suffering. Like a wife who had lost her husband, powerless, with no courage at all, bemoaning my fate, I let out a tragic cry. This was "Sinking," which stirred up so much criticism.
> (*Yu Dafu yanjiu ziliao* 1933: 1:217)

All critics agree that one of the most prominent characteristics of Yu Dafu's writing is its autobiographical tenor. Yu (1982: 7:180) is famous in China for his invocation that "literature is nothing but the autobiography of the author." His fiction tends to draw from the events of his own life and is peopled with characters resembling those he has known: his domineering mother; his arranged wife, Sun Quan 孙荃, whom he essentially abandoned but about whom he often wrote with a strong sense of guilt; members of the Creation Society; and Wang Yingxia 王映霞, his long-time lover and a famous Chinese beauty. Indeed, so autobiographical is his fiction that scholars often disagree in categorizing particular works fiction or autobiographical prose. Yu also wrote a great deal of explicitly autobiographical writing and published his letters and diaries. In its autobiographical nature, Yu's fiction is typical of his generation. Writers of all literary persuasions in the May Fourth period, those who saw themselves as romantics and those who saw themselves as realists, drew quite directly from their own lives for fictional material; indeed, the appeal and power of their works to contemporary readers derived precisely from that fact. Even the supreme ironist Lu Xun based much fictional material on his own experiences.

Although some have seen in Yu's stories parallels with traditional "scholar-beauty" (才子佳人) fiction, the psychological probing of the self makes them modern. They exhibit, moreover, a decadent quality in their obsession with sexual fetishes, masochism, masturbation, voyeurism, homosexuality, excessive drinking, and guilt. The minds revealed in his fiction are modern, wracked by contradictions and paradoxes, unable to recapture a sense of unity with the landscape of their pasts. Yu's characters can be read as emblems of modernity's tensions between desires for an autonomous self and traditional desires for stability defined within a shared cultural meaning system. What makes this experience of modernity so difficult and traumatic is that neither desire is, in and of itself, satisfying; the modern intellectual is psychologically homeless (Denton 1992).

Many of Yu Dafu's stories center on the return of male intellectuals to their homes, most often in small-town Jiangnan. These stories tell us much about the problem of leaving home, a common trope in modern Chinese literature that symbolizes a temporal separation from tradition and that began with Hu Shi's 胡适 translation of Ibsen's *A Doll's House*. Leaving home was the paradigmatic act of modernity for May Fourth writers and their fictional alter egos. Yu Dafu, by contrast, was far more obsessed with returning home. A good example of this is his autobiographical prose work called "Record of Returning Home" (还乡记, 1923). The story relates the narrator's feelings and fantasies as he awakens in the metropolis of Shanghai, takes the train to Hangzhou, where he stays overnight, and finally boards a boat for his hometown up the Qiantang River. As the story opens, he awakens suddenly in a "sensitive psychic state," bothered by lingering feelings from his early morning sleep, and vaguely recalls that he is supposed to go somewhere that day (return home). His room faces the Shanghai racetrack and the clock that looms above it, emblems of modernity in

Republican China (Lee 1999: 31), and the contrast between home as a disturbing memory and the space and time of modernity sets the story's theme as a conflict between tradition and modernity.

Yu's most famous story, "Sinking" (沉沦, 1921), displays many of the characteristics for which he was so notorious. The nameless hero in the third-person story is a student studying in a Japanese university. Wracked by sexual desires, he finds little pleasure and much guilt in daily masturbation and spying voyeuristically on his landlord's daughter as she bathes and on a couple making love in the woods. When an opportunity for real sexual intercourse with a Japanese prostitute presents itself, he gets drunk and passes out. Intertwined with this sexual insecurity is the protagonist's convenient blaming of his country's weakness for his own sexual inadequacies. Perhaps the most blatant example of sublimation in the history of modern Chinese literature, this deep-felt linking of the self to the state of the nation was shared by many young Chinese at the time. What makes this story modern is not its interest in sexuality or even deviant sexuality, for China had a long tradition of erotic literature, but describing that sexuality from a psychological perspective, through a tortured mind. But the story also enacts in spatial terms and through literary allusions the irresolvable modern tension between a radically alienated consciousness attempting to understand itself in social isolation and a nostalgic longing to return to the comfort of a traditional community of like minds in a unified moral cosmos (Denton 1992: 177).

Psychic conflict in Yu's characters is also played out in terms of human relations. "Wisteria and Dodder" (茑萝行, 1923), usually classified as a prose work (the story is in the form of a letter addressed to Yu's wife, Sun Quan), expresses the protagonist's misery in his marital relationship. Addressing his wife, the narrator writes, "Woman whom I must love and woman whom I cannot love! I despise the world because I despise myself for all my savagery to you" (Yu Dafu 1937: 247). Yu Dafu's characters also play out their psychic anxiety through others who are weaker and more powerless, often lower-class characters. The poverty and oppression experienced by these lower-class characters becomes a reflection of the first-person intellectual narrator's identity crisis. Perhaps the most famous examples are "Nights of Spring Fever" (春风沉醉的晚上, 1923) and "Humble Sacrifice" (薄奠, 1924), stories favored, not surprisingly, by leftist literary critics for their sympathetic portrayal of the working class.

Most of Yu Dafu's protagonists are loners who do not fit into society, alienated wanderers constructed through a filter of Western literary images of self borrowed from the likes of Rousseau, Oblomov, Turgenev, Ernest Dowson, and others. There is a marked tendency in Yu Dafu's fictional yet autobiographical writings toward confession, something that some critics have argued was absent in premodern times but that Yu may have discovered through reading works of Rousseau and Japanese naturalism. As Mau-sang Ng (1980) has discussed, Yu's characters are drawn after character types from the Russian literary tradition, in particular the superfluous man, a type seen most prevalently in Turgenev's fiction. Like the Russian model, the superfluous man in Yu's fiction both scorns society and is bothered by his out-of-placeness. So the awkward homelessness displayed by Yu's characters can be seen not only as a product of Chinese intellectuals' particular experience with modernity but also as a universal tendency in global literary modernism.

Some of Yu's characters indulge in a self-pity that makes them disagreeable companions for readers. It is often difficult to determine authorial attitude to these self-pitying characters. At times there seems to be a close identification between author and character; at others, the reader senses an ironic distance between the two, implying authorial criticism of the character's lack of self-awareness. Yu's stories lack the rigorous irony seen in the stories of Lu Xun, who seemed always to question intellectual self-indulgence, but this does not mean that we should dismiss the suffering of the characters in Yu's stories as mere self-pitying. Rather, the mawkish sentimentality and the confessional urge we see in Yu's prose reveal much about the traumatic nature of modernity for Chinese intellectuals, and these qualities had a freshness and authenticity that appealed greatly to young readers of the day.

Bibliography

Denton, Kirk A. "The Distant Shore: The Nationalist Theme in Yu Dafu's 'Sinking.'" *Chinese Literature: Essays, Articles and Reviews* 14 (1992): 107–123.

Doležalova, Anna. *Yu Ta-fu: Specific Traits of His Literary Creation*. Bratislava: Publishing House of the Slovak Academy of Sciences, 1970.

Egan, Michael. "Yu Dafu and the Transition to Modern Chinese Literature." In Merle Goldman, ed., *Modern Chinese Literature in the May Fourth Era*, 309–324. Cambridge, MA: Harvard University Press, 1977.

Feuerwerker, Yi-tsi Mei. "Text, Intertext, and the Representation of the Writing Self in Lu Xun, Yu Dafu, and Wang Meng." In Ellen Widmer and David Wang, eds., *From May Fourth to June Fourth: Fiction and Film in Twentieth-Century China*, 167–193. Cambridge, MA: Harvard University Press, 1993.

Ko, Dorothy. *Teachers of the Inner Chambers: Women and Culture in Seventeenth-Century China*. Stanford, CA: Stanford University Press, 1994.

Lee, Haiyan. *Revolution of the Heart: A Genealogy of Love in China, 1900–1950*. Stanford, CA: Stanford University Press, 2007.

Lee, Leo Ou-fan. *Shanghai Modern: The Flowering of a New Urban Culture in China, 1930–1945*. Cambridge, MA: Harvard University Press, 1999.

——. "The Solitary Traveler: Images of the Self in Modern Chinese Literature." In Robert Hegel and Richard Hessney, eds., *Expressions of Self in Chinese Literature*, 282–307. New York: Columbia University Press, 1985.

——. "Yu Ta-fu." In *The Romantic Generation of Modern Chinese Writers*, 81–123. Cambridge, MA: Harvard University Press, 1973.

Levan, Valerie. "The Meaning of Foreign Text in Yu Dafu's 'Sinking' Collection." *Modern Chinese Literature and Culture* 24, 1 (Spring 2012): 48–87.

Liu, Lydia. *Translingual Practice: Literature, National Culture, and Translated Modernity, China, 1900–1937*. Stanford, CA: Stanford University Press, 1995.

Ng, Mau-sang. *The Russian Hero in Modern Chinese Fiction*. Albany: State University of New York Press, 1980.

Prušek, Jaroslav. "Mao Tun and Yu Ta-fu." In *The Lyrical and the Epic: Studies in Modern Chinese Literature*, 121–177. Bloomington: Indiana University Press, 1980.

Schwarcz, Vera. *The Chinese Enlightenment: Intellectuals and the Legacy of the May Fourth Movement of 1919*. Berkeley: University of California Press, 1986.

Yu, Dafu. "Blood and Tears." In S. R. Munro, trans. and ed., *Genesis of a Revolution: An Anthology of Modern Chinese Short Stories*, 158–175. Singapore: Heinemann Educational Books, 1979.

——. "Class Struggle in Literature." Trans. Haili Kong and Howard Goldblatt. In Kirk A. Denton, ed., *Modern Chinese Literary Thought*, 263–268. Stanford, CA: Stanford University Press, 1996.

——. "Intoxicating Spring Nights." In Harold Isaacs, trans. and ed., *Straw Sandals*, 68–83. Cambridge, MA: MIT Press, 1974.

——. *Nights of Spring Fever and Other Writings*. Beijing: Panda Books, 1984.

——. "Sinking." Trans. Joseph Lau and C. T. Hsia. In Joseph Lau and Howard Goldblatt, eds., *Columbia Anthology of Modern Chinese Literature*, 44–69. New York: Columbia University Press, 1995.

——. "Wisteria and Dodder." In Edgar Snow, ed., *Living China*, 247–263. New York: Reynal and Hitchcock, 1937.

——. *Yu Dafu wenji* 郁达夫文集 (Collected writings of Yu Dafu). 12 vols. Guangzhou: Huacheng, 1982.

Yu Dafu yanjiu ziliao 郁达夫研究资料 (Research materials on Yu Dafu). 2 vols. Tianjin: Tianjin renmin, 1982.

17

FEMINISM AND REVOLUTION: THE WORK AND LIFE OF DING LING

JINGYUAN ZHANG

A major Chinese writer of the twentieth century, Ding Ling 丁玲 (pen name of Jiang Bingzhi 蒋冰之, 1904–1986) wrote in a period of great social and political upheaval, during which she and her literary reputation suffered many vicissitudes. She remains a highly controversial figure. Ding Ling is known especially as a feminist and a revolutionary. Yet many critics, especially Western feminists, believe that after Mao's "Yan'an Talks" in 1942 she betrayed feminism in favor of the socialist struggle. Indeed, when she emerged again in the early 1980s after more than twenty years of silence following her denunciation as a rightist in 1957, she decried Western feminism and showed remarkable faith in the future of socialism.

But it may be more accurate to say that Ding Ling's feminism grew away from the concern with individual self-expression that is central to most Western conceptions of the aim of feminism. She came to think of Western feminism as self-indulgent and to believe that the best interest of women (as of all people) lay in socialism, not in liberal individualism. Ding Ling's work raises many profound questions: How does it reflect the theme of feminism and revolution? Are there serious tensions between feminism and social progress in her writing? How does someone who begins as a champion for women's individuality and selfhood—as she was in her early writings and in her courageous challenge to the patriarchal order in Yan'an—change into a genuine believer that women's concerns are only part of the social issue and that the national interest should come before the personal?

Ding Ling's early life shares features with the lives of many writers of the May Fourth generation: she came from the declining gentry class in the countryside and fled her hometown in defiance of an arranged marriage to seek a new life in a big city, where she pursued a writing career. Quite unusual, however, was that Ding Ling was brought up by an unconventional and rebellious mother who, widowed when Ding Ling was three years old, earned a degree in education and made her own living by teaching at newly reformed schools. Such activities were virtually unthinkable for a gentry-class widow at that time. Thought to be drawn from the model of her own mother, Ding Ling's unfinished "Mother" (母亲, 1933) recounts the story of a mother and her sworn sisters who unbind their feet, abandon their gentry-class life, take part in a movement for social reform, and learn to put the nation's interest before their own. Growing up among reformers and young rebels in Hunan, a province vigorously pursuing educational reforms at the time, Ding Ling devoured Western books and new ideas about democracy and freedom. A rebel at heart, she published her first essay in the local newspaper, exposing the unsavory deeds of her maternal uncle, a local despot, and denouncing the social system to which he belonged. To avoid her prearranged betrothal to this man's son, she fled with the help of her mother to Shanghai.

In the early 1920s, the large treaty port of Shanghai was on its way to becoming an international metropolis. It had the allure of a modern city: uprooted people could remain anonymous and did not have to rely on clan networks. Here she adopted the name Ding Ling for its brevity and simplicity (the Chinese character *ding* has only two strokes) and began her life as a "modern girl." In 1921, she attended a women's college set up by Chen Duxiu 陈独秀 and Li Dazhao 李大钊, two of the founders of the Chinese Communist Party. A year later she and her friends enrolled in the Department of Chinese Literature at Shanghai University, a school known as a gathering place for left-wing intellectuals. Free from the watchful gaze of elders, she and her friends lived a bohemian life, spending most of their time in extracurricular activities. In 1924, Ding Ling went to Beijing and took private lessons in painting; a year later she met Hu Yepin 胡也频, a young poet whom she eventually married.

Ding Ling published her first short story, "Mengke" 梦珂 (a transliteration of the French *mon coeur*, my heart), in 1927. In the following year her second story, "Miss Sophie's Diary" (莎菲女士的日记), became an instant success. Many of Ding Ling's early works are about "modern girls"—educated young urban women—and their desires, frustrations, aspirations, and hopes. Critics praised Ding Ling for the psychological complexity and sexuality of her female characters. "Miss Sophie's Diary" touches on the forbidden topic of female erotic desire and records Sophie's tortured self-scrutiny. Mao Dun characterized it as "representative of the contradictory psychology regarding sexual love found in young women liberated since May Fourth" (in Feuerwerker 1982: 43).

"Miss Sophie's Diary" remains a landmark in Chinese women's writing. In the May Fourth generation of women's writing, platonic love was perhaps the dominant theme. Narratives tended to be sentimental, lyrical, and romantic, as in the writings of Bing Xin 冰心, Lu Yin 庐隐, and Su Xuelin 苏雪林. Feng Yuanjun 冯沅君 was the boldest of them all, but even she had not broken through the confines of traditional moral propriety. Although Ding Ling was not among the first May Fourth women writers to publish, she was perhaps the first to portray female sexual desire. Her literary success was achieved by moving beyond lyricism, introducing to the Chinese literary scene the autonomous and intelligent sensibility of someone like Nora in Ibsen's *A Doll's House* or Emma in Flaubert's *Madame Bovary*, two works that caused a splash in China at the time. Part of the success of "Miss Sophie's Diary" also lay in its use of the diary form, which diminished the sense of distance between the writer and the reader and appealed to readers' voyeuristic desires.

The influence of Western literary works is conspicuous in Ding Ling's early writings. For instance, many of the protagonists in her early stories have foreign names: Mon Coeur in "Mengke," Sophie in "Miss Sophie's Diary," Wendy in "A Woman and a Man" (一个女人和一个男人, 1928), and Mary in "Shanghai, Spring 1930" (一九三零年春上海, 1930). More substantive, her psychological approach to the construction of female characters bears a resemblance to those in Western and Russian novels. Ding Ling used Western themes and motifs to break new literary ground. For example, "Miss Amao" (阿毛姑娘, 1928) may be read as a Chinese version of *Madame Bovary* (and surely the protagonist's name is meant to suggest Emma). Amao, a country girl, is married into a middle-class family near the city of Hangzhou. Dissatisfied with the life of a housewife and dreaming of glamour, she leaves her husband's home and ventures into the city. But her dream is beyond her reach, and she eventually commits suicide. Amao's progression from innocence through insatiable desire to destruction parallels that of Emma. Still, Ding Ling's Amao is a psychologically convincing picture of a rural woman suffocated by a glamorous but small-minded urban society and her inability to rise above it. What is original and important about this story is the way Ding Ling brings Flaubert's Emma into play as a direct response to most previous constructions of rural women by May Fourth writers: miserable, helpless female figures largely devoid of inner life, such as Sister Xianglin 祥林嫂 in Lu Xun's "New Year's Sacrifice" (祝福, 1924). In contrast, Ding Ling creates an image of a Chinese rural woman with Westernized individuality. Ironically, this figure is destroyed by her passionate desire for material wealth in the city.

At the beginning of the 1930s, Ding Ling's writing began to shift from expressing the subjective life of her characters toward portraying their social milieu. This transition began with two stories, "Weihu" (韦护, 1930) and "Shanghai, Spring 1930." She brings together the two themes—the personal and the social—through the "love and revolution" formula so popular at that time among young leftist writers in Shanghai. This formula marked a modest politicization of the passion and subjectivism of 1920s romanticism, still focusing on the emotional conflicts and torments of the intellectual protagonists and very different from socialist realism. Nevertheless, the formula helped Ding Ling and other writers gradually transfer their literary focus from love to revolution.

As the 1930s progressed, Chinese writers shifted from portraying the lonely individual to depicting society at large, from personal psychological exploration to a focus on broad social and political issues. At the vanguard of this new kind of literature, Ding Ling became one of the most influential left-wing authors of the 1930s and worked as editor-in-chief of *Big Dipper* (北斗), an organ of the League of Left-Wing Writers. She also began to write stories in the social realist mode. "Water" (水, 1931), published in the first issue of *Big Dipper*, is representative of her work during this period and has been regarded as a leading work of social realist fiction in China. The story was inspired by the floods of 1931, but it focused on the impact of the natural disaster on the political consciousness of a rural community. Instead of viewing the event from a single protagonist's perspective, the narrative evokes the collective, the community as a whole, and sympathetically depicts its uprising against the corrupt local officials as inevitable.

With Ding Ling's deepening involvement in left-wing circles came political tragedies. In early 1931, Ding Ling's husband, Hu Yepin, and four other young league writers were captured and executed by the Guomindang. Ding Ling herself was kidnapped and put under house arrest in 1933. In 1936, she escaped from her imprisonment in Nanjing and arrived in Yan'an, where the Communist Party was based, and her writing career took another turn. There, she taught Chinese literature at the Red Army Academy and was given responsibilities for political training. Despite her efforts to conform to party ideology, and as a keen observer of her surroundings, she chose not to remain silent about the Communist treatment of women in the revolutionary base. Two stories published in 1941, "When I Was in Xia Village" (我在霞村的时候) and "In the Hospital" (在医院中), dwell on the dark side of the revolutionary experience and raise the question of women's position within the revolutionary community.

Ding Ling had her first taste of party criticism after she published an essay on the eve of International Women's Day, "Thoughts on March Eighth" (三八节有感, 1942). This feminist essay criticizes the unequal treatment of women in the "liberated areas." Ding Ling uses the official Communist policy that men and women are equal partners in the revolutionary cause to criticize the practice in Yan'an where women were subordinate to men in revolutionary organizations and were assigned social status according to the status of their husbands. Ding Ling thus points to the dilemma faced by revolutionary women: even where class oppression is lifted, gender oppression remains. Severely criticized for this essay, she was forced to retract its ideas and apologize for its potentially divisive effect. Her essay, along with others critical of life in Yan'an, including Wang Shiwei's 王实味 "Wild Lilies" (野百合花), prompted Mao Zedong to convene a forum on culture, at the end of which he presented two lectures (the Yan'an Talks) that laid down Communist Party cultural policy—namely, that literature and art should be subordinate to politics, writers should overcome their remaining petit-bourgeois subjectivism and write about and for the "masses" (workers, peasants, and soldiers) in order to mobilize them in the struggle against the Japanese, and writers should make use of Chinese national forms and folk traditions.

Guided by Mao's redefinition of the role of the writer, Ding Ling joined a reporters' group and later a propaganda team and went to the battlefront in the war against Japan. She wrote plays and performed on stage for soldiers and villagers. To communicate with the illiterate masses, the cultural workers utilized popular traditional forms such as drum songs, clapper talk, two-person acts, and comic cross talk. Ding Ling's own writing from this period shows a radical change of style and theme. No longer focusing on just one or two protagonists, her fiction begins to paint a broad picture of a village or other collectives. Her socialist realist novel *The Sun Shines over Sanggan River* (太阳照在桑干河上, 1948), which took second place in the 1951 Stalin Prize competition, was based on material collected when she took part in village land reform.

Ding Ling held a leading position in Beijing cultural circles after the founding of the People's Republic of China. During this period she wrote essays, literary criticism, and stories, primarily expressing her love for China's new socialist life. Even so, she did not escape persecution: labeled a chief member of two "antiparty cliques," she was sent to labor on a farm in a remote area of Northeast China, where she remained for twelve years. During the Cultural Revolution she was imprisoned in Beijing for five years. When the Cultural Revolution ended in 1976, Ding Ling was "rehabilitated" and finally resumed writing, focusing on essays, reminiscences, and reviews. The novella "Du Wanxiang" (杜晚香, written 1966, revised 1978) was the longest work of fiction she published during this time and her only work since Yan'an to focus on an individual woman. The story is a sketch of a model laborer whom Ding Ling had met during her stay on the farm in Northeast China. In this socialist parable, Ding Ling creates a model socialist woman: an ordinary farmer who wins the respect of others by leading a humble yet glorious life full of traditional womanly virtues: she is hardworking, selfless, considerate, accommodating, and unassuming. Here the rebellious, restless, and inquisitive modern girl in Ding Ling's early fiction has completely given way to the traditional feminine virtues that the socialist system reaffirmed.

Ding Ling's stories, essays, and speeches were often controversial and sometimes out of tune with their times, an indication of her nonconformist attitudes and strong convictions. In 1983, when many Chinese liberal intellectuals were abandoning Marxism and reevaluating their position in the global culture,

Ding Ling supported the Communist Party's campaign against "spiritual pollution"—the increasing Western influence on Chinese culture. Even though her behavior puzzled many people, it was consistent with beliefs she had publicly espoused for decades. Given her resilient fighting spirit, it is unsurprising that she remained controversial to the end. For the later Ding Ling, literature was never just pure art; it was a political vehicle by which to fulfill her deeply felt obligation to depict social changes and interpret their meaning for the community. For her, a woman's fate is always linked to that of her nation. In this sense, Ding Ling remained committed to the cause of revolution and feminism, a path on which she traveled and suffered, sometimes alone, sometimes with others, for more than sixty years, insisting to the end that in comparison with her cause, her personal sufferings were insignificant.

Bibliography

Alber, Charles J. *Embracing the Life: Ding Ling and the Politics of Literature in the PRC*. Westport, CT: Praeger, 2004.

——. *Enduring the Revolution: Ding Ling and the Politics of Literature in Guomindang China*. Westport, CT: Praeger, 2002.

Anderson, Jennifer, and Theresa Munford, eds. *Chinese Women Writers: A Collection of Short Stories by Chinese Women Writers of the 1920s and '30s*. Hong Kong: Joint Publishing, 1985.

Barlow, Tani. "Feminism and Literary Technique in Ting Ling's Early Short Stories." In A. Palandri, ed., *Women Writers of 20th-Century China*, 63–110. Eugene: Asian Studies Publications, University of Oregon, 1982.

——. "Gender and Identity in Ding Ling's 'Mother.'" *Modern Chinese Literature* 2, 2 (1986): 123–142.

Bjorge, Gary J. "'Sophia's Diary': An Introduction." *Tamkang Review* 5, 1 (1974): 97–110.

Chang, Jun-mei. *Ting Ling: Her Life and Her Work*. Taipei: Institute of International Relations, 1978.

Dien, Dora Shu-fang. *Ding Ling and Her Mother: A Cultural Psychological Study*. Huntington, NY: Nova Science, 2001.

Ding, Ling. "Day." In Amy D. Dooling and Kristina M. Torgeson, trans. and eds., *Writing Women in Modern China: An Anthology of Women's Literature from the Early Twentieth Century*, 267–273. New York: Columbia University Press, 1998.

——. *I Myself Am a Woman: Selected Writings of Ding Ling*. Ed. Tani Barlow and Gary Bjorge. Boston: Beacon Press, 1989.

——. *Miss Sophie's Diary and Other Stories*. Trans. W. J. F. Jenner. Beijing: Chinese Literature, 1985.

——. *The Sun Shines over the Sanggan River*. Trans. Yang Xianyi and Gladys Yang. Beijing: Foreign Languages Press, 1984.

Feng, Jin. *The New Woman in Early Twentieth-Century Chinese Fiction*. West Lafayette, IN: Purdue University Press, 2001.

Feuerwerker, Yi-tsi Mei. *Ding Ling's Fiction: Ideology and Narrative in Modern Chinese Literature*. Cambridge, MA: Harvard University Press, 1982.

Lau, Joseph S. M., C. T. Hsia, and Leo Ou-fan Lee, eds. *Modern Chinese Stories and Novellas, 1919–1949*. New York: Columbia University Press, 1981.

Tang, Xiaobing. "Shanghai Spring 1930: Engendering the Revolutionary Body." In *Chinese Modernism: The Heroic and the Quotidian*, 97–130. Durham, NC: Duke University Press, 2000.

Wang, Xiaojue. "Over Her Dead Body: Ding Ling's Politicization After the Socialist Revolution." In Wang, *Modernity with a Cold War Face: Reimagining the Nation in Chinese Literature Across the 1949 Divide*, 108–54. Cambridge, MA: Harvard University Asia Center, 2013.

Yan, Haiping. *Chinese Women Writers and the Feminist Imagination, 1905–1948*. London: Routledge, 2006.

18

THE DEBATE ON REVOLUTIONARY LITERATURE

CHARLES LAUGHLIN

Entering a literary field in the early 1920s in which "literary revolution" had become the principal rallying cry, young intellectuals of the time should nevertheless be excused for lacking a clear idea of what a "revolution" (革命) might be. At least it was understood, particularly in the wake of events leading from the New Culture movement in 1917 to the May Fourth movement of 1919, that it meant the introduction of something *new* and vital and the sweeping away of the *old* forces and norms of traditional Chinese culture. However, the literary revolution—advocating general use of a written vernacular (白话) and promotion of "new culture"—was already fading into the past, while youths shocked and tempered by the intensifying political violence of the mid-1920s were beginning to feel that merely to revolutionize literature would not be enough: the object of revolutionary change must be society itself. Although Chinese cultural norms determined that literature would be the crucial vehicle for such revolutionary change, passage from a "literary revolution" to a "revolutionary literature" meant reconceptualizing literature as no longer the end of a process of revolutionary change but a means to, an instrument of, social revolution. It was in this way that leftist writers of the 1920s, strong in impact but still a minority in literary circles, were to set themselves apart from what they were by then able to identify as a liberal humanist mainstream in modern Chinese letters.

Indications of the literary sea change that led to this debate on revolutionary literature pepper the 1920s. As early as 1923, prominent Creation Society writer Yu Dafu 郁达夫 published an article calling for a literature of proletarian struggle (Denton 1996: 263–268), and by 1925 Marxist critic Qu Qiubai 瞿秋白 was calling for mass literature and further reform of the modern written language to reach out to the working classes and vividly render their world. The violent suppression of anti-imperialist demonstrations in 1925 and 1926 made the younger generation disillusioned with older May Fourth writers, who begged their students and protégés to devote their energies to their studies and not take to the streets.

A crucial moment was the Creation Society's conversion to Marxism around 1925. Creationists such as Guo Moruo 郭沫若, Yu Dafu, and Cheng Fangwu 成仿吾 disdained what to them was the bland, pedestrian realism of the Literary Association that dominated the literary scene of the early 1920s and advocated a dynamic, vital literature more in step with current world literary trends. Their fiction and poetry emphasized the individualistic and romantic aspects of literary expression (see "Form and Reform"). In large part because of the influence of the contemporary Japanese literary scene, however, Guo Moruo rather ostentatiously embraced Marxism and launched the society on the path of "revolutionary literature." The rationale for this apparent reversal was vaguely evolutionary, with an emphasis on cleaving to literature's cutting edge in each succeeding era.

The debate on revolutionary literature, as it was called, took place in the early spring of 1928 in articles published by prominent writers in some of the leading literary magazines of the time. Cheng Fangwu's article, whose title, "From Literary Revolution to Revolutionary Literature" (从文学革命到革命文学), set the terms of the debate, echoed Yu Dafu's emphasis on bringing Chinese literature up to date on the world scene. Cheng especially faults the Threads of Talk (语丝) group of essayists, represented by Zhou Zuoren 周作人 and Lin Yutang 林语堂, for obstructing current literary progress with their apparent refusal to take burning social and political issues seriously. To the Creation Society, older May Fourth writers seemed to be settling back into quiet complacency as the world crumbled about them; if anything, the situation in China was more dire in 1928 than it had been in 1919. Cheng's article also makes the crucial point that what is required of a revolutionary literature is that it be a literature not of the individual but of the collective, of the masses.

The Sun Society (太阳社), which formed in 1928, also promoted revolutionary literature, but from a somewhat different perspective. In the debate on revolutionary literature, the Sun Society aimed its criticism at two major fiction writers of the time, Lu Xun 鲁迅 and Mao Dun 茅盾, whose works arguably manifested a revolutionary viewpoint and had inspired much of the younger generation in this very direction. Qian Xingcun 钱杏邨 launched the most vitriolic and iconoclastic of these attacks in his article "The Bygone Age of Ah Q" (死去了的阿Q时代, 1928). His main point, and one of the principal issues in the debate, was that May Fourth literature, of which Lu Xun's "The True Story of Ah Q" was taken to be a paradigmatic example, was hopelessly out of date. Qian's deepest concern seems to be with the pre–May Fourth settings of almost all Lu Xun's fiction. However, there is also the suggestion of another important point: that the *way* of writing was dated. A revolutionary literature had to differ not only in content but also in methodology (Denton 1996: 276–288).

In speeches given in the late 1920s, Lu Xun, for his part, maintained a strict distinction between literature and revolution; to him, writers who thought they could contribute to a revolution by writing were fooling themselves. Yet, Lu Xun often attacked the Crescent Moon Society (新月社), whose members included Xu Zhimo 徐志摩, Liang Shiqiu 梁实秋, and Shen Congwen 沈从文, for promoting what he considered a literature of escapism—love stories and lyrical poetry—because it was too detached from contemporary social reality. Thus, though not directly engaging in the debate, Lu Xun took a position somewhere in the middle.

In a different article, this time critiquing Mao Dun, Qian Xingcun asserts another of the principal points in the debate on revolutionary literature: that writers must begin to write forceful, positive literature that inspires readers to take action. Qian complains that Mao Dun's fiction is suffused with the melancholy and angst of petit-bourgeois intellectuals who cannot realize their revolutionary dreams. In a 1929 response to Qian's attack, "On Reading *Ni Huanzhi*" (读《倪焕之》), Mao Dun argues that Qian and other such radicals, in addition to misreading his works, are calling for propaganda, not literature (Denton 1996: 289–306). In perhaps the only firm defensive position in the debate, Mao Dun affirms one of the most important tenets of May Fourth realism: that petit-bourgeois writers like himself can write well only about the life they themselves know, narrow as that experience may be on the broad social horizon. This principle would haunt Chinese fiction throughout the century and would have to be dealt with seriously by the Communist Party and its writers before a convincing revolutionary literature could emerge in actual practice.

Liang Shiqiu joined the fray with an article entitled "Literature and Revolution" (文学与革命) in *Crescent Moon* (June 1928), asserting that writers need not always write revolutionary literature and that "revolutionary," being a political term, is not a coherent category of literature. "Human nature," he says, "is the sole standard for measuring literature" (Denton 1996: 310). He attacks Qu Qiubai's slogan Mass Literature, asserting that literature, revolutionary or otherwise, is always the product not of the masses but of "a few geniuses." Unlike Lu Xun's and Mao Dun's defensive positions, Liang's article totally rejects the emergent, class-based view of literature that lay at the heart of the debate. Ten years later, in the early months of the war against Japan, Liang reiterated this extreme position vis-à-vis "resistance literature," which a few years later got him ostracized from the literary community on the mainland.

Although it lasted only a few weeks in the spring of 1928, this public debate brought to the surface issues that remained at the center of Chinese letters throughout the century—namely, whether literature should reflect contemporary social reality or represent a broad social horizon and be written from the point of view of the working classes—indeed, whether this was possible at all—and whether it should be obliged to be positive, forceful, and dynamic. The debate was revisited in the 1930s in the more protracted battle over literary freedom, in which the very ideological independence of the writer was at stake.

Because these Creation and Sun Society writers emerged from the same literary conditions and practices of the Literary Association and other societies of the 1920s (see "Literary Communities and the Production of Literature"), these individuals were like-minded writers who would form an identifiable group, establish their own organs of publication, and cultivate a loyal readership, some of whom would become their protégés and literary successors. Although dominated by the bellicose voices of leftist ideologues, the debate also showed that within the conditions of the literary arena in the 1920s, simply attacking writers and telling them what to do did not begin to address the issue. But what would ultimately characterize Chinese revolutionary literature, making it stand apart from other modes of literary practice in China, was the crucial evolution of leftist literary organizations from the late 1920s to the early months of the war against Japan. It was during this period that leftists eventually came to dominate the literary scene, in part by redefining literary production as an instrument of mobilization and indoctrination, even as a training ground for new writers.

Bibliography

Chen, Jianhua. "Revolution: From Literary Revolution to Revolutionary Literature." In Ban Wang, ed., *Words and Their Stories: Essays on the Language of the Chinese Revolution*, 15–32. Leiden: Brill, 2010.

Denton, Kirk A., ed. *Modern Chinese Literary Thought: Writings on Literature, 1893–1945*. Stanford, CA: Stanford University Press, 1996.

Goldman, Merle. "Left-Wing Criticism of the Pai-Hua Movement." In Benjamin I. Schwartz, ed., *Reflections on the May Fourth Movement: A Symposium*, 85–94. Cambridge, MA: East Asian Research Center, Harvard University, 1973.

Hsia, C. T. *A History of Modern Chinese Fiction*. New Haven, CT: Yale University Press, 1971.

Hsia, Tsi-an. *The Gate of Darkness: Studies on the Leftist Literary Movement in China*. Seattle: University of Washington Press, 1968.

Pickowicz, Paul. "Qu Qiubai's Critique of the May Fourth Generation: Early Chinese Marxist Literary Criticism." In Merle Goldman, ed., *Modern Chinese Literature in the May Fourth Era*, 351–384. Cambridge, MA: Harvard University Press, 1977.

Tao, Donfeng, Yang Xiaobin, Rosemary Roberts, and Yang Ling, eds. *Chinese Revolution and Chinese Literature*. Cambridge: University of Cambridge Press, 2009.

Wong, Wang-chi. *Politics and Literature in Shanghai: The Chinese League of Left-Wing Writers, 1930–1936*. Manchester: Manchester University Press, 1991.

19

MAO DUN, THE MODERN NOVEL, AND THE REPRESENTATION OF WOMEN

HILARY CHUNG

Mao Dun 茅盾 (Shen Yanbing 沈雁冰, 1896–1981) was a leading figure in the development of the modern Chinese novel. By the time he began to write creatively in 1927, he already had a formidable reputation as a literary editor, critic, and translator. He is best known for his reformulation of nineteenth-century European realist theory and for putting this theory into practice in a series of novellas and full-length novels. His *Rainbow* (虹, 1929) was among the earliest novels in modern Chinese literature, and *Midnight* (子夜, 1933), a mature novel of nearly six hundred pages, is conventionally acknowledged as a high point of his literary theory in practice.

Three prominent intertwining elements contribute to Mao Dun's literary vision: his realist literary theory, his revolutionary commitment (as both a founding member of the Chinese Communist Party and an active participant in revolutionary campaigns during the 1920s), and his stance toward women's issues. The last of these significantly illuminates our understanding of the other two.

Provoked by the extent of educational and social disadvantage of women under traditional cultural norms, male intellectuals in late-modernizing nations such as China often committed themselves to fledgling women's movements. Young, modern male intellectuals like Mao Dun and his peers dominated the new discourses of modernity, nationalism, and cultural reconfiguration that evolved in the early decades of the twentieth century. Issues of national and individual identity, gender, women's emancipation, and so on were therefore mostly spoken with a male voice. A prolific contributor to contemporary journal-based debates on the "woman question" (妇女问题), Mao Dun wrote in general support of women's emancipation. For May Fourth intellectuals, issues such as the emancipation of the individual from such traditional patriarchal constraints as arranged marriage scarcely took on a gendered dimension: young men were just as much victims of such abhorrent practices as were their female comrades. From this easy assumption of advocacy, it was no difficult leap for May Fourth male intellectuals not only to identify with the new woman's quest for identity and meaning but also to appropriate it.

Mao Dun's fiction offers an insightful illumination into the problematic of May Fourth male feminism, both in his obsessive reconstructions and reconfigurations of the new woman and in the way these intersect with his interest in literary realism. His first short story, "Creation" (创造, 1928), a reworking of the Pygmalion myth, offers an allegory for the project of "writing woman." Junshi 君实, a modern educated intellectual, chooses a distant cousin, Xianxian 娴娴, "a piece of uncut jade," as a wife to "carve" into his ideal of modern womanhood. He attempts to do this by acquainting her with fashionable new books on culture and politics. But Xianxian is stirred by the radical message in these books, becomes actively involved in political work, and eventually leaves him out of frustration at his inertia and self-absorption. Although a third-person narrative, the story is recounted in flashback from the perspective of Junshi. One morning, Junshi wakes first and ponders the education and transformation of his wife sleeping beside him. He has created her to complete his own sense of self, but she has precipitated a crisis in him. She undermines his assumption of moral ascendancy over her by developing views of her own and, worse, even assumes a position of sexual dominance over him through her captivating sensuality. The portrayal of Xianxian is often read as an affirmation of both the realization of feminist aspirations and, as Mao Dun (1997: 1:393) suggests in his memoirs, a symbol of fulfilled revolutionary vocation. Yet, as a sexualized object and male construct, Xianxian is portrayed only through the consciousness of her creator. She has no inner identity. Any meaning her portrayal signifies has been inscribed by her creator in terms of his own crisis. All we learn of her is what she is not, that is, how she does not correspond to his ideal. Finally, Junshi, ironically the main obstacle to her becoming, is so unaware of who Xianxian has become, he scarcely notices her final departure. A deep-seated anxiety thus reveals itself whereby serious intellectual commitment to the cause of women's emancipation, which contains significant investment on the male intellectual's own behalf, is continually threatened by a fear of the sexually independent woman (see Chung 1998).

The conflict between sexuality and revolutionary commitment is a hallmark of May Fourth male discourses of feminism and emancipation. Mao Dun's own theorization of "writing reality" contributed to these discourses. Western nineteenth-century realism preoccupied itself with the accurate and objective depiction of reality. Mao Dun was theoretically attracted to Émile Zola's development of this practice, in which the writer as scientist—or naturalist—observes reality objectively and then uses the data to represent and analyze the human condition (see Wang 1992: 25–66). Such an approach only further elevates the narrative authority of the male novelist, whose position as a spokesman for the discourse of modernity is already privileged. As a novelist who consistently uses the experience of women as a vehicle for his representation and analysis of contemporary Chinese social reality, Mao Dun creates a hierarchy of power between the subject, who inscribes meaning, and the object of scrutiny upon whom meaning is inscribed. To inscribe meaning is to assign value, implying a position of empowerment that extends beyond the literary into the social sphere in a dynamic of mutual reinforcement.

Mao Dun inscribes the female body and psyche with meaning according to his own preoccupations and ideological commitments. In *Eclipse* (蚀, 1927–1928), a progression takes place through the three volumes of the trilogy: a psychological exploration of the response of modern educated bourgeois intellectuals to the failure of the Communist Party–led uprisings of 1926–1927 via the female characters in the first part is superseded by the mutilation of the physically alluring female body to signify the horror of the right-wing backlash in the second part; in the third part, the female characters, themselves objects of love pursuits, embody the quests for direction and meaning undertaken by their suitors. Throughout, there is an unstable interaction between the author's realistic approach and ideological impulses where the female body as an object of desire cannot readily be appropriated as a site of revolutionary signification without undermining the very process of signification. The sexual independence and empowerment of women simply undermines male discourses of revolution and emancipation by destabilizing their male-centered perspective. The only way for this process to succeed is to divest the female body of its sexuality. Thus a countercurrent of gender transvaluation also occurs in Mao Dun's fiction whereby women who assume a viable revolutionary role, or who seek to do so, become degendered.

The novel *Rainbow* gives greater play to this countercurrent. It traces the progress of Mei 梅, an emancipated young woman, toward an allegiance to leftist politics via a series of romantic or sexual encounters. Written during 1928–1929, the novel portrays the recent past, examining the growing intellectual and political awareness of the young modern Chinese intellectual. Familiar patterns of gendered appropriation are at work in this novel, narrated through the lens of a young woman who seems to be working her way through all the main themes of the "woman question" debate: arranged marriage, employment opportunity and economic independence, social mobility, and finally revolutionary commitment. These patterns of appropriation are highlighted by recent revelations that Mao Dun based the novel on the experiences of his lover Qin Dejun 秦德君. At every stage in Mei's life in Sichuan, the men whom she encounters inscribe meaning to her body. Her arranged husband in a graphic and quite disturbing wedding night scene inscribes her as "wife"; her teaching colleagues make allegations of sexual impropriety, for which she loses her job, and so on. Her departure from Sichuan by steamer to Shanghai marks a turning point in her development. Until this point in Mei's life, her fate, to which she has acquiesced, has been determined by her body and the sexually charged environment in which she has lived. But when she comes to Shanghai, her only ambition is to conquer her environment and overcome her fate. Under the political tutelage of Communist Party cadre Liang Gangfu 梁刚夫, she learns to rein in her strong feminine nature. Liang refuses her sexual advances. Indeed, when Mei dreams of Liang, he rejects her advances with physical violence, assailing her body, whose fate had been determined previously by its physical allure. He inscribes new meaning upon it: a commitment to revolution that transcends gender.

Mao Dun famously identified two master exponents of the nineteenth-century novel, Zola and Leo Tolstoy, as major sources of his creative inspiration:

> Zola explored human conditions because he wanted to be a novelist, while Tolstoy started to write novels only after experiencing the vicissitudes of life. Despite the two masters' different starting points, their works shocked the world equally. Zola's attitude toward life can be summarized as cool detachment, which is in sharp contrast to Tolstoy's warm embrace of it; but the works of both are criticisms of and reflections of reality. I like Zola, but I am also fond of Tolstoy. At one time I enthusiastically propagandized for naturalism. Yet when I tried to write novels, it was Tolstoy I came closer to.
>
> (in Wang 1992: 70)

The way in which Mei's existence is at first determined by her environment and later transformed by a new and all-encompassing vision illustrates how Mao Dun reinterprets both Zola and Tolstoy. Zola's scientific method examines the way in which heredity and environment shape the human condition. It is founded on a pessimistic determinism that allows no transcendence. Tolstoy offers an alternative humanistic vision. Concerned by the moral degradation of society, Tolstoy believed in the morally uplifting potential of art, offering the potential for growth and change in terms of Christian enlightenment. For Mao Dun, the guiding principle for change was Marxism, which offered the means to transcend both heredity and environment. Zola's existential determinism is replaced by the historical determinism of Marxism, whose vision is predicated on the necessary transcendence of heredity and environment (Wang 1992: 67–110). However, reminiscent of the pattern evoked in "Creation," significant tensions exist between the authoritative narrative stance and Mei's actual physical portrayal. Whereas Mei's political transformation has been achieved, the sexual power of her body still turns heads at the political meeting as Mei rushes in "like a nude mannequin" after having been caught in the rain (Mao Dun 1992: 220). Just like Xianxian's, Mei's body ultimately resists male inscription.

Anxiety at the disruptive yet irresistible potential of independent feminine sexuality remains at the heart of Mao Dun's novel *Midnight*. An epic portrait of industrial society in 1930s Shanghai, the novel explores in Zolaesque fashion the antagonistic class conditions engendered by heredity (class) and the environment of capitalism. The narrative ranges over all classes, including factory owners, stock traders, decadent bourgeois youth, and politicized youth active among the urban proletariat. In *Midnight*, the chimera of rampant, predatory feminine sexuality personifies the capitalist decadence of the city. Factory owner Wu Sunfu's 吴荪甫 elderly father, decrepit symbol of traditional patriarchy, dies of shock at his first encounter with it. Socialites beguile and manipulate their millionaire patrons; sex is used as a commodity to buy stock market information on which livelihoods depend. By contrast, the committed revolutionaries, particularly in the person of Ma Jin 玛金, who rejects the advances of her comrade Su Lun 苏伦, occupy the moral high ground. However, her "nice, firm little breasts" (Mao Dun 1957, 434) are just as threatening to *his* revolutionary commitment as the jutting, swelling curves of the women associated with the decadent classes. Ma Jin may embody revolutionary sublimation for the greater cause, but her body is still the locus of anxiety for her male comrade.

Defiance against the oppression of patriarchy by the modern woman is a beguiling metaphor for revolutionary vocation. Although Mao Dun identifies with the defiance, as soon as he appropriates it, by imposing *his own* interpretation on feminine experience, he colludes with the original problematic of sexual oppression. Thereafter, however much he seeks to inscribe new meanings onto the modern woman, in response to *his own* quests, beliefs, and crises, the sexual nature of metaphor disrupts and threatens his male-centered discourse.

Bibliography

Chan, Chingkiu Stephen. "Eros as Revolution: The Libidinal Dimension of Despair in Mao Dun's *Rainbow*." *Journal of Oriental Studies* 24, 1 (1986): 37–53.
Chen, Yu-shih. *Realism and Allegory in the Early Fiction of Mao Tun*. Bloomington: Indiana University Press, 1986.
Chung, Hilary. "Questing the Goddess: Mao Dun and the New Woman." In Raoul D. Findeisen and Robert H. Gassmann, eds., *Autumn Floods: Essays in Honour of Marián Gálik*, 165–183. Bern: Peter Lang, 1998.
Feng, Jin. "The Temptation and Salvation of the Male Intellectual: Mao Dun's Women Revolutionaries." In Feng, *The New Woman in Early Twentieth-Century Chinese Fiction*, 101–125. West Lafayette, IN: Purdue University Press, 2004.

Laughlin, Charles. "Mao Dun." In Thomas Moran, ed., *Dictionary of Literary Biography—Chinese Fiction Writers, 1900–1949*, 164–177. New York: Thomson Gale, 2007.

Lin, Sylvia Li chun. "Unwelcome Heroines: Mao Dun and Yu Dafu's Creations of a New Chinese Woman." *Journal of Modern Literature in Chinese* 1, 2 (January 1998): 71–94.

Mao, Dun. "Creation." Trans. Gladys Yang. In *The Vixen*, 5–35. Beijing: Panda Books, 1987.

——. "From Guling to Tokyo." Trans. Yu-shih Chen. *Bulletin of Concerned Asian Scholars* 1 (1976): 38–44.

——. *Midnight*. Trans. Meng-hsiung Hsu. Beijing: Foreign Languages Press, 1957.

——. *Rainbow*. Trans. Madeline Zelin. Berkeley: University of California Press, 1992.

——. *Spring Silkworms and Other Stories*. Trans. Sidney Shapiro. Beijing: Foreign Language, 1956.

——. 茅盾. *Wo zouguo de daolu* 我走过的道路 (Roads I have traveled). 2 vols. Beijing: Renmin wenxue, 1997.

Wang, David Der-wei. *Fictional Realism in Twentieth Century China: Mao Dun, Lao She, Shen Congwen*. New York: Columbia University Press, 1992.

20

BA JIN'S *FAMILY*: FICTION, REPRESENTATION, AND RELEVANCE

NICHOLAS A. KALDIS

Ba Jin 巴金 (1904–2005), whose style name was Li Feigan 李芾甘 and was born Li Yaotang 李尧棠, began to use the pen name Ba Jin, by which he is known today, in 1928. He first published the novel *Torrent*, or *Turbulent Stream* (激流), in serial form in the newspaper *Shibao* (时报) in April 1931. It created a sensation, and as *Family* (家), the title under which it would appear in book form in 1933, it became Ba Jin's most famous work. Although two earlier novels had been well received, *Family* established Ba Jin as one of the most popular of progressive Chinese writers of the 1930s and 1940s, second only to Lu Xun (Lang 1967: 3). The great success of *Family* eventually inspired Ba Jin to write a sequel, which he entitled *Spring* (春, 1938). Two years later a third novel, *Autumn* (秋), was added, forming a trilogy collectively entitled *Torrent* (the original title of the serialized version of *Family*). The trilogy received critical acclaim, but only *Family* has since been canonized as one of the masterpieces of modern Chinese literature. It has even been compared favorably with China's great literary classic *Dream of the Red Chamber* (红楼梦) (Lang 1967: 83–84; Mao 1978: 88–102), and Ba Jin's writing style has been likened to that of Balzac, Dreiser, and Thomas Wolfe (Mao 1978: 146). Since the 1958 English translation of *Family*, Ba Jin's literary output has earned him considerable recognition outside China; in 1975, he was nominated for the Nobel Prize in Literature.

Merited as such praise and comparisons with famous Western novelists may be, we gain a greater understanding of *Family*'s literary value by carefully analyzing and interpreting some of the novel's most important textual and contextual details. In other words, readers must still carefully and critically read *Family* to gain a deeper understanding of the novel and discover for themselves its contemporary relevance.

Family chronicles the breakdown of the house of Gao, a large and wealthy extended family of the scholar-gentry class. Three brothers, grandsons of the family patriarch, are the novel's main characters: the eldest is Gao Juexin 高觉新, followed by Gao Juemin 高觉民 and Gao Juehui 高觉慧. The three struggle against their family to gain control over their own lives and develop a sense of individuality. Theirs is a traditional Chinese multigenerational family living within the walls of a vast compound of residential quarters, meeting rooms, temples, kitchens, gardens, and servants' quarters. It is governed by a set of unbreakable rules that demand the subjugation of each individual in accordance with his or her predetermined role in the family and in Chinese society. The author portrays such a family structure as perfectly designed to crush the type of individual aspirations and personal dreams the three boys hold dear, chronicling their tortured and sometimes tragic experiences as they grow into young men.

Through the portrayal of the contemptible patriarch, Master Gao 高老太爷, Ba Jin shows how the traditional Chinese family structure is not an impersonal, abstract system but something tangible that is embodied in the conservative tyrants who uphold it. Master Gao rules the large household with an iron fist, tolerating neither debate nor dissension. The aging despot keeps an especially tight rein on Juexin, because Juexin is the eldest son of his own deceased eldest son and thus heir to the top post in the family hierarchy. Juexin and his brothers are being groomed for their future roles as leaders of the clan and pillars of society. As manager of their futures, their grandfather hands down decisions concerning every aspect of their private and social lives, and most of these decisions run counter to the boys' desires. The conflicts between the generations produce the dramatic events of the novel. Ba Jin focuses on the three brothers' various responses of rebellion, resistance, or acquiescence to Grandfather Gao's unwelcome dictums. In addition to this focus on the three grandsons (mainly Juexin and Juehui) are the novel's parallel plotlines depicting the suffering of women under the traditional Chinese family and social systems.

The story takes place between 1919 and 1923, when outside the walls of the Gao family compound the historical events of China's warlord era were taking place, including the student-led May Fourth movement (the editor's note in the 1989 translation erroneously places the events of the story in 1931, the year it was written [Ba Jin 1989: vi]). These larger, well-known historical events, though not described in great detail, provide the brothers with the critical awareness and "enlightenment" necessary to launch an attack against their family structure. Much of their new knowledge comes directly from the many journals such as *New Tide* (新潮) that disseminated the values of May Fourth iconoclasm. This relationship between literature, enlightenment, and the transformation of

Chinese society is reflected in the content of the story as well as in the novel's popular reception. Just as the youthful characters are inspired by the journal articles coming out of social and intellectual movements of the early 1920s, so were 1930s and 1940s readers of *Family* moved by its indictment of the traditional family system. For Chinese readers, the family of the title represented all Chinese families, seen as the bedrock of traditional values. The author himself claimed that in *Family* he "wanted to write . . . the history of a typical feudal family" and show the "inner struggles and tragedies inside those families—how lovable youths suffer there, how they struggle and finally do not escape destruction" (Lang 1967: 71). Ba Jin portrays the traditional Chinese family, ironically, as a hotbed of cruelty, corruption, greed, hypocrisy, misogyny, infighting, and other generally negative attributes.

Given Ba Jin's intentionally one-sided portrait, the traditional upper-class Chinese family in this book is certainly an easy target for exposure and ridicule. This sometimes leads to a partially justifiable yet oversimplified study of characterization in the novel. In this vein, Nathan Mao (1978: 90–96) describes characters who are "defenders of the status quo, victims of the status quo, and those who rebel against the status quo." Similarly, Olga Lang (1967: 78) divides members of the younger generations in *Family* into two main groups, either "victims" or "fighters." Lang (1967: 76), citing and supporting the author's own claim that "the root of evil lies not in personalities but in the family system itself," tends simply to malign the system and treat the characters as helpless victims. But of more importance to the author was the way his young characters responded to this decadent family, for their responses are a measure of their moral fortitude and, the author hoped, a model for readers.

A closer look at the text reveals a more ambivalent representation of character, for some of Ba Jin's male "victims" are clearly represented as not wholly innocent and at least partially to blame for their own fates. For example, the eldest of the three brothers, Juexin, is faulted for frequently bending to his grandfather's will. Consider the following:

> Indeed, Chueh-hsin [Juexin] found the "compliant bow" philosophy and the "policy of non-resistance" most useful. . . . They were a solace to him, permitting him to believe in the new theories while still conforming to the old feudal concepts. He saw no inconsistency.
>
> (Ba Jin 1989: 43)

> He had never disagreed with anyone in his life, no matter how unfairly they may have treated him. He preferred to swallow his tears, suppress his anger and bitterness; he would bear anything rather than oppose a person directly. Nor did it ever occur to him to wonder whether this forbearance might not be harmful to others.
>
> (Ba Jin 1989: 296–297)

The attitude toward Juexin has its origins in Ba Jin's attitude toward his eldest brother, on whom Juexin was closely modeled. Their lives are similar, except that Ba Jin's real brother committed suicide rather than have his dreams crushed by his family. News of his brother's suicide reached Ba Jin as he was finishing the novel's sixth chapter, which he had entitled "Eldest Brother" (Ba Jin 1993: 15). About a year after the novel was completed, Ba Jin wrote a short preface, entitled "Presented to a Certain Person," in which he accuses someone addressed only as "you" of "ruining your own splendid fantasies; destroying your own bright future," and becoming a "completely unnecessary sacrificial object and dying" (不必要的牺牲品而死了) (376–377). Clearly aware of his brother's complicity in his own misfortunes, Ba Jin is careful to demonstrate in the novel that much of Juexin's suffering is a result of his own spinelessness. That Ba Jin takes such a critical stance toward some characters' willful ignorance or passivity helps to temper criticism that his characters are "extremely sentimental" (Mao 1978: 98) and reveals that sometimes he is deliberately exaggerating a character's self-indulgent emotional sensitivity in order to contrast it with a necessary action or attitude that the character is neglecting. This is certainly the case with Juexin, but less so in the case of Gao Juehui, the youngest and most rebellious of the three brothers and the main protagonist of *Family*.

Juehui cannot be discussed outside Ba Jin's own thoughts and beliefs, for the character is somewhat an alter ego for the author. Like the youthful Ba Jin, Gao Juehui reads avant-garde journals and becomes politically aware at a young age. Combined with the events witnessed in his own home, these publications help to shape a strong determination to reject traditional vices and to believe in a better future for China's people. In this respect, Juehui and Ba Jin are almost stereotypical examples of the young (mostly male) Chinese intellectuals who came of age in the early twentieth century. They saw Chinese society and culture as decrepit, poisoned by the "feudal" ways of its past, and they viewed themselves as ultimately responsible for bringing about change and reform. However, although Juehui has been linked to the author himself, he is more accurately described as Ba Jin's *idealized* version of the rebellious youth he might have wished he had been: "I wanted to describe a rebel, a young but courageous rebel. I wanted to personify in him my hope. I wanted him to bring fresh air to us. . . . In those families we do not have much fresh air" (Lang 1967: 70). Ba Jin clearly felt that his imagination and creativity had to express and transmit his hope for change, for a better society. Such desires were common among Chinese writers of his time, partially inspired by literature and ideas from other cultures.

As noted earlier, the young Ba Jin (like Juehui) was an avid reader of May Fourth era journals, and his intellectual, political, and literary development were heavily influenced by the Western ideas and literary styles promoted in those journals. Lang (1967: 224–225) argues that "in the formation of his ideals three Western ideological complexes were of primary importance: international anarchism, Russian populism, and, to a lesser extent, the Great French Revolution." Among these three foreign influences, anarchism had by far the greatest impact on Ba Jin's beliefs and attitudes. Anarchism, as Emma Goldman said, is a belief in "a new social order based on liberty unrestricted by man-made law; the theory that all forms of government rest on violence, and are therefore wrong and harmful as well as unnecessary" (Lang 1967: 46). So influential was this philosophy on Ba Jin that he created his pen name from the Chinese transliterations of the surnames of the two anarchist thinkers he most admired, Mikhail Bakunin and Peter Kropotkin. By his own account, anarchism helped to give form and structure to his feelings of sympathy for the poor and downtrodden, which he had felt from an early age (his favorite childhood companions were the much-abused servants in and around his family's wealthy compound). In addition to favoring anarchist political writers, Ba Jin was also deeply impressed by Russian and French writers such as Turgenev, Zola, Maupassant, and Romain Rolland (Lang 1989: viii). He not only emulated the content of their work in his deeply emotional, realistic, and sympathetic descriptions of the poor and dispossessed but also tried to imitate their writing style, particularly "Europeanized sentences" (Ba Jin 1993: 17).

Aside from matters of imitation and grammatical style, Ba Jin's favored technique in *Family* is the didactic description of individual characters' responses to decisive events, through which he hopes to inspire his readers to act and think. For example, when Juehui magnanimously gives money to a poor beggar on a cold night, he is still haunted by a voice that criticizes the stopgap nature of individual acts of charity. The voice implies that only when collective, large-scale change is undertaken will Chinese society be reformed and China's people truly saved: "A voice seemed to shout at him in the silence: 'Do you think deeds like that are going to change the world? Do you think you've saved that beggar child from cold and hunger for the rest of his life? You—you hypocritical "humanitarian" what a fool you are!'" (Ba Jin 1989: 104). From a comparative perspective, as readers we are challenged to weigh the relative merits of Juehui's isolated act of kindness against our own responses to similar situations and reflect on the need for collective change that such deeds necessarily point toward.

The character Juehui is also held up as a negative example of those who privilege purely academic approaches to changing society over immediate, practical responses to events. Although Juehui is the "courageous rebel" of the story, his devotion to changing China through intellectual means, at the expense of concrete action, is shown to be a tragic flaw. In this sense, he is responsible for some of the very same willful ignorance that Juexin frequently displays. In one of the story's most tragic events, the servant Mingfeng 鸣凤 seeks out Juehui in desperation (she is to be married off as a concubine to a "lecherous old man"), but he is enthusiastically immersed in his editorial duties for a journal "introducing new ideas and attacking all that was unreasonable of the old" (Ba Jin 1989: 186). Absorbed in his own idealistic pursuits in the world of letters, Juehui ignores the very real crisis at hand. He is deaf to the passionate and urgently repeated pleas of Mingfeng (his secret love). With no one else to turn to, she commits suicide.

As Mingfeng's death demonstrates, although some of the young male characters in *Family* are shown to be partially responsible for the evils of the traditional patriarchal family system, the same cannot be said for the young female characters. The women and girls in the story are almost all victims, helpless to influence their own lives without a male character's intervention (even the enlightened and outgoing Qin 琴 ["Chin" in the Shapiro translation], the boys' cousin, needs Juemin's help in her quest for selfhood). This aspect of the novel—the one-sided and simplistic portrayal of women—has been singled out by some critics. Rey Chow (1991: 99), for example, has noted that a character like Mingfeng is sympathetically portrayed as a "sacredly human" being, but the economic and gender-specific conflicts that determine her fate are not adequately explored. In other words, the story glosses over the complicated personal, economic, social, and sexual specifics of Mingfeng's life; she becomes just another of the countless victims of the traditional patriarchal family and social system. Readers are instead encouraged to sympathize and commiserate with the man who could have saved her, Juehui. Chow (1991: 102) argues, "As [Juehui] mourns her, we feel that he is mourning the destructiveness of the 'system,' not the death of the woman who has devoted her life to him." Chow concludes that the rebellious young man's fight against the male-dominated family system takes center stage in *Family*. Women are just sympathetic grist for the mill.

Much like his attack on the traditional Chinese family, Ba Jin's portrayal of women was caught up in some of the most important issues of the day: How could Chinese women be liberated? How could male writers bring about that liberation? As Rey Chow's analysis makes clear, female characters in stories were often simply used by male writers as weapons in their own fight against the traditional Chinese cultural system. Women were excluded from the battle, not treated as complex human beings by either those upholding traditional patriarchal culture or the cultural iconoclasts. This raises an important question of contemporary relevance: How does the way male writers represent women affect their other literary goals, such as Ba Jin's goal of discrediting the traditional family system and modernizing Chinese society? In more cross-cultural terms, how are patriarchal attitudes and behaviors toward women related to larger social projects?

As evident in the foregoing discussion, a careful reading of Ba Jin's *Family* leads readers to explore the ways this novel deals with matters of gender, self and society, social reform, individual responsibility, and other issues that haunted Ba Jin and other modern Chinese authors. When a writer sees unfair conditions in his life and society, how does he turn that awareness into a fictional story?

Should he try to portray the situation accurately and objectively, exposing his culture's evils in a realistic fashion? Should he instead try to imagine a possible alternative to those conditions, such as characters who rebel against and change society, even if this rarely happens in real life? Or might there be some third alternative that gets beyond these two choices? Why are some people, like writers, compelled to respond to their experiences by creating fictional stories? And why do so many people feel the urge to read these stories? A discussion of these issues reveals that the novel deals with many experiences and questions that are as alive and relevant today as they were in Ba Jin's youth. A detailed and thoughtful analysis of *Family* thus leads readers to connect the events of the novel both to the specific historical circumstances of 1920s China and to experiences and questions concerning their own lives and society today.

Bibliography

Ba Jin 巴金. *Ba Jin xiaoshuo quanji: disi juan: Jia* 巴金小说全集：第四卷：家 (Ba Jin's collected fiction. Vol. 4, *Family*). Taipei: Yuanliu, 1993.

——. *Family*. Trans. Sidney Shapiro. Beijing: Foreign Languages Press, 1958 (Doubleday, 1972; Garden City, NJ: Anchor Books, 1972).

——. *Jia* 家 (Family). Shanghai: Kaiming shudian, 1933.

Chow, Rey. *Women and Chinese Modernity: The Politics of Reading Between West and East*. Minneapolis: University of Minnesota Press, 1991.

Kaldis, Nicholas A. "Ba Jin." In Thomas Moran, ed., *Dictionary of Literary Biography—Chinese Fiction Writers, 1900–1949*, 310–325. New York: Thomson Gale, 2007.

Lang, Olga. "Introduction." In Ba Jin, *Family*, vii–xxvi. Beijing: Foreign Languages Press, 1989.

——. *Pa Chin and His Writings: Chinese Youth Between the Two Revolutions*. Harvard East Asia Series, 28. Cambridge, MA: Harvard University Press, 1967.

Larson, Wendy. "Shen Congwen and Ba Jin: Literary Authority Against the 'World.'" In Larson, *Literary Authority and the Modern Chinese Writer: Ambivalence and Autobiography*, 61–85. Durham, NC: Duke University Press, 1991.

Mao, Nathan. *Pa Chin*. Boston: Twayne, 1978.

21

CHINESE MODERNISM: THE NEW SENSATIONISTS

STEVEN L. RIEP

The literary revolution that swept through China in the early twentieth century brought with it an openness to new modes of writing that drew on a wide variety of non-Chinese literatures. Writers enthusiastically responded to the depictions of urban life and psychological explorations found in the contemporary literatures of Japan, Europe, and America that were introduced by students studying overseas or by translators working in Shanghai and Beijing. One such approach was the modernism pioneered by the New Sensationists (新感觉派), the first group of self-consciously modernist writers in China. The group took shape in the late 1920s and flourished in the early to mid-1930s. Although initially their impact was limited, the New Sensationists and their revolutionary use of language, structure, theme, and style influenced later generations of writers in China and Taiwan.

During the 1930s, the conservative literary policies of the Nationalist government on the right and the radical Marxist literary program of the League of Left-Wing Writers (中国左翼作家联盟) on the left dominated the literary scene. By encouraging innovative attempts to depict the unique urban milieu of Shanghai, modernist writers created an alternative space for literature to develop outside the strict bounds established by the political left or right. Although the exigencies of war would end the movement in the late 1930s, it would leave a legacy of experimental writing for later modernist movements to follow.

The development of Chinese modernism has much to do with its point of origin, Shanghai, which was among the largest and most modern cities in the world in the late 1920s. As a semicolonial city with foreign concessions and a cosmopolitan flavor, it provided the rich material culture that would feature so prominently in modernist fiction: dance halls, cinemas, nightclubs, department stores, skyscrapers, and racetracks. Its abundance of Chinese and foreign bookstores and secondhand bookstalls gave writers ready access to books and periodicals from around the world. Residents of Shanghai could enjoy the latest Hollywood films at numerous movie theaters. The material trappings of modern life — cars, cigarettes, alcoholic beverages, and stylish clothes — appeared in magazines and on billboards and signs and would make their way into fiction. The metropolis pulsated with flashing neon lights and the rhythm of jazz music. Although the fast-paced lifestyle of the metropolis exhilarated, it also exhausted. A person could feel lonely amid the crowds (L. Lee 1999).

New Sensationism had characteristics that set it apart from modernism in other parts of the world. Its practitioners, unlike many European and American modernists, did not outright reject the city and the modernization and development it represented. On the contrary, the dynamic environment of the metropolis and its urban culture attracted them. Because many of these writers were newcomers to Shanghai, they had yet to experience the full forces of modernization and urbanization. Modernism became "a literary fashion, an ideal" rather than an "objective reality" for them (L. Lee 1999: 147). Thus the Shanghai modernists had mixed feelings for the metropolis and viewed it with a combination of excitement and fear. They reveled in the sensory stimuli (the sounds, sights, smells, tastes, and feelings) it provided and sought new ways to depict them in their writing, just as a group of Japanese writers that included Yokomitsu Rîchi and Kawabata Yasunari, known as the Shinkankakuha (New Sensationalists), had done a decade earlier. The Chinese term for New Sensationist derives from the name of the Japanese group; it signifies the common attempt by both Chinese and Japanese writers to "create a language that could account for the new sensations of modernity" (Shih 2001). Through reading Japanese and European literature, the Chinese New Sensationists were introduced to the psychological themes of repression, obsession, and eroticism, which allowed them to probe the loneliness, anxiety, and alienation of the city. The impact of cinema and popular music are apparent in the characterization, pacing, and structure of their works. Authors modeled their depictions of modern women on Hollywood film stars and used jazz to set the tempo for their stories (L. Lee 1999: 194–198, 220–223).

New Sensationism began with Liu Na'ou 刘呐鸥 (1900–1939), who had studied literature in Japan and came to Shanghai in the mid-1920s to study French. With the help of classmates Shi Zhecun 施蛰存 (1905–2003) and Dai Wangshu 戴望舒 (1905–1950), Liu published the journal *Trackless Train* (无轨列车, 1928). It introduced Chinese readers to modernist fiction, including translations of the work of the Japanese Shinkankakuha and the French writer Paul Morand, whose writing influenced both Japanese and Chinese New

Sensationists. It also featured fiction by Shi and poems by Dai. After *Trackless Train* was closed by the Nationalist government, the friends collaborated on a second journal, *La Nouvelle Littérature* (新文艺, 1929–1930), which included fiction by Shi and Liu, translations of French poetry by Dai, literary news from around the world, and a story by the young writer Mu Shiying 穆时英 (1912–1940), who was soon to become one of the luminaries of New Sensationism.

Experience gained from working on these publications prepared Shi to edit *Les Contemporains* (现代杂志, 1932–1935), the journal that showcased many of the mature New Sensationist works. It also introduced Chinese readers to the best contemporary Chinese literature, offered a wide selection of foreign literature in translation, and provided news of literary developments abroad. Unlike other journals of the day, *Les Contemporains* maintained an apolitical editorial position, and this neutrality attracted contributors from across the political spectrum. With a wide circulation, it introduced thousands of readers to modernist literature from China and around the world.

Two examples of New Sensationist fiction, an early work by Shi Zhecun and a later story by Mu Shiying, both focus on the seductive and repellent sides of the city. Shi's "One Evening in the Rainy Season" (梅雨之夕, 1929), a portrait of "urban eroticism," reveals the meandering of the narrator's imagination as he struggles with pent-up desire and the guilt it elicits (Y. Zhang 1996: 173). The story's straightforward plot (returning from work, a man encounters an attractive young woman whom he then escorts home before continuing on his way) is made more complex by using interior monologue to describe the narrator's thoughts in detail. The story begins with a vivid, sensory-rich description of Shanghai on a rainy evening. The narrator then meets a young woman stranded in the rain. He watches her for some time, imagining her thoughts and debating in his mind whether he should invite her to share his umbrella. After he issues an invitation and she accepts it, they walk along the street together. The narrator fantasizes that she is his first girlfriend, a woman he has not met in seven years and whom he believes he still loves. When she nears her destination and bids him farewell, his mind races to find a way to delay their parting. The narrator's barely concealed desire for the woman also stimulates his own guilt, which manifests itself in hallucinatory images of his wife, first in the face of a shopkeeper and then in the young woman herself. His initial attraction to and later repulsion from the woman symbolize the New Sensationists' attraction to and repulsion from Shanghai.

Whereas Shi explores the flights of imagination of a single character, in "Five in a Nightclub" (夜总会里的五个人, 1933), Mu Shiying focuses on a group of characters who struggle against the fast pace of city life. In Shi's story, the city retains a measure of beauty and glamour as it appears filtered through the spring rain. In Mu's work, however, the intoxicating nocturnal world of Shanghai, the "Heaven built on Hell," becomes a vortex that threatens to destroy the self-indulgent urbanites who populate it (Li 1988: 177). The opening section of the story offers a series of short scenes describing setbacks suffered by each of the five major characters that afternoon: a tycoon loses his fortune; a student is jilted by his girlfriend; a socialite discovers she has lost her youth; a scholar questions the significance of his work; a senior city clerk is unexpectedly fired from his job. A second section set that same evening captures the city in motion and sets the pace for the story. In this world rich in images of sight and sound, revolving glass doors become crystal pillars, automobiles rush onward, crowds of people become schools of fish, and all is bathed in the glow of myriad neon lights.

Mu (1992: 9) introduces the fundamental rhythm of the city and this story when he notes, "The world of Saturday night is a cartoon globe spinning on the axis of jazz." Jazz music, an essential part of Mu's "urban nocturnal landscape," leads the reader into and sets the pace of action for the third and longest section of the story, in which the five characters show up at a nightclub (L. Lee 1999: 141). The narrative cuts quickly from one character to another as they enter and leave the dance floor. They struggle but ultimately fail to make the pace of their personal lives match up with that of the city, as set by the blaring jazz music. The drummer for the club's band cannot get time off to be with his wife, who is about to give birth. Through a series of phone calls, he learns that she has gone into labor, given birth to a stillborn child, fainted, and died. The role of the drummer—the setter and keeper of time in both the music and the story—is vital: he cannot leave. His attempts to cheer up the nightclub's guests, as well as himself, through frenzied dancing and fast-tempo drumming fail to dispel the gloom of the characters, who are ironically referred to as "Five Happy People" in the title of this section. Time, signified by the jazz, the drumming, and the dancing, "beats a soft but steady tread into the heart[s]" of the characters (Mu 1992: 19–20). They share an inability to keep up with the city's time or gauge it correctly. The socialite is past her time, the tycoon missed the right time to sell his gold, and the student was too late to win his girl. The punctual and perfect senior clerk failed to anticipate his termination, and the scholar confronts the dilemma of the time-dependent concepts of being and existence. As the story concludes, the tycoon commits suicide in order to free himself from the fast pace of urban life and pressures of time. The story exemplifies the New Sensationists' ambivalent view of the city as both exciting and exhausting.

Although most often associated with experiments in fiction, the New Sensationists also included the pioneer modernist poet Dai Wangshu. Dai sought to describe sensations and depict the workings of the imagination and desire in his poetry much as Shi did in his stories. However, he only occasionally featured the city in his works and drew frequently on his knowledge of classical Chinese literature, something the fiction writers seldom did. "Rainy Alley" (雨巷, 1928) describes the poet-subject's seeing and then walking past a "lilac-like" woman in a lonely alley on a rainy evening, an image reminiscent of Shi Zhecun's story. The reference to lilacs suggests sadness and reveals Dai's knowledge of French symbolism and the work of Frances Jammes, whose poetry he had translated (G. Lee 1989: 144–148). It also shows his familiarity with traditional Chinese poetry and the work of Li Jing 李璟 (916–961) and Li Shangyin 李商隐 (813–858), who also referred to lilacs (G. Lee 1989: 148–150). Like Shi and Mu, Dai focuses on sensory imagery, including the lilac color and fragrance of the woman. Like Shi's narrator, Dai's poet-subject offers a rich psychological description of the perceived emotions of the woman: her resentment, melancholy, uncertainty, and apathy. The depiction of the dreamlike state of the poet-subject and his barely suppressed desires in the latter half of the poem are typical of the psychological probing of New Sensationist fiction. That the woman shares the poet-subject's own emotions and his dreamlike state and that he "hopes" to meet her suggest that she may be a projection of his imagination. In light of the poem's circular structure, wherein the poem ends as it begins, the work can be read as a meditation on poetry itself. The rainy alley "is a symbol of the poetic imagination," and the woman represents the fickle inspiration for the poet's work—his muse—whom he hopes to reencounter (Yeh 1991: 98). "Rainy Alley" exemplifies Dai's ability to draw on Chinese and Western literature to create original poetry in a modernist mode.

The flow of New Sensationist literature slowed significantly in the mid-1930s, and the group ultimately disbanded as a result of political critiques and the threat of war with Japan. Shi Zhecun abandoned his experimental writing because of criticism from the League of Left-Wing Writers. Trapped between leftist polemics, Nationalist censorship, and financial pressures from his publishers, he gave up his position as editor of *Les Contemporains* in 1934 (L. Lee 1999: 148–149). Both Liu Na'ou and Mu Shiying turned to editing and criticism and abandoned modernist fiction by the mid-1930s. The threat of war with Japan in the mid-1930s led to calls from both the left and the right for engaged, patriotic writing known as "national defense literature" (国防文学). With paper shortages and the destruction of printing plants due to the outbreak of war in 1937, modernist periodicals closed. By 1940 Shi had taken up the study of classical Chinese literature. Both Liu and Mu were dead. Dai had shifted his creative energies to translation in the mid-1930s and then moved to Hong Kong in 1938. There he edited several literary journals and supplements and published nationalistic and patriotic poetry. In 1949 he returned to China, where he died the following year.

In the early 1940s, modernist experimentation resumed briefly in Japanese-occupied Shanghai with the creative writing of Eileen Chang 张爱玲. Chang's short fiction and essays, like those of the New Sensationists, described Shanghai through sensory images. Like her predecessors, Chang depicted both the excitement and the strain of urban life. Yet she brought to modernist writing a probing exploration of everyday city life at a slower pace that contrasts with the glitz and fast rhythm of Mu Shiying's nightclubs and dance halls (L. Lee

1999: 270–271). Chang set many of her essays and stories in homes and apartments and analyzed the development of male-female relationships in these domestic spaces. She became one of the most popular and critically acclaimed exponents of urban modernist literature in China.

Just as the New Sensationists did in the 1930s, writers in Taiwan and China in the past five decades have used modernism to create space for literary experimentation. In Taiwan in the 1950s, Ji Xian 纪弦, a former associate of Dai Wangshu's, helped organize a revival of modernist poetry. The founding of literary associations, journals, contests, and publishing houses gave rise to a thriving, unofficial literary scene separate from the Nationalist government's promotion of anti-Communist literature. The journal *Modern Literature* (现代文学, 1960–1973) introduced the fiction of young writers such as Bai Xianyong 白先勇, Chen Ruoxi 陈若曦, Chen Yingzhen 陈映真, and Wang Wenxing 王文兴 and published translations of modernist literature from Europe and America. Available in Taiwan since the 1950s, Eileen Chang's fiction, with its focus on everyday life, domestic settings, and male-female relationships, has influenced such writers as Bai Xianyong, Wang Zhenhe 王祯和, and Yuan Qiongqiong 袁琼琼 (see also "Cold War Fiction from Taiwan and the Modernists").

With political liberalization in the People's Republic of China during the 1980s, writers there gained access to literature from overseas, including modernist literature from Europe, the Americas, and Japan as well as the fiction and poetry of the Taiwan modernists. Modernism contributed to the development of Misty poetry that emerged in the pages of *Today* (今天, 1978–1980). Avant-garde fiction writers, including Can Xue 残雪, Mo Yan 莫言, Su Tong 苏童, and Yu Hua 余华, experimented with decadence and desire in their stories and novels. Although modernist writing expanded the bounds of literature, it was also attacked by campaigns against "spiritual pollution" and "bourgeois liberalism" for what the government deemed to be its detachment from everyday life and its non-Chinese origins.

The recent modernist literatures of Taiwan and China have surpassed the New Sensationists in their sophisticated treatment of desire and repression and in their experiments with stream of consciousness and other linguistic and narrative innovations. However, like their predecessors, contemporary writers have also captured the sights and sounds unique to urban locales and have created new space for writing in spite of official literary policies and campaigns. Given the centrality of the unique cultural milieu of Shanghai in the 1930s and 1940s to the works of Shi Zhecun, Mu Shiying, and Eileen Chang, we should not be surprised that new modernist literature produced in urban settings with unique political climates had its own distinctive characteristics. New literature from the metropolitan cities of Hong Kong, Taipei, and Shanghai will bear traces of each locale's particular nexus of cultural forces and will expand the literary developments begun by the New Sensationists.

Bibliography

Braester, Yomi. "Shanghai's Economy of Spectacle: The Shanghai Race Club in Liu Na'ou's and Mu Shiying's Stories." *Modern Chinese Literature* 9, 1 (1995): 39–58.

Lee, Gregory. *Dai Wangshu: The Life and Poetry of a Chinese Modernist*. Hong Kong: Chinese University Press, 1989.

Lee, Leo Ou-fan. *Shanghai Modern: The Flowering of a New Urban Culture in China, 1930–1945*. Cambridge, MA: Harvard University Press, 1999.

Li Oufan. 李欧梵. "Zhongguo xiandai wenxuezhong de 'tuifei' ji qi zuojia" 中国现代文学中的"颓废"及其作家 ("Decadence" and decadent writers in modern Chinese literature). *Dangdai* 93 (1994): 22–47.

——— 李欧梵, ed. *Xinganjue pai xiaoshuo xuan* 新感觉派小说选 (Selected New Sensationist fiction). Taipei: Yunchen, 1988.

Liu, Jianmei. "Shanghai Variations on 'Revolution Plus Love.'" *Modern Chinese Literature and Culture* 14, 1 (Spring 2002): 51–92.

Macdonald, Sean. "The Shanghai Foxtrot—a Fragment by Mu Shiying." *Modernism/Modernity* 11, 4 (November 2004): 797–807.

McGrath, Jason. "Patching the Void: Subjectivity and Anamorphic Bewitchment in Shi Zhecun's Fiction." *Journal of Modern Literature in Chinese* 4, 2 (2001): 1–30.

Mu, Shiying. "Five in a Nightclub." Trans. Randolph Trumbull. *Renditions* 37 (1992): 5–22.

———. *Mu Shiying: China's Lost Modernist*. Trans. Andrew David Field. Hong Kong: Hong Kong University Press, 2014.

Rosenmeier, Christopher. "The Subversion of Modernity and Socialism in Mu Shiying's Early Fiction." *Frontiers of Literary Studies in China* 7, 1 (2013): 1–22.

———. "Women Stereotypes in Shi Zhecun's Short Stories." *Modern China* 37, 1 (January 2011): 44–68.

Shi, Zhecun. "One Evening in the Rainy Season." Trans. Gregory Lee. In Joseph S. M. Lau and Howard Goldblatt, eds., *Columbia Anthology of Modern Chinese Literature*, 2nd ed. New York: Columbia University Press, 2007.

Shih, Shu-mei. *The Lure of the Modern: Writing Modernism in Semicolonial China, 1917–1937*. Berkeley: University of California Press, 2001.

Wang, Yiyan. "Venturing into Shanghai: The Flâneur in Two of Shi Zhecun's Stories." *Modern Chinese Literature and Culture* 19, 2 (Fall 2007): 34–70.

Yan Jiayan 严家炎, ed. *Xinganjue pai xiaoshuo xuan* 新感觉派小说选 (Selected New Sensationist fiction). Beijing: Renmin wenxue, 1985.

Yeh, Michelle. *Modern Chinese Poetry: Theory and Practice since 1917*. New Haven, CT: Yale University Press, 1991.

Zhang, Jingyuan. *Psychoanalysis in China: Literary Transformations, 1919–1949*. Ithaca, NY: Cornell University Press, 1992.

Zhang, Yingjin. *The City in Modern Chinese Literature and Film: Configurations of Space, Time, and Gender*. Stanford, CA: Stanford University Press, 1996.

———. "Mu Shiying." In Thomas Moran, ed., *Dictionary of Literary Biography—Chinese Fiction Writers, 1900–1949*, 178–182. New York: Thomson Gale, 2007.

22

SHEN CONGWEN AND IMAGINED NATIVE COMMUNITIES

JEFFREY KINKLEY

Shen Congwen 沈从文 (1902–1988), whose works open a window on modern Chinese rural idealism, was one of the great Chinese writers of the first half of the twentieth century. Proscribed by mainland China and Taiwan after 1949 until both liberalized in the 1980s and exalted him as an independent writer, he was a reminder of how much had been lost of China's earlier cultural modernity. Revisionist critics in the People's Republic recast Shen Congwen as an eminent Other of revolutionary writing: a non-Lu Xun 鲁迅, neither socialist nor realist, treading his own anti-Confucian, pro-Western, yet nonurban and apolitical path. Taiwan, long open to the West but not to writers like Shen who remained on the mainland, reenvisioned him as a great modern "native" writer—rustic, non-Communist—*not* so Westernized. From 1982 until his death, Shen Congwen was in the running for a Nobel Prize in literature, though he had abandoned creative writing after attempting suicide in 1949. Having studiously avoided political front groups for writers before the revolution, under communism he found a new career in the less turbulent field of art history.

Shen Congwen as a writer favored craft, experimentation, and Western modernism, but the public loved his reimagining of China as a preindustrial moral community offering not the modern solaces of nation, race, or strength in unity, but the familiar comforts of home and local diversity of custom. Calling himself a country boy and recorder of life, Shen developed a tradition of impressionistically documenting local places and their culture that came to be conceptualized as *xiangtu* (乡土, native-soil, local, nativist, rural-native; cf. German *Heimat*). But many of his works blended that with a visionary cultural revivalism. It applied literary modernism to a far less "earthbound" Chinese tradition—that of frontier exoticism, primalism, and spirit journeys.

As a documenter of his native West Hunan 湘西, Shen Congwen brought the craft of the traditional literati-poet, gazetteerist, and travel writer into the twentieth century by using the colloquial language of the literary revolution. Avoiding set phrases for describing scenery and emotions and eschewing the rhythms of classical Chinese, he employed modern and often idiosyncratic grammar. Meanwhile he exploited the unique lexical resources of classical Chinese, whose building blocks were not words but a much vaster galaxy of morphemes (Chinese characters). The result was a very literary vernacular lyricism.

West Hunan was a mountainous internal frontier without many cities, literati, passable roads, or trappings of high culture. During the disorders of the early Republic, local warlords kept it autonomous from China and even the rest of Hunan. Southwestern non-Han "tribespeople," mostly Tujia (土家) and Miao (苗, Méo, Hmong), lived in the hills. Shen's forebears were military officers who intermarried with them. The crossing of that local equivalent of a color line was hidden from Shen Congwen in his youth, but ethnic-minority folklore, martial arts, and religion tinged the whole regional culture. He identified with his native region particularly after entering the local armies in adolescence and becoming personal clerk to Chen Quzhen 陈渠珍, the warlord of West Hunan from 1921 to 1935. Shen started to chronicle the demise of his region in *Long River* (长河, 1943). Had he completed the two sequels he intended to add to the single volume he published, the work might have been China's first sectionalist epic until the advent of the Taiwan independence writers (see "Nativism and Localism in Taiwanese Literature").

When he left West Hunan in 1923, Shen adopted Beijing as his home and hoped to become a new-style intellectual dedicated to social change and the new thought from Japan and the West. Homesick and living in genteel poverty at the margins of the old capital's student subculture, he discovered a literary atmosphere that favored dialect, folklore, and cultural diversity and enabled him to satisfy national curiosity about his "barbarous" region while writing to reform, de-Confucianize, and revitalize China. The initial result was short sketches and plays rich in vignettes of local custom, such as "Snow" (雪, 1927) and "The Celestial God" (霄神, 1925?). He wrote to show urban intellectuals the uncouthness and camaraderie of life in the warlord armies in "My Education" (我的教育, 1929). In "Ah Jin" (阿金, 1928) and "Long Zhu" (龙朱, 1929), he wove tales from legends and customs of the hill tribes. Their free-loving ways at festival gatherings, where boy met girl through alternating songs like those in "Songs of the Zhen'gan Folk" (筸人谣曲, 1926), fascinated Chinese urbanites enjoying their own sexual revolution.

The term "*xiangtu*" is said to have been first applied to Lu Xun's work in 1926. Shen credited Lu Xun's "Village Opera" (社戏, 1922) and Fei Ming 废名 (Feng Wenbing 冯文炳, 1901–1967) with teaching him how to write about country life; he also esteemed Wang Luyan 王鲁彦 (1901–1944). In an influential compendium of modern Chinese literature, Lu Xun deployed the term *xiangtu* in praise of regional works by recently urbanized writers such as Jian Xian'ai 蹇先艾 (1906–1994) of Guizhou. Peasants, rural themes, and even local color were a subsidiary concern of China's new literature until social science interest in peasants and rural reconstruction picked up in the 1930s, followed by the Communist movement to promote literature of, for, and eventually by "workers, peasants, and soldiers." Peasants made many intellectuals think solipsistically of their own elevated social status and mission.

In 1979 the newly exonerated former rightist writer Liu Shaotang 刘绍棠 (1936–1997) raised the banner of *xiangtu* literature. He admitted to inspiration from Taiwan, where the term had been hotly debated since the 1960s; on the mainland, Marxist-Leninist concepts had long overshadowed discourses of Lu Xun's era, although a textbook by Wang Yao 王瑶 (1914–1989) preserved the *xiangtu* concept. Because much Communist literature was already set in the countryside, featured peasants, and used dialect (typically northern), with Hao Ran's 浩然 (1932–2008) epics as the capstone, when Liu Shaotang and his friend Sun Li 孙犁 (1913–2002) sought status as *xiangtu* writers, they evidently meant to be more ruralist than Mao. Many critics considered the *xiangtu* formulation an attack on Western trends, as it had been in Taiwan, and Liu's and Sun's works still to be hackneyed revolutionary "realism," however much they focused on the authors' North China homes.

But both the mainland and Taiwan went on to hail the older, "rediscovered" works of Shen Congwen, and those of Lu Xun (another nostalgic nonnortherner), as model *xiangtu* literature steeped in local cultural sensitivities China had suppressed since 1949. Gu Hua 古华 (b. 1942), Sun Jianzhong 孙健忠 (b. 1938), He Liwei 何立伟 (b. 1954), Xiao Jianguo 肖建国 (b. 1952), Cai Cehai 蔡测海 (b. 1954), and other Hunanese writers took inspiration from Shen. Bai Xianyong 白先勇 (b. 1937), a displaced mainlander living and publishing in Taiwan, also claimed past influence. Shen's pre-1949 protégés were being rediscovered too—Xiao Qian 萧乾 (1910–1999), Wang Zengqi 汪曾祺 (1920–1997), and many poets. Some had written of common folk and colorful local trades, even if in Beijing—but then, Shen Congwen was now hailed as dean of a 1930s "Beijing school" that favored northern academism over "Shanghai school" commercialism, trendiness, and politicization, because in the 1930s he had polemicized against "Shanghai types."

Shen Congwen's classic 1930s stories, rich in mood and finely wrought in plot, language, and symbolism, are mostly about city people, but his most memorable characters are common country folk he wanted to defend from encroachment by outlanders and their commercial, bureaucratic, military, and moral and ritual worldliness. The country folk of *Border Town* (边城, 1934), "The New and the Old" (新与旧, 1935), "Sansan" (三三, 1931), "Guisheng" (贵生, 1937), and "Xiaoxiao" (萧萧, 1930) live quiet, "pastoral" lives amid natural beauty. They have their own rich life of the mind and seldom dwell on their poverty. Indeed, Sansan stands to inherit a mill, and Cuicui (翠翠, "Green Jade," in *Border Town*) a ferry. Guisheng is just a hired laborer, but he has a chance to marry up; he loses that chance only because of superstition. Even the regional backdrop acquires the density of a fictional actor. Although he mixed cultural criticism and nostalgia, often using his region as a foil for humanity's dark side as did Thomas Hardy, Shen Congwen was optimistic about human nature. Xiaoxiao, the powerless child bride of an infant boy, is seduced by an adult farmhand and bears his child (a capital offense), but she survives. Shen's failure to take a class stand and his distance from conventional urban nationalism with its absorption in anti-imperialism or neotraditionalism angered political critics of the day, yet this may explain why he, more than the engagé realists and satirists Zhang Tianyi 张天翼 (1906–1985), Mao Dun 茅盾 (1896–1981), Xiao Hong 萧红 (1911–1942), Zhao Shuli 赵树理 (1906–1970), Gao Xiaosheng 高晓声 (1928–1999), or even Wu Zuxiang 吴组缃 (1908–1994), retrospectively won accolades as a *xiangtu* writer—for Shen seldom wrote of place for its own sake either.

The more exotic tradition Shen Congwen plumbed begins with texts associated with Daoism and the *Chu ci* (楚辞, *The Songs of the South*), attributed to Qu Yuan 屈原 (ca. 343–277 B.C.), in which that Chu poet, misunderstood by his king, communes with shamans and female goddesses on a vision quest in the wondrous southwest of his day (West Hunan, Shen believed). After the Han dynasty fell and the Chinese people migrated south, poets and essayists further celebrated its exotic biota, landscapes, and customs, as did officials exiled there, like Shen's soldier-scholar hero Wang Yangming 王阳明 (1472–1529). A search for personal meaning in the southwest animates Han Shaogong's 韩少功 (b. 1953) "Homecoming" (归去来, 1985) and Gao Xingjian's 高行健 (b. 1940) *Soul Mountain* (灵山, 1990), which helped win that author the 2000 Nobel Prize in Literature. Preceding them were "manias" for Chinese culture, the Chinese West, ancient Chu (楚; by some calculations today's Hunan-Hubei), and a search for the "roots" of Chinese literature; in "Pa Pa Pa" (爸爸爸, 1985), Han Shaogong sought roots in West Hunan. Shen Congwen's achievement is another way station between Qu Yuan and Gao Xingjian. He assuredly influenced roots-seekers Han Shaogong, Han's colleagues A Cheng 阿城 (b. 1949) and Jia Pingwa 贾平凹 (b. 1952), and Wang Zengqi, who is also said to have inspired the roots movement.

The modern upward revaluation of China's frontier peoples, cultures, and lore is seen in the histories of Gu Jiegang 顾颉刚 (1893–1980), who theorized that China's diverse regional cultures took their distinctiveness from border peoples, and Fan Wenlan 范文澜 (1891–1969), who stimulated speculation about the role of the Miao in ancient Chu culture. Shen Congwen created beautiful modern myths about southwestern tribespeople in a similar spirit: his aboriginals bear a vital and unspoiled primal culture that the Han once possessed but lost through Confucian bureaucratism, puritanism, and urban worldliness. If his characters look like noble savages, Shen's concern was Social Darwinist—namely, that China, owing more to cultural than racial-national enervation, had lost the strength to survive in the modern world. Southwestern mores implicitly reprove Han high culture in "Seven Barbarians and the Last Spring Festival" (七个野人与最后一个迎春节, 1929). Bai Hua's 白桦 (b. 1930) *Remote Country of Women* (远方有个女儿国, 1988) echoes that theme.

China's spiritual and existential literary explorations in the late twentieth century recapitulated those of Shen Congwen and other modernists, much as the 1980s cult of "subjectivity" (主体) repeated the earlier generation's discovery of the self. Shen split himself and an imaginary female companion into conscious and subconscious personalities to explore desire, memory, and illusions of reality in "Gazing at Rainbows" (看虹录, 1941). In "Water and Clouds" (水云, 1943), a psychological autobiography contemplating how libido had shaped his romantic life and works, he cleaved his soul into mutually questioning narrative voices: ego, alter ego, and superego (cf. Zhang Xianliang's 张贤亮 [1936–2014] *Getting Used to Dying* [习惯死亡, 1989]). Shen's spiritual and philosophical quests converged with his southwestern regionalism in unfinished story cycles of the 1940s, which include "Qiaoxiu and Dongsheng" (巧秀和冬生, 1947) and the Seven-Color Nightmares—generically unclassifiable autobiographical meditations beginning with *Green Nightmare* (绿魇, 1944). In 1948 Shen Congwen felt he could not go on writing.

Noted for their style are *Recollections of West Hunan* (湘行散记, 1934) and *West Hunan* (湘西, 1938). They probe the meaning of Shen's regional roots in episodic travelogue form. *Border Town*, which analyzes the emotional and sexual awakening of a pubescent orphan girl, is his masterpiece in fiction. The limpid prose sculpting the novella's pastoral setting is a palimpsest for Freudian images. Regional ethos is evoked by local cultural images, but their meaning, like the alternative futures the heroine imagines, lies subconscious until fate brings on a tragedy. For all its local color, the novella sublimates *xiangtu* concreteness into a timeless myth.

Bibliography

Bai, Hua. *The Remote Country of Women*. Trans. Qingyun Wu and Thomas O. Beebee. Honolulu: University of Hawai'i Press, 1994.

Feuerwerker, Yi-tsi Mei. *Ideology, Power, Text: Self-Representation and the Peasant "Other" in Modern Chinese Literature*. Stanford, CA: Stanford University Press, 1998.

Han, Shaogong. *Homecoming and Other Stories*. Trans. Martha Cheung. Hong Kong: Renditions, 1992.

Hsia, C. T. *A History of Modern Chinese Fiction*. 3rd ed. Bloomington: Indiana University Press, 1999 [1961, 1971].

Kinkley, Jeffrey C. *The Odyssey of Shen Congwen*. Stanford, CA: Stanford University Press, 1987.

Ling Yu 凌宇. *Shen Congwen zhuan* 沈从文传 (Biography of Shen Congwen). Beijing: Shiyue wenyi, 1988.

Liu Hongtao 刘洪涛. *Hunan xiangtu wenxue yu Xiang Chu wenhua* 湖南乡土文学与湘楚文化 (Hunan nativist literature and the Chu culture of the Hunan region). Changsha: Hunan jiaoyu, 1997.

Liu Shaotang 刘绍棠. *Xiangtu wenxue sishi nian* 乡土文学四十年 (Forty years of nativist literature). Beijing: Wenhua yishu, 1990.

Peng, Hsiao-yen. *Antithesis Overcome: Shen Congwen's Avant-Gardism and Primitivism*. Taipei: Institute of Chinese Literature and Philosophy, Academia Sinica, 1994.

Shen, Congwen. *Border Town*. Trans. Jeffrey C. Kinkley. New York: HarperCollins, 2009.

———. *The Chinese Earth: Stories by Shen Ts'ung-wen*. Trans. Ching Ti and Robert Payne. New York: Columbia University Press, 1982.

———. *Genesis of a Revolution*. Trans. Stanley R. Munro. Singapore: Heinemann Asia, 1979.

———. *Imperfect Paradise: Stories by Shen Congwen*. Ed. Jeffrey Kinkley. Honolulu: University of Hawai'i Press, 1995.

———. *L'Eau et les nuages* (Water and clouds). Trans. Isabelle Rabut. Paris: Bleu de Chine, 1996.

———. *Recollections of West Hunan*. Trans. Gladys Yang. Beijing: Panda Books, 1982.

———. *Shen Congwen quan ji* 沈从文全集 (The complete works of Shen Congwen). 32 vols. Taiyuan: Beiyue wenyi, 2002.

———. *Shen Congwen wen ji* 沈从文文集 (The works of Shen Congwen). Ed. Shao Huaqiang 邵华强 and Ling Yu 凌宇. 15 vols. Hong Kong and Guangzhou: Sanlian and Huacheng, 1982–1985.

Wang, David Der-wei. *Fictional Realism in Twentieth-Century China: Mao Dun, Lao She, Shen Congwen*. New York: Columbia University Press, 1992.

———. *The Lyrical in Epic Time: Modern Chinese Intellectuals and Artists Through the 1949 Crisis*. New York: Columbia University Press, 2015.

Wang Runhua 王润华 (Wong Yoon Wah). *Shen Congwen xiaoshuo xinlun* 沈从文小说新论 (New perspectives on the fiction of Shen Congwen). Shanghai: Xuelin, 1998.

Wang, Xiaojue. *Modernity with a Cold War Face: Reimagining the Nation in Chinese Literature Across the 1949 Divide*. Cambridge, MA: Harvard University Asia Center, 2013.

Xiang Chengguo 向成国. *Huigui ziran yu zhuixun lishi: Shen Congwen yu Xiangxi* 回归自然与追寻历史：沈从文与湘西 (Return to nature and quest for history: Shen Congwen and West Hunan). Changsha: Hunan Shifan Daxue, 1997.

Zhang, Xianliang. *Getting Used to Dying*. Trans. Martha Avery. New York: HarperCollins, 1991.

23

XIAO HONG'S *FIELD OF LIFE AND DEATH*

AMY D. DOOLING

Few twentieth-century Chinese women writers have attained the canonical stature Xiao Hong 萧红 (Zhang Naiying 张乃莹, 1911–1942) now enjoys. Almost all her fiction, including two novels and numerous short stories and a major autobiographical work, have been translated into English, and she is currently one of only two modern woman writers whose life and writing have been extensively examined in English-language scholarship. Beyond her literary legacy, Xiao Hong's tumultuous personal life—from her strained family relationships and romantic entanglements to her tragic early death—have been the subject of enduring public fascination. Most recently, a feature-length film about the author's life was released in 2013, in commemoration of the centennial anniversary of her birth.

Field of Life and Death (生死场, 1934) was Xiao Hong's debut novel, written in Qingdao, where she and her lover, Xiao Jun 萧军, another young soon-to-be literary celebrity, had sought refuge from the Japanese occupation of their native Manchuria before moving on to Shanghai. Originally titled *The Wheat Field* 麦场, two installments of the work were serialized under the pen name Qiao Yin 悄吟 in the spring of 1934 in a Harbin newspaper. In 1935, after being rejected by the Literary Censorship Committee of the Central Propaganda Bureau, it was published in Lu Xun's semiunderground Slave Series (奴隶丛书), the third (and last) volume in the series that had also featured works by Ye Zi 叶紫 and Xiao Jun. Whether Lu Xun went so far as to personally finance the publication of Xiao Hong's novel is unknown, but there can be little doubt that his patronage was instrumental in the success the work was soon to have. Having taken the two Xiaos under his wing upon their arrival in Shanghai, he had already introduced the couple to intellectual luminaries such as Mao Dun 茅盾 and Hu Feng 胡风 and had helped Xiao Hong place several essays in journals such as *Wenxue* (文学) and *Taibai* (太白). He now personally endorsed her novel by writing its preface and recommending it to friends and colleagues. *Field of Life and Death*, as it was renamed at Hu Feng's suggestion, brought Xiao Hong overnight fame in Shanghai's literary world; despite Guomindang censorship, the novel underwent six consecutive printings within a year and continues to be regarded as one of the masterpieces of modern Chinese fiction.

Set in the Manchurian countryside on the eve of the war against Japan, *Field* owed much of its initial success to its timely treatment of subject matter that weighed heavily on the minds of the 1930s cultural left—namely, rural realities and the problem of national salvation. Qu Qiubai 瞿秋白 and others affiliated with the League of Left-Wing Writers had grown disenchanted with what they now saw as the elitism of May Fourth romanticism, and they called for a revolutionary literature attuned to the plight of China's collective masses (Anderson 1990). Xiao Hong's novel resonated with these concerns, and Xiao Hong herself, recently dislocated by the war, was hailed as an exemplar of this alternative literary voice. Xiao abandons the classical realist conventions of a tightly woven plot driven by individual protagonists, opting for a more fractured presentation of the peasant condition. Through a series of loosely related episodic vignettes involving locals such as Two-and-a-Half Li 二里半 and Mother Wang 王婆, she presents a montage of rural society mired in poverty, disease, and injustice. It is a profoundly unsettling vision: juxtaposed with unsentimental scenes of the desperation and drudgery of peasant life are lyrical glimpses of the regional landscape that bear a certain resemblance to the "nativist" (乡土) tradition of Shen Congwen 沈从文. With these jarring narrative shifts, the author accentuates the discordant relationship between the peasants and the land on which they labor.

If the novel dwells on the material hardships of the countryside, the subaltern figure inhabiting this fraught terrain cannot be understood in terms of economic oppression alone. As she does in much of her work, Xiao Hong brings a profoundly gendered consciousness to her account (Meng and Dai 1989; Lieberman 1998; Dooling 2005; Yan 2006). Rural men and women alike struggle under the numbing tyranny of poverty and deprivation, but women suffer the additional strain of male brutality. Over the course of the novel, we are confronted with graphic scenes that include the violent demise of an unwanted newborn daughter, a drunk who beats his wife during an agonizing childbirth, and the gruesome neglect of an invalid wife. In the final chapters, when Japanese soldiers are decimating the village, the rape of Golden Bough 金枝 by a Chinese compatriot in Harbin is a poignant reminder that women are subject to distinct forms of domination beyond those of their dispossessed class or nation.

Inevitably, however, given the heightened anxieties and patriotic fervor in the wake of the Mukden Incident of 1931, it was not Xiao Hong's sensitive representation of patriarchy but the theme of nationalist awakening as it emerges toward the end of her novel that contemporary critics privileged in their readings. Lu Xun, who stirred fresh memories of the bombing of Shanghai (1932) in his preface, promised readers that the novel would imbue them with "the strength to persevere and resist," while Hu Feng, who wrote the epilogue, lauded the work for its depiction of "a persecuted people in a pillaged land." For her part, Xiao Hong would remain aloof from the contentious literary politics of the years following the novel's publication (to the dismay of many critics), but she would never quite shake the legacy she acquired from this novel as a prescient voice of Chinese national resistance.

The nationalist significance of *Field* persists as the core issue around which contemporary commentators have focused their attention, though recent interpretations have shifted from acclaiming its patriotic spirit to analysis of how the text has been historically misread as an allegory of anti-imperialist struggle. In the view of Howard Goldblatt (1976: 123), the American scholar who resuscitated Xiao Hong's oeuvre in the 1970s, the novel is "seriously impaired by its forced anti-Japanese ending," a flaw he attributes to Xiao Hong's limited grasp of the circumstances engulfing Northeast China and to Xiao Jun's (alleged) influence over her writing at this stage in her career. Lydia Liu (1994), in a compelling feminist reading of the work, suggests that *Field* articulates an "ambivalent" nationalism through its unswerving scrutiny on the female body. Repudiating its canonical label as a patriotic novel, Liu contends that the life cycle of individual women, not the rise and fall of the nation, occupies the work's central concern. Thus, whereas the Japanese invasion is shown to mobilize new forms of national identity in male characters—even in villagers as apathetic as Two-and-a-Half Li—Xiao Hong reveals that for women the experience of male sexual violence can complicate an affective allegiance to the "homeland."

Insofar as Xiao Hong does little to foreshadow the theme of anti-Japanese resistance early in the narrative, it is not difficult to appreciate why the final scenes have been interpreted as either contrived or ironic. The first reference to the foreign threat looming along China's borders does not occur until chapter 11, when, without warning, "a flag never before seen by the villagers was raised" (1979: 73). Taken in the context of Xiao Hong's overall representation of the rural condition, however, the novel's resolution may not be so incongruous after all. To begin with, unlike many writers of the 1930s and 1940s, Xiao Hong is clearly not interested in enshrining the peasant as savior of China's historical predicament. Whether delineating the class awakening of the peasantry amid rural economic devastation (Mao Dun's "Spring Silkworms" [春蚕]), natural disaster (Ding Ling's "Flood" 水), or foreign incursion (Xiao Jun's *Village in August* [八月的乡村]), new narrative paradigms of Chinese fiction of this period reflected an emerging leftist discourse on the "masses" that invested the figure of the peasant (and worker) with extraordinary historical agency. In sharp contrast, Xiao Hong evokes a grim world of seemingly unceasing misery, hardly a breeding ground for the earthy heroism and solidarity celebrated by her contemporaries. Her novel does depict historical change, though change that issues not from the peasants themselves but violently from the outside.

Indeed, the bulk of the text explores the peasantry not as subjects of the national narrative but as marginal to that history, conditioned by rural realities that all but stifle a collective political consciousness and will. Most notable in this regard is Xiao Hong's extensive use of natural symbolism. Rather than visually evoke the regional landscape, Xiao Hung depicts animals and insects on the same narrative level as humanity itself, as if to challenge conventional distinctions between humankind and nature and to underscore the brute existence all living creatures endure. Consider, for example, the description of Mother Wang's mare:

> When there was work to be done, it worked with resignation. When ropes and chains were fastened onto its body, it obeyed its master's whip. The master's whip rarely fell on its body. But sometimes, when it was too exhausted and could not go on, its steps would slow down, and the master would beat it with a whip or with something else. Yet it would not rear wildly, because its future had already been determined by all the past generations.
>
> (Xiao Hong 1979: 16)

Like the old workhorse, the peasants who inhabit the novel have meekly surrendered to the harsh circumstances around them and evince little consciousness that things could be different. Life proceeds on the most elemental level, driven by basic physical needs (hunger, desire, and self-preservation). The narrator comments dispassionately: "In the village, one remained forever unaware. One could never experience the spiritual side of life; only the material aspects gave these people sustenance" (Xiao Hong 1979: 37).

Contributing to Xiao Hong's vision is her skillful manipulation of cyclical imagery: recurring references to the passing seasons, agricultural routines, the movement from day to night, and procreation. Time in the rural village is not the progressive, linear chronology of history but is a time suspended in a relentless natural rhythm. Her point is not that peasants lack the human capacity to protest their lot or to express joy or compassion, but that the continual grind of daily survival takes precedence. When Mother Wang and Fifth Sister 五姑姑 find the former town beauty, Yueying 月英, on the verge of death, her paralyzed body infested with maggots, they do not balk at providing her the comfort she so desperately craves. Yet in a world consumed with eking out a meager existence, the narrative does not linger on this poignant moment: "Three days later Yueying's coffin was borne swiftly over the desolate hill to be buried at the foot of the slope. The dead were dead, and the living still had to plan how to stay alive. In winter the women made ready the summer clothes; the men started scheduling the next year's crops" (Xiao Hong 1979: 41).

By immersing the reader within the circumscribed world of a peasant constituency and not simply furnishing the patronizing "cold glances from above" that Lu Xun deplored (Anderson 1990: 189), the text offers a sensitive analysis of this pivotal moment in modern Chinese history. For the pressing questions it poses are these: How can historically oppressed subjects surmount the material and mental circumstances that pin them down in order to break free from an entrenched cycle of poverty, sexual violence, and habitual apathy? And under what circumstances can an entity as inert and unconscious as the Chinese peasantry be transformed into a force of positive change?

One somewhat paradoxical answer the novel suggests is that war itself—and the destruction it spells for the village—may provide just such a catalyst for social transformation. Whereas in the conventional revolutionary bildungsroman, peasant (or worker) resistance materializes from either an innate insurgent spirit or gradual processes of education and collectivity, here the quiet misery of the insulated rural community is at first barely shaken by the horrors inflicted by the Japanese. The occupation accelerates the rate of death beyond peasant expectations as the Japanese routinely massacre and torture the local population. Despite the mounting piles of corpses and incidences of atrocity, however, most of the peasants are not immediately stirred to action or revolt. Yet, the violent disruption of age-old habits eventually forces open alternative patterns of human behavior from which new forms of consciousness might emerge. For example, whereas early in the novel the past is described as "a dead tree that can never be revived" (Xiao Hong 1979: 19), by the end memory begins to serve as a source of hope and resistance. The moment of resistance, in other words, simultaneously marks the beginning of a new kind of history for peasants: the past looked back upon nostalgically. Yet at the same time, the "patriotic awakening" that occurs in the village at the end of the novel is hardly romanticized. In contrast to the brigade of heroic peasant-guerillas in novels like Xiao Jun's *Village in August*, Xiao Hong's characters possess little more than a rudimentary understanding of the broader national implications of the struggle in which they are to become involved. More important, what still moves them to action is not lofty patriotic conviction (despite their undigested political rhetoric) but more basic concerns about material survival. Indeed, the looming image of barren wheat fields—where not even a few scattered kernels of grains can be scrounged—dominating the final pages reminds us what this is really all about. National liberation, in other words, is imbued with a radically different meaning: it is not a noble struggle to protect native soil or to safeguard traditional Chinese life; rather, for Xiao Hong it represents a historical opportunity to break the brutal cycle of contemporary existence itself.

Bibliography

Anderson, Marston. *The Limits of Realism: Chinese Fiction in the Revolutionary Period*. Berkeley, CA: University of California Press, 1990.

Dooling, Amy D. *Women's Literary Feminism in Twentieth-Century China*. New York: Palgrave Macmillan, 2005.

Goldblatt, Howard. *Hsiao Hong*. Boston: Twayne, 1976.

Huang, Nicole. "Xiao Hong." In Thomas Moran, ed., *Dictionary of Literary Biography—Chinese Fiction Writers, 1900–1949*, 241–249. New York: Thomson Gale, 2007.

Lieberman, Sally Taylor. *The Mother and Narrative Politics in Modern China*. Charlottesville: University of Virginia Press, 1998.

Liu, Lydia. "The Female Body and Nationalist Discourse: Manchuria in Xiao Hong's *Field of Life and Death*." In Angela Zito and Tani Barlow, eds., *Body, Subject, and Power in China*, 157–177. Chicago: University of Chicago Press, 1994.

Meng Yue 孟悦 and Dai Jinhua 戴锦华. *Fuchu lishi dibiao: Zhongguo xiandai nüxing wenxue yanjiu* 浮出历史地表：现代妇女文学研究 (Emerging on the horizons of history: Research on modern Chinese women's writing). Zhengzhou: Henan renmin, 1989.

Xiao, Hong. *The Dyer's Daughter: Selected Stories of Xiao Hong*. Trans. Howard Goldblatt. Hong Kong: Chinese University Press, 2005.

——. *The Field of Life and Death and Tales of Hulan River*. Trans. Howard Goldblatt and Ellen Yeung. Bloomington: Indiana University Press, 1979.

——. *Market Street: A Chinese Woman in Harbin*. Trans. Howard Goldblatt. Seattle: University of Washington Press, 1986.

——. *Selected Short Stories of Xiao Hong*. Trans. Howard Goldblatt. Beijing: Chinese Literature Press, 1982.

——. *Xiao Hong quanji* 萧红全集 (Complete works of Xiao Hong). 3 vols. Harbin: Harbin, 1998.

Xiao, Si. "Loneliness among the Mountain Flowers—Xiao Hong in Hong Kong." Trans. Janice Wickeri. *Renditions*, nos. 29–30 (1988): 177–181.

Yan, Haiping. *Chinese Women Writers and the Feminist Imagination, 1905–1948*. New York: Routledge, 2006.

24

PERFORMING THE NATION: CHINESE DRAMA AND THEATER

XIAOMEI CHEN

Early in the twentieth century, when China struggled to emerge from its imperial past and build a new republic, "performing the nation" was a theme shared by the traditional operatic theater (戏曲) and the emerging modern spoken drama (话剧). The latter was promoted by May Fourth men of letters as an alternative to the former, which they saw as too constrained to express the sentiments and concerns of modern times and as a vehicle for transforming China into a modern nation. Less known than their peers who promoted modern spoken drama, artists in operatic theaters initiated reforms to free traditional theater from its ancient rules so that opera could also play a significant role in constructing a new nation.

Liang Qichao 梁启超 initiated traditional theater reform (戏曲改良) in 1902 while in exile in Japan, where he published three operatic texts in *New Citizen* (新民丛报) to raise the spirit of the Chinese people to avenge their humiliation by foreigners. Between 1901 and 1912, as many as 150 new scripts of *chuanqi* (传奇) and *zaju* (杂剧) emerged in different magazines and newspapers. Some of these works dramatized the deeds of ancient national heroes who became models for patriotic resistance against the Qing. Other plays, in contrast, depicted significant contemporary events, such as the Hundred Days Reform in *Dreams of Reform* (维新梦). Another remarkable example is a biographical play about the life of Qiu Jin 秋瑾, a female revolutionary executed for her anti-Qing activities in 1907. In similar fashion, new Peking operas exposed foreign imperialist aggressions against China: Russia's incursion into Heilongjiang in

An Un-Russian Dream (非熊梦), the Eight Allied Armies' invasion of China in 1900 in *Wuling Spring* (武陵春), and the protest against America's Chinese immigration exclusion acts in *The Spring of Overseas Chinese* (海侨春).

To help depict an ideal new nation, foreign heroes and heroines also occupied center stage in these reform dramas. The French Revolution and the execution of Louis XVI are depicted in *Guillotine* (断头台), for example, and the Cuban student struggle against Spanish colonialism is shown in *Student Wave* (学海潮). *Resentment over the Lost Country* (亡国恨) portrays a heroic An Jung-geun, a Korean nationalist who in 1909 assassinated Itô Hirobumi, architect of the Japanese colonization of Korea. Chinese heroines also became popular symbols as victims of a patriarchal society and as champions for women's rights and liberation. Such figures are found in Liu Yazi's 柳亚子 late Qing text *New Daughter of Songling* (松陵新女儿), a remarkably well-written one-act play. Depicting women's resistance to arranged marriage in defense of women's rights, Liu allows his dramatic character, dressed in a Western suit, to speak her mind to the audience: "Asians are people. Europeans are people. But why does China, the great land, trample women's rights? Chinese women are still suffering every passing day while those white and fair foreign women enjoy equal rights with men; their names are even recorded in history." Liu's female protagonist expresses her deep admiration for Madame Roland, guillotined for her revolutionary activities during the French Revolution, and Sophia Perovskaya, executed for her abortive attempt to assassinate Tsar Alexander II. Liu Yazi's championing of Chinese women's rights, though in tune with the times, is not without problems, for it reflected an attitude of white supremacy common among the Chinese literati, who looked up to the West as the model for China's modernization.

Although Peking opera originated in the north, the center of operatic theater reform was Shanghai, a vibrant city in the south open to Western influence and innovative in artistic experience. Wang Xiaonong 汪笑侬, one practitioner of the "Shanghai school of Peking opera" (海派京剧), scripted new Peking operas that depicted the contemporary state of affairs. In 1908, Wang even introduced a new stage in Shanghai for producing Peking opera, using imported equipment and technology for stage design and lighting. To promote new Peking operas with contemporary themes, Wang and his cohorts successfully adapted *Black Slave Cries to Heaven* (黑奴吁天录), a "new drama" (新剧) adaptation of Harriet Beecher Stowe's *Uncle Tom's Cabin*. Influenced by the impact of modern drama at the beginning of the twentieth century, some theater reformers in the late Qing and early Republican period experimented with new Peking operas with contemporary costumes (时装新戏) in Shanghai.

One literary historian has recorded as many as two hundred reformed dramas tailored to the taste and concerns of contemporary audiences. Mei Lanfang 梅兰芳 performed five Peking operas with contemporary costume in Beijing after two visits, in 1913 and 1914, to Shanghai, where he had watched modern

Western dramas. His desire to reform traditional opera to reflect contemporary reality, however, found fresh expression in his new historical drama (新编历史剧), performed after Japan's invasion of China became imminent. His *Resisting the Jin Invaders* (抗金兵) and *Hatred in Life and Death* (生死恨) premiered in Shanghai in 1933 and represented the best of these dramas, which he continued to work on in the People's Republic of China (PRC). Mei, of course, was not alone in his attempt to reform Peking opera. Tian Han 田汉 also scripted *Jiang-Han Fishermen's Song* (江汉渔歌, 1940), a new Peking opera that depicted a fishermen's uprising to defeat Jin aggressors in the Song dynasty. Tian also wrote *Heroic Stories of New Sons and Daughters* (新儿女英雄传, 1940), which dramatizes a Ming dynasty hero fighting against foreign invaders. Similarly, Ouyang Yuqian 欧阳予倩 transformed *Peach Blossom Fan* (桃花扇, premiere 1937, originally a *chuanqi* text) into a new Peking opera, with a revised image of Li Xiangjun 李香君, the female protagonist who would rather die than see her lover turn into a traitor.

Unlike operatic theater, modern spoken drama was not constrained by its own indigenous tradition. Its dialogue-only form, moreover, was thought by its promoters to allow for greater freedom to express complicated ideas and plots than its traditional operatic counterpart. In spite of its marginal position in modern Chinese literary and cultural history, modern spoken drama played a significant role in constructing an image of a modern Chinese nation. Western drama became a weapon to battle traditional operatic theater as early advocates such as Hu Shi 胡适 introduced the plays of Ibsen and Shakespeare, for example, to create a "new drama" (新戏). Hu's own *The Greatest Event in One's Life* (终身大事, 1919) depicts a modern woman who elopes with her Japan-educated fiancé to avoid an arranged marriage. This Nora-like character heralded a series of female protagonists who leave home in search of free love and participation in public life. In female playwright Bai Wei's 白薇 *Breaking Out of Ghost Pagoda* (打出幽灵塔, 1928), for instance, a courageous daughter dies in the arms of her mother in her struggle against the patriarchal home, symbolized by her domineering and lustful father. The old and isolated rural village, as depicted in Tian Han's play *The Night a Tiger Was Captured* (获虎之夜, 1922), however, prevents its main character, Liangu 莲姑, from escaping her cruel father, who dictates that if a tiger is killed, he will use its sale for her dowry to marry a rich man. The tragic ending of the play, which features the death of Liangu's lover, signifies the hopeless fate of Chinese women, who in turn symbolize the plight of the suffering nation, also bound by Confucian doctrines of traditional society.

In contrast to these plays that foreground contemporary life, Guo Moruo's 郭沫若 trilogy of plays about women rewrote traditional stories. His *Zhuo Wenjun* (卓文君, 1923), for instance, depicts the title heroine as challenging the strong will of her father by eloping with her lover, Sima Xiangru 司马相如; she also confronts the Confucian ideology that expects a widow never to remarry. In a similar fashion, *Wang Zhaojun* (王昭君, 1923) creates its title heroine as a dignified courtesan who rejects the love of the Han emperor by willingly marrying an outsider from a "barbarous" tribe. More politically relevant to the reality of 1920s China, Guo Moruo's third play, *Nie Ying* (聶嫈, 1925), presents the title character as a martyr who stands by her patriotic brother against outside invaders. In Guo Moruo's father figures—the domestic father in *Zhuo Wenjun*, the imperial father in *Wang Zhaojun*, and the imperialist father in *Nie Ying*—we see the anti-Confucian and nationalist themes in May Fourth drama.

Anti-imperialist themes assumed a higher profile with Japan's encroachment on Chinese territory in the 1930s. This was a thriving period for Chinese spoken drama, which came to maturity with Cao Yu's 曹禺 plays (see "Cao Yu and *Thunderstorm*"), but it also witnessed the rise of "national defense drama" in 1935–1936, which connected dramatic performance even more closely to the defense of the Chinese nation. With the impending Japanese invasion, the Friendly Association of the Shanghai Dramatic Circle was organized in 1936 to unite dramatists of diverse political and ideological backgrounds to create a drama of national resistance. Most popular were Xia Yan's 夏衍 *Sai Jinhua* (賽金花, 1936) and *Under Shanghai Eaves* (上海屋檐下, 1937), representing, respectively, two distinct subgenres, the history play and the contemporary realist play. *Sai Jinhua* retells the story of the title character, a famous Qing dynasty courtesan who won over important Western men and persuaded them to lessen their demands on China during the Boxer Rebellion. According to PRC drama historians, this play's obvious allusion to the Guomindang's nonresistance policy toward the Japanese (reminiscent of the corrupt and cowardly Chinese officials' "kowtowing to Western powers" in the Qing dynasty) made the play a popular hit, with a record twenty-two full-house performances. Its immediate banning by the Guomindang and the subsequent public uproar (known as the "*Sai Jinhua* Incident") seemed only to have confirmed the genius of the playwright, whose allegorical use of a patriotic prostitute to save her nation at the time of crisis was not lost on either political camp.

Xia Yan's *Under Shanghai Eaves*, by contrast, presents a cross-section of a typical house in Shanghai, occupied by five poor families struggling for survival. The play focuses on a single event, the "homecoming" of Kuang Fu 匡复, who upon his release from prison after eight years finds Yang Caiyu 杨彩玉, his wife, living with and emotionally attached to his friend Lin Zhicheng 林志成. The originally scheduled premiere of *Under Shanghai Eaves* in Shanghai on August 15, 1937, was canceled because two days earlier war with Japan had broken out. Xia Yan later wrote that instead of feeling disappointed, he was excited about the turn of events: the war effort and its eventual victory should, he felt, bring an end to the sad stories presented in the play. In fact, he wished that the play would never have to be performed so that Chinese children would not be reminded of their parents' past suffering.

The period of war against Japan has been referred to as the "golden age of Chinese theater," when drama played a more significant and direct role than any other literary genre in promoting the war effort. The best-known performances include *In Defense of Lugou Bridge* (保卫卢沟桥, 1937), a play that represents the heroic efforts to resist the Japanese invasion. The play was written through the joint efforts of seventeen playwrights, its production made possible with the help of six musicians, nineteen directors, and a cast of close to a hundred actors and actresses. In August 1937, twelve National Salvation drama troupes organized in Shanghai to perform resistance plays in different parts of China. Their most frequently produced plays include *Put Down Your Whip* (放下你的鞭子, 1936), which depicts a starving daughter being whipped by her helpless, tearful father. Actors "planted" in the audience urge him to put down his whip and join the national effort to fight Japanese invaders. The stage lines from the actors and actresses elicited responses from the audience. Frequently performed outdoors, the play has been hailed as an important example of "street theater" (街头剧).

Stage production flourished from 1938 to 1945 in Chongqing and Guilin, where a series of drama festivals and exhibitions helped produce the most successful plays of the war period. During the "misty season" from October to May, when Chongqing was shrouded by heavy mist and sheltered from Japanese air raids, an annual Misty Season Drama Festival was held. The year 1944 witnessed 118 drama performances, written by diverse playwrights and performed by a variety of drama troupes. Among the best-known pieces produced in Chongqing were Cao Yu's *Metamorphosis* (蜕变, 1940) and *Peking Men* (北京人, 1941) and Guo Moruo's six history plays, including *Qu Yuan* (屈原, 1942). The last shows Qu Yuan as a tragic poet whose patriotic feelings and heroic spirit in fighting the corrupt status quo made this drama a hit.

Whereas wartime dramas featured the common theme of defending the nation, the dramas performed after 1949, under the guiding influence of Mao's "Yan'an Talks," present workers, peasants, and soldiers building a new socialist life. Jin Jian's 金剑 one-act play *Zhao Xiaolan* (赵小兰, 1950), for instance, dramatizes the courage of one woman's fight for free love against the will of her parents, a fight that contrasts sharply with the plight of her sister, who suffers greatly from an arranged marriage. In PRC drama, the fate of women is usually narrated in the larger context of "building a socialist motherland," which, according to state ideology, provided women a perfect stage for public performance. Such a feature can be found in Hu Ke's 胡可 *Huaishu Village* (槐树庄, 1959), the story of Mother Guo, a prototype of the loving "earth mother" now transformed into a "revolutionary mother." The loss of her only son to the Korean War only reinforces her determination to take the lead in numerous political events: the land-reform movement, the movement to support the Korean war effort, the collective farming movements, and, finally, the Great Leap Forward, aimed at boosting agricultural and industrial productivity.

Because Communist Party ideology promoted workers as pillars of socialist society, worker plays helped to validate the new PRC state. *Red Storm* (红色风暴, 1958), for example, portrays the famous Peking-Hankou railroad workers' strikes brutally suppressed on February 7, 1923, by the warlord Wu Peifu 吴佩孚 and his foreign supporters. Jin Shan 金山 wrote and directed the play and starred in the "unforgettable" role of Shi Yang 施洋, who supports the workers' strikes. Legend has it that Jin spent only seventy-two hours rehearsing the play before its highly successful premiere by the China Youth Art Theater in 1958. In the 1960s, the worker plays changed dramatically. Plays sought to educate the younger generation of workers "never to forget" such a revolutionary history and "never to forget class struggle," as expressed in the title of Cong Shen's 丛深 play *Never to Forget* (千万不要忘记). Premiered by Ha'erbin Theater in 1964 and soon followed by numerous productions throughout the country, *Never to Forget* depicts a young worker whose desire for a better material life is criticized as an example of a worker's family being "eroded" by bourgeois ideology. Such a theme culminated during the Cultural Revolution, when eight model revolutionary theatrical pieces dominated the Chinese stage for ten years. Most rehearsed past revolutionary war experiences to remind the audience never to forget class struggle (see "The Cultural Revolution Model Theater").

During the Cultural Revolution, a few spoken dramas were produced in the spirit of learning from model theater and creating proletariat art. *Battles at the Dockyard* (战船台), for example, depicts Shanghai workers' success in manufacturing China's first ocean-faring ship, while *Maple Tree Bay* (枫树湾) portrays a hero's return to his hometown in Hunan Province to organize a peasant militia and lead it to join Mao at the Chinese Communist Party military base in Jinggangshan in 1927. Developed from the tradition of workers' and soldiers' plays, *Mountains Astir* (沸腾的群山) is set in 1948 in Liaoning Province, where a group of People's Liberation Army soldiers restore production in a coal mine that had been controlled by the Nationalists during the civil war (1946–1949). These works were part of a 1974 "performance tour" (文艺调演) organized by the Cultural Group of the State Council to promote politically correct theater.

Spoken drama experienced a remarkable renaissance in the post-Mao period. Much of post-Mao theater was a reaction against the politics and culture of the Cultural Revolution. The popular anti–Gang of Four plays, for instance, depicted Jiang Qing and her followers as destroyers of the country, and the post-Mao regime as builders of a new nation moving toward democracy and modernization. An example is *Winter Jasmine* (报春花, 1979), which recounts the discrimination suffered by Bai Jie 白洁, a young female worker in a textile factory, because of her "politically incorrect" family origins: her father was declared a counterrevolutionary because he had worked for the Guomindang before 1949, and her mother charged a rightist for challenging the Communist

Party's radical policies in 1958. Xing Yixun's 刑益勋 *Power Versus Law* (权与法, 1979) portrays a party secretary, assigned to his post after the overthrow of the Gang of Four, who seeks to expose corruption and crimes within the party system and protect the wife and daughter of a rightist. Such a positive image of the party representative, however, is challenged in another highly controversial play entitled *If I Were for Real* (假如我是真的, premiered in 1979), written by Sha Yexin 沙叶新 and others. In this play, a young man from a worker's family with no connection to the privileged and the powerful finds himself impersonating the son of an important party official in order to get permission to return to his home city to marry his pregnant girlfriend before the child's delivery. The play's setting in post-Mao China made it politically suspect; its critique of party corruption was obviously not limited to the Gang of Four, who were no longer in power. Anti–Gang of Four plays include what drama historians term "revolutionary leader plays," which depict the wartime stories of high-ranking party and army officials, some of whom had, in real life, been persecuted during or even before the Cultural Revolution, such as Chen Yi, He Long, and Peng Dehuai. Meanwhile, female playwrights began to emerge. The best known among them, Bai Fengxi 白峰溪, distinguished herself with her women's trilogy, which depicts a post–Gang of Four society that fails to protect women, especially those living in rural China, from oppression. Female intellectuals and urban dwellers, likewise, struggle in Bai's plays to find their own identities and voices in an increasingly modernized China. Once again, women occupy a central position in the plays' construction of the nation.

Parallel with these developments, experimental plays such as *Bus Stop* (车站, 1983), by Gao Xingjian 高行健, and *WM*(我们, 1985), by Wang Peigong 王培公 and Wang Gui 王贵, experimented with elements of Western absurdist theater. In essence, however, these plays did not depart radically from the realist tradition of the Maoist era, although they critiqued Maoist ideology by exposing the effects of the Cultural Revolution. Wei Minglun's 魏明伦 Sichuan opera *Pan Jinlian: The History of a Fallen Woman* (潘金莲:一个女人的沉沦史, 1985) represents the best example of experimental theater. Wei attempted to reform Chinese traditional theater by combining elements of absurdist theater with the realist tradition. Unlike his Western counterparts, Wei believed that the play's "absurdity" resided only in its "absurdist form," in which characters from different countries and various historical periods appear on stage to comment on the tragic story of Pan Jinlian, one of the most notorious femmes fatales in Chinese literature. The play centers on the dramatic conflicts between Pan Jinlian and five men: the rich man, Zhang Dahu 张大户, who forces her into an arranged marriage with Wu Dalang 武大郎; Wu Dalang, the short and ugly man Pan marries; Ximen Qing 西门庆, the vicious playboy who sleeps with Pan and plots with her to kill Wu; Wu Song 武松, Wu Dalang's brother, who avenges his murder by killing Pan; and Shi Nai'an 施耐庵, the author of the *Water Margin* (水浒传), the original source of the story. Shi's misogyny is challenged by various fictional and historical characters from both the East and the West. This controversial play was so warmly received that it inspired numerous productions in other genres, such as modern spoken drama and local operas popular in Shanxi Province and Shanghai. At one point, fifty theaters in twenty cities were performing the work. Articles appeared in 130 newspapers and journals, ten of which dedicated special columns to discussion of the play. Wei's play reminds one of Ouyang Yuqian's earlier *Pan Jinlian* (1928), a modern spoken drama that borrowed formal features and plots from traditional operatic theater. At the same time, it presents a daring critique of the Confucian tradition that saw women as the source of evil. Like Ouyang's text, Wei's play portrays a sympathetic Pan Jinlian trapped by patriarchal society.

Other traditions such as Greek theater and Chinese folk dance and singing found their way into *Sangshuping Chronicles* (桑树坪纪事, 1988), about the sorrows of the local peasants in a small, isolated village in the northwestern part of China. Despite the reforms that have happened elsewhere, ignorance, illiteracy, sexual oppression, and patriarchal structure dominate this place that has remained unchanged for thousands of years. Once again, theater productions reflected a continued tension between individuals, their efforts to seek personal happiness, and the demands of the nation-state.

If domestic concerns still ruled the Chinese stage, global perspectives in which China redefined itself became increasing popular. Guo Shixing's 过士行 Bird Men (鸟人, premiered 1992) presents dramatic conflicts between a Chinese man, a Chinese American man, and an American-educated Chinese man. The play revolves around a group of bird-loving men who spend all their leisure time raising, examining, and talking about birds. Fascinated by this phenomenon, Dr. Paul Ding 丁保罗, a Chinese American psychiatrist, establishes Birdman Psychiatric Center in order to restore the mental health of the birdmen by retrieving their deeply buried memories of traumatic childhood experiences. Dr. Ding's experiment, however, proves frustrating and confusing. He does not always understand the literary and dramatic allusions his patients make under hypnosis. In the end, San Ye 三爷, a retired Peking opera star, easily masters Ding's psychiatric tricks. He rewrites, directs, and acts out a familiar scene from a Peking opera that puts Ding on trial and forces him to admit that he suffered from the very psychological problems he had attributed to his patients as a result of growing up in an American Chinatown. In an effort to show Ding up, San Ye performs his swan song as a Peking opera actor, a performance that helps him regain something of his previous power and heroic stature. In this role, he plays the wise, incorruptible Judge Bao 包公, a figure in traditional theater who never fails to protect the innocent and punish the criminal. He sentences Ding. He also condemns another defendant, Dr. Chen 陈博士, a Chinese bird expert admired globally for his dedication to animal protection, who has killed the last surviving bird of an endangered species to preserve it as a specimen for public display. This sarcastic commentary on hypocritical intellectuals reflects a fear of losing Chinese identity, which had rendered the Chinese economically and culturally vulnerable to imperialist powers. The use of Peking opera in the play-within-a-play comments on the decline of the opera and lends the entire play an unmatched charm. Lin Liankun 林连昆, the actor who played San Ye, displayed a great range of body movements, singing, and acting that he used to shuttle between the two dramatic genres. More than any other, this play needs to be seen on stage if one is to appreciate the beauty and depth of the diverse acting styles and local color, as well as the display of conventions from both modern spoken drama and traditional operatic theater.

Some theater in the twenty-first century expressed a socialist utopia of the bygone years in Maoist China, as seen in *Che Guevara* (切•格瓦拉, 2000) by Shen Lin 沈林 and others. Exploring the legacy of an enduring icon of the Communist revolution, *Che Guevara* evokes Maoist warnings against peaceful transformation from a socialist China into a capitalist and revisionist China— warnings that still give pause to those who resent the increasing gap between rich and poor in contemporary China. In the new millennium, in which many people are victimized by party corruption, exploitation from the new rich, and hopelessly polluted environments as the dangerous products of Chinese-brand capitalism, Che Guevara's summons to a new revolution to liberate the disadvantaged touches a deep chord. Just as Che declares on stage that as long as oppression and exploitation persist, he will never put down his gun, so one might conclude that as long as the dream of equality persists, both in and outside China, military heroes, heroines, and nationalist plays on the Chinese stage will continue to remind us of that dream of a modern and prosperous China, whose memory of the past and envisioning of the future have found their timely and artistic expressions in theater production and reception.

The twentieth-first century continues to witness a parallel development of three genres: (1) "main melody" or mainstream plays sponsored by state initiatives and state financial support; (2) experimental theater, which pushes the boundaries in theatrical innovations and realist traditions while imitating various schools of Western modernist theater; and (3) commercial theater operated by private theater producers (独立戏剧制作人) that gestures toward an emergent "independent theater" (民间戏剧) and a theater market, therefore providing a new challenge to the mainstream theater practices and their official culture. Coexisting with these three trends in spoken drama, traditional operas from numerous regions also flourish and share spoken drama's concern with social problems, such as corruption and bureaucracy in the Chinese Communist Party, and its representations of revolutionary leaders and war heroes as a strategy to remind the ruling powers never to forget the Chinese people who sacrificed their lives to put them in power. Realist, experimental, commercial, or other, contemporary theater in its various forms has attempted to relate to contemporary audiences in order to carve out a meaningful, albeit increasingly limited, cultural space.

Bibliography

Bai, Fengxi. *The Women Trilogy*. Trans. Guan Yuehua. Beijing: Chinese Literature Press, 1991.
Chen, Xiaomei. *Acting the Right Part: Political Theater and Popular Drama in Contemporary China*. Honolulu: University of Hawai'i Press, 2002.
———, ed. *Columbia Anthology of Modern Chinese Drama with a Critical Introduction*. New York: Columbia University Press, 2010.
———, ed. *Reading the Right Texts: An Anthology of Contemporary Chinese Drama*. Honolulu: University of Hawai'i Press, 2003.
Cheung, Martha P. Y., and Jane C. C. Lai, eds. *An Oxford Anthology of Contemporary Chinese Drama*. Hong Kong: Oxford University Press, 1997.
Eide, Elisabeth. *China's Ibsen*. London: Curzon Press, 1987.
Ferrari, Rossella. *Pop Goes the Avant-Garde: Experimental Theater in Contemporary China*. London: Seagull Books, 2012.
Gao, Xingjian. *The Other Shore: Plays*. Trans. Gilbert C. P. Fong. Hong Kong: Chinese University Press, 1999.
Goldstein, Joshua. *Drama Kings: Players and Publics in the Re-creation of Peking Opera, 1870–1937*. Berkeley: University of California Press, 2007.
Gunn, Edward, ed. *Twentieth-Century Chinese Drama: An Anthology*. Bloomington: Indiana University Press, 1983.
Guo, Moruo (Kuo Mo-jo). "Cho Wen-chün." In Harold R. Isaacs, trans. and ed., *Straw Sandal: Chinese Short Stories, 1918–1933*, 45–67. Cambridge, MA: MIT Press, 1974.
———. *Chu Yuan*. Trans. Yang Hsien-yi and Gladys Yang. Beijing: Foreign Languages Press, 1953.
———. *Five Historical Plays*. Beijing: Foreign Languages Press, 1984.
Liu, Siyuan. *Performing Hybridity in Colonial-Modern China*. New York: Palgrave Macmillan, 2013.
Luo, Liang. *The Avant-Garde and the Popular in Modern China: Tian Han and the Intersection of Performance and Politics*. Ann Arbor: University of Michigan Press, 2014.
Mackerras, Colin. *The Chinese Theatre in Modern Times: From 1840 to the Present Day*. Amherst: University of Massachusetts Press, 1975.
Shen, Lin, et al. *Che Guevara*. Trans. Jonathan Noble. MCLC Resource Center Publication (July 2006). http://u.osu.edu/mclc/online-series/noble.
Tung, Constantine, and Colin Mackerras, eds. *Drama in the People's Republic of China*. Albany: State University of New York Press, 1987.
Wagner, Rudolf G. *The Contemporary Chinese Historical Drama*. Berkeley: University of California Press, 1990.
Yan, Haiping, ed. *Theater and Society: An Anthology of Contemporary Chinese Drama*. Armonk, NY: M. E. Sharpe, 1998.
Yu, Shiao-Ling S., ed. *Chinese Drama After the Cultural Revolution, 1979–1989: An Anthology*. New York: Edwin Mellen, 1996.

25

CAO YU AND *THUNDERSTORM*

JONATHAN NOBLE

Cao Yu 曹禺 (1910–1966) is conventionally considered by literary historians and critics, in both China and the West, to be one of the leading modern Chinese playwrights. He is credited with bringing spoken drama to its maturity in the 1930s. Born Wan Jiabao 万家宝, Cao Yu grew up in Tianjin in an aristocratic family whose wealth and prestige was declining. His youthful experiences growing up in this milieu provided the material for most of his early dramas. He received a classical education in a private family school and had access to a large family library. His mother, an aficionado of the performing arts, introduced Cao Yu to various regional dramatic forms, folk performance arts, and Western-style spoken dramas. He entered Tianjin's Nankai Middle School in 1922, joining its renowned drama troupe and acting in such plays as Ding Xilin's 丁西林 *Oppression* (压迫, 1926), Ibsen's *A Doll's House*, and Hauptmann's *Weavers*. Frequently playing female roles, he earned the sobriquet "flower of the Nankai drama troupe." In 1930 he enrolled in Tsinghua University's Department of Western Languages and Literatures and assiduously delved into literary works from China and the West, in particular Western classical and modern plays.

Cao Yu's first spoken drama, *Thunderstorm* (雷雨), was written and published while he was still enrolled at Tsinghua. It is by most accounts the most famous spoken drama of the prewar era and the most frequently performed play in the history of Chinese theater. Initially published in *Literary Quarterly* (文学旬刊) in 1934, it was first performed later the same year at Ji'nan University.

With Cao Yu playing the lead, a 1936 production was a great commercial success. *Thunderstorm* was twice adapted for film in 1938 in productions by studios in Hong Kong and Shanghai.

The commercial success of *Thunderstorm* greatly increased the prestige and popularity of the new genre of spoken drama (see "Performing the Nation") and contributed to the play's subsequent canonization in China's modern literary history. One reason for the favorable reception of *Thunderstorm* was its articulation of the main political causes and artistic practices of the May Fourth generation. *Thunderstorm* adheres to the central mission promoted by May Fourth intellectuals—namely, the iconoclastic destruction of the shackles of tradition for the purposes of emancipating the individual and strengthening the nation. Set in the 1920s, *Thunderstorm* is a well-constructed four-act play that explores the themes of patriarchal capitalistic oppression and female emancipation through the dramatic conventions of tragic fate, revenge, and destined retribution. The dramatic conflict revolves around the complex three-decade entanglements between two economically disparate families: the Zhou family, headed by Zhou Puyuan 周朴园, a foreign-educated wealthy owner of a mine, and the Lu 鲁 family, all the members of which have at one time been employed by the Zhou family.

The action is triggered when Lu Shiping 鲁侍萍 arrives at the Zhou household at the behest of Fanyi 繁漪, the wife of Zhou Puyuan. Shiping comes to the horrifying realization that her daughter, Sifeng 四凤, is currently employed as a maid by the man whom she served thirty years ago and with whom she had a love affair. After bearing two of his sons, Shiping was abandoned by Zhou Puyuan due to her low station. Her first son, Zhou Ping 周萍, remained with his father, while Shiping was permitted to keep her younger son, Lu Dahai 鲁大海, because of his weak and sickly condition. Fearing that her daughter, Sifeng, will encounter a similar calamity, Lu Shiping willingly consents to Zhou Fanyi's request to have Sifeng discharged from the Zhou household's service. Fanyi is motivated in part by jealousy, wishing to have Zhou Ping to herself. Fanyi had previously been carrying on an affair with her stepson, but as of late, Zhou Ping has taken a fancy to Sifeng. Two triangular relationships emerge in the first act: among Zhou Puyuan, Fanyi, and Lu Shiping, on the one hand, and Fanyi, Sifeng, and Zhou Ping, on the other.

The laying bare of these triangular relationships, both past and present, is interspersed with scenes that highlight the ruthless oppression the Zhou patriarch inflicts on his subordinates, that is, his immediate family members and the workers at his mine. His past abandonment of Lu Shiping and his present actions toward his wife, Fanyi, reveal him as a cruel victimizer. Convinced of Fanyi's insanity, Puyuan orders her locked up in her room and forces her to take regular doses of medicine, a most poignant illustration of his callousness and symbolic of the hypocritical compassion of Confucian patriarchy. Another example of Puyuan's lack of compassion for or exploitation of the downtrodden is exemplified by his quashing and underhanded manipulation of a strike at his mine. The leader of the strike, ironically and unbeknown to Zhou Puyuan, is his own son, Lu Dahai. Representing the antithesis of the Confucian filial son and the hope for a proletarian revolution, Lu Dahai epitomizes the radical politics of the era.

The third act ends with Sifeng and Zhou Ping fleeing from the Lu residence, pursued by Lu Dahai, who is motivated by class hatred, and Shiping, who hopes to prevent Sifeng and Ping from unwittingly committing incest. When Zhou Ping returns home near the beginning of act 4, Fanyi begs Zhou Ping to take her with him to the mine, even if accompanied by Sifeng. At Zhou Ping's refusal, Fanyi declares that she has nothing to live for, and the stage is set for a desperate act of revenge. The denouement of the fourth act—composed of a sequence of revealed secrets, fated coincidences, and tragic deaths—is one of the most melodramatic in the history of modern Chinese drama. Fully aware of her daughter's love affair with Zhou Ping, Shiping continues to demand an end to the relationship. However, on learning that Sifeng is already pregnant, she resigns herself to wishing the couple well while concealing from them the reality of their incestuous relationship. Shiping blames only herself: "What have I ever done to bring such a calamity down on our heads? . . . Oh, God, if anyone has to be punished, why can't it just be me? It's my fault and no one else's: it all began when I took the first false step. They're my innocent children; they deserve a chance in life. The guilt here is in my heart, and I should be the one to suffer from it" (Cao Yu *Thunderstorm*: 142).

Shiping's compassionate and self-effacing support of her children's elopement, however, is compromised by Fanyi's need for revenge against Zhou Ping and her husband. To Fanyi's astonishment, Puyuan reveals Shiping's true identity as Zhou Ping's long-lost mother, thereby shocking everyone into realizing that Zhou Ping and Sifeng's relationship is incestuous. A horror-stricken Sifeng runs outside into the pouring rain and is electrocuted by a loose wire; Zhou Chong 周冲, Puyuan's son by Fanyi, is electrocuted in the process of trying to save her. Zhou Ping shoots himself in his father's study, leaving Zhou Puyuan with only one son, Lu Dahai, who runs off, according to some interpretations, to join the Communist cause. The epilogue and prologue, which are usually not performed or published with the script, reveal that years later Shiping is immobilized by grief and Fanyi has perhaps truly gone mad.

One of the overarching themes of *Thunderstorm* is the suppression of personal freedom by the patriarchal order of traditional Chinese society. Most critics interpret the Zhou household as a microcosm of the "old society" doomed to fade into obscurity. *Thunderstorm* can be viewed as a variation on the May Fourth critique of the oppressive, male-dominated family, a legacy of earlier May Fourth dramas, such as Chen Dabei's 陈大悲 *Ms. Youlan* (幽兰女士, 1921), Bai Wei's 白薇 *Breaking Out of Ghost Pagoda* (打出幽灵塔, 1928), and Ouyang Yuqian's 欧阳予倩 *Behind the Screen* (屏风后, 1919). However,

Cao Yu's drama has garnered its canonical status as the paragon of the doomed "feudal family" because it represents, according to many critics, a more profound and complete artistry. Zhou Puyuan, for example, could have been facilely sketched as a stereotypical archvillain, a symbol of feudalism and patriarchal hegemony, but his sentimental musings on the past complicate this reading. Likewise, Lu Dahai's dogmatic hatred for the Zhou brothers makes it difficult to wholeheartedly sympathize with him and adopt him as a humanistic hero.

The flip side of the oppressive social structure is the emancipation of the individual. Fanyi has conventionally been read as representing the May Fourth ideal of the individual's desire for liberation from an authoritarian stronghold. As stated in his preface, Cao Yu regarded her as a personal heroine: "She has a blazing passion and a dauntless heart which pushes her through all obstacles in her life-and-death struggles" (Lau 1970: 23). Female emancipation was another prominent trope during the May Fourth period, in part propelled by the fashion for Ibsenism, as articulated in other dramas such as Hu Shi's 胡适 *Greatest Event in Life* (终身大事, 1919) and Guo Moruo's 郭沫若 *Zhuo Wenjun* (卓文君, 1923) and *Wang Zhaojun* (王昭君, 1923).

Thunderstorm is Cao Yu's first exploration of the subject of female liberation, a theme as prominent as that of the oppressive, patriarchal family in his later plays. Fanyi's rebellion against patriarchal institutions is both motivated by personal desire and provoked by society's oppression. Whereas Fanyi challenges the patriarchal logic, Shiping and Sifeng are portrayed as victims of the system. This trope of female emancipation, however, is problematized within the drama. Fanyi's personal liberation is dependent on Zhou Ping's acceptance of her. She places herself in the hands of an incipient patriarch and is then left without hope when he deserts her: "I'd resigned myself to my fate, when along came someone who must need revive me—and then tire of me and cast me aside, and leave me to wither and slowly die of thirst" (Cao Yu *Thunderstorm*: 51). Despite Cao Yu's sympathetic interest in the fate of women in modern China, the convention of using the trope of female emancipation as a signifier for the emancipation of the individual may in fact have stripped women of their unique identity and subjectivity, unwittingly transferred from the rule of the old patriarch to the hands of their "enlightened saviors."

The 1936 preface to the play asserts that "cosmic cruelty" and "primitive passion," not class conflict and individual emancipation, were Cao Yu's main concerns in *Thunderstorm*. Cao Yu was familiar with Greek tragedy, but based on the notion that personal will is a prerequisite to "tragedy," the deaths of Sifeng and the fate of Shiping are better explained by Cao Yu's interest in exploring the mystery of heaven's will. The tight threads of blood relations and ethics create an inescapable "heaven's net" in *Thunderstorm*. The deaths of Zhou Chong and Zhou Ping recall the traditional Chinese concept of "retribution" (报应), inasmuch as their deaths leave Zhou Puyuan with his enemy, Lu

Dahai, as his only descendant. According to a reading based on traditional morals, the deaths of his sons are "retribution" for his illicit affair with and subsequent abandonment of Lu Shiping. In conjunction with a Marxist reading, the "retribution" is caused by his callous feudal behavior, of which his illicit relationship is only a symptom.

Two other plays written in the same decade, *Sunrise* (日出, 1936) and *Wilderness* (原野, 1936), continue to manifest the leftist agenda of opposing the feudal and patriarchal institutions of China and capitalist exploitation. Cao Yu's *Metamorphosis* (蜕变, 1940) and *Peking Man* (北京人, 1940) also articulate the theme of the superfluous and oppressive traditional family, although in a comical mode and in the Chekhovian dramatic style of indirect action.

Cao Yu held many academic and government positions in the fields of drama and the arts. From 1934 to 1935 he was employed at Tianjin's Hebei Women's Normal College, before moving on to teach at the National Academy of Dramatic Arts in Nanjing. In 1946, invited by the U.S. State Department, Cao Yu, along with Lao She, stayed in America for one year giving lectures. After the founding of the People's Republic of China, he held the positions of vice president of the Central Academy of Drama (1949), member of the board of directors of the All-China Dramatic Association (1952), president of the Beijing People's Institute of Drama and Art (1956), and deputy of the National People's Congress (1954, 1958, 1964). He also wrote several plays, including *Bright Skies* (明朗的天, 1954), *The Gall and the Sword* (胆剑篇, 1961), and *The Consort of Peace* (王昭君, 1978). In honor of Cao Yu's centenary, the Beijing People's Art Theatre restaged *Thunderstorm*, *Sunrise*, *Peking Man*, and *The Wilderness* in 2010.

Bibliography

Cao, Yu. *Bright Skies*. Trans. Pei-chi Chang. Beijing: Foreign Languages Press, 1960.
———. *The Consort of Peace*. Trans. Monica Lai. Hong Kong: Kelly/Walsh, 1980.
———. *Peking Man*. Trans. Leslie Nai-kwai Lo et al. New York: Columbia University Press, 1986.
———. *Sunrise*. Trans. A. C. Barnes. Beijing: Foreign Languages Press, 1978.
———. *Thunderstorm*. Trans. Wang Tso-ling and A. C. Barnes. Beijing: Foreign Languages Press, 1978.
———. *The Wilderness*. Trans. Christopher Rand and Joseph Lau. Hong Kong: Hong Kong University Press, 1980.
Galik, Marian. "Ts'ao Yu's *Thunderstorm*: Creative Confrontation with Euripides, Racine, Ibsen and Galsworthy." In Marian Galik, ed., *Milestones in Sino-Western Literary Confrontation (1898–1979)*, 101–122. Wiesbaden: Otto Harrassowitz, 1986.
Gunn, Edward. "Cao Yu's *Peking Man* and Literary Evocations of the Family in Republican China." *Republican China* 16, 1 (1990): 73–88.
Hu, John Y. H. *Ts'ao Yu*. New York: Twayne, 1972.

Lau, Joseph S. M. *Ts'ao Yu: The Reluctant Disciple of Chekhov and O'Neill—a Study in Literary Influence*. Hong Kong: Hong Kong University Press, 1970.

Robinson, Lewis S. "On the Sources and Motives Behind Ts'ao Yu's *Thunderstorm*." *Tamkang Review* 16 (1983): 177–192.

Wang, Aixue. *A Comparison of the Dramatic Works of Cao Yu and J. M. Synge*. Lewiston, NY: Edwin Mellen, 1999.

26

THE RELUCTANT NIHILISM OF LAO SHE'S *RICKSHAW*

THOMAS MORAN

Shu Qingchun 舒庆春 (1899–1966), who wrote under the pen name Lao She 老舍, is among the most widely read Chinese authors of the modern period. He was not typical of his generation of writers: he was from Beijing, not the south; he was Manchu, not Han Chinese; at the start of his career he wrote to entertain, not to reform society; his literary instinct was comic, not romantic; and until the war with Japan he was not involved with the left wing and its many feuds. He was also Christian, spent much time away from China, and had a nuanced understanding of the differences between East and West (Huang 2008: 99–109). From 1924 to 1929, he lived in London, where he wrote his first three novels. In the 1930s, he taught literature in Shandong Province and wrote prolifically. During the Japanese invasion of China from 1937 to 1945, he directed the All China League of Resistance Writers (中华全国文艺界抗敌协会). After the founding of the People's Republic of China in 1949, he continued to write and served in the cultural bureaucracy. He was attacked during the Cultural Revolution and committed suicide by drowning during the night or early morning of August 24–25, 1966.

Of Lao She's substantial output, which includes novels, stories, plays, poems, librettos for traditional Chinese opera, drum songs, comic dialogues, criticism, and essays, the novel *Camel Xiangzi* (骆驼祥子), translated by Jean James (Lao She 1979) as *Rickshaw*, is the work for which he is best remembered, especially outside China. *Rickshaw* appeared serially in the magazine *Cosmic Wind* (宇宙风) from September 1936 to October 1937 and was published as a book in 1939. Editions published in China from 1955 through the 1980s delete material that violates Maoist dictates of what is and is not permissible in fiction. Lao She was proud of the novel and not in the habit of tinkering with completed work, but he endorsed these revisions (Lao She 1980: 69–71; 1981: 231–236). James's translation follows the original.

The story is simple. An eighteen-year-old orphan named Xiangzi 祥子 comes to Beiping (Peking) from the countryside. He tries to make a living as a rickshaw puller but ends as a shuffling bum. First, Xiangzi is unlucky; his name, literally "fortunate son," is ironic. Second, his downfall is caused by a corrupt society, and to blame are the policeman Detective Sun 孙探长 and other unsavory characters who bully Xiangzi and represent the problems of early twentieth-century China, including class oppression and political thuggery. Third, Xiangzi is at fault; his "individualism" isolates him from allies. The ending of the novel comes as no surprise. We are warned at the beginning that "hopes for the most part come to nothing and Xiangzi's were no exception" (Lao She 1979: 10).

Rickshaw is an imaginary investigation of the real crisis facing China in the 1930s, and the city of Beiping, rickshaw men, and the rickshaw are symbols of this crisis. In 1928, the Nationalist government unified China, moved the capital to Nanjing, and changed the name of Beijing (northern capital) to Beiping (northern peace). Evidence in the novel suggests that when Xiangzi is press-ganged into a warlord's army, the first catastrophe to befall him, that army is in retreat from Beijing as Nationalist forces advance in the spring of 1928 (Shi 1980: 287). Each mention of "Beiping" in the novel is a reference to the tumultuous changes shaking Xiangzi's world. Modern China's new literature had given itself the task of writing about the exploited, and Beiping's rickshaw pullers were highly visible members of this group: stories about their difficult lives were ubiquitous in fiction and journalism. The rickshaw was a modern device, and the sight of poor men pulling foreigners and rich Chinese down city streets was a reminder of the painful cost of China's modernity, which arrived with foreign encroachment and national decline. Rickshaw pullers, David Strand (1989: 36) observes, dragged the machinery of the industrial age and their exploiters behind them. The novel suggests that the imperialist powers bullied the Chinese people, who were misled by the false promise of capitalist modernization and betrayed by corrupt government, the miscarried revolution of 1911, and their own disunity. Xiangzi's nickname, Camel, and his obsession with his rickshaw imply that the modern Chinese worker was reduced to the status of a beast of burden and a machine.

There is more to *Rickshaw*, however, than social critique. Readers value the novel for its enjoyable language, elegant narrative structure, vibrant characters, and vivid descriptive passages. When we move from appreciation to analysis, we find that any attempt to reduce *Rickshaw* to a single message leads to confusion because the novel is built around tension and contradiction. For example, the novel criticizes individualism, and so readers anticipate a call for collective revolutionary action; instead, toward the end of the novel, an old man tells Xiangzi the parable of the locusts ("grasshoppers" in James's translation), which suggests that mass revolution would be catastrophic (Lao She 1979: 229). While much revolutionary Chinese fiction places the hopes of the nation on the shoulders of robust young people, Xiangzi and the girl he loves, Xiao Fuzi 小福子, have venereal disease, a conventional symbol of China's "sickness." The character of Mr. Cao 曹先生 represents enlightened intellectuals, conventionally regarded as leaders of the campaign for national salvation, but Mr. Cao can do little to help himself, let alone Xiangzi. *Rickshaw* offers no hint as to how China might escape its predicament.

Critics have discussed the ways in which the novel is divided against itself. Frederic Jameson (1984: 69) says there are two narrative paradigms at work and at odds in *Rickshaw*. What Jameson calls the "outer" form is associated with Xiangzi and his "precapitalist view of money as hoard or treasure (or of value as the possession of the unique, quasi-sacred object)." The "inner" form is tied to Xiangzi's wife, Hu Niu 虎妞, and her values, which are those of "emergent capitalism and the market." Edward Gunn (1991) has argued that as Lao She wrote *Rickshaw*, his love of stylistic wordplay was at cross-purposes with his sense of obligation to write something socially progressive. David Der-wei Wang (1992: 119) has identified the tension in *Rickshaw* as that between melodrama and farce; the novel's melodrama contains "a longing for the return of a certain order," but its farce "ventures to laugh away such efforts."

Lydia Liu (1995) finds contradiction in the novel's language and mode of narration as well. Liu shows that the term "individualism" (个人主义) was important in late Qing and Republican China but did not refer to a single concept. Progressive thinkers defined individualism as a positive aspect of Chinese tradition; then they partially reversed themselves and promoted it as an antidote to a traditional society that placed constraints on individual freedom; and finally, they reversed themselves completely and attacked individualism as an obstacle to socialist revolution (Liu 1995: 88–99). All along they struggled to reconcile the need for individual liberation with the duty for patriotic self-sacrifice. In an essay published in 1936, the same year he started to write *Rickshaw*, Lao She (1936: 219) explains how this contradictory attitude toward individualism was resolved in modern Chinese literature: "social consciousness" (社会自觉), he said, led authors to renounce the creation of well-rounded, distinct fictional characters because to do so would be to give in to the "dregs of individualism" (个人主义的余孽). As a result, Chinese literature lacked memorable characters. Lao She wanted it both ways. *Rickshaw* is a novel of profound social consciousness, but it is built around a single memorable character. The novel's exploration of what Xiangzi thinks and feels is an implicit celebration of the same individualism the narrator condemns in the novel's final sentence. Liu (1995: 111–113) also demonstrates that the narration moves from the narrator's voice to Xiangzi's voice and back without marking the transitions (a strategy less evident in translation), and it is occasionally impossible to tell if a particular sentence is the narrator's thought, indirect representation of Xiangzi's thought, or direct quotation of what Xiangzi says to himself. Xiangzi does not understand many of the things that happen to him, and we cannot trust his interpretation of his story. There is, however, no reason to accept the narrator's judgment, especially given that every time Xiangzi starts to tell his life story, the story is broken off, often when the narrator interrupts and takes over (Lao She 1979: 36, 118, 141, 221–222, 228). Xiangzi cannot explain his life; he does not get to speak for himself; and the narrator is unreliable, and this, Liu (1995: 124) says, should encourage us to consider "alternative ways of looking at [Xiangzi's] situation." Readers must decide for themselves what Xiangzi's story means.

The novel contains one more tension. Lao She (1936: 219) believed that fully realized characters emerge through attention to their minds. Among the aspects of Xiangzi's psychological makeup that Lao She (1980: 68; 1985: 541–542) explores is sexual desire, which more than romantic love engaged his interests as a novelist. To think about what sex means in *Rickshaw*, we have to think about Hu Niu. For many commentators, Hu Niu is a wanton woman who ruins a good man. It is possible that Lao She's novel simply reflects the gender ideologies of its time. The women in the book are stereotypes. Xiao Fuzi is a prostitute with a heart of gold, and Hu Niu fits what publications of the time offered as the profile of the spinster who suffers from sexual frustration and a need for "invigorating male secretions" (Dikötter 1995: 47, 56). However, Hu Niu is too interesting a character to be so easily dismissed.

In the prodigality of her language, sex, and eating, Hu Niu is Xiangzi's opposite. She embraces sensual gratification; he denies himself debilitating pleasures. But neither Xiangzi's sober asceticism nor Hu Niu's exuberant licentiousness budges either from the course poverty dictates. The novel does not offer the irony that vice succeeds while virtue fails. Xiangzi becomes degenerate; Hu Niu dies. When we reproach Hu Niu for her bad behavior or ask whether we can forgive Xiangzi for his theft of the camels, we are forgetting that the novel disallows us the comfort of moralizing. The fictional world of *Rickshaw* is amoral. In the world of the novel, honesty, hard work, and chaste living get one nowhere; there is no possible appeal to a transcendent code of ethics because poverty and elemental desires render such abstractions as love and honesty irrelevant. Xiangzi learns this lesson from Hu Niu and sex. He does not want to want Hu Niu, but he does, and this undermines his dream of success through self-discipline (Liu 1995: 121). Xiangzi's desire for Hu Niu scares him because it is beyond his control, and his fear turns into loathing: "Hu Niu relied on her stinking X—to humiliate him!" (Lao She 1979: 85). Hu Niu is deceitful, mean, foulmouthed, gluttonous, promiscuous, and voyeuristic. Yet, by the logic of the novel, if virtue is its own reward, virtue is meaningless, and Hu Niu is smart for realizing it. Hu Niu functions to make as uncomfortable and therefore as powerful as possible *Rickshaw's* despairing recognition that the conventional morality shared by author and reader is made up out of thin air. In a discussion of Lao She's 1943 short story "Attachment" (恋), Rey Chow (2001) writes of an "impending nihilism" in the story. This notion that conventional values are empty and life senseless is even more strongly present in *Rickshaw*. The moral indignation the narrator rouses in us as we read about Xiangzi's unhappy end is canceled by nihilism.

Bibliography

Bernards, Brian. "From Diasporic Nationalism to Transcolonial Consciousness: Lao She's Singaporean Satire, *Little Po's Birthday.*" *Modern Chinese Literature and Culture* 26, 1 (Spring 2014): 1–40.

Chow, Rey. "Fateful Attachments: On Collecting, Fidelity, and Lao She." *Critical Inquiry* 28, 1 (Autumn 2001): 286–304.

Dikötter, Frank. *Sex, Culture and Modernity: Medical Science and the Construction of Sexual Identities in the Early Republican Period.* Honolulu: University of Hawai'i Press, 1995.

Gunn, Edward. *Rewriting Chinese: Style and Innovation in Twentieth-Century Chinese Prose.* Stanford, CA: Stanford University Press, 1991.

Huang, Alexander C. Y. "Cosmopolitanism and Its Discontents: The Dialectic Between the Global and the Local in Lao She's Fiction." *Modern Language Quarterly* 69, 1 (March 2008): 97–118.

Jameson, Fredric. "Literary Innovation and Modes of Production: A Commentary." *Modern Chinese Literature* 1, 1 (September 1984): 67–77.

Lao, She. "Attachment." Trans. William A. Lyell and Sarah Wei-ming Chen. In *Blades of Grass: The Stories of Lao She*, 211–225. Honolulu: University of Hawai'i Press, 1999.

——. "How I Came to Write the Novel *Camel Xiangzi.*" In *Camel Xiangzi*, 231–236. Trans. Xiaoqing Shi. Bloomington: Indiana University Press, 1981.

——. [老舍]. *Luotuo Xiangzi* 骆驼祥子 (Camel Xiangzi). Shanghai: Chenguang chuban gongsi, 1951.

——. "Renwu de miaoxie" 人物的描写 (On the description of character). *Yuzhou feng* 28 (November 1936): 219–222.

——. *Rickshaw: The Novel Lo-t'o Hsiang Tzu.* Trans. Jean M. James. Honolulu: University of Hawai'i Press, 1979.

——. "Wo zenyang xie *Da ming hu*" 我怎样写《大明湖》 (How I wrote *Da Ming Lake*). *Lao She yanjiu ziliao* 老舍研究资料 (Research materials on Lao She), ed. Zeng Guangcan and Wu Huaibin, 1:541–543. Beijing: Shiyue wenyi, 1985.

——. "Wo zenyang xie *Luotuo Xiangzi*" 我怎样写《骆驼祥子》 (How I wrote *Camel Xiangzi*). In Hu Jieqing, ed., *Lao She shenghuo yu chuangzuo zishu* 老舍生活与创作自述 (Lao She's essays on his life and work), 65–71. Hong Kong: Sanlian shudian, 1980.

Liu, Lydia H. *Translingual Practice: Literature, National Culture, and Translated Modernity—China, 1900–1937.* Stanford, CA: Stanford University Press, 1995.

Lyell, William A. "Lao She." In Thomas Moran, ed., *Dictionary of Literary Biography*. Vol. 328, *Chinese Fiction Writers, 1900–1949*, 79–94. Farmington Hills, MI: Thomson Gale, 2007.

Prado-Fonts, Carle. "The Anxiety of Fiction: Reexamining Lao She's Early Novels." *Modern Chinese Literature and Culture* 26, 2 (Fall 2014): 177–215.

Shi Chengjun 史承钧. "Shilun jiefang hou Lao She dui *Luotuo Xiangzi* de xiugai" 试论解放后老舍对《骆驼祥子》的修改 (Lao She's revisions of *Camel Xiangzi* since liberation). *Zhongguo xiandai wenxue yanjiu congkan* 4 (1980): 278–288.

Strand, David. *Rickshaw Beijing: City People and Politics in the 1920s*. Berkeley: University of California Press, 1989.

Wang, David Der-wei. *Fictional Realism in Twentieth-Century China: Mao Dun, Lao She, Shen Congwen*. New York: Columbia University Press, 1992.

Xu, Jian. "Retrieving the Working Body in Modern Chinese Fiction: The Question of the Ethical in Representation." *Modern Chinese Literature and Culture* 16, 1 (Spring, 2004): 115–152.

27

EILEEN CHANG AND NARRATIVES OF CITIES AND WORLDS

NICOLE HUANG

Eileen Chang (Zhang Ailing 张爱玲, 1920–1995) began her writing career in the early 1940s in the Japanese-occupied city of Shanghai and went on to become the most prominent author and public intellectual in the besieged city. Educated bilingually from an early age, she enrolled in the University of Hong Kong in 1939, only to see her college education brought to an abrupt end two years later by the bloody Battle of Hong Kong in 1941. She left the war-torn city and returned to the equally ravaged metropolis of Shanghai, an experience that would find recurrent expression in her fiction and essays.

When Eileen Chang started her literary career, she wrote in English for the Nazi-backed English-language journal *XXth Century*, contributing film reviews and social commentaries. She soon came to be known as "young Ms. Chang," who depicted Chinese life and customs in a witty, seasoned, and accessible prose style. Chang soon began to refashion her English essays into Chinese and publish them in popular literary journals. This practice of self-translation would define an entire writing career that straddled cities, continents, and cultural worlds.

Chang's most critically acclaimed works were published during the first few years of her career—that is, between 1941 and 1945. Many of her early works appeared in two volumes, a collection of short stories and novellas entitled *Romances* (传奇, 1944) and a book of prose entitled *Written on Water* (流言, 1945). Her best-known short stories and novellas include "Love in a Fallen City" (倾城之恋), "The Golden Cangue" (金锁记), "Traces of Love"

(留情), "Blockade" (封锁), "Red Rose and White Rose" (红玫瑰与白玫瑰), "Aloewood Ashes: The First Incense Brazier" (沉香屑: 第一炉香), and "Aloewood Ashes: The Second Incense Brazier" (沉香屑: 第二炉香). In adopting the title *Romances* (the Chinese title was used as a generic designation for both short "accounts of marvels" during the Tang dynasty and multiact dramas that flourished during the Ming and Qing dynasties), Chang seems to suggest reading her fiction as a modern appropriation and invocation of themes from China's long literary past. And by naming her prose as words "written on water," she highlights the brevity and immediacy that characterized the structure of the modern essay and the fragility and futility of human life in wartime. Chang sees herself as caught between a sense of despair over the destruction of war and a desire to emerge from the ruins of history and leave behind an enduring legacy.

Chang's early writing was deeply marked by her own time. Works from the first decade of her literary career constructed an alternative wartime narrative, one that contradicted the grand narratives of national salvation and revolution. In an age punctuated by horror and heroism, she highlighted the seemingly irrelevant details of daily life and stories of ordinary men and women caught in wars, revolutions, and drastic social transformations. In her fiction and essays from the war period, her impressionistic view of the modern era displays colors, lines, shapes, textures, and moods often crystallized in the rapidly changing styles of women's clothes. Chang is at her best when she juxtaposes fragments of an external reality (air raids, blockades, hunger, death, and scarcity) with the intricacies of a domestic and private life (love, loss, fantasy, emotional yearning, and artistic creativity). What shines through her highly stylized prose is the entanglement of a personalized inward journey and a persistent, though not always explicit, attempt to come to terms with a violent century.

"Blockade" (aka "Sealed Off"), a story written in August 1943, is representative of her wartime romances. The story depicts a brief encounter between a man (an office worker) and a woman (a college teacher) on a streetcar caught in the middle of an air raid, when the city comes to a standstill. As the story concludes, the brief "romance" draws to an abrupt end when the blockade is lifted and the streetcar moves again; both protagonists resume their original positions, and "everything that had happened while the city was sealed was a non-occurrence. The whole of Shanghai had dozed off, had dreamed an unreasonable dream" (Chang 1995: 197).

Here the concept of blockade is a metaphor for confined time and space that is particular to the besieged city during wartime occupation; the story is therefore an allegory of life in 1940s Shanghai. As in Chang's other works of the period, one senses the omnipresent threat of war—in the air raid and other manifestations of an extraordinary time—but is also reminded that life goes on, like the two streetcar tracks "never ending, never ending" (Chang 1995: 188). The threat of massive destruction lurks in the background, but what is foregrounded is a preoccupation with the immediate present and the everyday. The interior of a streetcar caught in the middle of a citywide blockade conveniently provides the spatial and temporal frame for the reader to imagine what it is like to live in a war-torn city. But the story depicts war only in a metaphorical sense, functioning more as a literary device to create a temporal and spatial suspension. Various borders and divisions that already cut across the cityscape are further sharpened because of this temporary suspension. Chang's narrative depicts individual experiences of war as integral to urban sensibilities.

In Chang's widely acclaimed novella "Love in a Fallen City," written just one month after "Blockade," war intrudes into the central romance in a different fashion—it ironically completes the narrative. In what is arguably Chang's best work of fiction, the protagonists travel between Hong Kong and Shanghai around the outbreak of the Pacific War. This is one of Chang's many "tales of two cities"—that is, narratives set in Hong Kong and Shanghai and written with Shanghai readers as her target audience. Its title alludes to an ancient Chinese tale in which the beauty of a woman is blamed for the collapse of a kingdom. Chang's modern narrative shares with the ancient legend a sense that war and turbulence are always lurking in the background and will eventually emerge as a substantial force that transforms individuals. As the story unfolds, the young and defiant widow Bai Liusu 白流苏 encounters Fan Liuyuan 范柳原, a wealthy dandy from an overseas Chinese aristocratic family. She decisively leaves the repressive house of her parents and travels to Hong Kong to be with Liuyuan. In Hong Kong, a city depicted as an exotic mirror image of Shanghai, Liusu gradually falls under the spell of Liuyuan's scheme of seduction. She would succumb to the fate of being Liuyuan's mistress if not for the outbreak of the war, which destroys the city but seals marital commitment between the two protagonists: "The demise of Hong Kong completes her. In this inexplicable world, who can say for sure what is the cause and what is the effect? Who knows.... Perhaps a metropolis is toppled precisely for the sake of fulfilling her romance" (my translation).

Like her female characters, Chang's agency and creativity are set against a violent context. And unlike many other writers of her time, Chang demonstrates no interest in composing a comprehensive account of war, resistance, or awakening of individual consciousness. Heroes and villains alike are absent in her narratives. In Chang's own explanation in "My Writing" (自己的文章, 1944), "Liusu escapes from a corrupt family, yet the baptism by war in Hong Kong does not change her into a revolutionary woman" (Chang 1996: 437). Her wartime narrative tells how individuals go on living and resuming their daily routines despite the intrusion of war. Chang's alternative wartime narrative actively responds to the immediate reality and, more important, challenges the way that war, history, and individual lives were represented in the master narrative of her time.

With the end of the Sino-Japanese War in 1945, Chang was politically stigmatized because of her brief marriage to Hu Lancheng 胡兰成 (1906–1981), a key intellectual player in Wang Jingwei's collaborationist government, and her professional association with the literary circle surrounding the *Miscellany Monthly* (杂志月刊) and several other Japanese-backed literary journals. She continued writing, though sparingly, during the postwar years, often under a pseudonym. Her first novel, *Eighteen Springs* (十八春), later reissued as *Destined for Half a Lifetime* (半生缘), was serialized under the pseudonym Liang Jing 梁京 in the entertainment newspaper *Yi bao* (亦报) in 1948. Her situation further deteriorated with the Communist takeover in 1949. In 1952, she left Shanghai for good and returned to Hong Kong, where she worked for the next three years at the United States Information Agency (USIA) as a translator. She translated Ernest Hemingway's *Old Man and the Sea* and Ralph Waldo Emerson's essays, among other English-language works, into Chinese. She also translated Chen Jiying's 陈纪滢 anti-Communist novel *Story of Di Village* (荻村传) and other propaganda materials into English for the agency to disseminate in Southeast Asia.

Chang's three years in Hong Kong were productive because she also completed two major novels, *The Rice-Sprout Song* (1955) and *The Naked Earth* (1956), which she wrote first in English and then translated into Chinese titled *Yangge* (秧歌) and *Chidi zhi lian* (赤地之恋), respectively. Both novels were anti-Communist works commissioned by the USIA and produced at the height of the McCarthy era in the United States. With the completion of these two novels, Chang secured a visa and moved to the United States in 1955.

Chang published little during her four decades of life in America. At the beginning, she tried to launch a literary career in the English-speaking world but met with little success. In 1977, more than three decades after her initial rise to fame in wartime Shanghai, Chang published a collection of Chinese essays on *Dream of the Red Chamber* entitled *Nightmares in the Red Chamber* (红楼梦魇). The volume was published by Crown Publishers, which also published the work of Qiong Yao 琼瑶 and San Mao 三毛 and would go on to publish Chang's sparse writings in later decades. But Chang's readers had come to believe that her creative energy had all but dried up, a belief significantly challenged well after her death when several unpublished manuscripts were discovered and published, fueling a resurgence of interest in her life and works on both sides of the Pacific and adding a new chapter to the long and winding history of the reception of Eileen Chang's works.

In the first three decades of the People's Republic of China, official literary histories made no mention of Chang and her work because of her association with the collaborationist regime during the war and the anti-Communist stance of her writing in the early 1950s. But Chang's reception outside mainland China is a completely different story. In the late 1960s and early 1970s, she was rediscovered by a generation of literary historians. Scholars such as

C. T. Hsia and Shui Jing recognized her significance and assigned her an unparalleled position in literary history. Her works became popular again among readers in Taiwan, Hong Kong, and the Chinese diaspora communities. Her literary legacy had an important impact on a host of writers in Taiwan, where a group of young women authors (including the Zhu sisters, Zhu Tianwen 朱天文 and Zhu Tianxin 朱天心) formed an "Eileen Chang school" in the 1970s.

With the rewriting of literary history in the post-Mao era (see "Modern Chinese Literature as an Institution"), an Eileen Chang "fever" also swept through cities on the mainland. Pirated editions of her early fiction and essays flooded the stalls of street vendors beginning in the late 1980s, a phenomenon that went hand in hand with a collective effort to uncover a cultural history of Shanghai from the prerevolutionary era and to redefine the city as a major metropolis on a new global map. As in Taiwan in the 1970s, in mainland China in the 1980s and 1990s, young authors emerged whose writings were strongly inspired by Chang. The name Eileen Chang came to stand for the glories of a bygone era, as well as for the healthy migration of Chinese narratives and voices across national borders.

Chang's popular reception has accompanied a growing body of scholarship on her works. Recent scholarship has, for example, taken a close look at the connection between Chang and transnational film culture. Chang's interest in film started in the early 1940s with a series of film reviews for *XXth Century* and matured with the writing of screenplays in postwar Shanghai, including the very successful *Long Live the Wife* (太太万岁), a film comedy directed by Sang Hu 桑弧 (1916–2004) in 1947. After Chang bid farewell to Asia by way of Hong Kong, her creative energy found an outlet in a series of film scripts written at the request of producer Stephen Soong 宋淇 (1919–1996) for the new Hong Kong MP & GI Company. Many of Chang's 1960s scripts were solid box office successes in Hong Kong, contributing to the transformation of Chang from a quintessential Shanghai writer to someone who envisioned and wrote for a Chinese-speaking readership across national and geographic divides. Recent scholarship on Chang also looks at how adaptable her works have been for the silver screen; the most successful of these adaptations is Ang Lee's thriller *Lust, Caution* (色戒, 2007), based on a once obscure story Chang first wrote in the 1950s and completed two decades later.

Recent scholarship on Chang also embraces the publication of a series of formerly unpublished manuscripts, all written during her American years. Three novels stand out among these "new" old works. Their excavation and formal publication were the results of the tireless efforts of Roland Soong, son of Stephen Soong, who inherited Chang's literary estate. Two novels were written in English—*The Book of Change* and *The Fall of the Pagoda*—and a third, the most highly anticipated of all, in Chinese, titled *Small Reunion* (小团圆). These works point to a writer caught in a state of constant rewriting, retelling, and incessant self-translation, as if forever haunted by memories of war, migration, and permanent loss. Research on these works has just begun, while adaptations of her works on screen, on stage, and through other multimedia venues continue.

When Eileen Chang died in 1995, she had lived long enough to witness how the legends surrounding her life had grown in the popular cultures of Taiwan, Hong Kong, mainland China, and other Chinese communities around the world. Although she watched from a safe distance, remaining unaffected most of the time, no cultural history of twentieth-century China would be complete without an account of how the Chang mythology took shape amid wartime turmoil and subsequently evolved and traveled across national and political boundaries in the following decades. The reception of Eileen Chang's writing is intertwined with experiences of war, revolution, migration, and urban transformations.

Bibliography

Chang, Eileen. *The Book of Change*. Hong Kong: Hong Kong University Press, 2010.
——. 张爱玲. *Chuanqi* 传奇 (Romances). Shanghai: Zazhishe, 1944.
——. *The Fall of Pagoda*. Hong Kong: Hong Kong University Press, 2010.
——. *Honglou mengyan* 红楼梦魇 (Nightmares in the red chamber). Taipei: Crown, 1977.
——. *Love in a Fallen City*. Trans. Karen Kingsbury. New York: New York Review of Books, 2006.
——. "My Writing." Trans. Wendy Larson. In Kirk A. Denton, ed., *Modern Chinese Literary Thought: Writings on Literature, 1893–1945*, 436–442. Stanford, CA: Stanford University Press, 1996.
——. *The Rice-Sprout Song*. Berkeley: University of California Press, 1998.
——. "Sealed Off." Trans. Karen Kingsbury. In Joseph S. M. Lau and Howard Goldblatt, eds., *Columbia Anthology of Modern Chinese Literature*, 188–197. New York: Columbia University Press, 1995.
——. *Written on Water*. Trans. Andrew F. Jones. New York: Columbia University Press, 2005.
——. *Xiao tuanyuan* 小团圆 (Small reunion). Taipei: Crown, 2009.
——. *Zhang Ailing: Dianmao juben ji* 张爱玲: 电懋剧本集 (Eileen Chang: Collection of film scripts for MP & GI). Hong Kong: Hong Kong Film Archive, 2010.
Chow, Rey. "Modernity and Narration—in Feminine Detail." In *Woman and Chinese Modernity: The Politics of Reading Between West and East*, 84–120. Minneapolis: University of Minnesota Press, 1991.
Deppman, Hsiu-Chuang. "Eileen Chang and Stanley Kwan: Politics and Love in *Red Rose (and) White Rose*." In *Adapted for the Screen: The Cultural Politics of Modern Chinese Fiction and Film*, 61–97. Honolulu: University of Hawai'i Press, 2010.
Huang, Nicole. *Women, War, Domesticity: Shanghai Literature and Popular Culture of the 1940s*. Leiden: Brill, 2005.

Lee, Leo Ou-fan. *Shanghai Modern: The Flowering of a New Urban Culture in China, 1930–1945*. Cambridge, MA: Harvard University Press, 1999.

Louie, Kam, ed. *Eileen Chang: Romancing Languages, Cultures and Genres*. Hong Kong: Hong Kong University Press, 2012.

Peng, Hsiao-yen, and Whitney Crothers Dilley, eds. *From Eileen Chang to Ang Lee: Lust/Caution*. New York: Routledge, 2014.

Shen, Shuang. "Ends of Betrayal: Diaspora and Historical Representation in the Late Works of Zhang Ailing." *Modern Chinese Literature and Culture* 24, 1 (Spring 2012): 112–148.

—— 沈双, ed. *Lingdu kan Zhang* 零度看张 (Eileen Chang degree zero). Hong Kong: Chinese University of Press, 2012.

28

LITERATURE AND POLITICS: MAO ZEDONG'S "YAN'AN TALKS" AND PARTY RECTIFICATION

KIRK A. DENTON

It may seem odd that Mao Zedong (1893–1976), head of the Chinese Communist Party (CCP), would give lectures on art and culture to cultural workers in Yan'an in the midst of the war against Japan (1937–1945) and an ongoing conflict with their erstwhile allies, the Nationalists or Guomindang (GMD). But just as during the war Mao developed major ideological writings that would become known as "Mao Zedong thought," he also shaped a cultural policy. The "Talks at the Yan'an Forum on Art and Literature" (延安文艺座谈会上的讲话), given in the spring of 1942, though not original or sophisticated literary theory, would become the theoretical basis for the rigid cultural policy implemented by the CCP after the revolution. It is as such among the most important texts in the cultural history of the People's Republic of China (PRC). Even today, in the freewheeling atmosphere of the PRC cultural market, their presence as a reminder of more oppressive times is keenly felt.

To understand the Talks it is important to know something of the history of their conception and dissemination. The early 1940s was a critical moment in CCP history. Party membership had increased dramatically since the war began, and most of these new recruits had little knowledge of Marxism. Although Mao had by this time begun to consolidate his control over the party leadership, he was not without opposition. Wang Ming and his supporters, who favored a more classically Marxist proletarian revolution over Mao's peasant focus and took a relatively conciliatory stance toward the GMD, were still in Mao's way. Moreover, partly with Mao's encouragement, writers had begun to turn their pens to exposing problems in Yan'an. Ai Qing 艾青, Ding Ling 丁玲, Wang Shiwei 王实味, and Xiao Jun 萧军 wrote essays and stories that cast the CCP paradise in a negative light, depicting it as a place of darkness in which women were unequal to men, party members had special privileges, and intellectuals were given little creative freedom. Ding Ling's "Thoughts on March Eighth" (三八节有感), for example, criticizes CCP patriarchal attitudes that existed beneath their official feminist rhetoric; Wang Shiwei's "Statesmen and Artists" (政治家与艺术家) called for an independent and vital role for the intellectual, and his "Wild Lilies" (野百合花) attacked CCP privilege and its alienation from the people.

In this atmosphere, Mao saw a pressing need for ideological and political uniformity in party ranks and so in early 1942 launched the Rectification Campaign, which set the pattern for most subsequent PRC campaigns against intellectuals: Mao calls for liberalization in cultural matters, encouraging writers to voice their dissent; writers respond; the party-led media attack the dissenting writers, who are then punished, typically by being sent to the countryside to engage in labor reform. Dissenting writers in particular had to be reined in with a clear party policy on art and literature. The Talks were thus part of the larger CCP program for the "rectification" (整风) of wayward intellectuals to offer them guidelines for accepting the authority of the party and their subservient roles in the revolution. Those writers who had spoken up were criticized and punished by being sent to the countryside to engage in labor reform. Wang Shiwei, the focus of the campaign, was tried and kept under house arrest until 1947, when he was apparently slowly poisoned to death (Dai 1994).

The Talks were presented in two lectures as part of a larger conference on literature and art. The more dogmatic tenor of the conclusion, as compared with the introduction, may indicate that there was oppositional debate at the conference and Mao saw a need to deepen his rationale for a political role for culture (McDougall 1980: 14). Most scholars agree that the ideas expressed in the Talks are not original but, rather, are the crystallization of ideas that date back at least to the late 1920s debate on revolutionary literature. Mao's debt to Qu Qiubai 瞿秋白, one of the first Chinese translators of Soviet literary theory and a former secretary of the CCP, is particularly strong. Through Qu, Mao was introduced to Soviet theory, particularly that of the Prolekult movement, formed after the 1917 revolution to create a purely proletarian culture void of bourgeois influence, and RAPP (All Russia Association of Proletarian Writers), founded in the 1920s to combat liberalism and absorb all cultural organizations under the banner of socialist realism.

The Talks were not published until more than a year later, in October 1943. According to one scholar, the long delay in publication reflected the political debate within the party leadership about how far to take the Rectification Campaign (Kondo 1997: 87). The Talks were republished in 1944 in Chongqing as the Rectification Campaign extended into the Nationalist-controlled areas, becoming the textual authority in the attack on such independent leftists as Hu Feng and his ideas on literary subjectivity. In the postrevolutionary period, the Talks quickly assumed a leading role in CCP cultural policy. They were referred to, for example, by Zhou Enlai in a July 1949 conference of representatives in literature and art. They were republished, with some revisions, in the 1953 four-volume *Selected Works of Mao Zedong* and thus became an essential part of the canonical Maoist corpus, required reading for all party officials and intellectuals. (See McDougall 1980 for a discussion of the differences between versions.) Calls for writers and intellectuals to accept the absolute authority of the Talks accompanied all the 1950s and 1960s cultural campaigns. As one of the signals of the launching of the Cultural Revolution, *Hongqi*, the official party organ, republished the Talks in its pages on July 1, 1966.

In the cultural liberalization of the post-Mao period, the Talks were the focus of heated debate. Many denounced them and saw an imperative for writers to escape the shackles of the politicized role for literature enshrined in them. Conservatives continued to appeal to the authority of the Talks even as they recognized that their dogmatic imposition on writers, especially during the Cultural Revolution, had seriously hindered literary creativity (Xia 1989). The Talks were blamed for a vacuous culture that eschewed the portrayal of complex characters, the themes of love and sexuality, difficult moral issues, and the depiction of real social problems in favor of a bright world of ideological simplicity. During the cultural crackdown of the early 1990s, following the violent suppression of the 1989 movement, the Talks were again invoked as conservative cultural figures attempted to restore socialist culture (Barmé 1999: 27–28). When Mo Yan 莫言 won the Nobel Prize in Literature in 2012, he was criticized in some camps for being a toady to the party, an attitude manifested in his participation in hand-copying part of the Yan'an Talks for a commemoration of their seventieth anniversary. In the post-Mao era, the legacy of the Talks is a controversial one.

Mao's ideas are not nearly as dogmatic as CCP cultural czars later interpreted them to be. Although the subservient role for literature is clearly expressed, one is struck by Mao's balanced approach to the use of both Chinese and Western literary models, for example, and the question of literature's role as satirical exposure or ideological extolling; he never unequivocally denounces Western literary models, nor does he completely erase a critical role for literature. This tension in Mao's ideas on literature is reflected in the schizophrenic cultural policy the CCP and its cultural czars implemented after 1949, which wavered from relative freedom to strict control, shifts invariably justified by calling on the authority of Mao's Talks.

In the introduction, Mao tackles the central question of the "class stand" (立场) of intellectuals. To write a literature in the interest of the laboring classes, writers, most of whom Mao recognized as coming from gentry or bourgeois families, had to embrace the class stand of the masses. This means, says

Mao in an elitist leap typical of Leninists, accepting the will of the party that represents the masses. To embrace the class stand of the laboring masses, "the thoughts and feelings of our writers and artists should be fused with those of the masses of workers, peasants, and soldiers. To achieve this fusion, they should conscientiously learn the language of the masses. . . . If you want the masses to understand you, if you want to be one with the masses, you must make up your mind to undergo a long and even painful process of tempering" (Denton 1996: 461–462). Mao then presents a personal anecdote, describing how in his youth his elitist disdain for the dirty peasant class was gradually transformed into deep respect: "I came to feel that compared with the workers and the peasants the un-remolded intellectuals were not clean and that, in the final analysis, the workers and peasants were the cleanest people, and, even though their hands were soiled and their feet smeared with cow dung, they were really cleaner than the bourgeois and petit-bourgeois intellectuals" (462). In accepting that the bourgeois writer needed to change consciousness in order to create a revolutionary literature, Mao is very much in line with late 1920s and 1930s mainstream leftist literary criticism, which sought a union of intellectuals with the masses, thereby giving voice to the unconscious desires of the masses and at the same time empowering intellectuals with a historical dynamism.

In the conclusion, Mao points to several negative examples of intellectuals who failed to accept the stand of the masses: Zhou Zuoren 周作人 (Lu Xun's 鲁迅 younger brother, who at the time Mao gave the Talks was working in the Ministry of Education in Japanese-occupied Beiping), Zhang Ziping 张资平 (a leftist writer also seen as a traitor for accepting a post in the Japanese government in Shanghai), and Liang Shiqiu 梁实秋 (a humanist essayist and translator who rejected the radicalism of his day and had often been criticized by Lu Xun). Liang in particular is shown to represent the humanist fallacy of a classless literature: in promoting a literature that depicts human nature, humanists like Liang actually contribute to the interests of the ruling minority over those of the oppressed majority. Instead, Mao urges, writers should self-consciously write for that majority, composed of workers, peasants, and soldiers.

Mao then looks at the question of literary form. He advises writers, on the one hand, to raise literary standards and, on the other, to popularize their language and style so that it is accessible to the masses. He qualifies his remarks on raising artistic standards, which might be interpreted as favoring aesthetic formalism, to mean raising artistic standards "in the direction in which the masses are moving." He maintains the usefulness of traditional Chinese and progressive foreign models of literature, which are connected to the will of the people, but urges writers not to blindly adhere to form but to "unreservedly and wholeheartedly go among the masses of workers, peasants, and soldiers, go into the heat of the struggle, go to the only source, the broadest and richest source, in order to observe, experience, study, and analyze all the different kinds of people, all the classes, all the masses, all the vivid patterns of life and struggle, all the raw materials of literature and art" (Denton 1996: 470). But Mao is no empiricist favoring a "critical realist" literature; he also sees art in a highly romantic and revolutionary mode: "Life as reflected in works of literature and art can and ought to be on a higher plane, more intense, more concentrated, more typical, nearer the ideal and therefore more universal than actual everyday life." As such, art can and should "help the masses propel history forward" (470). Again, this synthesis of empiricism with subjectivism is typical of Mao, but it was also something many literary critics who preceded him had attempted to do (51–53).

In the next section, Mao treats the essential question of the relationship between the CCP and the cultural worker. He shares Lenin's view that art is but part—the "cogs and wheels"—of the revolutionary machine: "Party work in literature and art occupies a definite and assigned position in Party revolutionary work as a whole and is subordinated to the revolutionary tasks set by the Party in a given revolutionary period" (Denton 1996: 474). Perhaps reflecting a traditional Chinese propensity for seeing culture's centrality to political life, but also trying pragmatically to enlist intellectuals' support for the revolution by assigning them an important role, Mao sees art "as an indispensable part of the entire revolutionary cause" (474).

Finally, after discussing the role of literary criticism in fusing political and aesthetic standards, Mao dissects and attacks views of literature commonly associated (though not explicitly by Mao) with the May Fourth literary tradition, particularly humanism and the role of literature in exposing the darkness of society. Mao is clearly trying to undermine the very notion of intellectual autonomy that the May Fourth intellectuals, particularly Lu Xun, sought to uphold. Ironically, just as he attacks much of what Lu Xun held dear, at the very end of the Talks Mao raises him as a literary ideal in what is perhaps a willful misreading of Lu Xun's famous classical couplet: "Fierce-browed, I coolly defy a thousand pointing fingers, / Head-bowed, like a willing ox I serve the children." Mao interprets "pointing fingers" as the enemy and the children (孺子) as the proletariat and the masses, while the ox is the revolutionary vanguard. In Mao's hands, the couplet demonstrates Lu Xun's willingness as a writer to serve the masses, whereas Lu Xun's intention was perhaps more a defiance of the status quo.

The Talks are as much a legacy of the Chinese literary tradition as they are a product of Leninist influence or the CCP/Maoist desire for political and ideological hegemony. When seen in the context of Confucian literary didacticism—from the "Great Preface" (大序) of the Book of Odes (诗经) to Liang Qichao 梁启超—Mao's view of a political/moral role for literature seems almost natural and normal. What is most obviously different between Confucian literary didacticism and Maoist literary politics is that Mao's ideas were implemented by a state apparatus far more powerful and interventionist than any seen before in Chinese history. Mao's ideas are also not as at odds with the

May Fourth tradition as they have been made out to be. The May Fourth liberal-humanist mode has often been pitted against the Yan'an legacy of cultural dogmatism and the imposition of literary models, a struggle between May Fourth enlightenment values and those of national salvation and collectivism, the former succumbing inevitably to the latter. The importance Mao placed on culture as a tool in political transformation is also a legacy of traditional and May Fourth views of writing's power to transform values. *Wen* (文, culture) was traditionally viewed as the fabric of society, inseparable from moral-political values. The Song neo-Confucian philosopher Zhu Xi 朱熹, for example, saw *wen* as arising out of the Dao, leaving no distinction between the two. In contrast to Zhou Dunyi's 周敦颐 slogan "Literature Conveys the Way," which saw *wen* as a vehicle for the propagation of the Dao, Zhu wrote, "Dao is the root of culture, culture is the limbs and leaves of the Dao" (*Zhu Zi yulei* 朱子语类, vol. 139). Literary critics in the May Fourth movement sought to create for literature, now termed *wenxue* (文学), an autonomous field separate from morality and politics. Yet even as they did this, they continued to ascribe a key moral-political function to literature. Mao inherited this traditional view via the May Fourth movement. In seeing literature as a tool of politics, Mao seems to share Zhou Dunyi's view that literature is a vehicle for the Way, but his view of the organic interrelationship of art and politics is more aligned with Zhu Xi's worldview. Given this traditional legacy and the extreme exigencies of the war period, it is not particularly surprising that Mao would adhere to a rigidly political role for literature.

Bibliography

Ai Ke'en 艾克恩. *Yanan wenyi yundong jisheng* 延安文艺运动纪盛 (Record of the rise of the Yan'an literary movement). Beijing: Wenhua yishu, 1987.

Apter, David, and Tony Saich. *Revolutionary Discourse in Mao's Republic*. Cambridge, MA: Harvard University Press, 1994.

Barmé, Geremie. *In the Red: On Contemporary Chinese Culture*. New York: Columbia University Press, 1999.

Cai Qingfu 蔡清富. "Zai Yan'an wenyi zuotanhui shang de jianghua zai Guomindang tongzhiqu de chuanbo"《在延安文艺座谈会上的讲话》在国民党统治区的传播 (The dissemination of the Yan'an Talks in the Nationalist areas). *Zhongguo xiandai wenxue yanjiu congkan* 1 (1980): 306–311.

Dai, Qing. *Wang Shiwei and "Wild Lilies": Rectification and Purges in the Chinese Communist Party, 1942–1944*. Armonk, NY: M. E. Sharpe, 1994.

Denton, Kirk A., ed. *Modern Chinese Literary Thought: Writings on Literature, 1893–1945*. Stanford, CA: Stanford University Press, 1996.

———. "Rectification: Party Discipline, Intellectual Remolding, and the Formation of a Political Community." In Ban Wang, ed., *Words and Their Stories: Essays on the Language of the Chinese Revolution*, 51–63. Leiden: Brill, 2010.

Kondo, Tatsuya. "The Transmission of the Yenan Talks to Chungking and Hu Feng: Caught Between the Struggle for Democracy in the Great Rear Area and Maoism." *Acta Asiatica* 72 (1997): 81–105.

Li Xin 黎辛. "Guanyu 'Yan'an wenyi zuotanhui' de zhaokai, 'Jianghua' de xiezuo, fabiao he canjia huiyi de ren" 关于延安文艺座谈会的召开, 讲话的写作, 发表和参加会议的人 (On the convening of the Yan'an Forum on Art and Literature, the writing and publication of the Talks, and the participants of the meeting). *Xin wenxue shiliao* 2 (1995): 203–210.

McDougall, Bonnie. *Mao Zedong's "Talks at the Yan'an Conference on Literature and Art": A Translation of the 1943 Text with Commentary*. Ann Arbor: University of Michigan Center for Chinese Studies, 1980.

Xia Zhongyi 夏中义. "Lishi buke bihui" 历史不可避讳 (History cannot be evaded). *Wenxue pinglun* 4 (1989): 5–20.

29

QIAN ZHONGSHU AND YANG JIANG:
A LITERARY MARRIAGE

CHRISTOPHER REA

By Yang Jiang's 杨绛 (b. 1911) account, it was not love at first sight. She first met Qian Zhongshu 钱钟书 (1910–1998) in March 1932 at Tsinghua University, where both were students in the Department of Foreign Languages and Literatures. Qian had a reputation as a brilliant but aloof undergraduate, never taking notes during lectures (often reading an unrelated book instead) but invariably coming in first at exam time. Yang was in the graduate program, having done a degree in political science at Soochow University before moving north to pursue her true passion, literature. Besides sharing this interest, both hailed from noted scholarly families in Jiangsu Province. Yang's father was a legal scholar and a judge; Qian's father, a literary critic and historian. When first introduced, by one of Yang's cousins, however, they did not even speak.

Three years later, they were married, graduated, and on their way to Oxford University, where Qian was to study at Exeter College (Oxford) on a Boxer Indemnity scholarship from 1935 to 1938, having earned the highest score on the English literature examination in three years of competition. By 1935, both were also published authors. In 1934, Yang's professor had submitted a story she wrote for class, "Don't Worry, Lulu!" (璐璐, 不用愁!) to one of China's largest-circulation newspapers, Tianjin's *L'Impartial* (大公报). Qian had published short book reviews in *Tsinghua Weekly*; after graduating from Tsinghua in 1933 and taking up a job teaching English at Shanghai's Kwang Hua University, he wrote occasional book reviews and critical essays for the leading English-language weekly, *The China Critic*. These gave Chinese readers an early taste of Qian's unsparing critical wit; one author's opinions he pronounced "provokingly dogmatic nonetheless for being expressed in a vague and drowsy language."

Their literary careers began in earnest several years after the couple's return to China in 1938. Yang took their one-year-old daughter, Qian Yuan 钱瑗, to Japanese-occupied Shanghai to live with family while Qian went to Nationalist-controlled Kunming to take up an appointment as full professor of English literature at Southwestern United University, an amalgamation of three northern universities (including Tsinghua). *Arriving at the Margins of Life* (写在人生边上), a collection of nine essays and one story that Qian wrote in the interior, appeared in 1941. Some essays explore the aesthetic significance of familiar things. In "Windows" (窗), for example, Qian notes that with a door "one *can* go out, but with a window one doesn't *need* to go out," since it brings nature inside. "Doors, which allow us to pursue things, signify desire, while windows, which allow us to dwell, signify enjoyment." Further, since not all rooms have windows, but all have doors, windows represent a higher state of evolution, from necessity to luxury. Other essays combine such imaginative conceits with satire of intellectuals. Writers who denigrate their own profession Qian likens to "those young women of good family in old novels who become prostitutes, it is said, due to circumstances beyond their control and the lack of any viable alternative." Critics who "confuse value with their own predilections" become "beasts in human form" and therefore do "a bit of an injustice to Darwin."

In his preface to *Margins*, Qian offered a tongue-in-cheek philosophy of "life as a book" that resonates with the subjective and pointed critical style he was to establish over the next forty years. The critic browses and jots down "piecemeal, spontaneous impressions" that illuminate without rendering "a verdict on the entire book." This critical focus on the discrete, penetrating insight, influenced by the tradition of "remarks on poetry" (诗话), is on display in critical works such as *On the Art of Poetry* (谈艺录, 1948; revised 1984) and *Limited Views* (管锥编, 1978). Yang Jiang, too, in her novel *Taking a Bath* (洗澡, 1987; translated as *Baptism*) and the essay collection *Arriving at the Margins of Life: Answering My Own Questions* (走到人生边上: 自问自答, 2007) endorsed the idea of the margins offering an advantageous critical perspective.

In 1941 the couple reunited for good in Shanghai, where they were neighbors of Chen Linrui 陈麟瑞 and Li Jianwu 李健吾, two prominent playwrights who had also studied abroad. At their encouragement, Yang wrote *Heart's Desire* (称心如意, 1943), the first of three comedies that made her famous and brought the family much-needed income. The play centers on an orphaned young woman, Li Junyu 李君玉, who arrives on the doorstep of rich relatives in Shanghai. Her aunt has summoned Junyu ostensibly out of concern for her plight, but really to replace her husband's sexy personal secretary. Having cold-shouldered the boyfriend who escorted Junyu from Beiping, her uncle and aunt soon dump her on other relatives, who also attempt to use her as a pawn in a domestic dispute. Eventually they too find a pretext to push her off on the eccentric grand-uncle whose fortune both families hope to inherit. This proves their undoing, as the old man makes Junyu his heir and blesses her union with the boyfriend the other relatives despise. *Forging the Truth* (弄真成假), an encore work staged later that year, similarly features intricate plotting, amusing caricatures of upper-class social types, and zingy dialogue. This time, though, the young couple outwit each other and the elder generation looks on in amusement at their shotgun wedding.

In Yang's and Qian's works alike, individual endeavor rarely leads to self-fulfillment. Even Junyu, who does get her heart's desire, does so thanks to a traditional patriarch (Dooling 1994). The narrative arc more often leads to self-frustration. In Qian's story "God's Dream" (上帝的梦), the Creator creates man and woman to be his companions only to have them pair off together. He kills them in jealousy. In "Cat" (猫), another story in his 1946 collection *Human, Beast, Ghost* (人兽鬼), an overbearing Beiping socialite wrangles away her husband's boy secretary only to lose them both. A character in "Inspiration" (灵感) known only as The Writer is so prolific that the weight of his books breaks open a hole in the earth's crust, and he falls to the underworld. Fang Hongjian 方鸿渐, the protagonist of Qian's novel *Fortress Besieged* (围城, 1947), alienates those around him with his quick and cutting wit.

Fortress Besieged, Qian's only novel, is the work on which his literary reputation primarily rests. (His erudite works of scholarly criticism, such as *On the Art of Poetry*, *Poems of the Song: An Annotated Selection* [宋诗选注, 1958], *Limited Views*, and *Patchwork* [七缀集, 1985], and his poetry are less accessible to the casual reader.) The novel follows the misadventures of Fang Hongjian, who has squandered several years of study in Europe and returns to Japanese-occupied Shanghai during the early years of the war with a purchased doctoral diploma. An eligible bachelor with the aura of a returned student, he becomes a desultory participant in a series of entanglements with a dead fiancée, a dark-skinned seductress, a comprador's spoiled daughter, and a bona fide PhD, turning earnest only when he falls in love with the latter's younger cousin, who eventually jilts him. The jilting, and his subsequent departure from Shanghai to take up a teaching position at an obscure university in the interior, is the first of a series of reversals that have Fang perpetually on the run from a poor situation partly of his own making. He escapes from the claustrophobic San Lü University into marriage with a colleague, which soon falls apart due to avoidable misunderstandings. The novel's continual comic liveliness and Fang's feelings of guilt and self-loathing make his final isolation both absurd and affecting. This attention to structure and tonal modulation, among other qualities, led the critic C. T. Hsia (1999: 441) to pronounce *Fortress* "the most delightful and carefully wrought novel in modern Chinese literature."

Yang Jiang's *Taking a Bath* has been called a companion novel to *Fortress Besieged* because it is a comedy of manners focusing on Chinese intellectuals' struggles with (and in) marriage and the academy. Unlike Qian, who set his novel in the recent past, Yang set hers thirty years back, during the early years of the People's Republic. It features an ensemble cast of intellectuals tasked with building a new academic institution in Beijing even as each is trying to figure out his or her place in the New China. The Literary Research Institute houses faculty members of dubious motivations and backgrounds, such as "the Hippo" Nina Shi 施妮娜, who brags of her time in Russia, and Yu Nan 余楠, who would have fled China and his marriage in 1949 if he had had the chance. Yao Mi 姚宓, a librarian and autodidact, and Xu Yancheng 许彦成, a professor of Western literature, two of the few decent people in this environment, form a close intellectual and emotional attachment. But the undertow of societal convention proves too strong: colleagues spurn Yao's self-taught scholarship due to her lack of credentials, and Xu Yancheng reluctantly returns to the wife he does not love. In the third and final part of the novel, the hermetic world of the institute is pried open by the Three-Antis and Five-Antis Campaigns (1951–1952), which force everyone to "take a bath in public" by making a self-criticism. A few take it as an opportunity for genuine self-examination; those who simply put on a show, ironically, emerge with fewer scars.

Yang had earlier explored the theme of self-possession in an adverse environment in *Six Chapters of Life in a Cadre School* (干校六记, 1981), a memoir about her and Qian's experiences during the Cultural Revolution (1966–1976). Like many intellectuals, they suffered various forms of harassment and persecution culminating in their being sent to the countryside for "reeducation." Yang tended vegetable plots, which local peasants regularly raided. Qian was assigned menial tasks in a men's camp a few miles away. The closest attachment Yang formed during this time was to a feces-eating dog. What distinguishes *Cadre School* from other post-Cultural Revolution memoirs of the period is its sparse prose style and lack of rancor. Victimization was the major theme of "scar literature," but Yang wrote that after all the tribulations she was "still the same old me."

By the mid-1980s, the couple were already famous. Both had recently published monumental works of scholarship—Yang's translation of *Don Quixote* (1978) and Qian's *Limited Views* (1979–1980)—and made brief overseas tours. Yang garnered public acclaim for *Cadre School*, as well as a steady stream of essays, and a new generation of Chinese readers discovered the delights of the republished *Fortress Besieged*. The novel attracted so much attention that Yang wrote a long essay, published as a book in 1986 (Yang 2011), responding to readers' curiosity about its author and their speculations about plot and character elements that seemed autobiographical. (Yang invited similar speculation by setting *Taking a Bath* in a research institute similar to the one where she and Qian had worked since the late 1940s.) Even more uninvited guests began knocking on their door after *Fortress* was made into a television serial in 1990.

The deaths of Qian Yuan in 1997 and Qian Zhongshu in 1998 precipitated one of the most remarkable comebacks in modern Chinese literary history. In

1999, Yang Jiang published a translation from English of *Phaedo*, a Platonic dialogue about the death of Socrates. This expression of grief also allowed Yang to adopt the persona of a "calm witness to death" who treats it as an opportunity for philosophical reflection before an "intimate public" (Field 2012). In 2003, at age ninety-two, Yang surprised the public again with *We Three*, a combination of dream-fiction, memoir, and family scrapbook inspired by her life with her husband and daughter. The book, an instant best seller, offered an unprecedentedly intimate portrait of a reclusive scholarly family. It also contained a mature writer's reflections on the surreal quality of bereavement and of a sense of self shrinking from three to one.

Arriving at the Margins of Life: Answering My Own Questions (2007), a self-dialogue drawing on philosophical classics East and West, is Yang's most existential work to date, one that explicitly confronts many of the themes raised in *We Three*. In 2014, Yang surprised her readers yet again with the novella "After the Bath" (洗澡之后), a coda to *Taking a Bath*, in which Yang sees its main characters safely and happily married. As the surviving member of a remarkable literary marriage, Yang has repeatedly testified—through her active stewardship of Qian's literary estate, her collaboration on an oral history of her family (Wu 2008), and her ongoing writing—to their joint devotion to literature, scholarship, family, and self.

Bibliography

Dooling, Amy D. "In Search of Laughter: Yang Jiang's Feminist Comedy." *Modern Chinese Literature* 8, 1–2 (1994): 41–68.
Field, Jesse L. "Writing Lives in China: The Case of Yang Jiang." PhD diss., Minneapolis, University of Minnesota, 2012.
Hsia, C. T. *A History of Modern Chinese Fiction*. 3rd edition. Bloomington, IN: Indiana University Press, 1999.
Huters, Theodore. *Qian Zhongshu*. Boston: Twayne, 1982.
Qian, Zhongshu. *Fortress Besieged*. Trans. Jeanne Kelly and Nathan Mao. New York: New Directions, 2004.
——. *Humans, Beasts, and Ghosts: Stories and Essays*. Ed. Christopher G. Rea. New York: Columbia University Press, 2011.
——. *Limited Views: Essays on Ideas and Letters*. Trans. Ronald C. Egan. Cambridge, MA: Harvard University Asia Center, 1998.
——. *Patchwork: Seven Essays on Art and Literature*. Trans. Duncan M. Campbell. Leiden: Brill, 2014.
Rea, Christopher G., ed. *China's Literary Cosmopolitans: Qian Zhongshu, Yang Jiang, and the World of Letters*. Leiden: Brill, 2015.
——, ed. "Yang Jiang." Special issue, *Renditions* 76 (Fall 2011).
——. "Yang Jiang's Conspicuous Inconspicuousness: A Centenary Writer in China's 'Prosperous Age.'" *China Heritage Quarterly* 26 (June 2011). http://www.china-heritagequarterly.org/features.php?searchterm=026_yangjiang.inc&issue=026.

Wu Xuezhao 吴学昭. *Ting Yang Jiang tan wangshi* 听杨绛讲往事 (Listening to Yang Jiang talk about the past). Beijing: Sanlian, 2008.

Yang, Jiang. *Baptism*. Trans. Judith Amory and Yaohua Shi. Hong Kong: University of Hong Kong Press, 2007.

——. "Indian Summer." Trans. Judith Armory and Yaohua Shi. MCLC Resource Center Publication (June 2014). http://u.osu.edu/mclc/online-series/indian-summer.

——. "On Qian Zhongshu and *Fortress Besieged*." Trans. Jesse Field. *Renditions* 76 (Autumn 2011), 68–97.

——. *Six Chapters from My Life 'Downunder.'* Trans. Howard Goldblatt. Seattle: University of Washington Press, 1984.

——. *Women sa* 我们仨 (We three). Beijing: Sanlian, 2003.

30

REVOLUTIONARY REALISM AND REVOLUTIONARY ROMANTICISM: *SONG OF YOUTH*

BAN WANG

Fiction from the period between the 1949 founding of the People's Republic of China (PRC) and the beginning of the Cultural Revolution (1966–1976) can be characterized as "revolutionary romanticism combined with revolutionary realism" (革命浪漫主义与革命现实主义相结合). This combination of seemingly paradoxical elements is the logical extension of paradoxes inherent in the practice of socialist realism, itself an outgrowth of the complex reception and practice of realism since the May Fourth New Culture movement.

Introduced from the West to China, realism was deployed by Chinese writers to fulfill a transformative mission in building a modern Chinese nation-state. Realism arose in the market-driven society of eighteenth-century Europe. Premised on an empirical epistemology and notions of the individual as a self-realizing, self-interested agent, realism signaled the hallmark of literary modernity by breaking with the religious, medieval worldview of the monarchical regimes. As Ian Watt (1957: 62) notes, "In the literary, the philosophical and the social spheres alike the classical focus on the ideal, the universal and the corporate has shifted completely, and the modern field of vision is mainly occupied by the discrete particular, the directly apprehended sensum, and the autonomous individual."

In the May Fourth period, literature was believed to be a potent agent for delivering progressive messages to a mass audience to effect social and political change. As Marston Anderson (1990: 3) points out, whereas Western realism seeks to mimic the world through language and verisimilitude, it was favored by

Chinese writers for its power to transform society. In the 1930s, some conceived of realism as the faithful observation and empirical registering of social ills and quotidian scenes. For others it also carried a moral imperative to deliver a message while heralding the future. Chinese realists were not content with the former—simply laying bare the nitty-gritty minutiae of everyday scenes and exposing life in the raw seemed inadequate—and so began to valorize the ethical impulse in their writing. The split between the realistic depiction of myriad everyday scenes and the expressive, moral impulse for social change was apparent in both the theory and the practice of the eminent realist Mao Dun 茅盾. He urged objective observation as a point of departure for the realistic writer, who should immerse himself or herself in the world's chaotic and murky details and reveal them with fine texture and authenticity. At the same time, Mao Dun also defended the intellectual organization of sensuous details into a coherent structure premised on truthful understanding of society. Influenced by European naturalism, he excelled, in Leo Lee's words, in "meticulous gathering and deployment of material" and portrayed his characters as "victims of socioeconomic forces" (Goldman and Lee 2002: 224). Although in his fiction Mao Dun offered panoramic visions of Chinese society in flux, he hardly indicated that society was to be altered by human agency.

In this early reception of realism in China, a moral thrust and aspiration for a romantically imagined world were interwoven with realistic portrayals. Western realistic authors, as Leo Lee writes, were "received 'romantically'" in China. Conversely, "romantically inclined Chinese writers" tended to be drawn to the realistic aspects of European romanticism and ignore its transcendent, mystical element "in favor of a humanistic, socio-political interpretation" (Goldman and Lee 2002: 184). This balance between showing and telling tipped toward the latter with the rise of socialist realism after Mao Zedong's (1893–1976) "Yan'an Talks" in 1942. The telling not only was to be an exposé of social conditions but also ought be more ideologically transparent and emotionally compelling. Realism was thus elevated to a higher, more intense emotional pitch and endowed with a forward-moving momentum: revolutionary realism driven by popular energy and romantic imaginations of a new world.

One key tenet of Mao's Yan'an Talks enjoined writers to serve the people. A new relationship between showing and telling is reflected in the relationship between consciousness and reality. In Mao's analysis, art and literature originate "realistically" from the richness and immediacy of social reality, and reality is the authentic source from which artists should draw inspiration. Artworks as mental forms are thus products of reflection on social experiences; revolutionary art is a reflection in the artists' minds of the people's life experience. But for Mao, only the reality envisioned by the party could meet the correct criteria for artistic treatment. From this assessment of realism emerged the imperative for writers to absorb the plain, everyday language of the peasants and to appropriate folk art forms because aesthetic forms and indigenous content would be real and authentic to the people (Mao 1967: 18). Yet if uninspired realism exposes only the harsh reality of peasant life, it does little more than mirror actual life conditions, which remain intact in all their sordidness and misery. Artworks, then, should look beyond reality and jolt the audience out of their lethargic acceptance of the status quo. Life reflected in realism should be on "a higher plane, more intense, more concentrated, more typical, near the ideal, and therefore more universal than actual daily reality" (19). Rather than staying on the level of actuality, revolutionary artists should "awaken the masses, fire them with passion, and impel them to unite and struggle in order to transform their environment" (19).

Mao's clarion call marked a shift toward a romantic conception of realism. Realism should recraft apparent reality, romantically and imaginatively, to invest it with utopian visions. To invest it with the power of emotional arousal and of raising consciousness, realism had to be married to a political form of romanticism—not a romanticism marked by subjective whims, fantasy, love, or imaginary freedom, but understood as a power to envision and to create alternative narratives and to project different images of the world, provoking the audience to identify with those visions and to participate in their realization.

This early romantic conception of realism became a full-fledged cultural mode in 1958, when Mao instituted the slogan "Revolutionary Romanticism Combined with Revolutionary Realism" during the Eighth Party Congress as the guiding principle for artistic work (Wang Geding and Chen Shijin 1992: 170). In that year, China was poised to make a "great leap forward," striving to catch up overnight with Great Britain and the United States in industrial, technological, and military power. The call for romanticism in literary production was thus a product of both cultural politics and economic policies.

Since 1949, writers, critics, and literary bureaucrats had argued back and forth about the significance of socialist realism. One camp advocated an honest, down-to-earth immersion in everyday life and free depiction of any aspect of social and psychic realities. Hu Feng 胡风 was one of the most important champions of this earthy realism (Denton 1998: 153–154). The other side, mostly Communist Party bureaucrats and ideologues, asserted that only party policy and socialist ideology should inform and shape literary images of reality. After Hu Feng was persecuted for his views in 1955, the doctrinaire camp got the upper hand. But with the advent of the Hundred Flowers campaign (1956–1957) to promote more imaginative and critical works, the issue was reopened. Unorthodox views, such as those of Qin Zhaoyang 秦兆阳, reappeared, only to be smothered with the consolidation of doctrinaire views in the Anti-Rightist Campaign (1957) and the elevation of romanticism in the Great Leap Forward (1958).

The ideological temper of the Great Leap Forward was marked by an impatience to accelerate socialist development. In this scheme, revolutionary realism can be seen in terms of the Marxist interpretation of history and its related notion of reality. This interpretation sees history as obeying a preconceived motive that propels society from the lower stages of feudalism and capitalism to the higher stages of socialism and communism. The driving force of this social advance is class struggle, and the final victor is the emergent class. Whoever participates in this historical current comes in touch with reality; whoever deviates from it will be swept into the dustbin of history. Coupled with this view of reality is the imperative to transform older modes of ideas and feelings in order to fashion members of a new society. Understanding the law of history, on the one hand, and constantly transforming traditional mentality and habits (自我改造), on the other, are the hallmark of fictional realism (Zhang 1997: 52).

Revolutionary realism therefore has more to do with a futuristic, romantic worldview than with literary techniques for representing nitty-gritty details of human experience. This worldview is an ideal, and revolutionary romanticism is a literary and fictional idealization of that ideal. At the bidding of this Marxist telos of history, revolutionary romanticism aims to transcend empirical reality in the very act of representing it. One of Mao's remarks in the Yanan Talks best illustrates this paradox. Literature and art, Mao (1967: 19) says, should draw on revolutionary practice and be realistic, but at the same time they should be "more intense, more concentrated, more typical, nearer the ideal and therefore more universal than actual everyday life." Revolutionary romanticism is not marked by the whims of authorial imagination, but it does possess an imaginative license that allows it to keep pace with goal-oriented history. It can exaggerate, elevate, emotionalize, and intensify; it creates mythical, heroic, and larger-than-life characters.

Song of Youth (青春之歌), by Yang Mo 杨沫, may be regarded as the exemplar of fictional works in the mode of revolutionary realism combined with romanticism. By no accident, the novel was published in 1958, when revolutionary realism and romanticism became the official guideline for artistic creation. Other novels of this period, such as *Red Crag* (红岩, 1961), *The Saga of Red Flag* (红旗谱, 1957), or *Three Family Alley* (三家巷, 1959), also belong to this mode, but *Song of Youth* more clearly traces the individual's coming-of-age in the revolutionary movement, thus illustrating the dual themes of history and of self-transformation.

Song of Youth follows the growth of the main protagonist, Lin Daojing 林道静, from a lonely and romantic young woman into a mature revolutionary. The narrative of her personal growth in the bildungsroman mode (Meng 1993: 126) can be read as an allegory of the nationalist project of saving an endangered China and transforming it into a strong, modern nation. The story is set from 1930 to 1935, a time of deepening national crisis that saw Japan's gradual occupation of Northeast China, concessions made by the Nationalist government, and the constant eruption of patriotic protests among the urban population. Like many of her generation, Lin's urgent problem is to find a way out of both personal and national desperation. She achieves this by joining the revolutionary ranks and becoming an active participant in history.

At first, Lin is out of touch with this "real" history in the making. She escapes her stepmother's scheme to sell her as mistress to a powerful official, but this spontaneous act of rebellion only lands her in further trouble. She finds herself stranded in a seashore village, with no human relation to turn to. Yu Yongze 余永泽, a student at Beijing University who becomes her first lover, saves her from a suicide attempt. Between them they form an emotional haven, spending their time in romantic musings and conversations laced with the poetry of Heine and Goethe. Their romance exemplifies the individualistic desire for self-fulfillment characteristic of the May Fourth generation, which favored Western romantic literature. But this desire appears far too individualistic, trivial, and petit bourgeois when Lin Daojing later meets Lu Jiachuan 卢嘉川, a student leader and underground party member. Lu and later Lin Hong 林红 and Jiang Hua 江华 are "true" characters at the vanguard of history. With their heroic deeds and self-sacrifice, they envision, write, and act out the real "romance" of Chinese revolution. In contrast, Lin's lover Yu Yongze is a self-centered and mediocre individual preoccupied only with personal advancement and totally unconcerned with the nation's destiny. History and politics—the stark reality of national salvation—become a dividing line that sets off good characters from the bad, the progressive from the retrogressive, the youthful from the prematurely aged. In her life trajectory, Lin Daojing encounters a spectrum of these characters and values. Her bildungsroman delineates the ascent from a weak and wavering bourgeois individual into a firm revolutionary fighter. In the beginning, Lin is physically and mentally homeless and fragile. She is helpless, abandoned in the wilderness. In utter despair, she contemplates suicide. In the closing scenes, by contrast, she emerges as a leader in the 1935 student protest against government pacifism in the face of Japanese encroachment. She is now a powerful figure who "merges into many other selves, forming a gigantic collective, which grants her identity, gives her life and meaning, and secures her emotional attachment and fulfillment. The collective seems to enable her to exercise to the full her energy and to fulfill her desire" (B. Wang 1997: 130).

Lin's story shows how crucial it is to get involved in history and how one can, in the process, transform oneself into the "subject of history." This is what is meant by realism in the Chinese socialist context. The romantic component of revolutionary realism, however, is much less obvious. In spite of the stark and painful reality of class and national struggle, one is struck by the exuberance of emotion and passion the positive characters display. A character like Lu Jiachuan is charming and youthful as well as dynamic and inspirational. He falls in love with Lin Daojing at first sight. His bombastic slogans and histrionic gestures may make for bad art, but this theatricality shows how important it is to elevate and dramatize and to inject transcendence and romance into a sordid reality and a dogmatic character.

The romantic motifs—love, affection, poetry, passion, and imagination—are not opposed to national and political concerns; they become intertwined with them. We may characterize this process as sublimation, a psychic and literary process of rechanneling one's desire, impulse, and affection into politically acceptable outlets. To put it more plainly, in revolutionary romanticism an individual can love politics as passionately and intensely as she loves another human being, sometimes even more fanatically.

Song of Youth is a textbook case of this romantic sublimation. Lin Daojing's life starts like those of many female characters in May Fourth fiction: she breaks away from the patriarchal family, seeks personal freedom, and falls in love, only to find herself economically dependent and psychologically disoriented when she finally marries and becomes a housewife. Lin's predicament is that diagnosed by Lu Xun 鲁迅 (1881–1936) in his celebrated essay "What Happens to Nora After She Leaves Home," which makes reference to Ibsen's play *A Doll's House* and the fate of many self-emancipated Chinese Noras. As Lin lives with Yu Yongze and busies herself with household chores, her romantic fervor lapses into domestic trivia. Her encounter on New Year's Eve, when she joins the patriotic students and hears Lu Jiachuan's inspiring talk, is nothing less than a turning point in her life, for it involves not just a political awakening but also a rekindling of romantic love for a really lovable person. A jealous Yu rightly senses in her sparkling eyes newly found love (Yang 1964: 115). Lin is in love with the revolution as much as she is with the gallant, inspirational, and devoted revolutionary Lu Jiachuan.

From this point on, Lin encounters other exemplary figures—including Jiang Hua, a sober-minded underground party member, and Lin Hong, a female party member and Lin's prison cellmate—who serve as signposts on her life's journey. Her growth is thus one of education, political involvement and experience, and consciousness-raising; it culminates in her joining the party and becoming a political activist. This political growth should not obscure the romantic undercurrent always present in her relationship with male revolutionaries. She not only identifies with these political figures but also becomes emotionally attached to them. In other words, her libidinal impulse is gradually purified of its private and primal stratum and becomes sublimated into "higher" objects of affection.

This libidinal stratum is not sublimated out of existence. It is not repressed for the sake of revolution, but appears in different form. Lin's attachment to male revolutionary figures is still couched in the name of love, even romantic love. Her love for Lu Jiachuan illustrates this "purer" form of love. When Lu is arrested and Lin is unsure that he has been executed, she writes him a love poem (Yang 1992: 424), gazing imaginatively at his image and awaiting him with heartfelt passion. Political identification and love become one. This sublimated desire can sustain itself without the presence of a real person; it readily dotes on a distant and abstract object, including a dead person, allowing it to be easily transferred. How she comes to love Jiang Hua also illustrates this point. Jiang Hua is clearly a substitute for Lu Jiachuan. At first, Jiang is just a comrade and friend (though he is secretly in love with Lin), but Lin gradually discovers that he and Lu have the same admirable qualities. This political affinity increases Jiang's lovability. Toward the end of the novel, Jiang Hua asks if they could be "more to each other than comrades" (548). Lin is overwhelmed by his expression of love, but the image of Lu intervenes and makes her hesitate. Yet this momentary hesitation quickly gives way to a new thought and new love for Jiang because she realizes how alike they all are—Lu Jiachuan, Lin Hong, and Jiang Hua.

Lin Daojing's love affair with revolutionary male figures may be seen as an allegory of romanticism married with realism. Revolutionary realism signifies the direction of history, the destiny of the nation, and the political and class identity of positive characters. Yet realistic portrayal of history can have emotional appeal, even sensual attraction, only when it is written as a romantic love story of a pretty young woman. If the reader believes that one can love one's nation and comrades as one loves one's beloved, then he or she is well prepared to accept and appreciate the marriage between revolutionary realism and revolutionary romanticism.

Bibliography

Anderson, Marston. *The Limits of Realism: Chinese Fiction in the Revolutionary Period*. Berkeley: University of California Press, 1990.

Button, Peter. *Configurations of the Real in Chinese Literary and Aesthetic Modernity*. Leiden: Brill, 2009.

Denton, Kirk A. *The Problematic of Self in Modern Chinese Literature: Hu Feng and Lu Ling*. Stanford, CA: Stanford University Press, 1998.

Goldman, Merle, and Leo Ou-fan Lee, eds. *An Intellectual History of Modern China*. Cambridge: Cambridge University Press, 2002.

Hang, Krista van Fleit. *Literature the People Love: Reading Chinese Texts from the Early Maoist Period (1949–1966)*. New York: Palgrave Macmillan, 2013.

King, Richard. *Milestones on a Golden Road: Writing for Chinese Socialism, 1945–80*. Honolulu: University of Hawai'i Press, 2010.

Mao, Tse-tung. *Mao Tse-tung on Literature and Art*. Beijing: Foreign Language Press, 1967.

Meng, Yue. "Female Images and National Myth." In Tani E. Barlow, ed., *Gender Politics in Modern China: Writing and Feminism*, 118–136. Durham, NC: Duke University Press, 1993.

Wang, Ban. *The Sublime Figure of History: Aesthetics and Politics in Twentieth-Century China*. Stanford, CA: Stanford University Press, 1997.

Wang Geding 王戈丁 and Chen Shijin 陈仕金, eds. *Lishi yu meixue de xuanze* 历史与美学的选择 (Choices of history and aesthetics). Nanjing: Guangxi jiaoyu, 1992.

Watt, Ian. *The Rise of the Novel*. Berkeley: University of California Press, 1957.

Yang Mo 杨沫. *Qinchun zhi ge* 青春之歌 (Song of youth). Beijing: Shiyue wenyi, 1992.

———. *The Song of Youth*. Beijing: Foreign Language Press, 1964.

Zhang Dexiang 张德祥. *Xianshizhuyi dangdai liubian shi* 现实主义当代流变史 (Contemporary history of the changing faces of realism). Beijing: Shehui kexue wenxian, 1997.

31

THE HUNDRED FLOWERS: QIN ZHAOYANG, WANG MENG, AND LIU BINYAN

RICHARD KING

The twin slogan "Let a hundred flowers bloom, let a hundred schools of thought contend" (百花齐放, 百家争鸣) was introduced by Communist Party chairman Mao Zedong in May 1956. The call for a "hundred flowers" was designed to inspire greater variety in the arts, and the "hundred schools," to encourage initiative and expertise, particularly on the part of scientists. This appeal to the nation's intellectuals, articulated on Mao's behalf by propaganda minister Lu Dingyi 陆定一, prompted vigorous debates over Communist Party policies in the arts and led to a brief outburst of literary works exposing a system of government that was autocratic and inefficient. The party's tolerance of such criticism was short-lived: following publication in June 1957 of a revised edition of Mao's "On the Correct Handling of Contradictions among the People" (关于正确处理人民内部矛盾的问题), a speech given in February of that year, the dissenting intellectuals were condemned as "antiparty" (反党) and labeled "rightists" (右派) in the subsequent Anti-Rightist Campaign (反右运动).

Those who view Mao as a duplicitous tyrant interpret the call for a more liberal approach as a trap he set to identify potential dissenters and then destroy them. More likely is that the decision to call for the blooming of a hundred flowers (a metaphor first used in the Warring States period more than two thousand years earlier) was a reaction to domestic realities and developments elsewhere in the Communist bloc. At home, the transformation of agriculture and industry from private to public ownership was virtually complete; the leadership was contemplating a second five-year plan and looking to the intellectuals, hitherto often reluctant partners in building socialism, for technical support and cultural enrichment. In the Soviet Union, the death of Stalin in 1953 had been followed by an ideological "thaw" (a term borrowed from the title of a novella by Ilya Ehrenberg) involving the dismantling of the personality cult that had surrounded Stalin and a relaxation of the party's demand for artists' absolute adherence to the whims of their political masters. Russian writers in the "thaw" years who influenced the Chinese Hundred Flowers included Valentin Ovechkin, creator of investigative reports on official malfeasance, and Galina Nikolaeva, author of *The Director of the MTS and the Chief Agronomist*. In Nikolaeva's novella, the newly appointed young female agronomist is an inspirational model, working with local activists to achieve higher production in a poor collective despite technical and organizational obstacles. Elsewhere in Eastern Europe, worker unrest in Poland and a Hungarian leadership proposing to secede from the Warsaw Pact showed the cracks in post-Stalin international Communist solidarity and left the way open for China to plot an independent course.

In China, much of the liveliest debate on the role of the arts in society and many of the reports and stories most critical of officialdom appeared in the pages of the journal *People's Literature* (人民文学), where they were published by the newly appointed associate editor Qin Zhaoyang 秦兆阳. Qin, who was forty in 1956, had impeccable revolutionary credentials: he came from an impoverished intellectual background, studied at the Lu Xun Academy in Yan'an, and began his career as editor and writer of fiction in the Communist-liberated areas. After 1949, in addition to holding editorial posts, he published short stories and a novel. Qin was no liberal dissident: his mission was to cultivate the hundred flowers required by the party leadership, and in pursuit of this goal he argued for greater scope for authors to write truthfully about problems in society rather than being bound by party-imposed idealism. In the September 1956 issue of *People's Literature*, Qin Zhaoyang published his own pseudonymous article "The Broad Road of Realism" (现实主义广阔的道路). In it he argued that the doctrine of socialist realism inherited from Stalin's Russia mandated slavish adherence to ephemeral party policies and stifled artistic creativity, resulting in formulaic and mediocre works. Qin advocated instead a new "realism of the socialist age" that would better reflect the complexities of society in transition.

Literary works published in *People's Literature* took Qin's "broad road" of critical realism; they included stories of young and idealistic intellectuals whose attempts to bring about much-needed change were frustrated by craven and bureaucratic superiors. Most celebrated at the time, and most notorious in the antirightist backlash, were the works of the young writers Liu Binyan 刘宾雁 and Wang Meng 王蒙; despite later accusations that they had formed a clique with Qin Zhaoyang, these were young authors whose connection to Qin was intellectual rather than personal. Liu Binyan, an admirer of Ovechkin who had met and interviewed the Russian author, contributed the investigative report "At the Bridge Construction Site" (在桥梁工地上) to the April 1956 issue of *People's Literature*, prefaced by an editorial note from Qin Zhaoyang calling for more such "pointed, critical, and satirical" works. In this report, an engineer attempts to speed up the construction of a bridge before rising water levels on the Yellow River halt work for the season. His plan is in the national interest, and the workers support him, but an incompetent local management denounces him for rashness, prevents his proposal from reaching the higher leadership, and waits for directives from above before making even the most trivial decisions; the journalist reporting the case can only lament such conservatism and the effect it will have on the achievement of state goals.

A frustrated journalist is also the focus of Liu Binyan's short story "Our Paper's Inside News," also known as "The Inside News of the Newspaper" (本报内部消息), published in the June 1956 issue of *People's Literature*, with a sequel appearing in the October issue. The story's young heroine is on assignment at a mine where skilled personnel are underemployed by a management unwilling to share them with other units. She supports the mine workers' protests against insufficient work and excessive meetings, only to be summoned back to her paper, where her report is suppressed and she is told that her application for party membership will be successful only if she is compliant and makes no trouble for her complacent superiors. Liu Binyan satirizes the working of the bureaucratic mind in the thoughts of the heroine's boyfriend and colleague: "Leadership, organization, and discipline are the most essential things ... no harm can be done in overdoing the essentials" (Liu 1981: 463).

Wang Meng's story "The Young Newcomer in the Organization Department," also known as "The Newcomer" (组织部新来的青年人), published in the same issue of *People's Literature* as Qin's "broad road" essay, repeats the theme of youthful idealism suppressed. Here the young newcomer, inspired by Nikolaeva's novella (a copy of which he carries in his pocket), seeks to clean up the party organization at a mismanaged factory. He is supported by a female colleague with whom he listens to Russian music and enjoys an innocent friendship, but his superiors, cynical men jaded by their years in the system, invent facts and couch them in officialese to assure the authorities that nothing drastic needs to be done. Wang Meng's conclusion is more optimistic than Liu Binyan's—even though his initiatives are stifled, the young newcomer remains determined to bring about change for the better.

To these stories Qin Zhaoyang added a short one of his own in January 1957. "Silence" (沉默) tells of an official's wife who objects when a line of carts is led by the slowest, with carts behind forbidden by the local district head to pass; she encourages the other carters to pull ahead. The district head tyrannically shouts at the carters who have disobeyed his orders and is abusive toward the woman when she protests. He changes his tune only when he finds that her husband outranks him; then he too is silenced. Qin's allegory was clear: Chinese society would develop at a snail's pace as long as officials jealous of their power continued to thwart the initiative of those activists wanting to bring about improvement.

The authors of these works were exercising an autonomy that had not been evident under Communist Party rule since the writings of the novelist Ding Ling 丁玲, the poet Ai Qing 艾青, and others in Yan'an in the early 1940s. Rather than accept Lenin's formulation, repeated by Mao in his 1942 "Yan'an Talks," that literature was "a cog and a screw" (齿轮和螺丝钉), a small component in the machinery of revolution, Qin Zhaoyang and the writers he published were giving themselves a less subservient role, characterized by Liu Binyan in his writing about Ovechkin as that of an army scout, loyal to the cause while acting independently to inform his commanders of the real situation in the field.

Complaints about the system in literary works were echoed in articles by academic, scientific, and professional intellectuals, especially after the party launched the brief Rectification Campaign (整风运动) to correct bureaucratic practices. If party leaders had been sincere in their call for criticism, that criticism was clearly more virulent than had been expected. The backlash was not long in coming. Those who had responded to Mao's appeal and voiced their objections found themselves denounced in the Anti-Rightist Campaign that began in the summer of 1957; by the time the campaign ended, a tenth of the nation's intellectuals, some half a million people, had been condemned. Many of China's most prominent scholars were denounced, along with well-known writers such as Ding Ling and Ai Qing—in the latter cases, as much for their writings at Yan'an fifteen years before as for any offenses committed during the Hundred Flowers period.

In the June 1957 revised version of his "Correct Handling" speech, Mao gave his ruling on the distinction between the "fragrant flowers" (香花) of socialist art and "poisonous weeds" (毒草) of the kind Qin Zhaoyang had cultivated, insisting that the arts should benefit socialism and strengthen the leadership of the Communist Party. Mao left the final word on the Hundred Flowers to Zhou Yang 周扬, the official charged with overseeing culture: in February 1958, Zhou likened the "rightists" to those who had incited the Hungarian uprising against the Soviet Union (the suppression of which the Chinese government had supported); Zhou also confirmed the party's commitment to the loyalist optimism of socialist realism.

At a meeting in the offices of *People's Literature*, Qin Zhaoyang was denounced and dismissed from his editorial post; his Communist Party membership was also revoked. Qin, Liu Binyan, Wang Meng, and many other condemned "rightists" were ostracized and banished to the countryside for two decades. They were to return to Beijing in the post-Mao rehabilitations, vindicated and remarkably unreconstructed by two decades of ideological remolding, to play their part in the second "Hundred Flowers" in the late 1970s.

Thereafter the three men's lives took different turns. Qin Zhaoyang continued his editorial work, this time at People's Literature Press, nurturing a new generation of writers before his death in 2001. Wang Meng resumed fiction writing, served briefly as minister of culture, and remains a respected public intellectual. Liu Binyan, unrepentantly combative and independent in more repressive times, was expelled a second time from the Communist Party in 1987 and died in exile in the United States in 2005.

Bibliography

Barmé, Geremie, and Bennett Lee, eds. *Fragrant Weeds: Chinese Short Stories Once Labelled as "Poisonous Weeds."* Hong Kong: Joint Publishing, 1983.

Børdhal, Vibeke. *Along the Broad Path of Realism: Qin Zhaoyang's World of Fiction.* London: Curzon Press, 1990.

Chen Sihe 陈思和. *Zhongguo dangdai wenxue shi jiaocheng* 中国当代文学史教程 (A course in the history of modern Chinese literature). Shanghai: Fudan daxue, 1999.

Fokkema, D. W. *Literary Doctrine in China and Soviet Influence, 1956–1960.* The Hague: Mouton, 1965.

Goldman, Merle. *Literary Dissent in Communist China.* Cambridge, MA: Harvard University Press, 1967.

Huang Weilin 黄伟林. *Zhongguo dangdai wenxue xiaoshuojiaqun lun* 中国当代小说家群论 (On groups of fiction writers in modern Chinese literature), 99–162. Beijing: Zhongyang bianyi, 2004.

Kraus, Richard. "Let a Hundred Flowers Blossom, Let a Hundred Schools of Thought Contend." In Ban Wang ed., *Words and Their Stories: Essays on the Language of the Chinese Revolution*, 249–262. Leiden: Brill, 2011.

Liu, Binyan. "The Inside News of the Newspaper." In Hualing Nieh, ed., *Literature of the Hundred Flowers, Volume II: Poetry and Fiction*, 411–464. New York: Columbia University Press, 1981.

Nieh, Hua-ling, ed. *Literature of the Hundred Flowers.* 2 vols. New York: Columbia University Press, 1981.

Qin, Zhaoyang. "The Broad Road of Realism." In Hualing Nieh, ed., *Literature of the Hundred Flowers, Volume II: Poetry and Fiction*, 121–144. New York: Columbia University Press, 1981.

——. "Silence." Trans. Bennett Lee. In W. J. F. Jenner, ed., *Fragrant Weeds—Chinese Short Stories Once Labeled as "Poisonous Weeds,"* 117–122. Hong Kong: Joint Publishing, 1983.

Wagner, Rudolf G. "The Cog and the Scout: Functional Concepts of Literature in Socialist Political Culture—the Chinese Debate in the Mid-Fifties." In Wolfgang Kubin and Rudolf G. Wagner, eds., *Essays in Modern Chinese Literature and Literary Criticism*, 334–400. Bochum: Brockmeyer, 1982.

Wang, Meng. "The Newcomer." Trans. Geremie Barmé. In W. J. F. Jenner, ed., *Fragrant Weeds—Chinese Short Stories Once Labeled as "Poisonous Weeds,"* 71–116. Hong Kong: Joint Publishing, 1983.

32

COLD WAR FICTION FROM TAIWAN AND THE MODERNISTS

CHRISTOPHER LUPKE

The Taiwan modernists emerged through a critical engagement with more ideologically motivated literature, such as the lengthy historical romances laden with anti-Communist rhetoric that dominated fiction writing in the immediate postwar period. To understand modernism, we need first to understand the Cold War era fiction it reacted against. Wang Lan's 王蓝 (b. 1922) popular novel *The Blue and the Black* (蓝与黑, 1958) typifies this period, while Peng Ge's 彭歌 (b. 1926) *Setting Moon* (落月, 1956) functions as a transition to modernism. Superficially, *The Blue and the Black* is pulp romance. It features Zhang Xingya 张醒亚, whose affections waver between a patriotic young nurse named Tang Qi 唐琪 and Zheng Meizhuang 郑美庄, the temperamental daughter of a Sichuan warlord. The predicament of a youth torn between two women of different temperaments is at least as old as *Dream of the Red Chamber* (红楼梦) and was replayed again in Mandarin Ducks and Butterflies (鸳鸯蝴蝶) fiction and the "love and revolution" model of leftist writers such as Mao Dun 茅盾. Wang Lan follows this latter model, but for him there is no dispute as to the hero's alliance—he is firmly entrenched in the Nationalist camp. Thus, more profoundly, *The Blue and the Black* is a politically charged narrative, first depicting the Japanese invasion and then the Communist takeover, seeking to legitimize the Nationalist position along the way. From Tianjin, the novel wends its way to Chongqing and eventually Taiwan, recounting the story of the mainlanders' flight to Taiwan in 1949. Xingya engages in armed combat with both the Japanese and the Eighth Route Army.

Staunchly anti-Communist, this work occasionally even paints the Japanese soldiers somewhat sympathetically, while the Communists are portrayed as sinister, soulless traitors to the Nationalist cause.

The slightly less ideological *Setting Moon* shares this loose narrative style. Although it also depicts idealistic youths dedicated to the resistance, it is foremost a romantic story of the heroine, Yu Xinmei 余心梅. In his mainly stylistic analysis of the novel, T. A. Hsia 夏济安 (1916–1965) almost single-handedly shifted the intellectual discourse in Taiwan from political ideology to literary form. *Literary Review* (文学杂志), where the article was published, served as a transitional venue between the two poles of ideologically informed historical romanticism and the more intricately wrought, less tendentious works of the *Modern Literature* (现代文学) group, established in 1960. Most premodernist authors were mainlanders by birth who had spent their youths on the mainland, not Taiwan nativists, who were born on the island. Because native Taiwanese intellectuals had to learn Mandarin as adults, having been educated in Japanese in the colonial era, they were hampered in their ability to enter Taiwan's literary milieu after the war when Japanese writing was banned.

Other important members of the generation of mainlander émigré authors were Jiang Gui 姜贵 (1908–1980), Pan Renmu 潘人木 (1919–2005), Meng Yao 孟瑶 (1919–2000), Lin Haiyin 林海音 (1918–2001), Ji Gang 纪刚 (b. 1920), Zhao Zifan 赵滋蕃 (1924–1986), and Zhu Xining 朱西宁 (1927–1998). Jiang Gui was the most controversial, least partisan, and best skilled at writing. His novel *Whirlwind* (旋风, 1957), set in Shandong, is an eviscerating dissection of internal relations in both the Chinese Communist Party and the Guomindang. Pan Renmu, Meng Yao, and Lin Haiyin were the best-known women writers of this era. Pan's *Little Cousin Lianyi* (莲漪表妹, 1952) provides insight into the travails of young women growing up on the mainland in a period of foreign incursion, civil war, and forced migration. The same sort of tragic impact of great national events like war and political oppression of personal and family relations is found in Meng's *Before the Sunrise* (黎明前, 1956). Lin's *Old Stories from the Southside* (城南旧事, 1960; aka *Memories of Peking*), set before the war, is somewhat different, articulating the various stories from the point of view of a young girl. Strictly speaking, Lin Haiyin was native Taiwanese, or at least the offspring of such people, but she was born in Japan, was raised in Beijing, and spoke with a northern accent. She subsequently became a highly influential editor and publisher in Taiwan. The sacrifice of a bright future by several promising students in Northeast China for the anti-Japanese cause is the main theme of Ji Gang's *The Rushing Liao River* (滚滚辽河, 1969). Zhao Zifan, best known for his fiction geared toward young adults, wrote *The Lower Half of Society* (半下流社会, 1953) as a record of those who did not escape mainland China until the 1950s and particularly to call attention to their rootlessness as refugees in Hong Kong. Zhu Xining's monumental work *The Jinmen Bombing Incident* (八二三注) focuses on the 1958 bombing incursion into Jinmen (also known as Kinmen or Quemoy). It was actually only published in its full form posthumously, in 2003, but was written in the early 1960s. Generally, all these works were long, loosely written, and plot driven.

Beyond fundamental stylistic differences with authors of the early Cold War era, the modernists had little appetite for recapitulations of the War of Resistance or the civil war. They were equally content to leave discussions of the Chinese Communist Party to the political scientists. They found a comfortable aesthetic haven in the academic environment provided by T. A. Hsia and others, such as Tai Jingnong 台静农, chair of the Chinese department at National Taiwan University from 1948 to 1968. *Modern Literature* was founded by Hsia's Taiwan University undergraduates from the Department of Foreign Languages, the most notable fiction writers of whom were Bai Xianyong 白先勇 (b. 1937), Wang Wenxing 王文兴 (b. 1939), and Chen Ruoxi 陈若曦 (b. 1938). They self-consciously adopted modernism from the dominant literary trends of Western Europe and the United States. Stylistically, they experimented with allegory, stream of consciousness, allusion, and alliterative description; thematically, they treated the emergence of individualism and the breakdown in relational forms of subjectivity, such as traditional filiality and the collective identity of communism. The emphasis on style over ideology is evident even in the juvenilia of these three writers.

In early works—for example, "Hong Kong—1960" (香港—1960, 1963)—Bai Xianyong used stream of consciousness and often depicted inexplicable suicides, such as that of a dejected youth in "Death in Chicago" (芝加哥之死, 1964). His "New Yorker" series focuses on Chinese suffering from alienation after relocating to the United States. *Wandering in the Garden, Waking from a Dream* (台北人, 1973), perhaps his most beloved work, is a collection of short stories, each portraying a different member of the "lost generation" of mainlanders who fled to Taiwan after the revolution. In contrast to the 1950s generation whose fiction recites their mainland experiences, the characters in *Wandering* are haunted by apparitions of the past. The stories are structured not as historical romance but as vignettes that highlight exquisitely mellifluous language and delicate yet complex psychological portraits. Though sympathetically rendered, the characters are seldom viewed as exemplars of the Nationalist cause.

Wandering begins with "The Eternal Snow Beauty" (永远的尹雪艳, 1965), in which mainland exiles attempt to reconstruct their lives in Taipei, even if only in an imaginary way. The use of interior space to evoke claustrophobia reminds one of Eileen Chang's 张爱玲 style, without the contemptuous tone. The protagonists of *Wandering* appear as small islands disconnected from each other, yet when connected in the mind of the reader their stories form a larger narrative of exile among these mainland refugees. Another one of the small islands is Taipan Jin 金大班, formerly a taxi dancer on the mainland. "The Last Night of Taipan Jin" (金大班的最后一夜, 1967) commingles moments from the present with recollections of the past. However, unlike the historical narratives of the 1950s, Bai Xianyong's more modernist approach avoids direct narrative, instead blending in recollections by way of interior monologue. He deploys supporting characters that enhance these reminiscences: the two men, Jin's Shanghai lover Moon Boy 月如 and Phoenix Zhu's 朱凤 Cantonese fling, serve as foils that illustrate the changes in Taipan Jin's attitude toward life with the passage of time. The predicament of the isolated émigré seeking refuge in historical imagination also gives rise to moments of poetic commentary. The reminiscence affords Taipan Jin's otherwise hardened character a soft pathos, contrasting her present unromantic view of men with her youthful naiveté. Such a pathos is also found in "Winter Nights" (冬夜, 1970), wherein two original participants in the May Fourth movement, one a specialist on Byron, the other an ancient Chinese history professor at Berkeley, find themselves marginalized fifty years later. Within the story are lyrical descriptions of the decrepit home, the ailing physical condition of the characters, and the incessant rain of the Taipei winter—each a memento of wasteland imagery, echoing the disillusioned tone of Bai's modernist master T. S. Eliot.

The most sophisticated work in *Wandering* is "Wandering in the Garden, Waking from a Dream" (游园惊梦, 1965). The heroine, Madame Qian 钱夫人, has come to a party from southern Taiwan, a double exile, first from her home in mainland China and second from her fellow mainlanders in Taipei. The story's drama hinges on her repressed memory reemerging during the course of the party in one of the finest examples of stream of consciousness in the Chinese language. Madame Qian's reverie is quilted together with allusions to *Dream of the Red Chamber, Peony Pavilion* (牡丹亭), Cao Zhi's 曹植 "The Goddess of Lo River" (洛神赋), and Li Shangyin's 李商隐 "Brocade Zither" (锦瑟). The intended effect cannot be appreciated without conversance with the literary tradition, which suggests that Bai is inscribing his work into that tradition as a means to textually resolve his political and cultural marginality. Bai Xianyong's later fiction includes the long novel *Crystal Boys* (孽子, 1983), which extends the theme of exile to the social issue of homosexuality in Taiwan (see "Homoeroticism in Modern Chinese Literature").

Wang Wenxing's novels *Family Catastrophe* (家变, 1973) and *Backed Against the Sea* (背海的人, 1981 and 1999) are more concerned with cultural critique than is Bai Xianyong's fiction; a cacophony of subversive linguistic experimentation, his works challenge the reader much more than Bai's relatively euphonic style. Wang Wenxing embraces and even accentuates his marginal status. His iconoclasm and avant-garde sensibility are demonstrated by his enthusiastic efforts to publish translations of many European modernists in *Modern Literature*, which he edited with Bai Xianyong, Chen Ruoxi, and others. Wang's early stories are often accounts of eccentric young boys. In "Flaw" (欠缺, 1964), for example, the young first-person narrator falls for a beautiful neighbor woman and is able to temper his feelings only by focusing on her flaws. The story ends ironically when she swindles all the neighbors, absconds with their money, and turns out indeed to be tragically flawed.

Family Catastrophe, Wang Wenxing's first novel, is one of the most uniquely structured novels in any language, composed of a bifurcated narrative with one part ordered alphabetically from A to O and the other numerically from 1 to 157. Focusing on the Fan family, the novel begins in the alphabetical narrative, with the flight of Fan Minxian 范闽贤, the family patriarch, from the home and the discovery that he is missing by his wife and the main character, son Fan Ye 范晔, who then spends the rest of the alphabetical narrative searching for him. The alternating numerical narrative recounts the family history from when the toddler Fan Ye begins reading to the present. The narratives converge at the end of the book when Fan Ye abandons his search and concedes that his father is gone for good. The two narrative modes are characterized by antithetical tones: the numerical one a bold rejection of filiality, the alphabetical one conciliatory and contrite. Together, the two narratives form a "split" psyche, a subjectivity divided against itself. The unfolding of the narrative seems like a futile attempt to suture the insurmountable fissure between a Western individual stance, on the one hand, and the more relational, respectful, and submissive stance of filiality, on the other. The double narrative also undermines any attempt to establish a stable, univocal reading of *Family Catastrophe*. It neither positions itself against the tradition nor endorses a resurgence of filiality. Although the family saga parallels the postwar flight from mainland China, the incorporation of history is effected obliquely. Direct references to history, such as the family's voyage to Taiwan in the bottom of a fishing vessel, are inserted almost parenthetically.

Backed Against the Sea, Wang's subsequent novel, extends the linguistic and structural experimentation of *Family Catastrophe*, heightening the ambivalent tone exhibited in the earlier work. However, in contrast to the first novel, *Backed Against the Sea* is a narrative of near pure isolation, featuring Lone Star 独星, the one-eyed, blathering soothsayer, on the lam from the police and in hiding from Taipei gangsters. His comical persona makes this work more playful and humorous, and while the themes dredged up—fate (命) and fortune telling, the Chinese political bureaucracy, and prostitution—are all standard themes in Chinese literature, the narrator's bantering tone foils attempts to discern whether Wang Wenxing employs Lone Star to satirize these institutions and rituals or whether Lone Star's participation in them is the principle object of ridicule. The novel is a tour de force of linguistic play—everything from double entendre and mixed metaphor to more visual escapades, such as the insertion of phonetic symbols, inverted characters, stuttering, and gaps in the text.

Bai Xianyong and Wang Wenxing deal with the inexorable weight of history elliptically, but in her mature work Chen Ruoxi directly addresses political and historical issues. Her early works were case studies combined with formal experimentation. "The Last Performance" (最后夜戏, 1961), for example, is a psychological portrait of Jin Xizai 金喜仔, a drug-addicted opera singer, on her last professional leg. It dramatizes the diminished life of the heroine, hopelessly smitten with a lover and left to raise his child. Chen uses symbolism in the description of the child's face, which resembles that of her lost love, along with clipped, economical dialogue, to articulate Xizai's predicament and achieve the literary ideals advanced by T. A. Hsia: to show rather than tell. Although somewhat similar to Bai Xianyong's depiction of the unseemly life of female singers, Chen's work contains more social commentary, foreshadowing her movement toward political concerns. Xizai initially admires the beauty of her own child, but his physical similarity to her lover gives the work an ironic twist.

Chen Ruoxi's best-known work is the collection *The Execution of Mayor Yin* (尹县长, 1976), which germinated from an ill-fated "return" to China on the eve of the Cultural Revolution. For many years, the stories in this collection were considered the literary word on the Cultural Revolution. Chen's ambiguous status as a returned overseas Chinese enabled her to carry out the project; such an account would have been unimaginable had she grown up in the People's Republic. *Mayor Yin* subjected the Cultural Revolution to a critique honed according to the methods she developed as a student of modernism. Her Taiwanese background was effaced, at least to English-speaking audiences, adding power to her voice. But her unique status was precisely what afforded her a position to speak out, even as it determined the form in which the critique would be delivered.

In the title piece, Chen Ruoxi's creation of Mayor Yin, the former Nationalist commander turned Communist exemplar who faces persecution during the Cultural Revolution with demure yet dignified resignation, represents a further development of her ability to project political and social commentary onto the description of individual characters. In his initial fervor to be absolved of all feudal sins, Mayor Yin proffers a false confession that he originated from the landlord class. His yearning for absolution can be satisfied only through confession, which eventually results in Red Guards exploiting the confusion over his class background. The narrator is a first-person observer of the situation, not unlike that found in Ding Ling's 丁玲 "When I Was in Xia Village" (我在霞村的时候). She relates the story in a tone of understated disbelief. Her own implicit biases are undercut by Mayor Yin's unwittingly poignant questioning of her political stance. Chen Ruoxi wages the critique not by frontal assault but by shaping the events of the narrative into dramatic irony. These stories solidify Chen's stature as a writer whose art emerges from the mixture of personal lives with cataclysmic political events.

"Chairman Mao Is a Rotten Egg" (晶晶的生日, 1976) uses humor to illustrate the absurdity of the Cultural Revolution. Here, pregnant Teacher Wen 文老师, the first-person narrator, finds herself implicated in a political situation: her toddler son has allegedly called Chairman Mao "a rotten egg." Chen uses dialogue to achieve ironic effect, for the embattled condition of the individual, pitted against state-sanctioned selflessness, is underscored by the little boy, who, rather than anticipating his birthday, asks his mother, "Mommy, what's a birthday?" The claustrophobia and domestic paranoia of Teacher Wen forced into tight living quarters with suspicious neighbors reveals a debt to the work of Eileen Chang.

Chen Ruoxi continued to compose social satire, exemplified by "The Tunnel" (地道, 1978). The story opens with the widower Master Hong 洪师傅, who seeks a relationship with a middle-aged divorcée named Li Mei 李妹, whom he admires for her diligence as a model worker. Friends and family members discourage their relationship, so they seek privacy in an air raid tunnel, only to be unintentionally locked inside and left to die. After settling in the United States in the late 1970s, Chen began exploring the contradictions overseas Chinese and China experts encounter in dealing with the People's Republic. The story "The Crossroads" (路口, 1980), for example, involves Yu Wenxiu 余文秀, a divorcée from Taiwan who lives near a busy intersection in Washington, D.C. The crossroads becomes a leitmotif in the story as she debates whether to embark on a new relationship with a Chinese economist from Taiwan who now leans toward China. Wenxiu's daughter, Ading 阿町, illustrates the generational differences among Chinese in the diaspora. The political subtext for "The Crossroads" is the imprisonment of Wei Jingsheng 魏京生 during the Democracy Wall Incident (1978), an issue as timely today as it was thirty years ago. Her ultimate decision not to pursue the relationship has personal as well as political implications and exemplifies how inextricably related these levels are.

Whether crafting lyrical descriptions of tragically marginalized characters (as in the case of Bai Xianyong), or rendering characters tormented by social conflict (with the formal experiments of Wang Wenxing), or confronting the historical problems of contemporary China (as in the psychological profiles of Chen Ruoxi), the Taiwan modernists share a devotion to individualism and respect for literary perfectionism, as well as antipathy toward broader historical narrative, making their work unique in Chinese literature during the time they flourished and affording them a prominent place in the history of modern Chinese literature.

Bibliography

Bai, Xianyong (Pai Hsien-yung). *Crystal Boys*. Trans. Howard Goldblatt. San Francisco: Gay Sunshine Press, 1990.

———. "Death in Chicago." Trans. Susan McFadden. *Tamkang Review* 9, 3 (1979): 344–358.

———. *Wandering in the Garden, Waking from a Dream*. Trans. Bai Xianyong and Patia Yasin. Bloomington: Indiana University Press, 1982.

——. "Xianggang—1960" 香港—1960 (Hong Kong—1960). *Xiandai wenxue* 21 (1964): 14–20.
Chang, Yvonne Sung-sheng. *Modernism and the Nativist Resistance: Contemporary Fiction from Taiwan*. Durham, NC: Duke University Press, 1993.
Chang, Yvonne Sung-sheng, Michelle Yeh, and Ming-ju Fan, eds. *The Columbia Sourcebook of Literary Taiwan*. New York: Columbia University Press, 2014.
Chen, Ruoxi. "The Crossroads." Trans. Hsin-sheng Kao. In *The Short Stories of Chen Ruoxi*, 16–75. Lewiston, NY: Edwin Mellen Press, 1992.
——. *The Execution of Mayor Yin and Other Stories of the Great Proletarian Cultural Revolution*. Trans. Nancy Ing and Howard Goldblatt. Bloomington: Indiana University Press, 1978.
——. "The Last Performance." Trans. Timothy Ross and Joseph S. M. Lau. In Joseph Lau, and Timothy Ross, eds., *Chinese Stories from Taiwan: 1960–1970*, 3–12. New York: Columbia University Press, 1976.
——. "The Tunnel." Trans. C. C. Wang. In Joseph S. M. Lau, and Howard Goldblatt, eds., *The Columbia Anthology of Modern Chinese Literature*, 289–303. New York: Columbia University Press, 2007.
Chi, Pang-yuan, and David Der-wei Wang, eds. *The Last of the Whampoa Breed: Stories of the Chinese Diaspora*. New York: Columbia University Press, 2003.
Chiang, Kuei (Jiang Gui). *The Whirlwind*. Trans. Timothy Ross. San Francisco: Chinese Materials Center, 1977.
Faurot, Jeannette, ed. *Chinese Fiction from Taiwan*. Bloomington: Indiana University Press, 1980.
Lee, Leo Ou-fan. "Dissent Literature from the Cultural Revolution." *Chinese Literature: Essays, Articles, Reviews* 1, 1 (1979): 59–80.
Lin, Haiyin. *Memories of Peking: South Side Stories*. Trans. Nancy Ing and Pang-yuan Chi. Hong Kong: Chinese University Press, 1992.
Lupke, Christopher. "(En)gendering the Nation in Pai Hsien-yung's (Bai Xianyong) 'Wandering in the Garden, Waking from a Dream.'" *Modern Chinese Literature* 6, 1–2 (1992): 157–177.
——, ed. *The Magnitude of Ming: Command, Allotment and Fate in Chinese Culture*. Honolulu: University of Hawai'i Press.
——. "Wang Wenxing and the 'Loss' of China." *boundary 2* 25, 3 (1998): 97–128.
Peng Ge 彭歌. *Luoyue* 落月 (Setting Moon). Taipei: Yuanjing, 1977.
Riep, Steven L. "Bai Xianyong." In Thomas Moran, and Ye (Dianna) Xu, eds., *Dictionary of Literary Biography: Chinese Fiction Writers, 1950–2000*, 3–17. Columbia, SC: Bruccoli Clark Layman, 2013.
Wang, Lan. *The Blue and the Black*. Trans. Michael Steelman. Taipei: Chinese Materials Center, 1987.
Wang, Wenxing. *Backed Against the Sea*. Trans. Edward Gunn. Ithaca, NY: Cornell University Press, 1993.
——. *Family Catastrophe*. Trans. Susan Wan Dooling. Honolulu: University of Hawai'i Press, 1995.
——. "Flaw." Trans. Chen Zhuyun. In Joseph Lau, and Timothy Ross, eds., *Chinese Stories from Taiwan: 1960–1970*, 15–27. New York: Columbia University Press, 1976.

33

NATIVISM AND LOCALISM IN TAIWANESE LITERATURE
CHRISTOPHER LUPKE

Lu Xun 鲁迅 and Mao Dun 茅盾 introduced the term *xiangtu wenxue* (乡土文学), or "nativist literature," to Chinese literary circles in the 1920s. Interest in the term, a loose translation of the German *Heimat Roman* (homeland novel), stemmed from a desire for writers from the provinces to express the local color of the places from which they originated (see "Shen Congwen and Imagined Native Communities"). In Japan, anthropologists adopted the term *kyôdo bungaku*, or "nativist art," to describe works that epitomize the national character of Japan by crystallizing the essence of particular localities. "Nativist literature" also gained currency among Taiwanese authors in the 1930s to highlight regionalist concerns in subject and language. "Nativism" is a term of layered ironies, for what has come to stand for the intrinsic features of a culture devoid of or hostile to foreign influence has in fact been imported twice over, from Europe via Japan. In addition, what was once a term employed to express national characteristics eventually came to represent the depiction of regional elements in Taiwanese society in contrast to modernism in Taiwan and literature from mainland China.

"Localist literature" (本土文学) is a term that came along much later and was heard with more frequency beginning in the 1980s. Its aim was to provide an additional level of distinction by contrasting those writers, mainly from outside the greater Taipei area and particularly the south, who most fervently touted their Taiwanese identity and in most cases repudiated their Chinese heritage. Most authors associated with the term nativism did not repudiate

Chinese culture and did not call for Taiwan's political independence from China. By contrast, localist authors tend to favor separatism.

Nativist literature movements and debates occurred in Taiwan during the Japanese occupation (1895–1945) and in the late 1940s, but the best known of the nativist writers are those who flourished in the 1960s and 1970s. Of them, three of the most prominent fiction writers are Huang Chunming 黄春明 (b. 1935), Wang Zhenhe 王祯和 (1940–1990), and Chen Yingzhen 陈映真 (b. 1937). Huang Chunming embarked on his writing career in 1962 by submitting short stories to the *United Daily News* (联合报) literary supplement, edited by Lin Haiyin 林海音 (1918–2001), a native Taiwanese of Hakka descent. As Huang developed confidence as a writer, he branched out and submitted works to numerous publications, including *Literary Quarterly* (文学季刊), the most important venue for nativist writers during the 1960s and 1970s. "The Fish" (鱼, 1968), a haunting work that evokes the poverty of Taiwanese in the countryside, begins with adolescent A Cang 阿苍 pedaling furiously toward home on an oversized bicycle, a fresh fish dangling precariously from the handlebars. The narrative shifts between the boy's eagerness to demonstrate his accomplishment to his grandfather 阿公 and flashbacks detailing his bitter childhood as an apprentice. "The Fish" is filled with suspense over what will happen when the boy meets up with his grandfather without the fish, which fell off the bike en route. The suspense turns to pathos as the grandfather, taunted by the boy's insistence that he did indeed bring home the fish, beats him. The dramatic tension hinges on the discrepancy between what each views as important: A Cang values the gesture of bringing home the fish, whereas the old man considers the act irrelevant if one fails to produce the fish. Poverty drives people to relinquish their sense of propriety.

For Huang, propriety is a combination of mutual respect and filial behavior, both of which have been undermined by global capitalism. In "His Son's Big Doll" (儿子的大玩偶, 1967), for example, Kunshu 坤树 makes his living wearing a sandwich board and clown makeup, transforming himself into a human advertisement. The torment Kunshu feels is enacted structurally by mixing a distanced third-person narrative voice with first-person comments made through interior monologue and with depictions and dialogue from supporting characters without access to this interiority. This reinforces the vividness of Kunshu's isolation from others and his own self-loathing. His facial makeup masks his identity, yet it is necessary for the job and thus for his economic survival. In a futile effort to escape humiliation, Kunshu secures the more dignified position of pedicab driver, which means he can shed the makeup. But his son, crying out in fright, ironically mistakes his true face for a stranger. His feelings are assuaged only by his father's reapplication of the clown makeup. Although a stirring critique of emergent capitalism in a client state of the Cold War era United States, the most remarkable feature of Huang's descriptive technique rests in his ability to penetrate the thoughts and feelings of lower-class, marginal figures such as the Sandwich Man. Revealing the interiority of characters who appear to mainstream society to be opaque and inaccessible is one of the hallmarks of Huang's craft.

This is equally true of "A Flower in the Rainy Night" (看海的日子, 1967), which remains oddly ambivalent about traditional Chinese values. Huang walks a tightrope between a maudlin rendering of the prostitute heroine Amei 阿梅 that celebrates traditional notions of nature, reproductivity, and filiality and a feminist critique that repudiates the patriarchal system. Amei, a foster daughter bonded into prostitution, abhors her lot. She paradoxically seeks deliverance from her fate through the birth of a son. Indeed, when she returns to her impoverished natal family in the mountains, the villagers all feel that the apportionment of government-owned potato fields to them is a result of her auspiciousness. Her reward is the birth of a son. However, Amei's conceiving with an inexperienced man and then leaving the trade to raise her child alone is a mark of agency seldom depicted in Chinese literature. Huang Chunming's work is distinguished by probing the bewildering middle ground between resignation and hope.

Huang's "Young Widow" (小寡妇) builds on this ambivalence. Beginning as a critique, the narrative voice ultimately cannot help but render the young American GIs in a sympathetic light, leaving war itself the ultimate villain. The story begins with Ma Shanxing 马善行 recasting a typical nightclub into something Confucian. His new creation, Young Widow, is predicated on fetishizing traditional Chinese feminine virtue, particularly chaste widowhood, as it plays libidinally on the psyches of American troops on furlough from Vietnam. The transgression of this Confucian virtue is supposed to forge a sense of the erotic and illicit. The ideal "young widow" would be "like an iceberg on the outside, but inside she is a seething volcano." The erotics of transgression are too subtle for the young GIs, who are more preoccupied with the trauma of fighting a war they do not understand. Huang's inclusion of the sexually impotent Louie 路易, for example, haunted by grotesque battle scenes that mix violence, sex, and guilt over the war effort, anticipates subsequent American literary and filmic psychodramas of the Vietnam War.

While Wang Zhenhe shares some concerns with Huang Chunming, such as the tensions between urban and rural, native Taiwanese and mainlanders, and the prostitution of women in both the war effort and the global capitalist economy, the tone of his work is quite different and very individualistic. Wang's early work was first published in *Modern Literature* (现代文学) and later in *Literary Quarterly*. Wang Zhenhe is fascinated with exploring the grotesque and unseemly side of the human character, in particular marginal figures who by nature transgress the social norms of cultured society. By flouting social etiquette, Wang's carefully drawn incendiaries illustrate the clash between high culture—that is, the literary apparatus—and the low culture of the common people (老百姓). His first story, "Ghost, North Wind, Man" (鬼,北风,人, 1961),

is just such an exploration; long before he acquired a penchant for social commentary, Wang was writing about bizarre figures. "Ghost" depicts Qin Guifu 秦贵福, the alcoholic, gambling indigent who desires to sleep with his sister Liyue 丽月. There is no silent dignity in the face of social pressures for Wang Zhenhe's literary cast. A modernist piece that exposes perversion, "Ghost" is a vignette that discloses human putrefaction through interior monologue and variable points of view, as well as flashbacks.

Wang's first mature work is the short story "An Oxcart for Dowry" (嫁妆一牛车, 1967), a scandalous, comical portrait of destitution. Exhibiting neither sympathy nor contempt, the narrator presents Wanfa 万发, a deaf peasant who farms an infertile plot of land with his wife. The remarkable feature of this story is not the subject matter—peasants abound in modern Chinese fiction. What is astounding is the manner in which the narrator subjects the characters to ridicule and the subtle juxtaposition of elements requiring great erudition, such as the Henry James quote at the beginning (decrying in English the limitations of Schubert), with the profanity of Wanfa and his ilk. Wang Zhenhe's clever intellect even mocks the reader, for in the end we cannot discern a stable moral tone but are left with an indelible image of the abjectly impoverished, forced to perform the unthinkable in order to survive. Rather than provide an opportunity for sympathy, Wanfa's deafness allows the narrator to carefully maneuver the narrative point of view in various directions.

"Xiao Lin Comes to Taipei" (小林来台北, 1973) represents a new stage for Wang. Though one of his finest social satires, the work is decidedly monologic in tone. The comic elements tend to serve the very serious goal of exposing the exploitative effects of capitalism on the daily lives of Taipei's urban workers. The theme of the Taiwanese rustic coming to the city to seek his fortune only to be disaffected by its commodified culture has since become pervasive in Taiwan literature and film. Wang is far more sympathetic to the protagonist in this story than he is in his previous work. In addition, he has developed his use of wordplay by inserting English words for humorous effect. The characters' names are homophonous with words for "Rotten Corpse" (烂尸), "Throw Out the Garbage" (倒垃圾), "Kick Ass" (踢屁股), and the like. Focusing on the comprador class in Taiwan, with Xiao Lin playing the role of observer, the work takes place in a travel agency, describing the sycophantic way Taiwanese workers toady to foreign clientele and sacrifice the well-being of others for material gain.

Wang extends his satiric voice in the campy burlesque *Rose, Rose, I Love You* (玫瑰, 玫瑰, 我爱你, 1984). Though it shares the theme of Huang's "Young Widow," both involving pimps who hawk their prostitutes to U.S. military personnel on leave from the Vietnam War, the tone of *Rose* could not be more different. Wang uses the theme of war and prostitution to exercise his boundless affinity for linguistic play. The characters all possess humorous or ironic names, with that of the main character, the pimp Dong Siwen 董斯文, meaning "refined or cultured." The novel centers on a few key scenes that feature Dong's scatological performance judging bar girls, goading a politician into a striptease for votes, and beholding a medical doctor's homosexual advances on a patient. Deft use of transliteration and double entendre for satirical effect turns this work into a cultural battleground, for it is reminiscent of a ribald Broadway musical comedy whose carefully choreographed theatricality forces the reader to contemplate what in Taiwanese society is the limitation of kitsch.

One does not typically associate humor with Chen Yingzhen. The most politicized of the nativist group, he spent years as a prisoner of conscience in Taiwan. His work has evolved greatly, given what he has encountered in life, but some themes have nevertheless remained constant. Chen has always been interested in the power of literature to conjoin seemingly unbridgeable experiences and relationships. The structure of his works is often self-consciously disjunct, compelling one to piece together the "mysteries" of the characters within them. In "A Race of Generals" (将军族, 1964), for example, one must ask why the two main characters are referred to as generals. What is the cause of their inexplicable deaths at the end? Triangle Face 三角脸 and Skinny Little Maid 小瘦丫头儿 are musicians in a funeral troupe thrown together by predicament—he a mainlander who has escaped to Taiwan during the civil war and left his wife behind, she a Taiwanese sold into prostitution, several years his junior. While fundamentally different in background, the two seem naturally drawn to each other. This unique bond combined with the jarring shift back and forth between past and present undermines the reader's attempt to make complete sense of the story. The oblique references to Taiwan's infamous Green Island political prison testifies to Chen's courage as a writer: a work, no matter how elliptical, that mixes images of dead generals, metaphorical or not, with references to Green Island could incite the ire of censors.

The difficulty of Taiwanese and mainlanders to fathom each other's identity resurfaces in Chen's existentialist classic "My First Case" (第一件差事, 1967). In this story, a young Taiwanese police detective must figure out why a middle-aged mainlander has committed suicide. Detective Du 杜警员 notes that the deceased Hu Xinbao 胡心保 has been pondering life's meaning, a story line that can be read as the general plight of the human condition. However, the references to his ethnic dislocation highlight the specificity to Taiwan and militate against a universalist reading. The story consists of splicing together Du's interviews with various characters. This paratactic narrative reveals as much about those characters as it does the mystery of Hu's untimely expiration.

Following his release from prison in 1975, Chen Yingzhen turned to exposing problems of Taiwan's economic dependence on the United States and Japan. "Night Freight" (夜行货车, 1978) is an intriguing accumulation of characters who all work in the Taipei office of a large American multinational firm. How they deal with their situation is very interesting: J. P. 林荣平, a Taiwanese executive, placates his American boss while biding his time until he can take over the office when Morgenthau 摩根索 retires. Morgenthau seems more preoccupied with his lust for Chinese women and derision of their culture than for maintaining a profit margin. Linda—Liu Xiaoling 刘小玲, born to mainlander parents—is hoping to find a husband someday but has given up on her longtime affair with J. P. in favor of the tempestuous "James" Zhan Yihong 詹奕宏, who loathes the American company and eventually takes umbrage at an off-color remark from Morgenthau. Linda is attracted to Zhan's anti-imperialistic fury, but she fears it too. She contemplates "escaping" to America, which functions in the story as an imaginary promised land. The notion of cultural ventriloquism, where one assumes the voice of the economic dominant and adopts a "slave" mentality, exhibiting no allegiances, no convictions, but only fetishes for "classy" automobiles and women, is counterpoised by the deep baritone of the freight train, Taiwan's bloodline running from the countryside to the city.

With the tacit relaxation of political censorship in the 1980s, Chen Yingzhen began to write stories detailing the political history of Taiwan. "Zhao Nandong" (赵南栋, 1987), about the way in which family and friends are rent asunder by the February 28 Incident of 1947, is the most important. It contains explicit reference to the Nationalist pacification campaign in which thousands of leftists were executed. Ye Chunmei 叶春美, a Taiwanese woman sentenced to life imprisonment (commuted after twenty-five years), seeks closure on her past by finding Zhao Nandong, the son of two political prisoners. His mother, Song Rongxuan 宋蓉萱, was executed after giving birth to him in prison. His father Zhao Qingyun 赵庆云 served twenty-five years. Each section of the narrative is told from the perspective of a major character. For Chen, the insurmountable cultural fissure created by political terror is healed only through literature.

Strictly speaking, "nativism" is a misnomer; all three aforementioned writers have at one time or another disavowed the term. It was assigned after the fact to describe the phenomenon of the authors' emergence in the 1960s and 1970s. "Localism," by contrast, is a term chosen self-consciously by the authors themselves, who seem to embrace it. Ye Shitao 叶石涛 (1925–2008), a creative writer and scholar based in the southern areas of Tainan and Gaoxiong, for example, sought to draw a clear distinction between his cohort and those who mainly lived in Taipei, such as Huang, Wang, and Chen. He also emphasized the continuities between writers of the Japanese colonial period, such as Lai He 赖和 (1894–1943), Yang Kui 杨逵 (1906–1985), Lü Heruo 吕赫若 (1914–1951), and Wu Zhuoliu 吴浊流 (1900–1976), and postwar literary figures such as himself, Zhong Zhaozheng 钟肇政 (b. 1925), Zhong Lihe 钟理和 (1915–1960), Liao Qingxiu 廖清秀 (b. 1927), Li Qiao 李乔 (b. 1934), and Zheng Qingwen 郑清文 (b. 1932). For most first-generation postwar Taiwanese authors, resurrecting their literary careers was an arduous task because they had been educated in and wrote in Japanese, which was banned after the war. An exception was Zhong Lihe, arguably the most important Taiwanese (Hakka) writer of the 1950s, whose tragic death cut short a prolific career. Because he had been educated in

Beijing during the Republican era, Zhong wrote in beautiful modern prose, mostly about the impoverished people in the southern Taiwan countryside. Liao Qingxiu, who wrote of the brutality of Japanese colonialism, was an early example of a Taiwanese author who learned Mandarin Chinese late and overcame the language barrier. Ye Shitao and Zhong Zhaozheng (another Hakka author) emerged later. Ye Shitao actually spent time in prison during the early years of the aforementioned pacification campaign in the 1950s. In addition to their literary writings, these two were stalwarts in the publication of major journals devoted to nativist literature such as *Taiwan Literary Arts* (台湾文艺). Li Qiao (also Hakka), whose long fiction is perhaps the most substantial expression of nativist consciousness, produced the monumental trilogy *Wintry Night* (寒夜) in the late 1970s and early 1980s. It is a saga, told through the frame of one extended family, depicting the history of the Hakka people's migration to Taiwan, their struggle to establish themselves agriculturally and economically, their resistance to the Japanese, their ultimate conscription by the Japanese, and their wartime survival. Li Qiao was also the first author in the 1980s, well before the 1987 lifting of martial law, to broach the subject of the White Terror pacification campaign. Zheng Qingwen, particularly admired for his short works, is highly adept at etching minute portraits of individual and ordinary people. The breadth of all the works these various authors have produced scarcely allows one to consider them as part of a single movement.

Bibliography

Chang, Yvonne Sung-Sheng. *Modernism and the Nativist Resistance: Contemporary Fiction from Taiwan*. Durham, NC: Duke University Press, 1993.

Chang, Yvonne Sung-Sheng, Michelle Yeh, and Ming-ju Fan, eds. *The Columbia Sourcebook of Literary Taiwan*. New York: Columbia University Press, 2014.

Chen, Yingzhen. "My First Case." Trans. Cheung Chi-yiu and Dennis T. Hu. In Joseph S. M. Lau and Timothy Ross, eds., *Chinese Stories from Taiwan: 1960–1970*, 26–61. New York: Columbia University Press, 1976.

——. "Night Freight." Trans. James C. T. Shu. In Joseph Lau, ed., *The Unbroken Chain: An Anthology of Taiwan Fiction from 1926*, 103–132. Bloomington: Indiana University Press, 1983.

——. "A Race of Generals." In Lucien Miller, trans. and ed., *Exiles at Home: Short Stories of Ch'en Ying-chen*, 69–82. Ann Arbor: University of Michigan Center for Chinese Studies, 1986.

——. "Zhao Nandong." Trans. Duncan Hewitt. *Renditions* 35–36 (1991): 65–86.

Faurot, Jeannette, ed. *Chinese Fiction from Taiwan*. Bloomington: Indiana University Press, 1980.

Goldblatt, Howard. "The Rural Stories of Huang Ch'un-ming." In Jeannette Faurot, ed., *Chinese Fiction from Taiwan*, 110–133. Bloomington: Indiana University Press, 1980.

Huang Chunming. "The Fish." Trans. Howard Goldblatt. In *The Drowning of an Old Cat and Other Stories*, 1–11. Bloomington: Indiana University Press, 1982.

———. "Flowers in the Rainy Night." Trans. Earl Wieman. In Joseph S. M. Lau and Timothy Ross, eds., *Chinese Stories from Taiwan: 1960–1970*, 195–241. New York: Columbia University Press, 1976.

———. "His Son's Big Doll." Trans. Howard Goldblatt. In *The Drowning of an Old Cat and Other Stories*, 37–60. Bloomington: Indiana University Press, 1980.

———. "Young Widow." In Rosemary Haddon, trans. and ed., *Oxcart: Nativist Stories from Taiwan, 1934–1977*, 221–304. Dortmund: Projekt Verlag, 1996.

Kinkley, Jeffrey. "From Oppression to Dependency: Two Stages in the Fiction of Chen Yingzhen." *Modern China* 16, 3 (1991): 243–268.

———. "Mandarin Kitsch and Taiwanese Kitsch in the Fiction of Wang Chen-ho." *Modern Chinese Literature* 6, 1–2 (1992): 85–113.

Lai, Ming-yan. *Nativism and Modernity: Cultural Contestations in China and Taiwan Under Global Capitalism*. Albany: State University of New York Press, 2008.

Lau, Joseph S. M. "Death in the Void: Three Tales of Spiritual Atrophy in Ch'en Yingchen's Post-Incarceration Fiction." *Modern Chinese Literature* 2, 1 (1986): 21–29.

———. "'How Much Truth Can a Blade of Grass Carry?': Ch'en Ying-chen and the Emergence of Native Taiwan Writers." *Journal of Asian Studies* 32, 4 (1973): 623–638.

Li, Qiao. *Wintry Night*. Trans. Taotao Liu and John Balcom. New York: Columbia University Press, 2001.

Lupke, Christopher. "Chen Yingzhen." In Thomas Moran and Ye Dianna Xu, eds., *Dictionary of Literary Biography: Chinese Fiction Writers, 1950–2000*, 36–46. Farmington Hills, MI: Gale Cengage, 2013.

———. "Huang Chunming." In Thomas Moran and Ye Dianna Xu, eds., *Dictionary of Literary Biography: Chinese Fiction Writers, 1950–2000*, 100–110. Farmington Hills, MI: Gale Cengage, 2013.

———. "Huang Chunming." In Sara Pendergast and Tom Pendergast, eds., *Reference Guide to World Literature*, vol. 1, 482–483. 3rd ed. New York: St. James Press, 2003.

Miller, Lucien. "A Break in the Chain: The Short Stories of Ch'en Ying-chen." In Jeannette Faurot, ed., *Chinese Fiction from Taiwan*, 86–109. Bloomington: Indiana University Press, 1980.

Russell, Terence. "Zhong Lihe." In Thomas Moran and Ye Dianna Xu, eds. *Dictionary of Literary Biography: Chinese Fiction Writers, 1950–2000*, 311–318. Farmington Hills, MI: Gale Cengage, 2013.

Scruggs, Bert. "Li Qiao." In Thomas Moran and Ye Dianna Xu, eds. *Dictionary of Literary Biography: Chinese Fiction Writers, 1950–2000*, 141–148. Farmington Hills, MI: Gale Cengage, 2013.

Wang, Zhenhe. "Ghost, Northwind, Person." In Nancy Ing, ed., *Winter Plum*, 413–436. Taipei: Chinese Materials Press, 1982.

———. "An Oxcart for Dowry." Trans. Joseph S. M. Lau and Jon Jackson. In Joseph S. M. Lau and Timothy Ross, eds., *Chinese Stories from Taiwan: 1960–1970*, 75–99. New York: Columbia University Press, 1976.

———. *Rose, Rose, I Love You*. Trans. Howard Goldblatt. New York: Columbia University Press, 1997.

Wu, Zhuoliu. *Orphan of Asia*. Trans. Ioannes Mentzas. New York: Columbia University Press, 2006.

Yee, Angelina. "Yang Kui." In Thomas Moran, ed. *Dictionary of Literary Biography: Chinese Fiction Writers, 1900–1949*, 264–271. Farmington Hills, MI: Gale, 2007.

Yip, June. *Envisioning Taiwan: Fiction, Cinema, and the Nation in the Cultural Imaginary*. Durham, NC: Duke University Press, 2004.

Zhong, Lihe. *From the Old Country*. Trans. T. M. McClellan. New York: Columbia University Press, 2014.

34

THE CULTURAL REVOLUTION MODEL THEATER
DI BAI

Revolutionary model theater (革命样板戏) first appeared on the Chinese cultural scene in 1966, the year the Great Proletarian Cultural Revolution started. The term "model theater" was coined to describe, loosely, a collection of revised performing arts productions guided by Mao Zedong's wife, Jiang Qing 江青 (1914–1991). The earliest official sources proclaiming the existence of the model theater were a special news report entitled "Carrying Out Chairman Mao's Line on Literature and Art: Brilliant Models" (贯彻毛主席的文艺路线: 光辉的样板). A short editorial on the same page celebrated the birth and significance of these works:

> Since 1964, under the brilliant radiance of Chairman Mao's line on literature and art, the high tide of revolutionary reform in the fields of Beijing opera, of ballet drama, and of symphonic music has swelled. The revolutionary model theater has been created, which consists of five Beijing operas: *Shajiabang* (沙家浜), *The Red Lantern* (红灯记), *Taking Tiger Mountain by Strategy* (智取威虎山), *On the Docks* (海港), *Raid on the White Tiger Regiment* (奇袭白虎团); two ballet dramas: *The White-Haired Girl* (白毛女), *The Red Detachment of Women* (红色娘子军), and the symphony *Shajiabang* (沙家浜).
>
> (*Renmin ribao*, December 6, 1966)

As the Cultural Revolution developed, the term "model theater" became a common designation for any Beijing opera or ballet production that had the exemplary qualities shown by the original eight. As the fame of the symphony *Shajiabang* faded—not a theatrical piece in the first place, it was adapted from the Beijing opera of the same name and equipped with costumed soloists and chorus—more popular newcomers such as the Beijing operas *Azalea Mountain* (杜鹃山, 1973) and *The Song of Dragon River* (龙江颂, 1972) took its place as models. Indeed, the model dramas underwent many revisions and productions (the dates given here indicate their official publications as "models" in the journal *Red Flag* [红旗]).

The model theater dominated the Chinese cultural stage from 1966 to 1976. During these ten years it was praised for its revolutionary reformation of the ideals for literature and art advocated by Mao Zedong in his 1942 "Yan'an Talks" (延安文艺座谈会上的讲话). Mao had established two criteria for revolutionary literature and art: political content and artistic form, with the former of primary importance. Because the overall purpose of literature and art, according to Mao, is to educate the people politically and ideologically, the content should carry the message. Model theater developed through a process of revising and reforming the already existing popular literary works that had not quite met the standard of Mao's ideals but nevertheless showed potential for reaching that standard.

In its content, model theater follows a central theme, which is to eulogize the victories of the Communist Party-led revolution and the socialist construction. Idealized characters—all party members—trumpet the virtues of Chinese Communist ideology. Selection of Beijing opera and ballet as the model forms was not accidental. One indigenous, one foreign, both forms require highly symbolic and suggestive performance, scant verbal exchanges, and exaggerated postures and choreography. They fittingly accommodate the contents, characterized by rigid plot structure, dogmatic language, and larger-than-life heroes and heroines. Model theater thus became a powerful weapon to educate the people, indoctrinating them into a standardized view of Chinese revolutionary history and class struggle.

Many of the model dramas are set during the revolutionary struggles. The model opera *The Red Lantern* (1970), for example, takes place during the war against Japan (1937–1945). Li Yuhe 李玉和, a seasoned underground party member, receives a mission to deliver a secret code to the guerrillas. Before he can fulfill his mission, however, he is betrayed and gets arrested by the chief of the Japanese gendarme, Hatoyama 鸠山. Li meets the enemy with unflinching courage. At his wit's end, Hatoyama executes Li and his mother. Li's daughter, Tiemei 铁梅, takes over the mission for her martyred father. Led by the party and helped by her neighbors, she succeeds in delivering the secret code to the guerrillas. *Taking Tiger Mountain by Strategy* (1970) centers on the shrewdness, skill, and nerve of Yang Zirong 杨子荣, a People's Liberation Army (PLA) scout during the War of Liberation (1946–1949). Disguised as a bandit with a convincing cover story, Yang infiltrates enemy headquarters on Tiger Mountain and wins its occupants' trust. When the Nationalist soldiers celebrate the chief's fiftieth birthday, Yang manages to get them all drunk. He has also managed to persuade them to light up the mountain with torches for the celebration of the birthday, a signal for the PLA to overrun the headquarters, which they do successfully, of course. *Raid on the White-Tiger Regiment* (1972) is a celebration of internationalism and the self-sacrifice of Chinese Communists during the Korean War (1950–1953). Yang Weicai 杨伟才, leader of a scout platoon of the Chinese People's Volunteer Army, successfully defeats the so-called indestructible White-Tiger Regiment of the South Korean army, advised by American military personnel.

Model theater is well known for its heroic female characters. These women resemble their male counterparts in always representing political and ideological correctness and serving as deus ex machina in critical situations. Stripped of most, if not all, feminine traces, these characters are not conventional women at all; they do not have families, are not wives and mothers, and most importantly are not sexual. In *Shajiabang* (1970), for example, Sister Aqing 阿庆嫂 is a splendid, dynamic party secretary during the war against Japan. She works underground to protect wounded soldiers of the New Fourth Army, providing them with food and medicine under extremely complicated political circumstances in which the Japanese aggressors, puppet troops, and Guomindang diehards conspire together to capture the wounded. In the end, she outwits these enemies and fulfills the task given her by the party. *Azalea Mountain* portrays another heroic woman, party member Ke Xiang 柯湘, who is sent by the Central Committee to provide much-needed leadership for a peasant self-defense corps in the 1920s. Having undergone many tests and difficulties, she eventually wins the trust of the peasants and leads them in victory over a reactionary armed force; more important, she has transformed the undisciplined peasants into an able fighting force with a proletarian worldview. *Azalea Mountain* and *Shajiabang* are also dramas about the relationship between a gendered identity and a political identity. Sister Aqing parades as a traditional woman, shielding her true political identity from the enemy behind a masquerade of femininity. Ke Xiang has to prove to the peasant corps she oversees that she is not a traditional woman and that her being a biological woman will not prevent her from being a worthy political and military leader.

On the Docks (1972) and *The Song of Dragon River* are sister dramas; both are set after the founding of the People's Republic (1949), and both deal with class struggle. In the former, a Shanghai Communist Party secretary, Fang Haizhen 方海珍, is in charge of the important operation of shipping rice seeds to Africa. She successfully fights the class enemy's attempt to spoil this internationalist activity and succeeds in shipping out the seeds in time for the sowing season. In *The Song of Dragon River*, set in rural China, Jiang Shuiying 江水英,

secretary of a Dragon River production brigade, sacrifices her own collective's interests by encouraging the construction of a dam to divert the water of Dragon River. This action will save a nearby and much larger drought-stricken area. A former landlord intervenes by convincing the brigade leader to breach the dam at the critical moment. Jiang Shuiying's timely entry saves the situation. She gives the order to open the gate and exposes the dark scheme of the class enemy.

The two plays are similar in many ways. Both dramas present ideological disputes between two contradictory classes. The nature of class struggle is less about economic divisions than moral conflicts. In their characterization, the proletarian class, represented by women, is dedicated to serving the public without any thought of self, whereas the class enemy of the proletariat seeks nothing but to destroy the cause of communism and internationalism. Between these two polarized positions is a more human group composed mostly of men; they are susceptible to the class enemy because they always put their own or their small groups' interests before those of the public at large. When they fall into the enemy's scheme, the proletarian women come to their rescue, rectifying their ideological positions and exposing the evil intentions of the class enemies, also usually male.

Model ballet dramas *The White-Haired Girl* and *The Red Detachment of Women* (1970) are stories about poor peasant girls becoming staunch Communists. Two themes overlap in both plays: class struggle and women's liberation. *The Red Detachment of Women* is about poor bondmaid Wu Qinghua's 吴清华 political maturation in the 1930s, when the Communists were fighting Nationalist rule. Wu manages to escape her abusive landlord's house and join a fighting force of "Red Women." Nurtured by the party and tested by the severe armed struggle, Wu finally transforms from a rash, naïve girl into a conscious proletarian fighter.

The masterpiece of Jiang Qing's radical feminism, *The White-Haired Girl* is arguably the most popular of the model dramas. This feminism is best illustrated by comparing the model ballet with the original opera on which it is based. First produced as a collective effort in 1945, the opera immediately gained unparalleled popularity in Communist-controlled areas. Set in the latter half of the 1930s, it relates the tragic story of a poor peasant girl, Xi'er 喜儿. Her father, Yang Bailao 杨白劳, works for the vicious landlord Huang Shiren 黄世仁. Unable to pay his rent and an accumulated cash debt, Yang is forced in his confusion and bewilderment to sign a contract that promises his daughter to the Huang family as payment. In desperation, he commits suicide, whereupon the Huang family forcefully takes Xi'er away. Wang Dachun 王大春, Xi'er's betrothed, runs away and joins the Communist Eighth Route Army. Xi'er is treated cruelly in the Huang family and is raped by Huang Shiren. Seven months later, with Xi'er now pregnant, Huang decides to sell her to a brothel to the surprise of Xi'er, who expects that Huang will marry her. On learning of Huang's scheme, she escapes from the landlord's household and flees into the wild mountains, where she gives birth to Huang's child, who later dies. For more than two years Xi'er exists like an animal in a mountain cave, hiding from the world. This hard life, and especially the lack of salt in her diet, turns her hair completely white. The villagers who encounter her take her to be an apparition. Finally, a detachment of the Eighth Route Army led by Wang Dachun comes to her rescue. The village is liberated, and the landlord Huang is executed. Liberated Xi'er marries Wang Dachun, and they live happily ever after.

The model ballet version keeps close to the original story line, but the plot is much thinner and the characters more abstract. The most obvious change is that Yang Bailao, the father, does not commit suicide; instead, in the spirit of revolt, he fights against his oppressors and is beaten to death. Similarly, Xi'er is changed into an embodiment of hatred, the spirit of revenge. She is treated cruelly but is not, as in the operatic version, sexually assaulted by Huang Shiren. Wang Dachun's significance fades, and he becomes just another of Xi'er's class brothers with no special romantic relationship. In the epilogue, Xi'er picks up a gun and joins the ranks of the Eighth Route Army to carry on the revolution. As such, she becomes a symbol of that class.

The simplification of the story, the politicization of the theme, and particularly the abstraction of characters reveal the centrality of the class dynamic concept in model theater. Class is the only social category within which the characters function. Traditional kinship relationships are eliminated. Relations between Yang Bailao and Xi'er and between Xi'er and Wang Dachun take on a class character. Most important, the model theater excludes the sexual. Huang Shiren's sexual assault of Xi'er in the original opera is deleted in the ballet; the two are only class enemies. Thus Xi'er's previous vulnerability as a woman, a female body, disappears. Her rape and pregnancy are excised: Xi'er is no longer a betrothed daughter to be raped, nor a mother giving birth to a dead child, nor a ghost waiting to be liberated. Structurally speaking, the elimination of the female body enables Xi'er to gain equality with the members of her class.

In the West, model theater has generally been regarded as the dead end of the Communist Party's political and ideological appropriation of art that began with Mao's "Yan'an Talks." Its critics have dismissed it as "artless and sterile, without depth, without truth, and without reality" (Meserve 1970: 1). Other scholarship analyzes the literary-artistic value in model theater and largely restricts its focus to form. This approach is interested in how the work is constructed as popular art and how it is a product of the party's manipulation of mass performing arts and popular culture. Even its obvious feminism looks suspicious: the nongendered women in model theater can easily be explained as a mere parodying of masculinity. Literary critics in China see model theater as not only being the evil products of a political and cultural disaster but also having partial responsibility for that turmoil. What's more, anti–Jiang Qing sentiment runs high when model theater is mentioned. The sole reason for the existence of model theater, some critics argue, was simply to satisfy Jiang Qing's personal ambition (Yan 1996). "Artless and sterile, without depth, without truth, and without reality," the model theatre does not deserve a place in the history of modern Chinese literature.

However, in the last twenty years or so, popular interest in model theater in China has been renewed as part of the nationwide nostalgia for the Mao era (1949–1976) that constitutes a backlash against the social woes brought about by the market reforms. New productions of *The Red Lantern*, *The Red Detachment of Women*, *Shajiabang*, and *The White-Haired Girl* were instant commercial successes, and their political messages, previously thought to be outdated, have seemed to regain vigor. In response to this renewed popularity, studies of model theater in China have taken a new turn. For instance, Hong Zicheng's 洪子诚 *A History of Contemporary Chinese Literature*, first published in Chinese in 1999, gives model theater a well-deserved place in the history of modern Chinese literature. Hong does not agree that model theater is a deviation from the norms of modern Chinese literature; rather, he writes, "historical stages of contemporary Chinese literature are demarcated by ruptures," and "model theater was the rupture with past literature and arts including the socialist literature of the 1950s and 1960s." These ruptures revolutionize literature and make it an important means to implement social change and establish new systems of meaning. In this sense, model theater deserves the name "red classics" (红色经典) in Chinese literature (Hong 2007: 226–229). In the West, Barbara Mittler (2012) and others have taken a sympathetic look at the art and creativity of these plays. Like Hong, Mittler argues that model theater should be seen not as a deviation but as part of a long process, beginning in the late Qing, of reforming traditional operatic drama. Model theater requires more in-depth studies so as to reach a fresh understanding of its complex cultural meaning, its position in the People's Republic political history, its artistic achievement, and its undying popularity.

Bibliography

"Azalea Mountain." *Chinese Literature* 1 (1074): 3–69.
Chen, Xiaomei. *Acting the Right Part: Political Theater and Contemporary Chinese Drama (1966–1996)*. Honolulu: University of Hawai'i Press, 2002.
Clark, Paul. *The Chinese Cultural Revolution: A History*. Cambridge: University of Cambridge Press, 2008.
Denton, Kirk A. "Model Drama as Myth: A Semiotic Analysis of *Taking Tiger Mountain by Strategy*." In Constantine Tung, ed., *Drama in the People's Republic of China*, 119–136. Albany: State University of New York Press, 1987.
Hong, Zicheng. *A History of Contemporary Chinese Literature*. Trans. Michael M. Day. Boston: Brill, 2007.
Mackerras, Colin. *The Chinese Theatre in Modern Times from 1840 to the Present Day*. London: Thames & Hudson, 1975.

Meserve, Walter J., ed. *Modern Drama from Communist China*. New York: New York University Press, 1970.

Mittler, Barbara. *A Continuous Revolution: Making Sense of Cultural Revolution Culture*. Cambridge, MA: Harvard University Asia Center, 2012.

"On the Docks." *Chinese Literature* 5 (1973): 22–48.

"Raid on the White-Tiger Regiment." *Chinese Literature* 3 (1973): 3–54.

"Red Detachment of Women." In Martin Ebon, ed., *Five Chinese Communist Plays*, 119–151. New York: John Day, 1975.

"The Red Lantern." *Chinese Literature* 8 (1970): 8–52.

Roberts, Rosemary. *Maoist Model Theatre: The Semiotics of Gender and Sexuality in the Chinese Cultural Revolution (1966–1976)*. Leiden: Brill, 2010.

"Shajiabang." *Chinese Literature* 11 (1970): 3–62.

"Song of the Dragon River." *Chinese Literature* 7 (1972): 3–57.

"Taking Tiger Mountain by Strategy." *Chinese Literature* 1 (1970): 58–74.

"The White-Haired Girl." In Martin Ebon, ed., *Five Chinese Communist Plays*, 27–117. New York: John Day, 1975.

Yan, Jiaqi, and Gao Gao. *Turbulent Decade: A History of the Cultural Revolution*. Trans. D. W. Y. Kwok. Honolulu: University of Hawai'i Press, 1996.

35

MARTIAL ARTS FICTION AND JIN YONG
JOHN CHRISTOPHER HAMM

Wuxia xiaoshuo (武俠小说), here loosely translated as "martial arts fiction," more literally means fiction (小说) whose subject matter is the intersection of the martial arts (武) with altruistic ideals and the figure of the "Chinese knight-errant" (侠). Martial arts fiction refers specifically to extended prose narratives on these themes written in vernacular Chinese during the twentieth century. Modern histories of martial arts fiction generally trace the genre's roots to the classical tales of the Tang dynasty or even the historical records of the Han period, and martial arts novels themselves often draw on such texts or cite them as predecessors.

There is good reason, nonetheless, to consider martial arts fiction a uniquely twentieth-century literary genre. The compound *wuxia xiaoshuo* did not appear in Chinese vocabulary until the first decade of the past century, apparently borrowed from the Japanese designation for a genre of contemporary adventure novels. Both the newness of the term and its transmission from the hands of China's forward-looking neighbor make it a fitting designation for a genre that, whatever its thematic and formal links with an ancient literary tradition, owes its modern form and popularity to the particular conditions of early twentieth-century China. Urbanization, changes in education and social structure, and the growth of commercial publishing all supported martial arts fiction as one element within the rising medium of mass-distributed entertainment literature. And the fundamental nostalgia and nativism of the genre—its setting in a pre-modern past, a moment of historical crisis, or a mythic antiquity and its celebration of the martial arts as a uniquely Chinese cultural practice—reflect the social disruptions of modernization and a self-consciousness nourished by cultural plurality and imperialist menace.

The Republican vogue for martial arts fiction is generally credited to Pingjiang Buxiaosheng 平江不肖生 (pen name of Xiang Kairan 向恺然, 1890–1957). His *Marvelous Knights of the Rivers and Lakes* (江湖奇侠传, 1923) interweaves local legends with a saga of warring sects of preternaturally powerful martial artists. The novel established some of the genre's key themes and narrative techniques and heralded its potential as a mass-culture phenomenon; *Marvelous Knights* not only sustained the journal in which it was serialized but also inspired China's first martial arts film, *The Burning of the Red Lotus Monastery* (火烧红莲寺, 1928), and its seventeen sequels. A sister novel, *Righteous Heroes of the Modern Age* (近代侠义英雄传, 1923), strings together tales of the historical figure Huo Yuanjia 霍元甲 and other martial artists of the late Qing and early Republic. Its comparatively realistic depiction of martial arts practice and actual martial lineages and its celebration of Chinese national spirit through fighters' encounters with foreign challengers reflect the institutionalization and nationalistic reimagining of the martial arts during the Republican decades and initiated a strain of martial arts fiction that was to attain periodic prominence in later decades—influencing, for instance, Bruce Lee and the "kung fu" films of the 1970s, as well as the patriotic martial arts fiction that emerged in the mainland in the early 1980s.

A number of Buxiaosheng's contemporaries and successors developed distinctive fictional voices. Bai Yu 白羽 (pen name of Gong Zhuxin 宫竹心, 1899–1966) is often noted for his strong characters and supple prose, and Wang Dulu 王度庐 (Wang Baoxiang 王葆祥, 1909–1977) for the wedding of martial themes with tragic romance and for the emotional intensity of his narration. Perhaps the most popular and influential (after Buxiaosheng) of the prewar authors was Huanzhulouzhu 还珠楼主 (Li Shoumin 李寿民, 1902–1961), whose most famous work, the mammoth *Swordsmen of the Mountains of Shu* (蜀山剑侠传, 1932), remained unfinished when its serialization came to an end in 1948. Some of its essential components are replicated in the shorter *Blades from the Willows* (柳湖侠隐, 1946): the protagonists, taking refuge from a conquering foreign dynasty in remote mountain realms, become involved in the quests and feuds of warring sects of flying swordsmen, eccentric immortals, and supernatural monsters. Huanzhulouzhu's rich prose, labyrinthine narratives, evocative descriptions of landscape, and incorporation of imagery and concepts from the Daoist and Buddhist heritages all contribute to his elaboration of what is sometimes described as a "Peach Blossom Spring" mode of martial arts fiction—the creation of a fantastic never-never land of martial adventure.

For literary and political reformers of the Republican era, martial arts novels represented the worst of "old-style" fiction, their alleged superstition, violence, and encouragement of the passive desire for an all-powerful savior exacerbating the faults (ideological backwardness, artistic inflexibility, and an unshakeable monopoly on the general population's affections) imputed to popular culture more generally. Critics, including Zheng Zhenduo 郑振铎, Qu Qiubai 瞿秋白, and Mao Dun 茅盾, penned bitter attacks on the genre during the 1930s, and after 1949 the writing and publication of this "poisonous weed" were prohibited. The emergence of what is sometimes called New School martial arts fiction in Hong Kong and Taiwan in the 1950s can be understood negatively as simply the corollary of the banning of this form on the mainland, but it can also be interpreted more positively as a reinvigoration of the genre through its responses to the recent and continuing crises of civil war, regime change, and exile from the ancestral homeland. In Hong Kong, the Communist victory, the experience of colonial rule, and the geopolitics of the Cold War era gave new resonance to such conventional plot elements as Ming loyalist resistance to the foreign Manchu dynasty. Writers in Taiwan, cautious under the Guomindang government's tight controls over cultural expression, avoided direct historical references but joined their Hong Kong colleagues in exploiting the genre's timely mix of violence, altruism, and romantic evocation of China's geography and cultural heritage.

Martial arts fiction gained momentum simultaneously and to some extent independently in Taiwan and Hong Kong during the 1950s, but it was developments in the British colony that have had the greatest impact upon the genre. In 1954 Liang Yusheng 梁羽生 (Chen Wentong 陈文统, 1922–2009) took advantage of the excitement generated by a match between local martial artists to begin serializing *Lion and Tiger Vie in the Capital* (龙虎斗京华, 1954). He followed this successful effort with more than thirty martial arts novels over the following decades. But Liang Yusheng's reputation was soon overtaken by that of one of his many successors and imitators—his colleague Jin Yong 金庸 (Zha Liangyong 查良镛, or Louis Cha, b. 1924), who by the end of the century emerged as not merely the most successful author of martial arts fiction but perhaps the most widely read of all twentieth-century Chinese novelists.

Like most of Jin Yong's works, his first novel, *The Book and the Sword* (书剑恩仇录, 1955, revised 1975), is set at a historical moment of China's conquest by a foreign power. Here Jin Yong employs the legend that the Qianlong emperor (r. 1736–1795) of the Manchu Qing dynasty was actually a Han Chinese by birth and makes him the brother of the leader of the anti-Qing resistance, Chen Jialuo 陈家洛. The resistance's political failure thus acquires the aspect of personal tragedy, which is further given a romantic dimension by the sacrifice of Chen Jialuo's Muslim lover, Princess Fragrance 香香公主. These political and personal tragedies are offset, however, by the first expressions of what will emerge in later novels as one of Jin Yong's hallmarks—the celebration of the martial arts as an epitome of the Chinese cultural tradition. The "culturalization" of the martial arts, a deepening exploration of characters' moral, psychological, and romantic lives, and a corresponding attenuation of the purely political aspects of the chosen historical settings can be traced through the course of the author's subsequent works. The epic *Legend of the Eagle-Shooting Heroes* (射雕英雄传, 1957, revised 1978), which solidified the author's reputation, is set against the Mongol conquest. Its protagonist, the slow-witted but indomitable Guo Jing 郭靖, represents the acme of ingenuous patriotism; at the same time, however, the novel's "Dispute of the Swords Upon Mount Hua" 华山论剑 and the fantastic characters associated with this episode create a milieu that is far more mythic than historical. *Fox Volant of the Snowy Mountain* (雪山飞狐, 1959, revised 1976) employs the Qing conquest primarily as a distant motivation for a tale whose primary focus is the conflict of personal loyalties. This novel also features a formal intricacy that testifies to the author's ambitions for expanding the aesthetic possibilities of the genre. In several late novels, the historical references disappear. The achievement of martial enlightenment through a classical poem encountered on an island in *Song of the Swordsman* (侠客行, 1966, revised 1977) epitomizes the identification of martial arts with a timeless and geographically decentered (diasporic?) essence of Chinese culture. And the absence of a dynastic setting in *The Proud and Gallant Wanderer* (笑傲江湖, 1967, revised 1978) allows the tale's venomously warring sects to mirror the contemporary politics of the Cultural Revolution or the nature of political life in the abstract. *The Deer and the Cauldron* (鹿鼎记, 1969, revised 1981), Jin Yong's last novel to date, returns to a concrete historical setting. It brings both culturalism and political cynicism to bear on the problem of the Qing conquest, justifying the reign of the Kangxi emperor (1662–1722) through his "Sinicization" or mastery of the Chinese cultural heritage. This reversal of the earlier novels' historical vision is accompanied by the jettisoning of many of the genre's conventions; its protagonist, the Yangzhou brothel urchin Wei Xiaobao 韦小宝, masters no martial arts at all but wins wealth, glory, and a harem of seven wives by devoting his skills in deceit, flattery, and invention to the service of his beloved alter ego, the Qing emperor.

Wei Xiaobao is Jin Yong's most famous and controversial creation, and it is tempting to read this worldly southerner's conquest of and service to the Manchu court as an allegory or omen of the author's career. Jin Yong's earliest works were serialized in Hong Kong papers sympathetic to the left, but most of his later novels appeared in his own *Ming Pao* (明报), established in 1959. The 1960s saw the mutual growth of the popularity of his fiction, his influence as a publishing magnate, and his reputation as a political commentator—the last forged in particular by his scathing reports on the Cultural Revolution. In the 1970s, Jin Yong devoted ten years to the revision of his novels and the production of the thirty-six-volume *Collected Works* (金庸作品集). In the 1980s, his works entered Taiwan (where they had been banned because of the author's early ties with the left) and the mainland (where Deng Xiaoping's economic and cultural policies fostered exchange with the outside world and a boom in entertainment culture) and quickly won immense readerships and increasing critical and scholarly attention. Zha Liangyong (Jin Yong) himself, meanwhile, became an influential supporter of Deng's pragmatic policies and a facilitator of Hong Kong's return to Chinese sovereignty. The success of Jin Yong's novels spurred debate and resistance on the mainland, to some extent echoing earlier critiques of martial arts fiction but more directly expressing intellectuals' distress at the commercialization of culture and the avant-garde's dismay at the lack of an audience for their own writing. Although debate continues, the awarding of an honorary degree by Beijing University in 1994 consecrated Jin Yong's status as a master of the art of fiction and a spokesperson for the glories of the Chinese cultural heritage. Jin Yong's elevation reflects popular culture's domination of the cultural sphere in the 1990s, but at the same time it reveals some critics' inclination to reinterpret his work as "high" culture and divorce it from its roots as genre fiction.

Jin Yong's contemporary Gu Long 古龙 (Xiong Yaohua 熊耀华, 1938–1985) wrote sensational martial arts sagas stripped of the historical references so central to Jin Yong's oeuvre. His works have been championed as a "Taiwanese" alternative to Jin Yong's Sinocentric vision and are seen by other scholars as representing a decentered Sinophone literature. Jin Yong and Gu Long's successors include Wen Ruian 温瑞安 (Wen Liangyu 温凉玉, b. 1954), known for his poetic style and formal experiments, and Huang Yi 黄易 (Huang Zuqiang 黄祖强, b. 1952), who mingles martial arts with science fiction. As a literary form, the genre has suffered the effects of the waning of full-length fiction as a primary form of popular culture, but its themes, conventions, and imagery circulate more widely than ever through the media of films, television serials, comic books, and videogames. Despite, or thanks to, its emphatic "Chineseness," martial arts fiction has proved popular throughout East Asia, and in translation and adaptation it can be found from Japan and Korea to Indonesia and Vietnam.

Bibliography

Cha, Louis (Jin Yong). *The Book and the Sword*. Trans. Graham Earnshaw. Hong Kong: Oxford University Press. 2000.

——. *The Deer and the Cauldron*. Trans. John Minford. Hong Kong: Oxford University Press, 1997–2000.

Chen Pingyuan 陈平原. *Qiangu wenren xiake meng: wuxia xiaoshuo leixing yanjiu* 千古文人侠客梦：武侠小说类型研究 (The literati's age-old dream of the knight-errant: A genre study of martial arts fiction). Beijing: Renmin wenxue, 1993.

Danjiang daxue Zhongwen xi 淡江大学中文系 (Chinese Department, Tamkang University), ed. *Xia yu Zhongguo wenhua* 侠与中国文化 (The knight-errant and Chinese culture). Taipei: Xuesheng shuju, 1993.

Hamm, John Christopher. "The Marshes of Mount Liang Beyond the Sea: Jin Yong's Early Martial Arts Fiction and Postwar Hong Kong." *Modern Chinese Literature and Culture* 11, 1 (Spring 1999): 93–123.

——. *Paper Swordsmen: Jin Yong and the Modern Chinese Martial Arts Novel.* Honolulu: University of Hawai'i Press, 2006.

Huanzhulouzhu. *Blades from the Willows.* Trans. Robert Chard. London: Wellsweep Press, 1991.

Huss, Ann, and Jianmei Liu, eds. *The Jin Yong Phenomenon: Chinese Martial Arts Fiction and Modern Chinese Literary History.* Amherst, NY: Cambria Press, 2007.

Jin, Yong. *Fox Volant of the Snowy Mountain.* Trans. Olivia Mok. Hong Kong: Chinese University Press, 1993.

Liu, James J. Y. *The Chinese Knight-Errant.* London: Routledge and Kegan Paul, 1967.

Liu, Petrus. *Stateless Subjects: Chinese Martial Arts Literature and Postcolonial History.* Cornell East Asia Series 162. Ithaca, NY: Cornell University East Asia Program, 2011.

Wang Hailin 王海林. *Zhongguo wuxia xiaoshuo shi lüe* 中国武侠小说史略 (A general history of Chinese martial arts fiction). Taiyuan: Beiyue wenyi, 1988.

36

TAIWAN ROMANCE:
QIONG YAO AND SAN MAO

MIRIAM LANG

From 1949 until the late 1980s, Chinese-language romantic writing (like other popular-entertainment literary genres, such as martial arts fiction) was dominated by authors from outside mainland China. The most famous writer of romance novels was the Taiwan author Qiong Yao 琼瑶, whose books have sold steadily for five decades. Her contemporary, San Mao 三毛, had a similar measure of fame. San Mao's writings were not romantic novels; rather, they were mostly quasi-autobiographical short stories or essays, the most famous of which narrated her life in Europe and Africa. Even so, San Mao and Qiong Yao have often been paired together as exponents of a culture of romance. Qiong Yao created a host of fictional romantic relationships, while San Mao wrote of—and appeared to embody in her own lifestyle—the ideals of a life in which romance and the quest for beauty were central concepts.

Both writers were born on the mainland and came to Taiwan with their families as children after 1949. Both began their writing careers in Taiwan's martial law period (1949–1987), Qiong Yao in the early 1960s and San Mao a decade later. Neither concerned herself with local Taiwanese issues in her writings. Both had significant social influence in martial law–era Taiwan and post-Mao China. With their emphasis on and beautification of personal emotional experience above all, Qiong Yao and San Mao provided a "softer" alternative to both the ever-present narratives of the state and the very demanding educational regimes that prevailed in both societies. Their romantic ideologies were particularly powerful for young readers, though their books were read not only by the young. In their heyday in the 1970s and 1980s, Qiong Yao and San Mao were two of the most widely read authors in the Chinese-speaking world, and overall they were two of the best-selling Chinese-language writers of the late twentieth century. Because popular romantic writing has been little valued by translators, academics, and other arbiters of literary canons, translations of their writing into English are few and secondary literature is relatively scarce. Thus, Qiong Yao and San Mao have not been accepted into prevailing Chinese literary canons, though a number of academic theses about both writers have been produced in Taiwan in recent years.

Qiong Yao (Chen Zhe 陈喆, b. 1938) made her mark on the Taiwan literary scene in 1963 with her first novel, *Outside the Window* (窗外). Ostensibly based on her own experience, the story concerns a lonely high school student struggling to cope with the pressures of schoolwork and high familial expectations. A romantic liaison develops between her and her teacher, a lonely, middle-aged man whose family was left behind on the mainland when he fled to Taiwan after the Communist revolution. After her mother breaks up the relationship, believing it to be destructive, the girl fails the all-important university entrance exams that would have ensured a secure future. Critics variously interpreted the story as a case of true and freely chosen adolescent love thwarted by an interfering mother and as a destructive relationship to which a wise mother rightly put an end. The fact that the novel attracted critical and scholarly discussion at all suggests that, initially at least, Qiong Yao was considered a serious author dealing with important social issues (Lin 1992).

In terms of productivity (more than sixty novels) and romantic subject matter (all her novels focus on romantic relationships), Qiong Yao has been likened to the English romance novelist Barbara Cartland; yet the scope of her work, the issues underlying her stories, and various structural aspects of her novels differentiate her markedly from the queen of the twentieth-century English-language romance. The plot construction of Qiong Yao's novels does not necessarily follow the axiomatic "boy-meets-girl, obstacle arises, obstacle is overcome, couple are united" pattern of English-language romantic fiction. "Obstacles" certainly arise, but they are meaningful elements in the plot rather than devices for delaying romantic reunion. Indeed, romantic union does not always take place; many of Qiong Yao's novels conclude with the couple being separated, either by death or by renouncing their relationship. In this regard, the stories have strong resonances with earlier Chinese romantic traditions from the Ming and Qing eras, including Cao Xueqin's mid-Qing classic vernacular romance novel *Dream of the Red Chamber* (红楼梦), Qing scholar-beauty fiction (才子佳人小说), and the Mandarin Ducks and Butterflies fiction of the Republican period. Narratives of suffering for the sake of love are important in the romantic ideology of Qiong Yao's novels. Sex scenes are generally few and not explicit.

Comparing the narrative structures of Qiong Yao's pre-1990 novels with Janice Radway's (1984) paradigms of American romance fiction, the Taiwan literary sociologist Lin Fangmei has noted the following features of Qiong Yao's writing: (1) the romantic encounter between hero and heroine tends to occur early in the narrative, with the realization and declaration of true love being immediate (the plot action does not hinge on the difficulties of recognizing true love); (2) obstacles to romance tend to be external (from parental opposition or illness to the more dramatic events of war, death, or suicide) rather than internal psychological and emotional dilemmas; (3) love scenes typically include a ritual in which the couple commemorate their love with a token of some kind (poems, letters, gifts, or items from nature such as flowers or leaves), and these tokens become significant to the subsequent action; (4) members of the romantic couple's family are usually vital to the plot; and (5) stories do not always end with the couple's being happily united (Lin 1992). The adoption of these features inherited from earlier forms of romantic writing in Chinese is reinforced by Qiong Yao's self-conscious drawing on the Chinese literary tradition for poetic and classical allusions.

Changes over time in the settings and plot constructions of Qiong Yao's novels may reflect trends or preoccupations in Taiwan society in general. Mostly set in the period of civil war and the flight of the Nationalists to Taiwan, her novels of the 1960s often feature dislocated families, straitened circumstances, and loneliness. Her 1970s novels tend to portray secure and stable family lives and are more likely to end happily (Lin 1992). In the 1980s and 1990s, more historical themes and settings emerged and happy endings were fewer. In the late 1990s and the early 2000s, Qiong Yao stepped away from contemporary Taiwan settings altogether, extending her historical reach further back in time and into portrayals of Manchu royal culture with her multivolume *Princess Huanzhu* (还珠格格) series, which was adapted for television and became extremely popular, especially in mainland China.

The portrayals of romantic love in Qiong Yao's writings have sometimes been referred to as "morbid," perhaps because the central romantic liaison in her novels is quite often a socially questionable one (teacher and student; guardian and ward; brother-in-law and sister-in-law). It has also been suggested that her sympathy for third parties in "love triangle" situations is connected with a long-standing extramarital liaison of her own (with Ping Xintao 平鑫涛, whom she would later marry). Some have praised her, however, for the quality of her prose, for her poetry (chiefly in her earlier works), and for the literary allusions in her book titles (Wang 2005). In addition to her many novels, Qiong Yao has also written a handful of short stories, an autobiography, and an account of a trip to China at a time when it was still relatively rare for people from Taiwan to travel there.

From the outset of her career, Qiong Yao has had very strong links with the mass media. Her novels were serialized in *Crown* (皇冠) magazine (owned by

Ping Xintao) before being published as monographs by Crown Press (also owned by Ping). Many of her stories were adapted as movies and television series, usually with either Qiong Yao herself or Ping Xintao writing the screenplays and supervising production. In fact, from the 1990s, Qiong Yao was perhaps more conspicuous as a writer of television drama series than as a novelist, with the release of her novels being timed to coincide with the television program. Over a writing career lasting from 1964 to 2002, her print and on-screen stories worked in seamless combination to bring her enormous visibility and fame not only in Taiwan and mainland China, where her novels first appeared in the mid-1980s in pirated editions, but all over the Chinese-speaking world.

San Mao (Chen Ping 陈平, also known as Echo Chen, 1943–1991) enjoyed—or suffered from—a measure of popularity and influence comparable to Qiong Yao's, though in San Mao's case the author's own person was just as important for her fame as her stories. She too was made famous by Ping's publishing house, Crown Press; indeed, stories by San Mao and Qiong Yao alternated for some years as the cover feature and prime selling point for *Crown* magazine.

San Mao's unique brand of writing contains characteristics of autobiography and travelogue, with a strong focus on personal encounters and emotions. Whereas Qiong Yao wrote romantic stories, it could be said that San Mao lived one, or narrated her life as one: opting out of high school and being educated at home; traveling to Europe (and studying there) and to Africa at a time when few in Taiwan had the means to do so; marrying a Spanish man (supposedly after he had waited faithfully for her for six years); living with him in exotic places that were very little known to her readers (the Sahara desert and the Canary Islands); widowed after six years of marriage when her husband died in an accident; returning to Taiwan a celebrity; and spreading her philosophy of happiness, beauty, love, and human concern wherever she went.

San Mao/Chen Ping consistently claimed that everything she wrote was based on her own life, and almost all her stories are narrated in the first person by a character named "San Mao." This led to a blurring of the identities of, and boundaries between, the person Chen Ping and the literary persona San Mao. As a result, many readers came to believe that they knew the "real" person from the stories, a tendency exacerbated by biographers, who reproduce events described in San Mao's stories as "facts" of her life (see, for example, Liu 2013). After her return to Taiwan, where her personal style as well as her fame made her identifiable, Chen Ping appeared to find the burden of being San Mao difficult to bear and expressed a wish to kill off the character and return to anonymity. When the real person Chen Ping died by suicide some years later, there was much bewilderment about how a person who had lived such a "beautiful life" could have died such an ugly death.

San Mao's fame began with "The Restaurant in the Desert" (沙漠中的饭店), a story about the character San Mao's creativity and resourcefulness in cooking Chinese food in the Sahara, published in Taiwan's *United Daily News* (联合报) in 1974. Further stories of the Sahara and of Europe followed, published in *Crown* magazine. Later stories dealt with San Mao's childhood, her return to Taiwan after her husband's death, her attitudes to and relations with family and work, her interest in community, her philosophies of life, her journeys to the Americas, her trip to China, and her passion for handcrafted things and folk-art objects. In addition to her stories, she wrote the screenplay for the award-winning film *Red Dust* (滚滚红尘, 1990) and the lyrics of a popular song, "The Olive Tree" (橄榄树); her list of complete works also contains recordings of her public storytelling, translations (of the Spanish "Mafalda" cartoons and of the U.S. missionary Jerry Martinson SJ's stories of Taiwan aboriginal communities), and two collections of readers' letters to her and her replies as an "agony aunt" in magazine columns.

It is for her Saharan stories, however, that San Mao is best known. Collected in *Stories of the Sahara* (撒哈拉的故事, 1976), *Crying Camels* (哭泣的骆驼, 1977), and *The Tender Night* (温柔的夜, 1979), the tales intersperse playful and ironic accounts of commonplace events, such as cooking, furnishing her home, or taking a driving test, with stories of the "exotic" (Sahrawi bathing customs), the "barbaric" (Sahrawi marriage customs or the keeping of slaves), the supernatural (an amulet that carries a curse), the adventurous (evading assailants and saving her husband from drowning in a freezing swamp), and the politically significant (friendship with Sahrawi independence activists). Several stories present San Mao as a whimsical supplier of medicines, basic education, and hygiene to Sahrawi individuals.

Though her romantic relationship and marriage is not the sole focus of San Mao's work, biographers have paid particular attention to this aspect of her writing and her life, depicting her relationship with her Spanish husband, José (荷西), as an ideal romantic union of two exceptional characters brought together by fate, in the manner of a Qiong Yao novel. The Taiwan critic Li Ao 李敖 viewed San Mao in a similar way, famously suggesting that the only difference between San Mao's writing and Qiong Yao's was "a handful of sand"—in other words, that San Mao wrote Qiong Yao–style romantic stories with herself as the heroine, then added the exotic setting of the Sahara Desert.

San Mao's writing about foreign countries provided readers with visions of exotic places; Qiong Yao's historical settings provided temporal exotica. Qiong Yao's chief preoccupation has been the heterosexual romantic bond, while San Mao's was the romantic individual in a world of wider connections (marriage, family, community, and the world). Both writers created worlds in which emotion was paramount, with an emphasis on the beauty and sincerity of that emotion. Thus a powerful romantic sensibility became available to Chinese readers of the late twentieth century in two different versions, both of which exerted a strong and long-lasting appeal.

Bibliography

Gu Jitang 古继堂. *Pingshuo San Mao* 评说三毛 (Evaluating San Mao). Beijing: Zhishi, 1991.

Lang, Miriam. "San Mao and Qing Yao: A Popular 'Pair.'" *Modern Chinese Literature and Culture* 15, 2 (Fall 2003): 76–120.

Lin Fangmei 林芳玫. *Jiedu Qiong Yao aiqing wangguo* 解读琼瑶爱情王国 (Reading Qiong Yao's kingdom of love). Taipei: Shangwu, 1994.

——. "Social Change and Romantic Ideology: The Impact of the Publishing Industry, Family Organization and Gender Roles on the Reception and Interpretation of Romance Fiction in Taiwan, 1960–1990." PhD diss., University of Pennsylvania, 1992.

Liu Lanfang 刘兰芳. *Yuedu jingdian nüren San Mao* 阅读经典女人三毛 (Reading the classic woman: San Mao). Taipei: Sixing wenhua chuanbo youxian gongsi, 2013.

Lu Shiqing 陆士清, Yang Youli 杨幼力, and Sun Yongchao 孙永超. *San Mao zhuan* 三毛传 (San Mao: A biography). Taipei: Chenxing, 1993.

Qiong Yao 琼瑶. *Chuang wai* 窗外 (Outside the window). Taipei: Huangguan, 1963.

——. *Huanzhu gege* 还珠格格 (Princess Huanzhu). Multivolume series in three main parts. Taipei: Huangguan, 1998–2002.

Radway, Janice. *Reading the Romance: Women, Patriarchy, and Popular Literature*. Chapel Hill: University of North Carolina Press, 1984.

San Mao 三毛. *Kuqi de luotuo* 哭泣的骆驼 (Crying camels). Taipei: Huangguan, 1977.

——. *Sahala de gushi* 撒哈拉的故事 (Stories of the Sahara). Taipei: Huangguan, 1976.

Wang Mingqi 王明琦. "Qiong Yao zuopin yu gudian shici" 琼瑶作品与古典诗词 (The writings of Qiong Yao and classical poetry). *Anhui shangmao zhiye jishu xueyuan xuebao* (shehui kexue ban), no. 4 (2005): 62–64.

Wenxue yanjiushe bianjibu 文学研究社编辑部, ed. *San Mao zuori, jinri, mingri* 三毛昨日今日明日 (San Mao—yesterday, today, and tomorrow). Hong Kong: Wenxue yanjiushe, 1983.

37

MISTY POETRY

MICHELLE YEH

Menglong shi 朦胧诗, variously translated as "Obscure poetry" or "Misty poetry," was originally used in a derogatory sense to describe the poetry that emerged during the "thaw" following Mao Zedong's (1893–1976) death and the arrest of the Gang of Four. First appearing in August 1980 in a short essay published in *Poetry Bimonthly* (诗刊), the largest official poetry journal in China, "misty" (朦胧) was defined by the critic Zhang Ming as a poetic style of opaqueness and incomprehensibility (Bi 1984: 151–153). The term quickly caught on and was—and still is—commonly used to refer to the work by a new generation of poets published from the late 1970s to the mid-1980s. As it attracted national attention, Misty poetry also took on positive meanings as fresh, new poetry distinguished from the formulaic, didactic verse endorsed by the cultural establishment. Among the best-known Misty poets were Bei Dao 北岛 (b. 1949), Shu Ting 舒婷 (b. 1952), Gu Cheng 顾城 (1956–1993), Jiang He 江河 (b. 1949), Yang Lian 杨炼 (b. 1955), Liang Xiaobin 梁小斌 (b. 1954), Wang Xiaoni 王小妮 (b. 1955), and Mang Ke 芒克 (b. 1951), among others.

The controversy over Misty poetry first erupted in 1980–1981, and then again in 1983–1984 during the Anti–Spiritual Pollution Campaign (Larson 1989; Yeh 1992). In both cases, the main charges mounted by the establishment can be summarized as follows. First, by indulging in obscurantism and individualism, Misty poetry separated itself from the people and deviated from the realist tradition, the officially espoused norm in People's Republic of China (PRC) literature. Second, the critical tone of much of the poetry expressed a skeptical, pessimistic outlook that ran counter to the spirit of the Four Modernizations, the national agenda for economic reform under Deng Xiaoping (1904–1997). Finally, obscurity, individualism, and skepticism were deemed the result of Western cultural influences, especially that of modernism; because China did not "face a crisis, either spiritual or material, that would produce modernism in literature" (Larson 1989: 51), Misty poetry was an anachronistic imitation of the West and suggested a loss of the Chinese cultural character. On the one hand, most establishment critics and veteran poets, such as the recently rehabilitated Ai Qing 艾青 (1910–1998) and Zang Kejia 臧克家 (b. 1905), were vehement in their attacks; on the other hand, the scholars Xie Mian and Sun Shaozhen, as well as the poets Xu Chi and Du Yunxie 杜运燮 (b. 1918)—the last a poet whose "Autumn" in 1979 was among the first poems to be criticized as "misty"—defended Misty poetry and advised tolerance.

The establishment's charges against Misty poetry are essentially political. According to the official ideology, poetry, like all cultural forms, should serve the people by being politically correct in content and easily comprehensible in language and form. Shu Ting's "Assembly Line" (流水线) and Gu Cheng's "The End" (结束), for example, were deemed unacceptable because of their contents. Based on the poet's personal experience as a worker in a light-bulb factory, "Assembly Line" depicts the erasure of individuality in an unnatural, dehumanizing environment of mechanized mass production. It was criticized for expressing discontent with modernization. "The End" compared the Jialing River to a soiled shroud and was accused of disrespect for the beloved motherland.

Even when a poem was devoid of political implications, obscure imagery constituted another reason for criticism. The most notorious examples are Gu Cheng's "Arcs" (弧线) and "Far and Near" (远和近). The second reads:

You
Sometimes look at me,
Sometimes look at the clouds.
I feel
You're so far away when you look at me
You're so close when you look at the clouds.

To most readers outside China, this poem would not come across as obscure, although it might lend itself to different interpretations. Ambiguity and polysemy, however, were alien to most Chinese readers, who had grown accustomed to the didactic, message-oriented poetry dictated by the Communist Party propaganda machine throughout Mao's era. The initial reaction of bewilderment and shock at poems like "Far and Near" reflected the bleak literary scene in the aftermath of the Cultural Revolution (1966–1976).

To trace the origins of Misty poetry, one must go back to the Cultural Revolution or even earlier in the 1960s, when young people organized poetry groups and published journals circulated among their own cohorts. Although the complete story will probably never be told owing to the loss of original material, we know, for example, that several poetry groups existed in the early 1960s, such as the X Poetry Club organized by Guo Shiying 郭世英 (1942–1968) and Zhang Heci 张鹤慈 (b. 1943) in Beijing, Wild Duck by Huang Xiang 黄翔 (b. 1941) in Guiyang, and Wild Grass by Deng Ken 邓垦 (b. 1944) and Chen Mo 陈墨 (b. 1945) in Chengdu. During the Cultural Revolution, despite the severe circumstances, poetry was widely circulated among dislocated young men and women in rural areas. Because underground poetry was typically short and relatively easy to commit to memory, it was very popular among so-called educated youth.

One poet who was to have a lasting impact on contemporary poetry is Shizhi 食指 ("index finger," the pen name of Guo Lusheng 郭路生, b. 1948). Shizhi's early association with Sun Column, a group of underground poets in Beijing (van Crevel 1996: 25–29), inspired his signature poems: "Believe in the Future" (相信未来) and "This Is Beijing at 4:08" (这是四点零八分的北京), both written in 1968. The title of the first poem allegedly memorializes the parting words of fellow poet Zhang Langlang 张郎郎 (b. 1943) when he tried to escape arrest for his underground literary activities in the Sun Column. (Unfortunately, he was caught and imprisoned from 1968 to 1977.) "Believe in the Future" expresses hope in the face of hopelessness and reportedly displeased Jiang Qing (1914–1991), or Madame Mao. The second poem was written when the poet was aboard the 4:08 train taking him away from home to an uncertain future. Political persecution might have contributed to the poet's mental breakdown in the early 1970s and intermittent hospitalization over the next two decades (van Crevel 1996: 28–34).

Although written mostly in a regular form with rhymes, Shizhi's early poetry is refreshingly different from the officially sanctioned "political lyric" for its natural cadence and intimate, introspective tone. The first stanza of "Believe in the Future" is a fine example:

When cobwebs ruthlessly seal off my cooking stove,
When smoldering smoke murmurs the sorrow of poverty,
I am determined to spread the ashes of disappointment on the floor
And write these words with beautiful snowflakes: Believe in the future.

Much of Shizhi's early work was published in *Today* (founded in 1978), an underground literary journal edited by two Beijing poets, Bei Dao and Mang Ke. In addition to publishing the work of the two editors, *Today* published such poets as Shu Ting, Fang Han 方含 (b. 1947), Yi Qun 依群 (b. 1947), Jiang He, Gu Cheng, Yan Li 严力 (b. 1954), Yang Lian, and Tian Xiaoqing 田晓青 (b. 1953), many of whom went on to become major Misty poets.

Misty poetry helped usher in a literary renaissance in post-Mao China. It arose from underground journals published in mimeograph all over China. *Today* also had an explicitly political presence: it was posted on a wall in Xidan in Beijing, later known as the Democracy Wall. In *Today*'s inaugural preface, the editors rejected the "cultural dictatorship" of the Gang of Four and identified the April Fifth populist demonstrations in 1976 as the beginning of a new era. In tune with the time, they sought to explore "the meaning of individual existence" and deepen "people's understanding of the spirit of freedom."

Misty poetry is both elegiac and forward-looking; it represents both the disillusionment and the hopefulness many felt in the wake of the Cultural Revolution. In a poem sequence titled "Sky," Mang Ke compares the rising sun—an unmistakable symbol of Chairman Mao—to a blood-dripping shield. Shu Ting refers to the "crown of thorns" she wears on her head. Gu Cheng's "A Generation" (一代人) is a succinct manifesto of the young men and women who went through the decade of devastation:

> Black night gave me black eyes,
> But I use them to look for light.

Acknowledging the darkness his generation has endured, the poet nevertheless refuses to portray himself as a victim. Instead, he asserts his agency and looks to a brighter future. Such optimism is reminiscent of Shizhi's "Believe in the Future" and finds countless echoes in other Misty poems. For example, the speaker in Liang Xiaobin's "China, I've Lost My Key" (中国，我的钥匙丢了) is determined to find the key—a symbol of the true self—that he lost in the political frenzy; Gu Cheng's "Feelings" (感觉) contrasts two children, one dressed in red, the other in green, against the surrounding grayness.

It is in this sense that Misty poetry may be seen as part of the "scar literature" (伤痕文学) that emerged in the late 1970s and early 1980s in the genres of fiction and drama. All of them reflect on the Cultural Revolution and critique its horrendous violence and injustices. Yang Lian's "From Our Own Footprints . . ." (我们从自己的脚印上) begins with these lines:

> From our own footprints
> We understand history
> From the age of ravished poetry
> From the age of guilty doves and flowers
> From the age of quietly weeping children
> From the age of unexpressed friendship and love . . .

In many of these poems, we detect a tone of confident defiance. For the post-Mao generation of writers, defiance also means reexamining the meaning of literature. After decades of subordination to political dictates, poetry reasserted its independence and creative freedom. Yang Lian hails the poet as Prometheus and declares, "Poetry is first of all *poésie*"; it "cleanses and purifies all" and "is above all" (*Today* 9:62). Romantic love between man and woman, nature as a consoling companion, personal memories and aspirations, tributes to the martyrs of the Cultural Revolution—all these themes would have been impossible in an earlier time, but they now appeared in abundance. Political correctness gave way to individual expression in form and content.

Despite the initial controversy, Misty poetry enjoyed unprecedented popularity among general readers in China; it was especially embraced on campuses of high schools and colleges. For many middle-aged Chinese today, their memory of poetry usually has to do with Misty poetry in the 1980s. It is difficult for us to imagine that the Misty poets were idolized like rock stars and famous Misty poems were lovingly memorized and recited in those days. By the mid-1980s, Misty poetry was no longer limited to underground outlets. In the liberalizing climate of post-Mao China, many new official journals were founded all over the country; some were more than happy to publish the popular poetry.

Misty poetry represented a promising beginning to a new, vital poetic movement in contemporary China. In retrospect, it had to overcome many disadvantages that were not only political but also educational and cultural. The Cultural Revolution deprived most Misty poets of a complete education; thus, their exposure to both traditional Chinese and world literature was rather limited. Not unaware of this historical contingency, Misty poets eagerly looked for inspiration to translations of foreign, predominantly European and Anglo-American, literature (van Crevel 1996: 35–41). Most Misty poets acknowledged having been directly influenced by Western poets and writers, but few Misty poets were proficient in Western languages, and their access to translations was haphazard; they ingested the foreign works with haste and often without an adequate understanding of the cultural context in which those works were written.

Furthermore, despite the intention of separating literature from politics, much Misty poetry remains firmly grounded in a political framework. The collective self, against whom the individual self struggles to find meaning, never really disappears from Misty poetry, as amply seen in the early work of Jiang He, Bei Dao, Shu Ting, and Yang Lian. With few exceptions, their language is not completely free of Maospeak. This is perhaps inevitable, as the Cultural Revolution was a major formative experience for their generation. In addition, some of the Misty poets' attempts "to change the inert components in the Chinese national character . . . also placed excessive stress on the role of literature" (Pan and Pan 1985: 215), which ironically undermines its stated ideal of pure literature.

It is in this sense that Misty poetry should be seen as a pioneer of contemporary Chinese poetry. Historical circumstances catapulted it to center stage and inducted it into the literary canon in a matter of a few years. By 1986, a second wave of new poetry began to challenge Misty poetry as a formidable predecessor. The generational differences between the Misty and post-Misty poets were striking. Commonly referred to as the "third generation" or the "newborn generation," the post-Misty poets were born in the late 1950s through the mid-1960s. Unlike the Misty generation, they were too young to be permanently imprinted with the scars of the Cultural Revolution. Moreover, most of them had complete formal schooling and were generally better educated; they held college degrees, and some were proficient in one or more foreign languages. Finally, in the economically developed and socially open environment in the second half of the 1980s, they had extensive exposure to other literatures and cultures, including those from other parts of the Sinophone world.

Misty poetry is an important chapter in the literary history of the PRC. It is also the only Chinese poetry since that of the May Fourth period in the 1920s to receive wide international recognition. Since the 1980s, some Misty poets have moved in new directions, and others have simply stopped writing and left the literary scene.

Bibliography

Barnstone, Tony, ed. *Out of the Howling Storm: The New Chinese Poetry*. Middletown, CT: Wesleyan University Press, 1993.

Bi Hua 壁华 and Yang Ling 杨零, eds. *Jueqi de shiqun—Zhongguo dangdai menglongshi yu shilun xuanji* 崛起的诗群—中国当代朦胧诗与诗论选集 (The rising poetry group: A collection of Chinese Misty poetry and poetic criticism). Hong Kong: Dangdai wenxue yanjiushe, 1984.

Emerson, Andrew G. "The Guizhou Undercurrent." *Modern Chinese Literature and Culture* 13, 2 (Fall 201): 111–133.

Finkel, Donald, ed. *A Splintered Mirror: Chinese Poetry from the Democracy Movement*. San Francisco: North Point Press, 1991.

Huang, Xiang. *A Lifetime Is a Promise to Keep*. Trans. Michelle Yeh. Berkeley: University of California at Berkeley, Institute of East Asian Studies, 2009.

Larson, Wendy. "Realism, Modernism, and the Anti-'Spiritual Pollution' Campaign in China." *Modern China* 15, 1 (January 1989): 37–71.

Morin, Edward, ed. *The Red Azalea: Chinese Poetry since the Cultural Revolution*. Honolulu: University of Hawai'i Press, 1990.

Owen, Stephen. "What Is World Poetry?" *The New Republic* (November 19, 1990): 28–32.

Pan, Yuan, and Jie Pan. "The Non-Official Magazine *Today* and the Younger Generation's Ideals for a New Generation." In Jeffrey Kinkley, ed., *After Mao: Chinese Literature and Society, 1978–1981*, 193–219. Cambridge, MA: Harvard University Press, 1985.

Tay, William. "'Obscure Poetry': A Controversy in Post-Mao China." In Jeffrey C. Kinkley, ed., *After Mao: Chinese Literature and Society, 1978–1981*, 133–157. Cambridge, MA: Harvard University Press, 1985.

Van Crevel, Maghiel. *Chinese Poetry in Times of Mind, Mayhem, and Money*. Leiden: Brill, 2008.

———. *Language Shattered: Contemporary Chinese Poetry and Duoduo*. Leiden: Research School CNWS, 1996.

———, comp. *Unofficial Poetry Journals from the People's Republic of China: A Research Note*. MCLC Resource Center Publication (2007). http://u.osu.edu/mclc/online-series/vancrevel2.

Wang, Ping, ed. *New Generation: Poems from China Today*. Brooklyn, NY: Hanging Loose Press, 1999.

Xu, Xing. "The Rise and Struggle for Survival of the Unofficial Press in China." In *Documents on the Chinese Democratic Movement, 1978–1980*, 33–45. Paris: Écoles des Hautes Études en Sciences Sociales, 1981.

Yeh, Michelle, ed. *Anthology of Modern Chinese Poetry*. New Haven, CT: Yale University Press, 1994.

Yeh, Michelle. "Light a Lamp in a Rock: Experimental Poetry in Contemporary China." *Modern China* 18, 4 (October 1992): 379–409.

38

SCAR LITERATURE AND THE MEMORY OF TRAUMA

SABINA KNIGHT

In November 1977, the official literary journal *People's Literature* (人民文学) published the first of a series of stories about suffering during the Cultural Revolution and about the spiritual state of the Chinese people who had survived it. In Liu Xinwu's 刘心武 "Class Counselor" (班主任, 1977), a devoted teacher, Zhang Junshi 张俊石, chooses to help a youth whose delinquency he sees as a consequence of his upbringing during the reign of the ultraleftist Gang of Four. As Zhang confronts his students' resistance to accepting the boy, he realizes the harm that "fascist cultural tyranny" (Barmé and Lee 1979: 157) has done to even the exemplary youth, most notably the well-intentioned Youth League branch secretary. Although tendentious passages condemn the Gang of Four and lecture on the need to cure the body politic, the story expresses impassioned faith in a teacher's ability to open his students' eyes to the wider achievements of human civilization. In this way, the story confronts the nation's "spiritual impoverishment" (161) while still proclaiming deep devotion to the cause of national salvation.

Liu's story was immediately followed by an outpouring of similar works testifying to the immeasurable trauma and dislocation of Mao's massive national campaign to unleash unending revolution. After the publication the following August of Lu Xinhua's 卢新华 story "Scar" (伤痕, 1978, English title "The Wounded"), such works became known collectively as "scar literature" or "literature of the wounded" (伤痕文学). By portraying the suffering endured by unjustly persecuted artists, intellectuals, common people, cadres, and educated youth "sent down" to the countryside (Cao 2003), these stories explicitly criticized the unrestrained implementation of political orthodoxy. Although scar literature did not yet question the revolutionary cause or challenge culture's instrumental subservience to it, it did reintroduce such humanist subjects as the importance of individual autonomy, the exercise of individual conscience, complex moral dilemmas, and literature's role in exposing the dark aspects of society. Its appearance within two years of Mao Zedong's death and the fall of the Gang of Four testifies to the authors' courage in reviving Chinese writers' traditional duty to expose injustice and corruption.

Scar literature thus holds great historical significance as the first stage in the liberalization of Communist Party literary policy in the post-Mao era. For the preceding three and a half decades, ever since Mao's "Yan'an Talks" (1942), literature had served politics more than at any other time in China's long literary history. With the Yan'an Talks as textual authority, the People's Republic of China (PRC) cultural bureaucracy implemented a rigid program centered around "revolutionary realism and revolutionary romanticism," making use of "rectification campaigns" (整风运动) to silence alternative voices. In 1953, Mao's culture czar, Zhou Yang 周扬 (1908–1989), solidified the rules for literary production by reiterating the tenets of socialist realism first developed in the Soviet Union. Thereafter, party literary doctrines lay an ever more hazardous minefield of taboos against "middle characters" (中间人物), psychological analysis, critical realism, or accounts of autonomous actions not dictated by party ideology. The persecution of writers in the Anti-Rightist Campaign (1957–1958) (see "The Hundred Flowers") and the Cultural Revolution taught writers the often fatal consequences they could face for unflattering portrayals of socialist society or for depictions of humanist principles or romantic love that might transcend class lines or overshadow social issues (Pollard 1978: 100–102).

By reaffirming the value of individuals and their inner struggles, scar literature broke decisively with the cultural paradigm of the Mao period. At the same time, the inclusion of an obligatory "bright tail" (光明尾巴) ending in these stories affirmed faith in the new regime under Deng Xiaoping (1904–1997) and thus limited these stories' censure to the wrongdoings of the past. By demonizing the Cultural Revolution and the Gang of Four, moreover, these works served a conservative ideological and political function: they reinforced the Deng regime's efforts to consolidate its power by distancing itself from Maoist ideology through its campaign of intellectual liberation (思想解放) and its creation of a "new era" (新时期) through the Four Modernizations economic program. In its implicit reassertion of individualism, scar literature might even have reinforced the party's new leniency toward the pursuit of profit and Deng's program of promoting a rational, progressive, and affluent society. By classifying recent literary production into categories such as "literature of the wounded" and its heirs the "literature of reflection" (反思文学) and "literature of reform" (改革文学), critics encouraged writers to repeat formulas. Official party endorsement of these new genres soon followed as the leadership announced the relaxation of thought control in late 1978 and ushered in the Beijing Spring of 1979. At the fall 1979 Fourth Congress of Writers and Artists, Deng Xiaoping and Zhou Yang relaxed literary policy and sanctioned all works helpful to realizing the Four Modernizations.

The literary significance of scar literature lies primarily in its potential to serve as a forum for moral reflection. Although many of the early stories denounce the Gang of Four for the country's ills and thus avoid issues of personal responsibility, soon bolder works broached characters' guilt over their participation in the persecution of their loved ones. The epithet "literature of the wounded" draws attention to the suffering of the victims, but these works increasingly hinted at their characters' roles as victimizers as well.

Such new attention to personal responsibility is evident in the story from which scar literature derives its name. One of the saddest stories of modern Chinese fiction, Lu Xinhua's "The Wounded" describes a former Red Guard's gradual coming to terms with her earlier disavowal of her mother after the latter is branded a renegade. The story opens nine years after Xiaohua's 晓华 departure from Shanghai as she travels back from Liaoning Province in the hopes of seeing her now-rehabilitated mother. Arriving only after her mother has passed away, Xiaohua finds a note in which her mother not only refuses to blame her daughter but also expresses concern for the ordeal she has lived through. "While she hasn't been as physically mistreated as I was by the Gang of Four," the note says, "the wound in her heart will be much worse than all the wounds on my body" (Barmé and Lee 1979, 23). This assertion of Xiaohua's position as a victim does not put to rest the issues raised by her earlier recollections and her pain upon seeing a mother and child together on the train. Xiaohua's remorse leads the reader to question how she came to believe official accusations against her mother in the first place. How would a daughter resolve to repudiate her mother and perceive her act as a matter of choice? "She had no choice but to criticize her own petit-bourgeois instincts and draw a line of demarcation between herself and her mother" (11).

Loath to identify with a criminal, had the sixteen-year-old Xiaohua abandoned her mother to pursue her own dreams and plans or to follow the party's program for what a good revolutionary's plans and dreams should be? In returning her mother's care packages, had she not become an instrument of the party's persecution of her mother? The barriers Xiaohua has erected to sever her love for her mother are further demonstrated when she doubts what her mother writes in her letter about her rehabilitation, illness, and concern that she may not live long enough to see her daughter. The possibility that Xiaohua could have acted otherwise, at least in not delaying her return, is implied by her boyfriend's suggestions that she enquire about her mother's status after the fall of the Gang of Four and by his own visit to Xiaohua's mother in her stead. The story's hopeful ending suggests Xiaohua's control over her emotions, but it leaves the reader to imagine the remorse left unexplored: "Dear mother, rest in peace. I will never forget who was responsible for your wounds and mine. I shall never forget Chairman Hua's kindness and [I shall] closely follow the Party's Central Committee headed by him and dedicate my life to the cause of the Party" (Barmé and Lee 1979: 23–24). Xiaohua's faith in her nation's progress toward a just and affluent society does not placate the deep sense of collective grievance brought out in other parts of the story.

The concrete depictions of trauma in much scar literature dispel some of the mystery surrounding the Cultural Revolution and testify to the peril that results when people are made into instruments of political movements. The senseless chaos that resulted from Mao's headlong pursuit of ideological purity and utopian ends is clearly depicted in such stories as Zheng Yi's 郑义 "Maple" (枫, 1979), which is about a young couple who find themselves on opposite sides of warring Red Guard factions. Such works may have helped renew readers' concerns for their own lives, souls, and families. For example, Chen Guokai's 陈国凯 "What Should I Do" (我应该怎么办, 1979) tells of the heartache, suffering, and near death of a woman after her husband suddenly disappears; one evening years later, having remarried, she answers the door to find her first husband freed from a labor camp. Kong Jiesheng's 孔捷生 "On the Other Side of the Stream" (在小河那边, 1979) also treats the trauma of a family's separation during the Cultural Revolution. Brought back together by coincidence, a brother and sister fail to recognize each other after years of separation and fall in love. "Neither wanted to open the other's wounds" (Link 1984: 185), and so they never ask about each other's families until they decide to marry and are thus forced to discover their original relationship.

If works of revolutionary romanticism had endorsed a Maoist version of history, scar literature often undermined Mao's faith in collective voluntarism. These stories revived the May Fourth tradition of critical realism in exposing China's social and economic problems, political corruption, and the disillusionment and utter exhaustion of a people still reeling from the anguish of the immediate past. Some authors used parody, as in Gao Xiaosheng's 高晓声 story "Li Shunda Builds a House" (李顺大造屋, 1979), about how shifts in official policy continually frustrate a peasant's attempts to build his family a home. Other authors portrayed the fraud, opportunism, and immorality of the bureaucracy, as in Liu Ke's 刘克 depiction of the rape of a young army recruit in "Feitian" (飞天, 1979), or of influence peddling, as in Xu Mingxu's 徐明旭 "Transfer" (调动, 1979).

Other works dramatized the self-destruction of youth so morally blinkered by Maoism that they lose even their own sense of survival. In Li Jian's 李剑 "Drunk in the Flowers" (醉入花丛, 1981), an idealistic young Red Guard finds herself stranded for the night with an older impoverished farmer. Reluctantly, she allows him to bed her and then to marry her, all in a blindly literal allegiance to Mao's slogan that denying peasants would be denying the revolution. As the story ends, she finds herself doomed and in a state of mental collapse. Such works overlap with the "literature of reflection" that not only condemned particular events and individuals but also questioned the ideological foundations of China's socialist system. Such questioning specially marked works that explored traumas of the "seventeen years" between 1949 and the onset of the Cultural Revolution in 1966.

Scholars differ in how widely they apply the label "scar literature." Some reserve the label for early works of 1977–1981 that despite traumatic testimony imply that honest analysis and individual responsibility will lead to reform. Even so narrowly defined, scar literature might still include early works of "prison literature" (大墙文学, literally "literature of the big wall") such as Cong Weixi's 从维熙 novella "Red Magnolias Beneath the Wall" (大墙下的红玉兰, 1979).

Scar literature also paved the way for the inward turn of psychological fiction that reemerged around 1980, such as in Dai Houying's 戴厚英 *Humanity, Oh Humanity* (人啊, 人!, 1980). In its function as cultural memory, scar literature may also be seen as a predecessor to later testimonial literature about the Cultural Revolution, some of which first appeared in English, such as Nien Cheng's 郑念 *Life and Death in Shanghai* (1986) and Gao Yuan's 高原 *Born Red: A Chronicle of the Cultural Revolution* (1987).

Other scholars thus extend the term "scar literature" to encompass such works, some presenting the injustices of the political system as ineluctable, and many dating well into the 1980s and even beyond. Among the most probing works are those about the labor camps, from Zhang Xianliang's 张贤亮 novella "Mimosa" (绿化树, 1984), his novel *Half of Man Is Woman* (男人的一半是女人, 1985), and later autobiographical writings, to memoirs such as Ma Bo's 马波 *Blood Red Sunset* (血色黄昏, 1987). Ma's harrowing novel-memoir describes how a Red Guard ransacks his own family home, denounces his mother, and himself suffers persecution as a counterrevolutionary. Ma's rough-hewn honesty astonished Chinese readers, who bought more than 400,000 copies.

Scar literature also broke ground for the "sketch" (特写) or "reportage" (报告文学) writings on the Cultural Revolution that began with journalist Liu Binyan's 刘宾雁 "People or Monsters" (人妖之间, 1979) and continued with writings such as Liao Yiwu's 廖亦武 searing essays collected in *Interviews with the Lower Strata of Chinese Society* (中国底层访谈录, English title *The Corpse Walker*).

Literature of the wounded is often criticized for formulaic and didactic content, but to write about suffering and not deliver a message is difficult. It deserves further consideration through comparison with other trauma literature, such as works about European genocides or the repression of intellectuals under Stalin. With greater hindsight, readers may also see significant continuity between scar literature and more mature Chinese trauma literature, such as Mo Yan's 莫言 *Life and Death Are Wearing Me Out* (生死疲劳, 2006).

Bibliography

Barmé, Geremie, and Bennett Lee, eds. *The Wounded: New Stories of the Cultural Revolution*. Hong Kong: Joint Publishing, 1979.

Berry, Michael. *A History of Pain: Trauma in Modern Chinese Literature and Film*. New York: Columbia University Press, 2008.

Braester, Yomi. "Disjointed Time, Split Voices: Retrieving Historical Experience in Scar Literature." In *Witness Against History: Literature, Film, and Public Discourse in Twentieth-Century China*, 146–157. Stanford, CA: Stanford University Press, 2003.

Cao, Zuoya. *Out of the Crucible: Literary Works about the Rusticated Youth*. Lanham, MD: Lexington Books, 2003.

Duke, Michael, ed. *Contemporary Chinese Literature: An Anthology of Post-Mao Fiction and Poetry*. Armonk, NY: M. E. Sharpe, 1985.

King, Richard. "'Wounds' and 'Exposure': Chinese Literature After the Gang of Four." *Pacific Affairs* 54, 1 (1981): 82–99.

Kinkley, Jeffrey, ed. *After Mao: Chinese Literature and Society, 1978–1981*. Cambridge, MA: Harvard University Press, 1985.

Knight, Sabina. "Historical Trauma and Humanism in Post-Mao Realism." In *The Heart of Time: Moral Agency in Twentieth-Century Chinese Fiction*, 162–190. Cambridge, MA: Harvard University Asia Center, 2006.

Lau, Joseph S. M. "The Wounded and the Fatigued: Reflections on Post-1976 Chinese Fiction." *Journal of Oriental Studies* 20, 2 (1982): 28–42.

Lee, Yee, ed. *The New Realism: Writings from China After the Cultural Revolution*. New York: Hippocrene Books, 1983.

Liao, Yiwu, *The Corpse Walker: Real Life Stories: China from the Bottom Up*. Trans. Wen Huang. NY: Pantheon, 2008. Rpt. New York: Anchor, 2009.

Link, Perry, ed. *Roses and Thorns: The Second Blooming of the Hundred Flowers in Chinese Fiction, 1979–1980*. Berkeley: University of California Press, 1984.

——, ed. *Stubborn Weeds: Popular and Controversial Chinese Literature After the Cultural Revolution*. Bloomington: Indiana University Press, 1983.

——. *The Uses of Literature: Life in the Socialist Chinese Literary System*. Princeton, NJ: Princeton University Press, 2000.

Liu, Binyan. *People or Monsters and Other Stories and Reportage from China After Mao*. Trans. Perry Link. Bloomington: Indiana University Press, 1983.

Ma, Bo. *Blood Red Sunset: A Memoir of the Chinese Cultural Revolution*. Trans. Howard Goldblatt. New York: Viking, 1995.

Pollard, David E. "The Short Story in the Cultural Revolution." *China Quarterly* 73 (March 1978): 99–121.

Wu Fengxing 吴丰兴. *Zhongguo dalu de "shanghen wenxue"* 中国大陆的伤痕文学 (Mainland China's scar literature). Taipei: Youshi wenhua, 1983.

39

CULTURE AGAINST POLITICS: ROOTS-SEEKING LITERATURE

MARK LEENHOUTS

The current of "roots-seeking literature" (寻根文学) dominated China's literary scene between 1985 and 1988. Although it is sometimes referred to as a literary movement guided by a manifesto, "roots-seeking" (寻根) is perhaps better seen as a pervasive theme that preoccupied writers during a certain period, stirring up lively debates in literary circles of the time. All these writers in some manner stressed the importance of their cultural identity for their creative work; they considered their Chinese or ethnic minority identity as a relevant or even decisive element of a successful Chinese literature.

The roots-seeking phenomenon was initially a theoretical affair that started with an essay, "Literary 'Roots'" (文学的"根", 1985), by the fiction writer Han Shaogong 韩少功 (b. 1953). Han's essay (Han 2001) immediately provoked a flood of articles that did not subside until the spring of 1988. This debate centered on one issue: how writers can renovate Chinese literature when they find themselves so cut off from their cultural tradition. In this call for revitalization, roots-seeking literature was clearly a reaction against, on the one hand, politically controlled or socially engaged literature—for example, the "scar literature" and "reform literature," respectively, of the early 1980s—and, on the other hand, the "pseudomodernists" (伪现代派), whose work, in the eyes of the roots-seeking authors, ran the risk of being a shallow imitation of Western literature. In the latter, they discerned a superficial focus on formal techniques borrowed from Chinese translations of Western literature. In reacting against these Western imitators, the roots proponents called for a return to China's indigenous cultures as the fountainhead for literary creativity.

Almost all theorists of roots-seeking literature mention May Fourth iconoclasm—and its culmination in the Cultural Revolution—as the main cause for their sense of cultural uprootedness. They oppose the May Fourth movement not only for its radical break with tradition in favor of the appropriation of Western literary techniques but also for its tendency to use literature for moral and sociopolitical engagement, to the detriment of art. The roots writers' stress on "culture" (文化) can also be seen as deliberately contrary to "politics," which Mao had put in command of the arts. This stress can also be seen in the language issue raised by the critic Li Tuo 李陀, a promoter of roots literature. Li opposed the Westernized May Fourth language and the so-called Mao style (毛文体), language colored by political ideology. These views of language were shared by writers not directly associated with roots literature. Gao Xingjian 高行健, for example, proposed that writers should return to basic characteristics of the traditional Chinese language to produce "modern literature imbued with an Asian spirit." The call for a "stronger national literature," as some writers put it, was thus based as much on artistic and aesthetic motives as nationalist ones.

It was to the countryside, either in the writer's home region or among the many minority cultures that lived there, that writers were to turn in search of their roots. That these writers looked to the countryside for their inspiration is perhaps not surprising, for almost all of them had been sent there as educated youth (知青) in the 1960s and 1970s and had spent many of their formative years living among the rural population. Roots writers and theorists saw the remote rural and minority areas, as preserves of cultures somehow untouched by the homogenizing influence of modernization, Westernization, and even the Chinese revolution, on the one hand, and of the Confucian or dominant Han Chinese culture, on the other.

Because of its subject matter, roots-seeking literature is often equated with, or treated as a subdivision of, "native soil literature" (乡土文学) (see "Shen Congwen and Imagined Native Communities" and "Nativism and Localism in Taiwanese Literature"). Although both draw material or inspiration from the countryside, however, they have little in common. The nostalgic mood of the native soil literature of the Republican period and the more ideological nature of Taiwanese nativist literature of the 1960s and 1970s, for example, cannot be called the main motives of roots-seeking literature. An exception is the native soil literature of Shen Congwen 沈从文, who served as an example to many roots-seeking writers because he shunned politics in favor of aesthetics and blended modern (Western) and traditional (Chinese) literary influences.

In the "Literary 'Roots,'" Han Shaogong (2001) points to Jia Pingwa's 贾平凹 (b. 1953) series of short stories *Records of Shangzhou* (商州初录, 1982) and A Cheng's 阿城 (b. 1949) novella "The King of Chess" (棋王, 1984) as early manifestations of roots literature. These works, along with Han's own work and

Mo Yan's 莫言 (b. 1956) internationally acclaimed *Red Sorghum* (红高粱家族, 1987), have since been labeled standard works of the roots-seeking current. The well-known film by Zhang Yimou 张艺谋 based on Mo Yan's novel (*Red Sorghum* 红高粱, 1988), as well as Chen Kaige's 陈凯歌 *Yellow Earth* (黄土地, 1984) and *King of the Children* (孩子王, 1987), based on a novella by A Cheng, represents a roots-seeking current in cinema around the same period. This current is further marked by films such as *Horse Thief* (盗马贼, dir. Tian Zhuangzhuang 田壮壮, 1986) and *Old Well* (老井, dir. Wu Tianming 吴天明, 1987), based on novels by the roots writers Zhang Chengzhi 张承志 (b. 1948) and Zheng Yi 郑义 (b. 1947), respectively. A current of roots-seeking in poetry has also been discerned in the work of Yang Lian 杨炼 and Jiang He 江河, among others, who employ imagery drawn from Chinese history, myth, and legends.

Jia Pingwa has declared that depicting the local customs of everyday people, as he does for his home district in rural Shanxi in his *Records of Shangzhou*, is the only way to revitalize Chinese literature, and he thereby explicitly agrees with the roots-seeking theory. Whereas his subject matter, the Cultural Revolution, is contemporary, Jia's style is said to hark back to the traditional prose sketch (笔记) (see, for example, "How Much Can a Man Bear" [人极, 1985]). The paradoxical and alienating effect of traditional style combined with modern content is a typical feature of roots literature.

A Cheng's "The King of Chess" has been noted for a linguistic style reminiscent of China's premodern novels. But more important is the story's attempt to link traditional Daoist spirituality with modern, everyday life. Set in the Cultural Revolution, it tells of a young man obsessed with food and chess. The protagonist's emphasis on eating marks his status as a poor commoner, whereas his craze for chess is enshrouded in Daoist philosophy. The story can be read as an attempt to show how the Daoist tradition has remained alive among the common folk, paradoxically even during the Cultural Revolution. "The Tree Stump" (树桩, 1984) also brings tradition and modernity together by recounting an aged folksinger's participation in a modern singing contest. In his essays, A Cheng has explicitly stated that literature, just like humanity, is conditioned by culture, as revealed in secular customs and language.

Han Shaogong shows great interest in marginal worldviews and local beliefs of the Hunan countryside that he traces to the ancient Chu culture. Another inspiration drawn from China's southern cultures is a spirit of Zhuangzi's relativity and ambivalence, which can be seen as a central governing aspect of Han's work, made manifest in his questioning the validity of various pairs of opposites. His best-known story, "Pa Pa Pa" (爸爸爸, 1985), set in a remote mountain hamlet, is a social satire in which primitive "nonrationality" (instinctive thought and superstition) is set off against the rationality (modern logic and scientific values) of the implied modern reader. If "Pa Pa Pa" focuses on social history, "Woman Woman Woman" (女女女, 1986) reflects the other side of the coin: individual action. The protagonist's love-hate relationships with his traditional, self-effacing, austere aunt and her hypermodern, emancipated, hedonist goddaughter reveal his ambivalent attitude toward modern as well as traditional values, in particular the issues of individual freedom and compliance to social norms. In the short story "Homecoming" (归去来, 1985), the first-person narrator comes to an unknown remote village where everyone takes him for someone else, an experience so haunting that he starts to question his own identity. The story's dreamlike atmosphere alludes to Zhuangzi's "butterfly dream" and the issue of the relativity of identity. Abundant depictions of strange local customs aim not to create an exotic effect or nationalistic identification but to evoke imagery in the service of the identity theme; they accentuate the alienating contrast between the individual and the outside world, the self and the Other. In addition, Han's interest in Hunan's local dialects has led him to a preoccupation with the use of language, notably in A *Dictionary of Maqiao* (马桥词典, 1996), his magnum opus, a novel written as a lexicon, in which many themes of his preceding work converge.

Besides the attention to regional customs, which all writers discussed here share, other related aspects of literary roots-seeking include the conflict between tradition and modernity, marginal cultures, magic realism, ethnic minorities, and nature. The conflict between tradition and modernity permeates the work of Li Rui 李锐 (b. 1950) and Zheng Yi. Li Rui has been noted for his series of short stories *The Solid Earth* (厚土, 1986), of which the title already speaks volumes, and his novel *Silver City* (旧址, 1992), a family saga set in a fictitious Chinese town in which modernity challenges traditional culture. Zheng Yi's novel *Old Well* (老井, 1985) portrays a man who is reluctant to leave the rural place where he has his roots, even if staying means forfeiting a chance to be with the modern, urban woman he loves.

Another pervasive aspect of roots-seeking fiction is its interest in marginal cultures as alternatives to the mainstream. In their essays, writers like Han Shaogong and Gu Hua 古华 (b. 1942) explicitly claim that orthodox culture is less conducive to artistic production than the unorthodox. They see Confucian tradition as more practical and less spiritual than, for example, Daoism, the *Songs of Chu* 楚辞, Song lyric meters, and Ming-Qing fiction, the influence of which can be seen in most roots-seeking works: for example, Daoism and Ming-Qing fiction in A Cheng, or the *Zhuangzi* 庄子 and Chu culture in Han Shaogong.

A conspicuous feature of roots-seeking fiction is magic realism, either influenced by its Latin American counterpart or derived from indigenous roots. Authors such as Han Shaogong and Mo Yan prefer to point to China's rich, persistent tradition of tales of the supernatural and the fantastic, the *zhiguai* 志怪 (records of anomalies) and the *chuanqi* 传奇 (accounts of the extraordinary); this influence is clear in Han Shaogong's short story "Embers" (余烬, 1994). Others such as Jia Pingwa and Zhaxi Dawa 扎西达娃 (b. 1959) have acknowledged their debt to Nobel Prize winner Gabriel García Márquez; after his *One Hundred Years* of *Solitude* was translated into Chinese in 1982, he had a great influence on them, not only in demonstrating literary techniques—specifically, his blending of local traditional culture with Western modernity—but also in offering a positive example of a writer from an economically disadvantaged nation who gained global recognition. Traits of magic realism can be detected in the work of the Han Tibetan writer Zhaxi Dawa, among others. In stories such as "A Soul in Bondage" (系在皮绳扣上的魂, 1985), traditional Tibetan values and modern Western culture exist side by side. Zhaxi Dawa and others also use notions of cyclical time in a subversive—call it postmodern—narrative. Han Shaogong often presents odd local customs, superstition, and violent primitivism in a way intended to convince us of their internal logic and maybe to hold up a mirror to modern culture; in this sense, his work can be superficially likened to that of García Márquez.

Minority cultures provide material for many roots works. For some writers, such as Zhaxi Dawa, this is a case of drawing from their own ethnic origins. But Han writers have also often written about minority cultures. The experimentalist Ma Yuan 马原 (b. 1953), for example, has often written about Tibetan culture, although his treatment of it is too casual to allow him to be included in the roots-seeking current. Zheng Wanlong 郑万隆 (b. 1944) is inspired by the Oroqen minority of Northeast China among whom he spent his youth. The title of his series of stories *Strange Tales from Strange Lands* (异乡异闻, 1985) evokes the sense of estrangement the writer apparently feels toward the culture of his home region, which he consciously portrays as exotic. This alienation of intellectuals in rural areas is a typical theme in the literary works and theoretical essays of most roots-seeking writers, who have more than once acknowledged that ethnic identity can be used as a metaphor through which to pursue personal identity.

Nature is another important element in roots-seeking literature. Many roots-seeking writers reveal a certain nostalgic longing for the authentic, natural life embodied in their rural characters and from which they feel alienated. A clear example of this is Mo Yan's work, perhaps most obviously his novel *Red Sorghum* (红高粱家族, 1986). Also evident is a tendency to see the regional environment and natural conditions as determinants of ethnic or personal identities. Zhang Chengzhi, a member of the Hui Muslim minority, has written extensively about the regional cultures of Inner Mongolia, Ningxia, and Xinjiang, the homelands of the Hui. The identity theme is apparent in his novella "Rivers of the North" (北方的河, 1984), for instance, where the protagonist likens the Yellow River to his father, just as in several short stories the grassy plains are likened to the protagonist's mother. Zhang's well-known novella "The Black Steed" (黑骏马, 1982; adapted for the screen by Xie Fei 谢飞 as *A Mongolian Tale* 黑骏马, 1997) is a pastoral love story that combines the typical oppositions of roots-seeking fiction: that between local and central (Han) culture, city and countryside, and intellectual and peasant.

Other writers more loosely belong to roots-seeking literature than do the writers discussed earlier. Wang Zengqi 汪曾祺 (b. 1920), for example, is an older writer who had published in the 1940s and made a comeback in the post-Mao era, when he was hailed as the inheritor of the legacy of Shen Congwen, whose pupil he had been. Younger generations of writers appreciated his stories, such as "Ordination" (受戒, 1980), for the language and cultural atmosphere that hark back to the pre-Communist period. Wang Anyi's 王安忆 (b. 1954) *Baotown* (小鲍庄, 1984) is often referred to as a roots-seeking work. Finally, Gu Hua's *A Small Town Called Hibiscus* (芙蓉镇, 1981) clearly also has a rural community as its subject, although it has mostly been appreciated for its political views.

Roots-seeking literature has been criticized for its hostility to foreign influence and its "inward turn" to its own culture. Critics have also disapproved of its "turning backward" to tradition, even glorifying tradition, while neglecting the issues of modernity and progress. Other critics, on the contrary, highlight the open-mindedness of the current: its treatment of Chinese culture from a modern point of view, absorbing Western culture as a frame of reference from which to understand Chinese culture better and more critically. They also agree with some writers in the movement that only a literature that is firmly rooted in its national soil can enter the stage of world literature.

Attention given to culture in this literary current formed part of the larger debates on culture in the sociopolitical sphere in the mid-1980s, known as a time of "culture fever" (文化热). In political as well as intellectual fields, Chinese felt the need to reestablish their national identity in the modern world after years of isolation. It can be argued that roots-seeking literature presents an alternative to the shallow nationalism of Communist Party orthodoxy; thanks to its aesthetic ambitions, the literary search for roots resulted in a much more subtle and even ambivalent attitude toward questions of cultural identity.

Although criticizing roots theory for its fixation on Chinese culture may be justified, in literary practice, as we have seen, many writers go beyond culture to delve into deeper questions of subjectivity and modernity. Roots-seeking literature was an important phase in the development of contemporary Chinese literature. One could say that it moved literature away from its narrow sociopolitical engagement by stressing literature's broad cultural aspects. By drawing attention to literature's aesthetic dimensions and delving into questions of identity and subjectivity, moreover, it paved the way for the avant-garde literature of the late 1980s and the 1990s.

Bibliography

A, Cheng. *Three Kings: Three Stories from Today's China*. Trans. Bonnie S. McDougall. London: Collins Harvill, 1990.

——. "The Tree Stump." In Jeanne Tai, trans. and ed., *Spring Bamboo: A Collection of Contemporary Chinese Short Stories*, 25–33. New York: Random House, 1989.

Feuerwerker, Yi-tsi Mei. "The Post-Modern 'Search for Roots' in Han Shaogong, Mo Yan, and Wang Anyi." In *Ideology, Power, Text: Self-Representation and the Peasant "Other" in Modern Chinese Literature*, 188–238. Stanford, CA: Stanford University Press, 1998.

Gu, Hua. *A Small Town Called Hibiscus*. Trans. Gladys Yang. Beijing: Panda Books, 1983.

Han, Shaogong. *A Dictionary of Maqiao*. Trans. Julia Lovell. New York: Columbia University Press, 2003; New York: Dial Press, 2005 (paperback).

——. "Embers." Trans. Thomas Moran. In Henry Zhao, John Rosenwald, and Yanbing Chen, eds., *Fissures: Chinese Writing Today*, 263–279. Brookline, MA: Zephyr Press, 2000.

——. "The Homecoming." In Jeanne Tai, trans. and ed., *Spring Bamboo: A Collection of Contemporary Chinese Short Stories*, 19–40. New York: Random House, 1989.

——. *Homecoming? and Other Stories*. Trans. Martha Cheung. Hong Kong: Renditions, 1992.

——. "The Leader's Demise." Trans. Thomas Moran. In Joseph Lau and Howard Goldblatt, eds., *The Columbia Anthology of Modern Chinese Literature*, 387–398. New York: Columbia University Press, 1995.

——. "Wenxue de 'gen'" 文学的"根" (Literary roots). In Han Shaogong, *Wenxue de gen* 文学的根 (Literary roots), 77–84. Jinan: Shandong wenyi, 2001.

Jia, Pingwa. *The Heavenly Hound*. Beijing: Panda Books, 1991.

——. "How Much Can a Man Bear?" and "Family Chronicle of a Wooden Bowl Maker." In Zhu Hong, trans. and ed., *The Chinese Western*, 1–52, 100–117. New York: Ballantine, 1988.

——. *Turbulence*. Trans. Howard Goldblatt. New York: Grove Press, 1991.

Leenhouts, Mark. *Leaving the World to Enter the World: Han Shaogong and Root-Seeking Literature*. Leiden: CNWS Publications, 2005.

Li, Rui. "Electing a Thief." Trans. Jeffrey C. Kinkley. In Helen F. Siu, ed., *Furrows: Peasants, Intellectuals, and the State: Stories and Histories from Modern China*, 201–211. Stanford, CA: Stanford University Press, 1990.

——. "Sham Marriage." Trans. William Schaefer and Fenghua Wang. In Howard Goldblatt, ed., *Chairman Mao Would Not Be Amused: Fiction from Today's China*, 90–98. New York: Grove Press, 1995.

——. *Silver City*. Trans. Howard Goldblatt. New York: Henry Holt, 1997.

Mo, Yan. *Red Sorghum*. Trans. Howard Goldblatt. New York: Viking, 1993.

Schiaffini-Vedani, Patricia. "The 'Condor' Flies over Tibet: Zhaxi Dawa and the Significance of Tibetan Magical Realism." In Lauran R. Hartley and Patricia Schiaffini-Vedani, eds., *Modern Tibetan Literature and Social Change*, 202–224. Durham, NC: Duke University Press, 2008.

Wang, Anyi. *Baotown*. Trans. Martha Avery. New York: Viking Penguin, 1985.

——. "Lao Kang Came Back." In Jeanne Tai, trans. and ed., *Spring Bamboo: A Collection of Contemporary Chinese Short Stories*, 41–55. New York: Random House, 1989.

Wang, Yiyan. *Narrating China: Jia Pingwa and His Fictional World*. New York: Routledge, 2006.

Wang, Zengqi. "The Love Story of a Young Monk" and "Story After Supper." Trans. Hu Zhihui and Shen Zhen. *Chinese Literature* 1 (1982): 58–96.

——. *Story After Supper*. Beijing: Chinese Literature Press, 1990.

Zhang, Chengzhi. *The Black Steed*. Trans. Stephen Fleming. Beijing: Chinese Literature Press, 1989.

——. "The Nine Palaces." In Jeanne Tai, trans. and ed., *Spring Bamboo: A Collection of Contemporary Chinese Short Stories*, 245–279. New York: Random House, 1989.

Zhaxi, Dawa (Tashi Dawa). *A Soul in Bondage: Stories from Tibet*. Beijing: Panda Books, 1992.

——. "Souls Tied to the Knots on a Leather Cord." In Jeanne Tai, ed., *Spring Bamboo: A Collection of Contemporary Chinese Short Stories*, 135–169. New York: Random House, 1989.

Zheng, Wanlong. "Clock." In Jeanne Tai, ed., *Spring Bamboo: A Collection of Contemporary Chinese Short Stories*, 3–18. New York: Random House, 1989.

——. *Strange Tales from Strange Lands*. Ithaca, NY: Cornell University Press, 1993.

Zheng, Yi. *Old Well*. Trans. David Kwan. San Francisco: China Books and Periodicals, 1989.

Zhong, Xueping. "Manhood, Cultural Roots, and National Identity." In *Masculinity Besieged? Issues of Modernity and Male Subjectivity in Chinese Literature of the Late Twentieth Century*, 150–170. Durham, NC: Duke University Press, 2000.

40

MO YAN

YOMI BRAESTER

Mo Yan 莫言, born Guan Moye 管谟业 in 1955, was awarded the Nobel Prize in Literature in 2012, and his prolific output and innovative style have earned him nearly every national award in the People's Republic of China (PRC) since he started publishing in 1981. He has also won international fame for the film script *Red Sorghum* (红高粱, 1987). In a close collaboration that has at times influenced Mo Yan's writing, Howard Goldblatt has masterfully translated many of his works into English.

Mo Yan has contributed to shaping the course of Chinese fiction by introducing a literary style that mixes reality and the supernatural, akin to the magic realism of Gabriel García Márquez. He acknowledges that García Márquez's *One Hundred Years of Solitude* triggered in him a "shock of recognition" (Mo Yan 1991: ix), although he did not read the novel until after writing his best-known work, *Red Sorghum* (红高粱家族, 1986). His first major work, the novella "A Transparent Carrot" (透明的红萝卜, 1984), won Mo Yan immediate renown for its crisp descriptions that blur into surreal fantasy. The novella contains themes and stylistic features that would become central to Mo Yan's writing, such as life in a backwater village and an outcast's point of view. Because the plot is set in a rural area during the Cultural Revolution, Mo Yan's work was identified as part of the contemporary "roots-seeking literature" (寻根文学) movement. Yet, unlike many other writers associated with the trend, Mo Yan was not a "sent-down" urban youth unfamiliar with the countryside. In fact, he was born to a peasant family, and many of his works depict life in his native

Gaomi 高密 County in Shandong Province. Mo Yan's work sets itself apart from fiction in the mid-1980s by emphasizing the surreal, a trait that would become popular only later in the decade with the rise of avant-garde literature.

During the Cultural Revolution, Mo Yan's schooling was interrupted and he was sent back to help in his family's fieldwork. In 1976 he joined the People's Liberation Army and served as political commissar and propaganda officer. While continuing his formal education (BA in literature from the People's Liberation Army Academy of Art, 1984–1986; MA from Beijing Normal University's Lu Xun Literary Institute, 1988–1991), Mo Yan developed a distinctive voice. His work reached an important landmark in 1986 with the publication of a series of novellas later compiled into *Red Sorghum*. What caught the eye of readers was the work's deviation from the accepted practice for the historical novel. The story takes place in 1939, in the heat of the anti-Japanese war. Since the late 1940s many novels have focused on the theme of resistance during the war, portraying Chinese fighters in heroic colors. Mo Yan's protagonists, too, win the narrator's admiration, yet they are as superhuman in their desires and faults as they are in their zeal to fight the Japanese. Yu Zhan'ao 余占鳌, a sedan-bearer, falls for a woman he carries in a wedding sedan. Having killed the bride's husband and father-in-law, he takes over the woman and her new property, including a sorghum-wine distillery. A boisterous, fearless man, he becomes a bandit leader and later the commander of a militia. After his two women—he has meanwhile established a second household—are murdered by the Japanese, he takes his fifteen-year-old son and continues to fight. In the same narrative breath one is told of Yu's valiant killing, his looting, and his defense of the country.

Red Sorghum reclaims historiography from the party-line version of heroic nationalism. For example, the third chapter, "Dog Ways" (狗道), recounts an epic military battle fought, ironically, not with the Japanese but against a pack of wild dogs. There is little bravery in slaughtering dogs with hand grenades, and the dogs' strategizing against the humans is equally inglorious. The novel's rich imagery also seems to undermine official nationalist narratives. The color red that pervades the story—from the red sorghum and the red dog leader to the blinding red light and the generous splashes of blood—is far different from the glorious red of the PRC flag, a color thought to have come from the blood of revolutionary martyrs. If Mo Yan's sensuous colors lend themselves to symbolic interpretation, it is one that goes against the grain of official PRC ideology.

In fact, as the text progresses it leaves behind all claim to redemption. The most heroic scene in the novel comes at the very beginning, when Yu Zhan'ao's company attacks a Japanese convoy; yet the attack is unsuccessful, and the Chinese troops, along with Yu's wife, perish. Later battles are senseless skirmishes suffused with brutality. Yu's servant, Uncle Arhat 刘罗汉, is skinned alive—few graphic details are spared—for fleeing from the Japanese; yet he brings the calamity upon himself as he is caught taking revenge on an innocent mule. Characters' motives are often reduced to basic needs and base desires that give rise to an all-encompassing violence, in turn depicted with disturbing indifference as a delicate ballet.

Mo Yan departs from the revolutionary realism that characterizes the literature of the 1960s and 1970s. *Red Sorghum* shuttles back and forth, in fuguelike form, between different points in time. Narrators and viewpoints change without warning until reality and fantasy fuse. As David Wang (1993: 125) notes, "Where facts and memory are incomplete, fantasy fills in." The novel satirizes what Li Tuo 李陀 (1993: 274) has mockingly called "the Mao style" (毛文体). Tonglin Lu (1993: 193) notices how frequent use of the superlative, which in Mao's jargon dictated the only course of action, serves in *Red Sorghum* to underline irony and contradiction.

The shunning of the heroic historical narrative is especially discernible in Mo Yan's use of narrative voice. The narrator, Yu Zhan'ao's grandson, returns to his ancestral village to compile a family chronicle. Yet instead of a genealogical epic, the result is an often unflattering account that identifies the narrator's father as "a bandit's offspring" (Mo Yan 1993: 3) and his village as "that sinful spot known as Northeast Gaomi Township" (327). Moreover, this is the history not of great national deeds but, rather, of individual actions in a private time and space. By describing in detail the sexual appetites of his ancestors, the narrator writes a history of desire. Rather than use an individual story as metonym for collective history, national events serve as metaphors for personal experience.

The narrator plays an important role in pointing to the troubled relationship between fact and fiction. Like Mo Yan, the narrator was born in Gaomi County in 1956, thereby bearing a slippery affinity with the author. Yet the authorial voice is misleadingly self-referential. It gives the lie to any attempt to reconstruct the past or establish a trusting relationship between author and readers. Mo Yan's fictional voice addresses the reader in an inscription before the novel begins: "I am prepared to carve out my heart, marinate it in soy sauce . . . and lay it out as an offering. . . . Partake of it in good health!" The passage implies that the relationship between Mo Yan and his readership is cannibalistic; readers consume the literary work, and the writer willingly provides them with gore. At the same time, both author and readers must accept the playfulness of such statements. The novel presents evidence contrary to the narrator's doubts toward the end of the novel: "Have I no voice of my own?"

The novel was popularized by Zhang Yimou's 张艺谋 award-winning film, which retains the basic plot of the first two chapters. The movie loses, however, the original work's epic proportions and alternative historical view. Upholding a clearer sense of patriotic heroism and narrating the story in a linear chronology, the film nevertheless echoes the modernist drive of the novel, and Mo Yan must share credit for the rise of "fifth-generation" Chinese cinema to world fame.

Mo Yan has continued to develop his style, invoking popular premodern romance and folk verse to create his particular modern myths. The novel *The Garlic Ballads* (天堂蒜薹之歌, 1988) targets the social unrest that accompanied the rural reform of the late 1980s. Representing the revolt of discontented villagers whose livelihood is threatened by a slump in garlic prices, the work contains Mo Yan's signature emphasis on the senseless violence that suffuses all realms of life, including family brutality and savage injustice by the legal and punitive systems. His next novel, *The Thirteen Steps* (十三步, 1988), reaches a new level of complexity as it presents multiple narrators who come to listen to a storyteller locked up in an insane asylum. As he weaves his own narrative, the storyteller devours chalk, which sticks to his lips.

The Republic of Wine (酒国, 1992) tells of a detective who travels to the town of Liquorland to investigate accusations that local officials have been eating human babies. The protagonist soon finds himself embroiled in the villagers' sexual vice and shares their culinary customs, including eating human "babies," allegedly made of pork and vegetables. The bout of ritual cannibalism and profuse drinking ends in murder and in the detective's drowning to death in a manure pit. The gory emphasis on infanticide and cannibalism may be attributed to the historical context of the novel's composition. As Xiaobin Yang (1998: 7) argues, *The Republic of Wine*, written soon after the Tiananmen Square massacre of June 4, 1989, designates the "historical destiny" of the text to "demonstrate the sanguinary ruins of national history."

The Republic of Wine owes its intricacy to a particular meshing of fiction and metafiction. The detective story is disrupted from time to time by correspondence between an author by the name Mo Yan, who is in the process of writing the detective plot, and another author, Li Yidou 李一斗. The correspondence shows the detective story to be the fruits of the two authors' collaboration, taking its material from Li Yidou's life. The reader who tries to trace the relationship between the fictitious author and his real-life namesake, Mo Yan, is bound to end up in drunken vertigo. One may conclude that the desire to distinguish fact from fiction, history from its representation, is a dangerous form of desire.

Mo Yan's concern with creating an alternative history through the role of the narrator is evident also in his later works, notably the novels *The Herbivorous Family* (食草家族, 1993) and *Big Breasts and Wide Hips* (丰乳肥臀, 1995). *Life and Death Are Wearing Me Out* (生死疲劳, 2006) explores the same themes by having the narrator undergo incarnations as a human, a donkey, an ox, a pig, a dog, and a monkey, experiencing the tribulations of China's modern history from these different viewpoints. Mo Yan continues to publish essays, short stories, scripts, and novels.

Mo Yan's work has drawn much critical attention for its direct, even sensationalist presentation of sexuality, as well as for its alternative version of historical writing. Some critics do not believe that Mo Yan's satire of party ideology goes far enough. They regard him as "pseudomodern" (伪现代), claiming that he privileges the consciousness of the whole nation at the expense of the individual. On the other end of the ideological spectrum, some see his emphasis on aesthetics as a sign of excessive individualism and accuse him of following trendy "imported" literary styles (J. Wang 1996: 186–189). In the aftermath of Mo Yan's winning the Nobel Prize, his political stance has come under attack. Critics of the Communist Party have deplored his role as vice president of the Chinese Writers Association, his gesture of producing a calligraphic copy of Mao Zedong's "Yan'an Talks" (a text that places art in the service of politics), and his failure to side with dissidents such as Liu Xiaobo 刘晓波. Mo Yan's detractors included Ma Jian 马建, Liao Yiwu 廖亦武, Ai Weiwei 艾未未, Herta Müller, and Salman Rushdie. Other writers and scholars noted, however, that Mo Yan had to make concessions to continue to write and that his novels paint an unflattering picture of Communist policies (Link 2012; Laughlin 2012).

Stylistically, Mo Yan has invented a unique literary idiom. He has brought to the fore the rupture between the claims of modernity and conditions in the Chinese countryside, especially the plight of misfits and women. The metafictional devices and self-mockery that make Mo Yan's texts seem insensitive might at times obscure the author's genuine humane concern. His bawdy language, humorous presentation, and riveting storytelling have created one of the most eloquent voices in contemporary Chinese fiction, despite the author's use of the pen name Mo Yan, literally "don't speak."

Bibliography

Chan, Shelley W. *A Subversive Voice in China: The Fictional World of Mo Yan.* Amherst, NY: Cambria Press, 2011.

Choy, Howard Y. F. *Remapping the Past: Fictions of History in Deng's China, 1979–1997.* Leiden: Brill, 2008.

Laughlin, Charles. "What Mo Yan's Detractors Get Wrong." *China File* (December 11, 2012). http://www.chinafile.com/what-mo-yans-detractors-get-wrong.

Li, Tuo. "Resisting Writing." In Liu Kang and Xiaobing Tang, eds., *Politics, Ideology, and Literary Discourse in Modern China*, 273–277. Durham, NC: Duke University Press, 1993.

Link, Perry. "Does This Writer Deserve the Prize?" *New York Review of Books* (December 6, 2012). http://www.nybooks.com/articles/archives/2012/dec/06/mo-yan-nobel-prize/.

Liu, Kang, and Xiaobing Tang, eds. *Politics, Ideology, and Literary Discourse in Modern China.* Durham, NC: Duke University Press, 1993.

Lu, Tonglin. "Red Sorghum: Limits of Transgression." In Liu Kang and Xiaobing Tang, eds., *Politics, Ideology, and Literary Discourse in Modern China*, 188–208. Durham, NC: Duke University Press, 1993.

Mo, Yan. *Big Breasts and Wide Hips.* Trans. Howard Goldblatt. New York: Arcade, 2002.

——. *Explosions and Other Stories*. Trans. Janice Wickeri. Hong Kong: Renditions, 1991.
——. *Frog*. Trans. Howard Goldblatt. New York: Viking, 2014.
——. *The Garlic Ballads*. Trans. Howard Goldblatt. New York: Viking, 1995.
——. *Life and Death Are Wearing Me Out*. Trans. Howard Goldblatt. New York: Arcade, 2012.
——. *Pow*. Trans. Howard Goldblatt. New York: Seagull, 2012.
——. *Red Sorghum*. Trans. Howard Goldblatt. New York: Penguin, 1993.
——. *The Republic of Wine*. Trans. Howard Goldblatt. New York: Arcade, 2000.
——. *Sandalwood Death*. Trans. Howard Goldblatt. Norman: University of Oklahoma Press, 2012.
——. *Shifu, You'll Do Anything for a Laugh*. Trans. Howard Goldblatt. New York: Arcade, 2011.
Stuckey, Andrew. "Memory or Fantasy? *Honggaoliang*'s Narrator." *Modern Chinese Literature and Culture* 18, 2 (Fall 2006): 131–162.
Wang, David Der-wei. "Imaginary Nostalgia: Shen Congwen, Song Zelai, Mo Yan, and Li Yongping." In Ellen Widmer and David Der-wei Wang, eds., *From May Fourth to June Fourth: Fiction and Film in Twentieth-Century China*, 107–132. Cambridge, MA: Harvard University Press, 1993.
Wang, Jing. *High Culture Fever: Politics, Aesthetics, and Ideology in Deng's China*. Berkeley: University of California Press, 1996.
Yang, Xiaobin. "The Republic of Wine: An Extravaganza of Decline." *positions* 6, 1 (1998): 7–31.

41

AVANT-GARDE FICTION IN POST-MAO CHINA

ANDREW F. JONES

Perhaps no other fictional moment epitomizes the sheer audacity and self-consciously provocative spirit of the literary avant-garde that transfigured the Chinese literary scene between 1987 and 1992 so well as the final scene of Yu Hua's 余华 (1960–) "One Kind of Reality" (现实一种, 1989). The story depicts a shocking and seemingly inexplicable spiral of domestic violence between two brothers, Shanfeng 山峰 and Shangang 山岗, in a nameless provincial town. When Shangang's son, Pipi 皮皮, accidentally kills Shanfeng's infant son, Shanfeng retaliates by killing Pipi. Shangang, in turn, ties his brother to a tree, coats him with stew, and allows him to be tickled to death by a voracious dog. Finally, in a scene reminiscent of Lu Xun's 鲁迅 classic allegorical treatment of the Chinese national character, "The True Story of Ah Q" (阿Q正传), a witless and somewhat bedraggled Shangang is apprehended and publicly executed by the local authorities.

Had Yu Hua's story ended simply with Shangang's execution, "One Kind of Reality" could well be understood as heir to the tradition of critical realism in modern Chinese letters, of which Lu Xun is the foremost representative, a tradition in which the writer shoulders the heroic task of exposing social and cultural ills and in so doing attempts to underwrite the making of a brighter world. But the conclusion of Yu Hua's tale veers off on an entirely different tack. Rather than provide readers with an epitaph or an explanation (be it political, social, cultural, or psychological) for the brutality they have just witnessed, Yu Hua places Shangang's lifeless body on an operating table and proceeds to narrate, in excruciating and sometimes excruciatingly funny detail, the process by which a team of doctors strip-mine his body for transplantable parts. The self-reflexive virtuosity of this passage—in which Yu Hua's language deftly slides between the clinical, the lyrical, and the ribald, sometimes within the space of a single sentence—signals a watershed in modern Chinese fiction. Social and political engagement is replaced by a subversive comment on the nature of fiction itself. At the same time that he dissects Shangang, in other words, Yu Hua also rather gleefully skewers the humanist pretensions and procedures of realist fiction, as well as the progressivist and nationalist ideals that have informed its use by Chinese writers since the 1920s.

Yu Hua (b. 1960) was only one of a talented group of young avant-garde writers who first burst onto the Chinese literary scene in the years directly preceding the Tiananmen Square student movement and its violent suppression of 1989, and whose work came to be collectively referred to as "experimental fiction" (实验小说). United by a spirit of restless experimentation with fictional forms and cultural norms, as well as a common generational and geographical provenance (almost all these writers were less than thirty years old and hailed from the prosperous and culturally sophisticated cities of China's southeastern seaboard), the emergence of writers such as Ge Fei 格非 (b. 1964), Su Tong 苏童 (b. 1963), Sun Ganlu 孙甘露 (b. 1959), and Bei Cun 北村 (b. 1965) was representative of a short-lived, highly significant, and somewhat anomalous cultural moment. Suspended between the "utopian fever and fascination with cultural roots" (Wang 1998: 4) of the 1980s and the massive globalization and commodification that characterized Chinese cultural production in the 1990s and the first decade of the twenty-first century, their appropriation of a host of techniques of international modernism, their deliberate subversion of their readers' expectations (be they ethical, ideological, or formal in nature), and their penchant for convoluted narrative labyrinths and thematic cul-de-sacs were enabled in part by the government-subsidized literary journals in which they published much of their work and were spurred on by the enthusiastic support of a number of prominent literary critics such as Chen Xiaoming 陈晓明 and Li Tuo 李驼.

As Jing Wang (1998: 5) points out, however, the story of the avant-garde begins with the pivotal contributions of two maverick figures not usually associated with the youthful demographic of the avant-garde. The first of these is Ma Yuan 马原 (b. 1953), a Han Chinese writer whose intricately constructed and sometimes enigmatic tales about an eponymous narrator's travels in Tibet insistently foregrounded the artificiality of storytelling itself. Ma Yuan's narrative innovations took place soon after the translation into Chinese of a number of works of European and American modernist fiction, including volumes by Jorge Luis Borges and William Faulkner, and his writings reflected their influence. His work was not, however, merely derivative in nature. It represented a deliberate use of modernism as a means of unseating the heretofore unquestioned authority of the omniscient narrator of socialist realism. Ma Yuan's efforts, moreover, signaled a desire for parity with the literary West and a place at the world literary table: in a characteristically self-referential gesture, Ma Yuan begins his "Fabrication" (虚构, 1986), the tale of a Han Chinese writer's affair with a leprous Tibetan girl, with the assertion that "I am the person known as Ma Yuan. . . . I take some satisfaction in being able to write in Chinese characters. None of the great figures of world literature were able to do this. I am the exception" (1993: 101). This drive for formal innovation and recognition on the world stage reflected a revolt against the constraints of the Maoist period and would be central to the concerns of the nascent avant-garde.

Can Xue 残雪 (b. 1953) is a second formative figure in the development of the avant-garde whose work is haunted by the Maoist legacy. A self-tutored former seamstress from Hunan Province, Can Xue emerged in 1986 as one of the most distinctive voices in post-Mao fiction with the publication of the short story "The Hut on the Mountain" (山上的小屋, 1986) and a longer novella entitled "Yellow Mud Street" (黄泥街, 1986). In both works, Maoist language and everyday life under socialism are refracted though a lens both scabrously grotesque— Can Xue is fond of insects, rats, dirt, disease, and rot—and relentlessly Kafkaesque. Populated by a cast of characters who speak to each other in non sequiturs that communicate little more than their own obsessive paranoia, Can Xue's claustrophobic fictional world represents a determined attack on the norms of realist fiction. And although it is clear that her work can be read as an attempt to grapple with the political violence and spiritual privation of the Maoist years, it is by no means a direct commentary on that experience. In Can Xue's work, recent history is oblique, fractured, and seen only through the eyes of protagonists whose vision is both irrational and partial. They are, indeed, little more than the sum of the physical decay and psychological delusions by which they are afflicted.

A similar disdain for conventional ways of writing history and representing humanity characterizes the work of the avant-garde writers who followed in Ma Yuan's and Can Xue's footsteps. They were, however, separated from these two older writers by a highly significant generational divide. Both Ma Yuan and Can Xue were born in 1953; as such, they were members of the first generation to grow up entirely under Communist rule. Schooled in revolutionary ideals and unquestioning devotion to Chairman Mao, these urban "educated youth" (知青), as they are still referred to in Chinese, served as the shock troops of the Cultural Revolution before ultimately being sacrificed by Chairman Mao at the altar of political expediency: when Red Guard factionalism escalated into armed conflict in 1968 and 1969, an entire generation was deported en masse to rural hinterlands for reeducation. And when these disenchanted revolutionaries finally began to filter back into the cities in the late 1970s, after nearly ten years of internal exile, they rapidly took leading roles in a wide range of literary and artistic efforts to dismantle the legacy of Maoist politics and culture.

The avant-garde writers, however, came of age in an era in which that legacy had already begun to crumble under the combined pressure of economic reforms, political liberalization, and the intense cultural ferment of the 1980s. Born too late to have participated in the Cultural Revolution and too young to have suffered the consequences of that participation, they began to attend high school (a luxury many of the previous generation had been denied) after Chairman Mao had already died. Significantly, they also grew up on a substantially different literary and intellectual diet. Whereas the educational staples of "educated youth" had consisted largely of socialist realism, translated Russian fiction, and other works of prose cast from the Maoist mold, the writers of the avant-garde were privy to a wealth of new literary translations that began to flow into Chinese book markets in the mid-1980s. Yu Hua, Ge Fei, Su Tong, and their contemporaries were well versed not only in the modernist fiction of Kawabata, Kafka, and Borges but also in Latin American magical realism, the French *nouveau roman*, and American postmodernist fiction.

Just as important, they were heirs of the deconstructive labors of the generation of "educated youth" that had preceded them. Beginning in the late 1970s, these returnees had launched movement after movement aimed at questioning the underlying causes of the tragic excesses of the revolutionary past, at the same time freeing themselves from the shackles of Maoist language and literary form. Among the many accomplishments of this generation number the Misty poetry of Bei Dao 北岛 and other writers who initially coalesced around the Beijing Democracy Wall in 1979, the fifth-generation cinema of directors such as Chen Kaige 陈凯歌 and Zhang Yimou 张艺谋, and the roots-seeking fiction of Han Shaogong 韩少功 and Mo Yan 莫言. All these authors and auteurs drew on the idiom of international modernism in order to create a new cultural space from which to launch critiques of Maoism. And all shared a common, humanistic faith in the redemptive power of art in the face of the ravages of a national history gone awry. In this sense, their work represented an attempt to revive the enlightened and exploratory spirit that they saw as characterizing the May Fourth era of the late 1910s and early 1920s.

The work of the avant-garde, then, can be understood in part as an extension of this critical project, but also as a generational revolt against it. In undermining the generic conventions of not only socialist realism but also critical realism itself, the avant-garde sought to knock down not just Maoist idols but those of the educated youth as well. Chief among these idols was the progressivist sense of patriotic mission embodied by intellectuals such as Lu Xun (or at least by the heroic image of Lu Xun erected by the socialist state and its literary establishment in the wake of the Communist Party's ascendancy in 1949). It is this sense of mission—one that profoundly informs the work of the roots-seekers whose fiction had electrified intellectual circles in China just two years before the emergence of the avant-garde—that is missing from the pages of these authors. Instead, they present their readers with a relentless (and sometimes playful) attack on history and humanist ideals. In practice this meant a fiction in which psychological depth is conspicuous by its absence and notions of progress are shattered by narratives that are anything but neatly linear.

This historical irreverence is a hallmark of avant-garde fiction. In the earliest short stories of perhaps the most popular and accessible of these writers, Su Tong, mythical family histories from the Republican era—his "Flying over Maple Village" (飞越我的枫杨树故乡, 1987) is one salient example—function as fractured mirrors that unevenly reflect, and thus call into radical question, official socialist historiography. In Ge Fei's fiction, historical episodes as disparate as the Nationalist Party's (GMD) Northern Expedition of 1928 ("The Lost Boat" [迷舟, 1989]), the turn-of-the-century "Great Game" of imperial diplomacy in Tibet ("Meetings" [相遇, 1993]), and the life of the Six Dynasties poet Ruan Ji ("Whistling" [呼哨, 1990]) are deliberately rendered enigmatic, even unintelligible, by way of narratives that loop back on themselves or omit crucial pieces of information. In Yu Hua's fiction, the past is conceived of as a site overflowing with extreme cruelty and seemingly gratuitous violence. Though readers of his "The Past and the Punishments" (往事与刑罚, 1989) and "1986" (一九八六年, 1986)—both of which touch on recent Chinese political history—may be tempted to read his work as a comment on the depredations of Maoism and the excesses of the Cultural Revolution, Yu Hua takes care to deflect just such an interpretation by pointedly deflating the reader's desire for an unambiguous, neatly resolved political allegory.

Yu Hua was also the avant-garde author most explicitly interested in collapsing the humanistic emphasis on character depiction in realist fiction. In his experimental fiction, as well as that of several of his contemporaries, characters represent nothing more than "props" (Yu Hua 1996: 274) or pawns to be guided by the author across a complex literary chessboard. Yu Hua's earliest and most provocative fiction thus lingers clinically over the surface of things, denying readers even the illusion of realistic, psychologically well-rounded characters.

The dense and often dreamlike mental landscapes that characterize the fiction of Sun Ganlu (for instance, "I Am a Young Drunkard" [我是少年酒坛子, 1987]) similarly dissolve any expectation of narrative coherence. Instead, Sun's fiction presents readers with a series of fragmentary images, oblique philosophical musings, and self-reflexive linguistic conceits. The work of Bei Cun is another case in point: his labyrinthine plotting and insistent repetition of scenarios within the same story (see, for example, "The Big Drugstore" [大药房, 1992]) play havoc with the conventions of realist fiction. And as with the fiction of Yu Hua, his is a fictional fabric prone to sudden and unexplained irruptions of the supernatural and the sordid.

It is these characteristics of avant-garde fiction—its refusal of historical causality and humanism, its determined avoidance of overtly politicized ways of writing and reading, its deadpan depictions of transgressive violence, its playful and self-referential experimentation with narrative form, and its preference for surfaces over psychological depths—that led many critics, both in China and abroad, to view the movement as heralding the advent of literary postmodernity in China. Although this contention remains a matter of debate, and cultural and literary developments of a more local nature have clearly been just as important as global cultural currents in the formation of the avant-garde, the claim itself was symptomatic of a desire for contemporaneity and literary parity with the developed world.

Ironically, the brief flowering of the avant-garde may also be remembered as one of the last unitary literary movements in twentieth-century Chinese history. The rapid commodification and consequent market segmentation that transfigured the Chinese cultural scene in the 1990s seem to have spelled the end of an era in which any one literary trend is able to occupy cultural center stage (see "Commercialization of Literature in the Post-Mao Era"). The rise of new media networks in the 2000s further destabilized the cultural authority of literary writing. Indeed, with the escalation of economic reforms in 1992, many of the movement's luminaries turned their attention to more conventional and commercially viable narrative fiction, to journalism, to film and television screenwriting, and eventually to blogging and social media. Authors such as Yu Hua, and to a lesser extent Su Tong, have gone on to enjoy considerable commercial success and celebrity throughout the Chinese-speaking world, and their work has been widely translated outside China. Yu Hua's best-selling epic of the excesses of the Cultural Revolution and reform era, *Brothers* (兄弟, 2005), is a particularly prominent example of this development. Indeed, the avant-garde as a viable and ideologically coherent movement ultimately fell victim not to censorship or official disapproval but to the vagaries of the market and the changing artistic agendas of its constituent members. Its artistic legacy, however—as well as the continuing creative efforts of authors such as Yu Hua and Ge Fei—remains vital to the ongoing articulation of contemporary Chinese literature and culture.

Bibliography

Cai, Yongchun. *Postmodernism and Contemporary Chinese Avant-Garde Fiction*. New York: Routledge, 2015.

Can, Xue. *Dialogues in Paradise*. Trans. Ronald R. Janssen and Jian Zhang. Evanston, IL: Northwestern University Press, 1989.

——. *The Embroidered Shoes*. Trans. Ronald R. Janssen and Jian Zhang. New York: Henry Holt, 1997.

——. *The Lost Lover*. Trans. Annelise Finnegan. New Haven, CT: Yale University Press, 2014.

——. *Old Floating Cloud*. Trans. Ronald R. Janssen and Jian Zhang. Evanston, IL: Northwestern University Press, 1991.

Goldblatt, Howard, ed. *Chairman Mao Would Not Be Amused*. New York: Grove Press, 1995.

Goldblatt, Howard, and Joseph S. M. Lau, eds. *The Columbia Anthology of Modern Chinese Literature*. New York: Columbia University Press, 1995.

Lu, Tonglin. *Misogyny, Cultural Nihilism, and Oppositional Politics: Contemporary Chinese Experimental Fiction*. Stanford, CA: Stanford University Press, 1995.

Ma, Yuan. "Fabrications." Trans. J. Q. Sun. In Henry Zhao, ed., *The Lost Boat: Avant-Garde Fiction from China*, 101–144. London: Wellsweep, 1993.

Su, Tong. *Raise the Red Lantern: Three Novellas*. Trans. Michael S. Duke. New York: Morrow, 1993.

——. *Rice*. Trans. Howard Goldblatt. New York: Morrow, 1995.

Tang, Xiaobing. *Chinese Modern: The Heroic and the Quotidian*. Durham, NC: Duke University Press, 2000.

Wang, Jing, ed. *China's Avant-Garde Fiction: An Anthology*. Durham, NC: Duke University Press, 1998.

——. *High Culture Fever: Politics, Aesthetics, and Ideology in Deng's China*. Berkeley: University of California Press, 1996.

Yang, Xiaobing. *The Chinese Postmodern: Trauma and Irony in Chinese Avant-Garde Fiction*. Ann Arbor: University of Michigan Press, 2002.

Yu, Hua. *Brothers*. Trans. Carlos Rojas and Eileen Cheng-yin Chow. New York: Anchor Books, 2008.

——. "One Kind of Reality." Trans. Jeanne Tai. In David Der-wei Wang and Jeanne Tai, eds., *Running Wild: New Chinese Writers*, 21–68. New York: Columbia University Press, 1994.

——. *The Past and the Punishments*. Trans. Andrew F. Jones. Honolulu: University of Hawai'i Press, 1996.

Zhang, Xudong. *Chinese Modernism in the Era of Reforms: Culture Fever, Avant-Garde Fiction, and the New Chinese Cinema*. Durham, NC: Duke University Press, 1997.

Zhao, Henry, ed. *The Lost Boat: Avant-Garde Fiction from China*. London: Wellsweep, 1993.

Zhao, Henry, and John Cayley, eds. *Abandoned Wine: Chinese Writing Today, Number Two*. London: Wellsweep, 1996.

——. *Under-Sky Underground: Chinese Writing Today*. London: Wellsweep, 1994.

42

CONTEMPORARY EXPERIMENTAL THEATERS IN THE PEOPLE'S REPUBLIC OF CHINA, TAIWAN, AND HONG KONG

ROSSELLA FERRARI

The late 1970s and early 1980s inaugurated a new chapter in the theater history of the People's Republic of China (PRC). As the ideological radicalism of the Cultural Revolution subsided, artists embarked on a critique of the stifling cultural policies of the Maoist era, paving the way for a phase of resurgence and revitalization. In the aftermath of a momentous national upheaval, alternative forms of expression were sought to make sense of a new society caught between fervid expectations for a future of economic and political modernization and the inevitability of coming to terms with a major collective trauma.

Experimental theater in the post-Mao period articulated a discourse of radical change, but also of critical reflection on the past in which national history and identity were addressed, and often questioned, in provocative new ways. There emerged a renewed pursuit of individualism and (re)discovery of the self; the instructional tenor of socialist writing was shunned in favor of existential introspection and humanistic investigation. The political became shrouded in allegory, while the subjective and the social, the public and the personal, were often intertwined.

Encouraged by a cultural climate of relative openness and liberalization, dramatists voiced dissatisfaction with the eulogistic tones and ossified conventions of dominant dramaturgical and directorial approaches. The rigid dictates of socialist realism and the propagandistic values of "revolutionary model theater" (革命样板戏) became a target, but dramatists also distanced themselves from the early twentieth-century "spoken drama" (话剧) tradition and the ubiquitous system of acting and mise-en-scène based on Konstantin Stanislavsky's principles of realistic illusion and psychological identification. In more or less radical fashion, dramatists began deviating from the realist-naturalist paradigm, contending that strict adherence to representational verisimilitude impeded innovation.

Theatrical orthodoxy was undermined by a concurrent adaptation, application, and—in various instances—amalgamation of previously proscribed modernist styles of foreign derivation and recently revived local legacies that had been sidelined or suppressed under Maoism. These included regional forms of "traditional theater" (戏曲) and folk genres such as puppet and shadow theater. Concomitant impulses toward avant-garde exploration and archaeological excavation of China's cultural heritage thus informed a substantial portion of the emerging repertoire.

The early works of Nobel Prize laureate Gao Xingjian 高行健 (self-exiled to France since 1987) provide a fitting illustration. On the one hand, in such plays as *Alarm Signal* (绝对信号, 1982) and the contentious *Bus Stop* (车站, 1983), a Beckettian tragicomedy about a group of people waiting for a bus that never comes, Gao evokes the Western modernist canon by experimenting with spatiotemporal indeterminacy, crisscrossing narratives, intersecting voices, and inner monologues. In contrast, in *Wild Man* (野人, 1985), about an ecologist who travels to a remote corner of southwestern China allegedly inhabited by the eponymous mythical creature, he merges the modernist lesson and contemporary concerns for ecological and ethnographic preservation with popular storytelling, ancient epics and rituals, and other facets of Chinese premodern culture and philosophy. The deliberate disruption of realism—the ecologist steps in and out of his role repeatedly, assuming different personae—and the pursuit of total theater through foregrounding of polyphony and performativity have been associated with the methods of Bertolt Brecht and Antonin Artaud. Jin Yun's 锦云 *Uncle Doggie's Nirvana* (狗儿爷涅槃, 1986); *Stories of Mulberry Village* (桑树坪纪事, 1988), by Chen Zidu 陈子度, Yang Jian 杨健, and Zhu Xiaoping 朱晓平; and Wei Minglun's 魏明伦 "Sichuan opera of the absurd" *Pan Jinlian* (潘金莲, 1986) are further examples of this intracultural effort at revitalizing tradition.

Brecht's epic theater, with its concern for detached observation, rational judgment, and nonrealistic presentation, was explored as an antidote to the melodramatic excesses of the previous decades. Introduced by Huang Zuolin 黄佐临 in the 1950s, Brechtian techniques resurfaced in the post-Mao period in Huang's own theorization and directorial practice—as in his production of Sun Huizhu 孙惠柱 and Fei Chunfang's 费春芳 *China Dream* (中国梦, 1987)—and in the works of younger dramatists such as Sha Yexin 沙叶新, Li Shoucheng 李守成, and Yao Mingde's 姚明德 *If I Were Real* (假如我是真的, 1979), which denounces official corruption and nepotism. Liu Shugang's 刘树刚 *The Dead Visiting the Living* (一个死者对生者的访问, 1984), Tao Jun's 陶骏 *Rubik's*

Cube (魔方, 1985), and Wang Peigong's 王培公 WM (我们, 1985) are further illustrations of innovative and sometimes controversial dramaturgy in this formative stage.

Shadowing the enthusiasm of the earlier period, "theater crisis" (戏剧危机) surfaced as a powerful catchword—but also a painful reality—in the late 1980s and through the 1990s, as rhetoric of exhaustion and emergency pervaded the field. Certainly, politics played a role: for a few years after the Tiananmen Square events of June 1989, state control heightened and experimental production decreased. Socioeconomic reform, however, posed a possibly greater challenge. While the implementation of a market economy made box office concerns more pressing, audience numbers declined because of competition from more accessible and crowd-pleasing forms of entertainment, such as television and cinema. In reaction to the double challenge from the state and from capital, the early 1990s marked an intense stage of experimentation in which aesthetics became more daring and critique more radical.

Mou Sen 牟森, founder of the independent Garage Theater (戏剧车间), came to prominence for formally trailblazing and semantically ambiguous productions such as the "postmodern verse drama" (后现代诗剧) *A Chinese Grammatical Discussion of "The Other Shore"* (关于《彼岸》的一回汉语词性讨论, 1993)—a deconstructive adaptation of Gao Xingjian's *The Other Shore* (彼岸, 1986)—and *File Zero* (零档案, 1994), both codevised with poet Yu Jian 于坚. Mou's work was applauded internationally as an articulation of dissent against party-state authority; domestically, however, it was perceived as overly provocative and obscure, leading to financial and institutional complications and his eventual withdrawal from the scene.

Shanghai playwright Zhang Xian 张献 has also attracted controversy for his unorthodox writings. Zhang emerged in the late 1980s with *The Owl in the Room* (屋里的猫头鹰, 1987), a psychodrama addressing the relationship between an agoraphobic woman and her impotent husband, and *Fashion Street* (时装街, 1988), a critique of social homogenization and cultural commoditization. His productions since the 1990s have alternated experimental scripts and more conventional dramas focusing on contemporary urban life and the new middle classes. However, several of his works have neither been published nor staged because of their politically inflected content. Zhang has also collaborated with various independent theater collectives that have emerged in Shanghai since the 2000s. Significant among these is Grass Stage (草台班), led by writer Zhao Chuan 赵川, whose community-based and socially oriented projects have strived to carve an alternative path between commercial and state-sponsored theater.

Guo Shixing 过士行, who has sometimes been compared to Lao She 老舍 because of his vivid depictions of Beijing life, is another noteworthy author, renowned for his penchant for paradox, allegory, and virtuosic use of language. His most celebrated works, which have been staged by Lin Zhaohua 林兆华, are *Fish Men* (鱼人, 1989), *Bird Men* (鸟人, 1991), and *Chess Men* (棋人, 1995),

collectively known as "The Loafers Trilogy." Directors-cum-playwrights Tian Qinxin 田沁鑫 and Li Liuyi 李六乙 have also been recognized for successfully combining modernist devices with traditional theater styles and elements of local cultures and history.

The career of director and dramatist Meng Jinghui 孟京辉 is possibly the most emblematic of experimental theater's progression from radicalism to reconciliation—namely, from an early avant-garde iconoclasm to a more negotiated approach toward audiences, institutions, and capital. Meng emerged in the early 1990s with highly stylized and politically suggestive reinterpretations of European classics (such as Samuel Beckett's *Waiting for Godot*, staged in 1991) and original scripts characterized by absurd and grotesque tones, mordant satire, and playfully deconstructive experiments with textual pastiche and wordplay. Representative plays include *Longing for Worldly Pleasures* (思凡, 1993), a collage of a Ming dynasty script and two novellas from Giovanni Boccaccio's *Decameron*, and the "antidrama" *I Love XXX* (我爱XXX, 1994), a plotless litany of over 600 lines, all beginning with "I love."

As with most practitioners, in the mid-1990s Meng was confronted with the twin challenge of market competition and institutional hostility. While the experimental arts were increasingly marginalized in the cultural field, his work was seen as contentious by authorities. However, by skillfully combining experiment and entertainment, since the turn of the century Meng has inaugurated a new mode of "pop avant-garde," which has allowed his theater to flourish in a competitive cultural environment without blunting its creative edge. Meng has directed the popular *Rhinoceros in Love* (恋爱的犀牛, 1999) and other plays by Liao Yimei 廖一梅, in addition to foreign adaptations and his own scripts, notably *Head Without Tail* (关于爱情归宿的最新观念, 2002), addressing tropes of identity manipulation and loss of self. His journey from the fringe to consecration epitomizes a paradigmatic shift in the relationship between experimentalism and establishment, margin and mainstream, in that experimental theater has progressively outshined the mainstream, becoming, somehow, a new kind of alternative establishment.

Since the 1980s, contacts between the theaters of mainland China, Hong Kong, and Taiwan have intensified. In these latter two localities, as in the PRC, aesthetic experiments were fueled by major historical events. In Taiwan, the lifting of martial law in 1987 stirred the advance of a diversified cultural environment and forms of theatrical expression connected to social movements and radical politics. In Hong Kong, the sanctioning by the Sino-British Joint Declaration (1984) of its retrocession to the PRC in 1997 spurred intensive interrogations of cultural identity and ambivalent visions of the city's future. In both places, this period saw an upsurge of localism, as testified by the increased stage presence of the Taiwanese and Cantonese languages.

A so-called Little Theater movement emerged in Taiwan in the 1980s, following pioneering experiments by innovators such as Yao Yiwei 姚一苇 and Ma

Sen 马森 in the 1960s and 1970s. Lanling Theater Workshop's (兰陵剧坊) *Hezhu's New Match* (荷珠新配, 1980), a farce about a prostitute posing as a wealthy couple's long-lost daughter, represented a trailblazing attempt to combine Beijing opera and group improvisation techniques. In 1984, Lai Shengchuan 赖声川, also famed for his improvisational approach, established the Performance Workshop (表演工作坊) and went on to become one of the most prominent Chinese-language playwrights. *Secret Love in Peach Blossom Land* (暗恋桃花源, 1986), a metadrama about two troupes compelled to share the same stage, is emblematic of his dramaturgy in that it investigates tropes of identity, nostalgia, and displacement while exploring the mainlander experience in Taiwan. Also significant is his "Crosstalk" series. Inaugurated by *The Night We Became Xiangsheng Comedians* (那一夜，我们说相声, 1985), it employs traditional stand-up comedy (相声) to comment on Chinese history, Taiwanese culture, and cross-straits relations. In 1986, Li Guoxiu 李国修 founded the Ping Fong Acting Troupe (屏风表演班), for which he authored satires and parodies such as *Can Three Make It* (三人行不行, 1987) and *Shamlet* (莎姆雷特, 1992).

As these early ensembles popularized their repertoires in the latter half of the 1980s, a more radical wave emerged, with works challenging repressed histories and political taboos. Critical Point Theater Phenomenon (临界点剧象录) tackled same-sex desire in Tian Qiyuan's 田启元 *Love Homosexuals in Chinese* (毛尸, 1988); U Theater (优剧团) exposed the violence of the February 28 Incident in Wang Keping's 王克平 *The Retrial of Wei Jingsheng* (重审魏京生, 1989); and Wang Molin's 王墨林 *Song of the Covered Wagon* (幌马车之歌, 1989), based on Lan Bozhou's 蓝博洲 eponymous novella, revived the White Terror persecutions. Several of these late-1980s avant-garde practitioners remained active in the ensuing decades, albeit in less militant fashion. Shakespeare's Wild Sisters Group (莎士比亚的妹妹们的剧团) founder Wei Yingjuan 魏瑛娟 has explored gender tropes and nonnormative sexualities in such works as *Emily Dickinson* (2003) and *Le Testament de Montmartre* (蒙马特遗书, 2000), based on Taiwanese lesbian novelist Qiu Miaojin's 邱妙津 writings. Wild Sisters Group director Wang Jiaming 王嘉明 has pursued intermedial strategies blending popular and avant-garde inspirations in *Zodiac* (2001), *Once, Upon Hearing the Skin Tone* (肤色の时光, 2009), and other productions.

The Hong Kong scene has witnessed a rise in political engagement since the 1980s as artists have probed the handover's implications for civil liberties. The transmedial collective Zuni Icosahedron (进念二十面体) has been a pioneering avant-garde force, confronting provocative gender and identity issues and questioning Beijing–Hong Kong relations in *Opium War . . . Four Letters to Deng Xiaoping* (鸦片战争—致邓小平的四封信, 1984), *Revolutionary Opera* (香港样板戏, 1991), and later works. Zuni has always been alert to—and often critical of—local politics, and their advocacy work has influenced cultural policies and censorship regulations. More recently, artistic director Danny Yung 荣念曾 has created experimental operas combining Chinese traditional performance with modern multimedia technologies, such as *Sigmund Freud in Search of Chinese Matter and Mind* (佛洛伊德寻找中国情与事, 2002), based on excerpts from Tang Xianzu's 汤显祖 *Peony Pavilion* (牡丹亭, 1598), while co-artistic director Mathias Woo 胡恩威 has investigated connections between theater and architecture in *Looking for Mies* (2002) and other productions. In 2003, together with former member Edward Lam 林奕华, Woo inaugurated the *East Wing West Wing* (东宫西宫) satirical series on local sociopolitical phenomena.

In anticipation of Hong Kong's retrocession, preoccupations with history and identity were voiced in a body of plays that critics have collectively categorized as "'97 theater." Among these is Hoyingfung's 何应丰 absurdist trilogy "Miss Julie of Yuen Chow Street" (元州街茉莉小姐三部曲, 1995–1997), which delves into the Hong Kong psyche through the investigation of a prostitute's murder on the eve of the handover. Chan Ping-chiu's 陈炳钊 *Hong Kong Archaeological Story: Fly, Fly, Fly* (香港考古故事之飞飞飞, 1996) and *Fly, Archaeology Bird, Fly!* (飞吧! 临流鸟,飞吧!, 1997) excavate Hong Kong's historical roots, individual and collective identities, and conflicting sentiments concerning 1997. Chan remains one of Hong Kong's most innovative authors. Noteworthy is his "Consumerist Era" series, comprising *Hamletmaxhine* (哈奈马仙, 2008), *My Favourite Time* (卖飞佛时代, 2009), and *Hamlet b* (2010).

Another important play of the late transitional period is *Two Men on a No Man's Land* (无人地带, 1996), a dark comedy about two wrongfully accused convicts coproduced by Jim Chim 詹瑞文 and Tang Shu-wing 邓树荣. Representative of Tang's dramaturgy is also the "Life and Death Trilogy," a mixed-media experiment involving puppets and human actors, composed of *Three Women in Pearl River Delta* (三级女子杀人事件, 1997), *Millennium Autopsy* (解剖二千年, 1999), and *My Murder Story* (我的杀人故事, 1999).

The Life and Times of Ng Chung Yin: A Hong Kong Story (吴仲贤的故事, 1997), jointly devised by theater activist Mok Chiu-yu 莫昭如 and filmmaker Evans Chan 陈耀成 (director of the eponymous 2002 film), provides a meaningful illustration of political playwriting; it reflects on the sovereignty transfer and celebrates the late leftist writer and prodemocracy activist.

In addition to landmark local developments, the past few decades have seen the emergence of transregional collaborative networks across the three territories, which bear implications not only at the level of practice but also with regard to historiography. These clusters of relational production suggest a critical shift from a singular and discrete notion of national theater to a rhizomic concept of transnational Chinese theater(s), prompting a reformulation of Chinese-language theater history as plural, interconnected histories encompassing a multiplicity of kindred yet diverse expressions and experiences.

Bibliography

Chen, Xiaomei, ed. *The Columbia Anthology of Modern Chinese Drama*. New York: Columbia University Press, 2010.

Cheung, Martha, and Jane Lai, eds. *An Oxford Anthology of Contemporary Chinese Drama*. Hong Kong: Oxford University Press, 1997.

Conceison, Claire. "China's Experimental Mainstream: The Badass Theatre of Meng Jinghui." *The Drama Review* 58, 1 (March 2014): 64–88.

Ferrari, Rossella. "Anarchy in the PRC: Meng Jinghui and His Adaptation of Dario Fo's *Accidental Death of an Anarchist*." *Modern Chinese Literature and Culture* 17, 2 (2005): 1–48.

——. *Pop Goes the Avant-Garde: Experimental Theatre in Contemporary China*. London: Seagull Books, 2012.

——. "Tang Our Contemporary: Twenty-First Century Adaptations of *Peony Pavilion*." In Paolo Santangelo and Tian Yuan Tan, eds., *Passion, Romance, and Qing: The World of Emotions and States of Mind in* Peony Pavilion 3, 1482–1518. 3 vols. Leiden: Brill, 2014.

Liao, Yimei. *Rhinoceros in Love*. Trans. Mark Talacko. MCLC Resource Center Publication (2012). http://u.osu.edu/mclc/online-series/rhinoceros-in-love.

Liu, Siyuan, Kevin J. Wetmore Jr., and Erin B. Mee. *Modern Asian Theatre and Performance 1900–2000*. London: Bloomsbury, 2014.

Meng Jinghui 孟京辉, ed. *Xianfeng xiju dang'an* 先锋戏剧档案 (Avant-garde theater archive). Beijing: Zuojia, 2000.

Quah, Sy Ren. *Gao Xingjian and Transcultural Chinese Theater*. Honolulu: University of Hawai'i Press, 2004.

Salter, Denis. "China's Theatre of Dissent: A Conversation with Mou Sen and Wu Wenguang." *Asian Theatre Journal* 13, 2 (Fall 1996): 218–228.

Tuan, Iris Hsin-chun. *Alternative Theater in Taiwan: Feminist and Intercultural Approaches*. Amherst, NY: Cambria Press, 2007.

Yu, Shiao-ling, ed. *Chinese Drama After the Cultural Revolution, 1979–1989: An Anthology*. Lewiston, NY: Edwin Mellen Press, 1996.

43

MODERN POETRY OF TAIWAN

MICHELLE YEH

An island is a paradox: it is simultaneously isolated and open, with the surrounding sea serving as both a protective barrier and a vital passage to other lands and cultures. Situated off the southeast coast of China, with Japan and Korea to the north and the Philippines to the south, halfway between Shanghai and Hong Kong, Taiwan is the nexus of diverse linguistic, economic, social, and cultural crosscurrents from Asia and other parts of the world. If its small size—comparable to Switzerland or Holland—has historically been a cause of Taiwan's marginalization, this is compensated for by openness and an ability to adapt to the new. Over a period of four centuries, Taiwan has evolved dramatically from a little-known island to an entrepôt, an outpost of the Qing empire, a colony first of Holland (1624–1662), then of Japan (1895–1945), and today a nation-state with twenty-three million people with a diverse culture and thriving economy. Over the years Taiwan has garnered international acclaim for its economic miracle and hard-won democracy. Equally deserving of worldwide recognition is that some of the best modern poetry written in Chinese comes from Taiwan. The history of Taiwanese poetry tells the story of how the periphery has transformed itself into the frontier.

Despite linguistic and historical connections, there are significant differences between Taiwan's modern poetry and that of post-1949 mainland China. The most obvious difference has to do with the relationship between poetry and politics. Whereas politics was *the* determining force in the People's Republic of China (PRC) from 1949 to 1978, it has never played a central role in Taiwan.

Although modern poetry in its formative period in May Fourth China was diverse and cosmopolitan, the dictates of Communist ideology during the Mao era produced politically correct verses in the formula of "classical + folk"—a hybrid of classical poetry and folk songs—leaving little room for free expression of the literary imagination. The situation began to change only in the late 1970s, with the arrival of the post-Mao New Era.

Despite censorship during the Japanese colonial period and under the Nationalist regime during the martial law era (1949–1987), Taiwan has had a relatively more open society and more cosmopolitan culture than that of the mainland. Even under the most repressive circumstances, political control was never pervasive; poetry always managed to carve out a space of its own outside the official discourse and to take advantage of being on the periphery. If "political poetry"—poetry written to critique a political situation or advance a political ideal—began to emerge in the liberalizing atmosphere in Taiwan after 1980, this category is simply inapplicable to mainland poetry before the late 1970s, since all of it is, by definition and in a quite direct way, political.

The second significant difference between Taiwan and the PRC is their cultural makeup. Historically, Taiwan has been exposed to and has assimilated elements of Chinese, European, Japanese, and American cultures, in addition to having a rich aboriginal culture. The first modern poetry in Taiwan was written in two languages, Chinese and Japanese. Many poets are fluent in two or more languages, and Chinese, Japanese, and English are the most commonly used languages in Taiwan today. With close to universal literacy, contemporary Taiwan boasts a level of education that is among the highest in the world. Most poets have college degrees, and quite a few hold master's degrees and doctorates from domestic or foreign universities. These highly educated, bilingual or multilingual poets move across national and linguistic boundaries with ease and confidence, tapping into their multicultural experience and knowledge—whether literature, music, art, philosophy, or religion—of other traditions as a resource for their poetry. Taiwan's poetry is a product of cultural hybridity in the best, fullest sense of the word.

Modern poetry in Taiwan has a dual origin. The earliest modern poems published in Taiwan were written in Japanese; authored by Zhui Feng 追风 ("chasing the wind," pen name of Xie Chunmu 谢春木, 1902–1967), the sequence of four poems under the title "Imitations of Poetry" (诗的模仿) was written in 1923 and published in *Taiwan* on April 10, 1924. At the same time, a young man from Taiwan named Zhang Qingrong 张清荣 (1902–1955) was studying at Beijing Normal College. Inspired by the literary revolution that had swept the mainland a few years earlier, he published "A Letter to the Youth of Taiwan," under the pen name Zhang Wojun 张我军 ("my army"), in *Taiwanese People's Journal* (台湾民报, April 21, 1924). In the letter, Zhang attacked classical poetry as decorative and decayed, and those who wrote it as slaves to archaic conventions. After returning to Taiwan in October of that year, Zhang wrote more critiques, which triggered heated debate between the old school of poets and the new. As editor of *Taiwanese People's Journal* from 1924 to 1926, he also introduced poetic theory and creative practice from the mainland. Finally, Zhang published a slim book of modern poetry in Chinese entitled *Love in a Chaotic City* (乱都之恋, 1925), which records his romantic relationship while living in Beijing. It is the first book of modern poetry published in Taiwan.

From the very beginning, then, modern poetry in Taiwan has drawn on two traditions: Japanese and mainland Chinese. These traditions should be seen not as diametrically opposed but as complementary and mutually reinforcing because they were often inspired by the same sources: romanticism, symbolism, and surrealism, to name but a few. If Yang Hua's 杨华 (1906–1936) *petits poèmes* were influenced by those of Bing Xin 冰心 (1900–1999) on the mainland, the immense popularity of the genre in China in the 1920s was itself the result of multicultural influences, including, at least, ancient Greek epigrams, Rabindranath Tagore's (1861–1941) short lyrics, Japanese haiku, and classical Chinese poetry. Though surrealism received only cursory mention in the Shanghai avant-garde magazine *Les Contemporains* (现代, 1932–1935), it exerted a major influence on the Le Moulin Poetry Society (风车诗社), founded in 1933–1934 by seven Taiwanese and Japanese poets in Tainan (Ye 1996).

When the island was returned to China in 1945 at the end of World War II, the difference between mainland China and Taiwan, especially in terms of linguistic background and cultural practices, was significant. Ironically, although Taiwan had identified with the motherland throughout the Japanese colonial period, the mother with whom she was finally reunited after fifty years was more or less a stranger whose language she could hardly comprehend. The February 28 Incident in 1947—when Nationalist troops violently suppressed local uprisings—aggravated the already difficult transition from Japanese colonialism to Chinese rule. The Nationalist regime stepped up its control as the civil war on the mainland worsened and its retreat to Taiwan seemed imminent, eventually ushering in the era of White Terror, which lasted from the 1950s to the 1970s.

The history of modern Taiwan presents an unusual case of postcolonial culture. Whereas many other countries in Asia, Latin America, and Africa that achieved independence have had to wrestle with the issue of using the colonizer's language, the situation was reversed in postwar Taiwan. In 1949 many Taiwanese writers were caught between two languages, neither of which they could identify with: Japanese, the colonizer's language they were no longer allowed to speak; and Mandarin Chinese, rightfully their mother tongue but a language they were unable to speak. In short, Taiwanese writers were in the unique quandary of having no language of their own. This condition of "cultural aphasia" was to have a significant impact on modern Chinese poetry.

Thus, Taiwanese writers who were in their twenties and thirties when the war ended were severely handicapped linguistically: they were unable to write and publish in either Japanese, which was banned, or Chinese, of which they had yet to achieve full command. For this reason, and perhaps also out of disenchantment with the Nationalist regime, some simply gave up writing, while a few would continue to write in Japanese for the drawer or publish their work in Japan. Most of those who persisted would need fully ten years to acquire enough proficiency in Chinese to write and publish in that language. This last group of writers constitutes "the translingual generation" (跨越语言的一代)—a term coined by the poet-critic Lin Hengtai 林亨泰 (b. 1924) in 1967—whereas we may call the group that chose to stop writing "the silenced generation."

The lacuna thus created was filled mainly by mainland poets who had recently sought refuge in Taiwan. Although a few native Taiwanese poets made a smooth transition from Japanese to Chinese, most of the poets active in the 1950s, notably Ji Xian 纪弦 (who previously used the pen name Luyishi 路易士, 1913–2013) and Qin Zihao 覃子豪 (1912–1963), had published on the mainland. With their credentials, some of them were able to obtain editorial positions in state-run print media, become teachers of writing workshops and state-sponsored correspondence courses, and found private poetry societies and publish journals. Among the most important magazines and societies were *Modern Poetry Quarterly* (现代诗季刊, 1953–1964) and the Modernist School founded by Ji Xian in 1956, Blue Star Poetry Society (蓝星诗社) by Qin Zihao in 1954, and Epoch Poetry Society (创世纪诗社) by Luo Fu 洛夫 (b. 1928), Zhang Mo 张默 (b. 1931), and Ya Xian 痖弦 (b. 1932), also in 1954. Although these journals and societies by no means excluded native Taiwanese poets, clearly the émigrés' linguistic skills in Chinese provided valuable cultural capital, which put them in an advantageous position.

In the nationalistic, conservative society of postwar Taiwan (Winckler 1994; Lee 1996), poets faced a dual challenge: the official anti-Communist discourse (which hindered the free development of poetic art) and classical Chinese poetry (which enjoyed a much higher social and cultural status than modern poetry). It was against these two forces that poets tried to carve out a new space in which to experiment relatively free from intervention by the political and cultural establishment. The Modernist School, above all, led in this pioneering effort. Ji Xian, Lin Hengtai, and Fang Si 方思 (b. 1925), for example, defended modern poetry by decoupling poetry from song and by defining poetry as an individual, spiritual endeavor. The decoupling of poetry from song meant that the proper medium of modern poetry was prose, not rhymed verse; it further led to the view that content should determine form, or that form and content were organically interrelated. The emphasis on poetry as a personal calling transcending worldly concerns sought to free the poet from political pressures and to affirm the autonomy and dignity of the poet, who was more often than not low in the economic and social hierarchy.

If leaders of the New Poetry movement in postwar Taiwan were direct in their criticism of the conservatives who upheld classical poetry as the only legitimate form of verse, they took a more subtle approach in dealing with the state discourse of anticommunism. Avant-garde poets, from Ji Xian to Ya Xian, were not averse to participating in state-sponsored writing competitions, which offered handsome prizes. These prizes in turn provided valuable resources for sustaining privately run journals, which in turn gradually transformed the literary scene. Poets in postwar Taiwan successfully positioned themselves by two principal means: challenging the venerated position of classical verse by redefining the nature of poetry; and participating in the official discourse of anticommunism in order to appropriate its abundant cultural capital to advance their own goals. As its following among the younger generation grew, the New Poetry movement was able to create new forms of symbolic capital, with which it remapped the literary field and further consolidated its own position (Yeh 2001).

As a result of these pioneering efforts, modern poetry flourished from the mid-1950s to the first half of the 1960s. An impressive range of styles from a large number of innovative poets abounded, including the modernist lyrics of Ye Shan 叶珊 (renamed Yang Mu 杨牧, b. 1940), Zheng Chouyu 郑愁予 (b. 1932), Lin Ling 林泠 (b. 1938), and Xiong Hong 夐虹 (b. 1940); the surrealist prose poetry of Shang Qin 商禽 (b. 1930) and Guan Guan 管管 (b. 1929); and the existentialist musings of Bai Qiu 白萩 (b. 1937), Ya Xian, and Luo Fu. These poets were intensely interested in avant-garde poetry from Europe, North America, and Latin America and at the same time drawn to the rich lyricism of classical Chinese and sensitive to the historical circumstances into which they were born. Ya Xian's (Yeh and Malmqvist 2001: 207) "Colonel" (上校) provides a good example of the complex genealogy of postwar Taiwanese poetry:

> that was another kind of rose
> born of flames
> in the buckwheat field they fought the biggest battle of the campaign
> and his leg bade farewell in 1943
> he has heard history and laughter
> but what is immortality?
> cough syrup, razor blade, last month's rent, et cetera, et cetera
> his wife's sewing machine engages in skirmishes
> while he feels that the only thing that can capture him
> is the sun

With a few simple but forceful strokes, the poem paints the pathos of war that few pay attention to: what happens to a war hero after the war? For the disabled colonel, war continues as his wife manages to eke out a living by taking on irregular sewing jobs. (The sewing machine makes a sound that resembles a machine gun.) Yet, there is no glory to the latter war. In contrast to the "history" and "immortality" associated with the rhetoric of war, the colonel struggles against poverty and illness—the petty but inescapable reality of daily life. (The razor blade is a diminished stand-in for the soldier's bayonet.) The adroit use of irony, understatement, ambiguity, and allusions, both Chinese and Western, showcases a mature poet, though Ya Xian was only twenty-eight when he wrote the poem.

"Colonel" and other memorable poems of the postwar generation have rightly come to be seen as contemporary classics. Although some poets have stopped writing or developed in new directions, their work from the 1950s and 1960s exerted profound influences on younger generations. The mid-1960s saw a hiatus in modern poetry in Taiwan, a result of the suspension of leading poetry journals and the departures, whether temporary or permanent, of many major players, including Qin Zihao, Fang Si, Ya Xian, Zheng Chouyu, Lin Ling, Fang Qi 方旗 (b. 1937), Ye Weilian 叶维廉 (b. 1937), and Ye Shan. In a positive vein, native Taiwanese poets who had lacked the linguistic facility or confidence in Chinese were now ready to publish.

In June 1964, a group of native Taiwanese poets founded a poetry society named Bamboo Hat (笠) and, under the same name, what remains to this day the longest-running journal in the history of Taiwanese poetry. The contributions of *Bamboo Hat* can be summarized as follows. First, continuing the tradition of the 1950s, it defended the legitimacy and importance of modern poetry as a genre. Like its predecessors, *Bamboo Hat* encouraged individual expression and bold experiments. Second, like the *Modern Poetry Quarterly*, it sought to remedy the absence of sound literary criticism in Taiwan by publishing in-depth analyses and fair-minded critiques of poems. *Bamboo Hat* also introduced a wide range of literary movements and theories from Europe, the United States, and Japan by publishing translations of creative and theoretical writings. In short, in the second half of the 1960s *Bamboo Hat* broadened the horizon and furthered the poetic movement of the 1950s. Composed almost entirely of native Taiwanese poets, *Bamboo Hat* included such established poets as Wu Yingtao 吴瀛涛 (1916–1971), Zhan Bing 詹冰 (b. 1921), Huan Fu 桓夫 (b. 1922), Lin Hengtai, and Bai Qiu, as well as several novices. Their styles varied but displayed a generally modernist orientation. This was to change in the 1970s and 1980s with the emergence of "Taiwan consciousness."

The Taiwanese poetry world underwent a fundamental transformation in the 1970s. The forces of change came from two quarters: the 1972–1973 debate on modern poetry and the nativist literature movement of 1977–1979. The debate was in many ways a literary response to nonliterary circumstances. From 1970 to 1972, Taiwan suffered a series of major diplomatic setbacks, including its loss of membership in the United Nations, territorial disputes with Japan over the Diaoyutai or Senkaku Islands, severance of formal ties with the United States and Japan, and President Richard Nixon's visit to Beijing, which led to the establishment of diplomatic ties with China in 1979.

The loss of political legitimacy in the international community and the economic boom, which depended heavily on American and Japanese capital, led to an explosion of nationalist sentiment. In the literary sphere, reflections on cultural identity triggered a series of harsh criticisms of the modernist poetry of the 1950s and 1960s. The experimental spirit of the earlier poetry was now condemned as shamelessly colonial and non-Chinese, its modernist orientation as decadent, solipsistic, and severed from local reality. The binary oppositions between China and the West, tradition and modernity, and the local and the cosmopolitan were nothing new; they had played a major role in previous cultural discussions, whether in May Fourth China or Taiwan in the 1950s. To be Chinese was to embrace the Chinese cultural and literary tradition and to identify with local reality (Yeh 1998).

In the debate on modern poetry, there was in fact little debate to speak of, with an overwhelming majority of views expressing opposition to modernist poetry. Faced with Taiwan's crisis in the international arena, few poets put forth an effective rebuttal against the critics of modernism. Insofar as it rejected cultural Westernization and emphasized local reality, the debate was a precursor to the nativist literature movement in 1977, in which fiction, not poetry, was the focal point (Wang 1980). There is, however, an important difference between the two literary events. With the surfacing of the opposition movement, which culminated in the Formosa Incident of December 1979, the identity of Taiwan was no longer unequivocal. "Taiwanese" identity, albeit still couched in the language of "the rural land" or "native land," emerged in contradistinction to "Chinese" identity. The long-unspoken tension between native Taiwanese, most of whose ancestors came from southern China, and post-1949 mainland immigrants, now regarded as non-Taiwanese, erupted in the open and was to become a highly politicized issue in the next two decades.

Nationalism, traditionalism, modernization, democratization, nativization—decades of social, cultural, and political movements have left indelible marks on Taiwan's poetry. The debate on modern poetry in the early 1970s led to much reflection on the relationship between the Chinese tradition and modern poetry. In the best scenario, it inspired poets to reevaluate tradition as a vital resource and led to a broad spectrum of neoclassicist experimentation. Poets sought to incorporate and transform traditional poetic language, imagery, and form with varying degrees of success. Similarly, the nativist emphasis ushered in a new range of themes that revolved around Taiwan, its present and past. Further, as the democracy movement gathered momentum in the 1980s, such political taboos as the February 28 Incident, White Terror, and ethnic tensions emerged as subjects. Once the orthodoxy fell, challenges to the center from the periphery multiplied. Poetry began to address a host of long-existing concerns, ranging from discrimination against women and homosexuals, to exploitation of and injustice to aborigines, and to impoverished veterans and environmental devastation. The rise of socially engaged poetry—whether feminist, queer, aboriginal, or ecological—along with sci-fi poetry, computer poetry, video poetry, and poetry written in Hokkien (Taiwanese) and Hakka—enlivened Taiwan's poetry scene.

Paradoxically, the impressive variety of poetry since the 1980s exists alongside the ascendancy of mass culture and digital culture. While Taiwan enjoys complete freedom of speech and freedom of the press, the intense competition on the cultural market has also resulted in considerable marginalization of poetry. Despite efforts to make it more accessible and more popular, poetry remains a "minority literature." Artistic experimentation has been going strong, however, and in a society where literature still commands a great deal of public respect, poetry continues to be read by people from all walks of life. In recent years, some poets and writers have also chosen to engage directly in social movements, such as protests against the construction of nuclear power plants and the 2014 Sunflower Student movement against Taiwan's trade agreements with China.

Modern poetry in Taiwan has traveled a long way from the 1920s to the present. It has drawn on multiple literary traditions and demonstrated a high level of originality and versatility. Pioneering literary modernism and postmodernism in the Chinese-speaking world, Taiwanese poetry has exerted an influence far beyond the island and is increasingly recognized globally. It is no exaggeration to say that Taiwan has given the world some of the best poetry written in Chinese. Taiwanese poetry has enriched the Chinese language and put its unique imprint on it. That, in the final analysis, is the only criterion for poetry, nothing more, nothing less.

Bibliography

Au, Chung-to. *Modernist Aesthetics in Taiwanese Poetry since the 1950s*. Leiden: Brill, 2008.

Chen Shaoting 陈少廷. *Taiwan xin wenxue yundong jianshi* 台湾新文学运动简史 (A short history of the new Taiwanese literature movement). Taipei: Lianjing, 1977.

Cheung, Dominic, ed. *The Isle Full of Noises: Modern Chinese Poetry from Taiwan*. New York: Columbia University Press, 1987.

Gold, Thomas B. "Civil Society and Taiwan's Quest for Identity." In Stevan Harrell and Chün-chieh Huang, eds., *Cultural Change in Postwar Taiwan*, 47–68. Boulder, CO: Westview Press, 1994.

Lee, Thomas H. C. "Chinese Education and Intellectuals in Postwar Taiwan." In Chun-chieh Huang and Feng-fu Tsao, eds., *Postwar Taiwan in Historical Perspective*, 135–157. College Park: University of Maryland, 1996.

Wang, Jing. "Taiwan Hsiang-t'u Literature: Perspectives in the Evolution of a Literary Movement." In Jeannette L. Faurot, ed., *Chinese Fiction from Taiwan: Critical Perspectives*, 43–71. Bloomington: Indiana University Press, 1980.

Winckler, Edwin A. "Cultural Policy on Postwar Taiwan." In Stevan Harrel and Chün-chieh Huang, eds., *Cultural Changes in Postwar Taiwan*, 22–46. Boulder, CO: Westview Press, 1994.

Yang, Mu. *No Trace of the Gardener: Poems of Yang Mu*. Trans. Michelle Yeh, with Lawrence R. Smith. New Haven, CT: Yale University Press, 1998.

Ye Di 叶笛. "Riju shidai Taiwan shitan de chaoxianshi zhuyi yundong—Fengche shishe de shi yundong" 日据时代台湾诗坛的超现实主义运动——风车诗社的诗运动 (The surrealist movement on Taiwan's poetry scene during the Japanese occupation: The Le Moulin Poetry Society movement). In *Taiwan xiandaishi shilun* 台湾现代诗史论 (Essays on the history of Taiwan's modern poetry), 21–34. Taipei: Wenxue zazhishe, 1996.

Yeh, Michelle. "On Our Destitute Dinner Table: Modern Poetry Quarterly in the 1950s." In David Der-wei Wang and Carlos Rojas, eds., *Writing Taiwan: A New Literary History*, 113–139. Durham, NC: Duke University Press, 2007.

—— (Xi Mi 奚密). "Taiwan xiandaishi lunzhan: zai lun 'Yi chang weiwancheng de geming'" 台湾现代诗论战: 再论"一场未完成的革命" (The debate on modern poetry in Taiwan: On "An Incomplete Revolution"). *Guowen tiandi* 13, 10 (March 1998): 72–81.

Yeh, Michelle, and N. G. D. Malmqvist, eds. *Frontier Taiwan: An Anthology of Modern Chinese Poetry*. New York: Columbia University Press, 2001.

Yeh, Michelle, N. G. D. Malmqvist, and Xu Huizhi, eds. *Sailing to Formosa: A Poetic Companion to Taiwan*. Seattle: University of Washington Press, 2005.

Yip, Wai-lim, ed. *Modern Chinese Poetry: Twenty Poets from the Republic of China, 1955–1965*. Iowa City: University of Iowa Press, 1970.

44

HOMOEROTICISM IN MODERN CHINESE LITERATURE

THOMAS MORAN

In imperial China, there were no notions of sexual identity that could be categorized as heterosexual or homosexual, and no notion that certain sexual behaviors violated religious doctrine. Men loving men was regarded with a range of attitudes: an expression of refined taste, an epicurean indulgence, blameworthy dissolution, or, if the infatuated party was a ruler distracted from ruling, dangerous. If homoerotic relations did not threaten the patriline—that is, if the man involved was also having sex with women and producing heirs—the homoeroticism was tolerated. Wah-shan Chou (2000: 7) provides the essential caveat: "The cultural tolerance of same-sex eroticism appeared only with a classist and sexist hierarchy of unequal social relations—it is the male elite who have enjoyed the class-gender privileges of sexually dominating their social inferiors of both sexes." Mention of female same-sex desire in traditional historiography is rare; emperors' dalliances with male "favorites" were within history's scope, but the lives of women were not. Female homoeroticism can be found in traditional fiction, but the record is "meager" (Shi 2013: 753). Men kept female same-sex relationships out of the written record because they perceived self-sufficient women as a threat (750) or regarded what women did on their own as trivial (Sang 2003: 21).

In the eighteenth and nineteenth centuries, it was the vogue among some men in Beijing to romance the boys who played female roles in opera. These actors and their roles were called *dan* (旦). The connection between *dan* and patron was the most prevalent and socially important form of homosexual relationship during the Qing dynasty (Wu 2004: 9). In a 1922 memoir, a man who worked in government in Beijing during the late Qing wrote that officials were prohibited from patronizing *dan* and from visiting female prostitutes, but they could get away with the former and did not need to be banned from the latter because it was held in general contempt anyway (Stevenson and Wu 2013: 263). The 1849 novel *Precious Mirror for Judging Flowers* (品花宝鉴) by Chen Sen 陈森 (c.1797–c.1870), which is about *dan* and their patrons, "represents the homoerotic sensibilities of the Qing dynasty taken to their romantic limit" (Wu 2004: 16). Chen Sen's novel appeared when everything in China began to change, including the discourse of "homosexuality," a word and concept that entered Chinese in the early twentieth century as *tongxing'ai* (同性爱), *tongxing lian'ai* (同性恋爱), or *tongxing lian* (同性恋) (Kang 2009: 41, 54).

In the early twentieth century, modern sexology, including the medicalization of sex and the definition of homosexuality as pathology, was imported into China from the West. Some argue that these notions were accepted in toto, replacing indigenous ideas about homoeroticism; an extreme form of this argument has it that traditional China had welcomed same-sex desire, but modern China learned homophobia from the West. More nuanced studies include those by Tze-lan D. Sang (2003) on modern Chinese female homoeroticism and Wenqing Kang (2009) on its male counterpart. Their work establishes that in premodern China there were prohibitions against same-sex desire, particularly between women; that the sexology translated into Chinese included works that express positive views toward homosexual love; that homegrown ideas and terms for same-sex desire circulated alongside imported ideas and terms; and that the Chinese who thought about these things had agency—they made up their own minds about what same-sex desire means. Sang and Kang agree that over the first four decades of the twentieth century, attitudes toward homosexuality turned negative. They show that the Chinese opponents of same-sex eroticism made conscious, selective use of foreign and domestic ideas to condemn homosexuality for reasons that, at the risk of oversimplification, come down to eugenics: the pursuit of sexual pleasure outside marriage did not strengthen the race or help build the nation, and strengthening the race and building the nation were seen as necessary for China's survival.

The history of homoeroticism in modern fiction (as opposed to popular fiction) in its early phase is not difficult to grasp: there is not so much of it, the 1920s flurry of stories about homosexual love notwithstanding; it appears less and less in a flattering light; and it disappears in 1949, not to reappear until the 1990s. Ye Shengtao 叶圣陶 (1894–1988) wrote about love between women in his "The Forgotten" (被忘却的), one of Ye's early stories about women suffering under class and gender oppression included in his collection *Conflagration* (火灾, 1923). Lu Yin's 庐隐 (c.1898–1934) autobiographical *Seaside Friends* (海滨故人, 1923) is about female college friends whose bond and dreams collapse after their marriages. Sang (2003: 139) reads Lu Yin's "Lishi's Diary" (丽石的

日记, 1923) as an "impassioned and self-conscious declaration of lesbian love." Ling Shuhua's 凌叔华 (1900–1990) "Once Upon a Time" (说有这么一回事, 1928) is about college women in love; after a summer vacation, Yingman 影曼 collapses in despair when she learns that her beloved Yunluo 云罗 has married a man. Ding Ling's 丁玲 (1904–1986) "Summer Vacation" (暑假中, 1928) treats the same-sex affairs, jealousies, and frustrations of female teachers at a girls' school. Sang argues that Yu Dafu 郁达夫 (1896–1945) novella "She Is a Weak Woman" (她是一个弱女子, 1932) uses female same-sex sex as a symbol of "social disintegration and chaos" (153).

New forms of social organization gave women opportunity for self-expression and at least temporary autonomy, which encouraged the exploration of female homosocial and homosexual bonds, as in Lu Yin's stories. Empowered women, especially those who could do without men, threatened male reformers, who were prepared to overthrow everything except the gender hierarchy. This explains the anxiety in Yu Dafu's novella and is why, Sang (2003, 132) argues, "female-female carnal desire is trapped between insignificance and ignominy in May Fourth fiction."

Kang (2009: 61, 83) argues that for a decade, beginning in the early 1920s, several writers presented male same-sex love "as a challenge to the constraints of social and sexual morality" and "an inspiration for an alternative human future." In Yu Dafu's "One Boundless Evening" (茫茫夜, 1922), two young men meet, become friends, and are separated. The men are not lovers, but Kang notes that the autobiographical protagonist Yu Zhifu 于质夫 compares his feeling for his friend to that between Verlaine and Rimbaud, who were lovers, as Yu Dafu likely knew (67). In Ye Lingfeng's 叶灵凤 (1905–1975) *Forbidden Zone* (禁地, 1931), the protagonist has a relationship with an older woman and is about to begin a sexual affair with a man when the novel breaks off (L. Lee 1999: 260–261). In his 1928 memoir, *My Childhood* (我的童年), Guo Moruo 郭沫若 (1892–1978) writes with disapproval about sex between classmates at an all-male boarding school but celebrates his emotional love for boys. According to Kang (2009: 79), Guo believed modernization required that traditional male same-sex relationships, "in which salacious men feminized beautiful male adolescents and forced them into sexual acts," be rejected and replaced by chaste intimacy among equals "based on mutual attraction and respect."

The negative half of Guo's message is what survived in the changing political environment of the war period: the endorsement of same-sex love vanished, replaced by heteronormativity. Wu Zuguang's 吴祖光 (1917–2003) play *Return on a Snowy Night* (风雪夜归人, 1942), for example, depicts the homoerotic bond between actors and opera patrons as a dirty habit of a decadent oligarchy in a world of class oppression and the exploitation (including sexual) of the powerless. Wu's play is evidence, according to Kang (2009: 116–117), that by the late Republican period the homoerotic subculture of opera was seen as "vulgar, inhuman, and unacceptable" and "un-modern."

The authors of Republican era fiction tended to be high-minded people with literary or revolutionary ambitions, or both. They wrote about sex, but not at length and never graphically; naturalism was not a mode they favored, and they withheld some of what they knew—and did—from their fiction. Accounts of same-sex love and desire in court documents and the tabloid press far outdo fiction in both inventiveness and detail (H. Lee 2007: 151–155; Kang 2009: 85–114). Fiction by the aforementioned authors aimed to instruct and elevate; it celebrated love, not sex; and eventually it taught that revolution required that romance wait. For their time, the stories by Lu Yin and others are entirely conventional in their narrative form and also in their exclusive focus on spiritual love. But Kang and Sang are perhaps justified in arguing that although fiction from the 1920s and 1930s describes the relationship among same-sex intimates in entirely spiritual terms, it does not preclude a homoerotic subtext. For example, *Seaside Friends* makes no explicit mention of sexual attraction between women, but this silence may be taken as evidence of repressed "lesbian physical desire" (Sang 2003: 138). Repression was the norm in these fictional works.

The official position in the People's Republic of China (PRC) from the 1950s through the 1970s seems to have been that homosexuality did not exist. It was almost never mentioned. Men who had sex with other men were subject to social, legal, and, in the workplace or party, administrative harassment or punishment for engaging in *liumang* (流氓, hooligan) activity—*liumang* being a term used to name behaviors deemed antisocial (Kang 2012). There have been men who loved men and women who loved women throughout Chinese history, and published memoirs prove this was true of the Maoist period as well. *Good Man Luo Ge* (好男罗格), a 1997 collection of fiction on male same-sex love by writer and scholar Tong Ge 童戈 (b. c.1951), includes stories set during the Cultural Revolution. Literature from and about the Maoist period that makes no mention of homoeroticism awaits rereading to uncover covert concern with same-sex desire. As A Cheng 阿城 (b. 1949) writes in a preface to a Taiwan edition of his work: "I only hope that twenty years from now, if anybody has the interest to go back to these stories, that their close readings turn up something new, like for example, the homosexual gaze in the stories. Under totalitarianism this gaze is at once very public and entirely secret" (A Cheng 2007: 5).

Bai Xianyong's 白先勇 (b. 1937) novel *Crystal Boys* (孽子, 1983) is the most well-known of several works that anticipated what became *tongzhi* (同志, comrade) or *ku'er* (酷儿, queer) literature, a body of writing on homoerotic themes that emerged in Taiwan in the 1990s. The terms *tongzhi* and *ku'er* were adopted by the Chinese gay community because they avoid the essentializing connotations and colonial associations of *tongxinglian* (同性恋, homosexual love). In Bai's novel, narrator A-Qing 阿青 is expelled from school and banished from home for having sex with a man. He goes to Taipei's New Park and joins the young men who flock around father figure and pimp Chief Yang 杨教头. Until the late 1980s, critics read *Crystal Boys* as a study of the causes of homosexuality or as a national allegory about Taiwan. Bai's favorite themes of exile and nostalgia suffuse *Crystal Boys* (see "Cold War Fiction from Taiwan and the Modernists"), but homosexuality is central to the novel, which assumes that male same-sex love is natural and that gay men epitomize masculinity. Chen Ruoxi's 陈若曦 (b. 1938) *Paper Marriage* (纸婚, 1986) and Li Ang's 李昂 (b. 1952) "A Romance about Forbidden Desire" (禁色的爱, 1989) are two other works from the 1980s that may, in retrospect, be considered to belong to Taiwan queer literature (Liou 2003; Liu 2010).

During the 1990s, the discourse of sexuality in Taiwan was transformed: a campaign for lesbian and gay rights was launched; the lesbian, gay, bisexual, transgender, and queer (LGBTQ) community cohered around new and active social organizations; and there was a "remarkable rise of the literature of transgressive sexuality," as Fran Martin (2003: 5) writes. An early example of this body of literature is Du Xiulan's 杜修兰 (b. 1966) *Unfilial Daughter* (逆女, 1993), which is sometimes regarded as a lesbian counterpart to *Crystal Boys*; it follows protagonist Ding Tianshi 丁天使 through high school, college, and after as she copes with poverty and her dysfunctional family and discovers Taipei's lesbian subculture. One of the most discussed works from the 1990s on a homoerotic theme is Zhu Tianwen's 朱天文 (b. 1956) *Notes of a Desolate Man* (荒人手记, 1994), in which the narrator, Shao 韶, a sophisticate tormented by self-doubt, tells the story of his life and loves and remembers his childhood friend Ah Yao 阿尧, a sexual adventurer confident in his identity as queer, who has died of AIDS. Zhu, a woman, was criticized for writing a novel in the voice of a gay man, but some in Taiwan's queer community defended her.

Qiu Miaojin's 邱妙津 (1969–1995) *Crocodile Notes* (鳄鱼手记, 1994) was published in the same year as *Notes*. The narrator falls in love with her female classmate Shuiling 水伶 but fears Shuiling will leave her for a man and so pushes her away. The crocodile of the title is introduced after the narrator represses her desire for Shuiling. The narrator reads reports in the newspaper about "crocodile" sightings all over Taiwan. She meets a "crocodile" and gives it a place to hide and a chance to tell its story. It is eager to make friends but shy about coming out. Sang (2003: 264) calls this part of the novel Qiu's "animal fable" and argues that it is a satire of the way the media sensationalize stories about lesbians. Another interpretation is that having internalized society's homophobia, the narrator believes herself to be a monster (怪物), and the "crocodile" is the monster externalized. Qiu committed suicide in 1995. Her novel *Last Words from Montmartre* (蒙马特遗书, 1996) was published posthumously and is a "cult classic" in the Taiwan queer community (Suher 2014).

Wuhe's 舞鹤 (b. 1951) *Gui'er and Ayao* (鬼儿与阿妖, 2000) and Luo Yijun's 骆以军 (b. 1967) *Expressions of Sorrow* (遣悲怀, 2001) are two works from Taiwan on homoerotic themes that attracted attention at the turn of the century. Wuhe's novel was criticized for its depiction of gay life (Payne 2013: 539). Luo's novel is told in letters between the narrator and Qiu Miaojin (Ying 2010: 128–129). By around 2000, the creative energy that produced Taiwan queer literature had waned somewhat or moved into other fields of art or into scholarship and activism; fictional works continued to be published, but not in the same volume. A writer who remained active is Hong Ling 洪凌 (b. 1971), also known as Lucifer Hung, "Taiwan's premier writer of queer gothic and vampire fiction" (Martin 2003: 189). Parry and Liu (2010: 354) argue that "in its difficulty, hybridity, and explicit violence, Hung's writing constructs a language that is capable of critiquing the totalizing aims" of heteronormative discourse that dismisses difference. Some of her work is science fiction, and she publishes online (see "Internet Literature").

By the early twenty-first century, most Chinese-language writing on homoerotic themes was published online, where the political boundaries that separate the different Chinese literatures disappear. Through the 1990s, however, writing on same-sex love in the mainland developed quite independently of that in Taiwan. Wang Anyi's 王安忆 (b. 1954) "Brothers" (弟兄们, 1989) revisits the theme of coed romance popular in 1920s stories and was one of the first post-Mao works of fiction to address, albeit gingerly, the subject of homoeroticism. *A Private Life* (私人生活, 1996) by Chen Ran 陈染 (b. 1962) and *A Self at War* (一个人的战争, 1997) by Lin Bai 林白 (b. 1958) include homoeroticism as an explicit, but not dominant, element. Both novels are semiautobiographical coming-of-age stories told in the first person, lack straightforward plotlines, and are preoccupied with the female narrators' psychology and the difficulties and traumas the narrators experience. Sang (2003: 194, 256) argues that Lin's work is concerned with her characters' "lesbian self-hatred," whereas Chen expresses in her writing a refusal to align with any socially determined sexual identity. Chen and Lin are associated with the writing of female same-sex love, but also with women's literature in general and the late 1990s genre of "personal writing" (个人写作).

Like Chen Ran and Lin Bai, Wang Xiaobo 王小波 (1952–1997) wrote about homoeroticism as part of a general challenge to social convention. Many of Wang's characters are driven by sexual desire, the strength and purity of which are celebrated in the narration. His antiheroes do not so much fight against society's power relations as they try to ignore them in pursuit of individual wants and needs, including sexual ones. One work that explicitly addresses homoeroticism is "Sentiments Like Water" (似水柔情), written first as a short story and a play and then as a screenplay for Zhang Yuan's 张元 film *East Palace, West Palace* (东宫西宫, 1996). (All three texts are included in *Everlasting and Unchanging: An Anthology of Fiction and Scripts by Wang Xiaobo* [地久天长: 王小波小说剧本集, 1998].) In the story, a policeman detains a man for cruising for gay sex in a park. They become lovers. The cop is a sadist, and his prisoner a masochist, and the story may be read as a political allegory about the relationship between the state and its people, but it is better understood as being about the mutability of libidinal energy, which cannot be defined and fixed by language, law, or convention. Before "Sentiments Like Water," Wang coauthored *Their World: A Look at the Chinese Male Homosexuality Community* (他们的世界: 中国男同性恋群落透视, 1993) with his wife, Li Yinhe 李银河, a sociologist and expert on sexuality, who as a member of the Chinese People's Political Consultative Conference has repeatedly but unsuccessfully proposed that same-sex marriage be made legal.

Prolific writer, director, critic, and queer activist Cui Zi'en 崔子恩 (b. c.1958) is one of the most high-profile members of mainland China's *tongzhi* community. Since the 1990s, he has published stories and novels and written and directed films, including a documentary on queer life in China. Cui's first novel, *Scarlet Lips* (桃色嘴唇, 1997), was published in Hong Kong and marketed as China's first homosexual novel.

In recent years, the most active venue for the publication of homoerotic fiction has been the Internet. Cristini (2005: 10) guesses that "thousands, if not tens of thousands of [comrade] stories, long and short" were put online in the decade beginning in the mid-1990s. Most of these stories are about men. Sang (2003: 170) notes that Chinese journalism and sociology on homoeroticism focus almost exclusively on gay men, and she discusses theories, beyond the general gender bias in Chinese society, that try to explain why this is so: gay subculture in China copies Western gay subculture and so is "recognizable," whereas lesbian subculture does not and is not; intimate relationships between women are so common that lesbian relationships are invisible.

In *Beijing Story* (北京故事, 1996), one of the first works of online comrade literature, Lan Yu 蓝宇 comes from the countryside to attend college in Beijing; he has no money and turns to prostitution. His first customer is Chen Handong 陈捍东, a successful businessman. Lan Yu falls in love with Chen, but Chen is inconstant. Chen eventually accepts his homosexuality and admits his love for Lan Yu, but Lan Yu dies, after which Chen moves to Canada. *Beijing Story* was the basis of Stanley Kwan's 2001 movie *Lan Yu*. There is speculation that the author of *Beijing Story*, known as Beijing Comrade 北京同志, is a woman born in the 1960s who also publishes under the name Xiaohe 筱禾. In 2013, Xiaohe published the online *danmei* (耽美) novel *Confusion* (混乱, "Xiaohe xin shu"). *Danmei*, or BL (for "boy love"), fiction is about romantic relationships between attractive men and is written by and for women (Feng 2009).

As is the case with popular genre fiction more generally, in recent years comrade fiction has splintered into subgenres. He Yaohui's 何要辉 (b. 1982) *More than Brothers* (兄弟之上, 2009), for example, belongs to the subgenre "campus comrade fiction" (校园同志小说) and depicts the lives of men who discover their sexuality in college, find support in the online queer community, experience love and sex, and after college resist or yield to pressure to marry (Huynh 2012: 5–6). The novel's online popularity led to publication in print in 2010. It is listed as a "classic comrade novel" (经典同志小说) on the website of danlan.org, which calls itself the largest gay portal website in mainland China. The website hosts thousands of works of fiction on homoerotic love.

The volume and variety of comrade fiction mirrors the general volume and variety in Chinese publishing since the late 1990s. Through the first decade of the twentieth-first century, most readers looked to fiction not for philosophy or art but for diversion, entertainment, excitement, sentiment, and inspiration, or for reflection or affirmation of their lives. Comrade fiction provides such sustenance for gay and lesbian readers. It is a product of—and also helped produce— the increased acceptance or tolerance of LGBTQ identities in Taiwan and China. This increased acceptance or tolerance is found, however, mostly or even exclusively in the more enlightened social circles in larger cosmopolitan cities. Chinese society has no history of homophobic violence, but *tongzhi* are under considerable pressure from families, schools, and workplaces, and their clubs and websites operate freely only at the unpredictable whim of the authorities. This is why some scholars who write on Chinese literature about homosexuality see their work as advocacy criticism: the point is to improve things for the *tongzhi* community (Liu 2010: 316). Chinese writers and Chinese critics continue the ongoing, unending project of fashioning *tongzhi* or *ku'er* identities that both borrow from global discourses and are specific to China and even to individual Chinese.

Bibliography

A Cheng 阿城. "Zixu (Taiwan ban)" 自序(台湾版) (Author's preface to the Taiwan edition). In *Qi wang, Shu wang, Haizi wang* 棋王, 树王, 孩子王 (King of chess, king of trees, king of children), 5. Taipei: Dadi, 2007.

Chou, Wah-shan. *Tongzhi: Politics of Same-Sex Eroticism in Chinese Societies*. New York: Haworth Press, 2000.

Cristini, Remy. "The Rise of Comrade Literature: Development and Significance of a New Chinese Genre." MA thesis, Leiden University, The Netherlands, 2005.

Feng, Jin. "'Addicted to Beauty': Consuming and Producing Web-Based Chinese 'Danmei' Fiction at Jinjiang." *Modern Chinese Literature and Culture* 21, 2 (Fall 2009): 1–41.

Huss, Ann. "Yu Dafu." In Thomas Moran, ed., *Dictionary of Literary Biography*. Vol. 328, *Chinese Fiction Writers, 1900–1949*, 282–289. Detroit: Thomson Gale, 2007.

Huynh, Tony. "The War Within: Queer Identity Formation in He Yaohui's *Beyond Brothers*." BA thesis, Middlebury College, Vermont, 2012.

Kang, Wenqing. "The Decriminalization and Depathologization of Homosexuality in China." In Timothy B. Weston and Lionel M. Jensen, eds., *China in and Beyond the Headlines*, 231–248. Lanham, MD: Rowman and Littlefield, 2012.

——. *Obsession: Male Same-Sex Relations in China, 1900–1950*. Hong Kong: Hong Kong University Press, 2009.

Lee, Haiyan. *Revolution of the Heart: A Genealogy of Love in China, 1900–1950*. Stanford, CA: Stanford University Press, 2007.

Lee, Leo Ou-fan. *Shanghai Modern: The Flowering of a New Urban Culture in China, 1930–1945*. Cambridge, MA: Harvard University Press, 1999.

Li Yinhe 李银河 and Wang Xiaobo 王小波. *Tamen de shijie: Zhongguo nan tongxinglian qunluo toushi* 他们的世界: 中国男同性恋群落透视 (Their world: A look at the Chinese male homosexual community). Hong Kong: Tiandi tushu youxian gongsi, 1993.

Liou, Liang-Ya. "At the Intersection of the Global and the Local: Representations of Male Homosexuality in Fictions by Pai Hsien-yung, Li Ang, Chu Tien-wen and Chi Ta-wei." *Postcolonial Studies* 6, 2 (2003): 191–206.

Liu, Petrus. "Why Does Queer Theory Need China?" *positions: east asia cultures critique* 18, 2 (2010): 291–320.

Martin, Fran. "Introduction: Taiwan's Literature of Transgressive Sexuality." In Martin, ed. and trans., *Angelwings: Contemporary Queer Fiction from Taiwan*, 1–28. Honolulu: University of Hawai'i Press, 2003.

Parry, Amie, and Liu Jen-peng. "The Politics of Schadenfreude: Violence and Queer Cultural Critique in Lucifer Hung's Science Fiction." *positions: east asia cultures critique* 18, 2 (Fall 2010): 351–372.

Payne, Christopher. "Queer Otherwise: Anti-Sociality in Wuhe's *Gui'er and Ayao*." *Archiv Orientální* 81, 3 (2013): 539–554.

Sang, Tze-lan D. *The Emerging Lesbian: Female Same-Sex Desire in Modern China*. Chicago: University of Chicago Press, 2003.

Shi, Liang. "Mirror Rubbing: A Critical Genealogy of Pre-Modern Chinese Female Same-Sex Eroticism." *Journal of Homosexuality* 60, 5 (2013): 750–772.

Stevenson, Mark, and Wu Cuncun, eds. and trans. *Homoeroticism in Imperial China: A Sourcebook*. London: Routledge, 2013.

Suher, Dylan. "Dylan Suher Reviews Qiu Miaojin's *Last Words from Montmartre*." Trans. Ari Larissa Heinrich. New York Review Books Classics, 2014. *Asymptote* (July 2014). http://www.asymptotejournal.com/article.php?cat=Criticism&id=78&curr_index=0.

Wu, Cuncun. *Homoerotic Sensibilities in Late Imperial China*. London: Routledge Curzon, 2004.

Xiaohe 筱禾. http://baike.baidu.com/view/2671386.htm#2.

"Xiaohe xin shu: Danmei xiaoshuo *Hunluan*" 筱禾新书: 耽美小说《混乱》. http://www.danlan.org/disparticle_45000.htm.

Ying, Li-hua. "Luo Yijun." In Ying, *Historical Dictionary of Modern Chinese Literature*, 128–129. Lanham, MD: Scarecrow Press, 2010.

45

CONTEMPORARY URBAN FICTION: REWRITING THE CITY

ROBIN VISSER AND JIE LU

In the late 1980s, writers in mainland China once again began writing on urban motifs that had been suppressed or used to promote Communist Party policy during the Maoist period. Mao Zedong's 1942 "Yan'an Talks," which favored "national forms" based on "folk customs" over foreign-influenced genres, became official policy in the 1950s. This formalized the primacy of rural literature until Deng Xiaoping's official statement on the arts in 1979, which effectively loosened strict party control over literary production. In the rapid urbanization starting from the late 1980s, however, urban experiences started to replace rural ones to represent Chinese national identity and postsocialist and postrevolutionary experiences. Instead of being defined as the Other of the rural, the city has gained its own characteristics. Urban writers began describing the city on its own terms, without reference to the dialectical values associated with urban and rural spaces that dominated the cultural production of the Mao era. Nevertheless, fundamental urban changes restructured urban life, culture, and experiences, which in turn both complicated urban representation and demanded new structures of vision and imagining.

The Beijing-based writer Wang Shuo 王朔 (b. 1958) was among the first to turn his attention to the city. Emerging as a literary force in the mid-1980s, he pioneered a trend labeled "hooligan literature" (痞子文学). With his literary influence on pop culture, critics single out "the Wang Shuo phenomenon" as the most salient epochal marker of the shift from the 1980s to the 1990s. Unlike the high-minded cynicism of avant-garde writers or the dark, neorealistic portrayal of everyday urban life, Wang Shuo writes about disenfranchised youth "playing" in the city to dispel their boredom, capitalizing on their ability to dupe members of the establishment. Wang Shuo has written more than twenty novels, selling more than ten million copies, and his ventures into television miniseries and film scriptwriting extended the Wang Shuo phenomenon into national mass media. *Masters of Mischief* (顽主, 1987) and *Playing for Thrills* (玩的就是心跳, 1988), two of his best-known works, portray unconventional characters who create elaborate games, such as the establishment of the Three T Company, specializing in "troubleshooting, tedium relief, and taking the blame." Many of his other works depict the ineffectuality of the intellectual class, instead valorizing "punks" (流氓), who are free from roots, bonds, and identities. Wang Shuo's works capitalize on the collapse of 1980s utopian ideals, presaging the 1990s siege of consumer culture and the resulting marginalization of intellectuals.

At roughly the same time in the late 1980s, another group of young writers, labeled "avant-garde" or experimental, emerged on the literary scene. Su Tong 苏童 (b. 1963), a Nanjing-based writer acclaimed for his 1980s experimental short fiction, uses a realistic narrative style in his first full-length novel, *Rice* (米, 1991), which contrasts urban and rural themes in depicting a peasant's coming of age in a southern town. Consistent with the avant-garde's attempt to subvert traditional connotations of city and countryside, Su Tong devalues both the impoverished village from which Five Dragons 五龙 has fled and the decadent town in which he makes his fortune and meets his demise. The benefit that the urban space promises the rural immigrant is demonstrably depleted, yet the rural space remains an equally ineffectual—indeed, inaccessible—grounding for modern identity. By draining both landscapes of their appeal, Su Tong displaces the familiar urban/rural terms in which the cultural debates over modernity have so often been waged. Though set in the 1930s, *Rice* speaks to the spiritual emptiness of Chinese life in the post-Mao era.

In many ways the realist style employed by Su Tong in *Rice* marked the appearance of "neorealist fiction" (新写实小说), represented by writers such as Wuhan-based Chi Li 池莉 (b. 1957) and Fang Fang 方方 (b. 1955), and Beijing-based Liu Heng 刘恒 (b. 1954) and Liu Zhenyun 刘震云 (b. 1958). Some of these neorealist works depict struggles of everyday urban life rather than create model characters and settings as prescribed for works of socialist realism. Liu Heng's *Black Snow* (黑的雪, 1988) is an early example of a post-Mao novel that reflects on urban estrangement. The narrative expresses the most intimate thoughts of Li Huiquan 李慧泉, a young man trying to negotiate the subtle complexities of modern urban life in 1980s Beijing after being released from incarceration in a labor-reform camp. The question of personal worth is foregrounded as it was in Su Tong's *Rice*, but whereas Five Dragons attempts to gain self-respect in the city by possessing women and wealth, Li

Huiquan is moderate in his financial pursuits and morbidly introspective about life. He goes through the motions of rehabilitating himself as an upright modern urbanite, peddling clothes in the new market economy, jogging to maintain his health, frequenting art museums and classical music concerts, and reading the daily papers to stay abreast of current events. Yet Li is primarily fixated on acquiring an unobtainable woman, an obsession that takes on morbid dimensions due to his extreme degree of social and psychological disaffection. As he wanders through the city, he is terrified by the aimlessness of the crowd and its implications for his own insignificance, recalling classic motifs of urban alienation. Liu Heng depicts 1980s alley (胡同) life from the perspective of "urban youth awaiting employment" (城市待业青年) who must work as street peddlers (个体户), and like Lao She's 老舍 portrayal of the underclass rickshaw pullers decades earlier, he invokes empathy for these marginalized city-dwellers. Chi Li's *Coming and Going* (来来往往) focuses on the rise of consumer culture and its gradual dominance over urban everyday life. The story grasps the complex cultural ethos of the late 1990s when global consumer culture was beginning to exert its powerful influence over the most intimate levels of everyday life and came into conflict with the revolutionary culture and traditional values that were still part of lived experience. This cultural change has also resulted from the formation of new bourgeois and middle classes—the social product of Chinese economic reform—whose cultural tastes have come to dominate the urban culture and lifestyle of contemporary China.

Jia Pingwa's 贾平凹 (b. 1952) novel *City in Ruins* (废都, 1993) was the best-selling novel in 1993 and gave rise to a series of heated cultural debates by intellectuals on the loss of "humanist spirit" (人文精神) in works such as those of Jia and Wang Shuo. Though Jia primarily writes about the rural, he was inspired to write about his urban home after a trip to the United States in order to rectify misperceptions there of an "authentic China" situated solely in the countryside. *City in Ruins*, which is set in Xijing (the western capital), a transparent reference to Xi'an, graphically recounts the sexual exploits of a famous author, Zhuang Zhidie 庄之蝶, drawing on many conventions of the traditional Ming and Qing novel. Jia's "deletion" of words in the midst of intense erotic scenes (replicating cleaned-up versions of erotic Chinese classics and mimicking socialist censorship) increased the novel's commercial value. An important subplot is a libel lawsuit by one of Zhuang's lovers, who sues Zhuang and the author of an article that recounts their love affair. The lawsuit forces Zhuang to confront his own identity through the words of others, and the notion of "authorial authenticity" is increasingly called into question throughout the novel as the classical literary allusion to the author's name (literally, "Zhuang's Butterfly") suggests. The ancient city wall also figures prominently in the novel as a symbolic demarcation between rural and urban space, locales that in turn figure the authentic self and the constructed self. Whereas some critics decry it as nothing more than pornography reflective of (and contributing to) the decadence of the 1990s, the novel remains a well-crafted commentary on the impotency of intellectuals in late twentieth-century society.

The Song of Everlasting Sorrow (长恨歌, 1995), by the Shanghai-based writer Wang Anyi 王安忆 (b. 1954), resembles *City in Ruins* in its depiction of a city in the shadow of the past. Wang, a prolific writer who gained critical acclaim with her rural-based "Three Loves" series from the mid-1980s, portrays Shanghai's historical vicissitudes by following the life of Wang Qiyao 王琦瑶 from beauty queen to empty nester. The most acclaimed work by one of China's most eminent and prolific writers, *Song* won the coveted Mao Dun Literary Award (茅盾文学奖) in 2000 and was adapted for the stage in 2003 and to the film and television screens in 2005. The novel is evenly divided into three parts, which correspond to Shanghai's Republican era in the 1930s and 1940s, the socialist modernization of the 1950s and 1960s, and the post-Mao 1980s. Throughout the novel Wang Anyi details the "petty urbanite" (小市民) yearnings that exude from Shanghai's alleyway courtyard (弄堂 or 里弄) neighborhoods. Shanghai's "feminine" qualities of superficiality, excess, decadence, and artificiality are dignified, its qualities portrayed as a necessary component in China's cultural configuration—the gossip of the alleys a counter to orthodox ideology, the charm of everyday life offsetting the weight of politics, the feminine excesses of the south balancing masculine northern starkness. Wang Qiyao is portrayed as a blend of the qualities of elegance and banality and thus is emblematic of the "essence" of Shanghai, a nostalgic acknowledgment that its everyday charm, embodied in the alleyways, is fading and destined to die, as Wang does, a fateful death. Like Eileen Chang 张爱玲, whose Shanghai love stories contrast the epic narratives of "loves that destroy cities" with the mundane sentiments of modernity, Wang Anyi characterizes Shanghai's pathos as something marginalized, trivial, and depoliticized. "This bottled-up pain differs from that which the Tang Emperor felt for Yang Guifei and the Chu Emperor felt for his beloved concubine," says the narrator. "It is not the kind of grand heroic pain that moves heaven and earth; but base and lowly like pebbles and dirt" (Wang Anyi 2008: 12). Writing in the mid-1990s, as Shanghai urban development was taking off with a vengeance, Wang Anyi mourns the intensely personal losses sustained by globalization, for Shanghai without its alleyways is no longer Shanghai. The ironic narrative voice undermines Shanghai's vaunted image as a glamorous global city, rejecting the utilitarian values that caused its urban aesthetic to be destroyed.

In the mid-1990s, several new forms of urban literature emerged in mainland China. Variously labeled "new urbanite fiction" (新市民小说), "new-state-of-affairs fiction" (新状态小说), or literature by a "belated generation" (晚生代) who came of age in the 1990s, these works portray contemporary urban life in the throes of the market economy, intense commercialization, and radically transforming urban space. Although the new economic configuration leaves some intellectuals at a loss, in search of a new position in society, others relish their freedom to explore previously taboo topics. Further, as the Communist

Party increasingly absolves itself of its previous role as moral standard-bearer and meaning-giver for the individual, these writers often explore themes of individual ethics and purpose in life.

He Dun 何顿 (b. 1958) is one of the best-known representatives of the "belated generation" of writers. He graduated from art school in the 1980s and taught art in a Changsha middle school for several years before quitting his job to do business in interior design. His lifestyle change from idealistic academic to practical businessman followed the pattern of many in the early 1990s who chose to "take the plunge [into business]" (下海). With his change in lifestyle came an evolution of values and worldview, and he began to write about the attitudinal changes accompanying the "new state of affairs" of the 1990s, where individual choices abounded and personal ethics were redefined and reexamined. He writes realistic accounts of Changsha closely based on personal experience, and he first gained critical acclaim for his novellas "Hello, Younger Brother" (弟弟你好, 1993), "Life Is Not a Crime" (生活无罪, 1993), and "I Don't Care" (我不想事, 1993).

"Hello, Younger Brother" depicts a young man who is a loser by most standards, disillusioned after failing to get into Beijing University and unmotivated by his subsequent job as an elementary school teacher. Married to one woman and impregnating another, Deng Heping 邓和平 is kicked out of his parents' house, quits his job, and joins a classmate selling cigarettes on the open market. He falls in love with the man's wife, whose contacts lead him to a job managing a nightclub. After his classmate is executed for dealing heroin and Heping divorces his wife, he marries his love and the couple start an extremely profitable business supplying decorating materials. However, the story ends on a shocking note: just as the protagonist has "found" himself in a profitable job with a lovely wife, fate intervenes and his wife and unborn child are killed in a motorcycle accident. The value of material success in the 1990s is shown to be as ephemeral as political or academic success proved in the 1980s.

He Dun's stories are peppered with references to fate, something striking to readers in the wake of twentieth-century campaigns to eradicate superstition in mainland China. The rise of superstitious practices in the 1990s is often directly related to the market economy. He Dun elaborates on this fact in one of his more ideologically explicit novels, *The Himalayas* (喜马拉雅山, 1998). His teacher-turned-businessman protagonist claims, "The majority of Chinese businessmen in the 1990s aren't controlled by faith or ideology, they don't talk about beliefs or politics or ideas, and they certainly don't talk about movies or art, what they talk about is superstition. That's what they believe!" (He Dun 1998: 358). In many of his later works, He Dun's protagonists search unsuccessfully for meaningful spiritual ideals, at odds with the decadent business environment of the city.

The Nanjing-based writer Zhu Wen 朱文 (b. 1967), like He Dun, writes new-state-of-affairs fiction based on his experiences in contemporary urban settings. Zhu Wen's comic story "I Love Dollars" (我爱美元, 1995) shook the literary establishment with the carefree manner in which the young male protagonist, a Nanjing author in his early twenties, has casual sex with prostitutes and even arranges for his father to join him in his escapades. This attempt to turn 1980s sexual conservatism on its head (while adding a twist to the notion of filial piety) is one of the hallmarks of 1990s urban literature—a celebration of individuality and social freedom often expressed through sexual licentiousness.

Zhu's novel *What's Trash, What's Love?* (什么是垃圾，什么是爱, 1998) is a more penetrating reworking of similar themes. Xiao Ding 小丁 is in his late twenties, a struggling Nanjing writer whose father brags about his son's nonexistent success and whose mother prays for her son to get a wife (to prevent him from contracting venereal disease). Zhu Wen depicts the angst and confusion plaguing Xiao Ding and his circle of friends that are not easily remedied by lucrative jobs, free love, drugs, or even self-sacrificing volunteer work. Rather than write about such aimlessness in a didactic, moralizing manner, new-state-of-affairs literature provides a plethora of realistic details, leaving readers to draw their own conclusions. Xiao Ding is frequently *fan* (烦, fed up, disgusted) with his life, and in the manner of Jiangnan stylists, Zhu Wen details the smallest aspects of Xiao Ding's troubles, right down to his lack of toilet paper after using a filthy public toilet. Xiao Ding refuses to assist a friend in his search for his missing daughter (who has been kidnapped and gang-raped, an increasingly common occurrence in the Chinese metropolis), but he stumbles into volunteer work in a futile attempt to find purpose. The novel closes with Xiao Ding, who is recovering from venereal disease, having sex with an old flame whose boyfriend died of a drug overdose, leaving him feeling more "disgusted" than ever. The novel ends as it opens, with the protagonist alone in a bar, his mouth gaping wide in a ludicrous silent scream—an appropriate coda for a literary mode that depicts existence as cyclical and meaningless.

The Beijing native Chen Ran (陈染 b. 1962) first gained critical acclaim with her short story "Sunshine Between the Lips" (嘴唇里的阳光, 1992), an experimental piece where dental work functions as a euphemism for childhood sexual abuse. Her controversial first novel, *A Private Life* (私人生活, 1996), is Ni Niuniu's 倪拗拗 interior monologue reflecting on her life in Beijing from her school days in the mid-1970s until her psychological breakdown at age thirty in the mid-1990s. *A Private Life* explores the usual topics of home life, school, friendship, romance, and sexuality, but in an avant-garde style that blends philosophical statements and poetic asides with idiosyncratic perspectives on events (or nonevents). The urban environment is described in a muted, understated fashion, and detailed descriptions of interior, psychic space serve to highlight the city's relative absence in the narrative. The claustrophobic, introspective tone of the novel is only temporarily alleviated by descriptions of walking in the city or an occasional drive to the rural suburbs. Niuniu repeatedly alludes to her ever-present sense of unease in the city's exterior space, often coded as male: dominant, suffocating, time bound, unfeeling. This is in contrast to inner spaces, which she associates with tropes of the female: obscure, eternal, sensitive, and sensuous. She augments her feminist analogies with pastoral sentiments—not unlike those of the 1930s Beijing school of literature (京派) that promoted rural values—by launching into diatribes of the rape of the pristine countryside by the colonizing city.

Niuniu's reclusion is a direct result of the city's encroachment on her private space. The ever-expanding boulevards of Beijing invade previously enclosed spaces, just as Baron Georges-Eugène Haussmann's boulevards of the nineteenth century broke down the hermetically sealed world of the old medieval enclaves of Paris. Commercial construction and residential developments systematically destroy Beijing's secluded alley communities and traditional courtyard houses (四合院). The intrusion of the city on Niuniu's already disjointed internal space results in her breakdown. Her bathroom, which she narcissistically decorates with mirrors so that she can gaze at herself in the bathtub, is seen as an ordered, hygienic place of wholeness and sanctity where she can integrate herself to offset the chaotic fragmentation she experiences within herself and outside in the city.

In a 1997 interview, Chen Ran noted that *A Private Life* had been criticized because it is *geren* (个人)—about an individual—"which is devalued by default since most value writing about larger state issues. The first 'mistake' according to Chinese cultural values is to write about something private, something individual. But my perspective is exactly the opposite—I think the more individual something is, the more universal it is." Chen Ran's writing on the city privileges female over male, local culture over global culture, and the private over the public sphere as a means of speaking to collective issues in the postmodern metropolis.

Qiu Huadong 邱华栋 (b. 1969) is one of the most ambitious writers of urban fiction in his self-proclaimed attempt to become "the Balzac of China" through rich descriptions invoking the ethos of the capital. Qiu revealed in an interview that his day job as a journalist for an economics journal affords him unique opportunities to explore a wide variety of Beijing lifestyles. As a relatively new resident of Beijing, raised in Urumqi and schooled in Wuhan, he expresses in many of his works, such as *City Chariot* (城市战车, 1997), the shock of trying to survive as an artist in an alienating commercial metropolis.

Fly Eyes (蝇眼, 1998) is one of Qiu's most successful works. In it he recounts five stories of Beijing residents whose lives are related by "six degrees of separation" and, in the tradition of John Dos Passos, depicts the complexity of the city through individual lives. Qiu's characters acknowledge that they are "two-dimensional people" (平面人) who resist plumbing the depths of existence. Yet while they indulge in every possibility urban life offers, they also admit they are bored and disgusted with it. What distinguishes this generation is their very awareness of the "flattening" process they have undergone. As in most new-state-of-affairs novels, Qiu's characters make abrupt lifestyle changes, often from idealist artists, poets, or scholars to businesspersons in every conceivable line of work. In recollecting the idealism of their pasts, some who are satiated with the get-rich materialistic lifestyle of the 1990s even attempt to return to a slower, simpler way of living. However, it soon becomes obvious that the thinkers and closet idealists in his stories are unable to survive, not only in the metropolis but also outside it. As one of his characters from *Fly Eyes* puts it, "We can't escape the city. As soon as we leave [Beijing] we'll want to return, because this is our stage, the place that nourishes dreams, and we depend on it for our very breath" (Qiu Huadong 1998: 250). Those characters who attempt to find a deeper sense of meaning and value in the city perish in the attempt, whereas the "survivors" live materialistic and banal middle-class lives.

In *City Chariot*, Qiu portrays a new kind of urban *flâneur* through the I-narrator, an artist who wanders around Beijing in search of excitement, self, and meaning for his life and art. His *flâneurie* constitutes a new form of vision and spectatorship to represent contemporary globalized urban space. The new structure of vision and representation is always partial because this fragmented postmodern urban space resists any form of totalization. Although this artist-*flâneur* tries to possess the city, he becomes possessed with its fascinating and shocking spectacles. This "being in the world" thus impedes his seeing and understanding. In many ways Qiu's stylistic collage, language games, and heteroglossia also epitomize the immense, complex, and bewildering metropolis.

Accompanying the formation of the glamorous commercialized and globalized urban space and culture represented in fiction by writers such as Chi Li and Qiu Huadong, there emerged another urban space of disenfranchised "lower-level people" (底层人). *Diceng* (底层) means the lower level, but its spatial connotation also refers to the foundation. *Diceng* people are the main force behind Chinese urbanization and modernization, but also the victims of this same process. The emergence of *diceng* literature as a socially engaged cultural praxis represents a new realist impulse that turns its attention to the social problems and contradictions created by Chinese economic development. In many ways *diceng* literature continues the neorealist tradition of zero-degree and antiallegorical writing by refusing to lyricize suffering, poeticize oppression, and sentimentalize poverty.

Among the representative works of *diceng* literature, *Loach* (泥鳅), by Qingdao-based You Fengwei 尤凤伟 (b. 1943), stands out for its broad picture of the hopeless and miserable life of rural migrants in the city. Guo Rui 国瑞, the protagonist, initially wants to find a job and live an honest life; however, his repeated efforts are thwarted by the cruel exploitation and unjust treatment he encounters in the city. First reduced to providing sex services to rich women, he is then used as a figurehead for a fake company, eventually becoming a scapegoat for a large fraud conspiracy organized by corrupt government officials and businessmen. Here the city is a dangerous and corruptive force that takes away Guo Rui's life and ruins many other migrants' hopes and lives. The new urban space is a glamorous façade that hides a vicious world of desires, power, and money. If contemporary Chinese economic development has created new bourgeois and middle classes, this same process has also created *diceng* people. The term "poor people," after its disappearance during the socialist period, has come back as a dominant socioeconomic phenomenon of postsocialist China. *Diceng* literature demonstrates the moral stance and social engagement of Chinese writers and raises the crucial and urgent question of how to solve this increasingly serious problem of socioeconomic inequality.

The city is both a physical topography and, to use James Donald's words, an "imagined community"—constellations of discourses, texts, symbols, and representations. This literary and cultural praxis therefore both represents and contributes to urban reality, experience, and culture, and it should be seen as an integral part of the city. Meanwhile the dialectical relationship between the built environment and semiotic representations opens up a critical space for cultural intervention, social engagement, and continued inquiry into the city.

Bibliography

Chen Ran 陈染. *Siren shenghuo* 私人生活 (Private life). In *Chen Ran wenji* 陈染文集 (Collected works of Chen Ran), vol. 4. Yangzhou: Jiangsu wenyi, 1996.

——. "Sunshine Between the Lips." Trans. Shelley Wing Chan. In Howard Goldblatt, ed., *Chairman Mao Would Not Be Amused: Fiction from Today's China*, 112–129. New York: Grove Press, 1995.

Chi Li 池莉. "Lailaiwangwang" 来来往往 (Coming and going). *Shiyue*, 4 (1997).

He Dun 何顿. *Shenghuo wuzui* 生活无罪 (Life is not a crime). Beijing: Huayi, 1995.

——. *Ximalaya Shan* 喜马拉雅山 (The Himalayas). Nanjing: Jiangsu wenyi, 1998.

Jia Pingwa 贾平凹. *Feidu* 废都 (City in ruins). Beijing: Beijing, 1993.

Kong, Shuyu. *Consuming Literature: Best Sellers and the Commercialization of Literary Production in Contemporary China*. Stanford, CA: Stanford University Press, 2005.

Liu, Heng. *Black Snow*. Trans. Howard Goldblatt. New York: Grove Press, 1990.

Lu, Jie, ed. *China's Literary and Cultural Scenes at the Turn of the 21st Century*. London: Routledge, 2008.

——. "Cultural Invention and Cultural Intervention: Reading Chinese Urban Fiction of the Nineties." *Modern Chinese Literature and Culture* 13, 1 (Spring 2001): 107–139.

McGrath, Jason. *Postsocialist Modernity: Chinese Cinema, Literature, and Criticism in the Market Age*. Stanford, CA: Stanford University Press, 2008.

Qiu Huadong 邱华栋. *Chengshi zhanche* 城市战车 (City chariot). Beijing: Zuojia, 1997.

——. *Ying yan* 蝇眼 (Fly eyes). Changchun: Changchun, 1998.

Su Tong. *Rice*. Trans. Howard Goldblatt. New York: William Morrow. 1995.

Tang, Xiaobing. *Chinese Modern: The Heroic and the Quotidian*. Durham, NC: Duke University Press, 2000.

Visser, Robin. *Cities Surround the Countryside: Urban Aesthetics in Postsocialist China*. Durham, NC: Duke University Press, 2010.

——. "Displacement of the Urban-Rural Confrontation in Su Tong's Fiction." *Modern Chinese Literature* 9, 1 (1995): 113–138.

——. "Privacy and Its Ill Effects in Post-Mao Urban Fiction." In Bonnie McDougall, ed., *Chinese Concepts of Privacy*, 229–256. Leiden: Brill, 2002.

Wang Anyi 王安忆. *Changhen ge* 长恨歌 (Song of everlasting sorrow). Beijing: Zuojia, 1996.

——. *The Song of Everlasting Sorrow: A Novel of Shanghai*. Trans. Michael Berry and Susan Chan Egan. New York: Columbia University Press, 2008.

Wang, Ban. "Love at Last Sight: Nostalgia, Commodity, and Temporality in Wang Anyi's *Song of Unending Sorrow*." *positions: east asian culture critique* 10, 3 (2002): 669–694.

Wang, Ban, and Jie Lu, ed. *China and New Left Visions*. Lanham, MD: Rowman and Littlefield, 2012.

Wang, Jing. *High Culture Fever: Politics, Aesthetics, and Ideology in Deng's China*. Berkeley: University of California Press, 1996.

Wang, Shuo. *Playing for Thrills: A Mystery*. Trans. Howard Goldblatt. New York: Penguin, 1997.

——. *Wanzhu* 顽主 (Masters of mischief). In *Wang Shuo wenji* 王朔文集 (Collected works of Wang Shuo), 2:106–167. Beijing: Huayi, 1995.

You Fengwei 尤凤伟. *Niqiu* 泥鳅 (Loach). *Dangdai*, nos. 3–4 (2002).

Zhang, Yiwu. "Postmodernism and Chinese Novels of the Nineties." Trans. Michael Berry. *boundary 2* 24, 3 (1997): 247–259.

Zhu, Wen 朱文. *I Love Dollars and Other Stories*. Trans. Julia Lovell. New York: Columbia University Press, 2007.

——. *Shenme shi laji, shenme shi ai* 什么是垃圾，什么是爱 (What's trash, what's love?). Nanjing: Jiangsu wenyi, 1998.

——. *Wo ai Meiyuan* 我爱美元 (I love American dollars). Beijing: Zuojia, 1995.

46

XI XI AND TALES OF HONG KONG

DAISY S. Y. NG

Xi Xi 西西 is the pseudonym of Zhang Yan 张彦, foremost among the first generation of writers to have grown up in Hong Kong. Xi Xi was born in Shanghai in 1938 to Cantonese parents. Shortly after the Communist takeover, at the age of twelve, she moved with her family to Hong Kong. She graduated from the Grantham College of Education in 1958 and became a primary school teacher until she gave up her career to become a full-time writer at age thirty-nine. Although Xi Xi won a number of literary prizes in Hong Kong in the 1960s and 1970s, her name became widely known only after she was awarded Taiwan's prestigious *United Daily* 联合报 prize for fiction in 1983. In the last three decades, Xi Xi has been one of Hong Kong's most prolific writers. Best known for her fiction, she is equally at home in poetry, scriptwriting, the occasional essay, translation, film review, and art criticism. She was also editor of two major Hong Kong literary journals.

Throughout her writing career Xi Xi has used numerous pen names. From the mid-1970s onward, however, she has published most of her fiction, including her collected works, under the name Xi Xi. The character *xi* (西) means "west," but Zhang Yan chose this pen name not because of its literal meaning but because of its graphic quality. She explains:

> When I was young I used to love playing a game similar to hopscotch, which we called "Building a House" or "Aeroplane Hopping." First you draw a series of squares on the ground. Then you tie a string of paper clips

into a knot and toss it into one of the squares and start hopping from one square to the next until you reach the square with the knot in it. Then you pick it up and hop your way back to where you started. . . . The Chinese character "xi" looks like a girl in a skirt, her two feet planted in a square. Put two of them side by side, and they are like two frames of a film, a girl in a skirt playing hopscotch in two squares.

(Xi Xi 1986: 84)

Stephen Soong (1986) suggests that this pseudonym reveals the childlike vision of the author, and other critics attribute Xi Xi's extraordinary use of narrative point of view in her fictional work, such as *My City: A Hong Kong Story* (我城, 1979), to the freshness of her childlike perception. Even more interesting is how Xi Xi wrenches the conventional and impersonal definition (west) from the pictograph and reinvests it with a new visual quality and a personal meaning. Moreover, by reduplicating the character, she makes the linguistic sign come alive with movement: a girl playing hopscotch. This semiotic creativity is indicative of a literary imagination unconstrained by narrative conventions.

Xi Xi's playful reinvention of the character *xi* is exemplary of the creative spirit behind her incessant exploration of new ways of storytelling. Her fiction is very often a reinterpretation of history, myth, legend, art, and literary works. She always strives to tell new stories through old ones, as suggested by the title of her collection, *Stories Within Stories* (故事里的故事, 1998). In this collection, Xi Xi rewrites well-known episodes from famous novels, making the reader see the familiar event with different eyes. For instance, in "Banana Fan" (芭蕉扇, 1987), by relating the incident in which Monkey King forces Princess Iron Fan 铁扇公主 to lend him the magical banana fan in *Journey to the West* (西游记, 1570s) from the perspective of Princess Iron Fan's cat, Xi Xi brings to light the injustice others suffered because of the hero's self-righteousness. In this story, Xi Xi uses first-person narrative to rupture the illusion of transparency and objectivity of the omniscient narrator in traditional Chinese novels. The first-person narrative voice of the cat allows the reader to see Princess Iron Fan as a woman who is mistreated by both her husband and the Monkey King, whereas in the original text she is simply cast as an unreasonable shrew whose refusal to lend them her precious fan constitutes another barrier the protagonists must overcome on their pilgrimage.

Xi Xi breaks down the monolithic discourse of heroism by using multiple first-person narrations in "Family Matters in the Chentang Pass Commander's Household" (陈塘关总兵府家事, 1987). This story retells the legend of Nezha 哪吒 in *Creation of the Gods* (封神榜), a reputed Ming novel built on folktales about the transition from the Shang dynasty (c.16–11 B.C.) to the Zhou (c.11–770 B.C.). Nezha is the third son of Li Jing 李靖, the garrison commander of Chentang Pass, and is said to be the reincarnation of the Pearl Spirit. He is sent down by a decree from the Jade Emptiness Palace to assist King Wu of the future Zhou dynasty in launching an attack on King Zhou, a notorious tyrant fated to become the last ruler of the Shang. Nezha's birth hour predestines him to break the commandment against killing; when Nezha is only seven years old, he stirs up trouble by killing the Yaksha Sea Patrolman and the third son of the East Sea Dragon King in a quarrel, and later by beating up the Dragon King. He also accidentally kills one of Lady Rock's disciples and assaults another. However, his master considers these deaths "a minor matter," for fate has dictated that Nezha is to lead the war against the Shang, and so the master helps Nezha avoid persecution from the Dragon King and Lady Rock. Nezha's killings nonetheless cause an irreparable rift in his relationship with his father, Li Jing, and he mutilates himself in front of his parents to cut ties with his family. After Nezha's death, on his master's advice, his spirit appears to his mother and begs her to build a temple for him so that he may be reincarnated into human form (which will happen after three years' worship by the people). When Li Jing finds out that Nezha has been worshipped as a god, he smashes Nezha's image and destroys the temple. Nezha's master, however, reincarnates Nezha, who then relentlessly seeks revenge against Li Jing until the immortals give the latter a magical pagoda to subdue Nezha and force the two to reconcile.

Against this mythical background of dynastic change, the title of Xi Xi's story is ironic. By calling Nezha's legend "family matters" (家事), Xi Xi relocates Nezha within a human and familial context. His actions are judged according to his roles as son and brother, not excused because of his predetermined role in the war against the Shang. By giving the first-person narrative voices to Nezha himself and to the numerous people involved with him, such as his parents, brother, servant, and especially innocent victims and witnesses of his whimsical violence, Xi Xi unveils the absurdity of the divinities' arbitrary indulgence in Nezha's egotistical and irresponsible behavior. The multiple narrative angles raise questions about the definition of heroism as well as the meaning of fate, and they challenge the reader to reflect on his or her conditioned response to the original text, which centers on Nezha and justifies his every act as simply predestined.

Through the use of first-person narration, Xi Xi gives voice to "minor" characters and puts "trivial" matters on center stage. Her fiction is never about the exceptional deeds of well-sung heroes, just about the ordinary life of common people. For instance, in her fiction about Hong Kong, Xi Xi is interested in presenting a polyphony of personal voices, not in weaving a grand narrative. She is not content with presenting things from a single perspective and a fixed position; instead, her narrative is volatile and diverse. The most acclaimed example is her first novel, *My City*. This novel does not have a conventional linear narrative that relies on emplotment. Rather, it consists of independent scenes, each with its own narrative style. Critics have compared the narrative technique in *My City* to the "scattered perspective" of traditional Chinese "long scroll" painting such as the famous Song dynasty *Along the River During the Qingming Festival* (清明上河图); instead of maintaining one focal point and a stationary position of observer, here the angles of perception are multiple and the viewer's position is mobile. In fact, Xi Xi herself also makes explicit her use of "scattered perspective" and mobile viewpoint in the short story "Hand Scroll" (手卷, 1987).

It is not coincidental that Xi Xi's narrative techniques in many of her fictional works have been compared to visual media such as painting and film. When *My City* was serialized in the literary supplement of *Hong Kong Express* (快报) in 1975, Xi Xi herself drew the illustrations for her novel. From 1974 to 1975, she also wrote a weekly column of essays on painting, some of which are collected in *Scrapbook* (剪贴册, 1991). Xi Xi is also well versed in film, having been a film critic, scriptwriter, and independent filmmaker in the 1960s. Her interest in experimenting with the film medium is most notable in her first novella, "Story of the Eastern City" (东城故事, 1966). The novella is divided into sections, each like a scene within a film. The narrative includes instructions such as "fade-in," "fade-out," "cut," "dissolve," "track," "span," "close-up," "medium shot," "background music," and "subtitle." The reader not only reads but must also visualize the scenes.

Xi Xi continues to explore textual relations between different media in her later work. The short story "Drinking with General Li among the Flowers" (陪李金吾花下饮, 1997) is a sophisticated attempt at connecting the poetry of Du Fu 杜甫 to the modern film medium. Another brilliant exercise not only in interdisciplinary but also cross-cultural reading is "Marvels of a Floating City" (浮城志异, 1988), one of Xi Xi's best-known fables about Hong Kong. This story can be seen as a creative interpretation of the paintings of the Belgian artist René Magritte. The text is based on visual images but is not contained by them. The synergy between Western painting and the Chinese text creates what the translator, Eva Hung (1997: xii) calls "a sense of indivisible heterogeneity which is representative of Hong Kong culture at its best."

The most successful example of intertextuality in Xi Xi's work is "The Fertile Town Chalk Circle" (肥土镇灰阑记, 1988), another of her allegories on Hong Kong. The story is based on a Yuan dynasty drama by Li Xingdao 李行道 about a court case of the legendary judge Bao Zheng 包拯 (999–1062). Judge Bao was a real official in the Northern Song dynasty, but he is elevated to a mythical stature in folklore and operas as the representative of justice in both the human world and the netherworld. The Yuan play is about two women fighting for a five-year-old child, the heir of his murdered father's fortune; both claim to be the biological mother. Judge Bao orders the son placed in the center of a chalk circle, with each claimant holding one of his hands; whoever succeeds in pulling the child to her side, declares the judge, will win parental rights. Judge Bao discovers the true mother, of course, as the one without the heart to pull her son apart.

Li Xingdao's play was the inspiration for *The Caucasian Chalk Circle* by the German dramatist Bertolt Brecht (1898–1956), who adapted the narrative form of traditional Chinese drama in his renowned Epic Theater. Brecht's idea of "alienation effect" in theater in turn informs Xi Xi's "The Fertile Town Chalk Circle." Critics have pointed out that although Xi Xi's story is based on the Yuan play, it is closer in form and spirit to Brecht's drama. The story is retold from the point of view of the child, who is at once the child in the play and the actor playing the child on stage. However, the narrator's voice is constrained by neither the role of the child character nor that of the actor. The narrator speaks not only in the voice of an unusually precocious child who has witnessed and understood the premeditated crimes against his parents but also as a commentator on issues in traditional Chinese society, such as legal injustice and the widespread corruption of government officials, the forced prostitution of poor women, and the psychological and practical constraints faced by scholars. Moreover, he undermines Judge Bao's authority by questioning the wisdom and effectiveness of using the chalk circle to settle the dispute. He even contests the way his future is decided for him without his testimony and freedom of choice. Unlike Li Xingdao's opera and Brecht's play, Xi Xi's story ends not with a resolved case but with a protest from the narrator: "I am standing here, in the court, at center stage. I ask you all, members of the audience, to listen, I have something to say. After six hundred years, are you still not going to let me grow up?" (*Marvels*: 106).

"The Fertile Town Chalk Circle" has been widely read as an allegory about Hong Kong's lack of representation in the 1980s Sino-British talks over its future. Other works of the "Fertile Town" series—"The Story of Fertile Town" (肥土镇的故事, 1982), "Apple" (苹果, 1982), "Town Mantra" (镇咒, 1984), "An Addendum to Cosmicomics" (宇宙奇趣补遗, 1988), and the novel *Flying Carpet* (飞毡, 1996)—have also been read as parables of Hong Kong. Though an allegorical interpretation can be readily supported by textual evidence, Xi Xi's fiction is never simply realism and always more than allegory. Whether using a fable to reconstruct the history of Hong Kong, as in "The Story of Fertile Town" and *Flying Carpet*, or describing facets of Hong Kong urban life, as in *My City* and *Beautiful Building* (美丽大厦, 1990), Xi Xi persists in representing the voices of common people at the margins of the grand historical discourse on Hong Kong. Her work poses an artistic challenge to preconceived notions of Hong Kong not only by presenting alternative voices but also by problematizing the relationship of the reader to the text in the way the audience is questioned in "The Fertile Town Chalk Circle":

> What have you really come to see? Have you come to see costumes, make-up, movement, set, and plot, to see a classical play, an epic, a narrative or a dialectical play? Or have you come to see me, just an insignificant little child on the stage, and to see how I must struggle along life's

road to gain some measure of dignity? Or did you come to see the *Chalk Circle*, to see Judge Bao once again act the part of the clever and just official?

(Xi, Xi, *Marvels*: 105)

Whatever the reader comes to see, Xi Xi (2000: 513) rejoins in the final words of *Flying Carpet*: "You want me to tell you about the story of Fertile Town. I believe I have already told you all that I know and all that you want to know." Just like her pseudonym, the story of Hong Kong told by Xi Xi resists a literal definition. It is through imaginative use of language that she represents the vibrant struggle of Hong Kong in fashioning a self-identity neither simply constrained by British colonialism nor purely impelled by Chinese nationalism.

Xi Xi's tales of Hong Kong have acquired even greater importance in the years following the return of Hong Kong to China in 1997. An anthology of Xi Xi's short fiction up to 1997 was published in 2008 — ten years after the handover — with the express intention to chronicle not only her representative works over four decades but also "how she writes about the various changes of China and Hong Kong and how she contemplates the interactions between the two places" (He 2008: 9). Also a local writer, the editor He Furen 何福仁 (2008: 10) frames his selection of short stories in *Floating City 1.2.3: New Analysis of Xi Xi's Fiction* (浮城1.2.3: 西西小说新析) with a table that maps Xi Xi's fictional works against the sociopolitical issues that have informed the subject matters of particular stories spanning the period from 1979 through 1997. He makes clear that the anthology was published with younger generations of readers in mind and gives a brief review of the historical milestones in the relationships of Hong Kong and mainland China as a background for reading Xi Xi's fiction, while taking care to add that Xi Xi's works are "neither history nor sociology" but "transformation of particular social issues into art through the form of fiction" (11).

Nowhere can the symbolic significance of Xi Xi's tales of Hong Kong be more manifest than in the social movements that arose in the years following the handover. During the Star Ferry Pier preservation protest in December 2006 and Queen's Pier protests in April 2007, which opposed the demolition of landmarks considered by many to be cultural heritage sites in which the collective memory of Hong Kong people resided, Xi Xi's *My City* was endowed with a new political meaning when demonstrators engaged in ritualistic readings of the book, tearing off and burning each page after it had been read aloud. Around the same time, a well-known local filmmaker named Qiu Litao 丘礼涛 made a short film on the issue of local identity in Hong Kong and sprinkled quotations from *My City* throughout the film. He recounts these passionate moments of reading *My City* in a 2014 documentary produced by another filmmaker, Jiang Qiongzhu 江琼珠. The film, titled *We Always Read Xi Xi* (我们总

是读西西), features people from different walks of life reading and appreciating selected works of Xi Xi. The collective but diverse reading experience of Xi Xi's works illustrates how a younger generation of readers invests new meanings in her tales of Hong Kong. As Liao Weitang 廖伟棠 (2012: 32) succinctly puts it in an interview with Xi Xi:

> This tenderness was what I felt when I first read Xi Xi's *My City* and her poetry collection *Bedrock* (石磬) over a decade ago, a decade later there were youths of our city who cited *My City* to support their resistance, and another decade later I re-read *My City* to reflect on how to reconstruct Hong Kong with them—Hong Kong, it has been named "my city" by Xi Xi and the idealists of her generation, and the young activists generations after them have verified this name by means of their attitudes and actions; now my city is no longer just the name of a work of fiction but a conviction put into practice by the new Ah Guo (阿果) and Happy Mak (麦快乐), and even inspiring the youths of the mainland and Taiwan—this is my reading in 2010.

Bibliography

Chen Jieyi 陈洁仪. *Yuedu Feituzhen: Lun Xi Xi de xiaoshuo xushi* 阅读肥土镇：论西西的小说叙事 (Reading *Fertile Town*: A discussion of Xi Xi's fictional narrative). Hong Kong: Oxford University Press, 1998.

Chen Qingqiao 陈清桥. "Lun dushide wenhua xiangxiang: bing du Xi Xi shuo Xianggang" 论都市的文化想象：并读西西说香港 (The cultural imagination of the city: Reading how Xi Xi speaks of Hong Kong). *Guodu* 1 (1995): 6–14.

Chen Yanxia 陈燕遐. "Shuxie Xianggang: Wang Anyi, Shi Shuqing, Xi Xi de Xianggang gushi" 书写香港：王安忆，施淑青，西西的香港故事 (Writing Hong Kong: The Hong Kong stories of Wang Anyi, Shi Shuqing, and Xi Xi). *Journal of Modern Literature in Chinese* 2, 2 (1999): 91–117.

Chen Zhide 陈智德. *Jieti wocheng: Xianggang wenxue 1950–2005* 解体我城：香港文学1950–2005 (Deconstructing Hong Kong: Hong Kong literature, 1950–2005). Hong Kong: Huaqianshu, 2009.

Dong Qizhang 董启章. "Chengshi de xianshi jingyan yu wenben jingyan: yuedu 'Jiutu,' 'Wo cheng' he 'Jian zhi'" 城市的现实经验与文本经验：阅读《酒徒》，《我城》，和《剪纸》 (Urban reality experience and textual experience: Reading *The Drunkard*, *My City*, and *Paper Cut*). *Guodu* 2 (1995): 15–22.

He Furen 何福仁, ed. *Fucheng 1.2.3.: Xi Xi xiaoshuo xinxi* 浮城1.2.3：西西小说新析 (Floating City 1.2.3: New analysis of Xi Xi's fiction). Hong Kong: Joint Publishing, 2008.

Huang Jichi 黄继持. "Xi Xi lianzai xiaoshuo: yidu zaidu" 西西连载小说：忆读再读 (Xi Xi's serialized fiction: Remembering, reading, and rereading). *Bafang wenyi congkan* 12 (1990): 68–80.

Liao Weitang 廖伟棠. *Fucheng shumengren: Xianggang zuojia fangtanlu* 浮城述梦人：香港作家访谈录 (Narrators of dreams in Floating City: Interviews of Hong Kong writers). Hong Kong: Joint Publishing, 2012.

Soong, Stephen C. "Building a House: Introducing Xi Xi." In Xi Xi, *A Girl like Me and Other Stories*, 127–134. Hong Kong: Chinese University of Hong Kong, 1986.

Xi Xi 西西. *Dongcheng gushi* 东城故事 (Story of the eastern city). Hong Kong: Mingming, 1966.

——. *Fei zhan* 飞毡 (Flying carpet). Hong Kong: Suye, 1996.

——. *Flying Carpet: A Tale of Fertilla*. Trans. by Diana Yue. Hong Kong: Hong Kong University Press, 2000.

——. *A Girl like Me and Other Stories*. Hong Kong: Chinese University of Hong Kong, 1986.

——. *Gushili de gushi* 故事里的故事 (Stories within stories). Taipei: Hongfan, 1998.

——. *Jiantie ce* 剪贴册 (Scrapbook). Taipei: Hongfan, 1997.

——. *Marvels of a Floating City and Other Stories*. Ed. Eva Hung. Hong Kong: Chinese University of Hong Kong, 1997.

——. *Meili dasha* 美丽大厦 (Beautiful building). Taipei: Hongfan, 1990.

——. *My City: A Hong Kong Story*. Trans. Eva Hung. Hong Kong: Chinese University of Hong Kong, 1993.

——. "A Woman like Me." Trans. by Howard Goldblatt. In Joseph S. M. Lau and Howard Goldblatt, eds., *Columbia Anthology of Modern Chinese Literature*, 303–313. New York: Columbia University Press, 2007.

Xu Diqiang 许迪锵, ed. 《*Women zongshi du Xi Xi*》 *shouying tekan* 《我们总是读西西》首映特刊 (We always read the Xi Xi premiere catalogue). Hong Kong: Step Forward Multimedia, 2014.

Yu Fei 余非. *Changduanzhang: yuedu Xi Xi ji qita* 长短章：阅读西西及其他 (Long and short movements: Reading Xi Xi and others). Hong Kong: Suye, 1997.

47

WRITING TAIWAN'S FIN-DE-SIÈCLE SPLENDOR: ZHU TIANWEN AND ZHU TIANXIN

LINGCHEI LETTY CHEN

Like the Brontës of England, the Zhu family of Taiwan produced three girls who would grow up to become writers. Like the Brontës, too, only two of the Zhu sisters became productive and successful writers: Zhu Tianwen 朱天文 (b. 1956), the eldest, and Zhu Tianxin 朱天心 (b. 1958), the second daughter. The Zhu sisters come from a prominent literary family; their father, Zhu Xining 朱西宁 (1927–1998), was a celebrated military writer and an important participant in the development of Taiwan's literature in the 1950s and 1960s, while their mother, Liu Musha 刘慕沙 (b. 1935), a Hakka Taiwanese, was a translator of many modern Japanese literary works.

Both Zhu Tianwen and Zhu Tianxin began their writing careers when they were only sixteen and immediately became best-selling authors in Taiwan. Their early works, produced in the 1970s and early 1980s, are mainly nostalgic short stories of childhood and sentimental essays about longings for "the motherland," China. The Zhu sisters' deep roots in the Chinese literary tradition and their patriotic passion for China—to them mostly an imaginary homeland, inasmuch as traveling to China was at that time prohibited—are influences from their father, who followed Chiang Kai-shek's retreat from China to Taiwan in 1949, and their mentor, Hu Lancheng 胡兰成, who was an accomplished scholar and philosopher of Chinese literature and thought. The Zhu sisters' early works are consistent with the official, mainstream ideology and the sentiment that Taiwan was the defender and torchbearer of China's long cultural tradition, which was being destroyed on the mainland. Their writings since the mid-1980s resonate with the political, social, and cultural changes Taiwan's society underwent right before the annulment of martial law in 1987 and later. What their later works reflect are remarkable changes in the literary development in Taiwan and shared concerns about Taiwan's cultural identity. People in Taiwan have collectively arrived at a point of political and cultural self-awareness about Taiwan's relation to China, as well as how Taiwan should position itself in the era of globalization. As participants in and observers of this dynamic society, the Zhu sisters have concerned themselves with the effects of multiple cultural influences and the question of how to conceive an authentic cultural identity in such circumstances.

Zhu Tianwen began her writing career with a series of short stories, the first collection of which, *New Stories of Minister Qiao* (乔太守新记), was published in 1977. In the following years, she continued to write short stories and published four more books: *Legends* (传说, 1981), *Most Memorable Season* (最想念的季节, 1984), *City of High Summer* (炎夏之都, 1987), and *Fin-de-Siècle Splendor* (世纪末的华丽, 1990). Aside from fiction, she also wrote a large body of essays that are collected in *Notes of Tamkang* (淡江记, 1979), *Stories of Xiao Bi* (小毕的故事, 1983), *Three Sisters* (三姐妹, 1985), and *Afternoon Tea Conversations* (下午茶话题, 1992). But Zhu Tianwen is probably best known for her collaboration with Taiwan's internationally renowned film director Hou Hsiao-hsien 侯孝贤, for whom she wrote several film scripts (see "Chinese Literature and Film Adaptation"). In 1994, she finally wrote her first full-fledged novel, *Notes of a Desolate Man* (荒人手记, 1994). Thirteen years later, she published her second novel, *Witchtalk* (巫言, 2007).

Most scholars and critics regard the short story "Fin-de-Siècle Splendor" as marking a turning point for Zhu Tianwen, a forerunner of a new style of writing that comes to dominate *Notes of a Desolate Man*. Remarkably more sophisticated than the sentimental, nostalgic style of her earlier writing, it is, as the critic Zhan Hongzhi 詹宏志 characterizes it, a style reflected through "an aging voice." It is more linguistically experimental, sharper, colder, and more nihilistic in portraying urban existence. In "Fin-de-Siècle Splendor" and other stories collected under the same title, Zhu Tianwen's primary interest is to depict Taiwan's complex cultural scene, especially in Taipei. She draws attention to the dominant presence of foreign cultural elements to critique the tendency of people in Taiwan to idolize as well as commercialize foreign popular culture, embracing such things as Hollywood movies and stars, popular singers from Japan and the West (mainly the United States), and European fashions. The foreign cultural presence in Taiwan is the direct product of Japanese colonization (1895–1945) and Taiwan's fast-paced economic expansion. Taiwan's culture today is a hybrid of Chinese, native Taiwanese, and various foreign cultural imprints. How one makes sense of such a cultural hybrid is a question central to Taiwan society, and one that is pursued in Zhu Tianwen's writing. Her use of exoticized language, such as inserting English or Japanese words in the

Chinese text or including difficult-to-read translated foreign terms and phrases, reflects that hybridized condition.

Set in 1992 Taipei, "Fin-de-Siècle Splendor" tells the story of a professional model, Mia 米亚, who at the age of twenty-five already feels old and is ready for retirement. She is the mistress of a much older man, Lao Duan 老段, and enjoys life outside the institution of marriage. She and her model friends live only for the present, chasing the glamour and fun of big city life. Narcissism dominates their lives, reflected in the story's endless description of clothes and the young models' obsession with self-image. The language of "Fin-de-Siècle Splendor" is laden with fashionable designer brand names, scents, perfumes, the intricate texture and colors of fabric, and exotic plants and herbs. Mia centers her life on experiences and memories of colors and fragrances from the ever-changing world of fashion and from the dried plants she collects; these concrete objects define the meaning of her existence. What prevails in Zhu Tianwen's later works is a sense of individuality that manifests itself in a flair for exotic linguistic practices. Zhu's characters, male and female alike, are narcissistic. Her fashion models, for example, are always conscious of the image they convey. They are individualistic in the ways they live, the self-image they project, and the performative nature of their behavior. But the celebration of narcissism is not without irony: Mia's obsession with sensuous exotic objects reflects a culture that is saturated with commodities and in which the individual is subsumed by commercialism.

In such a milieu, time and history are reduced to fashion. The history of Taipei is marked by each emerging new fashion: 1986, frankincense; 1987, irises; the summer of 1990, pale seaside colors. To Mia and her model friends, time does not become history; it simply flows through life, neither treasured nor lamented. As Mia and her fashionable gang gaze at Taipei at dawn from the top of Mount Yangming, the city appears like a rising mirage, its image reflecting in the water vapor. The ephemerality of Taiwan's social and historical existence cannot be described better than in this powerful and chilling image.

Mia intends to create a sense of eternity by collecting dried flowers and herbs and learning how to make paper. With her first two pieces of handmade paper, she believes that this paper-making skill will sustain her until the day the world built by men collapses. She will rebuild the world with her memories of scents and colors; the record of her rebuilding will be written on her own rose paper. In this new vision, her individual subjectivity can become complete and independent from all institutions. This is a new brand of existentialism conceived at the end of the millennium, in the late capitalist metropolis, and at the juncture of Taiwan's emerging cultural self-awareness. On an allegorical level, Zhu Tianwen also calls attention to the politics of the center (China) versus the marginal (Taiwan), the material versus the spiritual, and woman versus man.

Although the characteristics of exoticism and narcissism have been consistently present in Zhu Tianwen's fiction since the late 1980s, it is in *Notes of a*

Desolate Man that these two characteristics come to pervade the narrative and become significant elements in the formation of a coherent sense of the self for the novel's gay protagonist, whose sexual identity is not yet accepted by society (see "Homoeroticism in Modern Chinese Literature"). Before this novel, Zhu Tianwen's employment of exoticism and her characters' narcissism emerge only in a more performative and deliberate fashion: in these works, although exoticism serves as a mirror to reflect the image of the narcissistic self, it is mainly a tool of cultural critique. In *Notes of a Desolate Man*, the coalition of narcissism and linguistic exoticism is the means by which the gay protagonist's sexual and cultural identities are explored. The novel's provocative subject matter (male homosexual eroticism), unusual authorial perspective (a female writer assuming the voice of a gay man), excessively exoticized and floral language (mixed with Buddhist scriptural language, English words, transcribed foreign names, and borrowed texts), and the indeterminacy of its genre (prose? fiction? allegory? theoretical monograph?) all add to the intrigue and complexity of the protagonist's encyclopedic exploration on the subject of identity.

The novel is about a middle-aged gay man searching for true love and his struggle to come to terms with his sexuality. This journey takes him to the great books of East and West, to many far corners of the world, and to myriad cultural venues. Along his soulful search for his gender and cultural identities, he discovers that defining oneself is often a naming game, for only by being truly in touch with one's self can one establish a clear sense of one's subjectivity and an unambiguous sense of identity. By bringing so many cultures into the protagonist's search for identity, Zhu Tianwen also places us in the multicultural world and challenges us to think and imagine what a cultural identity is in a globalized world. At the center of this globalized world is the self; cultural identity is no loner defined by one's connection to a place or determined by a collective value system; rather, Zhu conceives of a new kind of individual subjectivity that is both in alliance with capitalist materialism and born of cultural globalism.

Zhu Tianxin began her writing career in high school in 1974. Her first publication of collected short stories was *Days on the Boat* (方舟上的日子, 1977). Subsequent publications include *Yesterday When I Was Young* (昨日当我年轻时, 1980), *Unfinished Affairs* (未了, 1982), *Passages of Things Past* (时移事往, 1984), *In Remembrance of My Buddies from Military Housing Compounds* (想我眷村的兄弟们, 1992), *The Old Capital* (古都, 1997), and *The Wanderer* (漫游者, 2000).

From her first works Zhu Tianxin has exhibited an unusual sensitivity to and passionate concern for history and her Chinese heritage. In her earlier works Zhu Tianxin, like her sister, uses an imaginary China as a necessary anchor for her sense of cultural heritage and identity. But as awareness of Taiwanese identity grew in the mid-1980s, Zhu Tianxin began to turn her attention toward social critique and politics. Discussions on the issue of national, cultural, and ethnic identities dominated the mass media, the arts, and academia during these formative years of Taiwan's democratization. A few years before the lifting of martial law in 1987, the Taiwan government finally allowed limited contact and communication with China, and activities between people on both sides of the Taiwan Straits accelerated. In the cultural sphere, such intensive contacts with the "motherland" have prompted Taiwan writers to reevaluate their place in the "Greater Chinese" literary tradition. Zhu Tianxin's fiction published in the 1990s reveals a serious attempt to articulate the cultural identity crisis that surfaced in this milieu. Like many writers who are her contemporaries, Zhu Tianxin seeks to understand the impact of political, social, and cultural changes and to find ways of articulating a coherent and independent cultural identity for people in Taiwan.

In her 1997 collection of stories *The Old Capital*, Zhu Tianxin reveals an obsession with the prevalence of foreign cultural influences in Taiwan. The collection is filled with references to foreign cities and countries, world literature, mythology, religion, the latest (thus most fashionable) theoretical jargon from various academic disciplines, and more popular artifacts such as pop music, fashion, and movies. Heterogeneous as they are, the references are all cultural icons signifying the nostalgic sentiments of the generation who grew up during the 1960s and the 1970s when Taiwan was culturally dominated by the United States. Zhu Tianxin appropriates bits and pieces of foreign cultures by freely making them a potent part of her narrative strategy to articulate the cultural identity crisis facing people in Taiwan.

The first short story in the collection, "Death in Venice" (威尼斯之死, 1992), recalls Thomas Mann's highly celebrated story of the same title. Zhu Tianxin's "Death in Venice" is about a writer who is unable to resist the effect his environment has on his creative process. For example, a café filled with the sounds of cell phones beeping and conversations buzzing influences him to change the protagonist of the novel he is writing from a simple villager into a reporter who decides to throw himself into the life of urban Taipei. Zhu is interested in exploring how transient information, including cultural imports from around the world, has possessed the psyche of the people in Taiwan, or at least of those who live in Taipei. In "Death in Venice," it is not just the incidental information we are barraged with daily that fades from view; even more enduring knowledge such as philosophy, psychology, or sociology faces the danger of being "out of fashion." Zhu treats both types of information equally as everyday cultural products.

In this story, Zhu Tianxin portrays an unusual writer who sees writing as both a passive activity and a manifestation of his nearly involuntary interaction with his environment. Writing is also a process of collecting and recalling minute experiences and observations from the past and the present. In this strange relationship between the writer, his surroundings, and the fiction he produces, Zhu Tianxin exposes the postcolonial predicament of a writer facing a hybrid literary heritage. Unable to draw from the past for authenticity, the postcolonial writer can find a meaningful identity only in the presently occupied space, manifested, for example, in exotically decorated cafés. Here, Zhu Tianxin uses her protagonist's penchant for processing his thoughts through Western high-culture formulations to expose his lack of a coherent cultural voice.

In the next story, "The Old Capital," Zhu Tianxin moves into history to find ways to resolve the problem of constructing cultural identity in an essentially hybrid culture. In this story, she delves into a space between past and present, the historical real and the imaginary, ideality and disillusionment, to find a balance between cultural hybridity and identity. To lay claim to a cultural identity, one must believe that this identity will be unique, that it is inherently original and authentic. "The Old Capital" digs deeply into the very core of what cultural identity means and what reconciliations one must make before construction of this identity can even begin.

Zhu Tianxin borrowed the title "The Old Capital" from Japan's Nobel Prize winner Kawabata Yasunari's 川端康成 canonical novel of the same title, *Koto* 古都. The plot of "The Old Capital" is linear, and the story parallels Kawabata's novel thematically. It begins with the narrator's remembering her high school years, spent with her best friend, A. But gradually, as they move into their adult years, they grow apart, until one day the narrator receives a fax from A inviting her to meet in Kyoto. The narrator thus begins her journey to Kawabata's old capital. While she awaits A's arrival, she takes a walks through the city's streets and alleys, remembering her stay there with her daughter some years before. After waiting for a day, she realizes that A will not show up and decides to return to Taipei earlier than scheduled. At the Taipei airport, she is approached by a cab driver who mistakes her for a Japanese tourist; without attempting to correct the driver, she gets into the cab and is driven into the city. As a "foreigner" in her home city, she begins to see everything differently. She finds in her bag a Japanese tourist map of colonial Taipei and is inspired to follow it and revisit the city as it was half a century ago. This map lays out Taipei the way it was designed by the Japanese, with streets, governmental buildings, and landmarks appearing under their previous colonial names. She thus experiences present-day Taipei through the filter of its colonial past. What makes this switch of perspective most intriguing is that she is pretending to be someone other than herself—a Japanese tourist. With this disguise she can remove herself psychologically from the immediacy of her surroundings and allow the map to guide her to see the city anew. The narrator begins a journey back to the past, only to realize at the end that she no longer knows where she is.

"The Old Capital" is also a story of remembering the history of Taiwan as a Japanese colony. References to foreign cultures constitute the narrative's cultural setting. In the first section of the story, before the narrator's trip to Kyoto, the cultural milieu is depicted through references to American popular music and movies. In this section, the narrator recalls her adolescent years and the way Taipei was at the time. Conflicts between the native and the foreign are apparent. As the narrator goes to Kyoto, anticipating a reunion with A, the scene shifts to the old capital, and Kawabata's *Old Capital* provides the narrator guidance in visiting the city. In the next section, where she pretends to be a foreign tourist back in Taipei, historical and cultural references alluding to the colonial period dominate the narrative, thus calling attention to the contrast between the historical and the contemporary. For each section, space and time are constituted by different sets of cultural references and structured by different principles.

This desire to see similarity between Taipei and Kyoto is itself a symptom of the very issue Zhu Tianxin wants to explore in her narrative—namely, the discontinuity in Taiwan's historical record and the disruption of the collective memory of Taiwan's people. Zhu Tianxin's recuperation of Kawabata's old capital thus is a sign not of her naiveté about history or mere romanticism for an ancient city but of her own sense of the lack of a coherent and continuous historical and cultural heritage. It is understandable that Zhu Tianxin's narrator finds in Japan and Kyoto the material necessary for constructing Taiwan's (via Taipei's) past. Kyoto's historicity is authentic, for the colonial connection between Japan and Taiwan provides her a reference to retrace the city of Taipei as it was built during the colonial period.

From dealing with culture in "Death in Venice" to investigating history in "The Old Capital," Zhu Tianxin recognizes that the essence of Taiwan's culture is a product of colonialism and capitalism. Although rooted in Chinese culture, Taiwan's culture has also absorbed tremendous Japanese and Western (mainly American) cultural influences. Maintaining cohesion among history, memory, and place, then, becomes a crucial way to assert an independent cultural identity.

Bibliography

Brown, Melissa. *Is Taiwan Chinese? The Impact of Culture, Power, and Migration on Changing Identities*. Berkeley: University of California Press, 2004.

Chang, Song-sheng Yvonne. *Modernism and the Nativist Resistance: Contemporary Chinese Fiction from Taiwan*. Durham, NC: Duke University Press, 1993.

Chen, Lingchei Letty. "Rising from the Ashes: Identity and the Aesthetics of Hybridity in Zhu Tianwen's *Notes of a Desolate Man*." *Journal of Modern Literature in Chinese* 4, 1 (July 2000): 101–138.

———. *Writing Chinese: Reshaping Chinese Cultural Identity*. New York: Palgrave Macmillan Press, 2006.

Gold, Thomas B. "Civil Society and Taiwan's Quest for Identity." In Stevan Harrell and Chün-chieh Huang, eds., *Cultural Change in Postwar Taiwan*, 47–68. Boulder, CO: Westview, 1994.

Kawabata Yasunari. *The Old Capital*. Trans. J. Martin Holman. San Francisco: North Point Press, 1987.

Liou, Liang-ya. "At the Intersection of the Global and the Local: Representations of Male Homosexuality in Fictions by Pai Hsien-yung, Li Ang, Chu Tien-wen and Chi Ta-wei." *Postcolonial Studies: Culture, Politics, Economy* 6, 2 (July 2003): 191–206.

Wang, David Der-wei. "Fin-de-Siècle Splendor: Contemporary Women Writers' Vision of Taiwan." *Modern Chinese Literature* 6, 1–2 (Spring–Fall 1992): 39–59.

——. *Fin-de-Siècle Splendor: Repressed Modernities of Late Qing Fiction, 1849–1911*. Stanford, CA: Stanford University Press, 1997.

Wang, David Der-wei, and Carlos Rojas, eds. *Writing Taiwan: A New Literary History*. Durham, NC: Duke University Press, 2007.

Zhu, Tianwen (Chu T'ien-wen). "Fin-de-Siècle Splendor." Trans. Eva Hung. In Joseph Lau and Howard Goldblatt, eds., *The Columbia Anthology of Modern Chinese Literature*, 388–402. 2nd ed. New York: Columbia University Press, 2007.

——. *Notes of a Desolate Man*. Trans. Howard Goldblatt and Sylvia Li-chun Lin. New York: Columbia University Press, 1999.

Zhu, Tianxin (Chu T'ien-hsin). "In Remembrance of My Buddies from the Military Compound." Trans. Michelle Wu. In Pang-yuan Chi and David Der-wei Wang, eds., *The Last of the Whampoa Breed: Stories from the Chinese Diaspora*, 242–270. New York: Columbia University Press, 2003.

——. "The Last Train to Tamshui." Trans. Michelle Yeh. *The Chinese Pen* (Spring 1988): 41–71.

——. *The Old Capital: A Novel of Taipei*. Trans. Howard Goldblatt. New York: Columbia University Press, 2007.

48

WANG ANYI

LINGZHEN WANG

Wang Anyi 王安忆 had only just graduated from junior high school in 1969 when she volunteered to join a commune in northern Anhui Province. Born in 1954 in Nanjing and brought up in Shanghai, this daughter of the noted writer Ru Zhijuan 茹志鹃 found her Anhui peasant life disappointing. She left in 1972 and was admitted to a local performing arts troupe in Xuzhou, Jiangsu, where she began writing and publishing short stories. She returned to Shanghai in 1978 to serve as an editor of a literary journal, beginning her professional writing career in 1980. She has since won many national literary prizes and remains one of China's most prominent and prolific writers.

"And the Rain Patters On" (雨, 沙沙沙, 1980) established Wang Anyi's literary promise. Influenced by other women writers of the early post-Mao era, such as Zhang Jie 张洁 and Zhang Xinxin 张辛欣, Wang emphasizes subjective perspectives, personal ideals, and daily experiences that were not aligned with the grand narrative advocated by the state, consequently challenging the dominant literary style around collectively validated and politically oriented topics (Lingzhen Wang 1998: 403). "And the Rain Patters On" tells the story of a young and innocent woman, Wenwen 雯雯, who falls in love with a young male bicycle rider when he helps her on a rainy night. Although her mother pressures her to accept the conventional view of love and consider an arranged marriage, Wenwen refuses to compromise or relinquish her memory of the young man. He stands in her mind for hope, courage, and ideal love. Wang's exploration of love shares much with that of her contemporaries, in her pursuit of the poetic, personal, and idealistic, but is also distinguished by her unusual emphasis on the ordinary, nonheroic, and daily urban experience.

In the early 1980s, Wang Anyi wrote many stories about people from various social groups and their attendant concerns, among which "The Destination" (本次列车终点, 1981) and *Lapse of Time* (流逝, 1982) were awarded national literary prizes. However, not until *Baotown* (小鲍庄, 1985) was Wang recognized as a self-transforming, mature, and successful writer. Wang wrote the novel after a four-month visit to the United States, where she attended an international writers' workshop in Iowa. She expressed shock at the dramatic cultural differences between the United States and China, which "led to the profound discovery that she was indeed Chinese and to the decision to 'write on China' when she returned" (Feuerwerker 1998: 227). More specifically, according to "Utopian Verses" (乌托邦诗篇, 1991)—an autobiographical novella detailing an unusual historical encounter between the famous Taiwan literary figure Chen Yingzhen 陈映真 and Wang herself—the creative impulse for *Baotown* originated from these two writers' spirited conversations in the United States and Wang's subsequent longing for Chen and his idealistic, socially committed vision of universal love (Lingzhen Wang 2009: 4–7).

Drawing from history, legend, humanistic and utopian senses of universal love (Chen Yingzhen's influence), personal imagination, and her experiences in the countryside, Wang presents in *Baotown* a mythical, timeless China, but she depicts in detail the crises, heterogeneous voices, and fragmentation that contradict any claim of a homogeneous and stable Chinese tradition. She presents the Confucian ideal of *renyi* (仁义, benevolence and righteousness) as the defining characteristic of Bao village, but at the same time this village is shown to be poverty-stricken, conservative, passive, and fatalistic. Furthermore, coexisting with the ideal of *renyi* and embodied by Laozha 捞渣 (Dregs), a young child who sacrifices his own life to save an old man in a catastrophic flood, are the ordinary lives of rural folk full of prejudice, selfishness, and cruelty, to which most women and outsiders fall victim. The death of Dregs symbolizes the traditional ideal of *renyi* and announces its demise; Bao village benefits from Dregs's death, and its inhabitants live completely different lives afterward.

Wang's ambivalent attitude toward the death of Dregs parallels ambivalence toward representing China in her works: she is at once sanguine and skeptical about the validity of such a project. Her conscious problematization of the reliability of writing itself, through the figure of Bao Renwen 鲍仁文, the peasant writer in Baotown, further destabilizes the act of representation and thus resists "the rationalized interpretations of society promoted by modern ideologies defining nation-state" (Gunn 1991: 176). Set up at the beginning of the story as the ideal origin of Chinese civilization, *renyi* becomes a fantasy challenged by the lives of the marginalized, and it breaks down by the end as different narratives compete in appropriating the death of Dregs. Claimed as one of the most representative works of roots-seeking literature, *Baotown* questions the value of traditional origin and challenges the political and cultural significations of the literary movement.

Wang Anyi returns to a subjective mode of writing in her famous "romance trilogy" (三恋): *Love on a Barren Mountain* (荒山之恋, 1986), *Love in a Small Town* (小城之恋, 1986), and *Brocade Valley* (锦绣谷之恋, 1987). *Love on a Barren Mountain* tells the story of two people growing up in different regions, with different backgrounds, who fall into a transgressive, extramarital relationship and then end their lives in a tragic double suicide. *Love in a Small Town* depicts two adolescents' awakening to libidinal desire too powerful for them to control. That desire remains the sole basis of their relationship for years, until the girl becomes a mother and suddenly transcends her sexual restlessness. *Brocade Valley* describes a narcissistic young wife, suffocated by her uneventful marriage and her indifferent and boring husband. At a conference held on Lu Mountain, she seeks to create a new self through a brief romantic liaison with a famous male writer. Although critics claim Wang's romance trilogy successfully breaks socialist taboos on carnal love and sexuality, the three novels, with their foregrounded psychological activity and subjective perspectives, center on the roles of sex and desire in the formation of subjectivity. Wang's trilogy thereby "tackles the problematic of sexual difference as an immediate reality rather than as a signifier of social and ideological entities" (Chen 1998: 93).

Wang Anyi's popular story "Brothers" (弟兄们, 1989) explores the tenuousness of a same-sex love relationship (see "Homoeroticism in Modern Chinese Literature") built without sexual, material, and institutional grounds. After years of separation, two married women, Lao Li 老李 and Lao Wang 老王, resume an intimate relationship developed during their years in art school. In order to help Lao Li give birth to her son, Lao Wang moves out of Nanjing and into Lao Li and her husband's Shanghai apartment. Just as their relationship develops and demands new terms, an unexpected incident—the fall of Lao Li's newborn son from his stroller—tears them apart. Their relationship ends in frustration for want of a new set of terms for understanding and defining it. As Lydia Liu (1993: 56) puts it, "The fragility and rupture of the female bond testify to the difficulty a woman encounters in sorting out her desire in a society that privileges patriarchal heterosexuality," including institutionalized marriage and motherhood.

In *Brocade Valley*, Wang Anyi experiments with metafiction, a trend she further develops in "The Story of Uncle" (叔叔的故事, 1990), a critically acclaimed novella that "ushers in a new logic of literary creation, the premise of which is no longer referential experience or reality but the independent technique of crafting fiction" (Tang 1997: 181). "The Story of Uncle" is recounted by a narrator whose own recent experience prompts his desire to tell a story. Unwilling to disclose his own story, he decides instead to recount that of Uncle, an established writer from the older generation of rehabilitated rightists, whose recent insight into his own unhappy fate corresponds to that of the narrator's. With Uncle at the center of his story, the narrator not only maximizes the effect of the emotion he recently experienced in his own life but also intentionally undermines the romantic, optimistic, idealized, and heroic narrative of Uncle's generation. To reconcile Uncle's story with the views of the narrator's generation, which embraces a more cynical, pragmatic, and nihilistic attitude toward history and life, the narrator candidly fabricates Uncle's story, piecing together multiple and conflicting threads of information, including pure speculation. If the process of fabricating and narrating serves to debunk the cultural myths of Uncle's generation, this method simultaneously undermines the validity of the narrator's generation; in the end, the two generations share profound despair over their unfortunate fates.

In her writing of the early 1990s, Wang Anyi probes into questions regarding the intrinsic logic and technique of storytelling, as well as the nature and status of literature in contemporary China. She believes that literature, fiction in particular, is an autonomous field independent of historical reference and utilitarian function. Yet from another perspective, literature remains a personalized activity for Wang; she insists on linking individual minds, emotions, moods, temperaments, experiences, and desires to the act of writing. Over her more than three-decade career, Wang consistently returns to a personal mode of writing, focusing on her characters' internal worlds throughout her many autobiographical stories and novels.

Documentation and Fabrication: One Method of Creating the World (纪实与虚构: 创造世界方法之一, 1993) demonstrates two major principles of Wang's writing. This novel consists of two interwoven parts: in the first, the narrator reconstructs her lost maternal genealogy with well-researched public and historical materials that may or may not be relevant to her mother; in the second, the narrator connects her isolated life with its immediate physical environment, urban Shanghai in socialist China. The latter part contains many references to Wang's life, even rewritings of earlier autobiographical stories. Searching for maternal roots and self-identity, Wang Anyi employs the most accurate and concrete materials, both historical and personal, only to construct imagined entities, thus bearing testimony to the irretrievability of the past and the instability of the self. *Documentation and Fabrication* dispenses with literary conventions that differentiate fiction from autobiography, creating a distinctive world and logic that are both independent from and dependent on history and reality.

Wang Anyi won the fifth Mao Dun Literature Award for her novel *The Song of Everlasting Sorrow* (长恨歌, 1995). Originally named *The Shanghai Story* (上海故事), the novel demonstrates both the binding relationship between place and narrative invention and Wang's desire to recreate the city of Shanghai. In this novel, Wang paints a portrait of the city through its historical and social changes over the past forty years. Unlike her other Shanghai stories, which are set in post-1949 Communist China, this novel begins in the early 1940s, thus connecting to other Shanghai fiction of the time by such writers as Eileen Chang 张爱玲 and Su Qing 苏青. (See also "Contemporary Urban Fiction.")

Shanghai is the primary subject of this novel; Wang Anyi devotes much textual space to depicting the city, its alleys, the gossip (or street talk), the girls' inner chambers, the doves, and the vicissitudes of ordinary city-dwellers, of whom Wang Qiyao 王琦瑶, the female protagonist, remains but one. Wang Anyi thus defines Shanghai through its ordinary *shimin* (市民, city residents) and their daily lives. Born into a *shimin* family in the alleyways, Wang Qiyao grows up to be Miss Shanghai of 1946, after which she becomes involved with numerous men at different stages of her life. Wang Qiyao survives all the turmoil of modern Chinese history only to be murdered by a thief, in a fight over a box of gold bars, in the 1980s. Despite her somewhat extraordinary life, Wang Qiyao is the quintessential *shimin*; she embodies the down-to-earth, shrewd, pragmatic, and flexible lifestyle of Shanghai people, who both indulge in and resist the dominant ideological currents this city embodies.

The Song of Everlasting Sorrow may be read as part of the 1990s nostalgia wave, which capitalized on the commercialization of Shanghai culture, particularly of the 1930s and 1940s. Wang Anyi also indirectly participated in the late 1990s "privacy fever" (隐私热), a process of ongoing reconfigurations of the private space and private self, and the growing mass production and consumption of self-narratives. Among the categories that constituted this new ideal of the private self, private emotion was particularly emphasized. Women were seen as central to privacy fever; femaleness itself evoked the sense and meaning of privacy and aroused the public's desire to consume it (Lingzhen Wang 2004: 172–175).

The publication of Wang Anyi's autobiographical novella, "Years of Sadness" (忧伤的年代, 1998), is inseparable from this late 1990s consumerist mode of privacy, which foregrounded intimacy, memory, and gendered emotions. Wang's novella in fact reaches an extreme; its irreducible personal voice challenges contemporary cultural consumption and resists total market consumerism. The narrator sorrowfully recounts seemingly trivial yet humiliating childhood episodes from the mid-1960s, revealing deep emotional scars. She realizes she has unconsciously suppressed her childhood memories when a sobbing woman in a dark movie theater triggers their recollection. Her early experiences include: twice losing movie tickets right before entering the theater and her subsequent humiliation; secret admiration for and embarrassingly overdone imitation of a girl in her neighborhood; disappointment over her appearance; public betrayal by her sister in front of a math teacher; fear of loneliness and darkness; and—her most unspeakable and shameful experience—being sent to the hospital for examination and treatment of a genital infection caused by an insect sting. From these private and emotional episodes, readers see a shy and sensitive young girl who in her early years was confused, ignored, unprotected, and deeply hurt. She is lonely, lacking the means to communicate even with her own mother, and feels awkward and inadequate, rejected by people and excluded from the external world.

Among Wang's autobiographical works, "Years of Sadness" ventures deepest in exploring her early emotional and psychic experiences, revealing a hidden, affective core of personal identity and her continuous drive to negotiate the self through writing. At the societal level, this novella questions socialist gender ideology by detailing children's psychic "trauma" as caused mostly by the absence of the mother (a revolutionary figure) in the home. Wang's work also illustrates how women writers could appropriate the market to reclaim their personal sense of self and literature (Lingzhen Wang 2009: 7–9).

Wang Anyi has continued to be productive in the new millennium, further expanding her literary themes and styles. Two novels in particular have drawn critical attention as well as popular debate: *Age of Enlightenment* (启蒙时代, 2005) and *Scent of Heaven* (天香, 2011), the latter of which won the fourth Dream of the Red Chamber Award from Hong Kong Baptist University in 2012.

In *Age of Enlightenment*, Wang turns against the trend of popular literature, attempting to recapture important historical moments in the socialist period that led to the thought transformations of the younger generation. Set in a relatively quiet phase of the Cultural Revolution, after the high wave of the movement had passed and the educated urban young were to be "sent down" to the countryside (1967–1968), the novel portrays a sixteen-year-old middle school student, Nanchang 南昌, who is the son of revolutionaries. In response to his father's marginalization during the Cultural Revolution, and to their troubled relationship, Nanchang searches for new ideas and self-identity. Wang configures Nanchang's search through his encounters with different types of people all active in Shanghai during the Cultural Revolution, such as the city's *shimin* class (which itself encompasses a wide variety of backgrounds and perspectives), newly privileged "red descendants" like himself whose families did not move to Shanghai until the 1950s, a Christian doctor with firm beliefs in the light of truth and science, and a pre-1949 capitalist who vividly remembers the past. Nanchang grows through his engagements and entanglements with this cast of characters, and his transformation is punctuated by revolutionary ideals, bodily and sexual desires, Shanghai urban life, and reason and secular thought, as well as the *shimin* self-sustaining spirit.

Debate provoked by this novel largely centered on the meaning of "enlightenment," including whether enlightenment ideas and experiences had been possible during the Cultural Revolution. *Age of Enlightenment* provides no single answer to such questions. Instead, Wang shows that multiple "nonrevolutionary" elements contained in the urban center facilitated Nanchang's thought transformation during the revolutionary era, thus she indirectly reveals how this generation came to embody reformist ideas immediately after the Cultural Revolution. Yet the novel also clearly situates the origins of thought transformation in the anarchic and chaotic moments of the Cultural Revolution. For

Nanchang, "enlightenment light" refers to the light of both revolution and reason. Moreover, in the end, Nanchang's growth does not repudiate his revolutionary spirit and ideals. Linking her conceptualization of enlightenment to the stages of individual growth, Wang Anyi seems to suggest that enlightenment is a dialectic process that embraces passion and reason, abstract idealism and the concreteness of daily life (Zhang 2012: 130–137).

Wang's fictional writing had always been set in modern China until *Scent of Heaven* (2011), which takes place in late Ming and early Qing dynasty Shanghai. The novel has been compared to Cao Xueqin's 曹雪芹 *Dream of the Red Chamber* (红楼梦), a Qing masterpiece, for its narrative structure, general theme of the decline of a prominent family, focus on domestic details and material objects, and extraordinary women characters in their inner chambers. However, the overall tone, ultimate goal, and social and cultural concerns of the two novels diverge significantly. *Scent of Heaven* is a historical novel about Shanghai's famous Gu 顾 family, which developed a distinctive style of embroidery. Through her depictions of the rise and fall of Heavenly Scent Garden (天香园), home of the fictional Gu family, Wang Anyi traces the changing significance of Heavenly Scent embroidery, which first develops into "high art" as practiced by the elite women in their inner chambers and then serves as a practical necessity deployed by those women after the loss of the family fortune. Rather than lamenting the irreversible disintegration of a prominent family, *Scent of Heaven* centers on survival and how elite women employ their embroidery skills to endure extraordinary hardship.

Wang Anyi's turn to this late imperial setting occurred in the context of contemporary China's ongoing popularization and commercialization of the history of dynastic China. But as in previous works, Shanghai and women remain her twin foci. Changing the Gu family name to Shen 申, a historical term for Shanghai, Wang attempts to recreate a cultural and material history of the city. *Scent of Heaven* is a tale of Shanghai, celebrating its cultural and material splendor as well as its pragmatic realism. This novel is also a tale of gender. Presenting women's embroidery as high art, comparable to men's writing, and tracing the development of Heavenly Scent embroidery from imperial inner chambers back to common folk, Wang emphasizes women's agency throughout the cultural, artistic, and economic production of late imperial China.

Bibliography

Chen, Helen H. "Gender, Subjectivity, Sexuality: Defining a Subversive Discourse in Wang Anyi's *Four Tales of Sexual Transgression*." In Yingjing Zhang, ed., *China in a Polycentric World: Essays in Chinese Comparative Literature*, 90–109. Stanford, CA: Stanford University Press, 1998.

Feuerwerker, Yi-tsi Mei. *Ideology, Power, Text: Self-Representation and the Peasant "Other" in Modern Chinese Literature*. Stanford, CA: Stanford University Press, 1998.

Gunn, Edward. *Rewriting Chinese: Style and Innovation in Twentieth-Century Chinese Prose*. Stanford, CA: Stanford University Press, 1991.

Liu, Lydia H. "Invention and Intervention: The Female Tradition in Modern Chinese Literature." In Tani Barlow, ed., *Gender Politics in Modern China: Writing and Feminism*, 33–57. Durham, NC: Duke University Press, 1993.

Tang, Xiaobing. "Melancholy Against the Grain: Approaching Postmodernity in Wang Anyi's *Tales of Sorrow*." *boundary 2* 24, 3 (Fall 1997): 177–200.

Wang, Anyi. *Baotown*. Trans. Martha Avery. London: Viking, 1989.

——. *Brocade Valley*. Trans. Bonnie S. McDougall and Chen Maiping. New York: New Directions, 1992.

——. "Brothers." Trans. Diana B. Kingsbury. In Diana B. Kingsbury, ed., *I Wish I Were a Wolf: The New Voice in Chinese Women's Literature*, 158–212. London: New World Press, 1994.

——. 王安忆. *Jishi yu xugou: chuangzao shijie fangfa zhiyi* 纪实与虚构: 创造世界方法之一 (Documentation and fabrication: One method of creating the world). Beijing: Renmin wenxue, 1993.

——. *Lapse of Time*. San Francisco: China Books, 1988.

——. *Love in a Small Town*. Trans. Eva Huang. Hong Kong: Renditions, 1988.

——. *Love on a Barren Mountain*. Trans. Eva Hung. Hong Kong: Renditions, 1991.

——. "Shushu de gushi" 叔叔的故事 (Story of Uncle). In *Xianggang de qing yu ai* 香港的情与爱 (Love and sentiment in Hong Kong), 1–77. Beijing: Zuojia, 1996.

——. *The Song of Everlasting Sorrow: A Novel of Shanghai*. Trans. Michael Berry and Susan Chan Egan. New York: Columbia University Press, 2008.

——. *Years of Sadness: Autobiographical Writings of Wang Anyi*. Ed. Lingzhen Wang. Trans. Lingzhen Wang and Mary Ann O'Donell. Ithaca, NY: Cornell East Asian Series, 2009.

Wang, Lingzhen. "Consumption, Shame, and the Imaginary in Contemporary Autobiographical Practice." In *Personal Matters: Women's Autobiographical Practice in Twentieth-Century China*, 167–200. Stanford, CA: Stanford University Press, 2004.

——. "Introduction." In Wang Anyi, *Years of Sadness: Autobiographical Writings of Wang Anyi*. Ithaca, NY: Cornell East Asian Series, 2009.

——. "Retheorizing the Personal: Identity, Writing, and Gender in Yu Luojin's Autobiographical Act." *positions* 6, 2 (Fall 1998): 394–438.

Zhang, Xudong. "In Light of Concreteness: Wang Anyi and the Bildungsroman of the Cultural Revolutionary Generation." *Frontiers of Literary Studies in China* 6, 1 (2012): 112–137.

49

WANG SHUO

JONATHAN NOBLE

Although many literary critics disparage Wang Shuo 王朔 (b. 1958) as a profiteering purveyor of insipid tales about the sordid urban underworld, few deny that he poignantly represents the transformation that Chinese culture experienced during the late 1980s and early 1990s. Wang Shuo has become a household name referring to an epochal "cultural attitude" associated with his status as one of China's best-selling authors and media-savvy writers of television series and popular blockbusters. The emergence of his widespread yet controversial popularity, known as the Wang Shuo "phenomenon" (现象), reveals the contradictions between a "brave new world" generated by market reforms and China's gradual opening to outside capital, ideas, technology, and images. He also represents the potential for Chinese writers to become rich and famous, especially as producers of content for television and film, within a commercialized domestic market.

When Wang Shuo began writing in the early 1980s, China was experiencing tremendous social and economic change. The casting away of the "iron rice bowl" (铁饭碗) system, which guaranteed lifelong employment, in tandem with the introduction of profit as a key economic and social logic, created new economic possibilities as well as social unrest, alienation, and uncertainties. On the streets and in literature, new social roles emerged, such as the "sugar daddies" (大款) who successfully navigated the new market and emerged as emblems of a new era of materialism and money worship. Slipping through the cracks of the new market, however, were the *liumang* (流氓), a multifaceted cultural term referring to a spectrum of lowlifes, riffraff, vagrants, hooligans, and slackers, who negotiated the market terrain by designing cunning scams and running ostensibly criminal operations.

Depending on one's point of view, Wang Shuo can be seen as *liumang* culture's self-appointed spokesperson, the lucky commercial benefactor of a topsy-turvy world, or as an insincere hack parasitic on those morally adrift in the brave new world. Regardless, Wang Shuo's works and pop image are best understood in relation to this *liumang* culture. Wang Shuo himself shares much in common with the *liumang* featured in his works. As by-products of the rapidly changing economy, most *liumang* were dismissed or resigned from their government-assigned jobs—in particular, the military—before sinking into a life of drifting, slumming, conniving, or scamming.

Although the market reforms are central to the social formation of the *liumang*, the violence and chaos of the Cultural Revolution played an equally influential role. As part of the Red Guard generation, the *liumang* were trained at an early age in street violence and inculcated in the attitude of collective rebellion. Wang Shuo, as a prototypical *liumang*, entered the People's Liberation Army (PLA) as a sailor after finishing middle school at the end of the Cultural Revolution. The submission of his first story, "Waiting" (等待, 1978), to *Liberation Army Literature and Art* (解放军文艺) earned him a job as editor with the magazine, but this failed to bring an end to his *liumang* activities: he started a smuggling operation in the south. After being demobilized and fined for illegal trade, he loafed about working for a pharmaceutical company for three years and continued writing while living off his female companions, many of whom became celebrated characters in his works. Even after he made it big in the late 1980s, Wang Shuo was unable and unwilling to shed his reputation as a *liumang*. In fact, it became one of his great selling points.

The Wang Shuo phenomenon is, in part, the story of the commercialization of culture in post-Mao China. From one perspective, Wang Shuo is just one of many profit-minded entrepreneurs who emerged with the market reforms. Wang supports the role of the market in cultural production and admits that he strives to appeal to a large audience: "What I am most interested in and pay the closest attention to is popular lifestyles. This includes violence, sex, mockery, and shamelessness. I just reproduce these in my works" (Zhang and Jin 1993: 67). He is accused of promoting a "bestseller consciousness" (Wang Jing 1997: 262) or condemned as a panderer to vulgar, popular tastes. But Wang is unrepentant: "I'm not interested in dreams that are painted all rosy, thought by all as so wonderful.... I tell people the way things really are to make them laugh and relieve their tedium, to let them live a bit more relaxed and more true to themselves and life itself. Is this really so irresponsible?" (Zhang 1993: 76).

Wang's unfettered pursuit of making a buck in catering to the public's taste for profane cynicism and voyeuristic pleasure has certainly contributed to his commercial success. His works portray the vagrancies of the *liumang* in a pseudorealist style, similar to the more serious reportage literature that was gaining prestige and widespread popularity during the 1980s. However, Wang Shuo clearly rejects the heroic models—intellectuals, students, rustic peasants, and so on—offered in some post–Cultural Revolution literature. His characters, as the dregs of society, pursue unethical and illegal activities, such as racketeering and pimping, or more innocuous activities, such as slacking off, "shooting the breeze" (侃大山), swindling, seducing women, and "living aimlessly" (混). The merging of author, narrator, and protagonist in Wang's fiction, moreover, heightens readers' sense of peering into the life of a *liumang*, vicariously experiencing their self-indulgent idleness and the urban underworld they inhabit.

The neorealist first-person mode combined with such popular genres as the love story, detective story, and comical satire have contributed enormously to Wang Shuo's commercial success. Love was the major theme of his early stories. His first story to gain notoriety, "The Stewardess" (空中小姐, 1984), which is semiautobiographical, tells of a young girl who irrationally falls for the romantic image of the story's protagonist. After the protagonist is relieved from his duties with the navy some years later, adopting a rootless lifestyle, he attempts to carry on a relationship with his former idolater, Ah Mei 阿眉, who is now a flight attendant. The relationship fails, with Ah Mei becoming disillusioned by the protagonist's slothfulness and social indifference, including his inability to express affection for her. After Ah Mei dies in a plane crash, the protagonist searches to find out what she truly thought of him before her tragic death. Although a callow work, "The Stewardess" foreshadows Wang Shuo's focus on irreconcilable and usually tragic love relationships, the emergence of the *liumang* type, and a nostalgic, albeit implied, intellectual pursuit of a system of values or morality, often represented by the image of an innocent girl.

Wang Shuo's fiction also includes similarly sentimental love stories. In "Lost My Love" (永失我爱, 1989), which was also adapted into film in 1994, the protagonist is unwilling to disclose his terminal illness to his fiancée, leading her to marry another. However, in general, the male protagonists in his stories become increasingly misogynist; innocent and pure women are symbolically deflowered by the *liumang*'s decadent and immoral lifestyles, emotional indifference, and licentious womanizing. For example, in *Half Hot, Half Cold* (一半是火焰，一半是海水, 1986), adapted into film in 1988, Wu Di 吴迪, originally a wholesome college student with a bright future, is led to join the cold-shouldering protagonist's racketeering scam as a prostitute, leading to her eventual suicide.

Another major genre in Wang's oeuvre is comical satire, of which *Masters of Mischief* (顽主, 1987) is a masterpiece. It tells the story of enterprising *liumang* who start a shady business called "Three T Company," providing three services: "troubleshooting, tedium relief, and taking the blame." The company's employees are hired as surrogates, standing in for a client's date or providing a target for a housewife's frustrated harangues. The appeal of this story lies not only in the slapstick and irreverent antics but also in the mockery of official culture.

Serious official functions are subject to absurd parodies in much of Wang Shuo's fiction. In the film adaptation of *Masters of Mischief*, a phony literary award ceremony hosted by the Three T Company concludes with a performance in the style of a fashion show accompanied by a disco beat. This farcical yet highly symbolic performance juxtaposes sacred images, such as that of the PLA soldier, with the popular and vulgar, as embodied by a scantily clad female weightlifter. One of Wang Shuo's trademarks is his subversion of political rhetoric. In "An Attitude" (一点正经没有, 1989) the protagonist, Fang Yan 方言, provides a mocking rendition of Deng Xiaoping: "I have repeatedly said with all sincerity and concern that under no circumstances should we ever forget the masses, 99 percent of the population. So long as the 800 million peasants and 3 million PLA members are at peace, the empire will be stable" (Barmé 1999: 78). It is no exaggeration to say that Wang Shuo's mockery of official slogans and speeches has infiltrated the Chinese popular imagination, making it virtually impossible not to snicker at hackneyed official rhetoric and jargon. However, as Dai Jinhua (1995: 52) points out, although Wang Shuo mocks and deconstructs the sacrosanct official discourse, he also at times promotes the government's official agenda of pursuing material wealth.

In the history of contemporary Chinese literature, the Wang Shuo phenomenon represents the arrival of a commercialized cultural cynicism and the ebbing of serious cultural questioning of identity as well as a sanguine view of literature's role in shaping society. Despite Wang Shuo's popular appeal and his condemnation by academics and supporters of elite culture for pandering to vulgar tastes, he cannot be entirely disassociated from elite culture. Intellectuals make up a large part of his readership, his fiction contains important elements of an elite literary discourse, and his engagement with elite culture increases as he becomes a more significant public icon. In fact, in his controversial collection of essays published for the new century, Wang Shuo diffidently owns up to the trend toward intellectualization in his fiction while maintaining his trademark sardonic repartee: "What I would like to say is that over the years I have become an intellectual through my works.... In my view, the course of intellectualization is one of abstraction, in which the living is made machine-like.... I don't know how to free myself from the shackles of abstraction and whether this direction can be reversed. I feel repulsed by the tendency toward intellectualization in my writing's train of thought and style" (Wang Shuo 2000: 107–109).

In the development of Wang Shuo's literary career, his "literature of escape and sublimation" (Barmé 1999: 63) is gradually tainted by the very elitist discourse and intellectuality previously scoffed and derisively ridiculed in his fiction and public statements. The shameless pursuit of making a buck through lawless or unethical endeavors is gradually obscured by a proclivity for waxing witticisms and falling prey to the pursuit of meaning. *Playing for Thrills* (玩的就是心跳, 1989) is a transitional work displaying both the vivid lifelike portrayal of *liumang* culture of his earlier works and his later interest in language games and philosophical musings, not so different from those of avant-garde experimental writers. *Playing for Thrills* narrates the concoction of a fictitious murder by idle, spent *liumang* for the purpose of relieving their tedium. Mockery of intellectuality gives way to a mental pursuit of solving a whodunit puzzle. "Fooling around" (玩儿) serves as a bridge between Wang Shuo's earlier fiction, in which the *liumang* irreverently mess about town, and his later works, in which "to play at writing literature"(玩儿文学) is created through garrulous banter (侃) verging on existential or absurdist language games. Wang Shuo's *Vicious Beasts* (动物凶猛, 1991) and *Seemingly Beautiful* (看上去很美, 1999), adapted for the screen in 1995 and 2005, respectively, attempt a greater balance between a realist style and the play of cynicism, wit, and language games. Moreover, as both of these works explore the childhood environment of the *liumang*, they search for the root causes of China's current historical predicament in its recent socialist past.

Much of Wang Shuo's fame, however, has been garnered from producing and writing scripts for films and television miniseries. In 1988, dubbed the "year of Wang Shuo's films," four of his short stories were adapted into films, including *Troubleshooters* and *Samsara* (轮回). Following this success, Wang Shuo established the Seahorse Studio and collaborated on producing or writing some of China's most popular television miniseries during the early 1990s, including *Yearnings* (渴望, 1989), *Editorial Office* (编辑部的故事, 1992), *Seahorse Night Club* (海马歌舞厅, 1993), *Satisfied* (过把瘾, 1994), and *Beijinger in New York* (北京人在纽约, 1994). Despite his success in the television industry, Wang Shuo unabashedly mocks his market promiscuity. For example, television miniseries scriptwriters, he states, are "goods for sale . . . no different from prostitutes" (Wang Shuo 1992: 65). Nonetheless, Wang Shuo built his team of collaborators in the television business; his ongoing relationship with blockbuster director Feng Xiaogang 冯小刚, as well as with leading actor Ge You 葛优, since the late 1980s, continues to be one of the most celebrated creative and commercial teams in China's film industry. Collaborations include, for example, the blockbusters *Be There or Be Square* (甲方乙方, 1998), *A Sigh* (一声叹息, 2000), *If You Are the One 2* (非诚勿扰 2, 2010), and *Personal Tailor* (私人订制, 2013). These hit comedies thematically and stylistically maintain Wang Shuo's trademark satirical humor.

Since 2000, Wang Shuo's fictional output has been minimal, but he has turned to writing more essays about literature, culture, philosophy, and religion. For example, *The Ignorant Fear Nothing* (无知者无畏, 2000) is a collection of more than twenty essays that discuss his own creative work as an author and his critique of China's contemporary literature. *Millennium* (我的千岁寒, 2007), a collection of adaptations, essays, and a film script, retains Wang Shuo's playful experimentation with the Beijing dialect. As the majority of the collection includes interpretations of religion and philosophy, however, most critics assert that the collection represents a more profound direction for the author. For example, the collection's title work, "Millennium," a reworking of the premodern Chan Buddhist scripture *The Platform Sutra of the Sixth Patriarch* (六祖坛经) in the Beijing dialect, represents the author's stylistic and philosophical engagement with Buddhism. Similarly, the collection also includes Wang Shuo's new interpretation of the Buddhist Diamond Sutra and an essay engaging Hegelian thought and Marxism entitled "Concise History of Materialism." The only piece in the collection that is original fiction is the short story adapted by director Xu Jinglei 徐静蕾 for her film *Dreams May Come* (梦想照进现实, 2006). Wang Shuo has also become an irreverent public intellectual; he has criticized many authors, including engaging in highly publicized clashes with authors Jin Yong 金庸 and Han Han 韩寒, for example, about their literary work and cultural representation.

Because his works are replete with Beijing colloquialisms and slang, Wang Shuo can be considered a major force in exploring a Beijing indigenous style in the tradition of the dramatist and novelist Lao She 老舍. His works also have ties to martial arts (武侠) fiction. The *liumang* adhere to an unofficial pact of collective camaraderie and to a common ideology, even if that ideology amounts to lackadaisical lethargy, sedition, seduction, and sardonic banter. The disintegration of the work unit (单位) as the basic structure of society in the 1980s provided the impetus for forming new solidarities based on shared values or lifestyles. The emergence of clans of "buddies" (哥们儿) is a symptom of these social changes, even as it draws on cultural memory and shared values of community and loyalty. The clans of *liumang* in Wang Shuo's works are as such not so far removed from the bands of lawless heroes in the tradition of martial arts fiction (Barmé 1999: 85). It is perhaps not coincidental that during the period of Wang Shuo's greatest commercial success, Jin Yong's martial arts novels were becoming best sellers in China. Essentially entertainment genres that provide a myth of individual emancipation either through heroic feats or subversive behavior, both appealed to readers in an era of new economic anxieties, angst, and alienation. Any analysis of Wang Shuo, however, would not be complete without recognizing his enormous impact on creating popular television miniseries and films that focus on everyday life, albeit usually exaggerated for comic effect, and defy the industry's predominance of historic costume dramas and patriotic melodramas.

Bibliography

Barmé, Geremie. *In the Red: On Contemporary Chinese Culture*. New York: Columbia University Press, 1999.

Dai Jinhua 戴锦华. *Jingcheng tuwei: nuxing, dianying, wenxue* 镜城突围: 女性, 电影, 文学 (Breaking out of the mirrored city: Woman, film, literature). Beijing: Zuojia, 1995.

Wang, Jing. *High Culture Fever: Politics, Aesthetics, and Ideology in Deng's China*. Berkeley: University of California Press, 1997.

Wang Shuo 王朔. *Kanshangqu hen mei* 看上去很美 (Seemingly beautiful). Beijing: Huayi, 1999.

——. *Playing for Thrills*. Trans. Howard Goldblatt. New York: William Morrow, 1998.

——. *Please Don't Call Me Human*. Trans. Howard Goldblatt. New York: Hyperion, 2000.

——. *Wang Shuo wenji* 王朔文集 (Collected works of Wang Shuo). Beijing: Huayi, 1996.

——. *Wo de qiansuihan* 我的千岁寒 (Millennium). Beijing: Zuojia, 2007.

——. *Wo shi Wang Shuo* 我是王朔 (I am Wang Shuo). Beijing: Guoji wenhua, 1992.

——. *Wuzhizhe wuwei* 无知者无畏 (The ignorant fear nothing). Beijing: Chunfeng wenyi, 2000.

Zhang Dexiang 张德祥 and Jin Huimin 金惠敏. *Wang Shuo pipan* 王朔批判 (Critique of Wang Shuo). Beijing: Zhongguo shehui kexue, 1993.

50

COMMERCIALIZATION OF LITERATURE IN THE POST-MAO ERA: YU HUA, BEAUTY WRITERS, AND YOUTH WRITERS

ZHEN ZHANG

Starting in 1992, as economic marketization intensified, the commercialization of literature in post-Mao China gained momentum. Writers were greeted with an era in which literature was, for good and for bad, "liberated" from the goal-oriented, morally serious, socially responsive intellectual elitism that had hitherto been the norm. As a secular, market-embracing mass culture has increasingly gained sway in post-1992 China, the commercialization and commodification of everyday life have undermined state control of the production and dissemination of literature; literary writers are now also subject to the rules of the marketplace.

Wang Shuo's 王朔 novels, with their kitsch, parody, and hooligan (流氓) heroes, appeared in tandem with the initial emergence of commercialization in the 1980s. Beyond the cultural cynicism emblematized by Wang Shuo's works and playful personas, the commercialization of literature in the post-Mao era manifested itself in diverse ways and can be understood by looking at a handful of writers/public figures, such as the avant-garde writer Yu Hua 余华, the eye-catching but often scandalizing "beauty writers" (美女作家), and the youth writers Guo Jingming 郭敬明 and Han Han 韩寒. Each of these figures has pursued and enjoyed commercial success while breaking free, in various ways, from the confinements of commercialization. Their writings not only reflect the social milieu and articulate new modes of self in the market era but also engage in complex negotiations with and at times assert agency against the forces of commercialization.

Before publishing his two-volume bestselling novel *Brothers* (兄弟) in 2005 and 2006, Yu Hua (1960–) was mostly regarded as an avant-garde writer who earned his literary fame by creating hyperbolic and even surreal stories delineating the material hardships and ethical dilemmas of the Mao era. *Brothers* was Yu Hua's first major work in a decade, and it turned out to be a distinct shift away from his earlier avant-garde stance toward mainstream consumerist tastes. Even as he critiques unabashed commercialization in the novel, Yu Hua avails himself of commercial tactics in its narrative and its marketing.

Brothers tells the story of two siblings growing up through the turbulent days of the Cultural Revolution and how their destinies diverge in the "new era" when marketization leads to a national obsession with money. The brothers weather the storms of the Mao era together. They commiserate with each other on their father's persecution to death and successive family misfortunes. The battle for survival as orphans tightens their bonds. In the era of the market economy, however, they part ways. The brazen and sly Baldy Li 李光头 becomes an entrepreneur and makes a fortune, while his upright and trustworthy stepbrother Song Gang 宋钢 ends up as a laid-off worker in a state-owned enterprise. The allegorical nature of the story, the biting commentaries on market mentalities, the dark and sardonic depiction of Baldy Li as a "successful person" (成功人士), and the age-old theme of tragic virtue (in the case of Song Gang) contribute to the duality of the novel.

One of China's runaway best sellers of the early twenty-first century, *Brothers* marked the conversion of Yu Hua the writer into Yu Hua the brand. The branding is actualized through a marketing schema comprising advertisements, book tours, public readings, and TV appearances that have turned Yu Hua into a celebrity. As such, Yu Hua's avant-garde reputation as a "serious" writer was a form of cultural capital that converted into monetary gain. *Brothers* also caters to popular taste as well; with its excessive use of voyeurism, sensation, absurdity, bodily fluids, and repetition, the story is told in an entertaining way that fully considers readers' tastes and expectations.

However, the novel's commercialization and entertainment value are not the whole story. *Brothers* also tackles contemporary social ills and offers a sharp critique of the advent of capital in China. Whereas Yu Hua's peers, such as Mo Yan 莫言 and Su Tong 苏童, have in their fiction mostly focused on historical narratives predating the People's Republic of China (PRC) or on the Mao era, Yu Hua was among the first prominent Chinese writers to depict what is happening in China today. With the novel's freakish protagonist Baldy Li, Yu Hua portrays and ridicules the new subject of the consumerist age—the successful person. Portraits of contemporary China's social and ecological devastation brought by the onset of capital are rarely sharper or more scathing than in *Brothers*, particularly in the second half of the novel. Baldy Li's success comes from removing himself from the sociohistorical, moral, and environmental dimensions of life. He turns himself into a *homo economicus* (经济人), who valorizes himself by his purchasing power and measures his success by his conquest of women. His behavior undermines long-standing community values and ethics. In the figure of Baldy Li, Yu Hua satirizes China's exaltation of the successful person, his supermanly image, and his power to redefine life by recategorizing self, dignity, status, taste, beauty, success, happiness, and freedom in accordance with the standard of consumption and material life defined by the logic of capital.

The beauty contest section of the novel and the subsequent demolition of Liu Town best illustrate Yu Hua's critique of commercialization. Newly rich through his scrap trading, Baldy Li sets his mind on finding China's most beautiful virgin. He launches the "Inaugural National Virgin Beauty Competition," which attracts blatant and covetous sponsors, necessitates the leveling and rebuilding of a town to receive guests, and ends with the winning contestants sleeping with the judges. The empty commercial tactics that necessitate Liu Town's demolition and rebuilding are described:

> Our Liu Town was turned upside down. The big-shot Baldy Li and County Governor Tao Qing 陶青 now spoke as one and jointly announced that they were going to tear down the old Liu Town and build a new one. Everyone said that this was a classic case of collusion of business and government, with Tao Qing providing the official documents and Baldy Li providing the capital and labor. They demolished one street after another, gradually transforming the face of the entire town. For five full years, Liu Town was covered in dirt and dust from dawn to dusk. Everyone complained that they were inhaling more dust than oxygen and that the layer of dirt permanently caked on their necks was thicker than a scarf. They said that Baldy Li was like a B-52 bomber, carpet-bombing the formerly beautiful town. A few educated townspeople became more embittered than the rest; they remarked that the classic novel *Romance of Three Kingdoms* had a scene that was set in Liu, *Journey to the West* had a scene and a half, while *Water Margin* had two entire scenes—but now Baldy Li had demolished the town and its landmarks.
>
> (Yu Hua 2010: 429)

Liu Town is clearly a microcosm of China, which has experienced such destruction on a vast scale, sweeping away the venerated past and cherished memories merely to satisfy the lust of the wealthy.

Another notable facet of literary commercialization was the emergence of the "beauty writers" in the late 1990s. Two Shanghai writers, Mian Mian 棉棉 (1970–) and Wei Hui 卫慧 (1973–), caught public attention by vividly celebrating uninhibited sex, drugs, and urban decadence in their novels, such as *Candy* (糖, 2000) and *Shanghai Baby* (上海宝贝, 1999). The beauty writers were so named because most of them were young, attractive women writing in styles that publicly called attention to the female body.

Without the cultural capital enjoyed by older writers such as Yu Hua, the beauty writers capitalized on their own youthful attractive bodies and invented a style called "body writing" (身体写作), literally writing with or about one's body. By foregrounding female sexuality, body writing is intended to produce shock value and caters to the commercial logic that "sex sells." In an interview, Wei Hui claims that her main goal in experimenting with writing about the female body was to test how commercially successful it would be. The beauty writers distinguish themselves by their acute awareness of market forces and active participation in commodifying themselves, as well as in the way their writing embodies the need to surrender to market forces.

Beauty writers are highly conscious of commercialism's logic and how its far-reaching tentacles can generate new ways of life and new truths and also silence and obliterate them. In fact, one can argue that beauty writers assert their agency by successfully promoting and profiting from the commodification of their own bodies and subjectivities, fully aware that they will be cast away once their short-lived literary spotlight dims.

Beauty writers represent a type of consumerist subjectivity in the age of commercialization. They focus on the forces of globalization and the shocks and sensations of the modern metropolis, allowing readers to contend at once with its allures and repulsions. Body writing's confessional mode reveals how the female body is caught between local and global economic forces, both subject to marketing of high-end consumer goods and aware of the need to self-commodify in all aspects of personhood to assert the self. In other words, beauty writers call attention to the fact that women's social value is reduced to their bodies; indeed, women can claim their subjectivity only by flaunting themselves and self-commodifying while ironically calling attention to the complex process of their objectification and commodification.

Set in Shenzhen and Shanghai in the late 1980s and mid-1990s, *Candy* is told from the first-person perspective of a "problem" girl, Hong 红. *Candy* depicts Hong's loss of self-control and her spiritual journey for meaning and freedom through the senses. Early in the novel Hong proclaims: "I had lost faith in everything. I was only sixteen, but my life was over. Fucking over" (Mian Mian 2003: 8). Dropping out of high school at the age of seventeen in Shanghai, Hong floats to Shenzhen, the showcase city of reform era China, where she enters a youth subculture of rock music, alternative lifestyles, drug addiction, petty crime, and casual sexual encounters. Hong falls in love with Saining 赛宁, through whom she learns about drugs and rock music. Both have overbearing parents whose expectations they refuse to live up to. Addicted to drugs, Hong returns to Shanghai to enroll in a drug rehabilitation program. Although the promiscuous Saining remains her object of true love, Hong also tries marriage and experiments with sexual partners, but she finds herself going back to where she started. In the end, however, Saining dies. It is through these failures that Hong finally finds herself. Hong represents a generation lost in China's rapidly globalizing cities. Throughout the novel, Hong uses an airy subjective voice and a wantonly flowing, interior-focused style to convey how she has sex so as to find something to believe in. In this universe of pub hopping, drug use, and rock 'n' roll, bodily sensations and experiences give validity to her existence, whereas all ideological structures seem hollow and dysfunctional.

Wei Hui's *Shanghai Baby* focuses on the struggle between body and soul in globalizing Shanghai. The female protagonist, Nikki 倪可, is known by her friends as Coco because of her passion for Coco Chanel. A café waitress and an aspiring writer who has written some short stories in a sensual, sexually detailed style, Nikki is working on her first novel. She meets the young and artistic Tian Tian 天天, for whom she feels tenderness and love, but Tian Tian grows reclusive and impotent as a result of his troubling relationship with his mother. Nikki later gravitates to Mark 马克, a tall, blond businessman from Germany with whom she starts a highly charged sexual relationship. As a result of Nikki's infidelity, Tian Tian seeks escape in drugs. Nikki's great awakening arrives when she returns to Tian Tian after some passionate final days with the departing Mark, only to have Tian Tian die next to her in bed from a drug overdose.

Shanghai Baby's world of drugs, ennui, and luxury brands reflects a small group of well-to-do but rather parasitic youth. The parasitic spectacle-hungry mistress is a new subject in the consumerist age, a far cry from the female character types of the socialist era, such as the "woman soldier" (女战士), the "iron girl" (铁姑娘), or the "model woman laborer"(女劳模). In Wei Hui's and Mian Mian's writings, commodity and genital gratification work together seamlessly, testifying to the amoral and apolitical stance of capital, even though capital often poses as an indispensable catalyst undermining state control as well as spurring sexual liberation.

Since the turn of the century, "youth literature" (青春文学) has flourished, with Han Han (1982–) and Guo Jingming (1983–) its most influential representatives. Participants in the "New Concept Composition Contest" organized by a literary journal, Han Han and Guo Jingming gained huge market success with the publication of their winning novels *Triple Gate* (三重门, 2000) and *City of Fantasies* (幻城, 2003), respectively. In addition to managing their public images to enhance their fame, these two writers-turned-entrepreneurs make extensive use of the Internet and mass media to propel their literary careers and cultivate their celebrity. With the rise of the Internet and the use of advertisements, interviews, blogs, and videos for market promotions, the boundaries between literature, business, and entertainment have melted. Beauty writers and youth writers alike profited through public-image management: the beauty writers flaunted their youthful bodies in their writing and promotional activities, whereas Guo and Han have invested in and cultivated prominent brand images.

Guo and Han appear more lifelike, more personal, and more well rounded—in other words, more like real people—than public figures of the pre-Internet era. Among other things, the Internet enables Guo and Han to have more direct connections with potential readers and allows them to control their image by inundating those readers with text and video links. Besides being a race car driver and product endorser, Han Han is also a blogger whose provocative postings made him the most popular blogger in the world in 2010. Likewise, Guo uses the Internet to directly market his work and personality to his readers; he publishes extracts of his work on the web as a teaser to draw in readers.

Guo and Han have also been influential in shaping the new characters of the current era. In Guo Jingming's case, his characters live in a historical vacuum in which personal career aspirations and private relationships mean everything. In his twenties, Guo was already ranked among China's richest writers. All his novels are best sellers, and the *Tiny Times* (小时代) film series, which he directed and adapted from his own novels of the same name, was a huge box office success in 2013 and 2014. The *Tiny Times* novels accurately define a new China, where the logic of capital invades all dimensions of personhood. Set in Shanghai, it is a trilogy about four women who leave college and enter the corporate world. Using a descriptive style that paints a world dominated by economic pursuits, Guo writes in a slightly melancholic but aesthetically pleasing manner. His descriptive prose makes the narrow compass of private life infinitely grand. Guo's style renders the fierce corporate world rosy, and his deep narrative of private struggles has struck a chord with a generation of young urban Chinese. Guo's prose creates a world of pretty boys and girls who forego all grand narratives and live in a weightless here and now; in their lives, there are only career ambitions, relationships, and brand-name possessions.

Guo Jingming's writings emerge out of the special historical circumstances of the market-oriented 1990s, where *homo economicus* was the new ideal. The novels are filled with luxury fashion brands, such as Hermes, Birkin, Prada, and LV. Guo's protagonists want to live the "China dream" of the new century: owning cars and houses, graduating from elite universities, working at transnational corporations, leading a fashion-savvy, cosmopolitan, middle-class life. None of the young protagonists in *Tiny Times* are "laborers" in the traditional sense. Inheriting all they have from their families, these youngsters gradually grow into consumer subjects; capital and commodities permeate their everyday lives and their emotional experiences. Beyond the "ideology-free," anti-intellectual gesture that appeals to many young urban readers, Guo Jingming's works bespeak a complete affirmation of the mainstream values of a market society. His writings bridge commodity fetishism and a euphoria centered on capital.

As a contrast to Guo Jingming's highly abstract and dehistoricized works, Han Han's writings suggest that for the post-1980s generation, the individual experience as well as one's personal destiny remains fundamentally rooted in concrete historical circumstances. Han Han dropped out of high school at seventeen and published *The Triple Gate*. Through the voice of its rebellious hero, the high school student Lin Yuxiang 林雨翔, *Triple Gate* portrays a problem-ridden high school life by crystallizing how the ineffectiveness and absurdity of the education system manifest in concrete social relations, such as teacher-student relationships and the relationships among students. Like the self-taught Han Han, who quit the world of schooling and high-stakes exams out of utter disillusionment, Lin Yuxiang shows a maturity beyond his years.

Youth writers emerge at a moment when the marketization of education forces them to define and express a unique experience under the weight of an education system that aims to reduce them to nothing more than a career path. In such a system, youth need an outlet to speak; lonely and alienated, they hunger for a literature that gives expression to a new existential state. Meeting the needs of both, the publishing industry found and profited from these young authors. If teenage novels like Yu Xiu's 郁秀 *Bloom During the Rainy Season* (花季雨季, 1996) spelled out the ennui, the hidden sorrow and subtle lamentation of blossoming youth trapped by and wasting away in a career-oriented, prison-like school system, Han Han's writing follows this trend but is more rebellious and more overtly critical. Han Han's biting social criticism and acute social observations conveniently provide the publishing industry with a spicier, rowdier, rockier, more scandalous, more sensational product, which equals more profit.

In a drastically changing China, despite its commercialization, Han Han's writing unequivocally spells out the loss of certainty in everyday life. In novels such as *Triple Gate*, *A City* (一座城池), and *Days of Glory* (光荣日), Han Han's characters wander about in a world of absurdity and hypocrisy without a definite goal. They express sober criticism of and discontent with the status quo; passive resistance is their dominant mode of life. Often going through a process of helplessness, compromise, or resistance, the characters experience a spiritual odyssey, but they find that their path leads nowhere.

Literary commercialization of the post-Mao era has also led to significant changes in the structure of readership, in modes of literary production, and in ideologies. One example is market fragmentation, most prominently featuring the development of the niche market and the compartmentalization of readerships. Whereas some low-brow works may mindlessly repeat a marketable formula, others can unveil the logic and tension of capital and demonstrate complex negotiation with capital. Although the marketing of Yu Hua's *Brothers* demonstrates that the high-brow can captivate a low-brow readership, the works of beauty writers and youth writers suggest further fragmentation of the high-brow and low-brow divide. New modes of literary production, such as fee- or subscription-based Internet fiction and blog literature, resonate with the emergence of new styles, new languages, new social outlooks, and new senses of personhood. Ideologically, commercialized literature tends to celebrate and promote individual eccentricity, demonstrating a "liberalization" of personality and the importance of commodity consumption in personality expression. A cult of personality marks both authors' self-marketing and the characters they create. However, the ideological shift to consumerist values does not mean that socialist ideas have all but vanished: new "red classics" (红色经典) also emerge in response to commercialization and are commercially viable.

Commercialization of literature remains an ongoing process. Established as well as aspiring writers now find themselves absorbed by the ebb and flow of the here and now. Unlike in the 1980s, when literature was endowed with aspirations to produce high-minded visions for Chinese society or for literature itself, after the market reforms of the 1990s it lost some of its luster. Literature was no longer placed on a pedestal, nor did it take itself too seriously, content with capturing the present, with being entertaining, profitable, and even fleeting. As commercialization brings about new attitudes toward literature, new channels of expression, new modes of living, and new kinds of personhood, however, the people emerging from such historical conditions will find ways to assert their agency against the myriad fantasies and illusions generated in literary production in the era of commercialization.

Bibliography

Coderre, Laurence. "Meaningful Mobility and the Ties That Bind: 1988 as Postsocialist Road Story." *Modern Chinese Literature and Culture* 26, 2 (Fall 2014): 1–37.

Fumian, Marco. "The Temple and the Market: Controversial Positions in the Literary Field with Chinese Characteristics." *Modern Chinese Literature and Culture* 21, 2 (Fall 2009): 126–166.

Henningsen, Lena. *Copyright Matters: Imitation, Creativity and Authenticity in Contemporary Chinese Literature.* Berlin: Berliner Wissenschafts-Verlag, 2010.

Knight, Sabina. "Self-Ownership and Capitalist Values in 1990s Chinese Fiction." In *The Heart of Time: Moral Agency in Twentieth-Century Chinese Fiction*, 222–258. Cambridge: Harvard University Asia Center, 2006.

——. "Shanghai Cosmopolitan: Class, Gender and Cultural Citizenship in Weihui's *Shanghai Babe*." In Jie Lu, ed., *China's Literary and Cultural Scene at the Turn of the 21st Century*, 43–58. New York: Routledge, 2008.

Lu, Hongwei. "Body-Writing: Cruel Youth, Urban Linglei, and Special Economic Zone Syndrome in Mian Mian's *Candy*." *Chinese Literature Today* (Winter/Spring 2011): 40–47.

Mian Mian. *Candy*. Trans. Andrea Lingenfelter. Boston: Little Brown, 2003.

Wei, Hui. *Marrying Buddha*. Trans. Larissa Heinrich. London: Constable and Robinson, 2005.

——. *Shanghai Baby*. Trans. Bruce Humes. New York: Simon and Schuster, 2001.

Yu Hua. *Brothers*. Trans. Carlos Rojas and Eileen Cheng-yin Chow. New York: Anchor Books, 2010.

51

POPULAR GENRE FICTION: SCIENCE FICTION AND FANTASY

MINGWEI SONG

Genre fiction regained popularity in mainland China over the past two decades as literature went through a rapid process of marketization (see "Commercialization of Literature in the Post-Mao Era"). Some genres have existed in Chinese literature for a long time; martial arts (武侠) and romance (言情), for example, prevailed in Hong Kong and Taiwan for decades before becoming popular again on the mainland. Fantasy (奇幻), science fiction (科幻), and mystery (悬疑), three of the most prominent new genres, have been heavily influenced by contemporary Western popular literature. Other genres or subgenres are domestically cultivated and are often characterized by the thematic, stylistic, and narrative conventions formulated in recent best sellers. For example, "grave robbery" (盗墓) fiction came into existence as a subgenre that combines horror and adventure following the success of two novel series, *Ghost Blows Out the Lamp* (鬼吹灯, 2006) and *Grave Robbers' Chronicles* (盗墓笔记, 2007–2012), and the plot patterns of "struggle in the palace" (宫斗) fiction are largely defined by best sellers such as the time travel romance *Suspense at Every Step* (步步惊心, 2011).

Genre fiction production has differed from both state-supported and author-centered literary practices. Many of these popular novels first emerged as serials on the Internet, written by amateur authors, closely followed by fans who often post comments, and later published in book form when a substantial readership was generated. Active online interactions among netizens often further develop the world system outlined in a certain set of novels, motivating the creations of spinoffs and fan fiction, as well as creating communities of imagination based on readers' shared interest, knowledge, and identification.

Escapism dominates many genres that are popular in China today, though social exposés still exist and appeal to relatively older readers. For the young generation growing up as netizens, the pleasure of reading often comes from imaginative engagements in fictional worlds far removed from mundane reality. The majority of the popular genres share elements of fantasy ranging from the sensational to the supernatural to the utopian/dystopian. This phenomenon may, as many critics believe, suggest an unwillingness to engage reality directly, but it can, as in some science fiction, also nurture imagination of alternative worlds that reflect negatively on this world.

One of the most influential fantasy novels published in recent years is *City of Fantasies* (幻城, 2002) by Guo Jingming 郭敬明 (b. 1983), a "youth writer" who later became one of the most widely admired and iconic figures in Chinese popular culture (see "Commercialization of Literature in the Post-Mao Era"). *City of Fantasies*, Guo's debut novel, is full of clichés. Populated by magicians, mermaids, and princes, the novel borrows heavily from Western epic fantasies, Japanese manga, and Chinese martial arts romances. The "illusory snow empire" (幻雪帝国), where most of the story takes place, is a purely imaginary realm that lacks the clarity and complexity of a carefully constructed fictional world such as J. R. R. Tolkien's Middle-earth or Ursula K. Le Guin's Earthsea. Guo's style is a combination of intense hyperbole and pretentious sentimentalism, which converge in a dreamlike text that foregrounds surreal visuality at the cost of narrative coherence. In many ways, *City of Fantasies* establishes a model for later fantasy novels by authors of Guo's generation: fragmented narrative, introverted characters, lyrical prose, and shallow sentimentalism.

A more ambitious project for constructing a unique Chinese fantasy world has been carried out by authors who formed the "Jiuzhou" (九州) community. An archaic name for China's nine territories, which are supposed to have existed since the legendary Xia dynasty, Jiuzhou was revived by contemporary writers to refer to an imaginary world consisting of twelve stars, nine lands, and six human or anthropomorphic races. First conceived by authors such as Pan Haitian 潘海天 (b. 1975) and Jiang Nan 江南 (b. 1977), Jiuzhou came into existence in 2002 as a common setting for online stories and novels. Over several years of collective efforts by nearly one hundred authors, Jiuzhou gradually evolved into a sophisticated enterprise that saw the publication of dozens of novels and two major magazines as well as the creation of online games and virtual communities. Diversely and loosely constructed, the world of Jiuzhou is nevertheless meant to center Chinese fantasy novels on a unique set of Chinese elements derived from traditional mythologies, geographies, astrology, ethnographies, and historical writings. Jiuzhou is a landmark phenomenon in contemporary Chinese popular literature because it has not only popularized the idea of creating a particularly Chinese form of fantasy but also gained for fantasy a large number of faithful readers and devoted authors.

Popular-genre fiction has also witnessed overlapping between fantasy and science fiction author and reader communities. The two genres have reached unprecedented popularity in tandem, but for the diehard Chinese fans who began to populate the Internet at the turn of the twenty-first century, science fiction remains distinct from fantasy. These fans promote the idea of "hard science fiction" (硬科幻) to highlight the genre's validations of its technological "nova" in scientific discourse, which echoes a general trend of scientism in the popular consciousness of contemporary China, though the scientific discourses in science fiction can, of course, be imaginary and fictional. Another widely circulated argument for a clear division between science fiction and fantasy has to do with gender: the former is a "masculine" genre and the latter a "feminine" one. Whereas some works of popular-genre fiction can be highly stereotypical in their gender representation, other works of fantasy and science fiction offer radical experiments in writing about transgender and transspecies in imaginary and allegorical contexts.

A genre first promoted by Liang Qichao 梁启超 (1873–1929) at the very beginning of the twentieth century, science fiction experienced a boom in the late Qing period and then again in the early post-Mao reform era. Earlier science fiction authors wrote tales of political utopianism, with optimism about the power and potential of technology. When the new wave of Chinese science fiction emerged online at the turn of the twenty-first century, it appropriated and parodied those earlier themes in a changing context of globalization and fast-paced technological advances.

One of the first major science fiction novels to signal the arrival of a new wave in Chinese science fiction is Liu Cixin's 刘慈欣 (b. 1963) *China 2185* (中国2185). Published only on the Internet, the novel was drafted, according to the author, in the spring of 1989. It describes the resurrection of Mao's consciousness in cyberspace, where it triggers a cybernetic popular uprising that paralyzes the authorities in the real world. Liu does not glorify the cybernetic uprising or denigrate Mao's political legacy but instead creates an ambiguous utopian/dystopian vision reflecting on the effects of cybernetic democracy and technologized governance. The novel holds social criticism at bay while concentrating on experiments of conceiving "alterity" in terms of the social and scientific future of humanity. A political cyberpunk novel, *2185*, though largely unknown until Liu became a best-selling author much later, anticipated a radically different future for Chinese science fiction that was less idealistic and optimistic. A dark version of science fiction—the new wave—gradually came into existence in the decades after 1989.

The new wave of Chinese science fiction is both popular and subversive. It mingles utopianism with dystopian anomalies, challenges conventional ideas of humanity through posthuman images, and questions key concepts of Chinese modernity, such as progress, development, nationalism, and scientism. Compared with fantasy fiction, the new wave of science fiction has engaged seriously with social, political, and philosophical themes. The world systems created by authors like Liu Cixin are at once sublime and provocative, characterized by wild imagination beyond the mundane as well as the uncanny estrangement of the familiar.

Wang Jinkang 王晋康 (b. 1948), Han Song 韩松 (b. 1965), and Liu Cixin are the three most prominent authors of this new wave. They each have a distinctive style and a set of unique themes. Wang Jinkang is particularly interested in exploring the ethical effects of the biological and political reengineering of humanity, evident in many of his novels and stories. One of his most bizarre stories, "The Regenerated Giant" (转生的巨人, 2006), published under a pen name, addresses the theme of China's hunger for unlimited economic development through a story about a business tycoon's regeneration into a giant baby whose uncontrollable growth eventually causes his own demise. *Ant Life* (蚁生, 2007), Wang's most widely acclaimed novel, envisions an experiment in a utopian society conducted by a sent-down youth during the Cultural Revolution. The protagonist seeks to create an ideal society by spraying people with an "altruistic element" extracted from ants. His utopian community of altruists quickly collapses when its members are seized by an antlike submission to the collective will. *Ant Life* is one of several Chinese science fiction novels set against the backdrop of the Cultural Revolution, which looms large in contemporary writers' visions of utopian experiments and their dystopian results.

Compared with Wang Jinkang, Han Song's style is darker, and his writings show an obsession with the uncanny posthuman condition. Several of his novels, including *Red Ocean* (红色海洋, 2004), *Subway* (地铁, 2010), and *High-Speed Rail* (高铁, 2012), delineate the future histories of human degeneration. For his allegorical depictions of absurd, nightmarish scenes, Han Song's style is called "Kafkaesque." In his unpublished short story "My Fatherland Does Not Dream" (我的祖国不做梦), at night all citizens of Beijing turn into restless, sleepwalking construction workers. The first chapter of *Subway* depicts the horror and bewilderment of an old clerk witnessing the secret removal of human bodies from the midnight train. Han Song's literary images also clearly refer to some of Lu Xun's 鲁迅 famous metaphors, such as the "iron house" and cannibalism. One of his short stories, "The Passengers and the Creator" (乘客与创造者, 2006), for instance, depicts a group of Chinese people stuck in a new type of "iron house": the main cabin of an airplane where they are fed the flesh of those who died on the plane. The characters in this story have to go through the process of being enlightened and making a revolution that ends in a plane crash. A journalist working for the Xinhua News Agency, Han Song has repeatedly said that China's reality is more science fictional than science fiction. His imagination often thrives on the reconstruction of China's reality into fantasy that poignantly amplifies the pains and sorrows behind the myth of China's development. The 2008 Sichuan earthquake inspired him to compose one of his most enchanting stories, "The Regenerated Bricks" (再生砖, 2010). It depicts how artists and developers create humanized, intelligent bricks by recycling earthquake remains in which is embedded human flesh. The "miracle" of the regenerated bricks eventually enables the Chinese to conquer the universe, but what they build with these bricks is forever haunted by the whispers and weeping of the dead.

While Wang Jinkang's and Han Song's novels have sold modestly, Liu Cixin is the unrivaled best-selling author of science fiction in China today. Having published dozens of short stories and two novels (excluding *China 2185*, which remains unpublished), Liu's magnum opus, *The Three-Body Trilogy* (三体, 2006–2010), has sealed his reputation as China's foremost science fiction writer. The last volume of the trilogy was on the best-seller lists of several major newspapers and became a topic for nationwide discussions on TV and the Internet. The trilogy has been viewed as the Chinese equivalent of Isaac Asimov's *Foundation* series and as a landmark in Chinese science fiction's "golden age." *The Three-Body Trilogy* tells an epic story that begins with the Cultural Revolution when a secret mission launched by Mao made contact with a hostile alien civilization living in an unstable Trisolaran system and concludes with the end of the universe. It centers on the question of whether morality is necessary in a universe that thrives on the law of the jungle. Filled with sublime and awe-inspiring images of space wars, technological utopia, and wondrous mutations of the rules of physics, Liu Cixin's narrative is cold-bloodedly realistic in portraying the moral dilemma of its characters when confronted with catastrophic threats from alien civilizations. A dramatic conflict unfolds between the moral instincts of humanity and the necessity for survival. Although many characters choose to follow the former at crucial moments in the story, the latter prevails in a universe with limited resources. In the second volume, one of the main characters establishes the principles of "astrosociology," combining social Darwinism with the Maoist mandate for self-defense and preemptive attack, which is described as a key to unlocking the darkest secret of the universe. But the narrative remains ambiguous with regard to the conflicts between morality and survival, humanism and scientism, hope and despair. Through the overall plot development Liu clearly shows that the universe is a cold place with little room for morality, but the most powerful and stirring aspect of the trilogy may come from the inextinguishable humanity that can be found even in the coldest moments and places.

Fans and critics have announced that Chinese science fiction entered the "post–*Three Body* era" after Liu's success. Although there has perhaps not been another novel that can compete with *The Three-Body Trilogy*, the market for science fiction has opened up substantially. Since 2010, dozens of younger science fiction writers have published their first books, and this third boom of Chinese science fiction seems to be enduring.

Bibliography

Feng, Jin. *Romancing the Internet: Consuming and Producing Chinese Web Romance.* Leiden: Brill, 2013.

Han Song 韩松. *Ditie* 地铁 (Subway). Shanghai: Shanghai renmin, 2011.

———. "Zaisheng zhuan" 再生砖 (Regenerated bricks). *Wenyi fengshang* 1 (December 2010): 59–71.

Huss, Mikael. "Hesitant Journey to the West: SF's Changing Fortunes in Mainland China." *Science Fiction Studies* 27, 1 (March 2000): 92–104.

Isaacson, Nathaniel. "Science Fiction for the Nation: Tales of the Moon Colony and the Birth of Modern Chinese Fiction." *Science Fiction Studies* 40, 1 (2013): 33–54.

Jia, Liyuan. "Gloomy China: China's Image in Han Song's Science Fiction." *Science Fiction Studies* 40, 1 (2013): 103–115.

Jones, Andrew. *Developmental Fairy Tales: Evolutionary Thinking and Modern Chinese Culture.* Cambridge, MA: Harvard University Press, 2011.

Liu, Cixin. *The Dark Forest.* Trans. Joel Martinsen. New York: Tor Books, 2015.

———. *The Three-Body Problem.* Trans. Ken Liu. New York: Tor Books, 2014.

Song, Mingwei. "Preface." Special issue on "Chinese Science Fiction: Late Qing and the Contemporary," *Renditions* 77/78 (Spring/Autumn 2012): 6–14.

———. "Variations on Utopia in Contemporary Chinese Science Fiction." *Science Fiction Studies* 40, 1 (2013): 86–102.

Wagner, Rudolf. "Lobby Literature: The Archaeology and Present Functions of Science Fiction in the People's Republic of China." In Jeffrey Kinkley, ed., *After Mao: Chinese Literature and Society, 1978–1981,* 17–62. Cambridge, MA: Harvard University Press, l985.

Wang, David Der-wei. *Fin-de-Siècle Splendor: Repressed Modernities of Late Qing Fiction, 1849–1911.* Stanford, CA: Stanford University Press, 1997.

Wang Jinkang 王晋康. *Yisheng* 蚁生 (Ant life). Fuzhou: Fujian renmin, 2007.

Wu, Yan. "'Great Wall Planet': Introducing Chinese Science Fiction." *Science Fiction Studies* 40, 1 (2013): 1–14.

52

WORD AND IMAGE: GAO XINGJIAN
MABEL LEE

Gao Xingjian's 高行健 (b. 1940) creative endeavors embody word and image and, moreover, the literary and the visual are simultaneously present in his work. As in traditional Chinese literati practice, Gao's paintings exude a sense of poetry, while his literary creations are replete with imagery, and this represents the strongest link with his Chinese cultural heritage. In traditional China, word and image were not antagonistic binaries as in the modern West and, subsequently, in modern China. Plays, of course, are written for actualization by performers in a theater space and by definition involve a written text as well as its visual presentation on the stage. Gao has written nineteen works for the theater, and in the playwright-directed Taipei and Marseille productions of his grand opera *Snow in August* (八月雪, 2000), his ink paintings are in fact a dominating presence as stage background. His unique style of Chinese ink painting that incorporates texture, sensuality, and poetic suggestion developed in tandem with his extensive innovations in the writing of narrative fiction during the early 1980s, and striking visual images can be found in the short stories of his *Buying a Fishing Rod for My Grandfather* (给我老爷买鱼竿, 1989) and in his autobiographical novels *Soul Mountain* (灵山, 1990) and *One Man's Bible* (一个人的圣经, 1999), which complement each other in presenting aesthetic portrayals of Gao's life. Both novels are lengthy works providing the author with ample space to implement his strategies for expanding the expressive potential of the written language and for challenging conventionally accepted models of narration. The most striking feature of both novels is the sustained use of various pronouns to probe the protagonists' psyches. That his painting and narrative fiction indicate similar sensibilities is not coincidental, because their common wellspring lies deep in the hinterland of Gao's unconscious, where a wealth of inchoate sensations demand concrete expression. If words fail to express these sensations, he resorts to images. He is cognizant of both his ecstasy during the creative process and his total exhaustion afterward.

Many of China's finest writings in premodern times were inspired by the ancient Daoist literary masterpiece known as *Zhuangzi*, which espoused the idea that the individual who attains oneness with the cosmos is insignificant, but through the free roaming of the untrammelled self in creative pursuits he or she is able to attain great heights of ecstasy. The advent of Western modernity in China denigrated traditional culture with increasing intensity beginning in the second decade of the twentieth century, and in this period literature and art became two separate disciplines, as in the West. The antitraditional modernist thrust was soon appropriated by politics, and during the Cultural Revolution (1966–1976) any person clinging to traditional culture could be persecuted or even hounded to death. The *Zhuangzean* notion of joy in creative activities was erased from memory and practice. Gao's creative impulses in writing and painting were nurtured through childhood and early adolescence, but thereafter he encountered a succession of harsh political campaigns aimed at stifling individuality in thought and action to coerce the entire population into obedience. As the Cultural Revolution drew to an end, Gao embarked on a rigorous study of premodern writings that connected him with *Zhuangzi*, but with a clear understanding that he lived in modern times. Over many centuries alcohol and various drugs were commonly used to induce a state of Daoist nonbeing that would release creative energies, but in Gao's case it is by listening to music that he attains a state of primordial transcendence for his creative process: Mozart's *Great Mass*, Mahler's *Eighth Symphony*, Shostakovich's *Eleventh, Fourteenth, and Fifteenth Symphonies*, Messiaen's *L'Ascension*, and some dirges sung by folk Daoists that he had recorded while in China are among the many works he has mentioned.

Gao was born in 1940 in the Republican era, but he received most of his formal education in the People's Republic. The prospect of painting propaganda posters for life led him to abort his original plan to become an artist, and he instead enrolled as a five-year major in French literature at the Foreign Languages Institute, Beijing, graduating in 1962. He worked in Beijing as editor and translator at the Foreign Languages Press until he was assigned work as playwright for the People's Art Theater in 1981. His reading of French writings as an undergraduate ignited his desire to write, but it was a time when writers were being persecuted, and it was impossible for him to show anyone the "politically incorrect" works he was writing in secret. Nonetheless, he carried out an intensive self-study of world writings by systematically reading through the library's holdings. At the outbreak of the Cultural Revolution he burned a suitcase of unpublished manuscripts rather than risk having them found and suffer the consequences of being branded a counterrevolutionary.

When the political situation relaxed after the Cultural Revolution, Gao emerged among a cohort of unpublished writers who suddenly rose to prominence. His short stories, poems, and criticism frequently appeared in literary publications. His book *Preliminary Exploration Into the Art of Modern Fiction* (现代小说技巧初探, 1981) came under the scrutiny of the authorities. He had proposed that literary characters should have human characteristics and literature should not be written to "educate," posing a direct challenge to Mao Zedong's guidelines for cultural production. However, the enthusiastic response of audiences to the staging of his first plays validated what he had proposed. His first play, *Absolute Signal* (绝对信号, 1982), instantly turned him into a celebrity. His second play, *Bus Stop* (车站, 1983), created even greater excitement but was banned after the tenth staging: the "Anti–Spiritual Pollution" campaign of 1983 had begun, and he fled for his life to parts unknown until the campaign died out toward the end of that year. The staging of his third play, *Wild Man* (野人, 1985), also won high critical acclaim in literary circles, and during the period the play was being performed he took the opportunity to hold an exhibition of his ink paintings in the theater foyer. His 1986 play *The Other Shore* (彼岸) was banned after a few rehearsals, and from then on he found himself subjected to various insidious forms of harassment that are detailed in his memoir, "Wilted Chrysanthemums" (隔日黄花, 1991).

In late 1987, Gao relocated to Paris, where he resolutely worked to recoup the lost decades of his creative life. He gradually found theaters for his plays—sometimes with him as the director—and publishers and galleries to represent him. Unencumbered by politics, he submitted to the demands of his creative self in exploring and articulating in word or image the rich terrain of his unconscious. His contribution to literature and the arts was acknowledged in France, where he was awarded the Chevalier de l'Ordre des Arts et des Lettres (1992), and he received the Nobel Prize in Literature on December 7, 2000. At the time many of his major works had been translated into French, Swedish, and English, and his plays had been performed on five continents. In the one-hundred-year history of the Nobel Prize, his award was the first for a body of works originally created in the Chinese language. He received the award as a French citizen, having taken up citizenship in 1997.

In his Nobel lecture, "The Case for Literature" (文学的理由, 2000), Gao states that literature is the solitary act of the individual and as such has its own rationale for existence: "Literature can only be the voice of the individual and this has always been so." He claims to write for himself and to be his own reader and critic; moreover, as literary creation is primarily for the writer's own aesthetic fulfillment, he feels no strong need for readers to read what he writes. He warns: "Once literature is contrived as the hymn of the nation, the flag of the race, the mouthpiece of a political party, or the voice of a class or group, it can be employed as a mighty all-engulfing tool of propaganda. However, such literature loses what is inherent in literature, ceases to be literature, and becomes a substitute for power and profit." The repression of individual autonomy during the Cultural Revolution had given him unique insights into the substance and intrinsic value of literature, and he advocates a form of writing akin to Chinese "recluse literature" of the past—often writers and artists would "recluse" themselves in a metaphorical sense even while living in the midst of the hustle and bustle of society.

Addressing a world audience in his Nobel lecture, Gao took the opportunity to indict the baleful influence of Nietzsche (1844–1900) for having unleashed destructive megalomania everywhere during the twentieth century. In his view, Nietzsche's pronouncement "God is dead!" had led to the proliferation of countless lesser "supermen" who saw their heroic role as saviors of humankind, nation, or race. In the year leading to his departure from China, Gao read in Chinese translation all Nietzsche's major works, and an intense loathing began to manifest itself in his essays and creative works from 1990 onward. His first major attack on Nietzsche appears in his play *Escape* (逃亡, 1990), which he wrote in late 1989 a few months after the military crackdown on student demonstrators in Tiananmen Square on June 4. He had not failed to note that the student movement of 1989 was inspired by celebrations for the seventieth anniversary of the May Fourth student movement of 1919 or that on both occasions a Nietzsche craze was raging in China. The play is critical of student leaders for naively thinking that plastic bottles and bricks were a match for tanks and live ammunition, as well as for failing to have worked out an exit strategy in advance.

However, the primary concern of *Escape* is the exploration of human psychology and behavior: the prospect of imminent death can arouse sexual lust because of a primeval instinct to continue the species, and the mind can race back to events of one's childhood; a person who joins group action abrogates individual autonomy and is instead directed by the group; mass hysteria can be induced by mesmerizing music and frenzied dancing, such as that seen all over the world in television footage of Tiananmen protesters dancing to rock music played on ghetto-blasters; the worship of totems—even those as noble as democracy, the revolution, the nation, and the race—can have an anesthetic effect on rational thinking, and "supermen" heroes will willingly sacrifice themselves for the cause. Many of these issues are probed further in his second novel, *One Man's Bible*, which recounts what he had witnessed during the Cultural Revolution. He also makes a sustained attack on Nietzsche throughout his long treatise on art, "Another Kind of Aesthetics" (另一种美学, 1997), and gives a stark and ironic visual representation of what he perceives as Nietzsche's pernicious impact on art in his play *The Man Who Questions Death* (Le Quêteur de la Morte, 2003; 叩问死亡, 2004).

Gao employs word and image in interpenetrative ways to create works that will gratify his own multidimensional aesthetic sensibilities. In the early 1980s, he also carried out extensive research on the Chinese language and devised strategies to ensure that the musicality inherent in spoken Chinese was replicated in the plays and fiction that he began to write at that time: audio appeal is as important as visual appeal in his writings. His ink paintings, which he describes as being "between figurative and abstract," have been familiar in the international art world since the mid-1980s and have been exhibited in galleries in the United States, in Asia, and throughout Europe. More recently, he has produced three art films, each of which abandons conventional modes of filmmaking: *La Silhouette sinon l'ombre* (侧影或影子, 2007), *Après le déluge* (洪荒之后, 2008), and *Requiem for Beauty* (美的葬礼, 2013). Each of these films variously seeks to expand the limitations of the screen, and he regards his films as "cinematic poems." It is Gao's intense intellectual curiosity that drives him to interrogate the internal dynamics of genres and media; the theoretical underpinnings of his resulting innovations are elucidated in detail in the essays collected in *Aesthetics and Creation* (论创作, 2008). In 2012, he published his first collection of poetry, *Wandering Spirit and Metaphysical Thoughts* (游神与玄思), and in 2013 his black-and-white photography reproduced on silk was exhibited for the first time at iPreciation Gallery in Singapore and then at the University of Maryland. A large number of his artworks were exhibited simultaneously at the Belgium Museum of Fine Art and at the Museum of Ixelles from February 26 to May 31, 2015.

Bibliography

Chen, Xiaomei. "A Wildman Between Two Cultures: Some Paradigmatic Remarks on 'Influence Studies.'" *Comparative Literature Studies* 29, 4 (1992): 397–416.

Gao, Xingjian. *Aesthetics and Creation*. Trans. Mabel Lee. Amherst, NY: Cambria, 2012.

——. "Another Kind of Aesthetics." Trans. Mabel Lee. In Gao, *Aesthetics and Creation*, 89–158. Amherst, NY: Cambria, 2012.

——. *Ballade Nocturne*. Trans. Claire Conceison. Lewes, UK: Sylph Editions and the American University of Paris, 2010.

——. "*Bus Stop*: A Lyrical Comedy on Life in One Act." Trans. Kimberly Besio. In Haiping Yan, ed., *Theater and Society: An Anthology of Contemporary Chinese Drama*, 3–59. Armonk, NY: M. E. Sharpe, 1998.

——. *City of the Dead*. Trans. Gilbert C. F. Fong. In Gao Xingjian, *City of the Dead and Song of the Night*, 1–61. Hong Kong: Chinese University Press, 2015.

——. *City of the Dead and Song of the Night*. Trans. Gilbert C. F. Fong and Mabel Lee. Hong Kong: Chinese University Press, 2015.

——. "Contemporary Technique and National Character in Fiction." Trans. Ng Mausang. *Renditions* 19–20 (1983): 55–58.

———. *Escape & The Man Who Questions Death*. Trans. Gilbert C. F. Fong. Hong Kong: Chinese University Press, 2007.

———. "*Fugitives*: Translation of a Play by Gao Xingjian." Trans. Gregory B. Lee. In Gregory B. Lee, ed., *Chinese Writing and Exile*, 89–138. Chicago: University of Chicago Center for East Asian Studies, 1993.

———. "Literature as Testimony: The Search for Truth." Trans. Mabel Lee. Stockholm: Swedish Academy, 2001.

———. "Nobel Lecture: The Case for Literature." Trans. Mabel Lee. Stockholm: Swedish Academy, 2000.

———. *One Man's Bible*. Trans. Mabel Lee. New York: HarperCollins, 2002.

———. *The Other Shore: Plays by Gao Xingjian*. Trans. Gilbert C. F. Fong. Hong Kong: Chinese University Press, 1999.

———. "The Other Side: A Contemporary Drama Without Acts." Trans. Jo Riley. In Martha P. Y. Cheung and Jane C. C. Lai, eds., *Oxford Anthology of Contemporary Chinese Drama*, 149–183. New York: Oxford University Press, 1997.

———. *Song of the Night*. Trans. Mabel Lee. In Gao Xingjian, *City of the Dead & Song of the Night*, 64–84. Hong Kong: Chinese University Press, 2015.

———. *Soul Mountain*. Trans. Mabel Lee. New York: HarperCollins, 2000.

———. "The Voice of the Individual." Trans. Lena Aspfors and Torbjörn Lodén. *Stockholm Journal of East Asian Studies* 6 (1995): 71–81.

———. "*Wild Man*: A Contemporary Chinese Spoken Drama." Trans. Bruno Roubicek. *Asian Theater Journal* 7, 2 (1990): 184–249.

———. "Wilted Chrysanthemums." Trans. Mabel Lee. In Gao Xingjian, *The Case for Literature*, 140–154. Sydney: HarperCollins, 2006.

———. "Without Isms." Trans. Winnie Lau, Deborah Sauviat, and Martin Williams. *Journal of the Oriental Society of Australia* 27–28 (1995–96): 105–114.

———. *Youshen yu xuansi* 游神与玄思 (Wandering spirit and metaphysical thoughts). Taipei: Lianjing, 2012.

Kuo, Jason C. "On Gao Xingjian's Films, Paintings, and Photographs." In *Gao Xingjian: After the Flood*, 10–18. Singapore: iPreciation, 2013.

Łabędzka, Izabella. *Gao Xingjian's Idea of Theatre: From the Word to the Image*. Leiden: Brill, 2008.

Lackner, Michael, and Nikola Chardonnens, eds. *Polyphony Embodied: Freedom and Fate in Gao Xingjian's Writings*. Berlin: DeGruyter, 2014.

Lee, Mabel. "Aesthetic Dimensions of Gao Xingjian's Fiction, Theatre, Art, and Filmmaking." Trans. Mabel Lee. In Gao Xingjian, *Aesthetics and Creation*, vii–xxiii. Amherst, NY: Cambria, 2012.

———. "Gao Xingjian: Autobiography and the Portrayal of the Female Psyche." Trans. Mabel Lee. In Gao Xingjian, *City of the Dead and Song of the Night*, vii–xxvii. Amherst, NY: Cambria, 2012.

———. "Gao Xingjian dui Nicai de pipan" 高行健对尼采的批判 (Gao Xingjian's antagonism toward Nietzsche). In Chiu-yee Cheung 张钊贻, ed., *Nicai yu huawen wenxue lunwenji* 尼采与华文文学论文集 (Essays on Nietzsche and Chinese literature), 21–32. Singapore: Global Publishing, 2013.

———. "Gao Xingjian on the Issue of Literary Creation for the Modern Writer." *Journal of Asian Pacific Communication* 9, 1–2 (1999): 83–96.

—. "Gao Xingjian's Dialogue with Two Dead Poets from Shaoxing: Xu Wei and Lu Xun." In R. D. Findeisen and R. H. Gassman, eds., *Autumn Floods: Essays in Honour of Márian Gálik*, ed., 401–414. Bern: Lang, 1998.

—. "The Writer as Translator: On the Creative Aesthetics of Gao Xingjian." In Kwok-kan Tam and Kelly Kar-yue Chan, eds., *Culture in Translation: Reception of Chinese Literature in Comparative Perspective*, 1–18. Hong Kong: Open University of Hong Kong Press, 2012.

—. "Two Autobiographical Plays by Gao Xingjian." Trans. Gilbert C. F. Fong. In Gao Xingjian, *Escape & The Man Who Questions Death*, vii–xviii. Hong Kong: Chinese University Press, 2007.

—. "Without Politics: Gao Xingjian on Literary Creation." *Stockholm Journal of East Asian Studies* 6 (1995): 82–101.

Liu Jianmei 刘剑梅. "*Lingshan*: Xiandai Zhuangzi de kaixuan" 灵山：现代庄子的凯旋 (*Soul Mountain*: The triumph of modern Zhuangzi). In Liu Jianmei, *Zhuangzi de xiandai mingyun* 庄子的现代命运 (The modern fate of Zhuangzi), 296–320. Beijing: Shangwu yinshuguan, 2012.

Liu Zaifu 刘再复. *Gao Xingjian lun* 高行健论 (Essays on Gao Xingjian). Taipei: Lianjing, 2004.

—. *Gao Xingjian yinlun* 高行健引论 (Introductory essays on Gao Xingjian). Hong Kong: Dashan wenhua, 2011.

—. *Lun Gao Xingjian zhuangtai* 论高行健状态 (On the Gao Xingjian state of mind). Hong Kong: Mingbao, 2000.

Lodén, Torbjörn. "World Literature with Chinese Characteristics: On a Novel by Gao Xingjian." *Stockholm Journal of East Asian Studies* 4 (1993): 17–40.

Ma, Sen. "The Theatre of the Absurd in Mainland China: Gao Xingjian's *The Bus Stop*." *Issues and Studies* 25, 8 (1989): 138–148.

Quah, Sy Ren. *Gao Xingjian and Transcultural Chinese Theater*. Honolulu: University of Hawai'i Press, 2004.

—. "Searching for Alternative Aesthetics in the Chinese Theatre: The Odyssey of Huang Zuolin and Gao Xingjian." *Asian Culture* 24 (2000): 44–66.

Special issue on Gao Xingjian. *Modern Chinese Literature and Culture* 14, 2 (Fall 2002). http://u.osu.edu/mclc/journal/back-issues.

Tam, Kwok-kan. "Drama of Dilemma: Waiting as Form and Motif in *The Bus Stop* and *Waiting for Godot*." In Yun-Tong Luk, ed., *Studies in Chinese-Western Comparative Drama Hong Kong*, 23–35. Hong Kong: Chinese University Press, 1990.

—, ed. *Soul of Chaos: Critical Perspectives on Gao Xingjian*. Hong Kong: Chinese University Press, 2001.

Tay, William. "Avant-Garde Theatre in Post-Mao China: *The Bus Stop* by Gao Xingjian." In Howard Goldblatt, ed., *Worlds Apart: Recent Chinese Writing and Its Audiences*, 111–118. Armonk, NY: M. E. Sharpe, 1990.

Yeung, Jessica. *Ink Dances in Limbo: Gao Xingjian's Writing as Cultural Translation*. Hong Kong: Hong Kong University Press, 2008.

Zhao, Henry Y. H. *Towards a Modern Zen Theatre: Gao Xingjian and Chinese Theatre Experimentalism*. London: SOAS Publications, 2000.

53

HONG KONG VOICES: LITERATURE FROM THE LATE TWENTIETH CENTURY TO THE NEW MILLENNIUM

ESTHER M. K. CHEUNG

Hong Kong literary critic Wong Wai-leung claims that Hong Kong literature integrated with modern Chinese literature during World War II, when Hong Kong became the stopover for refugee writers from the mainland. It is true that for a few decades Hong Kong literature was mainly produced by writers either passing through or residing temporarily in Hong Kong. However, this mainland-based view of Hong Kong literature has been altered by the emergence of a generation of writers born and raised in Hong Kong, whose voices are distinguishable from those in earlier times and those from mainland China and Taiwan. From the late twentieth century to the new millennium, some among them have, with the benefit of Western-style education and opportunities of traveling or studying abroad, started to translate or "cotranslate" their own work. It is a fortuitous coincidence that Dung Kai-cheung's 董启章 (b. 1967) *Atlas: The Archeology of an Imaginary City* appeared in 2012 as a full-length book in English translation, and *City at the End of Time: Poems by Leung Ping-Kwan* (1949–2013) was reprinted in 2013 as an expanded volume with new critical material. Unlike earlier writers who either ignore Hong Kong's existence or simply denigrate it as an uninteresting commercial enclave, Dung and Leung turned to the city as their major subject matter. Partly triggered by the looming 1997 turnover, this new literary attention to Hong Kong was more than an uncritical celebration of the city; it marked a generation of voices aiming to negotiate with clichéd images, to rediscover the colonial process, and to rewrite local history. This momentum continued after 1997 when another generation of younger writers came of age in the new millennium. Collectively these writers are preoccupied with the need to consider the paradoxical nature of the Hong Kong urban space through which the notion of home is addressed. They are interested in forging a postcolonial identity for Hong Kong through the process of writing and rewriting Hong Kong history as well as engaging with the dynamic power of what more recent critics in Sinophone discourse might call "place-produced" literature.

To discuss Hong Kong urban space, it is important to start with Liu Yichang 刘以鬯 (b. 1918), an older émigré writer who came to Hong Kong from the mainland before the Communist takeover in 1949 and whose dedication to Hong Kong literature—as both author and editor—has earned him the status of "institution" (Liu Yichang 1995: vii). Unlike other émigré writers who fled to Hong Kong in 1949, Liu demonstrates genuine interest in writing about the Hong Kong experience. Although Liu is a prolific writer, not many of his works are available in English translation. "Intersection" (对倒), a novella representative of his perspective on Hong Kong, inspired Wong Kar-wai's 王家卫 famous film *In the Mood for Love* (花样年华, 2000). Originally serialized in a Hong Kong newspaper in 1972 and then translated into English in 1988, the story traces the crisscrossing paths of a middle-aged man and a young woman who have never known or spoken to each other. Their brief encounter in the cinema is a natural prelude to their final divergence—something all passersby in the city experience. The man, an immigrant from Shanghai, heads north, while the woman, a Hong Kong–born youngster, heads south. These directional markers figuratively signify the different cultural identities in Hong Kong. The mature man's memories of the "north" (Shanghai) often flit by, creating some sense of his cultural displacement living in Hong Kong. In contrast, the young woman's emotional engagement is with her here and now in Hong Kong, but her social alienation is as intense as the man's cultural estrangement. Told in a stream-of-consciousness style, the story depicts both characters in a prolonged moment of personal crisis. The author subtly implies the impossibility for such identities to converge, and the story ends with two birds taking off in different directions, one eastward, the other westward. To Liu, such cultural identities, intertwined with personal and gendered desires and dreams, maintain an uneasy coexistence in Hong Kong.

Liu's recognition of the paradoxical nature of the Hong Kong urban space finds echoes in Leung Ping-kwan 梁秉钧 (Liang Bingjun, pen name of Ye Si 也斯, 1949–2013). Famous for his "poetics of the everyday" in *City at the End of Time* (Esther M. K. Cheung 2013: 2), Leung's verse and prose bring readers to almost every corner of Hong Kong: from the most representative, such as Victoria Harbor and Lan Kwai Fong, to the most mundane, such as Ap-liu Street and Ladder Street; from the historic, such as the Main Building at the University of Hong Kong, to the seemingly exotic Walled City in Kowloon. Born in China but educated in Hong Kong, Leung is particularly interested in exploring the tactics of negotiating with this contradictory space he calls home. In an analysis of "North Point Car Ferry," in the same poetry volume, Ackbar Abbas (1997: 131) describes Leung's urban images as "surreal," turning "the familiar sights of Hong Kong into a post-apocalyptic landscape." His poems vigorously work against clichés, particularly clichéd images of Hong Kong. His poetic world conveys a strong sense of urgency about the end of time; not a mere lamentation over the destructiveness of modernity, his urgency was fueled by an earnest determination to find fresh images for Hong Kong as the city contemplated its "end," its reintegration with China in 1997. In another poem, "Images of Hong Kong," he pleads for "a new angle / for strictly visual matters," because in this "sign" city "history" has diminished into "a montage of images, / of paper, collectibles, plastic, fibers, laserdiscs, buttons," erasing contradictions and differences. Similarly, in "In Fabric Alley," which weaves a world of colorful yet trite patterns and fabrics, Leung expresses a strong desire for "tailoring something new, / to make it so it wears the body well" (Leung 2013: 29). Driven by a sense of belonging to Hong Kong, Leung constantly explores new angles and new patterns to negotiate with hackneyed stories of Hong Kong imposed mainly from the outside.

Wong Bik-wan 黄碧云 (b. 1961) is less interested in dealing with cultural images than Leung, but she is also concerned with the condition of homelessness. As the title of her second collection of short stories, *Tenderness and Violence* (温柔与爆裂, 1994), indicates, homelessness is experienced through contradictions that are an existential and cultural condition. "Losing the City" offers a good example of this treatment of homelessness. Written in the thriller mode, the story is set on the eve of the 1997 turnover, invoking home as an uncanny trope with a strong sense of displacement and desperation. The story is about a middle-class Hong Kong Chinese who feels an immense threat to his capitalist way of life because of the turnover and so resorts to emigration with his wife. However, the sense of homelessness is felt everywhere, and he ends up "tenderly" killing his family when they return to their birthplace, Hong Kong, after years of bitter isolation in North America. Another character, an Irish inspector in Hong Kong, cannot but sense his uprootedness with the approaching end of colonial Hong Kong. Apart from this historical background, Wong seems to suggest that this contradictory experience is also partly an existential crisis: both characters demonstrate their inability to negotiate with fear, pain, and despair. It is only through two other characters, an ambulance driver and his wife (a funeral agent), who witness the bloody aftermath of the murder, that we realize how people can cope with trauma through "the principle of hope." The story ends with an ironic actualization of this principle. By pouring red wine into the bathtub and turning the water into blood, the two make love in the "blood pool," trying to reenact violence "tenderly" and to "exorcize" their fear and despair.

The 1997 turnover triggered the emergence of various literary voices seeking to grasp this important historical change. Dung Kai-cheung chose to rewrite the history of colonial Hong Kong, which he calls "the city of Victoria," in *Atlas: Archaeology of an Imaginary City* (地图集：一个想象的城市的考古学, 1997). Together with the new edition of Leung's *City at the End of Time*, the English rendition of *Atlas* in 2012 has ignited international interest in what Sebastian Veg (2013) calls Hong Kong "cultural activism" through Sinophone literature. The appearance of these literary works in English translation in the new millennium coincided with growing social movements centered on Hong Kong's civic culture. As a younger generation of writers and activists came of age to seek greater freedom in defining Hong Kong, the "place-produced" works of Leung and Dung and others have become sources of inspiration for their cultural activism. Set in the future when the city no longer exists, Dung's *Atlas* demonstrates that history is a matter of interpretation; instead of writing history as a grand narrative, Dung resorts to a fragmented microhistory of Hong Kong's local streets. Taking the readers on a spatial and temporal journey through Possession Street, Aldrich Street, and so on, he writes the histories of the streets through a blending of fact and fiction. In his "atlas" of this imaginary city, the local streets are less like static remains of the past than dynamic processes of cultural translations and of domination and resistance. The story of Possession Street is a case in point. Named by the British as a sign of their military achievements in Hong Kong, the street became associated with a story about how fear of the colonizers gave rise to an imaginary local resistance in the form of ghostly vengeance. The British ultimately restored the original Chinese name, Shui Hang Hau 水坑口, to "exorcise" evils and avoid being "possessed."

Many other writers who similarly write the history of Hong Kong through the stories of the common people and the mundane practices of everyday life share Dung's preoccupation with the past. Xi Xi 西西 (b. 1938) is perhaps the writer most dedicated to this project. She makes use of microhistorical details (legends, myths, oral narratives, and local social customs) to weave a collection of stories that critics call the "Fertile Town" series, among which is the novel *Flying Carpet* (飞毡, 1996). To turn to the past, Leung Ping-kwan also seeks to demythologize the Walled City as a common place, "the place in which we live, the space which we all share" ("Walled City," 39). Hong Kong citizens have known the Walled City in Kowloon, now demolished and turned into a park, as a dirty, dangerous no man's land without law and jurisdiction, a place of prostitution, drug trafficking, illegal dental and medical services, and so on. Without denying any of this, Leung describes the place as "messy, complicated, intriguing," and "frightening," but it is where "most people continued to lead normal lives. Just like Hong Kong" (37).

Unlike Leung and others who aggressively demythologize dominant cultural representations of Hong Kong, Xin Qishi 辛其氏 (b. 1950) is more interested in telling the stories of common people. Her major work, *The Red Chequers Pub* (红格子酒铺, 1994) depicts the experience of some Hong Kong activists who participate in social and nationalistic movements—namely, the

Protect Diaoyu Islands Campaign and the prodemocratic movement of 1989. By setting the story against this historical backdrop, Xin demonstrates how the collective experience of living in Hong Kong is inextricably and inevitably bound up with a sense of Chineseness. In "The Ghost Story," Xin's interest in the Chinese roots of Hong Kong culture is also evident. This story of a garbage collector depicts life in the public housing estates, and the local custom of the Ghost Festival expresses the writer's preoccupation with the past. But as in the work of other writers, fact blends with gossip and legends in Xin's writing of the past.

Xin's literary activism and low mimesis are echoed in the emerging writers of the new millennium. The increased importance of place in Hong Kong literature is particularly notable. Since 1997, the Hong Kong government has busied itself with the branding of the city as "Asia's World City." In the new millennium, urban developments have come into direct confrontation with widespread demands for preserving cultural heritage sites. Threatened by the gradual disappearance of historical buildings and old neighborhoods, the new writers—many of whom are also social activists—share a common urge to express their sense of belonging through poetry, fiction, and prose writing. In the wake of the demolitions of the Star Ferry Pier and the Queen's Pier in 2006 and 2007, respectively, a host of writers—Liu Waitong 廖伟棠, Uncle Hung 雄仔叔叔, Lui Wing Kai 吕永佳, and Tang Siu Wa 邓小桦—have written poems with explicit references to the two piers and their demolitions. In "The Ballad of Queen's Pier" (皇后码头歌谣), Liu Waitong laments the loss of the pier by conjuring up a ghostly space of solidarity between the dead and living when the city's fate is subject to the forbidding bulldozer: "'Cloaked by moon and capped by stars, with you' / Tonight I burn letters on the pier / Demons rise on the thousand spires of the city / I boil rain and burn wind with you / calling out for flying frost in a melting pot." Liu also published a volume of poetry titled *With a Ghost Roaming in Hong Kong* (和幽灵一起的香港漫游, 2008), which gives prominence to Hong Kong's topography. In this collection, the city of Hong Kong is frequented by nameless, ordinary people from society's lowest stratum as well as by deceased known writers such as Eileen Chang 张爱玲, Xiao Hong 萧红, and Dai Wangshu 戴望舒. Chan Chi Tak's 陈智德 *Topographies* (地文志, 2014), a volume of prose writings that blends his own personal memoir and poetry with archival material and literary criticism, breaks new grounds in Sinophone literature. With lucid prose, informative research, and creative tropes, Chan delineates the city of Hong Kong as a memorable home. From vanished entertainment parks and the old airport to small attic bookstores and city spaces charged with political activism, Chan's work accentuates the importance of literary conscience and cultural memories in the contested, public space of a city in transformation.

William Tay (2000: 37) notices that the ideological struggles between Taiwan and mainland China during the Cold War turned Hong Kong into a space for literature to flourish and to speak from the margins. From the late twentieth century to the new millennium, partly due to historical events such as the 1989 Tiananmen Square massacre, the 1997 turnover, and more recent urban developments that have uprooted people's cultural memories, Hong Kong writers have been embarking on a long soul-searching journey into Hong Kong as a marginal place at the edge of the nation-state. Thanks to institutional support, such as the establishment of the Hong Kong Arts Development Council and the development of Hong Kong literature and culture programs in tertiary education institutions, more and more literary voices are heard. Some are gentle, some humorous, some indignant, but they share an urgent need to represent Hong Kong at a time when the city has undergone drastic political and cultural transformations. Whether writing before or after the handover of sovereignty, the notion of home has been central to their representations of the city. Rewriting Hong Kong history and reimagining the city space can be seen as attempts "to seize hold of a memory as it flashes up at a moment of danger, . . . at an instant when it can be recognized and is never seen again" (Benjamin 1969: 255).

The future of Hong Kong literature remains to be seen. Perhaps one direction, the signs of which are already visible, is Hong Kong's active interaction with the larger world outside. While the momentum of internationalization ushered by Dung's and Leung's timely translations in recent years is likely to continue, some writers working in English are already publishing their work. What lies ahead may be the production of new voices writing about new concerns through various media and languages, spreading across visible and invisible boundaries. Among the different thematic concerns, perhaps Hong Kong as home is a long-lasting topic that will engage writers when they attempt to reinvent the complex postcolonial history of Hong Kong.

Bibliography

Abbas, Ackbar. *Hong Kong: Culture and the Politics of Disappearance*. Hong Kong: Hong Kong University Press, 1997.

Benjamin, Walter. "Theses on the Philosophy of History." In *Illuminations*, 253–264. New York: Schocken, 1969.

Chan Chi Tak 陈智德. *Diwen zhi* 地文志 (Topographies). Taipei: Lianjing, 2014.

Cheung, Esther M. K. "New Ends in a City of Transition." In Cheung, ed., *City at the End of Time: Poems by Leung Ping-kwan*, 1–19. Trans. Gordon Osing. Hong Kong: Hong Kong University Press, 2013.

Cheung, Martha P. Y., ed. *Hong Kong Collage: Contemporary Stories and Writing*. Hong Kong: Oxford University Press, 1998.

Dung, Kai-cheung. *Atlas: Archeology of an Imaginary City*. Trans. Dung Kai-cheung, Anders Hansson, and Bonnie S. McDougall. New York: Columbia University Press, 2012.

Leung, Ping-kwan. *City at the End of Time: Poems by Leung Ping-kwan.* Ed. Esther M. K. Cheung. Trans. Gordon Osing. Hong Kong: Hong Kong University Press, 2013.

———. "The Sorrows of Lan Kwai Fong." Trans. Martha Cheung and P. K. Leung. In Martha P.Y. Cheung, ed., *Hong Kong Collage: Contemporary Stories and Writing*, 85–95. Hong Kong: Oxford University Press, 1998.

———. "The Walled City in Kowloon: A Space We All Shared." Trans. Janice Wickeri. In Martha P. Y. Cheung, ed., *Hong Kong Collage: Contemporary Stories and Writing*, 34–39. Hong Kong: Oxford University Press, 1998.

Liu Waitong 廖伟棠. *He Youling yiqi de Xianggang manyou* 和幽灵一起的香港漫游 (With a ghost roaming in Hong Kong). Hong Kong: Kubrick, 2008.

Liu, Yichang. *The Cockroach and Other Stories.* Hong Kong: Chinese University of Hong Kong, 1995.

———. "Intersection." Trans. Nancy Li. *Renditions* 29–30 (1988): 84–101.

Shih, Shu-mei, Chien-hsin Tsai, and Brian Bernards, eds. *Sinophone Studies: A Critical Reader.* New York: Columbia University Press, 2013.

Tay, William. "Colonialism, the Cold War Era, and Marginal Space: The Existential Conditions of Five Decades of Hong Kong Literature." Trans. Michelle Yeh. In Pang-yuan Chi and David Der-wei Wang, eds., *Chinese Literature in the Second Half of a Modern Century: A Critical Survey*, 31–38. Bloomington: Indiana University Press, 2000.

Veg, Sebastian. "Putting Hong Kong's New Cultural Activism on the Literary Map: Review Essay." MCLC Resource Center Publication (May 2013). http://mclc.osu.edu/rc/pubs/reviews/veg.htm.

Wang, David Der-wei. "Late Twentieth-Century Chinese Fiction: Four Discourses." *Literature East and West* 28 (1995): 63–88.

Wong Bik Wan 黄碧云. *Wenrou yu baolie* 温柔与爆裂 (Tenderness and violence). Hong Kong: Cosmos Books, 1994.

Wong, Wai-leung. *Hong Kong Literature in the Context of Modern Chinese Literature.* Hong Kong: Centre for Hong Kong Studies, Chinese University of Hong Kong, 1987.

Xi Xi. *The Flying Carpet.* Hong Kong: Hong Kong University Press, 2000.

Xin, Qishi. "Excerpts of *The Red Chequers Pub.*" Trans. Cathy Poon. *Renditions* 47–48 (1997): 73–82.

———. "The Ghost Festival." Trans. Cathy Poon. In Martha P. Y. Cheung, ed., *Hong Kong Collage: Contemporary Stories and Writing*, 107–121. Hong Kong: Oxford University Press, 1998.

54

AVANT-GARDE POETRY IN CHINA SINCE THE 1980S
MAGHIEL VAN CREVEL

Global connotations of "avant-garde" include such notions as radical experimentation and provocation, the quality of being peripheral *within* the periphery that encompasses modern literature and art, and eminent unfitness for canonization in one's own time. In China, "avant-garde poetry" (先锋诗歌), a category now almost half a century old, covers an ever-expanding variety of texts. Their genealogy dates back to underground literary activity during the Cultural Revolution and continues to diversify to this day. Whether they fit the foregoing description is a matter of perspective. What counts as radical, and as canonized, to whom? Where lies the center against which the margins, the periphery, are defined? What if the very notion of a center is problematic, given a history of politics from the 1940s through the 1970s telling literature and art what to be and mean, with little space for individual positioning? What if, to the contrary, in the next few decades just about everybody who is anybody in modern poetry turns out to be part of the "avant-garde"? How can an avant-garde encompass so much?

This reflection on terminology is motivated by local literary history. Early in the reform era (from 1978), avant-garde poetry and all that came with it—authors, critical and popular discourse, aesthetics, events, publication channels—were mostly negatively defined. That is, the avant-garde was *not* like the orthodox poetry that had been produced by the politically sanctioned literary establishment (官方) in the People's Republic to date. As such, the concept of the avant-garde displays considerable overlap with that of "unofficial" (非官方) poetry. But the latter term has become less commonly used over the years, and the poetry in question is increasingly experienced on its own terms, rather than as a deviation from something else. In this scheme of things, the early "Misty poetry" (朦胧诗, aka Obscure poetry), which defied the establishment in the pages of Today (今天, 1978–1980), has come to be seen as complicit with the very official discourse it claimed to resist and with the language of that discourse, "Maospeak" (毛文体). As such, early Misty poetry constitutes the transition to an avant-garde that truly emerged only in later years, in a rapid diversification of styles from the early 1980s onward, with growing autonomy from politics. Incidentally, while the label has predictably clung to the Misty poets, profound changes occurred in the later work of poets associated with the Misty group such as Bei Dao 北岛, Yang Lian 杨炼, Wang Xiaoni 王小妮, and Duoduo 多多. In this sense, they were no less part of emancipation from political control than were the younger authors who followed on their heels.

In the 1980s, developments in poetry were typical of an ebullient cultural life with close links to higher education and public debate, often referred to as "high-culture fever" (文化热). The violent suppression of the protest movement in June 1989 ushered in what is widely perceived as a time of all-pervading materialism, during which poetry lost the social prominence it had enjoyed in the 1980s. In the 1990s and beyond, the distinction between official and unofficial became increasingly blurred. Throughout the history of the avant-garde, somewhat similar to "new poetry" (新诗) from the 1910s through the 1930s, poetry has grappled with its relationship to the massive tradition of classical Chinese poetry and to foreign literatures. Notably, an opposition of two literary aesthetics—here summed up as the "elevated" and the "earthly"—is of particular relevance for the avant-garde, even if it is by no means unique to China. I return to this point in the following sections, which touch on salient trends and authors in loosely chronological order.

THE 1980s

High-culture fever held across literary and artistic media and genres. Because the genre needs little in the way of infrastructure and lends itself well to performance and dissemination, and because the poet had enjoyed high social status in the classical and Maoist traditions, poetry played a leading role in reclaiming space for literature and the arts after the "cultural desert" (文化沙漠) of the Mao era. This was most clearly so for Misty poetry, but it was also true for subsequent trends. And trends there were aplenty. In an atmosphere of cheerful, collective activism, a single poem, idea, or event could suffice for the formal launch or the critical identification of a new style, school, or movement.

Literally hundreds were listed by Xu Jingya 徐敬亚 in survey anthologies in 1986 and 1988.

This intense poetry activism is visible in the histories of unofficial or "popular" (民间, literally "among-the-people") avant-garde poetry journals of the kind that had been pioneered by *Today*. These publications were produced outside the state-directed and -controlled publishing industry and disseminated through personal networks. Also known as "collegial journals" (同仁刊物 or 同人刊物), they were often held together by a small number of authors-cum-editors who came from or lived in the same place, maintained personal ties, or subscribed to a shared aesthetic. They were hugely significant at a time when, for all the avant-garde's cultural capital, its opportunities for publication through formal channels were severely limited.

One of the most accomplished and enduring among the unofficial journals was the Nanjing-based *Them* (他们, 1985–1995), with Han Dong 韩东 as its driving force and contributors from various parts of the country. Another signature voice in *Them* was that of Yu Jian 于坚, himself a resident of Kunming. *Them* was the fountainhead of a so-called colloquial poetry (口语诗) that had emerged in the early 1980s as one of several trends among younger authors who dissociated themselves from Misty poetry. In their view, Misty poetry was divorced from reality and daily life and suffered from a penchant for grandiloquence and tragic heroism. In their turn, Han Dong, Yu Jian, and others advocated a poetics of the everyday, with minimal use of high-modernist metaphor and symbolism, low-key language usage, and much room for humor and irony.

Very different players in the early 1980s published in *Macho Men* (莽汉, 1984), out of Chengdu. In what may be termed a poetics of the vulgar, the Macho Men made a point of transgressing social decorum. Li Yawei's 李亚伟 "The Chinese Department" (中文系, 1984) is a notorious example extending to the realm of education, parodying academic power games and the worship of hallowed names in literary history in scenes that include various antics of student love life, the discovery of a modernist in the toilet, and urination by the poet/protagonist. In the abstract, the Macho Men shared with *Not-Not* authors (非非, 1986–1993), out of Xichang and Chengdu, a rambunctious, daredevil iconoclasm seen as typical of the hotbed of poetry that Sichuan was in the 1980s and 1990s. *Not-Not*, however, with Zhou Lunyou 周伦佑 and Yang Li 杨黎 as central contributors, carried much theoretical and critical discourse in addition to poetry and was ultimately much more political than *Macho Men*. A third trend out of Sichuan, with activities in Chengdu and Fuling and ties with Beijing-based authors, including Yang Lian and Haizi 海子, is best summed up as "nativist" (本土) in that it drew heavily on indigenous history and culture at a time when many Chinese cultural producers and consumers uncritically embraced foreign, especially Western, literatures and cultures. Authors included the brothers Song Qu 宋渠 and Song Wei 宋炜, Shi Guanghua 石光华, and

Liao Yiwu 廖亦武, and journals included *Han Poetry* (汉诗, 1986–1988) and *Modern Poetry Groups of Ba and Shu* (巴蜀现代诗群, 1987), Ba and Shu being ancient kingdoms of present Sichuan.

Another major author from Chengdu was Zhai Yongming 翟永明. The reception of her work has focused not on her Sichuanese provenance but on her work's groundbreaking role in the establishment of a discourse of "women's poetry" (女性诗歌), in which her early series "Woman" (女人, 1984) is invariably cited as a key text. Zhai herself has not displayed the activism required for producing journals, but women's poetry, too, was institutionalized in journal form in *Women's Poetry Journal* (女人诗报, 1988–1994), out of Xichang, edited by Xiaoyin 晓音, and later in *Wings* (翼, 1998–2002), out of Beijing, edited by Zhou Zan 周瓒.

As trends and journals mushroomed in urban centers, including Beijing, Chengdu, Guangzhou, Hangzhou, Kunming, and Shanghai, there was much happy crossing-over in terms of personnel, textual contributions, and so on. Also, as noted, physical location sometimes codetermined literary groupings so that single journals could accommodate poets of divergent persuasion. This made for considerable eclecticism, *Not-Not* being a case in point.

More generally, if an overarching opposition of elevated and earthly runs through the avant-garde's history, this is not to say that every poem, poet, or publication is either of the elevated or the earthly kind. The category of women's poetry, generically and in its manifestations in the 1980s, is a prime example. Some trends and journals, however, definitely count as landmarks of the elevated and the earthly. Colloquial poetry and the Macho Men, for instance, clearly come under earthly, and so does the mid-1980s, Shanghai-based "coquetry school" (撒娇派), with Jingbute 京不特 and Momo 默默 among its members. An important example from the elevated end of the spectrum is the poetry of "intellectual" (知识分子) inclination published in *Tendency* (倾向, 1988–1990), out of Beijing and Shanghai, with Chen Dongdong 陈东东 and Xi Chuan 西川 among its proponents, and consciously set against the colloquializing and vulgarizing trends discussed earlier. *Tendency*'s second issue commemorated Haizi, whose poetics and godlike status following his suicide in March 1989 illustrate a widespread "cult of poetry" that is also very much a cult of poet-*hood* and is widely seen to embody the elevated aesthetic (Yeh 1996).

The relevance of the opposition of the elevated and the earthly for contemporary mainland Chinese poetry can be gleaned from the frequent use in critical discourse of such dichotomies as heroic/quotidian, utopian/realist, sacred/mundane, elitist/ordinary, and formal/colloquial, with the first term in each pair helping to constitute the elevated aesthetic, and the second, the earthly. This is not to present an image of poetry as solely binary by nature on either individual or collective levels. Elevated and earthly are coordinates, not pigeonholes — but they matter.

THE 1990s AND BEYOND

The June 1989 massacre on and around Tiananmen Square in Beijing, remembered as June Fourth, dealt a terrible blow to the bustling cultural scene. The next few years saw reintensified ideological control in the cultural realm, until Deng Xiaoping's 1992 Southern Tour depoliticized things by focusing the nation's attention on making money. Among those who heeded the call were poets who made it big as "book brokers" (书商) and would later return to the poetry scene as wealthy sponsors. In the meantime, several authors had gotten in trouble after June Fourth. Wang Jiaxin 王家新 lost his job as editor at the official *Poetry Monthly* (诗刊), which had enabled him to support up-and-coming avant-garde authors. Bei Dao, Yang Lian, and Duoduo, who found themselves abroad, faced the credible threat of harassment or worse by the authorities if they returned. Liao Yiwu and several other Sichuan poets were arrested and jailed over the production of an audiocassette containing a recital of Liao's long poem "Slaughter" (大屠杀, 1989). At the same time, the avant-garde showed its resilience, and the significance of unofficial poetry was reaffirmed through the establishment of new journals with the unmistakable determination to safeguard the hard-earned space for a poetry with real literary autonomy. Outside China, an exile poetry scene emerged, institutionalized from 1990 by the resurrection of *Today*, with Bei Dao as editor-in-chief.

June Fourth was not the root cause of major changes in poetry from the 1980s to the 1990s, but it certainly acted as a catalyst. If the 1980s had been a time of idealism and exaltation, the early 1990s were one of disillusionment and cynicism. The avant-garde appeared as irrelevant as it was vulnerable, vis-à-vis politics but especially vis-à-vis the market. This was manifest in a certain atomization of the poetry scene, with the collectives and the programmatic banner-waving that had marked the 1980s disappearing, and poetry events becoming less frequent. If there was one general trend that characterized the 1990s, it would have to be "individual(ized) writing" (个人[化]写作). Its straightforward surface meaning aside, this notion was at the same time linked to the trauma of 1989, explicitly so in an influential essay by poet Ouyang Jianghe 欧阳江河, published in the new *Today* in 1993. To be sure, new authors and trends emerged. Provocateur and polemicist Yi Sha 伊沙 burst on the scene with "Starve the Poets" (饿死诗人, 1994); the absolutely unclassifiable Che Qianzi 车前子 continued producing his "alternative" (另类) writings; and the work of authors such as Zhang Shuguang 张曙光, Xiao Kaiyu 肖开愚, and Sun Wenbo 孙文波 generated a sustained discussion on "narrativity" (叙事性) in poetry. But to many critics and scholars, the avant-garde had entered a crisis because, simply put, it had ceased to matter.

Arguably, these concerns were unwarranted, on two counts. First, the doomsayers proceeded from an unspoken assumption that this poetry was still answerable to the age-old poetics of "literature conveys the Way" (文以载道)—or, in a crude simplification, that this poetry had to engage in a type of social positioning that established a connection, ultimately, with the well-being of the nation. This had, however, stopped being the case after the earliest specimens of Misty poetry and their indictment of the Cultural Revolution. As such, one might argue that literature to convey the Way was in trouble, not the avant-garde. Second, they failed to relate poetry's situation to radical changes in China's sociocultural ecology—namely, the rapid rise of a multimedia consumer society and popular culture, with poetry being a single niche in a vast array of possibilities for cultural production and consumption. Further to the second point, in the 1990s book and journal publication opportunities for avant-garde poetry increased enormously, in official and unofficial circuits alike, as the authorities relaxed their grip on the publishing world. What's more, the 1990s saw the emergence of many successful poets whose works outshone 1980s poetry from a literary-critical point of view. Xi Chuan, Yu Jian, Zhai Yongming, Ouyang Jianghe, and many others come to mind. Inadequate as they are, nutshell characterizations are tempting—so let's call Xi Chuan's poetry pseudophilosophical, humorous, and melancholy; Yu Jian's, absurdist and inimitably down to earth; Zhai Yongming's, physical and daringly imaginative; and Ouyang Jianghe's, angrily sophisticated.

In sum, the avant-garde's striking visibility in society at large in the 1980s had been an anomaly, occasioned by circumstance. Its relative invisibility in the 1990s was a situation common to modern poetries in many national literatures, serving as disruptions of culture rather than the repositories of stable, affirmative values often found in classical texts and popular culture. Describing such poetries as peripheral or marginal in other than purely quantitative terms makes little sense because, inherently, they *cannot* be at the center.

And yet, issues of social relevance and centrality resurfaced with a vengeance during a major polemic in 1998–2000 involving scores of poets and critics. The polemic juxtaposed so-called popular and intellectual writing, roughly representing the earthly and the elevated aesthetics, respectively. It raises questions about the "horizontal" generalizability of modernity across cultural traditions, but this lies outside the scope of the present essay. What matters here is that contemporary poetry's "vertical" relationship to the legacy of Chinese poethood through the ages and to Chinese cultural identity was at stake—coupled with mundane matters such as the perceived obstruction of popular publications by editors with intellectual loyalties. Leading activists in the popular camp included Yu Jian, Yang Ke 杨克, Shen Haobo 沈浩波, and Han Dong, and important intellectual voices were those of Wang Jiaxin and Cheng Guangwei 程光炜. As with many other metatextual moments in the avant-garde's history, the polemic was a male-dominated affair. By and large, the popular camp was on the offensive throughout. Opinions differ with regard to the effect on the poetry scene, but the polemic reaffirmed that in today's China poethood continues to *matter* in complicated, energetic ways that are taking shape anew in the twenty-first century. As such, it also showed that upon closer inspection, the cult of poetry extended to earthly quarters as much as to poets and critics of elevated persuasion.

THE WEB

The Internet, generally available in China from around the year 2000, has had far-reaching effects on the poetry scene. First, the web is perfect for doing what unofficial journals did in the 1980s and 1990s—and, indeed, for retroactively taking them to larger audiences than the print editions could ever have dreamed of reaching. More generally, it has provided nationwide poetry platforms through forums, blogs, microblogging (微博), and other social media. Second, even though political control of China's cyberspace is highly effective, online publication has allowed for the modest exploration of taboos such as June Fourth. Third, it has connected poetry to new generations of authors and readers who basically live online. In the 2000s, born-digital poetry included extreme manifestations of the earthly aesthetic such as the "lower body" (下半身), with Shen Haobo and Yin Lichuan 尹丽川 as its most prominent authors, and the "trash school" (垃圾派) and the wider "Low Poetry movement" (低诗歌运动). Significantly, beyond their *succès de scandale*, trends such as these also bespoke a social concern with vulnerable groups in society, such as prostitutes and migrant workers. Finally, the web has further spurred the discursive hyperactivity that has characterized the avant-garde ever since the controversy over Misty poetry in the late 1970s. The quantities of online poetry, criticism, and debate, digitized and born digital alike, are breathtaking. Just as in other national literatures, print publication continues to count as a marker of quality, but it is no longer the only, or the ultimate, criterion for success.

HOW AVANT-GARDE IS THAT?

Amid the intense commodification, commercialization, and consumerism of the 1990s and the early twenty-first century, *and* as compared to best-selling fiction, film, and art, poetry stands out as being unmarketable in financial terms. This, conversely, generates much cultural capital, in what Bourdieu calls the reversal of the economic world. Yet, the contemporary mainland Chinese poetry scene is remarkable in that it has seen a number of unlikely, only mildly contentious alliances between the avant-garde and ultracapitalist enterprises such as real estate development companies, with poets and poetry in well-paid advertising roles. Also, there are many examples of businesspeople funding institutional endeavors such as journals, book series, and indeed entire academic centers at well-respected universities for the study of modern poetry, emphatically including the avant-garde. Some write poetry themselves and are clearly trying to pay their way into recognized poethood, with modest success and amid modest controversy.

A striking instance of Bourdieu's "reversal" occurred in 2013 when the Shanghai Library published an exquisitely produced book called *Poetry Manuscripts* (诗稿), containing facsimiles of poetry handwritten by Ouyang Jianghe, Xi Chuan, Zhai Yongming, and Wang Yin 王寅, in a mere two hundred numbered copies. Yet again, this goes to show how the tenacious industry that is the avant-garde somehow manages to hold its own in spite of, and because of, its marginality and quantitative irrelevance. Splendidly dismissive of the idea that numbers matter, *Poetry Manuscripts* signals the ultimate canonization-through-exclusiveness. How avant-garde is that?

Bibliography

Crespi, John. *Voices in Revolution: Poetry and the Auditory Imagination in Modern China*, 168–188. Honolulu: University of Hawai'i Press, 2009.

Day, Michael Martin. *China's Second World of Poetry: The Sichuan Avant-Garde, 1982–1992*. Leiden: DACHS poetry chapter, 2005. http://leiden.dachs-archive.org/poetry/md.html.

Hong Zicheng 洪子诚 and Liu Denghan 刘登翰. *Zhongguo dangdai xinshi shi* 中国当代新诗史 (A history of China's contemporary new poetry). Rev. ed. Beijing: Beijing daxue, 2005.

Inwood, Heather. *Verse Going Viral: China's New Media Scenes*. Seattle: University of Washington Press, 2014.

Kunze, Rui. *Struggle and Symbiosis: The Canonization of the Poet Haizi and Cultural Discourses in Contemporary China*. Bochum: projektverlag, 2012.

Luo Zhenya 罗振亚. *20 shiji Zhongguo xianfeng shichao* 20世纪中国先锋诗潮 (The avant-garde trend in 20th-century Chinese poetry). Beijing: Renmin, 2008.

Lupke, Christopher, ed. *New Perspectives on Contemporary Chinese Poetry*. New York: Palgrave MacMillan, 2007.

Manfredi, Paul. *Modern Poetry in China: A Verbal-Visual Dynamic*. Amherst, NY: Cambria Press, 2013.

van Crevel, Maghiel. *Chinese Poetry in Times of Mind, Mayhem and Money*. Leiden: Brill, 2008.

———. Three online bibliographies on contemporary Chinese poetry. MCLC Resource Center Web Publications (2007 and 2008). http://u.osu.edu/mclc/online-series.

———. "Underground Poetry in the 1960s and 1970s." *Modern Chinese Literature* 9, 2 (1996): 169–219.

Wong, Lisa Lai-ming. "Voices from a Room of One's Own: Examples from Contemporary Chinese Women's Poetry." *Modern China* 32, 3 (2006): 385–408.

Yeh, Michelle. "The 'Cult of Poetry' in Contemporary China." *Journal of Asian Studies* 55, 1 (1996): 51–80.

Zhang, Jeanne Hong. *The Invention of a Discourse: Women's Poetry from Contemporary China*. Leiden: CNWS, 2004.

55

TAIWAN LITERATURE IN THE POST–MARTIAL LAW ERA

MICHAEL BERRY

While the martial law period in Taiwan witnessed the dominance of popular literary genres and forms—the *wuxia* (武侠) novels of Liang Yusheng 梁羽生 and Bai Yu 白羽, the romance novels of Qiong Yao 琼瑶 and later San Mao 三毛, inspirational prose by writers like Wang Dingjun 王鼎钧, Qi Jun 琦君, Zhang Xiaofeng 张晓风, and Lin Qingxuan 林清玄, and nostalgic poetry by Zheng Chouyu 郑愁予 and Yu Guangzhong 余光中—the 1980s witnessed a major shift in the level of political engagement seen in Taiwan literature. In the years leading up to the 1987 lifting of martial law, Taiwan saw an increasing number of writers intent on pushing the limits of government censorship, giving voice to the repressed, and excavating lost pages from modern Taiwan's often contested history. If there is a single overarching theme that best captures literature from the era immediately preceding the lifting of martial law, it would be the tide of political engagement and iconoclasm. The end of martial law is thus a pivotal moment in the transition from largely apolitical popular forms to intense political engagement during the 1980s and early to mid-1990s, ultimately leading to a much more vibrant and diversified engagement with new styles, genres, and trends in the late 1990s and the 2010s.

WRITING POLITICS AND THE POLITICS OF WRITING

Although after 1949 the Republic of China (ROC) on Taiwan was widely referred to internationally as "Free China," under martial law there remained widespread censorship, suppression, and imprisonment of writers and intellectuals who voiced dissent. Political fiction that probed sensitive historical traumas through an often thinly veiled fictional lens became one of the few outlets for readers to peek into the darker side of Taiwan's modern history. One of the most notable examples is Chen Yingzhen 陈映真, whose short fiction did not shy away from the February 28 Incident (2/28)—a violent suppression of Taiwanese resistance to the Nationalist government in 1947—and other taboo topics under the Nationalist regime. Two of the most high-profile examples of literary dissent during the martial law era are the cases of Li Ao 李敖 and Bo Yang 柏杨, both highly productive writers of cultural criticism, history, and fiction who spent many years in prison during the height of the White Terror for their political views and published writings.

When the emergency decree was finally lifted on July 15, 1987, thirty-eight years after it was first put into effect, a new social space where literary dissent would seem to become the norm rather than the exception emerged. One of the first shots fired was a collection of essays by Long Yingtai 龙应台 entitled *The Wild Fire* (野火集, 1985). Although published before the end of martial law, the collection anticipated the unprecedented social outpouring that would follow once the decree was formally lifted. *The Wild Fire* provided a forum for the author's criticisms, ranging from problems in the Chinese educational system to the Chinese national character. By voicing her own strong iconoclastic views in such pieces as "Chinese, Why Don't You Get Angry?" (中国人, 你为什么不生气?), Long initiated the phenomenon that would come to be known as the "Long Yingtai Tempest," in the wake of which a new space for social critique, literary dissent, and critical engagement was encouraged. Although Bo Yang, Li Ao, and Long Yingtai are all published authors of fiction, their social and political views were largely expressed in their essays. In the late 1980s, however, this trend began to change, and suddenly readers found it increasingly difficult to separate fiction from politics and politics from fiction.

In the immediate aftermath of martial law during the late 1980s and early 1990s, the shadow of political iconoclasm in literature continued to loom large as older writers, as well as a younger generation, produced a deluge of politically inspired fiction. The floodgates had opened, and while the old vanguard of writers like Li Ao and Bo Yang continued to write incendiary work, other veteran writers like Dongfang Bai 东方白 and Li Qiao 李乔 produced sprawling multivolume fictional chronicles of modern Taiwan's history. Works like Dongfang's *Waves Breaking on the Sand* (浪淘沙), Li's *Burying Injustice 1947*, *Burying Injustice* (埋冤 1947, 埋冤), and other examples of the epic "long river novel" (长河小说) attempted to position the horrors of 2/28 and political suppression as a key chapter in modern Taiwan's formation story. From another angle, the reportage fiction of Lan Bozhou 蓝博洲 excavated other forgotten crimes carried out under the White Terror. With these works and others, political iconoclasm turned mainstream. Writers born in the 1950s like Dong Nian 东年, Yang Zhao 杨照, and Zhang Dachun 张大春 turned to the political in their fiction. It was as if during the decade from 1987 to 1996, when the first true democratic presidential election was held, the entire Taiwan literary scene embarked on a radical political turn, purging the demons of its past and exploring the frontiers of its newfound political freedom.

Among this group of writers, the figure who best embodies this political turn is Zhang Dachun. Through the 1980s and 1990s, Zhang published a series of highly political novels that would help establish his career as one of Taiwan's leading fiction stylists. His novels *The Grand Liar* (大说谎家) and *No One Wrote to the Colonel* (没人写信给上校) were highly satiric political works that blended current events and fiction. A prolific and versatile writer, Zhang also introduced the world to his adolescent alter ego in the form of a highly successful trilogy revolving around the adventures and misadventures of Datou Chun 大头春, or Big Head Spring. The first volume of the series, *The Weekly Journal of Young Big Head Spring* (少年大头春的生活周记, 1992), was a fictionalized collection of weekly journal entries written in the tone and style of a middle school student. The novel is filled with whimsical, entertaining, and often sharp critical observations about Taiwanese society in the early 1990s. In just a few short years, Long Yingtai's "tempest" of serious, highbrow social commentary had transformed—or rather, degenerated—into the grammatically flawed complaints and ramblings of a rebellious punk teenager. Whereas in 1985 it seemed as if only the voice of an American-educated professor at a prestigious European university could ignite the kind of social criticism found in *The Wild Fire*, by 1992 delinquent teenagers could offer equally profound visions of contemporary Taiwanese politics and society. Zhang Dachun was offering not only an iconoclastic subversion of politics but also a metacritical commentary on Long Yingtai's project. Zhang would continue his iconoclastic bent in the two follow-up volumes of his trilogy, *My Kid Sister* (我妹妹) and *Wild Child* (野孩子), which would take on corrupt government officials, the Taiwan underworld, dirty businesspeople, and the educational system, all through the eyes of semidelinquent teenagers. By the time *Disciples of the Liar* (撒谎的信徒), Zhang's unofficial biography of former Taiwanese president Lee Teng-hui, made its appearance just in time for the 1996 presidential election, political fiction was clearly one of the most important genres in contemporary Taiwanese literature. *Disciples of the Liar* is a good example of this rather bombastic political turn, but also of the calculated, almost opportunistic, marketing of fiction to capitalize on political events.

And while Zhang's work from this period stands out, many others also followed suit. In 1994, novelist Zhu Tianxin 朱天心 published her collection of political essays *The Weekly Political Journal of a Novelist* (小说家的政治周记), which bore such a striking resemblance to Zhang Dachun's *Weekly Journal* in both title and form that she was forced to begin her book with a short disclaimer. Yang Zhao published a series of novels and short story collections, from *The Great Love* (大爱) to *Dark Souls* (黯魂), that delved deeply into once-suppressed chapters of Taiwan history, while veteran writer Dong Nian pursued political issues in works such as *Last Winter* (去年冬天), which documents the plight of former victims of the White Terror.

But the crowning example—and perhaps inadvertently a contributor to the decline—of this trend in political writing is Li Ang's 李昂 fictional biography of Taiwan female politician Chen Wenqian (Sisy Wen-hsien Chen). A controversial writer who first caused a stir on the Taiwanese literary scene in the late 1960s for her sexually charged short stories and who later gained international recognition for her powerful feminist novel *The Butcher's Wife* (杀夫), Li Ang returned to the public eye in 1997 with her *Everybody Sticks the Beigang Incense Burner* (北港香炉人人插). Flirting with the ethical and legal limits of political fiction, Li's novel was a best seller, but it also led to lawsuits and intense controversy. Li followed this work with other highly political works like her ambitious attempt to rewrite Taiwan history in *The Lost Garden* (迷园) and yet another fictionalized biography of a Taiwanese female political figure, 2/28 heroine Xie Xuehong 谢雪红. *Autobiography: A Novel* (自传の小说), Li Ang's latter novel, appeared in the midst of a large-scale fictional excavation of the long-forgotten tragedy of 2/28, which a host of writers, including Lin Yaode 林耀德 and WuHe 舞鹤, have reexamined, recreated, and reimagined.

DIVERSIFICATION, EXPERIMENTATION, AND NEW VOICES

The newfound political openness of the post–martial law era also opened new space for a broad array of literary schools and forms to take root and flourish. Among the trends that went from being highly marginalized—or in some cases, nearly invisible—to being embraced by the mainstream were queer fiction, indigenous fiction, Chinese Malay fiction, and the new avant-garde. When veteran modernist stylist Bai Xianyong 白先勇 (Kenneth Pai Hsien-yung) published his first full-length novel *Crystal Boys* (孽子) in 1987, it was one of the few works of Taiwan fiction that frankly addressed homosexual themes. Often touted as the first modern Chinese-language queer novel, *Crystal Boys* may have been groundbreaking, but it was still a lone voice on the Taiwan literary scene. Most remarkable is that a decade later Taiwan began to witness the flowering of rich and diverse queer fiction (see "Homoeroticism in Modern Chinese Literature").

Younger writers, many inspired by Bai, began to publish highly regarded works, including Ji Dawei's 纪大伟 *Membrane* (膜) and Qiu Miaojin's 邱妙津 *Crocodile Notes* (鳄鱼手记) and *Suicide Note from Montmartre* (蒙马特遗书). Over the next several years, Ji and Qiu would go on to publish many other works that would become cornerstones of Taiwan queer literature, including Ji's *The Realm of the Senses* (感官世界) and Qiu's posthumous *Qiu Miaojin's Diary, 1991–1995* (邱妙津日记, 1991–1995), which has gained cult status in Taiwan. Other writers like Chen Xue 陈雪 have also emerged as major voices in Taiwan's queer literature movement, amassing huge followings on social media, inspiring film adaptations, and often taking on a public role in queer rights movements, such as the 2013 gay marriage debate in Taiwan. With a string of more than fifteen books, Chen has demonstrated productivity, literary imagination, and influence that have clearly positioned her as one of the most important voices on the queer literary scene. Of course the interaction of queer activism and literature can be traced back much earlier: in 1996, writer Xu Yousheng 许佑生 held the very first public gay marriage ceremony in Taiwan. And while queer fiction is clearly the domain of younger writers, veteran figures on the literary scene, such as Zhu Tianwen 朱天文 and Wuhe, have made important contributions to Taiwan queer fiction, such as Zhu's award-winning exploration of queer identity, loss, and AIDS in *Notes of a Desolate Man* (荒人手记) and Wuhe's *Ghost and Goblin* (鬼儿与阿妖). Writers like Su Weizhen 苏伟贞, Cheng Yingshu 成英姝, and Wu Jiwen 吴继文 also challenged and transgressed traditional conceptions of gender and sex in the mid- to late 1990s.

With a total population estimated at around 500,000—making up approximately 2% of Taiwan's total population—the indigenous tribes of Taiwan have been marginalized not only politically and in terms of social status and educational opportunities but also in terms of their literary presence. Since the 2000s, however, indigenous Taiwan literature has taken on a markedly stronger profile and seen a blossoming of styles and genres. Literature about Taiwan's native tribes was once dominated by ethnic Han writers, and there continues to be an ever-increasing number of literary works about them by Han writers, notable examples being Wuhe's experimental meditation on the 1930 Musha Incident *Remains of Life* (余生), not to mention an increasing body of more popular historical books, anthologies, and graphic novels by writers such as Deng Xiangyang 邓相扬. To some degree, this renewed interest in indigenous culture can be seen as a direct result not only of new cultural policies of inclusiveness but also of political policies attempting to capitalize on Taiwan's indigenous cultural history as a means of articulating a national identity distinct from mainland China.

As a result of these shifts, there has also been a highly visible increase in the number of literary works written by indigenous authors. Besides veteran figures, such as Sun Dachuan 孙大川 (Paelabang danapan), who has been a leader in this area thanks to his numerous books and journal *Culture of the Mountain and the Seas* (山海文化), and Walisi Yougan 瓦历斯 诺干 (Walis Nokan), who has published more than eighteen volumes of essays, reportage literature, and poetry, there is also a younger generation of writers ranging from Ligelale Anuwu 利格拉乐 阿乌 (Liglave A-wu) to Tuobasi Tamapuma 拓拔斯 塔玛匹玛 (Topas Tamapima). The relative absence of indigenous literature during the martial law era can partly be attributed to indigenous groups' emphasis on oral traditions over written traditions, a lack of written form for many tribal languages, and inferior economic and educational opportunities on many reservations. The Taiwan indigenous rights movement of the past few decades has begun to improve many of these conditions, resulting in a new generation of indigenous writers writing in Chinese, but also experimenting with romanized versions of aboriginal languages (not unlike the approach taken by some Taiwan writers experimenting with Taiwanese writing).

Roughly paralleling the rise of indigenous literature was a rapid expansion of fiction written in Chinese by ethnic Chinese who immigrated to Taiwan from Malaysia. While Li Yongping 李永平, author of such sprawling experimental works as *The Green East Sea* (海东青), *Zhu Ling in Wonderland* (朱鸰漫游仙境), and *When the Great River Comes to an End* (大河尽头), has long been the most important figure in Chinese Malay literature of Taiwan, the 1990s and 2000s saw an incredible surge of creativity from writers like Zhang Guixing 张贵兴, Huang Jinshu 黄锦树 (Ng Kim Chew), He Shufang 贺淑芳, and Zeng Linglong 曾翎龙. Further, Taiwan publishers have remained a key portal for Chinese Malay writers not based in Taiwan, such as Li Zishu 黎紫书, whose novel *The Age of Farewells* (告别的年代) offers not only a new take on Malaysian Chinatown life during the 1960s but also a fresh use of the Chinese language, tinged with a neoclassical style, and a complex metafictional narrative. From the rich diversity of new voices that have emerged since 2000, it is clear that Chinese Malay literature continues to play a crucial role in the continuing evolution of the Taiwan literary scene.

Intricately tied into many of the aforementioned movements and trends has been the rise of a new literary avant-garde in Taiwan. This trend, marked by uncompromising experimentation of style, form, and structure, can be seen in the work of many writers across a wide generational spectrum. The origins of this tradition can be traced, in part, to the groundbreaking work of Wang Wenxing 王文兴 and his classic novels *Family Catastrophe* (家变) and *Backed Against the Sea* (背海的人) (see "Cold War Fiction from Taiwan and the Modernists"), both of which radically challenged the literary conventions of their day. One of contemporary Taiwan's foremost experimentalists is Wuhe, author of the aforementioned *Remains of Life*, who has written numerous short stories and novels, such as *Chaos and Confusion* (乱迷), that make use of radically different narrative voices and literary forms. Zhu Tianwen, who began her career with rather conventional narrative form in the late 1970s, went in a markedly more challenging direction with her *Notes of a Desolate Man* (荒人手记)

in 1994, but by the time she published her novel *Witchtalk* (巫言) in 2008, Zhu was again pushing the limits of literature in an entirely new direction. Luo Yijun 骆以军 (Lo Yi-chin), one of the most creative and prolific writers of the past twenty years, also experiments with a wide array of literary styles, structures, and forms in both his fiction and his prose. Luo has built up a loyal readership with his unorthodox and twisted tales, such as his award-winning two-volume novel *The Western Xia Motel* (西夏旅馆). Egoyan Zheng 伊格言 (Yigeyan) is another younger writer who is expanding Taiwan's literary horizons with breakthrough works like the deconstructionist *The Dream Devourer* (噬梦人) and the postapocalyptic novel *Groundzero* (零地点).

Another side of this experimentalism can be seen in writers and publishers who push the boundary of literary forms by integrating elements from design, architecture, and other disciplines. These multigenre works include the publications of architecture professor Yan Zhongxian 颜忠贤, whose work, like *design: a bad master* (坏设计达人), combines fiction, photography, architecture, and design; or Wu Mingyi 吴明益, a science fiction writer best known for his *Man with the Compound Eyes* (复眼人) and author of such books as *Above Flame* (浮光), which interweaves his photographs with his essays. Another example is architect and professor Ruan Qingyue 阮庆岳, whose numerous publications, such as *Mountains Beyond the Door* (开门见山色), stretch traditional genres and open up new possibilities by combining literary experimentalism, photography, and architecture with bold innovations in book design.

Just as some writers have continually pushed the boundaries of literature through formal experimentation, others have become part of an alternative trend best described as a return to traditionalism. Veteran writers who were truly the cutting edge of Taiwan literature from the 1960s through the 1980s, such as Bai Xianyong and Huang Chunming 黄春明, have gradually turned away from fiction in order to concentrate on traditional arts like *kunqu* (昆曲) opera and children's theater, respectively. The former bad boy of Taiwan literature Zhang Dachun has become a calligrapher, has written a four-volume martial arts novel, and in 2013 wrote a fictional biography of Tang poet Li Bai in classical Chinese. Younger novelists have returned to tradition in more playful ways: for example, Zhang Wankang's 张万康 *Record of the Good Deeds of a Daoist* (道济群生录) reinvigorates the traditional "linked-chapter fiction" (章回小说) style with a snappy, comic postmodern edge.

From queer fiction and indigenous literature to the new avant-garde and fiction inspired by older Chinese literary traditions, the contemporary Taiwan literary scene is indeed a diverse market where writers and publishers are not afraid to take risks. Of course, at the end of the day, the most startling sign of the Taiwan literary market's diversity is not the variety of its writers, schools, styles, and genres, but the global openness of the market itself. Major works by (formally banned) mainland Chinese writers are now widely available, and there are close ties between many Taiwan writers and their counterparts in the mainland. And unlike in the United States, where translated fiction makes up a mere 3 percent of the annual book market, in Taiwan translated works made up more than 20 percent of the total Taiwan book market and as much as 60 percent of the market for fiction in 2013.

In the new millennium, Taiwanese writers are no longer persecuted for voicing iconoclastic political views through literature. At the time of his death in 2008, Bo Yang considered himself the last victim of the Chinese literary inquisition; Li Ao, who once claimed the honor of having the most books banned of any author worldwide, not only began hosting his own television show but was even a marginal candidate in the 2000 Taiwan presidential election. As well, *The Wild Fire* author Long Yingtai has not only maintained her status as a best-selling writer but also served as minister of culture. Once ostracized pioneers of literary iconoclasm have found a place in the market and in politics.

I do not mean to suggest by the foregoing narrative of Taiwan fiction from the 1990s to the 2010s a turn away from political literature—after all, the rise of queer literature, indigenous fiction, and other forms have clear political subtexts and can even be read as a form of activism through literature. But there has been a very pointed diffusion from intense interest in pure politics and repressed political incidents to a much broader and diverse set of concerns ranging from the body and gender, to questions of ethnicity and national identity, to radical literary experimentation. Naturally, the political is ever present—it has just continued to transform.

Bibliography

Balcom, John, and Yingtsih Balcom, eds. *Indigenous Writers of Taiwan: An Anthology of Stories, Essays, and Poems*. New York: Columbia University Press, 2005.

Berry, Michael. *A History of Pain: Trauma in Modern Chinese Literature and Film*. New York: Columbia University Press, 2008.

Bo, Yang. *The Ugly Chinaman and the Crisis of Chinese Culture*. Ed. and trans. Don J. Cohn and Jing Qing. Sydney: Allen and Unwin, 1992.

Chang, Sung-sheng Yvonne. *Literary Culture in Taiwan: From Martial Law to Market Law*. New York: Columbia University Press, 2004.

Chang, Sung-sheng Yvonne, Michelle Yeh, and Ming-ju Fan, eds. *The Columbia Sourcebook of Literary Taiwan*. New York: Columbia University Press, 2014.

Chang, Ta-chun. *Wild Kids: Two Novels about Growing Up*. Trans. Michael Berry. New York: Columbia University Press, 2000.

Chu, Tien-wen. *Notes of a Desolate Man*. Trans. Howard Goldblatt and Sylvia Li-Chun Lin. New York: Columbia University Press, 1999.

Lin, Sylvia Li-chun. *Representing Atrocity in Taiwan: The 2/28 Incident and White Terror in Fiction and Film*. New York: Columbia University Press, 2007.

Martin, Fran, ed. *Angelwings: Contemporary Queer Fiction from Taiwan*. Honolulu: University of Hawai'i Press, 2003.
——. *Situating Sexualities: Queer Representations in Taiwanese Fiction, Film and Public Culture*. Hong Kong: University of Hong Kong Press, 2003.
Qiu, Miaojin. *Last Words from Montmartre*. Trans. Ari Larissa Heinrich. New York: New York Review Books Classics, 2014.
Wang, David Der-wei, and Carlos Rojas, eds. *Writing Taiwan: A New Literary History*. Durham, NC: Duke University Press, 2007.
Wu, Ming-Yi. *The Man with the Compound Eyes*. Trans. Darryl Sterk. New York: Vintage Books, 2015.
Wu, Yenna, ed. *Li Ang's Visionary Challenges to Gender, Sex, and Politics*. Lanham, MD: Lexington Books, 2014.

56

SPEAKING FROM THE MARGINS: YAN LIANKE

CARLOS ROJAS

Although most Chinese literary production from the Maoist era (1949–1976) hewed closely to the ruling regime's ideological center, the post-Mao period has witnessed the emergence of a variety of new voices and literary configurations. Deng Xiaoping's 1978 reform and opening up set in motion a series of cultural and economic transformations that not only permitted a broader range of literary works to be approved for publication but also had far-reaching implications for the ways in which such works could be disseminated to the public. In particular, works published during the post-Mao era began to address a much wider array of topics, including formerly proscribed issues of sexuality, mental illness, and criminal delinquency. The period also saw a large influx of translations of Western literature, inspiring local authors such as Yu Hua 余华, Ma Yuan 马原, Gei Fei 格非, and Can Xue 残雪 (see "Avant-Garde Fiction in Post-Mao China") to pursue innovative experimentations with narrative form. At the same time, the rapid growth of the Chinese economy granted popular authors like Wang Shuo 王朔 greater freedom to rely on their royalties rather than on the monthly stipends they would otherwise have received from the official Chinese Writers Association. Moreover, the rapid development of the Chinese Internet beginning in the mid-1990s provided an important avenue for authors to release works that had not been officially approved for publication (see "Internet Literature"), just as the gradual regularization of ties between China and both Hong Kong and Taiwan offered new opportunities for works that could not be published easily in China.

Spanning more than twenty novels and volumes of short fiction over the past three decades, Yan Lianke's 阎连科 literary oeuvre to date exemplifies several of these overlapping trends. Born in 1958 in rural Henan, Yan joined the army in 1978 at the beginning of the reform era, and it was with the army that he began his professional writing career in the 1980s. In the mid-1990s, Yan began writing a series of increasingly provocative works. In contrast to the realism (现实主义) that characterized many works from the May Fourth period and the emphasis on socialist realism (社会主义现实主义) that dominated the Maoist era, Yan has increasingly come to write in a style he calls "mythorealism" (神实主义), which he describes as the use of patently fantastic elements in order to comment on actual social concerns. Over time, Yan has emerged as one of China's most critically acclaimed authors, but also one of its most controversial. In China he has been awarded the prestigious Lu Xun and Lao She literature prizes, while internationally he was a finalist for the Man Booker International Prize and was the first Chinese author to win the Franz Kafka Prize. At the same time, however, a number of his recent books have been either banned or recalled in China due to his focus on politically sensitive topics.

One early example of Yan Lianke's fictional exploration of social concerns can be found in his 1998 novel *Time's Passage* (日光流年), which centers on a remote village whose inhabitants have long suffered from physical ailments resulting from excessive levels of fluorine and more recently have begun suffering from a mysterious throat swelling that invariably kills them before they reach the age of forty. Although the precise cause of this new condition is never specified, the novel suggests that the disease is a result of a toxic environmental contaminant, and a key plotline centers around the villagers' decision to sell strips of their own skin to a hospital for burn victims in order to raise money for an aqueduct that would pipe in uncontaminated water. The villagers' struggle to survive in the face of a health crisis apparently caused by harmful contaminants prophetically anticipates the recent attention to so-called Chinese cancer villages, in which industrial pollution is believed to be responsible for high rates of cancer.

Yan Lianke returns to a similarly isolated community in his 2004 novel *Shouhuo* (受活). Published in English translation as *Lenin's Kisses* (2012), the work revolves around a remote Henan village called Liven (受活庄), almost all of whose residents are physically disabled. To compensate for their disabilities, many of the villagers have developed an unusual "special skill"—for instance, a blind girl develops an unusually acute sense of hearing, and a boy missing a leg acquires exceptional strength in his one good leg. The novel opens in the summer of 1998 with a visit to the village by the county chief, Liu Yingque (柳鹰雀), who has become obsessed with the idea of purchasing Lenin's embalmed corpse from Russia and bringing it to China. To raise the vast sum of money needed for this purpose, he proposes to have villagers form a troupe that would travel the country performing their "special skills." The village matriarch agrees, but only on the condition that the village then be allowed to withdraw again from the county's administrative oversight and regain the independence, and thus relative anonymity, it had enjoyed before the Mao era. The result is a compelling exploration of the legacy of communism (symbolized by Lenin's corpse), contemporary China's fascination with economic development (symbolized by the attempt to use the corpse to establish a profitable tourist site in Liven), and a pattern of exploiting vulnerable populations (symbolized by the decision to have the Liven villagers form a troupe to perform their disabilities).

Liven's geographic and sociopolitical isolation also contributes to the novel's innovative structure in that the work employs many unusual local words and phrases. On the assumption that most readers will be unfamiliar with this local vocabulary, the novel includes a series of explanatory footnotes, beginning with the term from which the novel takes its title, *shouhuo* (the footnote explains that this is a dialectal word meaning "enjoyment, happiness, and passion, [with] connotations of finding pleasure in discomfort, or making pleasure out of discomfort" [Yan 2012a: 4]). While some of these footnotes contain only a short definition, others provide longer explanations that constitute an important backstory on the history of the village and its residents. In several instances, the footnoted text is so long that it contains additional footnotes in its own right. The result is a situation in which, like some of Nabokov's works, the footnoted text is almost more important than the main story. As a result, the text that is literally positioned at the work's textual margins is granted central importance within the work as a whole.

The year after publishing *Lenin's Kisses*, Yan completed the novella *Serve the People!* (为人民服务), which describes an illicit romance between a young soldier and the attractive young wife of his commanding officer during the Cultural Revolution (1966–1976). The adulterous couple develop a system wherein the general's wife leaves a placard bearing Chairman Mao's trademark dictum "serve the people" (为人民服务) out of its usual position to signal to the soldier to join her in her bedroom. The couple then discover that they derive an intense erotic thrill from destroying Maoist icons, thus inverting the Cultural Revolution's Maoist injunction to "destroy the Four Olds" (namely, old customs, old culture, old habits, and old ideas). In this way, the covert affair between the soldier and the general's wife dramatically illustrates the closely imbricated relationship between Maoist era political fervor and libidinal desires, and it therefore should be no surprise that the novel was never approved for publication in China, though an abridged version was published in the Chinese literary journal *Huacheng* (花城). A complete version published in traditional characters in Taiwan was made available on the Internet, and the novel has also been translated into numerous foreign languages.

After *Serve the People!*, Yan Lianke published a novel, *Dream of Ding Village* (丁庄梦, 2006), whose origins can be traced back to 1996, when the Chinese medical activist Gao Yaojie 高耀洁 introduced Yan to his first AIDS patient. Over the next several months, a medical anthropologist escorted Yan to visit several AIDS villages where Yan was able to see firsthand the effects of the invisible HIV/AIDS epidemic raging in many rural areas of central China, and particularly in Yan's home province of Henan. The epidemic's primary vector of infection was subsequently revealed to have been rooted in the blood-selling practices that became increasingly popular in rural China in the 1980s and 1990s, though in 1996 there was still little public recognition of the cause—or even the existence—of the epidemic. After a long struggle over how to render this health crisis in fictional form, Yan settled on the idea of narrating the story through the voice of a dead boy who had been murdered by villagers seeking retribution for the actions of the boy's father, a prominent "blood-head" who profited from encouraging others in the region to sell their blood. That much of the novel is narrated from a theoretically impossible position "beyond the grave" is figuratively apropos, given that not long after the book's publication in China it was officially recalled (though individual booksellers were permitted to sell their remaining stock). In this way, the author's own voice was figuratively silenced in China (or "buried"), even though by that point the existence of China's rural HIV/AIDS epidemic was already officially acknowledged, and its link to blood-selling practices was well recognized.

Yan Lianke explores related themes in his 2010 novel *The Four Books* (四书). Set in a "reeducation" compound for intellectuals accused of being rightists that is overseen by a boy known simply as "the Child," this work describes how the compound's political "criminals" get drawn into China's Great Leap Forward campaign's (1958–1961) call to increase steel and agricultural production beyond plausible limits, to the point that the accused rightists in the novel even begin using their own blood to irrigate their crops. Throughout the work, meanwhile, the Child attempts to confiscate all the books he perceives to be ideologically problematic, including Western novels, religious texts, and even Chinese classics. Although he announces that he intends to burn the books, it is subsequently revealed that he has actually kept most of them for his own enjoyment and has burned only the ones he had duplicated. At the conclusion of the work, the Child returns most of the confiscated books to their original owners, suggesting a complicated relationship among literary production, consumption, and state censorship.

In an essay he initially wrote to serve as afterword for *The Four Books*, "Betrayer of Literature" (写作的叛徒), Yan describes how he decided not to attempt to write the novel simply to satisfy the censors but instead composed it as he wished. It is, therefore, not surprising that when he subsequently shopped the manuscript to a dozen or so Chinese publishers, none was willing to take it on—though the novel has circulated widely abroad. The result is an acute commentary on what Yan Lianke describes elsewhere as the challenge of "performing in chains" as an author writing under China's censorship apparatus, wherein "if you praise brightness you will be rewarded with brightness, while if you (artistically) reveal darkness you will be rewarded with darkness. Because things have been like this for a long time, literature has therefore learned how to perform in chains" (Yan, "Performing in Chains").

Bibliography

Liu, Jianmei. "Joining the Commune or Withdrawing from the Commune? A Reading of Yan Lianke's *Shouhuo*." *Modern Chinese Literature and Culture* 19, 2 (Fall 2007): 1–33.

Tsai, Chien-hsin. "In Sickness or in Health: Yan Lianke and the Writing of Autoimmunity." *Modern Chinese Literature and Culture* 23, 1 (Spring 2011): 77–104.

——. "The Museum of Innocence: The Great Leap Forward and Famine, Yan Lianke, and *Four Books*." MCLC Resource Center Publication (May 2011). http://u.osu.edu/mclc/online-series/museum-of-innocence.

Yan Lianke 阎连科. *Dingzhuang meng* 丁庄梦 (Dream of Ding Village). Taipei: Maitian, 2006.

——. *Dream of Ding Village*. Trans. Cindy Carter. New York: Grove/Atlantic, 2011.

——. *Faxian xiaoshuo* 发现小说 (Discovering fiction). Tianjin: Nankai daxue, 2011.

——. *The Four Books*. Trans. Carlos Rojas. New York: Grove/Atlantic, 2015.

——. *Lenin's Kisses*. Trans. Carlos Rojas. New York: Grove/Atlantic, 2012a.

——. "Performing in Chains." Trans. Carlos Rojas. English PEN, April 12, 2012b. http://www.englishpen.org/performing-in-chains.

——. *Riguang liunian* 日光流年 (Streams of time). Shenyang: Chunfeng wenyi, 1998.

——. *Serve the People!* Trans. Julia Lovell. New York: Grove/Riverside, 2008.

——. *Shouhuo* 受活 (Livening; translated as "Lenin's Kisses"). Shenyang: Chunfeng wenyi, 2004.

——. *Shuo Yan Lianke* 说阎连科 (Discussing Yan Lianke). Ed. Lin Yuan 林源. Shenyang: Liaoning renmin, 2014.

——. *Sishu* 四书 (Four books). Taipei: Maitian, 2011.

——. *Wei renmin fuwu* 为人民服务 (Serve the people). Taipei: Maitian, 2005.

——. "Xiezuo de pantu: Sishu de houji" 写作的叛徒：四书的后记 (A traitor to writing: Afterword to *Four Books*). In Lin Yuan, ed. *Shuo Yan Lianke* (Discussing Yan Lianke), 1:10–11. Shenyang: Liaoning renmin, 2014.

57

INTERNET LITERATURE: FROM YY TO MOOC

HEATHER INWOOD

The founding of China's first Internet Literature University (网络文学大学) in October 2013 was a sign of how far online literature had come since the earliest Chinese-language creative writings were circulated via email in the late 1980s. Established by a consortium of literary websites, including 17K.com and Chinese Online (中文在线), the university describes its mission as "inheriting five thousand years of Chinese culture, training a million writers of Internet literature, allowing newcomers to gain faster entry into the profession, helping Internet literature become part of the social mainstream, and encouraging it to walk from China toward the world" ("Banxue beijing"). Its choice of president, the 2012 Nobel Prize in Literature winner Mo Yan 莫言, was shrewd if a little unexpected, given his past admissions that he had no idea how to use a computer. The most well-known of a group of writers hired by the university to teach Massive Open Online Courses (MOOCs), Mo Yan (2013) now views the web as the modern equivalent of the village walls of his childhood, a place where aspiring writers can "freely release their inner emotions" in an "expansive and unrestrained" manner.

Many observers of Chinese Internet literature have shared Mo Yan's idealism over the past two decades. As visual forms of culture have eroded the market for print literature, the Internet has been welcomed as a source of fresh talent, innovative genres of writing, and increased readerships and income for not only established authors but also writers once confined to fan or amateur status. The history of Chinese Internet fiction is usually traced to the hit romance novel

The First Intimate Contact (第一次的亲密接触) by the Taiwanese author Pizicai 痞子蔡 (pen name of Cai Zhiheng 蔡智恒), released in installments online in 1998 before being published in print in 1999. Nowadays, writings that can be found only on niche fan-fiction sites elsewhere in the world have, in China, gone mainstream. According to statistics from the China Internet Network Information Center (CNNIC), literature ranks just inside the top ten online activities, with a user base of over 290 million in 2014. The Chinese Internet has rapidly turned into a vast literary marketplace where fortunes can be made, fandoms born, and fantasies realized.

Many writers have seen their lives transformed as a result of writing and publishing online, with those at the top of the pyramid (known as "big gods" 大神) becoming millionaires and thousands of others maintaining a regular salary. The financial viability of Internet literature can be attributed to the implementation of VIP pay-per-view reading systems in the mid-2000s, in which novels are published in installments and readers pay a small amount to receive regular updates from their favorite authors. Another source of income results from publishing houses bringing works of Internet fiction under contract and then releasing them as physical books once a solid fan base has been established online. Although the more stringent censorship regulations that govern print publishing ensure that they have usually been stripped of their most salacious and supernatural tendencies, these books still sell in the millions and have helped position authors such as Nanpai Sanshu 南派三叔 (Third Uncle of the Southern School, pen name of Xu Lei 徐磊, an author of "tomb-robbing fiction" [盗墓小说]) and Dangnian Mingyue 当年明月 (Bright Moon of Yesteryear, pen name of Shi Yue 石悦, author of a popular retelling of Ming dynasty history) among the top ten highest-grossing Chinese authors of recent years, with annual earnings of over seven million renminbi.

Television and film adaptations of Internet novels also augment earnings via royalty agreements that go some way to counteract the negative effects of online piracy. One example is the 2012 television series *The Legend of Zhenhuan* (甄嬛传), adapted from the Internet novel of the same name by Liu Lianzi 流潋紫 (pen name of Wu Xuelan 吴雪岚) and representative of the historically themed genre of "rear palace" (后宫) fiction. Especially close commercial ties between Internet fiction and computer games have given rise to the category of "web-game literature" (网游文学), fiction that narrates the triumphs and tribulations of online gamers as they attempt to work their way to the top of the leaderboard. Web-game novels contribute to a symbiotic cultural ecosystem in which writers inspire and educate gamers by setting their novels in the worlds of existing games and companies respond by developing new games that draw on the stories and game settings dreamed into being by online authors.

The commercialization of Internet literature has created economic incentives for authors to write as quickly and engagingly as possible; fierce competition means that readers will look elsewhere if a novel is not updated regularly or fails to entertain. In order to maintain readers' attention, authors often preface chapters with self-reflexive comments on their progress or latest thoughts about characterization or plot. In turn, readers make their opinions heard in the comments section, thus forming an interactive feedback loop that has given audiences unprecedented power to shape the content of what they read. Market pressures have been a central concern of critics who speak out against the commercial excesses of Internet literature. In November 2013, an article in the *People's Daily* warned that demands placed on writers to churn out tens of thousands of words each day have turned them into cogs in a huge, high-pressure literary machine. When Nanpai Sanshu announced earlier that year that he was quitting his writing career for mental health reasons, many fans blamed the psychological stress of producing epic works such as his first series of novels, *Grave Robbers' Chronicles* (盗墓笔记), the abridged print version of which was published over nine volumes between 2007 and 2011.

Another criticism of Internet literature relates to its low literary quality, described as being full of "water" (水) or as "little white writings" (小白文) in reference to its audience of "little whites" (小白), the name given to a generation of young netizens who are constantly immersed in online media. According to estimates, several hundred thousand Chinese novels are serialized on the Internet each year, compared to the thousand or so full-length novels published in print; the sheer volume of texts on the Internet means that a certain amount of pulp is unavoidable. The term that has caught on the most in descriptions of Internet literature, however, is "YY," an abbreviation of the pinyin term *yiyin* (意淫), or "mental porn." YY is essentially wish-fulfillment fiction that allows the subjective fantasies of authors and readers to be realized through plot devices such as time travel, gender swapping, futuristic technologies, magic and the supernatural, and sheer good luck. The word *yiyin* was first used in Cao Xueqin's 曹雪芹 classic eighteenth-century novel *Dream of the Red Chamber* (红楼梦) in reference to Jia Baoyu's 贾宝玉 romantic desires or "lusts of the mind." Some critics now see YY as the default mode of Internet literature, closely connected to its tendency to revel in fantasy worlds that are "built upon air" (架空) and only tenuously rooted in the "real" world.

Many YY genres of Internet fiction draw heavily on existing texts and belief systems; they challenge the limits of reality and offer vicarious pleasures to their readers. A typical example is the hit novel *Legend of Immortals* or *Stars Change* (星辰变) by Wo Chi Xihongshi 我吃西红柿 (I Eat Tomatoes), which began serialization on Qidian.com in 2007. Set in a fantasy world that owes much to martial arts fiction as well as to Daoist philosophy and mythology, *Legend of Immortals* narrates the journey of a young boy warrior who has been isolated due to his apparent inability to cultivate his "inner force" and thus denied the opportunity to find happiness among the immortals as he so desires. Despite its fantasy setting, the novel can be read as an archetypal coming-of-age story that inspires its readers to follow their dreams: if only they put their minds to it, they too can change what is written in the stars. Other YY genres include "infinite fiction" (无限流小说), which inserts its protagonists into the diegesis of well-known horror films and blends science fiction with elements of fantasy, web-game literature, horror, and the various subgenres of "time travel fiction" (穿越小说), many of which transport modern men and women back in time to the imperial households of former dynasties where they become embroiled in scandalous love affairs. Novels set in more everyday contexts such as "workplace" (职场) and "officialdom" (官场) fiction also contain YY characteristics, making their protagonists' steady rise through the career ranks seem as easy and predictable as the process of leveling up in a computer game.

While the term "Internet literature" is often assumed to refer solely to genre fiction of the kind that dominates China's major literary portals, poetry too has also seen its fate altered by the popularization of the Internet in China. Poetry was, in fact, among the earliest forms of Chinese literature to be published online in the early 1990s. By the 2000s, thousands of websites dedicated to the publication and discussion of both modern and classical poetry had sprung up. Internet forums (论坛) in particular helped bring about an explosion in the number of active poetry communities in China, free from the limits of geography and social connections. Many poets have taken advantage of the Internet's textual liberties to produce the kind of poems that could never be published in print. In an effort to go "even lower" than the sexually explicit poetics of the "lower body" (下半身) group created by Shen Haobo and Yin Lichuan in 1999, a number of poetry schools organized themselves around the philosophy of "worshiping of the low" (崇低), writing poems about "trash" (垃圾), or the dark and dirty side of contemporary life. At the other end of the poetic spectrum, the Internet is home to more high-minded poets who write in search of an elusive poetic beauty and use online forums as a means of inviting feedback on their writings from other poets and critics. It is also awash with the poetic equivalent of "water," mundane poems dashed off in seconds using everyday language. Such writings could serve as the best support for Mo Yan's view of the Internet as a place where aspiring writers can freely release their inner emotions, even if the results do not always meet with the most positive reception—for example, the "colloquial" poet Zhao Lihua was famously spoofed on the Internet in 2006 for her "pear blossom form" (梨花体) poems, making her China's most famous contemporary poet for all the wrong reasons.

After more than two decades in which growing numbers of Chinese citizens have taken to writing, publishing, and consuming literature online, what might the future hold for Chinese Internet literature? Mo Yan's new role as the president of the Internet Literature University offers some clues. The university's goal of "inheriting five thousand years of Chinese culture" reflects hopes that the Internet might serve as more than a breeding ground for derivative genre fiction designed for fast-food-style consumption. As China looks to culture as a driver for economic growth and conduit for soft power, the Internet is seen as a tool for nurturing new generations of talented writers who can help communicate the central tenets of Chinese culture to a global audience. November 2013 also saw the inauguration of a new branch of the Chinese Writers Association called the Internet Writers Association (网络作家协会), a sign that gentrification may be the next stage to follow the commercialization of Internet literature. At the same time as traditional cultural organizations attempt to absorb the biggest stars of online writing, literature websites have contracted best-selling print authors such as Hai Yan 海岩, Mai Jia 麦家, and Guo Jingming 郭敬明 to release future novels in installments online. With institutional co-option and growing mediatization of everyday life blurring the boundaries between "online" and "offline," one cannot help wondering how much longer the category of "Internet literature" will exist.

Bibliography

"Banxue beijing" 办学背景 (Background to setting up a school). http://daxue.17k.com/bxbj.html (accessed September 2, 2015).

Feng, Jin. *Romancing the Internet: Consuming and Producing Chinese Web Romance*. Leiden: Brill, 2013.

Hockx, Michel. *Internet Literature in China*. New York: Columbia University Press, 2015.

——. "Links with the Past: Mainland China's Online Literary Communities and Their Antecedents." *Journal of Contemporary China* 38 (February 2004): 105–27.

——. "Virtual Chinese Literature: A Comparative Case Study of Online Poetry Communities." *The China Quarterly* 183 (September 2005): 670–691.

Inwood, Heather. *Verse Going Viral: China's New Media Scenes*. Seattle: University of Washington Press, 2014.

——. "What's in a Game? Transmedia Storytelling and the Web-Game Genre of Online Chinese Popular Fiction." *Asia Pacific: Perspectives* 12, 2 (Spring/Summer 2014): 6–29.

Mo Yan 莫言. "Wangluo wenxue daxue mingyu xiaozhang Mo Yan zhici" 网络文学大学名誉校长莫言致辞 (An address from Mo Yan, renowned president of the Internet Literature University) (October 30, 2013). http://daxue.17k.com/news.html.

Ouyang Youquan 欧阳友权, ed. *Wangluo xiaoshuo mingpian jiedu* 网络小说名篇解读 (Famous novel interpretation of the network [sic]). Beijing: Zhongguo shehui kexue, 2011.

Yu Yang 于洋, Tang Aili 汤爱丽, and Li Jun 李俊. *Wenxue wangjing: wangluo wenxue de ziyou jingjie* 文学网景：网络文学的自由境界 (Literary webscapes: The free state of Internet literature). Beijing: Zhongyang bianyi, 2004.

INDEX

Abbas, Ackbar, 409
aboriginals (indigenous peoples), 187, 333; aboriginal literature, 21, 74–75, 284, 328, 426–27; oral literature of, 32
Above Flame (Wu Mingyi), 428
Absolute Signal (Gao Xingjian), 402
Account of the Future of New China, An (Liang Qichao), 100
A Cheng (b. 1949), 81, 186, 300, 301, 302, 339
adaptations. *See* films; Internet; theater
"Addendum to Cosmicomics, An" (Xi Xi), 359
Aesthetics and Creation (Gao Xingjian), 404
Afternoon Tea Conversations (Zhu Tianwen), 364
Again the Palm Tree, Again the Palm Tree (Yu Lihua), 66
Age of Enlightenment (Wang Anyi), 376–77
Age of Farewells, The (Li Zishu), 427
"Ah Jin" (Shen Congwen), 184

AIDS/HIV, 340, 426, 434
Ai Qing (1910–1998), 225, 248, 287
Ai Weiwei, 311
Alai, 76
Alarm Signal (Gao Xingjian), 321
Alexander II (Tsar of Russia), 196
alienation, 346–47, 359, 392
All-China Dramatic Association, 209
All China League of Resistance Writers, 12, 42, 211
All Russia Association of Proletarian Writers. *See* RAPP
"Aloewood Ashes: The First Incense Brazier" (Chang, E.), 117, 218
"Aloewood Ashes: The Second Incense Brazier" (Chang, E.), 218
Along the River During the Qingming Festival (lscroll painting), 358
Analects, 146
"AnAn's Vacation" (Zhu Tianwen), 83
anarchism, 173
ancient-style prose, 5–6
Anderson, Benedict, 100

Anderson, Marston, 33, 237–38
"And the Rain Patters On" (Wang Anyi), 371
An Jung-geun, 196
"Another Kind of Aesthetics" (Gao Xingjian), 403
Anthology of Famous European and American Short Stories (Zhou Shoujuan), 114
Anthology of Taiwan's Sinophone Indigenous Literature (Sun Dachuan), 75
Anti-Rightist Campaign (1957–1958), 14, 43, 239, 245, 248, 294
Anti-Spiritual Pollution Campaign, 286, 402
Ant Life (Wang Jinkang), 397
Anuwu, Ligelale, 427
"Apple" (Xi Xi), 359
Après le déluge (film), 404
architecture, 325, 428
"Arcs" (Gu Cheng), 287
Arrayed Marvels, 140
Arriving at the Margins of Life: Answering My Own Questions (Yang Jiang), 232, 235
art, 202, 209, 228, 232, 258, 264, 295, 380, 402, 403; art films, 404; China Youth Art Theater, 200; Deng Xiaoping on, 345; Hong Kong Arts Development Council, 412; Mao Zedong and, 238–39, 240, 248, 268, 300. *See also* martial arts fiction; paintings; photography
Artaud, Antonin, 321
Ascension, L' (Messiaen), 401
Asimov, Isaac, 398
"Assembly Line" (Shu Ting), 287
assimilation policy, 52
"Assorted Quatrains on Japan" (Huang Zunxian), 93
Atlas: The Archeology of an Imaginary City (Dung Kai-cheung), 407, 410
"Attachment" (Lao She), 215
"At the Bridge Construction Site" (Liu Binyan), 247

"Attitude, An" (Wang Shuo), 382
autobiography, 33, 67, 115, 132, 283, 374; literature as, 147–48, 149; psychological, 187
Autobiography: A Novel (Li Ang), 425
Autumn (Ba Jin), 169
"Autumn" (Du Yunxie), 287
avant-garde fiction, 16, 18; Can Xue and, 315; Ma Yuan and, 314–15; urban fiction and, 346; violence and, 317; Yu Hua and, 313–14, 316, 317, 318
avant-garde poetry (since 1980s): canon, 421; with commercialization, 420–21; connotations, 414–15; Internet and, 420; 1980s, 415–18; 1990s and beyond, 418–20
A Ying, 28, 29
Azalea Mountain (opera), 268, 269

Backed Against the Sea (Wang Wenxing), 253, 254, 427
Bai Fengxi, 201
Bai Hua (b. 1930), 187
baihua journals, 39
Bai Jingrui, 81
Bai Qiu (b. 1937), 331, 332
Bai Wei (1894–1987), 132, 197, 207
Bai Xianyong (b. 1937), 19, 65, 77, 82, 181, 185, 428; with homosexual themes, 253, 339–40, 425; with Taiwan and Cold War fiction, 252–53, 254, 255
Bai Yu, 275, 422
Ba Jin (1904–2005), 10, 32, 63, 169–75
Bakunin, Mikhail, 173
Balcom, John, 75
"Ballad of Queen's Pier, The" (Liu Waitong), 411
ballets, 15, 267, 268, 270–71, 272
Bamboo Hat (poetry group), 332
Bamboo Hat (poetry journal), 332
"Banana Fan" (Xi Xi), 356
Bao Tianxiao (1876–1973), 80, 111, 113
Baotown (Wang Anyi), 304, 372–73
Bao Zheng (999-1062), 358, 360
Barmé, Geremie, 17

Battle of Mount Dingjun, The (film), 80
Battles at the Dockyard (play), 200
beauty, 74, 115–16, 148, 262, 281, 404
beauty writers, 386, 388–89, 390
Beckett, Samuel, 321
Bedrock (Xi Xi), 361
Before the Sunrise (Meng Yao), 251
Behind the Screen (Ouyang Yuqian), 207
Bei Cun (b. 1965), 314, 317
Bei Dao (b. 1949), 43, 53, 67, 286, 288, 290, 316, 415, 418
Beijing, 29, 212; Democracy Wall movement (1978–1979), 289; operas, 267, 268–70, 272; "This Is Beijing at 4:08," 288
Beijing Comrade, 342
Beijinger in New York (television drama), 383
Beijing People's Institute of Drama and Art, 209
Beijing Spring of 1979, 295
Beijing Story (Beijing Comrade), 342
"Believe in the Future" (Shizhi), 288, 289
Be There or Be Square (film), 383
"Betrayer of Literature" (Yan Lianke), 434–35
Bewitching Words (Zhu Tianwen), 364
Bible, the, 92
bifurcated narrative, 254
Big Breasts and Wide Hips (Mo Yan), 310
Big Dipper (literary magazine), 155
Bing Xin (1900–1998), 8, 9, 40, 130, 154, 329
Bird Men (Guo Shixing), 202–3. 322
Bi Yihong (1892–1926), 111
Black Slave Cries to Heaven (opera), 196
Black Snow (Liu Heng), 346–47
"Black Steed, The" (Zhang Chengzhi), 303
Blades from the Willows (Huanzhulouzhu), 275
"Blockade" (Chang, E.), 218–19
Blood Red Sunset (Ma Bo), 297
Bloom During the Rainy Season (Yu Xiu), 392

Blue and the Black, The (Wang Lan), 250–51
Blue Star Poetry Society, 330
Boccaccio, Giovanni, 323
body writing, 30, 389
Book and the Sword, The (Jin Yong), 276–77
Book of Change, The (Chang, E.), 221
Book of History, 140, 142
Book of Odes, 228
Book of Poetry, 123
Border Town (Shen Congwen), 186, 187
Borges, Jorge Luis, 314, 316
Born Red: A Chronicle of the Cultural Revolution (Gao Yuan), 297
Bourdieu, Pierre, 420, 421
Boxer Rebellion (1900), 56, 57, 104, 109, 114, 198
Bo Yang, 423, 429
boy love (*danmei*) fiction, 342
branding, 365, 387, 390–91, 411
Breaking Out of Ghost Pagoda (Bai Wei), 197, 207
Brecht, Bertolt (1898–1956), 321, 359
Brief History of Modern Times, A (Li Boyuan), 106
Bright and Sunny Days (Hao Ran), 15
Bright Skies (Cao Yu), 209
"Broad Road of Realism, The" (Qin Zhaoyang), 246
Brocade Valley (Wang Anyi), 373
"Brocade Zither" (Li Shangyin), 253
Brothers (Yu Hua), 318, 387–88
"Brothers" (Wang Anyi), 341, 373
Buddhism, 76, 92, 275, 384
Builders, The (Liu Qing), 14
Bulwer-Lytton, Edward, 100, 105
Burning of the Red Lotus Monastery, The (film), 275
Burying Injustice 1947, Burying Injustice (Li Qiao), 423
Bus Stop (Gao Xingjian), 201, 321, 402
Butcher's Wife, The (Li Ang), 425
Butterfly fiction. *See* entertainment fiction
Butterfly Lovers, The (Li Hanxiang), 81

Buying a Fishing Rod for My Grandfather (Gao Xingjian), 400
"By Chance" (Xu Zhimo), 125
"Bygone Age of Ah Q, The" (Qian Xingcun), 160–61
Byron, George Gordon (Lord), 114, 146

Cai Cehai (b. 1954), 185
Call to Arms (Lu Xun), 8, 136
Camel Xiangzi. *See Rickshaw*
camps, labor. *See* labor
campus comrade fiction, 342
Candy (Mian Mian), 388, 389–90
cannibalism, 136–38, 310, 397
canon: avant-garde poetry (since 1980s), 421; literary history and, 27–34; Misty poetry and, 290–91; revision of, 29–30
Can Three Make It (Li Guoxiu), 324
Can Xue (b. 1953), 43, 181, 315, 431
Cao Xueqin, 101, 169, 220, 250, 253, 376; influence, 281, 377; "YY" and, 438
Cao Yu (1910–1966), 10, 198, 199, 205–9
Cao Zhi, 253
Cartland, Barbara, 281
"Case for Literature, The" (Gao Xingjian), 402–3
"Cat" (Qian Zhongshu), 233
Caucasian Chalk Circle, The (Brecht), 359
CCP. *See* Chinese Communist Party
"Celestial God, The" (Shen Congwen), 184
censorship, 99, 106, 263, 325, 434, 437; GMD, 19, 180, 189, 190; with literature, production of, 14, 51–53; in Taiwan, 52, 53, 328, 423
Central Academy of Drama, 209
Cervantes, Miguel de, 234
"Chairman Mao Is a Rotten Egg" (Chen Ruoxi), 255–56
Chan, Evans, 325
Chan Chi Tak, 411
Chang, Eileen (1920–1995), 12–13, 17, 23, 31, 44, 411; with cities and worlds, narratives of, 217–22; film and, 80, 82–83, 221; immigration to U.S., 220; influence, 32, 117, 220–22, 348; Shanghai and, 180–81
Chang, Yvonne, 32
Chang Ta-Chun, 60
Chan Ping-chiu, 325
Chaos and All That (Liu Suola), 67–68
Chaos and Confusion Wuhe, 427
Che Guevara (Shen Lin, et al.), 203
Che Qianzi, 418
Chekhov, Anton, 209
Chen, Joan, 84
Chen Baibing, 133
Chen Dabei, 207
Chen Diexian (1879–1940), 111
Chen Dong-dong, 417
Chen Duxiu (1880–1942), 7, 50, 145, 146, 153
Chen Fangming, 31
Chen Guofu, 84
Chen Guokai, 296
Chen Hengzhe (1893–1976), 9
Chen Jialuo, 276
Chen Jianzhong, 31
Chen Jiying, 220
Chen Kaige, 81, 301, 316
Chen Kunhou, 81
Chen Linrui, 232
Chen Mo (b. 1945), 288
Chen Pingyuan, 29
Chen Quzhen (Hunan warlord), 184
Chen Ran (b. 1962), 18, 341, 350–51
Chen Ruoxi (b. 1938), 20, 66, 181, 252, 253, 254–56, 340
Chen Sanli (1859–1937), 56–57, 59
Chen Sen (c.1797–c.1870), 337
Chen Shaoting, 31
Chen Sihe, 30
Chen Xiaoming, 30, 314
Chen Xiefen (1883–1923), 129
Chen Xiying, 142
Chen Xue, 426
Chen Xuezhao (1906–1991), 132, 133
Chen Yan (1856–1937), 55–57, 60
Chen Yi, 201

Chen Ying (1907–1986), 132
Chen Yingzhen (b. 1937), 20, 31, 181, 259, 262–63, 372, 423
Chen Yinke (1890–1969), 59
Chen Zidu, 321
Chen Zizhan (1898–1990), 89
Cheng, Eileen, 141
Cheng Bugao, 81
Cheng Fangwu, 147, 160
Cheng Guangwei, 419
Cheng Xiaodong, 82
Cheng Xiaoqing (1893–1976), 111
Cheng Yingshu, 426
Chess Men (Guo Shixing), 322
Chi, Pang-yuan, 32
Chiang Kai-shek, 363
children, 43, 63, 81, 109, 138, 198, 207, 289, 301; children's fiction, 132; children's theater, 428
Chi Li (b. 1957), 346, 347, 352
Chim, Jim, 325
"China, I've Lost My Key" (Liang Xiaobin), 289
China 2185 (Liu Cixin), 396
China Critic, The (newspaper), 231
China Dream (Sun Huizhu and Fei Chunfang), 321
China Internet Network Information Center (CNNIC), 437
China Youth Art Theater, 200
"Chinese, Why Don't You Get Angry?" (Long Yingtai), 423
Chinese Communist Party (CCP), 10, 13, 15, 48; Rectification Campaign, 12, 224–29, 248, 294
"Chinese Department, The" (Li Yawei), 416
Chinese Ghost Story, A (film), 82
Chinese Grammatical Discussion of "The Other Shore," A (play), 322
Chinese Online, 436
Chinese People's Political Consultative Conference, 342
Chinese Women's Paper (literary magazine), 129

Chinese Writers Association, 14, 48, 52, 311, 431, 440
Chou, Wah-shan, 336
Chow, Rey, 33, 174, 215
Chu ci (Qu Yuan), 186
ci (song lyrics), 57, 58, 121–22
cinema. *See* films
cities: with foreign culture, 363–69; metropolis, 176–79; narratives of worlds and, 217–22; as subject matter, 18, 22, 82, 302, 329, 356, 360, 390, 395, 407, 409; urban fiction and, 345–53; Walled City, 408, 410. *See also* Beijing; Hong Kong; Shanghai
City at the End of Time (Leung Ping-kwan), 22, 407, 408, 410
City Chariot (Qiu Huadong), 351–52
City in Ruins (Jia Pingwa), 18, 347–48
City of Fantasies (Guo Jingming), 390, 395
City of High Summer (Zhu Tianwen), 364
civil service examination system, 5, 56, 106
"Class Counselor" (Liu Xinwu), 293
classical poetry, contested, 55–60
Classic of Mountains and Seas, 140, 141
CNNIC. *See* China Internet Network Information Center
Cold War fiction, 250–57
Collected Works (Jin Yong), 277
Collection of Modern Poetry (Chen Yan), 55
"Colonel" (Ya Xian), 331–32
Coming and Going (Chi Li), 347
commercial culture, 17, 21
commercialization, of literature: beauty writers and, 386, 388–89, 390; branding, 387; Internet and, 390–93, 437–38; youth writers, 386, 390, 391–92
commercialization, of poetry, 420–21
Common Sense (literary supplement), 118
communities. *See* literary communities

Compendium of Modern Chinese Literature, 113
computer games, 437
comrade fiction, 342–43
"Concise History of Materialism" (Wang Shuo), 384
Confessions of Love (Zhou Shoujuan), 116
Conflagration (Ye Shengtao), 337
Confucianism, 4, 7, 16, 131, 133, 302, 372; criticism of, 93, 145, 146, 198; with literature and the Way, 8, 27, 105, 229, 418
Confucius, 4, 142
Confusion (Xiaohe), 342
Cong Shen, 200
Cong Weixi, 297
Consort of Peace, The (Cao Yu), 209
consumer culture, 17–18, 346–47
"Consumerist Era" (Chan Ping-chiu), 325
Contemporains, Les (journal), 10, 11, 178, 180, 329
"Correct Handling" (Mao Zedong), 248
Cosmic Wind (literary magazine), 211
costume dramas, 12, 13, 384
"Creation" (Mao Dun), 164, 166
Creationists, 29, 160
Creation Society (1921–1930), 48, 141, 142, 160, 162; formation of, 147; with Marxism, 160; romanticism and, 8, 10, 147, 148
Crescent Moon, 161
Crescent Moon Society, 121–26, 161
"Critical Discussion of *The Dream of the Red Chamber*, A" (Wang Guowei), 101
Critical Point Theater Phenomenon, 324
Crocodile Notes (Qiu Miaojin), 340, 426
"Crossroads, The" (Chen Ruoxi), 256
Crown (magazine), 282–83, 284
Crown Press, 283
Crown Publishers, 220
Crying Camels (San Mao), 284
Crystal, The (literary magazine), 113
Crystal Boys (Bai Xianyong), 253, 339–40, 425

Cui Zi'en (b. c.1958), 342
Cultural Revolution (1966–1976), 43, 226, 376; "Four Olds," 15, 433; Gang of Four and, 16, 200, 201, 286, 289, 293, 294, 295; historical overview, 15–16; Misty poetry and, 288, 289, 290; persecution during, 52, 57, 155, 156, 201, 211, 225, 234, 239, 248, 255, 288, 293–95, 297, 401, 418, 429; revolutionary model theater and, 15, 267–72; roots-seeking literature and, 301; scar literature and, 293–97; science fiction and, 397, 398
culture, 32; commercial culture, 17, 21; consumer culture, 17–18, 346–47; cultural policy, 13; "high-culture fever," 304, 415; *liumang* culture, 17, 379–81, 383, 384; Mount Culture, 142; New Culture movement, 7, 40, 122–23, 159, 237; politics and, 299–304; print culture, growth of, 5, 111–18; Taiwan with foreign culture, 363–69; *wen* culture, 6, 56, 229
Culture of the Mountain and the Seas (Sun Dachuan), 426–27
"Curbing the Flood" (Lu Xun), 141, 142
cyclical imagery, 192–93

Dai Houying, 297
Dai Jinhua, 382
Dai Wangshu (1905–1950), 11, 177–78, 179–80, 411
Dame aux camélias, La (Dumas), 106, 115
dan, homoeroticism and, 336–37
dance, 202, 403. *See also* ballets
Dangnian Mingyue, 437
danlan.org, 343
danmei (boy love) fiction, 342
Daoism, 186, 229, 275, 301, 302, 401, 428
Dark Souls (Yang Zhao), 425
Darwin, Charles, 4, 187, 398
David Copperfield (Dickens), 101
Days of Glory (Han Han), 392
Days of Traveling Afar, The (Liu Zaifu), 68
Days on the Boat (Zhu Tianxin), 366

Dead Visiting the Living, The (Liu Shugang), 321
"Death in Chicago" (Bai Xianyong), 252
"Death in Venice" (Zhu Tianxin), 367–68, 369
Decameron (Boccaccio), 323
Deer and the Cauldron, The (Jin Yong), 277
Defense of Lugou Bridge (play), 199
Democracy Wall movement (1978–1979), 17, 256, 289, 316
Deng Ken (b. 1944), 10, 288
Deng Xiangyang, 426
Deng Xiaoping (1904–1997), 142, 278, 287, 324, 418, 431; on art, 345; criticism of, 382; Four Modernizations and, 294–95; PRC and, 67
Denton, Kirk, 33, 63
design: a bad master (Yan Zhongxian), 428
"Destination, The" (Wang Anyi), 372
Destined for Half a Lifetime (Chang, E.), 220
detective fiction. *See* fiction
Dewey, John, 122
"Diary of a Madman" (Lu Xun), 3, 136–43
diaspora: exile and, 63–65, 67–68; Hong Kong and, 65; immigrants and, 68–70; nation and, 62–63; PRC and, 66, 67; Sinophone literature and, 62; Taiwan and, 64, 65–66
diceng (lower level) literature, 352–53
Dickens, Charles, 101, 106, 114, 146
Dictionary of Maqiao, A (Han Shaogong), 302
Ding Ling (1904–1986), 13, 131, 225, 255, 338; with feminism and revolution, 152–57; persecution of, 155, 156, 248
Ding Ning (1902–1980), 58
Ding Xilin, 205
Ding Yi, 28
Director of the MTS and the Chief Agronomist, The (Nikolaeva), 246
Disciples of the Liar (Zhang Dachun), 424

Discussion of China (reform journal), 92
Disraeli, Benjamin, 100, 105
diversification: literary diversification (1920s and 1930s), 9–11; literary history and, 30–31; Taiwan with experimentation, new voices and, 425–29
Documentation and Fabrication: One Method of Creating the World (Wang Anyi), 374
Doll's House, A (Ibsen), 148, 154, 205, 242
domestic violence, 313
Donald, James, 353
Dongfang Bai, 423
Dong Nian, 424, 425
Don Quixote (Cervantes), 234
"Don't Worry, Lulu!" (Yang Jiang), 231
Dos Passos, John, 351
Dowson, Ernest, 149
Doyle, Arthur Conan, 106, 114
drama, 40; ballet, 267, 270–71, 272; costume, 12, 13, 384; national defense drama, 198; spoken drama, 10, 197–203, 205–9, 320; television, 283, 383; theater and, 195–203
"Dream and Poetry" (Hu Shi), 123–24
Dream Devourer, The (Zheng, E.), 428
Dream of Ding Village (Yan Lianke), 433–34
Dream of the Red Chamber (Cao Xueqin), 101, 169, 220, 250, 253, 281, 376, 377, 438
Dream of the Red Chamber Award, 376
Dreams May Come (film), 384
Dream of Ding Village (Yan Lianke), 18
Dreams of Reform (play), 195
"Drinking with General Li among the Flowers" (Xi Xi), 358
drugs, 255, 350, 388, 389, 390, 401, 410. *See also* Opium War
"Drunk in the Flowers" (Li Jian), 296–97
Du Heng, 142
Dumas, Alexander, 106, 115
Dung Kai-cheung (b. 1967), 22, 407, 409–10

Duoduo, 415, 418
"Du Wanxiang" (Ding Ling), 156
Du Xiulan (b. 1966), 340
Du Yunxie (b. 1918), 287

early postrevolutionary period (1949–1966), 13–15, 237–48
Eastern Times (Bao Tianxiao), 111
East Palace, West Palace (film), 341–42
East Wing West Wing (play), 325
Eclipse (Mao Dun), 165
Editorial Office (television drama), 383
education, 28, 39, 50, 114, 184, 401; Internet and, 436, 439; in Taiwan, 51, 328; for women, 9, 46, 130, 153
"Eight Don'ts" (Hu Shi), 122
Eighteen Springs (Chang, E.), 220
Eighth Symphony (Mahler), 401
eight-legged essays, 9, 39, 42, 98
Eleventh Symphony (Shostakovich), 401
Eliot, T. S., 253
"Embers" (Han Shaogong), 302
Emerson, Ralph Waldo, 220
Emily Dickinson (Wei Ying-juan), 324
"End, The" (Gu Cheng), 287
entertainment (Mandarin Ducks and Butterflies) fiction, 8, 80, 250; popularity of, 10, 33; Zhou Shoujuan with love stories and, 111–18
"Entrails of Nüwa, The" (Lu Xun), 141–42
Epic Theater, 321, 359
Epoch Poetry Society, 330
Escape (Gao Xingjian), 403
essays. *See* eight-legged essays
Essays on the History of Taiwan Fiction (Chen Jianzhong), 31
"Eternal Snow Beauty, The" (Bai Xianyong), 252
Everybody Sticks the Beigang Incense Burner (Li Ang), 425
Evolution and Ethics (Huxley), 5
examination system. *See* civil service examination system; imperial examination system
Execution of Mayor Yin, The (Chen Ruoxi), 255

executions, 57, 139, 155, 196, 255
exile: diaspora and, 63–65, 67–68; exile literature, 17, 65
experimentation: experimental phase, literary history, 27–28; fiction, experimental, 314; Taiwan, literature in post-martial law era, 425–29; theater, experimental, 320–25
Experiments (Hu Shi), 123–24
Expressions of Sorrow (Luo Yijun), 340–41

"Fabrication" (Ma Yuan), 315
Fall of the Pagoda, The (Chang, E.), 221
family, 240, 310
Family (Ba Jin), 10, 169–75
Family Catastrophe (Wang Wenxing), 253, 254, 427
"Family Matters in the Chentang Pass Commander's Household" (Xi Xi), 356–57
Fang Fang (b. 1955), 346
Fang Han (b. 1947), 288
Fang Qi (b. 1937), 332
Fang Si, 332
Fang Xiu (1970–1972), 73
Fan Si (b. 1925), 330
fantasy, 390, 394–98, 438–39
Fan Wenlan (1891–1969), 186–87
"Far and Near" (Gu Cheng), 287
fashion, 365, 391
Fashion Street (Zhang Xian), 322
Fate in Tears and Laughter (Zhang Henshui), 113
Faulkner, William, 314
Faurot, Jeannette, 32
February 28 Incident, 19, 21, 263, 324, 329, 333, 423
"Feelings" (Gu Cheng), 289
Fei Chunfang, 321
Fei Ming. *See* Feng Wenbing
Fei Mu, 81
"Feitian" (Liu Ke), 296
female homoeroticism, 336, 337–38, 339, 340, 341, 342, 373

feminism: revolution and, 152–57, 164–67, 270–71; with sexuality, 164–67
Feng Wenbing (Fei Ming) (1901–1967), 11, 185
Feng Xiaogang, 383
Feng Yuanjun, 131, 154
"Fertile Town Chalk Circle, The" (Xi Xi), 358, 359–60
"Fertile Town" series (Xi Xi), 410
fiction, 32, 360, 402; avant-garde fiction, 16, 18, 313–18, 346; Cold War, 250–57; detective fiction, 6, 8, 105, 109, 111, 262, 310, 381; entertainment fiction, 8, 10, 33, 80, 111–18, 250; late Qing (1895–1911), 104–9; Liang Qichao (1873–1929) and, 6, 97–102, 105, 106, 111, 396; martial arts, 22, 33, 274–78, 384, 394; metafiction and, 310, 311, 373, 427; newspapers and, 104, 105, 106, 113, 114, 118, 284, 358; with representation and relevance, 169–75; Republican era (1911–1949), 18, 49, 317, 339; science fiction, 6, 18, 105, 278, 394–98, 428, 439; Taiwan with modernists and Cold War, 250–57; types of, 18, 132, 281, 314, 342–43, 346, 348–49, 394, 425–26, 439; urban fiction, 18, 33, 345–53
Field of Life and Death (Xiao Hong), 189–94
Fifteenth Symphony (Shostakovich), 401
File Zero (Gao Xingjian), 322
films, 117, 177, 189, 275, 284, 316, 379, 404; adaptations, 80–85, 221, 303, 307, 309, 341–42, 348, 358, 364, 381, 383, 384, 391, 408, 437; Chang, E., and, 80, 82–83, 221; roots-seeking literature and, 43, 301; Xi Xi and, 358, 360–61
Fin-de-Siècle Splendor (Zhu Tianwen), 364
"Fin-de-Siècle Splendor" (Zhu Tianwen), 364–65
First Intimate Contact, The (Pizicai), 437
"Fish, The" (Huang Chunming), 259
Fish Men (Guo Shixing), 322

"Five in a Nightclub" (Mu Shiying), 178–79
Flaubert, Gustav, 154
"Flaw" (Wang Wenxing), 253–54
"Flight to the Moon" (Lu Xun), 141
Floating City 1.2.3: New Analysis of Xi Xi's Fiction (He Furen), 360
Flower in a Sea of Retribution (Zeng Pu), 107–8
"Flower in the Rainy Night, A" (Huang Chunming), 260
Flower of Love, The (Zhou Shoujuan), 115
Flowers of Shanghai, 44
Flowers of the Women's Prison (Wang Miaoru), 129
Fly, Archaeology Bird, Fly! (Chan Ping-chiu), 325
Fly Eyes (Qiu Huadong), 351–52
Flying Carpet (Xi Xi), 359, 360, 410
"Flying Over Maple Village" (Su Tong), 317
"Fooling around" (Wang Shuo), 383
Forbidden Zone (Ye Lingfeng), 338
Forest of Fiction (magazine), 106
"Foreword to the Publication of Political Novels in Translation" (Liang Qichao), 99
Forging the Truth (Yang Jiang), 233
"Forgotten, The" (Ye Shengtao), 337
"Form in Poetry" (Wen Yiduo), 125–26
Fortress Besieged (Qian Zhongshu), 13, 233, 234
Foundation series (Asimov), 398
Four Books, The (Yan Lianke), 434
Four Modernizations, 294–95
"Four Olds," 15, 433
Fourteenth Symphony (Shostakovich), 401
Fourth Congress of Writers and Artists, 295
Fox Volant of the Snowy Mountain (Jin Yong), 277
Franz Kafka Prize, 432
freedom, 142. *See also* personal freedom; War of Liberation

Free Talk (literary magazine), 113, 114, 117
Friendly Association of the Shanghai Dramatic Circle, 198
"From Literary Revolution to Revolutionary Literature" (Cheng Fangwu), 160
"From Our Own Footprints" (Yang Lian), 289

Gall and the Sword, The (Cao Yu), 209
Gang of Four. *See* Cultural Revolution
Gao Changhong, 140–41
Gao Xiaosheng (1928–1999), 186, 296
Gao Xingjian (b. 1940), 17–18, 186, 201, 321, 322; on literature, 402–3; with word and image, 400–404
Gao Yaojie, 434
Gao Yihan (1885–1968), 7
Gao Yuan, 297
Garage Theater, 322
García Márquez, Gabriel, 302–3, 307
Garlic Ballads, The (Mo Yan), 310
"Gathering Vetch" (Lu Xun), 141, 142
"Gazing at Rainbows" (Shen Congwen), 187
Ge Fei (b. 1964), 20, 314, 316, 317, 318
gender, 324, 340, 343, 396; inequality, 155–56, 174, 196; revolution and, 165
"Generation, A" (Gu Cheng), 289
Ge Qin (b. 1907), 133
Ge You, 383
"Ghost, North Wind, Man" (Wang Zhenhe), 260–61
Ghost and Goblin (Wuhe), 426
Ghost Blows Out the Lamp, 394
"Ghost Story, The" (Xin Qishi), 411
global Chinese literature. *See* Sinophone literature
GMD. *See* Guomindang
Goddesses, The (Guo Moruo), 124
"Goddess of Lo River, The" (Cao Zhi), 253
"God's Dream" (Qian Zhongshu), 233
Going to America, Going to America (Zha Jianying), 67
Goldblatt, Howard, 191, 307
"Golden Cangue, The" (Chang, E.), 217
Golden Lotus, 101
Golden Mountain Blues (Zhang Ling), 69
Golden Road, The (Hao Ran), 15
Goldman, Emma, 173
Gong Zizhen (1792–1841), 92
Good Man Luo Ge (Tong Ge), 339
"Gramophone Record, A" (Zhou Shoujuan), 115
Grand Liar, The (Zhang Dachun), 424
graphic novels, 426
Grass Stage, 322
Grave Robbers' Chronicles (Nanpai Sanshu), 394, 438
grave robbery fiction, 18, 394
Greatest Event in One's Life, The (Hu Shi), 197, 208
Great Leap Forward (1958), 14, 199, 239, 434
"Great London Fog, The" (Huang Zunxian), 94
Great Love, The (Yang Zhao), 425
Great Mass (Mozart), 401
Greek theater, 202, 208
Green East Sea, The (Li Yongping), 427
Green Nightmare (Shen Congwen), 187
Groundzero (Zheng, E.), 428
Growing Up (film), 81
Guan Guan (b. 1929), 331
Gu Cheng (1956–1993), 286, 287, 288, 289
Gu Hua (b. 1942), 185, 302, 304
Gui'er and Ayao (Wuhe), 340
Guillotine (play), 196
"Guisheng" (Shen Congwen), 186
Gu Jiegang (1893–1980), 142, 186
Gu Jitang, 31–32
Gu Long (1938–1985), 81, 278
Gunn, Edward, 33, 213
Guo Jingming (b. 1983), 386, 390–91, 395, 440
Guomindang (GMD), 31; censorship and, 19, 180, 189, 190; Nationalists, 177, 178, 180, 200, 212, 263; with Northern Expedition of 1928, 9, 317

Guo Moruo (1892–1978), 8, 124, 147, 160; homoeroticism and, 338; spoken drama and, 197–98, 199, 208
Guo Shixing, 202–3, 322–23
Guo Shiying (1942–1968), 288

Ha'erbin Theater, 200
Haggard, H. Rider, 101, 106
Hai Yan, 440
Haizi, 416, 417
Half Hot, Half Cold (Wang Shuo), 381
Half of Man Is Woman (Zhang Xianliang), 297
Hamlet b (Chan Ping-chiu), 325
Hamletmaxhine (Chan Ping-chiu), 325
Han Bangqing, 98
Han Dong, 416, 419
"Hand Scroll" (Xi Xi), 358
Han Han (b. 1982), 384, 386, 390–92
Han Poetry (poetry journal), 417
Han Shaogong (b. 1953), 186, 299, 300–303, 316
Han Song (b. 1965), 397–98
Hao Ran (1932–2008), 15, 185
Hardy, Thomas, 186
Hatred in Life and Death (Mei Lanfang), 197
Hauptmann, Gerhart, 205
Head Without a Tail (Meng Jinghui), 323
Heart of Women, The (Lu Yin), 130–31
Heart's Desire (Yang Jiang), 232–33
Heavenly Hound (Guo Moruo), 124
He Dun (b. 1958), 18, 349
He Furen, 360
Heimat Roman (homeland novel), 258
He Lei, 30
He Liwei (b. 1954), 185
"Hello, Younger Brother" (He Dun), 349
He Long, 201
Hemingway, Ernest, 220
Herbivorous Family, The (Mo Yan), 310
Herder, Johann Gottfried, 121
Heroic Stories of New Sons and Daughters (Tian Han), 197
He Yaohui (b. 1982), 342–43

He-Yin, Zhen (1884–1920?), 129
Hezhu's New Match (play), 324
"high-culture fever," 304, 415
High-Speed Rail (Han Song), 397
Hill, Michael, 6
Himalayas, The (He Dun), 349
"His Son's Big Doll" (Huang Chunming), 259–60
history, 106, 140, 142, 201, 202, 272, 321, 384. *See also* literary history
History of Contemporary Chinese Literature, A (Hong Zicheng), 272
History of Hong Kong Fiction (Yuan Liangjun), 32
History of the Development of New Poetry in Taiwan (Gu Jitang), 31
HIV/AIDS, 340, 426, 434
Hockx, Michel, 8
"Homecoming" (Han Shaogong), 186, 302
homeland novel (*Heimat Roman*), 258
homelessness, 138, 148, 149–50, 241, 409
homoeroticism: female, 336, 337–38, 339, 340, 341, 342, 373; Internet and, 342–43; male, 336, 338–43, 366; queer fiction and, 425–26
homophobia, 337, 340, 343
homosexuality, 253, 324, 336–37, 339–40, 342, 343, 425–26
Hong Kong, 17, 48, 51, 65, 81, 219, 276; experimental theater and, 323, 324–25; historical overview, 21–22; literary history of, 31–32; literature, late twentieth century to new millennium, 407–12; Xi Xi and tales of, 355–61, 410
"Hong Kong—1960" (Bai Xianyong), 252
Hong Kong Archaeological Story: Fly, Fly, Fly (Chan Ping-chiu), 325
Hong Kong Express (newspaper), 358
Hong Kong MP & GI Company, 221
Hong Ling (Hung, Lucifer) (b. 1971), 341
Hong Zicheng, 272
hooligan literature, 17, 30, 345
Horse Thief (film), 301
Horse Thief (Zhang Chengzhi), 301

Hou Hsiao-hsien, 364
Hou Xiaoxian (b. 1947), 81, 83–84
Hoyingfung, 325
Hsia, C. T., 32, 33, 221, 233
Hsia, T. A. (1916–1965), 19, 251, 252, 255
Huacheng (journal), 433
Huainanzi, 140, 141
Huaishu Village (Hu Ke), 199
Huan Fu (b. 1922), 332
Huang Chunming (b. 1935), 20, 259–60, 428
Huang Jinshu, 31, 427
Huang Xiang (b. 1941), 288
Huang Xinmian, 133
Huang Xiuji, 30
Huang Yi (b. 1952), 278
Huang Zunxian (b. 1848), 6, 89, 92, 93–96
Huang Zuolin, 321
Huanzhulouzhu, 275
Hu Feng (1902–1985), 12, 190, 191, 239
Hugo, Victor, 106, 114
Hui, Ann (b. 1947), 81, 82–83
Hu Ke, 199
Hu Lancheng (1906–1981), 220, 363
Human, Beast, Ghost (Qian Zhongshu), 233
Humanity, Oh Humanity (Dai Houying), 297
"Humble Sacrifice" (Yu Dafu), 149
Hundred Days Reform (1898), 57, 90, 195
Hundred Flowers (1956–1957), 14, 239, 245–49
Hung, Eva, 358
Hung, Lucifer. *See* Hong Ling
Hu Shi (1891–1962), 7, 8, 27, 50, 56, 124, 130, 148; poetry revolution and, 89, 122–23; spoken drama and, 197, 208
"Hut on the Mountain, The" (Can Xue), 315
Huxley, Thomas, 5
Hu Yepin, 153, 155

Ibsen, Henrik, 148, 154, 197, 205, 242
"Ice River in the Jungle" (Zha Jianying), 67

"I Don't Care" (He Dun), 349
If I Were for Real (Sha Yexin), 201
If I Were Real (Yao Mingde), 321
If You Are the One 2 (film), 383
Ignorant Fear Nothing, The (Wang Shuo), 383
Illustrated Fiction (magazine), 106
"I Love Dollars" (Zhu Wen), 350
I Love XXX (Meng Jinghui), 323
imagery, 192–93, 400–404, 426. *See also* paintings; photography
"Images of Hong Kong" (Leung Ping-kwan), 409
"Imagist Credo" (Lowell), 122
"Imitations of Poetry" (Zhui Feng), 328
immigration, 68–70, 73, 220
Immigration Exclusion Act (1882), 94, 196
imperial examination system, 9, 47
imperialism, 4, 9, 146, 186
Imperially Reviewed Encyclopedia of the Taiping Era, 140
income, for writers, 5, 431, 437
indigenous peoples. *See* aboriginals
individualism, 213
inequality. *See* gender
"In Fabric Alley" (Leung Ping-kwan), 409
In Remembrance of My Buddies from Military Housing Compounds (Zhu Tianxin), 366
"Inside News of the Newspaper, The" (Liu Binyan), 247
"Inspiration" (Qian Zhongshu), 233
Internet, 48, 53, 318, 431, 433; adaptations, 437; education and, 436, 439; homoeroticism on, 342–43; Internet Literature University, 436, 439; Jiuzhou community, 395–96; literature and, 18, 50, 390–93, 436–40; MOOCs, 436; poetry and, 60, 420, 439; popular-genre fiction and, 394–96, 398; "YY" or mental porn, 438–39
"Intersection" (Liu Yichang), 83, 408
Interviews with the Lower Strata of Chinese Society (Liao Yiwu), 297

"In the Hospital" (Ding Ling), 155
In the Mood for Love (film), 83, 408
"In the Nine-Flower Curtain" (Zhou Shoujuan), 115
"In the Wine Shop" (Lu Xun), 136, 139–40, 143
"Intimate Beauty, The" (Zhou Shoujuan), 115–16
Isolation (Ma Sen), 66
Itô Hirobumi, 196

Jade Pear Spirit (Xu Zhenya), 111, 112
James, Jean, 211, 212
Jameson, Frederic, 213
Jammes, Frances, 180
Japan, 3, 9, 93, 177, 332–33; Sino-Japanese War (1894–1895), 4, 19, 84, 90; Sino-Japanese War (1937–1945), 11–13, 41, 193, 198–99, 201, 220
Jiang Gui (1908–1980), 251
Jiang-Han Fishermen's Song (Tian Han), 197
Jiang He (b. 1949), 286, 288, 290, 301
Jiang Nan (b. 1977), 395
Jiang Qing (Madame Mao) (1914–1991), 15, 200, 267, 271–72, 288. *See also* Cultural Revolution
Jiang Qiongzhu, 360–61
Jiang Wen (b. 1963), 81
Jiang Ziyou (1865–1929), 92–93
Jian Xian'ai (1906–1994), 185
Jia Pingwa (b. 1952), 18, 186, 300, 301, 302, 347–48
Ji Dawei, 426
Ji Gang (b. 1920), 251
Jiling Chronicles, The (Li Yongping), 74
Jingbute, 417
Jin Jian, 199
Jinmen Bombing Incident, The (Zhu Xining), 251–52
Jin Shan, 200
Jin Yong (b. 1924), 22, 33, 274–78, 384
Jin Yun, 321
Jiuzhou community, 395–96
Ji Xian (1913–2013), 181, 330, 331

journals, 18, 39; poetry journals, 17, 67, 181, 286, 288, 289, 330, 332, 415, 416–17, 418; reform journals, 92, 123, 137, 195; travel, 67–68; underground, 289. *See also specific literary journals*
Journey to the West (Xi Xi), 356
Ju Dou (film), 84

Kafka, Franz, 316, 397, 432
Kang, Wenqing, 337, 338, 339
Kangxi emperor (1622–1722), 277
Kang Youwei (1858–1927), 4, 91
Kawabata Yasunari, 176–77, 316, 368, 369
"King of Chess, The" (A Cheng), 300, 301
King of the Children (film), 43, 81, 301
Ko, Dorothy, 9
kominka literature, 19, 52
Kong Jiesheng, 296
"Kong Yiji" (Lu Xun), 136, 138–39, 143
Korean War (1950–1953), 199, 269
Koto (Kawabata Yasunari), 368
Kropotkin, Peter, 173
Kwan, Stanley (b. 1957), 81, 82, 83, 342

labor: labor camps, 156, 225, 234, 296, 297, 346; strikes, 200, 246
Lai He (1894–1943), 19, 31, 263
Lai Shengchuan (Stan Lai), 324
Lam, Edward, 325
Lan Bozhou, 324, 424
Lang, Olga, 171, 172–73
languages, 7–8, 9, 19, 56, 290, 300, 415; with modern writing, forms of, 38–40; regional speech and fracture of, 43–45; revolutionary, 40–43; Sinitic, 72, 74, 76–77; Taiwan and, 329–30, 334; vernacular, 9, 56, 73
Lanling Theater Workshop, 324
Lan Yu (film), 81, 342
Lao She (Shu Qingchun) (1899–1966), 23, 42, 63–64, 209, 322, 384; on individualism, 213; influence, 32, 347; nihilism and, 211–15
Lao She literature prize, 432
Laozi, 142–43

Lapse of Time (Wang Anyi), 372
"Last Hunter, The" (Tamapima), 75
Last Night of Madame Chin, The (film), 81
"Last Night of Taipan Jin, The" (Bai Xianyong), 252–53
"Last Performance, The" (Chen Ruoxi), 255
Last Winter (Dong Nian), 425
Last Words from Montmartre (Qiu Miaojin), 340
late Qing (1895–1911): fiction, 104–9; historical overview, 4–6; poetry revolution, 6, 89–96, 122
League of Left-Wing Writers (1930–1936), 10, 41, 48, 155, 176, 180, 190
"Leaving the Pass" (Lu Xun), 142–43
Lee, Ang, 81, 84, 221
Lee, Bruce, 275
Lee, Leo, 146, 147, 238
Lee, Leo Ou-fan, 32–33, 58
leftist literature, historical overview, 9–11
Legend of Immortals (Stars Change) (Wo Chi Xihongshi), 438–39
Legend of the Eagle-Shooting Heroes, The (Jin Yong), 277
Legend of Zhenhuan, The (Liu Lianzhi), 437
Legend of Zhenhuan, The (television series), 437
Legends (Zhu Tianwen), 364
Le Guin, Ursula K., 395
Lenin, Vladimir, 248
Lenin's Kisses (Yan Lianke), 18, 432–33
lesbian, gay, bisexual, transgender, and queer (LGBTQ) community, 340, 343
lesbians, 337–38, 339, 341, 342
"Letter to the Youth of Taiwan, A" (Zhang Qingrong), 328
Leung Ping-kwan (1949–2013), 22, 32, 407, 408–9, 410
LGBTQ community. See lesbian, gay, bisexual, transgender, and queer community
Li Ang (b. 1952), 340, 425

Liang Qichao (1873–1929), 39, 145, 228; fiction and, 6, 97–102, 105, 106, 111, 396; influence, 6, 50; with late Qing poetry revolution, 6, 89–92, 94, 95–96; "new style" prose and, 6, 8; print culture and, 5; science fiction and, 396; with theater reform, 195
Liang Shiqiu, 161, 227
Liang Xiaobin (b. 1954), 286, 289
Liang Yusheng (1922–2009), 276, 422
Li Ao, 284, 423, 429
Liao Qingxiu (b. 1927), 263, 264
Liao Weitang, 361
Liao Yimei, 323
Liao Yiwu, 297, 311, 417, 418
Liberation Army Literature and Art (magazine), 380
Li Boyuan (1867–1906), 106, 107
Li Dazhao, 153
Life and Death Are Wearing Me Out (Mo Yan), 297, 310
Life and Death in Shanghai (Nien Cheng), 297
"Life and Death Trilogy" (plays), 325
Life and Times of Ng Chung Yin: A Hong Kong Story, The (play), 325
"Life Is Not a Crime" (He Dun), 349
Li Guoxiu, 324
Li Hanqiu (1874–1923), 111
Li Hanxiang, 81
Li Helin, 28
Li Huiying, 29
Li Jian, 296–97
Li Jianwu, 232
Li Jinfa (1900–1976), 11, 63
Li Jing (916–961), 180
Li Liuyi, 323
Limited Views (Qian Zhongshu), 232, 234
Lin Bai (b. 1958), 341
Lin Fangmei, 282
Ling Shuhua (1900–1990), 9, 338
Lin Haiyin (1918–2001), 251, 259
Lin Hengtai (b. 1924), 330, 332
Link, Perry, 33, 112
Lin Liankun, 203

Lin Ling (b. 1938), 331, 332
Lin Qingxuan, 422
Lin Shu (1852–1924), 5–6, 101, 105–6, 115, 146
Lin Yaode, 425
Lin Yutang, 23, 142, 143, 160
Lin Zexu, 105
Lin Zhaohua, 322
Lion and Tiger Vie in the Capital (Liang Yusheng), 276
Li Qiao (b. 1934), 263, 264, 423
Li Rui (b. 1950), 302
Li Shangyin (813–858), 180, 253
"Lishi's Diary" (Lu Yin), 337–38
Li Shoucheng, 321
"Li Shunda Builds a House" (Gao Xiaosheng), 296
Literary Association (1920–1947), 8, 40, 48, 160, 162
literary communities, 46–53
Literary Culture in Taiwan (Chang, Y.), 32
literary form, 38–45
literary history, 3, 137; canon and, 27–34; experimental phase, 27–28; PRC and, 28, 29–30; of Taiwan and Hong Kong, 31–32; West, developments in, 32–34
Literary History of Chinese Women (Xie Wuliang), 128
Literary Quarterly, 205, 259
Literary Review (journal), 19, 251
"Literary 'Roots'" (Han Shaogong), 299, 300
literary schools. *See* schools
literary supplements, 5, 100, 118
literature, 3, 32, 56, 113, 160, 249, 272, 380, 432, 434–35; as autobiography, 147–48, 149; commercialization of, 386–93, 437–38; with Confucianism and the Way, 8, 27, 105, 229, 418; Gao Xingjian on, 402–3; Hong Kong, late twentieth century to new millennium, 407–12; Internet and, 18, 50, 390–93, 436–40; New Literature movement (1920s–1930s), 29, 31, 49,

59; politics and, 224–29; in Taiwan, post-martial law era, 422–29. *See also specific types of literature*
literature, production of: censorship, 14, 51–53; Internet and, 392–93; literary communities and, 46–53. *See also* printing
"Literature and Revolution" (Liang Shiqiu), 161
Li Tianji, 81
Little Cousin Lianyi (Pan Renmu), 251
Little Theater movement, 323–24
Li Tuo, 300, 309, 314
Liu, Jen-peng, 341
Liu, Lydia, 33, 191, 213, 373
Liu Binyan, 246–47, 248–49, 297
Liu Cixin (b. 1963), 396–97, 398
Liu Daren, 66
Liu Denghan, 32
Liu E (1857–1909), 108–9
Liu Guangdi (1859–1898), 57
Liu Heng (b. 1954), 18, 81, 346–47
Liu Ke, 296
Liu Lianzhi, 437
liumang culture, 17, 379–81, 383, 384
Liu Musha (b. 1935), 363
Liu Na'ou (1900–1939), 10–11, 177, 180
Liu Qing, 14
Liu Shaotang (1936–1997), 185
Liu Shousong, 28, 29
Liu Shugang, 321
Liu Suola (b. 1955), 67–68
Liu Waitong, 411
Liu Xiaobo, 311
Liu Xinhuang, 29
Liu Xinwu, 293
Liu Yazi, 196
Liu Yichang (b. 1918), 21–22, 83, 408
Liu Zaifu (b. 1941), 68
Liu Zhenyun (b. 1958), 346–47
Liu Zijie, 84
Lives of Shanghai Flowers (Han Bangqing), 98
Li Xingdao, 358, 359
Li Yawei, 416
Li Yinhe, 342

Li Yongping, 20, 74, 427
Li Zishu, 427
Loach (You Fengwei), 352–53
"Loafers Trilogy, The" (Guo Shixing), 322–23
localism, nativism and, 258–64
Longing for Worldly Pleasure (Meng Jinghui), 323
Long Live the Wife (film), 221
Long River (Shen Congwen), 184
long scroll painting, 357–58
Long Yingtai, 423, 424, 429
Long Yusheng (1902–1966), 58
"Long Zhu" (Shen Congwen), 184
Looking for Mies (play), 325
"Losing the City" (Wong Bik-wan), 409
Lost Daughter of Happiness (Yan Geling), 69
Lost Garden, The (Li Ang), 425
"Lost My Love" (Wang Shuo), 381
Louie, Kam, 33
Louis XVI (King of France), 196
love, 81, 82, 83, 147, 217, 261–62, 323, 324, 371, 408, 425; boy love or *danmei* fiction, 342; as escapism, 161; love stories, 111–18, 381; sexual love, 153; urban fiction and, 348, 350. *See also* entertainment fiction; romanticism
Love Eterne, The (film), 81
Love Homosexuals in Chinese (Tian Qiyuan), 324
Love in a Chaotic City (Zhang Qingrong), 329
Love in a Fallen City (film), 82
"Love in a Fallen City" (Chang, E.), 82, 217, 219
Love in a Small Town (Wang Anyi), 373
Love on a Barren Mountain (Wang Anyi), 373
love stories. *See* entertainment fiction
Lowell, Amy, 122
Lower Half of Society, The (Zhao Zifan), 251
Lü Bicheng (1883–1943), 58
Lu Dingyi, 245
Lü Heruo (1914–1951), 263

Lui Wing Kai, 411
Lu Jingqing (1907–1993), 132, 133
Lu Ling (1923–1994), 12
Luo Fu (b. 1928), 330, 331
Luo Guangbin, 14, 240
Luo Shu (1903–1938), 132, 133
Luo Yanbin (1869–?), 129
Luo Yijun (b. 1967), 340–41, 428
Lust, Caution (film), 84, 221
Lu Xinhua, 293, 295–96
Lu Xun (1881–1936), 3, 7, 8, 9–10, 12, 15, 28, 49, 154, 228; influence, 32, 40, 48, 107, 128, 185, 242, 313, 316, 397; patronage of, 189–90, 191; poetry and, 58–59; with revolutionary literature, 160–61; with tradition and modernity, 136–43
Lu Xun Prize, 49, 432
Lu Yin (1898–1934), 9, 130–31, 132, 154, 337–38, 339

Ma and Son (Lao She), 63–64
Ma Bo, 297
Macho Men (poetry journal), 416, 417
Madame Bovary (Flaubert), 154
Madame Mao. *See* Jiang Qing
magazines. *See specific literary magazines*
magic realism, 302, 303, 307, 316
Magritte, René, 358
Mahler, Gustav, 401
Mai Jia, 440
Ma Jian, 311
Malaysia, 73–74, 75, 427
male homoeroticism, 336, 338–43, 366
Man Booker International Prize, 432
Mandarin Ducks and Butterflies fiction. *See* entertainment fiction
Mang Ke (b. 1951), 286, 288, 289
Mann, Susan, 9
Mann, Thomas, 367
Man Who Questions Death, The (Gao Xingjian), 403
Man with the Compound Eyes (Wu Mingyi), 428
Mao, Nathan, 171

Mao Dun (1896–1981), 10, 81, 112–13, 147, 186, 238, 276; criticism of, 160, 161; influence, 32, 190; on sexual love, 153; with women and modern novel, 163–67
Mao Dun Literary Award, 49, 348, 374
Maoism, 3, 42–43
Mao Zedong (1893–1976), 50, 143, 245, 255–56, 402, 433; art and, 238–39, 240, 248, 268, 300; Maospeak, 290, 415; modernity, post-Mao (1977–1989), 16–17; poetry and, 59, 286, 289; rehabilitation, post-Mao, 248, 287, 295; on writers, 156, 224–25, 238; with "Yan'an Talks," 13, 28, 30, 52, 199, 224–29, 238, 240, 248, 268, 271, 294, 311, 345. *See also* Cultural Revolution
"Maple" (Zheng Yi), 296
Maple Tree Bay (play), 200
Marconi, Lara, 76
marriage, 340, 342, 426
martial arts fiction, 22, 33, 274–78, 384, 394
martial law. *See* Taiwan
Martin, Fran, 340
Marvelous Knights of the Rivers and Lakes (Ping-jiang Buxiaosheng), 275
"Marvels of a Floating City" (Xi Xi), 358
Marxism, 160, 166, 185, 224, 384
Ma Sen (b. 1932), 66–67, 323–24
Massive Open Online Courses (MOOCs), 436
Masters of Mischief (Wang Shuo), 346, 381–82
Maupassant, Guy, 114, 173
May Fourth movement (1915–1925), 3, 63, 106, 161, 403; historical overview, 7–9, 137; influence, 73, 112, 113, 229; roots-seeking literature and, 300; writers, 8, 12, 15, 16, 128–33, 160
Ma Yuan (b. 1953), 303, 314–15
McDougall, Bonnie, 33
"Medicine" (Lu Xun), 136, 138, 139
Mei Lanfang, 196–97
Membrane (Ji Dawei), 426
Mencius, 140

"Mending Heaven" (Lu Xun), 141
Meng Jinghui, 323
"Mengke" (Ding Ling), 153, 154
Meng Yao (1919–2000), 251
mental porn ("YY"), 438–39
Messiaen, Olivier, 401
metafiction, 310, 311, 373, 427
Metamorphosis (Cao Yu), 199, 209
metropolis, 176–79. *See also* cities
Mian Mian (b. 1970), 388, 389–90
Miao Xiu, 73
Midnight (Mao Dun), 163, 167
"Military Songs" (Huang Zunxian), 95–96
Mill, John Stuart, 5, 105
Millennium (Wang Shuo), 383
"Millennium" (Wang Shuo), 384
Millennium Autopsy (play), 325
"Mimosa" (Zhang Xianliang), 297
Ming Pao (journal), 277
Mingxing Studio, 80
Miscellany Monthly (journal), 220
"Miss Amao" (Ding Ling), 154
"Miss Julie of Yuen Chow Street" (Hoyingfung), 325
"Miss Sophie's Diary" (Ding Ling), 131, 153–54
Misty poetry, 16, 43, 181; canon and, 290–91; politics and, 287–89, 290, 415; PRC and, 286; scar literature and, 289
Misty Season Drama Festival, 199
Mittler, Barbara, 15, 272
"Mixed Emotions" (Huang Zunxian), 93
model theater. *See* theater
modernism: historical overview (1920s and 1930s), 9–11; New Sensationists and, 10, 176–81; Taiwan with modernists and Cold War fiction, 250–57
Modernism and the Nativist Resistance (Chang, Y.), 32
Modernist School, 330
modernity: May Fourth (1915–1925), 7–9; poetry revolution and, 89–96; post-Mao (1977–1989), 16–17; tradition and, 136–43

Modern Literature (journal), 19, 181, 251, 252, 253
"Modern Parting" (Huang Zunxian), 95
Modern Poetry Groups of Ba and Shu (poetry journal), 417
Modern Poetry Quarterly, 330, 332
Mok Chiu-yu, 325
Momo, 417
Mongolian Tale, A (film), 303
Monroe, Harriet, 122
Montesquieu, 5
Monthly Fiction (magazine), 106
MOOCs. *See* Massive Open Online Courses
Morand, Paul, 177–78
More than Brothers (He Yaohui), 342–43
Morning in Shanghai (Zhou Erfu), 14
Most Memorable Season (Zhu Tianwen), 364
"Mother" (Ding Ling), 153
Moulin Poetry Society, Le, 329
Mountains Astir (play), 200
Mountains Beyond the Door (Ruan Qingyue), 428
Mount Culture, 142
Mou Sen, 322
Mo Yan (b. 1956), 18, 84, 226, 297, 302, 436, 439; influence, 181, 301, 303, 316; legacy, 307–11, 387; Nobel Prize and, 18, 311, 436
Mozart, Wolfgang Amadeus, 401
Mozi, 140
Mozi (philosopher), 142, 143
Ms. Youlan (Chen Dabei), 207
Mulberry and Peach: Two Women of China (Nie Hualing), 64–65
Müller, Herta, 311
Mu Shiying (1912–1940), 178–79, 180, 181
music, 177, 179, 267, 268, 272, 401, 403
My Childhood (Guo Moruo), 338
My City: A Hong Kong Story (Xi Xi), 356, 357–58, 359, 360, 361
"My Education" (Shen Congwen), 184
"My Fatherland Does Not Dream" (Han Song), 397

My Favourite Time (Chan Ping-chiu), 325
"My First Case" (Chen Yingzhen), 262
My Kid Sister (Zhang Dachun), 424
"My Lifelong Worship of Violet" (Zhou Shoujuan), 116
My Murder Story (play), 325
My South Seas Sleeping Beauty (Zhang Guixing), 74
mystery, 394
"mythorealism," 18, 432
"My Writing" (Chang, E.), 219

Nabokov, Vladimir, 433
Naked Earth, The (Chang, E.), 220
Nanpai Sanshu, 394, 437, 438
narratives: bifurcated, 254; of cities and worlds, 217–22; techniques of Xi Xi, 356–58
nation: diaspora and, 62–63; with late Qing (1895–1911), 4–6; national defense drama, 198; national salvation, 11–13; selfhood and, 146, 147; Sinophone literature and, 72
"national forms," 12, 13, 41, 156, 345
Nationalists. *See* Guomindang
nationalization, of publishing industry, 13, 39
National People's Congress, 209
native soil literature, 300
nativism: historical overview (1920s and 1930s), 9–11; influence, 190; Taiwan and, 20, 258–64
Nazis, 217
neorealist fiction, 346, 352, 381
Never to Forget (Cong Shen), 200
"New and the Old, The" (Shen Congwen), 186
New Citizen (reform journal), 92, 195
"Newcomer, The" (Wang Meng), 247
"New Concept Composition Contest," 390
New Culture movement, 7, 40, 122–23, 159, 237
New Daughter of Songling (Liu Yazi), 196

New Fiction (magazine), 97, 106
New History of Taiwan Literature (Chen Fangming), 31
New Literature movement (1920s–1930s), 29, 31, 49, 59
New Poetry movement, 330, 331
New School martial arts fiction, 276
New Sensationalists (Shinkankakuha), 10, 177
New Sensationists: modernism and, 10, 176–81; music and, 179; Shanghai and metropolis, 176–79
newspapers, 5, 39, 41, 98, 100, 220, 231, 247, 259, 355, 438; fiction and, 104, 105, 106, 113, 114, 118, 284, 358; with revolutionary model theater, 267
New Stories of Minister Qiao (Zhu Tianwen), 364
New Tide (journal), 170
new urbanite fiction, 348–49
New Woman, The (journal), 133
"New Year's Sacrifice" (Lu Xun), 154
New Yorkers (Bai Xianyong), 65, 77
"New Yorker" series (Bai Xianyong), 252
New Youth (reform journal), 123, 137
Ng, Mau-sang, 149–50
Ng Kim Chew, 73–74
Nie Gannu (1903–1986), 59
Nie Hualing, 64–65
Nien Cheng, 297
Nietzsche, Friedrich (1844–1900), 403
Nie Ying (Guo Moruo), 198
Night a Tiger Was Captured, The (Tian Han), 197
"Night Freight" (Chen Yingzhen), 262–63
Nightmares in the Red Chamber (Chang, E.), 220
"Nights of Spring Fever" (Yu Dafu), 149
Night Wandering (Ma Sen), 66–67
Night We Became Xiangsheng Comedians, The (play), 324
nihilism, 211–15
Nikolaeva, Galina, 246, 247
Ningxia, 303
Nixon, Richard, 332

Nobel Prize, 18, 169, 183, 186, 226, 307, 311, 402–3
No One Wrote to the Colonel (Zhang Dachun), 424
Northern Expedition of 1928, 9, 317
"North Point Car Ferry" (Leung Ping-kwan), 409
Notes from Drifting (Liu Zaifu), 68
Notes of a Desolate Man (Zhu Tianwen), 340, 364, 365–66, 426, 427–28
Notes of Tamkang (Zhu Tianwen), 364
"Notes on False Freedom" (Lu Xun), 142
Not-Not (poetry journal), 416, 417
Not One Less (film), 81
Nouvelle Littérature, La (journal), 178
novels, 425; graphic novels, 426; *Heimat Roman* or homeland novel, 258; in late Qing (1895–1911), 6; political, 6, 99, 100–101, 105, 424; role of, 97–100; with women, representation of, 163–67. *See also* fiction

"Of Mixed Race" (Woeser), 76
Old Capital, The (Zhu Tianxin), 366, 367
"Old Capital, The" (Zhu Tianxin), 368–69
Old Man and the Sea (Hemingway), 220
Old Stories from the Southside (Lin Haiyin), 251
Old Tales Retold (Lu Xun), 136, 140–41, 143
Old Well (film), 81, 301
Old Well (Zheng Yi), 301, 302
"Olive Tree, The" (song), 284
Once, Upon Hearing the Skin Tone (play), 324
"Once Upon a Time" (Ling Shuhua), 338
"On Climbing the Eiffel Tower" (Huang Zunxian), 94
On Contemporary Women Writers, 131
"One Boundless Evening" (Yu Dafu), 338

"One Evening in the Rainy Season" (Shi Zhecun), 178
One Hundred Years of Solitude (García Márquez), 302–3, 307
"One Kind of Reality" (Yu Hua), 313–14
One Man's Bible (Gao Xingjian), 400, 403
On Liberty (Mill), 5
"On New Poetry" (Hu Shi), 123
"On Reading *Ni Huanzhi*" (Mao), 161
On the Art of Poetry (Qian Zhongshu), 232
"On the Correct Handling of Contradictions among the People" (Mao Zedong), 245
On the Docks (opera), 267, 269
"On the Other Side of the Stream" (Kong Jiesheng), 296
"On the Relationship Between Fiction and the Government of the People" (Liang Qichao), 97, 99
operas. *See* Beijing; Peking operas; Sichuan opera; theater
Opium War (1839–1842), 21, 73, 104
Opium War . . . Four Letters to Deng Xiaoping (play), 324
"Opposing Aggression" (Lu Xun), 142
"Opposite Window, The" (Zhou Shoujuan), 117
Oppression (Ding Xilin), 205
oral literature, aboriginals, 32
"Ordination" (Wang Zengqi), 304
organizations. *See* writers
Other Shore, The (Gao Xingjian), 322, 402
"Our Paper's Inside News" (Liu Binyan), 247
Outside the Window (Qiong Yao), 281
Ouyang Jianghe, 418, 419, 421
Ouyang Yuqian, 197, 202, 207
Ouyang Zi (b. 1939), 19–20
Ovechkin, Valentin, 246, 248
"Overseas Merchants" (Huang Zunxian), 94
Owl in the Room, The (Zhang Xian), 322
"Oxcart for Dowry, An" (Wang Zhenhe), 261

pacification campaign, 263, 264
paintings, 358, 400–401, 404
Pan Guangdan, 142
Pan Haitian (b. 1975), 395
Pan Jinlian (Ouyang Yuqian), 202
Pan Jinlian: The History of a Fallen Woman (Wei Minglun), 201, 202, 321
Pan Renmu (1919–2005), 251
"Pa Pa Pa" (Han Shaogong), 186, 301
Paper Marriage (Chen Ruoxi), 340
Parry, Amie, 341
Passages of Things Past (Zhu Tianxin), 366
"Passengers and the Creator, The" (Han Song), 397
"Past and the Punishments, The" (Yu Hua), 317
Pathlight (journals), 18
patriarchy, 173–74, 207–8
patronage, 189–90, 191, 418
pay-per-view reading systems, 437
Peach Blossom Fan (Ouyang Yuqian), 197
Peking-Hankou railroad workers' strike, 200
Peking Man (Cao Yu), 199, 209
Peking operas, 15, 195–97, 203
Peng Dehuai, 201
Peng Ge (b. 1962), 250, 251
Penguin, 18
Peony Pavilion (Tang Xianzu), 325
"People or Monsters" (Liu Binyan), 297
People's Daily (newspaper), 438
People's Literature (journal), 246, 247, 248, 293
People's Literature Press, 249
People's Republic of China (PRC), 3; diaspora and, 66, 67; exile literature and, 17; experimental theater and, 320–23; homosexuality and, 339; literary history and, 28, 29–30; Misty poetry and, 286; Taiwan and, 327–28; theater and, 200
Performance Workshop, 324
periodization, 4, 28, 30, 31, 50
Perovskaya, Sophia, 196

persecution. *See* Cultural Revolution
personal freedom, 207–8, 213
Personals, The (film), 84
Personal Tailor (film), 383
Phaedo (Plato), 235
photography, 47, 95, 117, 404, 428
Ping Fong Acting Troupe, 324
Ping-jiang Buxiaosheng (1890–1957), 275
Ping Xintao, 283
Pizicai, 437
"place-produced" literature, 408–9, 410
Platform Sutra of the Sixth Patriarch, The, 384
Plato, 235
Playing for Thrills (Wang Shuo), 346, 382–83
Poems from the Hut in the Human World (Huang Zunxian), 95
poetry, 31, 232, 301, 407; avant-garde poetry (since 1980s), 414–21; classical poetry, contested, 55–60; Crescent Moon Society and new poetry, 121–26; groups, 288, 329, 330, 332; Internet and, 60, 420, 439; journals, 17, 67, 181, 286, 288, 289, 330, 332, 415, 416–17, 418; language reform and, 7–8; Misty poetry, 16, 43, 181, 286–91, 415; New Poetry movement, 330, 331; poetry revolution, 6, 89–96, 122–25; politics and, 56, 59, 287–89, 290, 415; songs and, 330; Taiwan and, 181, 327–34
Poetry (U.S. journal), 122
Poetry Bimonthly, 286
Poetry Manuscripts (Shanghai Library), 421
Poetry Monthly, 418
"Poetry Talks from the Ice-Drinking Studio," 92
Poland, 246
politics: culture and, 299–304; literature and, 224–29; poetry and, 56, 59, 287–89, 290, 415; political correctness, 28, 43, 50, 290; political novels, 6, 99, 100–101, 105, 424; Taiwan, writing politics and politics of writing, 423–25; women and, 58, 152–57, 342
popular-genre fiction, 18, 394–98
Postcolonial Taiwan (Chen Fangming), 31
post-Mao literature (1977–1989), 16–17
Power Versus Law (Xing Yixun), 201
PRC. *See* People's Republic of China
Precious Mirror for Judging Flowers (Chen Sen), 337
Preliminary Exploration Into the Art of Modern Fiction (Gao Xingjian), 402
Princess Huanzhu (Qiong Yao), 282
printing, 100; print culture, 5, 111–18; printing industry, late Qing (1895–1911), 106
prison literature, 297
privacy fever, 375
Private Life, A (Chen Ran), 341, 350–51
Prolekult movement, 225
prose, 5–6, 8, 39
protest movements, 360, 411. *See also* Tiananmen Square
Proud and Gallant Wanderer, The (Jin Yong), 277
Průšek, Jaroslav, 32, 58
psychological autobiography, 187
publishing industry, 18, 220, 283; nationalization of, 13, 39; in war period (1937–1945), 41. *See also* literature, production of; printing
puppet theater, 321, 325
Put Down Your Whip (play), 199

Qian Liqun, 29
Qianlong emperor (r. 1736–1795), 276
Qian Xingcun (1900–1977), 9–10, 160–61
Qian Xuantong (1887–1939), 112
Qian Yuan, 232, 234
Qian Zhongshu (1910–1998), 13, 32, 63, 231–35
"Qiaoxiu and Dongsheng" (Shen Congwen), 187
Qidian.com, 438
Qi Jun, 422
Qin Dejun, 165

462 Index

Qing. See late Qing
Qin Zhaoyang, 239, 246, 247–49
Qin Zihao (1912–1963), 330, 332
Qiong Yao (b. 1938), 17, 20, 80–81, 220, 280–84, 422
Qiu Fengjia (1864–1912), 92
Qiu Huadong (b. 1969), 18, 351–52
Qiu Jin (1875–1907), 129, 195
Qiu Litao, 360
Qiu Miaojin (1969–1995), 324, 340, 341, 426
Qiu Miaojin's Diary (Qiu Miaojin), 426
Qu Bo, 14
Queen's Pier protest, 360, 411
queer fiction, 425–26. See also homoeroticism
Qu Qiubai (1899–1935), 9, 41, 160, 161, 190, 225, 276
Qu Yuan (ca. 343–277 B.C.E.), 141, 186
Qu Yuan (Guo Moruo), 199

"Race of Generals, A" (Chen Yingzhen), 262
Radway, Janice, 282
Raid on the White Tiger Regiment (opera), 267, 269
Rainbow (Mao Dun), 163, 165–67
"Rainy Alley" (Dai Wangshu), 179–80
rape. See violence
RAPP (All Russia Association of Proletarian Writers), 225
realism, 8, 12, 246; magic realism, 302, 303, 307, 316; "mythorealism," 18, 432; neorealist fiction, 346, 352, 381; revolutionary realism and romanticism, 237–43
Realm of the Senses, The (Ji Dawei), 426
rebellions: Boxer Rebellion (1900), 56, 57, 104, 109, 114, 198; Taiping Rebellion (1851–1864), 104
Recollections of West Hunan (Shen Congwen), 187
"Record of Returning Home" (Yu Dafu), 148–49
Record of the Good Deeds of a Daoist (Zhang Wankang), 428

Record of Travels (Liang Qichao), 89, 90–91; exile and, 63–65, 68; PRC and, 66, 67
Records of Shangzhou (Jia Pingwa), 300, 301
Records of the Grand Historian, 141, 142
Records of the Search for Spirits, 140
Rectification Campaign, 12, 224–29, 248, 294
Red Army, 42, 155
Red Chequers Pub, The (Xin Qishi), 410–11
Red Crag (Luo Guangbin and Yang Yiyan), 14, 240
Red Detachment of Women, The (ballet drama), 267, 270, 272
Red Dust (film), 284
Red Guards, 15, 255, 295–97, 315, 380
Red Lantern, The (opera), 267, 268, 272
"Red Magnolias Beneath the Wall" (Cong Weixi), 297
Red Ocean (Han Song), 397
"Red Rose and White Rose" (Chang, E.), 83, 218
Red Sorghum (film), 81, 84, 301, 307, 309
Red Sorghum (Mo Yan), 84, 301, 303, 308–9
Red Storm (Jin Shan), 200
reform: education, 39; fiction and national reform, 6; Hundred Days Reform, 57, 90, 195; language, 7–8; reform journals, 92, 123, 137, 195; theater, 195–97
"Regenerated Bricks, The" (Han Song), 398
"Regenerated Giant, The" (Wang Jinkang), 397
regional speech, 43–45
rehabilitation: drug, 389; labor camps and, 156, 225, 234, 296, 297, 346; post-Mao, 248, 287, 295
Remains of Life (Wuhe), 426, 427
Remote Country of Women (Bai Hua), 187
Renaissance (reform journal), 123
Ren Qingtai, 80

reportage, 15, 41, 132, 297, 381, 424, 427. *See also* newspapers
Republican era (1911–1949), 275, 348, 401; fiction, 18, 49, 317, 339; writers, 15, 17, 48, 264, 339
Republic of China (ROC). *See* Taiwan
Republic of Wine, The (Mo Yan), 310
Requiem for Beauty (film), 404
Resentment over the Lost Country (play), 196
Resisting the Jin Invaders (Mei Lanfang), 197
"Restaurant in the Desert, The" (San Mao), 283–84
Retrial of Wei Jingsheng, The (Wang Keping), 324
Return on a Snowy Night (Wu Zuguang), 338
revolution: feminism and, 152–57, 164–67, 270–71; with language and literary form, 40–43; poetry revolution, 6, 89–96, 122–25; revolutionary literature, 10, 159–62; revolutionary model theater, 15, 267–72; revolutionary romanticism and realism, 237–43; romanticism in early postrevolutionary period (1949–1966), 13–15. *See also* Cultural Revolution
Revolutionary Opera (play), 324
Rewriting Taiwanese Literary History (Zhang Jinzhong and Huang Jinshu), 31
Rhinoceros in Love (Liao Yimei), 323
Rice (Su Tong), 346
Rice-Sprout Song, The (Chang, E.), 220
Rickshaw (*Camel Xiangzi*) (Lao She), 211–15
Righteous Heroes of the Modern Age (Ping-jiang Buxiaosheng), 275
Rimbaud, Arthur, 338
"Rivers of the North" (Zhang Chengzhi), 303
ROC (Republic of China). *See* Taiwan
"Rocking-and-Rolling on the Road" (travel journal), 67
Rojas, Carlos, 32

Rolland, Romain, 173
romance, Taiwan, 280–84
"Romance about Forbidden Desire, A" (Li Ang), 340
Romance of the Three Kingdoms, 80, 101, 388
Romances (Chang, E.), 12–13, 217, 218
romanticism, 12; Creation Society and, 8, 10, 147, 148; in early postrevolutionary period (1949–1966), 13–15; revolutionary romanticism, 237–43; romantic sentiment, 145–50; *Song of Youth* and, 240–43 roots-seeking literature, 16, 43, 299–304, 307
Rose, Rose, I Love You (Wang Zhenhe), 261–62
Rouge (film), 82
"Rousseau" (Jiang Ziyou), 92–93
Ruan Ji, 317
Ruan Qingyue, 428
Rubik's Cube (Tao Jun), 321–22
rural life, 185, 190, 191–93, 197, 303
Rushdie, Salman, 311
Rushing Liao River, The (Ji Gang), 251
Russia, 195–96, 225, 246
Ru Zhijuan, 371

Saga of Red Flag, The, 240
Sai Jinhua (Xia Yan), 198
same-sex marriage, 342, 426
Sandwich Man, The (film), 81
Sang, Tze-lan D., 337–38, 339, 341, 342
Sang Hu (1916–2004), 221
Sangshuping Chronicles (play), 202
San Mao (1943–1991), 17, 20, 220, 280–84, 422
"Sansan" (Shen Congwen), 186
Satisfied (television drama), 383
Saturday (literary magazine), 111, 114
"Scar" (Lu Xinhua), 293
Scarlet Lips (Cui Zi'en), 342
scar literature, 16, 234, 289, 293–97
Scent of Heaven (Wang Anyi), 376, 377
Schiaffini, Patricia, 75–76
scholar-beauty fiction, 148, 281

schools, 5, 221, 234, 276; literary schools, 6, 29, 30; Modernist School, 330
science fiction. *See* fiction
Scott, Walter (Sir), 106
Scrapbook (Xi Xi), 358
Seahorse Night Club (television drama), 383
Seahorse Studio, 383
Sea of Regret, The (Wu Jianren), 109
Searching for Homeland Westward (Liu Zaifu), 68
"Seaside Friends" (Lu Yin), 337, 339
Secret Love in Peach Blossom Land (Lai Shengchuan), 324
Seemingly Beautiful (Wang Shuo), 383
Selected Works of Mao Zedong, 226
Self at War, A (Lin Bai), 341
self-consciousness, 56, 133, 146–47, 176, 227, 263, 275, 338
"Self-Encouragement" (Liang Qichao), 90
selfhood, 146, 147, 152
Semi-Monthly (literary magazine), 114, 117
sentiment. *See* love; romance; romanticism
"Sentiments Like Water" (Wang Xiaobo), 341, 342
"Separation" (Feng Yuanjun), 131
Serve the People! (Yan Lianke), 433
Setting Moon (Peng Ge), 250, 251
"Seven Barbarians and the Last Spring Festival" (Shen Congwen), 187
Seven Days in Heaven (film), 84
17K.com, 436
sex, 149, 153–54, 213, 281, 380, 439; body writing, 30, 389; feminism with sexuality, 164–67; homoeroticism and, 336–43, 366, 373, 425–26; homosexuality, 253, 324, 336–37, 339–40, 342, 343, 425–26; licentiousness and, 350, 403; revolutionary model theater without, 271; same-sex marriage, 342, 426; sexual desire, 214; Taiwan and sexuality, 340; urban fiction and, 347–48; violence and, 190, 270–71, 296, 350–51

shadow theater, 321
Shajiabang (opera), 267, 269, 272
Shajiabang (symphony), 267, 268, 272
Shakespeare, William, 197
Shakespeare's Wild Sisters Group, 324
Shamlet (Li Guoxiu), 324
Shanghai, 14, 44, 98, 198, 219, 297; bombing of, 191; depictions of, 180–81, 374–77; New Sensationists and, 176–79; theater and, 196, 199; urban literature and, 348
"Shanghai, Spring 1930" (Ding Ling), 154–55
Shanghai Baby (Wei Hui), 388, 390
Shanghai Library, 421
Shang Qin (b. 1930), 331
Sha Ting (1904–1992), 12
Sha Yexin, 201, 321
"She Is a Weak Woman" (Yu Dafu), 338
Shenbao (newspaper), 98, 114, 118
Shen Congwen (1902–1988), 11, 17, 32, 161; with native communities, imagined, 183–87; native soil literature and, 300
Shen Haobo, 419, 420, 439
Shen Lin, 203
Shen Zufen (1909–1977), 58
Shibao, 169
Shi Guanghua, 416
Shih, Shu-mei, 23, 76–77
Shi Nai'an, 100, 101, 201–2, 388
Shinkankakuha (New Sensationists), 10, 177
Shi Pingmei (1902–1928), 131, 132, 133
Shi Tuo (1910–1988), 13, 32
Shi Zhecun (1905–2003), 141, 143, 177–78, 180, 181
Shizhi (b. 1948), 288, 289
Short Story Magazine, 112–13, 130
Shostakovich, Dmitri, 401
Shouhuo (Yan Lianke), 432–33
Shui Jing, 221
Shu Qingchun. *See* Lao She
Shu Ting (b. 1952), 286, 287, 288, 289, 290
Sichuan opera, 201, 202, 321

Sigh, A (film), 383
Sigmund Freud in Search of Chinese Matter and Mind (play), 325
"Silence" (Qin Zhaoyang), 247–48
Silhouette sinon l'ombre, La (film), 404
Silver City (Li Rui), 302
Sima Changfeng, 29
Sima Zhen, 141
Sinitic languages, 72, 74, 76–77
"Sinking" (Yu Dafu), 59, 63, 147, 149
Sino-British talks (1980), 359
Sino-Japanese War (1894–1895), 4, 19, 84, 90
Sino-Japanese War (1937–1945), 11–13, 41, 193, 198–99, 201, 220
Sinophone literature (global Chinese literature), 72, 76–77; diaspora and, 62; historical overview, 22–23; Malaysia and, 73–74, 75; Taiwan and, 74–75
Sinophone Malaysian Literature and Chineseness (Ng Kim Chew), 73
Six Chapters of Life in a Cadre School (Yang Jiang), 234
"Sky" (Mang Ke), 289
"Slaughter" (Liao Yiwu), 418
Slave Series, 189
Small Reunion (Chang, E.), 221
Small Town Called Hibiscus, A (Gu Hua), 304
Smith, Adam, 5
"Snow" (Shen Congwen), 184
Snow in August (Gao Xingjian), 400
Social Darwinism, 187, 398
social media, 318, 420, 426
Solid Earth, The (Li Rui), 302
"Solitary Reaper, A" (Wordsworth), 59
"Some Modest Proposals for the Reform of Literature" (Hu Shi), 56
Song dynasty, 5, 197, 358
"Song for the Twentieth Century on the Pacific Ocean, A" (Liang Qichao), 90
"Song of Cherry Blossoms, A" (Huang Zunxian), 94
Song of Everlasting Sorrow, The (Wang Anyi), 348, 374–75

Song of the Covered Wagon (Lan Bozhou), 324
Song of the Covered Wagon (Wang Molin), 324
Song of Dragon River, The (opera), 268, 269–70
Song of the Swordsman (Jin Yong), 277
Song of Youth (Yang Mo), 14, 240–43
Song Qu, 416
songs: poetry and, 330; song lyrics or *ci*, 57, 58, 121–22
Songs of Chu, 302
"Songs of the Zhen'gan Folk" (Shen Congwen), 184
Song Wei, 416
Soong, Roland (son), 221
Soong, Stephen (1919–1996), 221, 356
"Soul in Bondage, A" (Zhaxi Dawa), 303
Soul Mountain (Gao Xingjian), 186, 400
Southeast Asia, 73–74, 220, 427
speech, regional, 43–45
Spirit of Laws, The (Montesquieu), 5
spoken drama. *See* drama
Spring (Ba Jin), 169
Spring in a Small Town (film), 81
Spring of Overseas Chinese, The (play), 196
"Spring Silkworms" (Mao Dun), 81
"Stagnation" (Wen Yiduo), 126
Stalin, Joseph, 246
Stalin Prize, 156
Stanislavsky, Konstantin, 321
Star Ferry Pier preservation protests, 360, 411
Stars Change. *See Legend of Immortals*
"Starve the Poets" (Yi Sha), 418
"Statesmen and Artists" (Wang Shiwei), 225
"Stewardess, The" (Wang Shuo), 381
Stones of the Jingwei Bird (Qiu Jin), 129
Stories of Mulberry Village (Chen Zidu), 321
Stories of the Sahara (San Mao), 284
Stories of Xiao Bi (Zhu Tianwen), 364
Stories Within Stories (Xi Xi), 356
Story of Di Village (Chen Jiying), 220

"Story of Fertile Town, The" (Xi Xi), 359
"Story of the Eastern City" (Xi Xi), 358
"Story of Uncle, The" (Wang Anyi), 373–74
Stowe, Harriet Beecher, 196
Strand, David, 212
Strange Events Eyewitnessed over Twenty Years (Wu Jianren), 107
Strange Tales from Strange Lands (Zheng Wanlong), 303
stream of consciousness, 181, 252, 253
strikes, labor, 200, 246
students, 137, 196, 334, 342. *See also* May Fourth movement; Tiananmen Square
Student Wave (play), 196
Subway (Han Song), 397
"Suez Canal, The" (Huang Zunxian), 94
suicide, 211, 252, 340, 417
Suicide Note from Montmartre (Qiu Miaojin), 426
Su Manshu (1884–1918), 115, 146
Summer at Grandpa's, A (film), 83
"Summer Vacation" (Ding Ling), 338
Sun Column (poetry group), 288
Sun Dachuan, 75, 426–27
Sunday (literary magazine), 113
Sunflower Student movement of 2014, 334
Sun Ganlu (b. 1959), 314, 317
Sun Huizhu, 321
Sun Jianzhong (b. 1938), 185
Sun Li (1913–2002), 185
Sun Liaohong (1897–1958), 111
Sun Quan, 148, 149
Sunrise (play), 209
Sun Shaozhen, 287
"Sunshine Between the Lips" (Chen Ran), 350
Sun Shines over Sanggan River, The (Ding Ling), 156
Sun Society, 160, 162
Sun Wenbo, 418
Sun Yat-sen (1866–1925), 91
superstition, 139, 186, 275, 301, 303, 349
supplements. *See* literary supplements

Supplement to the Records of the Grand Historian (Sima Zhen), 141
Suspense at Every Step (time-travel romance), 394
Su Tong (b. 1963), 18, 20, 314, 316, 317, 318; influence, 181, 387; urban fiction and, 346
Su Weizhen, 426
Su Xuelin (1897–1999), 132, 154
Swordsmen of the Mountains of Shu (Huanzhulouzhu), 275
symphonies, 267, 268, 272, 401

Tagore, Rabindranath (1861–1941), 124, 125, 329
Taibai (journal), 190
Tai Jingnong, 252
Taiping Rebellion (1851–1864), 104
Taiping Yulan, 141
Taiwan, 17, 48, 340; aboriginals, 21, 32, 74–75, 284, 328, 426–27; censorship in, 52, 53, 328, 423; diaspora and, 64, 65–66; diversification, experimentation and new voices, 425–29; education in, 51, 328; experimental theater and, 323–24; film and Taiwan New Cinema, 81; with foreign culture, 363–69; historical overview, 19–21; languages and, 329–30, 334; literary history of, 31–32; literature in post-martial law era, 422–29; localism and, 258–64; martial law and, 19, 20, 21, 31, 81, 280, 367; with modernists and Cold War fiction, 250–57; nativism and, 20, 258–64; New School martial arts fiction and, 276; poetry and, 181, 327–34; population, 426; PRC and, 327–28; queer fiction, 425–26; ROC and, 44, 75, 423; romance, 280–84; Sinophone literature and, 74–75; White Terror (1950s–1970s) and, 21, 329, 333, 423; writing politics and politics of writing, 423–25
Taiwan, 328
Taiwan Chengwen Books, 29

Taiwanese People's Journal, 328–29
Taiwan Literary Arts, 264
Taiwan's Imagined Geography (Teng), 32
Taking a Bath (Yang Jiang), 232–33, 235
Taking Tiger Mountain by Strategy (opera), 267, 268–69
Talks on Verse in the Human World (Wang Guowei), 101
Tamapuma, Tuobasi (Topas Tamapima), 75m 427
Tang dynasty, 121, 218, 274
Tang Shu-wing, 325
Tang Siu Wa, 411
Tang Tao, 29
Tang Xianzu, 325
Tan Sitong (1865–1898), 4, 89, 92, 145
Tao Dongfeng, 30
Tao Jun, 321–22
Tashi Dawa, 76
Tay, William, 411–12
television, 283, 348, 379, 383, 398, 429, 437
Tendency (poetry journal), 417
Tenderness and Violence (Wong Bik-wan), 409
Tender Night, The (San Mao), 284
Teng, Emma, 32
Testament de Montmartre, Le (Wei Ying-juan), 324
theater, 41, 200; adaptations, 322, 323, 324; children's, 428; drama and, 195–203; Epic Theater, 321, 359; experimental, 320–25; Greek theater, 202, 208; operas, 15, 185, 195–97, 201, 202, 203, 267, 268–70, 272, 321, 324, 336–37; reform, 195–97; revolutionary model, 15, 267–72; war period (1937–1945) and, 198–99, 201
Their World: A Look at the Chinese Male Homosexuality Community (Wang Xiaobo and Li Yinhe), 342
Them (poetry journal), 416
Thirteen Steps, The (Mo Yan), 310
"This Is Beijing at 4:08" (Shizhi), 288
"Thoughts on March Eighth" (Ding Ling), 155, 225

Threads of Talk essayists, 160
Three-Body Trilogy, The (Liu Cixin), 398
Three Family Alley, 240
"Three Loves" (Wang Anyi), 348
Three Sisters (Zhu Tianwen), 364
Three Women in Pearl River Delta (play), 325
Thunderstorm (Cao Yu), 205–9
Tiananmen Square, 7; historical overview, post-Tiananmen (1989–), 17–18; violence in, 59, 68, 84, 226, 310, 314, 322, 403, 412, 415, 418
Tian Han, 147, 197
Tian Qinxin, 323
Tian Qiyuan, 324
Tian Xiaoqing (b. 1953), 288
Tibet, 75–76, 314, 317, 349
Time's Passage (Yan Lianke), 432
time travel fiction, 18, 394, 438, 439
Tiny Times (film series), 391
Tiny Times (Guo Jingming), 391
Today (poetry journal), 17, 67, 181, 288, 289, 415, 416, 418
Tolkien, J. R. R., 395
Tolstoy, Leo, 114, 166
Tongcheng school, prose and, 5
Tong Ge (b. c.1951), 339
Tongguang style, poetry, 57, 58
Tonglin Lu, 309
Topographies (Chan Chi Tak), 411
Torrent (Ba Jin), 169
"To the Tune Zhe Gutian" (Zhu Zumou), 57
"Town Mantra" (Xi Xi), 359
"Traces of Love" (Chang, E.), 217
Trackless Train (journal), 177, 178
Tracks in the Snowy Forest (Qu Bo), 14
tradition, modernity and, 136–43
"Transfer" (Xu Mingxu), 296
translation: Hong Kong and, 407; in late Qing (1895–1911), 105–6; role of, 5–6, 40, 99, 101, 114, 125, 431; Taiwan with, 429; translation journals, 18; USIA with, 220
"Transparent Carrot, A" (Mo Yan), 307
trauma, 376. *See also* scar literature

travel journals, 67–68
Travels of Lao Can, The (Liu E), 108–9
"Tree Stump, The" (A Cheng), 301
Triple Gate, The (Han Han), 390, 392
Troubleshooters and Samsara (Wang Shuo), 383
"True Story of Ah Q, The" (Lu Xun), 49, 136–43, 160–61, 313
Tsinghua Weekly (newspaper), 231
"Tunnel, The" (Chen Ruoxi), 256
Turbulent Stream (Ba Jin), 169
Turgenev, Ivan, 149, 150, 173
Two Men on a No Man's Land (play), 325

Uncle Doggie's Nirvana (Jin Yun), 321
Uncle Hung, 411
Uncle Tom's Cabin (Stowe), 196
underground journals, 289
Under Shanghai Eaves (Xia Yan), 198
Unexpected Encounters with Beauties (Liang Qichao), 100
Unfilial Daughter (Du Xiulan), 340
Unfinished Affairs (Zhu Tianxin), 366
United Daily News, 259, 284, 355
United Nations, 332
United States (U.S.), 77, 94, 220, 239, 332, 367, 372. *See also* West, the
United States Information Agency (USIA), 220
Un-Russian Dream, An (play), 196
urban fiction, 18, 33; cities and, 345–53; encroachment and, 350–51
USIA. *See* United States Information Agency
U Theater, 324
"Utopian Verses" (Wang Anyi), 372

van Crevel, Maghiel, 18
Veg, Sebastian, 410
venereal disease, 213, 350
Verlaine, Paul, 338
vernacular, 9, 56, 73. *See also* languages
Vicious Beasts (Wang Shuo), 383
Village in August (Xiao Jun), 193
"Village Opera" (Lu Xun), 185

violence, 380, 409; avant-garde fiction and, 317; domestic violence, 313; labor strikes and, 200; rape, 190, 270–71, 296, 350–51; theater and, 324; in Tiananmen Square, 59, 68, 84, 226, 310, 314, 322, 403, 412, 415, 418; in war period (1937–1945), 193. *See also* rebellions
Violet, The (literary magazine), 113, 114, 116, 117, 118

"Waiting" (Wang Shuo), 380
Walisi Yougan, 427
Walled City, 408, 410
Wanderer, The (Zhu Tianxin), 366
Wandering in the Garden, Waking from a Dream (Bai Xianyong), 65, 252, 253
"Wandering in the Garden, Waking from a Dream" (Bai Xianyong), 253
Wandering Spirit and Metaphysical Thoughts (Gao Xingjian), 404
Wang, David, 32, 33, 309
Wang, David Der-wei, 213
Wang, Jing, 314
Wang Anyi (b. 1954), 304, 341, 348, 371–77
Wang Dingjun, 422
Wang Dulu, 275
Wang Dungen (1888–1950), 111
Wang Gui, 201
Wang Guowei (1877–1927), 101
Wang Jiaming, 324
Wang Jiaxin, 418, 419
Wang Jingwei (1883–1944), 59, 220
Wang Jinkang (b. 1948), 397, 398
Wang Keping, 324
Wang Lan (b. 1922), 250–51
Wang Luyan (1901–1944), 185
Wang Meng (b. 1934), 17, 246, 247, 248–49
Wang Miaoru, 129
Wang Ming, 224
Wang Molin, 324
Wang Peigong, 201, 322
Wang Pengyun (1849–1904), 57–58
Wang Shiwei, 156, 225

Wang Shuo (b. 1958), 17, 81, 379–84, 431; commercialization and, 386; urban fiction and, 345–46, 347
Wang Wenxing (b. 1939), 19, 20, 181, 252, 253–54, 427
Wang Xiaobo (1952–1997), 341–42
Wang Xiaoni (b. 1955), 286, 415
Wang Xiaonong, 196
Wang Yangming (1472–1529), 186
Wang Yao (1914–1989), 28, 29, 185
Wang Yin, 421
Wang Yingxia, 148
Wang Yulin, 84
Wang Zengqi (1920–1997), 185, 186, 303–4
Wang Zhaojun (Guo Moruo), 198, 208
Wang Zhefu, 27–28
Wang Zhenhe (1940–1990), 20, 181, 259, 260–62
Wang Zhongqi, 100–101
"Warning to Novelists, A" (Liang Qichao), 99
War of Liberation (1946–1949), 269
war period (1937–1945), 41, 193, 220; historical overview, 11–13; theater and, 198–99, 201. *See also* Sino-Japanese War
"Water" (Ding Ling), 155
"Water and Clouds" (Shen Congwen), 187
Water Margin (Shi Nai'an), 101, 201–2, 388; Wang Zhongqi's defense of, 101
Wang Zhongqi, 101
Watt, Ian, 237
Waves Breaking on the Sand (Dongfang Bai), 423
Way, the. *See* Confucianism
Wealth of Nations (Smith), 5
We Always Read Xi Xi (film), 360–61
Weavers (Hauptmann), 205
"web-game literature," 437
Weekly Journal of Young Big Head Spring, The (Zhang Dachun), 424, 425
Weekly Political Journal of a Novelist, The (Zhu Tianxin), 425

"Weihu" (Ding Ling), 154
Wei Hui (b. 1973), 388, 389, 390
Wei Jian, 30
Wei Jingsheng, 256, 324
Wei Minglun, 201, 202, 321
Wei Yingjuan, 324
wen culture, 6, 56, 229
Wen Ruian (b. 1954), 278
Wenxuan school, prose and, 5, 6
Wenxue (journal), 190
Wen Yiduo (1899–1946), 63, 125–26
"We Shall Meet Again" (Zhou Shoujuan), 114–15
West, the, 152, 356; influence, 5, 154, 287, 372, 395, 401; literary history and developments in, 32–34
Western Xia Motel, The (Luo Yijun), 428
West Hunan (Shen Congwen), 187
We Three (Yang Jiang), 235
"What Happens to Nora After She Leaves Home" (Lu Xun), 242
"What Should I Do" (Chen Guokai), 296
What's Trash, What's Love? (Zhu Wen), 350
"When I Was in Xia Village" (Ding Ling), 155, 255
When the Great River Comes to an End (Li Yongping), 427
Whirlwind (Jiang Gui), 251
White-Haired Girl, The (ballet drama), 267, 270–71, 272
White Terror. *See* Taiwan
Whitman, Walt, 124
"Why Our Newspaper Will Print a Fiction Supplement" (Xia Zengyou and Yan Fu), 100
Wild Child (Zhang Dachun), 424
Wild Duck (poetry group), 288
Wilderness (play), 209
Wild Fire, The (Long Yingtai), 423, 424, 429
Wild Grass (Deng Ken), 10
Wild Grass (poetry group), 288
Wild Lilies (Wang Shiwei), 156
"Wild Lilies" (Wang Shiwei), 225

Wild Man (Gao Xingjian), 321, 402
"Wilted Chrysanthemums" (Gao Xingjian), 402
"Windows" (Qian Zhongshu), 232
Wings (poetry journal), 417
Winter Jasmine (play), 200–201
"Winter Nights" (Bai Xianyong), 253
Wintry Night (Li Qiao), 264
"Wisteria and Dodder" (Yu Dafu), 149
Witchtalk (Zhu Tianwen), 428
With a Ghost Roaming in Hong Kong (Liu Waitong), 411
WM (Wang Peigong), 201, 322
Wo Chi Xihongshi (Internet novelist), 438–39
Woeser, 76
Wolfe, Thomas, 169
"Woman" (Zhai Yongming), 417
"Woman and a Man, A" (Ding Ling), 154
"Woman Woman Woman" (Han Shaogong), 301–2
women, 64–65, 187, 267, 272, 297, 325; education for, 9, 46, 130, 153; female homoeroticism, 336, 337–38, 339, 340, 341, 342, 373; feminism and, 152–57, 164–67, 270–71; literary history and, 28–29; novels and representation of, 163–67; politics and, 58, 152–57, 342; portrayals of, 174, 208, 214, 269, 270–71; violence and, 190–91, 270–71, 296, 313, 350–51; "women's problems," 130, 133; writers, 9, 16, 29, 58, 117, 128–34, 152–57, 189–94, 201, 251, 280–84, 363–69, 371–77, 389, 410–11, 417, 423, 425, 427–28, 439; writing of women, origins, 128–34. *See also* entertainment fiction
Women's Bookstore, 133
Women's Poetry Journal, 417
Wong Bik-wan (b. 1961), 409
Wong Kar-wai, 83, 408
Wong Wai-leung, 407
Woo, Mathias, 325
word, image and, 400–404
Wordsworth, William, 59

"workplace" fiction, 439
worlds, narratives of, 217–22
"Wounded, The" (Lu Xinhua), 295–96
writers: beauty writers, 386, 388–89, 390; income for, 5, 431, 437; Internet and, 53; with literary history, 28–29; Mao Zedong on, 156, 224–25, 238; May Fourth writers, 8, 12, 15, 16, 128–33, 160; organizations, 10, 12, 14, 41, 42, 48, 52, 155, 176, 180, 190, 211, 225, 295, 311, 395–96, 431, 440; Republican era (1911–1949), 5, 17, 48, 264, 339; women, 9, 16, 29, 58, 117, 128–34, 152–57, 189–94, 201, 251, 280–84, 363–69, 371–77, 389, 410–11, 417, 423, 425, 427–28, 439; youth writers, 386, 390, 391–92, 395
writing, 5, 6, 31, 219; language and forms of modern, 38–40; Taiwan, writing politics and politics of writing, 423–25; types of, 30, 74, 297, 389; women's writing, origins of, 128–34
Writing Taiwan (Wang, David, and Rojas), 32
Written in the Margins of Life (Qian Zhongshu), 232
Written on Water (Chang, E.), 217
Wuhe (b. 1951), 340, 425, 426, 427
Wu Jianren (1866–1910), 106, 107, 109
Wu Jiwen, 426
Wuling Spring (play), 196
Wu Mingyi, 428
Wu Nianzhen (b. 1952), 81
Wu Peifu, 200
Wu Tianming, 81
Wu Yingtao (1916–1971), 332
Wu Yu (1871–1949), 7
Wu Zhuoliu (1900–1976), 263
Wu Zuguang (1917–2003), 338
Wu Zuxiang (1908–1994), 10, 186

Xiang Kairan (1890–1957), 111–12
xiangtu literature, 185, 186, 187. *See also* nativism
Xiaobin Yang, 310
Xiaofei Tian, 59

Xiaohe, 342
Xiao Hong (1911–1942), 132, 186, 189–94, 411
Xiao Jianguo (b. 1952), 185
Xiao Jun, 189, 191, 193, 225
Xiao Kiayu, 418
"Xiao Lin Comes to Taipei" (Wang Zhenhe), 261
Xiao Qian (1910–1999), 185
"Xiaoxiao" (Shen Congwen), 186
Xiaoyin, 417
Xia Yan, 198
Xia Zengyou (1863?–1924), 39, 89, 92, 100, 104
Xi Chuan (b. 1963), 17, 417, 419, 421
Xie Bingying, 132
Xie Fei, 303
Xie Mian, 287
Xie Wuliang, 128
Xing Yixun, 201
Xinjiang, 303
Xin Qishi (b. 1950), 410–11
Xiong Hong (b. 1940), 331
Xiu Xiu: The Sentdown Girl (film), 84
Xi Xi (Zhang Yan) (b. 1938), 22; Hong Kong and, 355–61, 410; with narratives techniques, 356–58
X Poetry Club, 288
Xu Chi, 287
Xu Jinglei, 384
Xu Jingya, 416
Xu Mingxu, 296
Xu Yousheng, 426
Xu Yunuo (1893–1958), 8
Xu Zhenya (1889–1937), 111, 112
Xu Zhimo (1897–1931), 8, 63, 125, 142, 161
Xu Zhuodai (1880–1958), 111
XXth Century (journal), 217, 221

"Yan'an Talks." *See* Mao Zedong
Yan Fu (1854–1921), 5, 39, 100, 104
Yan Geling (b. 1958), 68–69
Yang Hua (1906–1936), 329
Yang Jian, 321
Yang Jiang (b. 1911), 13, 231–35

Yang Ke, 419
Yang Kui (1906–1985), 263
Yang Li, 416
Yang Lian (b. 1955), 286, 288, 289–90, 301, 415, 416, 418
Yang Mo, 14, 240–43
Yang Yi, 30
Yang Yiyan, 14, 240
Yang Zhao, 424, 425
Yan Jiayan, 29–30
Yan Li (b. 1954), 288
Yan Lianke, 18, 431–35
Yan Zhongxian, 428
Yao Mingde, 321
Yao Yiwei, 323
Ya Xian (b. 1932), 330, 331–32
Yearnings (television drama), 383
"Years of Sadness" (Wang Anyi), 375–76
Ye Lingfeng (1905–1975), 338
Yellow Earth (film), 43, 301
"Yellow Mud Street" (Can Xue), 315
Ye Shan (b. 1940), 331, 332
Ye Shengtao (1894–1988), 40, 337
Ye Shitao (1925–2008), 31, 263, 264
Yesterday When I Was Young (Zhu Tianxin), 366
Ye Weilian (b. 1937), 332
Ye Zi, 189
Yi Baisha (1886–1921), 7
Yi bao (entertainment newspaper), 220
Yin Lichuan, 420, 439
Yi Qun (b. 1947), 288
Yi Sha, 418
Yi Zhen, 131–32
Yokomitsu Rîchi, 177
Yoshikawa Kōjirō, 57
You Fengwei (b. 1943), 352–53
Young China (reform journal), 123
"Young Newcomer in the Organization Department, The" (Wang Meng), 247
"Young Widow" (Huang Chunming), 260
youth, 14, 123, 137, 200, 240–43, 328; popular-genre fiction, 394–98; youth writers, 386, 390, 391–92, 395

Yuan Liangjun, 32
Yuan Qiongqiong, 181
Yuan Shikai, 111
Yu Dafu (1896–1945), 8, 58–59, 63, 338; revolutionary literature and, 159–60; with romantic sentiment, 145–50
Yu Daxiong, 113
Yu Guangzhong. *See* Yu Kwang-chung
Yu Hua (b. 1960), 18, 20, 43, 181, 431; avant-garde fiction and, 313–14, 316, 317, 318; commercialization and, 386, 387–88, 392
Yu Jian, 322, 416, 419
Yu Kwang-chung, aka Yu Guangzhong (b. 1928), 22, 422
Yu Lihua, 65–66
Yung, Danny, 325
Yu Pingbo (1899–1990), 8
Yu Xiu, 392
"YY" (mental porn), 438–39

Zaifeng (Qing prince) (1883–1951), 59
Zang Kejia (b. 1905), 287
Zeng Pu (1872–1935), 106, 107–8
Zhai Yongming, 417, 419, 421
Zha Jianying (b. 1959), 67
Zhang Bing (b. 1921), 332
Zhang Chengzhi (b. 1948), 301, 303
Zhang Dachun, 424, 425, 428
Zhang Guixing, 74, 427
Zhang Heci (b. 1943), 288
Zhang Henshui (1895–1967), 10, 112, 113
Zhang Jie, 371
Zhang Jinzhong, 31
Zhang Langlang (b. 1943), 288
Zhang Ling (b. 1957), 68–69
Zhang Ming, 286
Zhang Mo (b. 1931), 330
Zhang Qingrong (Zhang Wojun) (1902–1955), 328–29
Zhang Shuguang, 418
Zhang Tianyi (1906–1985), 10, 186
Zhang Wankang, 428
Zhang Wojun. *See* Zhang Qingrong
Zhang Xian, 322
Zhang Xianliang, 297
Zhang Xiaofeng, 422
Zhang Xiguo, 21, 66
Zhang Xinxin, 371
Zhang Yan. *See* Xi Xi
Zhang Yimou (b. 1951), 81, 84, 301, 309, 316
Zhang Yuan, 341
Zhang Ziping, 147, 227
Zhan Hongzhi, 364
Zhao Chuan, 322
Zhao Lihua, 439
"Zhao Nandong" (Chen Yingzhen), 263
Zhao Qingge, 133
Zhao Shuli (1906–1970), 186
Zhao Xiaolan (Jin Jian), 199
Zhao Zifan (1924–1986), 251
Zhaxi Dawa (b. 1959), 302, 303
Zheng, Egoyan, 428
Zheng Chouyu (b. 1932), 331, 332, 422
Zheng Qingwen (b. 1932), 263, 264
Zheng Wanlong (b. 1944), 303
Zheng Xiaoxu (1860–1938), 56–57
Zheng Yi (b. 1947), 296, 301, 302
Zheng Zhenduo (1898–1958), 113, 276
Zhong Lihe (1915-1960), 263–64
Zhong Zhaozheng (b. 1925), 263, 264
Zhou Dunyi, 229
Zhou Enlai, 226
Zhou Erfu, 14
Zhou Jin, 29
Zhou Lunyou, 416
Zhou Shoujuan (1884–1968), 111–18
Zhou Yang (1908–1989), 248, 294, 295
Zhou Zan, 417
Zhou Zuoren (1885–1967), 8, 27, 33, 50, 112, 133, 160, 227
Zhuangzi, 140, 301, 302, 401
Zhu Defa, 30
Zhui Feng (1902–1967), 328
Zhu Ling in Wonderland (Li Yongping), 427
Zhuo Wenjun (Guo Moruo), 197–98, 208
Zhu Shuzhen, 131–32

Zhu Tianwen (b. 1956), 365–66, 427–28; film and, 81, 83–84, 364; homoeroticism and, 340, 426
Zhu Tianxin (b. 1958): foreign culture and, 363–64, 366–69; politics and, 424–25
Zhu Wen (b. 1967), 349–50
Zhu Xi, 229
Zhu Xiaoping, 321
Zhu Xining (1927–1998), 251–52, 363
Zhu Zumou (1857–1931), 57–58
Zodiac (play), 324
Zola, Émile, 114, 165, 166, 173
Zuni Icosahedron, 324–25